12-0

W. R. STARK

C000285515

THE RIVER IS WITHIN US

A Maritime History of Lymington

Written and Edited

by

JEAN CHITTY

BELHAVEN

AUTHOR OF

PAPER IN DEVON

To

My Mother

T. S. ELIOT – THE FOUR QUARTERS: SALVAGE

*"The River is within us,
the Sea is all about us."*

© Jean Chitty   All rights reserved

First Published in 1983 by BELHAVEN
8 King's Saltern Road, Lymington, Hants SO4 9QF

Printed in Great Britain by
Printwise, High St, Lymington, Hampshire

British Library Cataloguing in Publication Data
Chitty, Jean   The River is Within Us
1. Lymington (Hampshire) – History
I. Title 942.2'75   DA690.L89

ISBN 0-9505869-1-9

CONTENTS

ACKNOWLEDGEMENTS

I would like to convey my warmest thanks to all those people who have assisted me in compiling this maritime history of Lymington. I spoke to many in their homes, offices and even on board their boats and needed all their patience with my temperamental tape-recorder! Others wrote to me, kindly loaned me photographs and suggested more contacts.

These include: Jim Arnold, John Atkins, Richard Bagnall, A. L. Baigent, Maurice Bailey, Sandy Balfour, David Balme, Ted Barraclough, David Barrow, Doug Baverstock, Roger Bayzand, Horace and Catherine Bashford, Peter Bevan, Stuart Beck, Patrick Beesly, J. A. Bell, Jack Blachford, Bob Blunt, Denys Brook-Hart, Larry Brown, Erroll Bruce, Graham Butler, Lionel St. Clare Byrne, Mary Campbell-Ross, Wendy Carrington, Peg Carruthers, Eileen Caulcutt, L. T. Chapman, Anna Chitty, John Claridge, Joey Cleall, Christine Cobb, David Cobb, Bob Cook, Roy Coombs, James Crawford, Maureen Davin, Chris DeVeulle, Tom Doe, George Downing, Hyacinth Duplessis, Alastair Easton, Nicholas Edmiston, George Edwards, Sgt. Feist, Clare Francis, Norman Gannaway, Richard Gatehouse, Mark Goodhart, Buster Hallett, Henry Harris, Charles Hay, John Hayter, Tony Hibbert, Don Howard, Rob Humphreys, Freda Inman, Peter Johnson, Kirk Kalis, Mary King, Monty Knight, Chris Lawn, Jack Lowis, Gowan McAlister, Arthur McDonald, Colin McMullen, Brian Manby, Hugh Marriott, Bill Martineau, Ray Milward, Kay Mitchell, Tom Morris, Colin and Rosemary Mudie, Charles Munro, William Payne, P. W. Penny, Roger Pinckney, Pat Pocock, George Power, Bert Rand, Fiona Rogers, Helen Russell, Joe Sanders, Derry Seaton, Bill Smith, Jim Smith, Rob Smith, Ken Stone, Dick Stower, David Strang, Alasdair Terras, Ian Thurgood, Charles Turner, Tom Turrell, Jean Vernon-Jackson, Barbara Webb, Frank Webster, John Webster, Peter and Pat Webster, Hugh Wilson, Eddie Wiseman and Fred Woodford. SCATS, Shell and B.P., Travis & Arnold and Whitbread searched their records for me and Wellworthy kindly presented me with a copy of John Howlett's autobiography *The Guv'nor*.

On reading the list of contributors it must be obvious that many names are not included in it. There are so many interesting people in Lymington that it was just not possible for me to have talked to any more in the time available. Their omission is our loss.

I am indebted to: The Centaur Press Ltd. of Fontwell, Arundel, Sussex for permission to include extracts from William Allingham's Diary (with an introduction by Geoffrey Grigson); Lord Montagu of Beaulieu, Chairman of Pioneer Publications, Beaulieu for material from *Verderers of the New Forest – A History of the New Forest 1877-1977* by Anthony Pasmore; Captain F. T. O'Brien of Bramshaw for information taken from his book *Early Solent Steamers*, published by David and Charles of Newton Abbot, Devon; A. P. Watt Ltd., Literary Agents, London, acting for the Estate of Nevil Shute Norway to quote from *Requiem for a Wren* by Nevil Shute and published by William Heinemann; Maldwin Drummond for extracts from *Conflicts in an Estuary*, published by Ilex Press; and in particular to Nautical Publishing Ltd., Lymington.

I would also like to thank the RCC Press Ltd., 4 Coval Lane, London for permission to use material from *A History of the Royal Cruising Club 1800-1980* by Alasdair Garrett and Trevor Wilkinson; Arthur Lloyd, Chairman of the Lymington Historical Records Society for access to papers presented to the Society by Members and listed in the Bibliography; Colin Tubbs of the Nature Conservancy Council for extracts from his Report of 3rd December 1979, *The Future of the North West Solent Coast – Proposals for the coast from Pitts Deep to Hurst Spit*; also to Charles Cuthbert, Conservation Officer of Hampshire County Council Recreation Department for material from its Report dated March 1982, *The Lymington-Keyhaven Coast – Policies for future management*, and two maps from the Nature Conservancy Report; Stanford Maritime Ltd. to quote from *Blue Water – Green Skipper* by Stuart Woods; Leo Cooper to quote from John Howlett's autobiography *The Guv'nor*, and especially to Miss Mary King for the research by her great-grandfather, Edward King, in *Old Times Revisited in the Parish and*

Borough of Lymington, and her father, Edward King in *A Walk through Lymington.*

I am grateful to Radio Solent for the transcript of an interview of Captain Hugh Wilson, RN, by Bill Lyon on 13th March 1982 for the programme *Open Waters*; and acknowledge and thank C. S. Curry, Editor of *The Lymington Times,* W. M. Hill, Editor of *Bournemouth Evening Echo,* J. D. Sleightholme, Editor of *Yachting Monthly* and Peter Cook, Editor of *Yachts and Yachting* for permission to use material from articles; and also thank Group Captain Howard Lewis, Secretary of the Royal Lymington Yacht Club for allowing me to use the Club library.

I must thank all those who have given me permission to reproduce photographs in this book: Denys Brook-Hart for *A View of Lymington River* by Alfred Vickers on the cover; Robert H. Wark, Curator of the Art Collection in the Henry E. Huntington Library and Art Gallery in San Marino, California, USA for the four drawings by Rowland-son; Peter Woolass for the photograph of Jack Laurent Giles and an appreciation of him by Jack Lowis in his book *Vertue* and for kindly presenting me with a copy; Tom Pocock for the portrait sketch of Captain Thomas Johnstone, David Cobb, the marine artist and Brian Manby and William Payne, marine photographers for examples of their work; and also to Marcus Associates for their *View of Lymington River.*

Finally, my warmest thanks to my mentor, James O'Donald Mays, the Burley author and publisher, for his help and encouragement.

June 1983

PREFACE

We came to Lymington in 1951 but I only returned to live here permanently in 1978. My mother was attracted to Lymington because the river and the heather in the New Forest reminded her a little of her beloved Scotland. In a letter written in 1807, after he had landed at Lymington in rough weather, Sir Walter Scott made the same comparison. "The Forest was looking absolutely beautiful and quite surpasses Scottish woods in depth and variety but was lacking in burns and glens."

Our house in King's Saltern Road was formerly called "Isle View" – and one can still just glimpse the Island past the Mayflower Hotel opposite. The house belonged to Mrs. Ellen Doe, a widow who died at the age of 83 and whose husband was drowned rowing a passenger to Yarmouth late at night who had missed the ferry. We changed the name to "Belhaven" because that is exactly what it became for us after all the travelling around we had done in the services.

The first time I saw the Solent was in 1929 when I came home from India in a trooper, the *Dorsetshire*, at the age of five, but I can only remember being met at Southampton by a car and chauffeur sent by my great-grandmother to take us to Eastbourne.

The next time was in 1945 and I was also on board a trooper, the *Athlone Castle*, returning from Colombo as a Leading Wren at the end of World War Two. She dropped anchor off Cowes and it was very dramatic and extremely moving hearing the rattle of the anchor chain, during the two minutes silence of the Armistice Day service at the Cenotaph, which was broadcast over the ship's loudspeakers. This was all the more poignant as we had so many ex prisoners-of-war from Burma and Malaya on board. It was a perfect sunny autumn day and I was conscious of the soft beauty of the Hampshire countryside and the feeling of peace. I never imagined that we would be living down here so soon afterwards. Incidentally, there was no chauffeur and car to meet me this time and I had to carry all my luggage off the boat – there was a dock strike!

In July 1978 when I returned to Lymington from Exeter, I was fortunate enough to get a job with the Royal Ocean Racing Club Rating office at No. 8 Station Street. By a happy coincidence Commander Erroll Bruce, whom I had worked for in 1960–61, when he was Southern Area Officer of the Sea Cadet Corps, was Chairman of the sub-committee responsible for the Rating Office.

He worked next door to us in the Nautical Publishing Company until the sad death of Richard Creagh-Osborne, another Director, was ultimately responsible for the firm being taken over by Macmillans. The farewell party in their office made me feel that another fleeting chapter in the marine history of Lymington had come to a close. This feeling increased daily every time I cycled the mile to work beside the river, past yacht clubs, boatyards, sailmakers, chandleries and marine engineering firms, all of them facing up to the current recession, until I felt compelled by a sense of urgency to tell their story now.

Jean Chitty

April 1983

"THE PAST WILL NOT SLEEP"

*The past will not sleep, it works still, with every new fact a ray of light shoots up from
the long buried years.*

RALPH WALDO EMERSON

'Caer Lym', or 'water city,' is the beautiful name
that the Celts gave to Lymington when they came
here from their refuge on the Isle of Wight in 200–300
B.C. They called the river 'Boldre' or full river, as in
those days it was deeper than it is now, and in addition
the strong double tides kept the water clear. The
Romans called the river 'Alainus' but it is the Celtic
name that remains – the 'Ing' and 'Ton,' the latter
meaning small settlement or town, being added in
Saxon times. The lovely motto of the Borough coat of
arms is so appropriately 'By Sea and Forest
Enchanted.'

War

But our history goes back even further than the
settlement of the Celts. Although no documentary
evidence exists, Arthur Lloyd, the New Milton his-
torian, is convinced that salt was being evaporated
from sea water all along the South Coast of
Hampshire from at least as far back as the Iron Age.
Heaps of wood ashes found in the marshes are said
to come from these ancient workings.

The Celts then built a small town on the first piece
of firm ground on the side of the river near where it
could be forded. To protect their salt workings they
raised earthworks two miles upstream at Buckland
Rings. In 1935 Hawkes excavated the fort, and the
great gateposts contained so little decayed wood that
he came to the conclusion they must have been constructed at about the time of Julius Caesar's two raids
(55 and 54 B.C.). Then in A.D. 43 during the reign of
Claudius (of TV fame), the Roman general Vespasian
set about the conquest of Britain and a Roman army
from the West of the Isle of Wight, almost certainly
from Yarmouth, invaded at Lymington. They
captured and destroyed the fort as, due to the marshy
ground, there were no defences at the river mouth.
This invasion was confirmed when in 1939
F. C. Bennett found a Roman coin, a Dupondius of
the Emperor Claudius dated 41–54 A.D., in a sand
pit close to the railway bridge near the earthworks.

Little is known of the Saxon occupation which
followed and Lymington is not mentioned again
until Norman times when the name 'Lentune'
appears in the Domesday Book.

The Abbey of Beaulieu, founded in 1204, used
Lymington as its port and market. The Abbot and
his vassals were bound to come from Sowley and
Norley to help the local countrymen in the defence
of Lymington. Even so, the town was sacked and
burnt three times by the French. In 1338 during the
Wars of the Roses there was a very heavy raid by
French, Sicilian, and Genoese pirates under
Grimaldi, and another in 1370 in the reign of
Richard II. The last time it was destroyed was in 1565,
when a vast French fleet under Francis I sailed into
the Solent. After the *Mary Rose* tragically capsized
and sank, the French entered Portsmouth harbour
and then continued westward raiding and burning
farms and even Lymington itself.

But it was not all one way. In 1345 in the early years
of the 100 Years War, Edward III assembled a vast
fleet for the invasion of France. This was called the
South Fleet and was drawn from 50 ports and maritime towns from the Thames along the South Coast
to Wales, and comprised 493 vessels and 9,030
mariners. Twenty-five ships and 576 mariners were
raised by Southampton and 9 ships and 194 mariners
from Lymington, compared with 5 ships and 96
mariners from Portsmouth.

When the Civil War broke out in 1642 loyalties in
Lymington, as in the rest of the country, were divided
between the two sides: the gentry remained pro-
Royalist but the townsfolk firmly supported the
Parliamentarians.

Towards the end of the war when Charles I was
imprisoned in Carisbrooke Castle, a fleet of 19 ships
and 2,000 men appeared in the Solent, under the
command of the Prince of Wales. While the royal
fleet was in Yarmouth Roads it was supplied with
provisions free of charge from the inhabitants of
Lymington "who were warmly disposed to the royal
cause and the mayor engaged to take an inferior
command in the Prince's army should it gain a
footing on the Island." (This would seem to belie the
previous statement that the townsfolk firmly
supported the Parliamentarians.)

In a bid to rescue the King, a landing was made at
Yarmouth which was defeated by the Parliamentarians and the fleet withdrew. Parliamentarian

sympathies or else shrewd thinking – the Royalists were always short of funds – are indicated by the fact that, possibly anticipating an invasion of the mainland, it was thought advisable for the town valuables to be sent to Hurst Castle for safekeeping until the moment of danger had passed. An entry in 1647 shows a charge of £0 2s. 0d. to bring the Towne Chest back to Lymington!

On 30th November 1648 King Charles was brought to Hurst Castle as a prisoner and remained in a dungeon there until 21st December. He was taken to London and executed a month later. I have been told that his ghost has been seen walking in shackles at Vicar's Hill!

In 1789 the French Revolution erupted and Lymington was to play a prominent part in its aftermath. There was an unsuccessful insurrection in La Vendee in 1792 by its inhabitants, who had remained loyal to the imprisoned Louis XVI and that same year France became a Republic. The King was executed a year later followed by the Reign of Terror which was to continue until the fall of the Jacobin Republic in 1794.

All along the South West coast royalists of both sexes, nearly all from the nobility, landed on our shores seeking refuge from the excesses of the French Revolution. These were followed by an even larger number of officers and civilians, who had also managed to escape from the massacres in France, and still more were brought back by Lord Howe, when he captured Toulons in the South in 1793. These emigrés had no means of support at all, but everywhere they were accorded sympathetic and friendly hospitality, particularly in Lymington.

On 1st June 1794, 'The Glorious First of June', Lord Howe defeated the French fleet and this was celebrated by much bell ringing in the town. The battle continued to be celebrated for many years afterwards by an old sailor, who had fought in the action, "by regularly getting most gloriously drunk. His favourite tale was how he and his comrades had fired the tailor's goose into their opposing vessel and how they found it, after the engagement, embedded in the stump of her mast!" The ship in which he served was most appropriately called the *Glory*.

The English government formed the emigrants into several corps, both in order to supply them with a living and to assist them in their war against France. The first corps, known as 'The Loyal Emigrants' soon saw active service in Flanders. They were billeted in Lymington, "their officers occupying lodgings at various tradesmen's houses where they were both liked and respected." Another corps, commanded by Count d'Hector (formerly Governor of Brest) and numbering 600 officers and sailors

from the French (Royalist) Navy were known as the 'Royal Marine' and their quarters were at Buckland. The Third Corps was known as the 'French Artillery' and they were formed principally from the gunners brought back by Lord Howe when he captured Toulons, together with those inhabitants who were able to escape. They occupied the present Malt House in New Lane, since then called Cannon Lane. The Acting Chief here was the Comte de Soulange, who lived here with his family. His daughter died in Lymington and his widow later got a pension from the government in 1809.

In 1795 a naval victory off L'Orient left the coast clear for an invasion of Brittany, and a fleet assembled off Lymington In Yarmouth Roads in June of that year, under the overall command of the Earl of Moira. (Rowlandson sketched some of his troops when he visited Southampton but fortunately for him he did not accompany the Expedition.) The French commander of the Lymington forces was the Comte de Puisaye, an emigré who lived in Plymouth but who stayed occasionally in Lymington.

The first attack failed, and a second attempt was made, which was disastrous and is vividly described in *Old Times Revisited*. The English fleet managed to save about 1300 but altogether 1200 men and 102 officers were either slaughtered or drowned. Many of the officers threw themselves in despair on their swords, and those who surrendered in good faith, were taken away to Vannes and shot there. All but one of the de Puisaye family perished at Quiberon and so did many others, who had once lived in our town. So Lymington was emptied of its foreign guests and with the rise of Napoleon no further invasion attempt was made.

In fact the very reverse could now be expected. In 1803, when invasion was imminent, "all the waggons at the neighbouring farms were registered and numbered, so as to carry off the non-combatant population into the Forest in case of the enemy landing."

The places of the emigrés were taken by "the debris of various armies and troops that had fought on the Continent" (mostly German and Dutch), and they were a rough and turbulent lot. The sailors from the gunboats and cutters in the Solent were the causes of frequent tumult and riots.

It is interesting to note that locally a pike corps was so hurriedly raised from our own volunteers, that there was no cannon available and instead a pump barrel (simulating a cannon) was used. So they became known as 'Pump Corps' (or Dad's Army of that day!). They were dissolved at the Peace of Paris in 1814. All the foreign troops left for their own countries only to fight for or against us at the Battle of Waterloo, following Napoleon's escape from Elba.

Smuggling

In the late eighteenth and early nineteenth century smuggling was rife, and was probably connived or winked at by most of the inhabitants. Indeed when Napoleon put a ban on English trading, smuggling was considered legitimate trade, and even the magistrates regarded smuggling with complacency. There is a tradition that the belfry tower of the Church of St. Thomas was used by poachers or smugglers. Cargoes landed at Lymington, Milford and Milton were often taken up the Boldre River to the New Ford.

Closely involved with them was a young fisher lad, called Tom Johnstone (1772–1839), whose colourful and exciting life can be read in a little book called *Smuggling Days*. It mentioned that from the age of 9 he used to watch the 'free traders' take their ponies and carts to Pennington Marsh Gate. There they loaded the brandy which the rest of the men had dragged across the mud in 'mud pattens,' or flat-bottomed boats to the firm land. He warned them if he saw the Preventive Officers approaching and they would hurriedly tread the kegs into the soft mud. He may not have been Lymington's first smuggler but he was most certainly its first naval architect, frogman and submariner (see Appendix 1)!

The *Hampshire Chronicle* of 6th February 1773 reported that "On Friday were brought to H.M. Warehouse in this port (Southampton) 285 casks of foreign brandy, rum, geneva, white wine and near 3 cwt of tea, all of which were lately seized at Lymington by Mr. Sparrow, Riding Surveyor of that place, assisted by some other officers and a party of the military quartered there."

That the smugglers were usually armed is shown by entries from the Burial Register in Lymington:

1781 Thomas Hanson, who died of his wounds received on board a smuggling lugger in an engagement with the *Rose* cutter. The *Rose* cutter is commemorated on a tablet inside the church and on a stone in the churchyard.
1798 Pierre Bougre, of the *Terror* gunboat, in the river.
1799 Charles Colborne, shot in the custom-house boat by smugglers.

During the latter part of the 18th Century and early 19th Century the work of the Preventive Service was hampered, as few men could be spared for this service from the armed forces fighting against the French. On the other hand the militia could be of tremendous help, not only in guarding the coast against the enemy, but assisting the local Preventive men in their work.

At sea the Revenue Service found it difficult to catch a fast lugger with their guard ships, usually of the frigate type. For customs and preventive purposes, Southampton was the Mother Port; Christchurch and Lymington being called 'Creeks.' Lymington was the only creek in Hampshire where "not only coal duties but all other coast duties were received and a coastal waiter was stationed there for that purpose. The duty of the coast waiter stationed at Lymington was to supervise the loading and discharging of coasting vessels at 'Bewley,' Keyhaven, Redbridge, Christchurch, Heath Leap and Hamble. An additional duty was that of Riding Officer, and with 4 others formed a guard from Southampton to Christchurch."

There was a guard cutter of 100 tons with a commander, and 30 men called the *Batt*. An entry for 1st October 1894 shows that the skipper of the boat at Lymington reported that smugglers were seized with their boat and the contraband was impounded in the King's Custom House on Poole Quay.

Although Pitt lowered the duties and reduced the number of goods liable to Excise it was not until after the Battle of Waterloo in 1815 that the large-scale free trading industry began to dwindle. There were then more men available to man the coast, and gradually coastguards replaced the Riding Officers and Revenue Cutters. The coastguard officers and their men were housed at strategic places on the coast; in Lymington at King's Saltern Road.

The coming of steam in place of sail and the establishment of long distance communications combined to make smuggling more difficult. One of the last smuggling runs to take place was at Christchurch in 1876 when tubs of brandy were brought by road from Lymington on Christmas Eve of that year. A Mr. Tom Clark said that he could not remember any Christmas when Christmas carols were sung so fervently!

Press Gangs

The best description of press gangs is to be found in Chambers Encyclopaedia: "Impressment was the method under which the deficiency of seamen in the navy after all other means of recruitment had been tried, was made good. The practice had not only the sanction of custom but the force of law. It may be traced back to legislation in the reign of Edward I and many Acts of Parliament from the reign of Mary Tudor to that of George III were passed to regulate the system of impressment. Under the laws, all eligible men of seafaring habits were liable between the ages of 18 and 55; but exceptions were made in favour of apprentices, who had not been 2 years apprenticed, fishermen at sea and a proportion of able seamen in each collier and many others. Mitigations of these harsh laws were frequently introduced, and as early as 1563 the naval authorities had to secure the sanction of the local justices of the peace to operate a press gang. The law on pressing was in fact never repealed but the practice died out when continuous service was introduced into the navy in 1853."

There are three references to press gangs in Lymington. From the burial register is recorded in 1781 the death of Hugh Baggs, a sailor belonging to the press gang from H.M. Storeship *The Robinson* commanded by Lieutenant Nath. Phillips. The second is a plaque on Press Gang Cottage in Bath Road, formerly the Harlequin Inn, stating that it was their headquarters about 1800. Finally, in 1803 there is a Press Gang Warrant addressed to the Mayor (who was probably a justice of the peace) which proves that the town did not escape the attentions of the Admiralty in this respect. The press gangs were particularly active throughout the Napoleonic Wars, and it may well be that men pressed into service with the navy under this warrant fought under Nelson at the Battle of Trafalgar on 21st October 1805.

French Privateer

A narrow escape from capture by the French is excitingly narrated by Edward King in *Old Times Revisited*. Yachting had started to become popular and in 1806 a Mr. Fullerton of Lymington was sailing in his yacht *Zephyr* with Mr. Weld of Lulworth, and two other friends outside the Needles when, "to their consternation they espied a French privateer bearing down upon them. This was an awkward position, indeed, for at that time we were at war with France, and to be taken prisoner by the French conveyed anything but pleasant thoughts to the minds of the occupants of the gallant little yacht: with all speed therefore they sailed away, and were fortunate in reaching Hurst Castle, and thus escaping the threatened danger." One of those on board was John Bird Sumner, a future Archbishop of Canterbury and his brother, Charles Richard Sumner was to become a Bishop of Winchester! An example of the church not so militant?

PEACE

Salt

Salt has, from earliest times, been a staple manufacture at Lymington. It was her chief asset and the source of her prosperity. Salt was used not only for culinary purposes but also for the tanning industry, preserving fish and meat and later even as a cure. Salt and salterns forming a conspicuous feature along the coast from Pylewell to Hurst, recognised by the winding, riverlike indentations or short canals used for removing salt, and bringing in stone, bricks and later, coal to and from the works.

By courtesy of Henry E. Huntington Library

Inside a Saltern at Lymington, with the manner of making salt – Rowlandson

The salt houses were of all sizes and had from one boiling pan to twenty-eight pans at work. The earliest record is a Grant of Tithe of all the Lymington salt by Richard de Redvers to the Abbey of Quarr near Tyde in A.D. 1147. Edward King, in *Old Times Revisited*, wrote that in 1743 there were in Lymington 4 pans at Pylewell, 5 pans near the Elms, 22 pans at King's Saltern (where the Lymington baths are now), 12 pans opposite the Town Quay, 3 pans at Vienna Saltern (Lymington Bridge), 4 pans at the Saltern (Inman's shipyard), 1 pan adjoining it and 3 pans (formerly the Coastguard Station), 2 pans at Little Oxey and 20 at Stone and Rowe salterns, Woodside. There were 163 pans in use in the whole Lymington area and this was the time of her greatest prosperity.

In 1694 the government of William III imposed a Salt Tax and although this was repealed by Walpole in 1730 it had already started to have an adverse effect. However, the main reason for the total decline of the salt industry in Lymington was the advent of the railway.

Mined salt in Cheshire was infinitely quicker and cheaper to produce than evaporated salt, where 16 weeks boiling was the general seasonal average, and each pan only made about 3 tons of salt per week. As the railway network spread and roads improved, it was now possible for Cheshire rock salt to be sold anywhere in the country, and in particular to the port of Liverpool. Evaporated salt could not compete financially, and in addition Liverpool had taken over the Newfoundland market from Lymington. To add insult to injury, Cheshire salt was actually brought in cargo ships from Liverpool to Lymington (the Hampshire equivalent of carrying coals to Newcastle). This was the death knell of the salterns and the last salt house was closed in 1835.

Maritime Trade

The maritime trade of Lymington developed in the 14th century as a result of the export of salt – a figure as much as 4,000 quarters of salt has been given. She imported at one time 3,000 fish caught off the deep sea fisheries of Northern Ireland and 1,880 tuns of wine from the Continent. She also imported cloth, canvas, iron and figs from there as well as wool from the Isle of Wight for Somerset clothiers.

In 1507 Lymington, with its weavers, tanners and merchants, was at that time a self-contained commercial town. In 1661 there is an entry of 3 rolls of tobacco and syrup of lemons. From the end of the century her main import was now coal from the Tyne which she needed for her salt industry.

The earliest references to Lymington expanding her trade to the New World are contained in the Petty Customs book of the early 18th century. The Salterns were then exporting salt to North America, Newfoundland, Holland and the Channel Islands and West Country cloth. Timber was shipped to Portsmouth for the Navy and vessels of 50–60 tons used to carry bricks from Walhampton brickyard.

In 1723 Lymington ships were carrying salt and other commodities regularly to Newfoundland and returning with cargoes of oil, seal skins, beaver skins, fox skins and otter skins. Occasionally they called at the West Indies and Barbados, and in 1730 were exporting large quantities of salt to the American colonies. This latter was to be curtailed by the War of Independence. Ships also sailed to Ireland with purging salts, oak bark and oak timber, bricks, tiles and strong beer. Was this latter commodity responsible for the curative salts!

Incidentally, as early as 1606 there was a Town Beer Brewer, who was a very important personage. He had to serve seven years apprenticeship before the burgesses granted him the sole right to brew beer and ale. An ale-taster was regularly appointed each year, "usually some respectable old burgess qualified by long experience for this important duty"!

Occasionally ships from Lymington sailed to the North Coast of France with bricks, tiles, wheat and salt. Scandinavian ships, principally from Norway, brought large quantities of timber, partly for the ship-building yard at Bucklers Hard.

By the middle of the 18th Century, although Lymington continued to trade with Newfoundland, part of the trade was taken over by Poole and London. Later Liverpool, with the Cheshire salt, was to capture what was left of that market. Lymington as a commercial port no longer existed.

However, a new chapter in the maritime history of Lymington was to start. In 1819 a man moved with his family from Hastings to Lymington, who would be responsible for altering the whole character of the river and who would once again bring prosperity and international recognition to the town. His name was Thomas Inman.

Maritime Law

In 1199 King John had granted a Charter to Southampton, enabling them to collect all royal dues, customs and port revenue in its vicinity in return for a payment of £200. Lymington was not specifically mentioned, and Southampton claimed the entire coast from Hurst to Langstone; this was to cause friction between the two ports for many centuries to follow. In 1324 Lymington refused to pay customs on salt, fruit, barley and oats, but a jury found against them. This law suit was only one of many disputes recorded in the Southampton Borough archives.

The first Admiralty Court sat in 1361 and its authority was increased by the Charter of 1447 which made the Mayor of Southampton the Admiral of the whole area until 1835, when the Admiralty jurisdiction was abolished by Act of Parliament.

The courts administered three kinds of maritime law: Common law, Roman law and Statute law. Common law included harbour dues, regulation of fishing, obstructions to navigation, and even control of swans. The Admiral was also entitled to seize and sell to his own use all flotsam, jetsam and pirate goods. Roman law was accepted by all Christian countries for settling international disputes. Statute law started in 1536, when Commissioners were appointed to try traitors, pirates, thieves and murder upon the sea. Courts were also held for profit from wrecks.

As Admiral, the Mayor of Southampton held Courts at 5 meeting places: Southampton, Lepe, Lymington, Keyhaven and Hamble. Apart from Southampton they were usually held on the Quay (as in Lymington) and even on the sea shore. Once when a court was held on the shore at Keyhaven, there was such violent opposition to it that the Town Clerk only just prevented the Elizabethan Admiralty Court book from being thrown into the river!

A month before a Court was held, the Water Bailiff summoned all fishermen and sailors in the area to attend the Court and jurors were elected from them. Questions were asked and the answers recorded. They fell into four main groups: wrecks, navigational obstructions, trade offences and regulations of fishermen.

Wrecks included entries in 1573 of French boats abandoned by English pirates and in 1566 a boat with 5 men overturned in the harbour and 2 drowned but sadly there were no goods except "a jerkin and a pair of sops."

Navigational obstructions were usually ballast being thrown overboard, which caused a lot of trouble, and "poles for nets were restricted."

Three interesting examples of trade offences are the illegal export of leather and horses in 1579; "engrossing and forestalling salt" with fines of 6/8d., 13/4d., 20s. and even pillory and banishment. In 1675 mention is made of one Charles Gudott, gent., who was accused of "keeping boats to take over poor men's employment."

Under the regulation of fishermen in 1569 were complaints of over-fishing oysters and using nets with too small a mesh (still a major international problem today). In 1571 2 porpoises taken for the Mayor were seized by the Earl of Arundel and in 1648 there was a further complaint that "eel pots were pulled down unseasonably."

In 1707 an Admiralty Court at Lymington was held in a booth set up on the Quay to consider outstanding disputes, and others followed in 1714 and 1727. On these occasions there was always plenty of ceremonial. A silver oar, symbol of Southampton's dominance, was carried upright through the town. This was followed by a salvo which asserted the rights of Lymington.

In 1730 Lymington petitioned to be made a member of the port of Southampton and, as a result, a Branch Customs House was set up in Lymington. This saved the great inconvenience to cargo ships of having first to pay duties in Southampton. In the same year Lymington also petitioned to be made a separate port but nothing came of it.

In 1793 the circuit was suspended and Southampton did not visit Lymington again until 1947 to celebrate the 500th Anniversary of the granting of the Admiralty Charter of 1447.

Poor Law

From earlist times the monasteries had always protected and helped the poor and at their dissolution by Henry VIII this relief came to an end, and bands of beggars began to terrorise the countryside. This forced the government of Queen Elizabeth I to introduce the Poor Law, when it became the duty of every parish to provide, through the rates, for the poor in its boundaries. The parish officers could also send back to his place of birth a man and his family who were chargeable to the rates. The relief of the poor was the responsibility of the Church Wardens and later new officers called the 'Overseers of the Poor' were elected to help them. Entries were made in the Poor Book.

Our first maritime entry was in 1780, when an order was made that if James Alexander did not contribute to the maintenance of his child, the parish would endeavour to get him on board a man of war. It cost them 19/- to ship a prisoner over to the Island, accompanied by the local barber, who acted as a constable. Poor sailors, including an American, were usualy given a shilling, but some suffering from smallpox were put in a carriage and driven to Ringwood, at a cost of 3/- for horse hire and probably an extremely uncomfortable journey. Incidentally, in 1617 any seaman taking on freight on the Sabbath day had to pay a fine to the Mayor, which would be distributed to the poor.

Dam

A disastrous happening occurred affecting the river in 1731, whose repercussions and the problems it created continue to this very day. Captain William Cross, a merchant captain of Boldre parish, erected a dam or bank 500 feet in length, 30 feet in breadth and 20 feet in depth. He had acquired an interest in a grant made by Charles I to Robert Pamlyn and his two daughters "in consideration of a great debt and faithful service done" of all the mudlands on the coast of Hampshire. On the strength of that title he dug the common and built the bridge.

The Corporation, realising the effect this would have on a tidal river, and the accumulation of mud, consulted Counsel and brought an action against Captain Cross for trespass, which they lost. He died in 1737 and that year his widow was accused of repairing the dam and levying a toll on all who passed over it, through William Lyne, a tailor. The Corporation went to law again, this time on the grounds that the dam was a "common nuisance" and their acts were "to the evil example of others and against the Peace of the Realm." The case was heard at Winchester Assizes on 11th July 1778, and a second hearing took place in 1739. Unfortunately the defendants were acquitted and the dam has remained to this day.

In 1832 there was an imaginative plan to replace the dam with a suspension bridge, but unfortunately nothing came of it, probably due to lack of funds.

The last word on the tollbridge rests with Canon John Hayter who wrote an article in *The New Forest Magazine,* December 1963 issue, about it:

"The toll bridge is a thorn in the flesh – and a drain on the pockets – of most Walhamptonians and many others living on the eastern edge of the parish and beyond. Taking the long view, in seven years, which may be more, there is to be an end to this inequitable tax. But seven years is a long time and a very large number of sixpences will have been handed over before those years are done – £105's worth at no more than one return trip a day.

"On the short view, the users are not so well off under the new regime. Gone is the cheerful wave of the British Railways collector who waved his regulars on for, say, one journey in four. Now under the new owners, the Hampshire County Council, there are no concessions – no free trips – no cries of "back in a few minutes" . . . It has been estimated that some £80,000 must be collected in tolls before the bridge is freed, of which the local users of Walhampton, South Baddesley, Portmore, Norleywood, etc. will have paid between £15,000 and £20,000. This is quite clearly a most unfair proportion. There is no other way of lightening it except by the introduction of season tickets." No season tickets were introduced but thankfully the tollbridge ceased to exist in 1970.

By courtesy of Henry E. Huntington Library

Lymington Quay with the method of shipping cattle to the Isle of Wight – Rowlandson

By courtesy of Henry E. Huntington Library

Lymington River near the Quay. Going on board the vessel to carry us to the Isle of Wight – Rowlandson

Harbour Dues

In the first half of the 19th Century the activities of the Corporation were very limited, due to lack of funds. Its main sources of income were from the ancient right to levy tolls on visiting fairs and markets held in the Borough and the collection of harbour dues from vessels using the river and quay.

In April 1816, there is an entry showing that the Town Quay itself was actually let to John West for 7 years, at an annual rent of £32, but this was later reduced to £21. There was also a long list of charges that vessels, anchoring in the river down to Jack in the Basket, had to pay as harbour duty, according to size of vessel up to a maximum of 3/-.

The Mayor also claimed the right to 1 cwt. of coal from every coaling vessel discharging in the port. This caused some controversry and in 1868 it was changed to one bushel from each ship unloading. This was normally collected by the Town Sergeant and used for heating the Town Hall! He could also claim sixpennyworth of fish from every fishing vessel unloading in the port but it is not known how long ago these rights ceased to be exercised!

Pollution

Our forefathers also suffered from problems of pollution, but much worse than they are today. Cattle used to be slaughtered in the High Street, and the garbage was washed down by showers and rolled in a torrent into the river. When Dean Swift visited Lymington, it made such an impression on him that he described it all in the following humorous verse:

"Now from all parts the swelling kennels flow,
And bear their trophies with them as they go.
Sweepings from butchers' stalls, dung, guts and blood,
Drown'd puppies, stinking sprats all drenched in blood,
Dead cats and turnip-tops come tumbling down
    the flood."

In 1830 an attempt was made to drain the lower end of the town, and a small sewer was put in, which drained Captain's Row (then South Street) and the parts adjacent to the quay. Owing to non-ventilation, this proved injurious to health and cases of typhoid arose from time to time. In 1928 this drain was traced by the surveyor, in a search to see what caused the water to collect in the cellars of adjoining houses.

Sewer

About the turn of the century, when public health services began to show results, the Lymington Local Board had undertaken a disposal scheme which enabled sewage to be discharged into the sea at Pennington Marshes and apart from expected complaints by a few local residents it worked quite well.

However, during a storm in 1893 a small vessel called *The Daring* fell foul of the seaward end of the sewer and became a total loss. Her owners sued, claiming that the sewer had been negligently constructed so as to be a hazard to shipping. The Council, who were now responsible for it, then appealed to the High Court, and lost, even though it transpired that the sewer had in fact been built in a different position to the plans. It had to pay damages and costs totalling £750 to the ship owners. Finally the Council decided to shorten the sewer by some 600 ft. to prevent further accidents.

Railway

In 1858 the railway reached Lymington and passengers for Yarmouth had to embark from a pier on the west side of the river. Later in the 1870s, the Council proposed to extend the railway to the mouth of the river and to build docks there. An appeal for assistance from the Home Office was unsuccessful and the plan was shelved until 1875, when a further approach was made to the Treasury. This fared no better. A local resident, Captain Wilson, was the chief protagonist of this scheme but the cost factor was too much and nothing further was heard of it.

However, in 1880 the Railway Company complained of obstruction due to silt and mud, which often prevented the ferry from reaching the pier, and the Council agreed to the extension of the railway across the river in 1882. But it claimed damages for loss of dues because of the upper part of the river being cut off by the railway bridge and their claim was eventually settled at 250 guineas plus 25 guineas costs.

Once the new ferry station was established the Council then claimed the right to charge the Railway Company river dues on all steamers using it. After many years of dispute the Company eventually paid the Council £25 towards the upkeep of the river and the question of river dues has remained undetermined.

Spa

One usually associates the word "spa" with Bath, but it is interesting to note that one of its protagonists was Dr. Thomas Guidott, who was in fact born in Lymington in September 1638. He edited the 3rd edition of Dr. Edward Jordan's *Discourse of Natural Baths and Mineral Waters,* to which he added an Appendix and wrote many treatises such as *A Brief Account of the Nature and Virtues of the Hot Waters there* and later published a tract on *Reflections on Fresh Cold Bathing, Bathing in Sea Water and Dipping in Baptism,* which perhaps was influenced by Lymington. It was only in the late 18th Century that Lymington started to become known as a pleasant

Lymington, April 1856

By courtesy of E. M. Knight

Lymington River, 1893

9

By courtesy of Henry E. Huntington Library

Mrs. Beeston's Bath at Lymington – Rowlandson

watering place. In Southampton a spa also developed, which was visited in 1750 by Frederick, Prince of Wales, who found the waters "most salubrious and invigorating." He set a fashion for the nobility and local gentry to follow.

Skelton's Guide of 1777 described Lymington as a small but maritime town, an appendange of the port of Southampton and in 1810 it stated: "the library furnished a tolerable invitation to reading in a place which boasts few amusements which can engage the gay or relieve the languor of the old." The popularity of Southampton as a spa waned by 1820 when the Royal Family found Brighton more entertaining.

However, in Lymington new Baths were opened in 1830, and its position, with lovely views of the Island, and its fresher air enabled it to continue longer as a spa. To maintain its image as a watering place, a public company was formed on 10th March 1833 called the 'Lymington Bath and Improvement Company' which built more commodious baths, enclosed a considerable tract of mudland and improved the approaches to the bathing establishment. It provided hot, cold or vapour bathing for both ladies and gentlemen in strictly separate wings. Upstairs there was a large circular room for social gatherings, on the west side were large swimming baths and the grounds outside were used for archery and other sports.

Unfortunately, a few years later Lymington's popularity as a spa declined too and the Company got into financial difficulties. The building is now the Lymington Town Sailing Club and the swimming baths are still being used today.

Yachting

The sheltered situation of the river and its close proximity to Cowes, the headquarters of the yachting world, caused our town "to be much frequented by those gentlemen who are attached to that fashionable amusement!" The reputation of the town was further enhanced by having Mr. Inman, a "shipwright of the first rank" whose yachts had "borne away the palm in all the yachting clubs of England." Yachting and Lymington from now on were to be synonymous. There would be plenty to occupy both gay youth and languorous old age in the century that followed!

By courtesy of E. M. Knight

Bath House, Lymington

CHAPTER 2

WILLIAM ALLINGHAM (1824 – 1889)

"Fortune not choice fixed my abode at Lymington."

W. ALLINGHAM

One of the most interesting characters to live in Lymington was William Allingham, who started his famous diary when he was posted here as a Customs and Excise Officer on the 8th May 1863. "Fortune not choice fixed my abode at Lymington," he wrote and he never really settled down here but was always hankering after London, his literary Mecca. His diary gives us considerable insight into life in Lymington in the latter half of the nineteenth century and is worth studying in some detail for that reason alone. I am most indebted to Centaur Press Ltd. for permission to quote from it.

Allingham was born in Ballyshannon in County Donegal, Ireland in 1824, the son of a small merchant there. He felt isolated from his parents (his invalid mother died when he was nine and was succeeded by a stepmother, and his father was short-tempered) and also from his siblings, and so he escaped at an early age into dreams and writing.

He became a bank clerk and, at the age of 22, after seven long, tedious years, he managed to change his occupation to that of Customs and Excise. He was sent to Belfast for training in the duties of Principal Coast Officer of Customs, with a salary of £80 a year. He trudged daily along the docks learning to measure logs, piles of planks, "bread stuffs" (chiefly maize) and ships for tonnage. Perhaps the most interesting side of his new job was examining the fittings and provisions of emigrant ships, and calling over the passenger lists when they were ready for sea. There were also visits to coastguard stations, navy and other pensioners and occasionally to wrecks. Indoors he would do book-keeping, receive notice of the arrival of a vessel and sign her papers if outward bound, make out a lighthouse bill for each light-house passed on the way and engage and pay off seamen.

Allingham had a great love of nature and was a keen observer of all its forms and recorded his impressions in a note book. He obviously had an artist's eye as later Rossetti said to him: "You ought to have been a landscape painter: you notice everything." "Sometimes to the length of boredom, perhaps he meant," wrote Allingham.

Although delicate as a child, he had tremendous physical energy and was a rider, skater, swimmer and a great walker. He was particularly fond of children and always showed them great kindness as well as participating in their games.

He still managed to read incessantly – often at his work – and would discuss poetry and literature with his fellow clerks at every opportunity. He longed to meet all the poets whose works he had read and with whom he had corresponded and later met such eminent Victorians as Carlyle, Browning, Leigh Hunt, Rossetti, Coventry Patmore and, above all, Tennyson. He wrote a poem, *The Fairies,* when he was 25 and published a book of poems the following year in 1850.

Unsuccessful in his attempts to settle in London he transferred to Lymington. "I was Lymington's Custom-House Officer, the only one," he wrote in his diary, "my office being a small first-floor room over the Coastguard Station, looking upon the little harbour (muddy at low water, occupied by pleasure yachts) and the woods of Walhampton beyond. A little higher up a Ferry-Boat rowed by a big man in a jersey, a Blue Giant, kept crossing to and fro, and higher still a toll-bridge to which the Boldre Water or Lymington River ran down its green valley, a quiet rural stream, from the oaks, beeches and brackens of the New Forest."

His first lodgings were in Prospect Place, but he later moved to Wellington Place, where he wrote on the chimney piece of his bedroom:

I hope that in this house I may
No evil do, no evil say."

but whether it is still there, I do not know.

"Depressed though I was," he continued, "I felt a great deliciousness in the quiet green lanes and hedges, thickets, woods and distances; and the evening after my arrival, standing at the field gate close to the Town, I heard four nightingales." A month later he was still depressed by his move and wrote on 28th June 1863: "In the evening walked sadly along the shore of the Solent eastwards by Pylewell – returning brought home a glow-worm and put it in a white lily through which it shone."

As Carlyle had told him, when trying to cheer him up about coming to Lymington, he would be close to Tennyson, living 5 miles away on the Isle of Wight, and Allingham took every opportunity of seeing him. This was sometimes in Lymington as "From Customs-House window see Tennyson on board the steamer as she passes and hurry to the station," or on the Isle of Wight: "Ned and I crossed to the Island and visited Tennyson, who received us very friendlily and took us up to his den." On 14th July 1866 he returned to his lodgings to find a telegram had arrived and was frightened that it was about his father but it turned out to be very pleasant. "Crown Hotel Lyndhurst. A. Tennyson to W. Allingham. Will you come to us here?" "Dine hastily and rush to train!"

When over at Farringford on 3rd April 1867 on one of his many visits there he describes how: "Tennyson and I buried ourselves in the shrubberies, transplanting primroses with spade, knife and wheel-barrow. After dinner T. concocts an experimental punch with whiskey and claret – not successful! Talks of publishers; anon of higher things . . . T. is the most delightful man in the world to converse with even when he disagrees. . . ." He did not stay the night with them this time but went "To my inn, where I wrote in the dark, bitten, and improvised –

Who in a country Inn lies ill at ease
On fozy feathers fill'd with furious fleas."
Pace, the Isle of Wight pubs!

In return for his hospitality he obviously did what he could to help them and looked for a house near Lymington for the father and sister (Mrs. Weld) of Mrs. Tennyson and found Aubrey House for them.

He has left a vivid description of a fair in Lymington on the 12th and 13th May 1863. "Booths in the streets with toys and sweets, noise and clatter. Shows – some monkeys and a wild boar, a 'Zulu Caffir'; fat woman (leaving her baby behind the scenes) does conjuring tricks – Dancing-booth – shooting galleries. Gypsies – black-eyed girls in tawdry bright attire, brown old witches, gypsy young man lithe and tall, wonderfully handsome animal, a black panther – and about as trustworthy? How oriental these people keep! The English rustic, getting drunk, bellows discordant, tumbles down and snores, the Irishman quarrels and strikes. Perhaps the kind of drink has something to do with it. Pothouse beer is bad, but raw public house whisky is a frightful potation . . ." Then three months later there is mention of another circus in the cricket field with a boxing content.

An entry in his diary for 5th October 1865 shows his feeling for beauty. "Walked up and down Lymington High Street and examined the forms of the separate houses, some seventeenth – most eighteenth century? One may live long in a town and never do this. Old bricken chimneys are often

beautiful – new, in the same class of buildings, never." A Founder Member of the Lymington Society perhaps!

He gives us a watercolour sketch of Lymington when crossing to the Island. "Lymington – Fine and vernal. Ferry to steamer – delightful colours of earth, sky and sea, a bloom upon the landscape. From the Solent see the woody background of Lymington recede, the Island approach with a welcome; a boat with red sails passes in the sunshine."

He was a great traveller, and it is perhaps surprising, in this age of the motor car, just how much he got around without one and how much free time he seemed to have from his work. Perhaps most of all he enjoyed taking the ferry to Yarmouth and visiting Tennyson but he did many other trips as well. On 31st August 1865 he took the "steamer *Solent* to Portsmouth to see the French Fleet now at Spithead, *Solferino* and other iron-clads; black brutal hulks. We carry a tricolour and cheer the French ships in passing." A fortnight later he was to visit Gosport and see more of the French 'invasion' and on to Portsmouth Hard with French and English sailors drunk together, some arm-in-arm, mutually friendly and unintelligible."

On September 14th he took another excursion, this time to Swanage, and had quite an adventure on the return journey. "Passengers got out at Bournemouth and Yarmouth; then we ran for Lymington by starlight, missed the channel and stuck in the mud. We had to land by boat, some of the women frightened; one, a smooth fair woman 'going to Leicester tomorrow,' threw her arms around me which was some compensation. The oars sparked as they dipped. Landed at the Bath, with wet feet; to Custom-House and home to dinner."

Despite all these excursions and the beauty of his surroundings, he still seemed unreconciled to both his work and living at Lymington. On 23rd October 1863 he wrote: "I go on studying old Ballads. Customs-House daily. Yachts, steamers, pensioners, accounts, Coastguard. Periodical visits to Pitts Deep, Bucklers Hard, Keyhaven and Hurst Castle, walking or riding; boat and punt – sailing etc. Measuring vessels is the most troublesome duty" (*pace* the Royal Ocean Racing Club Rating Office!), "boarding yachts and examining their stores the most disagreeable." He continued in the same vein on Wednesday, 30th December: "Walked to Pitts Deep and visited the Coastguard Station; returned at dusk, dirty road, starry sky. Be content: what folly in a poor man to wish for an easy life and at the same time for much that he could only get by hard work."

This was followed by a revealing description of the Civil Service which could have been written today. "I have been an 'Official' all my life, without the least turn for it. I never could attain a true official manner, which is highly artificial and handles trifles with ludicrously disproportionate gravity. True that ordinary men are thus kept in order and the dull work of the world got through; but for my own part, I always get back to the question, is it really necessary that men should consume so much of their bodily and mental energies in the machinery of civilised life? . . . In the Government offices of which I know something by experience, I believe the clerks could do all they really do in half the allotted time, and, moreover, that much of their work when done is itself useless."

On 12th October 1868 we read: "Dissatisfied: life slips by – to what purpose? Lindley on plants. Walk to Keyhaven Marsh." Apart from his entries in his diary he must have also confided his discontent to a sympathetic listener in a Miss Dickson. On Tuesday, 21st January 1868: ". . . Walk to Lyndhurst, vernal, call at Miss Dickson's, poorly; friendly chat. She says 'I thought you surly at first, – like you now, – thrown away at Lymington.' Hurry to Brockenhurst, hot, catch train. Dine 7 – rain – sleep better." A year later Tuesday, 3rd August 1869: "Internal gloom. To Lyndhurst (invited) Whitehorn meets me with Miss Dickson's carriage: Bird's Nest, Miss D. and Mrs. Aide. I walk off over moor, Matley wood – nothing good! Begin to feel better. Mem. 'Songs of despair, O Poet, only songs of despair.' Return by road. Dinner at 8.0. Miss Dickson and I talk gloom, Lymington, etc. She speaks wisely and kindly as usual, but agrees that Lymington is no abiding place."

On his return from a visit to the Isle of Wight, on 29th July 1865, he was extremely critical about yacht owners. "The privileges granted to pleasure yachts appear to me utterly absurd and unjust. They pay no lighthouse dues, no Port or Harbour Dues, no fees on engaging or discharging men, all of which must be paid by every merchant vessel. They are allowed to have their 'stores' of dutiable goods, wine, tobacco, etc., free of duty. So are merchants vessels, but on oversea voyages only, and in restricted measure. Why should the rich owners of Pleasure Yachts be thus favoured. The only reason I have heard given is that yachting is a 'nursery for the navy.' Is it?

"There are at least 7000 men and boys, all picked, engaged in Yachts. From all I have observed and heard here on the Solent, the most Yachtish piece of water in the world, nobody that can possibly help it ever goes from the idler and better paid Yachting into either the Navy or the Merchant Service. The gentlemen in livery who abound Rotten Row and elsewhere might almost as well be supposed a nursery for the Army as yachting a nursery for the Navy."

On 27th September 1865, he was present at the death-bed of old Mr. Rice – perhaps one of the pensioners he used to visit and pay. He described him as: "A quiet, silent man (employed in Portsmouth Harbour in youth – afterwards Rope Spinner by trade), who has gone steadily and I believe honestly along his humble track in life. He is over three score and ten, his old wife is gone before him, his family are grown up (three of his sons are Masters of yachts, one keeps a tavern." Edward King, in his book *A Walk through Lymington,* does mention a Mr. H. Rice as landlord of the Crown & Anchor in Captains Row, originally No. 1 then No. 2 in the year 1861.

November 4th 1865: "Measured yacht *Stella* by girting. Then rowed round by ferry and bridge in the sunshine and felt as if it was shining out of old times. I seldom care to row in this shallow, muddy river." But it wasn't all work on the yachts and he was entertained on board as well. An entry for 22nd January 1868 reads: "Sir Percy Shelley runs after me, and takes me aboard his yacht *Enchantress,* pleasant chat with Lady Shelley: 'Come to us tomorrow evening, if we're not gone.' But *Enchantress* had left and I walked instead to Pennington on a fine, frostyish day. August 30th 1867: Yacht *Mirella.* Faraday is gone."

Allingham was obviously an outgoing personality, as well as a cultured and interesting companion, as is illustrated in this note of a crossing to Yarmouth when a servant girl said to him: "I took your advice, sir, not to go to London.' Had forgotten it but it was good advice – wonder whether my habit of talking with everybody ever does real good. Perhaps."

On 31st October 1865: "Rev. William Barnes comes to me by invitation. I go up from the Custom House and find him sitting by my fire in Prospect Place. We dine at 6.30; to the Literary Institution where B. lectures on 'House and House Life' – caves, huts, tents, etc., wives (laughter). Praise of the Good Wife. Odd lecture – rather puzzled everybody."

He was visited by the Jones family, Ned and Madam and Pip and Baby, who stayed at Stanwell House for three weeks from 15th August 1866. So it was used as a hotel or lodging house as long ago as then.

September 5th: "Joneses packing up – They would like, they say, to some again to the same lodging . . ."

He even attended a seance on 16th May 1869: "Lymington. Mrs. S's – table turning. Mrs. S. attacks my want of faith – we know, etc. 'celebration' etc. (What can one say in such a case? and silence offends). We try a table; and it does tilt and knock and spells out a message to myself, 'You will be much loved!' After which it runs about, we dodging it up and down. What tiresome nonsense!" August 11th 1868: "Charles Darwin expected but comes not. Has been himself called 'Missing Link'."

Dante Gabriel Rossetti stayed from 11th to 20th September 1867 with Allingham in his lodgings. "My landlandy grumpy – 'Didn't tell me of a gentleman'." Rossetti would never do anything he didn't like, as can be seen from the following entry in the Diary. "September 17th – I try to get Rover to the Island and coax him as far as the pier, but it is rather windy, and he entirely objects to be sea-sick, and doesn't want to see either Mrs. Cameron" (the famous photographer) "or Tennyson. He takes no interest whatever in the sea, ships, boats, etc. . . . ."

Allingham had a rather dangerous experience when out riding to Hurst. "Returning I rode by the edge of the sea, till in one place the horse suddenly sank to his belly in the muddy sand. I had a real fright for half a minute and then we scrambled out, I don't know how. At Keyhaven I got the horse well wisped."

The next extracts from his Diary illustrate how easily Allingham would converse with everyone he met and at an erudite level too in the country. "20th February 1868 – Walk Efford, poor little moles executed, hanging on twigs. Talk with gamekeeper, who is considerably like Carlyle in person: grouse – pheasants. I try to explain something of Darwin's researches. Keeper's dog had to be trained to fly at a man, so as to be ready for poachers. 'I likes a good savage dog'," and the next his sense of outrage by a member of the local aristocracy. "April 23rd walk to Sowley Pond. Lord Henry Scott, after trying illegally to close the path (charming shady short-cut from the dusty road) and failing has now cut down the trees and grubbed up all the hazels and hollies, and left it a path through a bare field. The magistrates decided against his claim to shut the path, the judges at Winchester decided against it, and now, instead of humbly apologising, his Lordship does this!"

On Friday July 30th 1869 he was commissioned by Longman to write verses to a set of fairy drawings by Doyle, which he agreed to do somewhat reluctantly, and it was not a success. However they were later to offer him the post of sub-editor of *Fraser's Magazine,* and with it the chance to live in his beloved London, in the literary milieu that he so admired and enjoyed. In April 1870 he gave up the customs in Lymington and went to live there. Four years later he became Editor and on 22nd August 1874, at the age of 50 he was married to Helen Patterson and had three children. He died in 1889 and his ashes were returned rather surprisingly to Ireland for burial in the churchyard at Ballyshannon.

"No funeral gloom, my dears, when I am gone,
Corpse-gazings, tears, black raiment, grave-yard
*   grimness;*
Think of me as withdrawn into the dimness,
Yours still, you mine, remember all the best
Of our past moments, and I forget the rest;
And so to where I wait, come gently on."

WAR

Here lie we, because we did not choose
To live, and shame the land from which we sprang.
Life to be sure is not too much to lose
But young men think it is, and we were young.

A. E. HOUSMAN

In tracing the history of Lymington at war, I have followed the river up past Brockenhurst, where it changes its name to 'Highland Water' right up to its source at Ocknell Enclosure near Stoney Cross. In this way I can include the contributions made to the war effort by the Forest, vital and complementary to that of the lower reaches of the Lymington River and the banks and marshes of its estuary. In both wars the Forest was occupied by the military; mainly as an important staging post for troop movements to France.

I am indebted to Pioneer Publications for permission to use material from *Verderers of the New Forest* by Anthony Pasmore for information on World War One.

WORLD WAR ONE

The Forest was also used extensively for training and in 1915 the Agisters were asked to assist by marking on military maps the sites of dangerous bogs to be avoided during manoeuvres. They also outlined the bogs with red flags supplied by the army. But if bogs were a hazard other natural resources of the Forest were put to great use.

A massive amount of timber was supplied for various purposes and there was actually a Portuguese lumberjacks' camp situated at Millyford Green. Charcoal was another interesting and important commodity to be provided by the Forest. The traditional art of making it had all but died out but was fortunately revived by the Cull brothers. The charcoal was sent to France for use in water filtration and possibly in the form of activated charcoal for gas masks.

As well as the hard wood used for charcoal, in the summer of 1917, the acorns of the oak trees were needed for the manufacture of cordite, "much to the chagrin of the New Forest pigs, as it was a bad year for mast anyway!" Heather too, played its part and in the winter of 1914/1915 large quantities were sent from Beaulieu for use in the saturated camps around Winchester. In the spring of 1916, hand-picked heather tops were supplied for packing munitions and as bedding.

Animals too were needed, and in 1914 many forest ponies were requisitioned for active service in France. "In August 1918 a War Dog Training School was set up at Matley, with some 200 canine recruits to be trained in message-carrying under battle conditions. Unfortunately some of them, when released at various places, were side-tracked by the interesting scent of forest fauna and the messages and the messengers did not always return to base very promptly!"

A hospital for wounded Indian troops was set up in Balmer Lawn which was later visited by King George V and Queen Mary in 1917. Agisters acted as outriders to the royal coach. The crematorium in Perry Wood was in danger of being defiled by forest pigs (an unclean animal to Mahommedans) and at the end of the visit the Agisters had to spend the rest of the day putting up wire to keep the pigs out.

The army also had a grenade school at Bolton's Bench and an artillery range at Matley Wood as well as a grenade school at Whitemoor, east of Lyndhurst. It applied for forest land to be used as an airfield and the site chosen was one at Beaulieu which had been developed as a private flying school as long ago as 1910 by a Mr. McArdle.

Down river now to Lymington where the Lymington River Sailing Club had been founded in the early part of 1914 only to be closed down a few months later when 'the balloon went up.' Talking of balloons, Bill Morgan has a photograph of a German zeppelin coming up river and a friend to whom he showed it actually remembered seeing it.

Boom defences were set up in the Western Solent, examination vessels anchored off Yarmouth and Fort Victoria and Hurst Castle were re-fortified. Berthon Boatyard, whose famous collapsible boats had been widely used by the Royal Navy as well as by private yachtsmen, now turned to war production. One of the vessels they built was a hospital launch.

WORLD WAR TWO

A few months preceding the outbreak of World War II in September 1939 the Verderers had approved the construction of anti-aircraft gun sites in the

By courtesy of E. M. Knight

Boat built at Berthon, 1914 - 1918

By courtesy of E. M. Knight

Hospital Launch built at Berthon, 1914 - 1918

Forest. Later 8,700 acres were to be requisitioned by the War Office and the Air Ministry. Anthony Pasmore, in his book *Verderers of the New Forest*, from which most of this history has been taken, goes on to record that: "In addition to the three airfields, two bombing ranges and cultivated areas, there were numerous lesser service installations and sawing sites. The whole area had been parcelled up into different military training and firing zones, and damage by tanks was extensive. The military had destroyed many of the bridges and dug thousands of slit trenches and a number of anti-aircraft landing traps. Barbed wire littered the heath and live explosives made areas such as Acres Down perilous to animals and humans alike. A large prisoner-of-war camp disfigured Setley Plain and sprawling camps and depots had sprung up at several sites...."

The Royal Lymington Yacht Club 50th Anniversary Souvenir recorded that: "A controlled minefield stretched across the Western Solent from Sowley Sluice to Hamstead Ledge. The barrage was protected by a boom defence vessel and ships theoretically could not pass through without clearance from the Extended Defence Officer (West) in the George Hotel, Yarmouth.

A continuous nightly Channel Patrol operated from Yarmouth. Whilst waiting for the German invasion these little craft steamed 30 miles south every night, winter and summer, their duty being to sit on the wireless transmitter key at the first enemy sighting.

Wellworthy was now a fortress making rings and aircraft pistons for the war. Both Ampress and Stamford Road factories had been camouflaged since the beginning of the war and even cars left outside were sprayed with green and khaki paint and a decoy aerodrome was set up at Sowley Pond. It did not deceive the Germans, or they failed to spot it, as not one bomb landed there. However when a garage light showed at Brockenhurst they dropped a load of bombs which hit a petrol supply. John Howlett, the founder and owner of Wellworthy, gave the impression that his factory had been destroyed by using a London address for the rest of the war.

A decoy that was successful was recalled by Mrs. Teresa Rumsey, of 6 Fairlea Road, Lymington, who wrote to the Editor of *The Lymington Times* of 6th June 1981. She thought that the war-time bomb found on Pennington marshes on 21st May had probably been dropped on a mock runway that had been built on the marshes to deceive and mislead the Germans into thinking it was the runway at Beaulieu. For this reason, she said, Woodside village suffered many bombing attacks but fortunately without loss of life. She remembers as a child going out to collect shrapnel after a raid and in most cases it was still hot when it was picked up!

John Howlett had tried to join up in World War I and had been told that he had not had the education for an officer and would have to serve in the ranks. He served for four years with the Norfolk Volunteer Regiment, known as the 'Saturday Butterfly Shooters,' and although he volunteered for South Africa he never got there.

He started in the ranks again in World War II when he formed the Wellworthy's Volunteers as part of the LDV, later to become the Home Guard. He recalls that 450 men were under arms and they would "spend Friday or Saturday nights swarming over the marshes out on exercise with their rifles and ammunition slung on their backs; or making long route marches over the moorland in the dark." The men got so hungry out on these night exercises that food was always laid on at the works for them, together with eighteen gallons of beer and they were nick-named 'The Beer and Cheese Brigade.' John Howlett then recruited a doctor and also nurses from the canteen making a virtually self-contained unit. Most of them had already put in long hours in the daytime, where production had speeded up, as well as doing other voluntary war work.

The staff had increased from 800 in 1939 to nearly 4,000, many of them drafted from munitions work. When Sir Cyril Deverill inspected them he was amazed to discover that they even had an old elephant gun and ammunition for it! Sir Cyril warned John Howlett against using it on the enemy, as it fired 'dum-dum,' which was against the Geneva Convention, and would bring reprisals if the enemy ever discovered it. There was also a machine-gun nest outside the factory at Stanford Hill. This had been taken from a crashed aeroplane. Unfortunately, a patriotic youth removed all the factory's iron railing with oxyacetylene cutting equipment, which left the machine-gun exposed for anyone to use, much to John Howlett's fury. Later when it was discovered that his rank in the Home Guard as commander of this large unit was that of a private, he was hastily promoted to the rank of major!

Many Canadians were stationed on John Howlett's land and some were at the manor. There were thousands of them camped on a hill behind Rhinefield, "tall lads most of them, always ready for a laugh." But sadly they took part in the ill-fated Dieppe landing where they suffered heavy casualties. It had been suggested that maples should be planted in the forest in their memory.

When he started organising his farm and used a bulldozer on the hedges, it got stuck in the soft mud, and it took a Canadian tank to get it out again, with the best part of a unit from the Canadian Tank Regiment. They were stationed at Bucklands Manor waiting for the balloon to go up, and it was an armed camp there, with a couple of 'ack-ack' guns in the fields and sentries in amongst the rhododendrons. That was the regiment that went to France within a week of D-Day and they too suffered terrible casualties.

Surprisingly no bombs were dropped on Well-worthy, but Mrs. Russell recalled that they had a near miss, when an American plane blew up close to them. High explosives and incendiaries were dropped on Lymington. She was serving in the Red Cross at the time and was on leave during one of the air raids, and she remembers her father and mother saying to her: "Trot along back to your safe military objective!" That was Tidworth Camp! She had a charmed life where bombs were concerned and her presence anywhere seemed to guarantee immunity to them. "Ah, it is all right now. They won't drop any more bombs, Miss Corbet has come back!"

Her mother used to give out tea at Wellworthy before they got a canteen. Her father was considered too old for the Home Guard, much to his annoy-ance, but was kept very active in Civil Defence. There were plenty of alarms as well as raids, as the Needles was such a landmark for the German planes. A high explosive landed in the marshes doing little damage and another where it is now Courtenay Place. Ford's linoleum store was hit by incendiaries and made quite a bonfire!

Fred Woodford, the Harbour Master, was born in Lymington at Burrard Grove and was a small boy here at the outbreak of war. He remembered that most of the yachts were moved behind the black railway bridge, but larger yachts, such as *Foxhound* and *Bloodhound* (later Prince Philip would sail in the latter) were laid up in pens on mud berths off Berthon. A bomb landed on craft at the railway bridge when German aircraft were returning from a bombing raid on Southampton. Several boats were damaged, including *Vixen (Dulcibella* in *The Riddle of the Sands)* at Bill Smith's yard and one of the Sea Scouts' 16-footers which was moored by the bridge. Another bomb hit Syd Cooper's greenhouse in Waterloo Road.

When war broke out Bert Rand was a Rover Sea Scout and was attached to the Coastguards. They kept two whalers always available and used to relieve the coastguards, carrying out patrols along the beach every night. One night they saw a head swimming in and thought it was a German. They hid behind a bank and watched it coming closer and closer and were all set to hit it on the head; it was not until it got within 10 feet of the bank that they could

see it was a seal!

Another night there was a plane coming over and a bit of 'ack-ack' going up from the Island and bursting all round, perhaps from John De Mowbray's unit. Bert and his fellow scouts were near the sewage pipe at the time so they nipped into it and waited until the raid was over. "It protected us from the shrapnel anyway," he said.

The marshes between Lymington and Keyhaven were covered with encampments with searchlights. Fred Woodford used to walk across the marshes and saw soldiers cleaning the searchlights and anti-aircraft guns. The Germans did drop some bombs near Platoff, the home of the Martineaus.

Once one of our Mosquito aircraft flew over and exploded in mid-air and crashed in Elay Lane off Lower Pennington Lane. The pilot was killed but the navigator baled out and was caught up in a Scotch fir tree. In the ploughed field nearby, Fred saw an airforce jacket, which must have belonged to the pilot. It contained all the aircraft papers and some secret documents and he took them to the Police station in Gosport Street, now Il Palio Restaurant, and was given 2/6d. reward (a princely sum in those days) and a really good recommendation from the sergeant.

The Berthon Boat Company constructed MLs, MTBs, minesweepers and water ambulances on Admiralty contract. Some of these 110 ft. craft were fitted with auxiliary sail for their intended passages across the Atlantic.

I went to see Bob Blunt at his home in 45 Waterford Lane, Lymington on 12th January 1982, only a few months before his death, and he told me about the work carried out in Berthon during the war. Bob Blunt had signed to join up in the early 1940s but probably, in view of heavy losses at sea, anyone who had worked in a boatyard was ordered to report to one immediately. He went to see Mr. Fairford at Berthon and was given a job there straight away. "There were about 120 or 130 of us then," he recalled, "and most of them painters although there were a few shipwrights. Then about 15 women joined us. The old foreman, Mr. Parker, could never get used to women working in the yard and taking so long in the powder room!" he chuckled.

The largest craft they worked on then was a 72 ft. Harbour ML and it soon reached the stage when one was going off the slip nearly every month, more like a car production line. There were four berths where they were built and they kept the same men doing the same job. One gang would lay the keel, the transom and all the frames, and then another gang would plank her and put in the beams and deck. A gang consisted usually of four men, but sometimes it was only two, the unskilled men being put to finishing off inside the boat and general joinery work. When Bob Blunt first joined them the yard was building assault craft about 40 ft. long for personnel and more launches, which were on the secret list and he thought were for the Marine Commandos.

One really interesting and secret boat built at the yard was a sort of Q ship, her topsides were more or less on the lines of a fishing boat but she was different from our ones. He remembered that the parts that mattered were built of balsa wood and men would go into the yard carrying perhaps 10 ft. of balsa on their shoulders. She was intended to pass as a Spanish fishing boat so that she could mingle with the Spanish fishing fleet. At the time it was believed the German U-boats were surfacing beside the boats and getting information from the fishermen.

At Berthon they had a man on the roof to spot aircraft, a Mr. Shaw. There were shelters to go to but they could not be dug down into the ground very deep because of filling with river water. The alarm could go off eight or nine times a day and they would break off work – sometimes it was for ten minutes and sometimes for as long as a couple of hours. In the early part of the war bombs were dropped right by the pier.

I visited Freda Inman when I was over in Chichester in March 1981. She is the great great granddaughter of Thomas Inman of Lymington and her father was a cousin to Miss Alice Cook. Her father worked in Berthon too for part of the war and they moved into a grey house facing the boatyard in Bath Road. She too remembered some of the bombing. 'Lord Haw-Haw' had given it out on the radio from Germany that Lymington would be bombed and she supposed the targets were Wellworthy and the bridge. Her immediate concern, womanlike, was for the jars of home-made jam which bounced around on the shelves when the bombs fell!

Bob Blunt takes up the story again. He told me that when the Americans had an airstrip at Pylewell some of the American fighter bombers, if they had not dropped their bombs, used to jettison them over the marshes "by waggling their wings in some way." Of course there were no warnings of that! He used to see quite a lot of the Americans during the war because he lived over at Norley. He had the tenancy of a bungalow belonging to old Mr. Duplessis at Newtown. Once a 1,000 lb. bomb dropped just up the road and when they went to see the crater it was 60 odd feet across, nearly 30 feet deep and the blast had "picked up an old oak tree with a large trunk and tossed it right over the hedge into a nearby field."

One Saturday night he heard a plane flying low that did not sound right; it was a Liberator that had just come back from patrol in the Bay of Biscay. She was in real trouble and just as he got outside, she touched the top of an oak tree and there was a terrific bang and a flash followed by smoke. She was carrying depth-charges and there was no hope for any of her crew. Bob Blunt confided that the Americans worried him far more than the Germans! You expected danger from German planes but there was often more from American ones, which would sometimes crash on take-off early in the morning, but whether this was due to overloading he did not know.

Fred Woodford recalled that the Town Quay was shut off completely for security reasons and for the first time the right of way along by Berthon on the side of the river was closed to the public – and has remained so ever since. When preparations were being made for D-Day, there were sentries posted on duty outside the Rowing Club and Ship House. Quite a number of river marks were put in for craft going out to service ships that were too big to come into the river. At the same time many mediaeval ones were replaced by new ones, such as 'American Post,' so named perhaps because so many American craft ran aground on the mud there!

The Americans stationed at Elmer's Court built a pontoon for their own amusement out of packing cases and they used to swim off there. There was an aerodrome at Pylewell (as Bob Blunt has confirmed) and he used to watch "chubby-nosed aircraft" taking off and flying behind the trees which stretch to the foreshore on the east bank of the river. He remembered walking along the shore with some other boys, and looking into the woods, and they suddenly met an enormous negro, the first they had ever seen, and they were so frightened that they all ran away. The Americans were very friendly and used to give them 'cookies,' chewing-gum and candy. They also used to hold Christmas parties for the children.

A very detailed description of Lymington River in April 1944, just before the invasion of Normandy, is given by Nevil Shute in his book *Requiem for a Wren,* and I am most grateful to the Estate of Nevil Shute Norway to quote from it. Although the characters are fictional his description of the D-Day preparations is probably entirely factual, and I am convinced that this is so, and that they were witnessed first hand by Nevil Shute (the Alan Duncan of the story). I therefore have no hesitation in including them here as 'faction'.

Those of you who have read the book will recall that Leading Wren Prentice, Bill and Alan spent a Sunday in April 1944 in Lymington and she managed to produce a motor-boat to take them on a trip down the river to the Solent.

"It was a little grey painted naval boat fifteen or sixteen feet long, a fishing boat that had been taken over by the navy, I should think. She had it at the quay by the Ship Inn when I got back from Beaulieu aerodrome at about half past ten. The WAAF driver took me to the quay and there was Bill in battledress and gumboots with his dog, and Janet Prentice in rather dirty blue serge slacks and gumboots and a blue jersey and a greasy duffle coat. I dismissed my car and went down to the boat."

Then followed a very detailed description of the craft they saw on their way down river. "There were no civilian boats or yachts afloat upon the South Coast at that time, but the river was full of landing craft, box-like grey, painted things of steel with ramps to let down by the bow, with diesel engines thumping away inside them to charge the batteries as they lay moored bow and stern to the buoys, with soiled white ensigns drooping at the stern with bored ratings fishing over the side and staring at us as we threaded our way past. I did not know the function or the name of any of these ships, but Janet and Bill knew them all and told me shortly what they were, and what they were to do, as we chugged past.

"This was the LCT Mark 4, the standard rank landing craft, British built and shipped to England on the decks of ships, an unpleasant and relatively unseaworthy little craft that would go in first in the assault, bearing the Sherman tanks that were to swim ashore, and the work tanks, the armoured vehicles RE that were to clear the beach of obstacles so that the landing craft could come in safely and detonate the mines, and bridge the trenches in the sandhills on the other side. This was an obsolete mark of LCT converted as a rocket ship to fire a salvo of nine hundred rounds at one push of the button to blast the shore defences. This, bristling with Bofors guns and Oerlikons, was a gunnery support craft, manned and commanded by marines. This fast powerful open landing craft coming up the river towards us at speed, manned by American sailors in white, upturned caps, and with the name *Dirtie Gertie* proudly painted on her bow, was an LCVP, an American infantry landing craft so powerful and well designed that ratings with a minimum of training could handle her.

"All these were known to Janet and Bill, but there were other things afloat upon the Solent that they knew nothing of, great box-like things of concrete bigger than a cross channel steamer floating moored or building on the shore, things like a monstrous reel of cotton fifty or sixty feet in diameter floating on the water, flat rafts with grotesque girders sticking up in the air . . ."

This was 'Pluto,' 'Pipe Line under the Ocean,'

which was to lay pipes from England to France, to carry petrol to supply the armies which were due to land in Normandy. David Strang, who lived on the Isle of Wight during the war, and who crossed to and fro at school holidays, told me that he had seen lots of landing barges before they left for D-Day. "We also saw Pluto drums wandering around and wondered what the hell they were!" he said.

Returning to *Requiem for a Wren* again, there follows a fascinating description of preparations being carried out in the Beaulieu River and in particular the activities at Lepe House, HMS *Mastodon* and at Lepe Hard. But for Lymington we take up the story in the last month before the invasion.

"Every two or three hundred yards along each lane hard stands were made, which were parking places for tanks and vehicles. Temporary airstrips paved with hessian and steel units appeared almost overnight and crowded thickly one on top of another. The U.S. Air Force moved in to these with Thunderbolts and B.25s and Lymington became thronged with American soldiers and American trucks. Overhead it was a common sight to see fifty of their aircraft flying in formation at one time . . ."

Finally to the start of the invasion itself: "The whole stretch of water between the Isle of Wight and the mainland was crowded with landing craft and ships of every sort, and all in turn were getting short their anchors, weighing, and moving off. In the deep channels were the Infantry landing ships, cross-channel steamers and small liners with landing craft hanging on to their davits; in the shallows were the LCTs loaded with vehicles and tanks and men, moving off towards the eastern entrance of Spithead with great flotillas, shepherded by their MLs. Coming down Southampton Water was a great fleet of Tank Landing Ships, big American vessels with a double door that opened in the bow. Overhead the fighters circled in the evening light, the inner patrol positioned to catch any German aircraft that penetrated the outer guard of fighters over the Channel. The evening was thunderous with the roar of engines on the sea and overhead. . . . They were looking at a mass of ships that nobody might ever see again assembled in one place. Viola told me that she had tried to count the ships that were in sight that evening; she counted over four hundred and then failed to separate the hulls massed together in the east down by Spithead. Gradually, as they crossed the Solent, weaving in and out between the landing craft, the Western Solent cleared. The craft that had been lying between Lymington and Beaulieu passed them going to the east and by the time they reached the river entrance there were few left to westwards."

As Bob Cook so succintly put it: "The craft were so tightly packed together that it would have been possible to have walked from Lymington to Yarmouth without getting your feet wet." The Longest Day had begun!

*   *   *   *   *

At the very time when I was on board the *Athlone Castle* at 11.0 a.m. on Armistice Day 1945 at anchor off Ryde, Bert Rand, serving in an aircraft carrier out in the Indian Ocean also had a moving experience. In honour of the first Armistice Day in peace time, the Royal Marine Band turned out in full dress uniform and came on deck by the flight lift. At the two minutes silence the aircraft carrier turned off her engines and even with 3,000 men on board the only sound to be heard was the swish of the water. It was very dramatic and watching HMS *Invincible* leave with the Task Force for the Falklands reminded him of it.

Three young men from Lymington went to the Falklands: Andrew Glennie in HMS *Hermes,* Colin De Mowbray in HMS *Alacrity* and Charles Thornton in HMS *Broadsword* and they were remembered each Sunday in prayer at Boldre Church. They all came back. Andrew Glennie is the grandson of the late Admiral Glennie, who commanded HMS *Hood* up to a few weeks before she was sunk, in the North Atlantic in 1941, with the loss of 1,416 officers and men.

In the far corner of the North Chapel of the Church of St. John the Baptist, Boldre, stands the Book of Remembrance and beside it, on the left hand wall, is a picture of HMS *Hood* painted for the church and given by the eminent marine artist, Montague Dawson. A copy of the account of the last action of HMS *Hood*, beautifully executed by Mrs. Bond, a talented illuminator, may be seen in the porch together with a photograph of the ship. The Dedication of the Hood Memorial was held on Trinity Sunday in May 1949 and today the annual memorial services are recognised nationally, and survivors and relatives come from all over the country to attend them. Ten years later in May 1959, John Hayter, the Vicar of Boldre, wrote in the *New Forest Magazine* (the forerunner of the present *Bridge*):

"There are many in our community in whose lives the sea has played a major part. There are still more who now find in it their greatest enjoyment and relaxation. It is for this reason that, on one of the Sundays nearest to the anniversary of the loss in action of HMS *Hood*, besides remembering those who died, we offer our praise and thanks to God for all that the sea means to us. It is fitting too, that we should make our "Thanksgiving for the Sea" on Trinity Sunday, for then the thoughts of Christians are turned to the wonder and majesty of God. Where more than in the side reaches of the sea, in its power and its beauty, do we see the glory and the might of God."

THE WORKING RIVER

"It was still a working river and most of its traffic consisted of the ferries to the Isle of Wight and the great red-sailed barges that carried bricks and beer to Lymington."

JOHN HOWLETT

Wellworthy Ltd.

John Howlett, the founder of Wellworthy Limited, was born in 1883 and left school at the age of 13. When he was 29 he received a telephone call from his old boss, who was in charge of the Siddeley-Deasey Organisation, telling him that his company had garages in Lymington and Bournemouth and were thinking of expanding and would he be interested in the post of General Manager.

So it was that John Howlett came here and his *Walk through Lymington* on that Easter Monday of 1912, described in his autobiography *The Guv'nor,* gave us a newcomer's impression of the Edwardian Lymington of that time. Income tax was one shilling in the pound and the large country houses were still occupied by the familes of Duplessis of Newtown Park, the Whitakers of Pylewell, the De Courcys of Lisle Court and the Keppel-Poulteneys of St. Austins.

He arrived by train at Lymington Station, where a brass band was tuning up in readiness for the Easter Parade through the High Street. "The air was as exhilarating as the music, and both gave a jaunty encouragement to my euphoria. I humped my cases up the steep hill of the main street and tried to discount the looks of blank incomprehension which met enquiries for the offices of the South Coast Garages. I passed a great number of public houses – there must have been over thirty in the town – and several butchers' shops which gave evidence of slaughtering animals on their back premises. I passed many great houses, with pillars and gardens and windows which looked down the High Street with more than enough aristocratic disdain to ignore the presence of butchers and pubs. I passed the High Street garage which was part of our concern, but it was closed up and deserted. Further along the road was a fine Norman church with a graveyard surrounded by chestnut trees. I walked on and presently I realised that I had passed right through the town and would soon be emerging into the countryside.

"It was then that I noticed the main place of business of South Coast Garages. It had originally been a livery stable where shire horses were bred. There was a tank on the roof for watering the horses and a clock tower in which the clock still went, its face besmeared with pigeon droppings. The blue-tiled floor of the old stables was still littered with straw." He put up at the Anglesea Hotel. Two of his first customers were Mr. Klitz, whose motorbike kept breaking down and a dealer in old tyres.

The old Town Clerk, who was an authority on local history, told John Howlett that South Coast Garages was on the site of an old Saxon Fort known as 'Priestlands Well.' Apparently in Wessex the title of 'Worth' or 'Worthy' had been given to such fortifications, and the name 'Priestlands Worthy' immediately sprung to his mind. However it seemed "cumbersome and rather popish" so he decided on the neater and more memorable 'Wellworthy.' So July 1919 marked the inauguration of Wellworthy Limited as we know it today. The new board was entirely a Lymington one and 30 local people were employed in the works under Mr. Gray, the works manager.

John Howlett was very civic-conscious and joined the Council two years later in 1921 at the age of 38. He was Mayor in 1930, and on the creation of the greater Borough of Lymington in 1931 was asked to continue as Mayor for another term, November 1931 to April 1932. He stood for Parliament as an Independent Liberal but the Conservative candidate, Sir Oliver Crosthwaite-Eyre was elected as M.P.

John Howlett was awarded the OBE in 1950 and was made a Freeman of the Borough in 1955. He also served on the committee of the Annual Hospital Ball, a fund-raising event which provided Lymington with the biggest single event in its social calendar. He organised a supplementary appeal by running a special market selling, amongst other things, large quantities of elderberry wine and elderflower champagne – now very popular again.

He believed that wealth brought with it responsibility and that others should benefit from it as well as himself. "I had already taken an active part in seeing that the hospital had its new wing, that the town had sea-water baths and that the Masonic Hall was built, because I considered it important that people should have a place to gather in, and that kids could swim in safety. That is the great pleasure of wealth, as I see it – to know an area well enough to be able to appreciate that an Old People's Home needs a laundry, that a new Town Hall needs a rather special Mayor's Parlour and to be in a position, not only to do something about it, but to watch the results being enjoyed."

He achieved his ambition of becoming a land-owner himself, and owned about 165 acres in all, his land reaching from the gates of Ravenscourt to Battramsley Cross and well back into the Forest. He ran a model dairy farm with a magnificent herd of pedigree Guernseys, and those of us who came to Lymington more recently will remember with what pride they were shown at the New Forest Show, where he won many of the top awards.

John Howlett also became a keen sportsman. "It was a genuine need in all of us, and almost a craving in me. I was now finding ways of satisfying it, nothing very sophisticated. Just a share in a rough shoot near Romsey and the purchase of a fairly elderly boat called *Albatross* which I kept on the Lymington River." He enjoyed nothing better than spending long days out on the moors shooting with his friends, even going as far afield as the mud flats of the Caspian.

It was in the Caspian that just before dawn one morning his friend Dev and himself were rowed out to their hides by a ghilly and something made him go and check to see if Dev was all right, because he was unfamiliar with the ways of mud. He himself had gained plenty of experience of it from the Lymington marshes during the war, and he could tell where the spear, or salt grass, would hold and where it would not. It was fortunate that he did so, as he was just able to rescue Dev from sinking into the mud by levering him up with an oar while the ghillies wrapped their arms round him and pulled him out.

He went out sailing in *Albatross*. "Before the days when the river was developed as a marina; it was still a working river, and most of its traffic consisted of the ferries to the Isle of Wight and the great red-sailed barges that carried bricks or beer to Lymington. On the Island, Cowes was, of course, the centre of the smart yachting world; but my yachting was not particularly smart and it certainly was not competitive. I liked the sense of space and the feel of the river slipping past us and the complete lack of urgency as we came home in the evening, with the wind and tide behind us and Harry Bell telling stories. He was the man who skippered the boat for me; he had been a bookie's clerk in his time and had a very philosophical outlook on the ups and downs of all things, and the sea in particular. 'I take it as I find it,' he would say. 'And I reef in when I need to.' As a means of conducting life, or a boat, it seemed to work very well on the whole."

Another skipper who worked for John Howlett was Albert Edward (Bert) Woodford who died on 31st May 1982 at the age of 69. He was the son of William (Nim) Woodford who began his sailing career as deckhand for Major H. W. Hall of Downton and then Mr. Russell of Grove Road, Lymington. When his father was skipper of John Howlett's yacht *Happy Lass,* Bert Woodford joined the crew while he studied for his Master's certificate and then took over from his father when he retired. John Howlett bought a new yacht, *Happy Lass II* and Bert Woodford sailed it until 1960, except during the war when he was in charge of the women workers at the Wellworthy plant at Ampress. When the Admiral of the Fleet visited Lymington for the Town's eighth centenary, he was brought up the river by Bert Woodford in *Happy Lass I.* After retiring as a skipper, Bert Woodford worked for the Berthon Boat Company as a rigger until he retired in 1978.

John Howlett himself died in 1976. He had seen Lymington develop from a small yachting centre into one with a international reputation and perhaps not all to the good. We leave him with this envoi. "I have seen the life go out of many of the great houses, and the families pack and go away, and soon their very names will be forgotten. I have seen changes in the cottages, all central heating and stripped pine and prinked out by people from London with hanging baskets of geraniums. The town itself is being changed by means of something known as Neo-Georgian town houses, and on the quay where the men of Lymington used to fight with men from the Island, the old brothel has been developed out of all recognition."

He would have been saddened to see the buildings today on the Ravenscourt Estate and yet he would have understood that they were necessary and filled a need.

Travis & Arnold Limited

Travis & Arnold Ltd., the timber merchants in Grove Road, have been trading in Lymington for just over 50 years. A former employee, J. E. Matthews, wrote to me of their close links with the Lymington River.

"I was employed at the timber yard when on 1st February 1922 Travis & Arnold Ltd. took over from E. Loxton & Sons, who had been running the business for many years with many vessels coming direct into the river. Early that year we had a small sailing barge with timber which I believe came round here from either Sutton Bridge or Kings Lynn. After that and between 1923 and 1928 we had three vessels direct from abroad which, as far as memory serves, came from Finland.

"It was not so much the silting of the river that caused my Company to stop importing direct, but mainly through lack of help by the ruling people of the river, and particularly the Harbour Master at that time. It was made very obvious that they did not want the river commercialised but left for yachting only.

"It was mainly through bad piloting that a serious mishap nearly happened with the last vessel; she ran onto a mud bank almost opposite the pier, and there was some concern that the vessel might break its back. However, with the high tide, she refloated and eventually arrived at the Town Quay. But news of this near mishap soon got around and the Ship-owners refused to entertain Lymington River afterwards.

"From then on the ships went into Southampton where the timber was transhipped into flat bottom barges and were then towed to Lymington by tug; it brought three barges each trip. We continued to use this method right up to the outbreak of the War, in fact we had three barges moored at the Town Quay at that time and were given seven days to off load, after which they would have to return to Southampton with any cargo still on board. However, by working long hours the off loading was completed on time.

"Timber barges were always 'in the way' at the Town Quay and continually had to be moved to permit the yachts to come in for water, etc. which of course delayed our working; so much so that after the War it was decided to try other methods and for a time the timber came by rail. However this method was not a success and now the ships come either into Southampton and/or Portsmouth and the timber carted to Lymington by road."

Another employee of Travis & Arnold was Roy Prince, who collapsed at work and died in July 1981 at the age of 52. He was born in Coastguards Cottages at Waterford, the son of George Prince who had worked for King's the printers for 50 years. On leaving school he became Assistant Harbour Master to Bert Thomas. He spent his national service in the Royal Navy, serving aboard coastal protection vessels, which sometimes visited Scandinavia. He was a keen sportsman and used to shoot or fish at most weekends.

Mew Langton & Co. Ltd.

In England in the Middle Ages there was a large number of small breweries owning a few inns and taverns, a number of these brewing their own ale and beer. Such a one was Mew Langton. Old records show that in 1643 a 'Mr. Mewes' held five plots of land in Newport, Isle of Wight and brewing had probably been going on much earlier than that.

In the latter part of the 18th Century Benjamin Mew formed the partnership of Mew & Co. and it thrived. On his death he left the Lymington brewery to his eldest son Tom and the Isle of Wight business to his second son, William Baron. Tom preferred to hunt and shoot so William rented the Lymington brewery for £400 a year from his brother and lived in style at Walhampton.

The firm expanded still further and soon had branches in Aldershot, London, and abroad in Malta, the Mediterranean and as far away as India and China. To raise more capital, the firm then offered a partnership to a Walter Langton. In 1850 William Baron was granted a Royal Warrant to supply Queen Victoria in Osborne House and the firm continued to supply the Royal Household until the death of King George V in 1936, when his beloved racing cutter *Britannia* was scuttled off St. Catherines.

In 1887 it became a limited liability company, and in 1898 a new malthouse was built, using the modern method of pneumatic malting, which enabled malting to be carried out throughout the year. Another new venture was started that year, the manufacture of mineral waters, and a factory was built on the Island with the most modern plant. To trade with the mainland sailing barges were chartered from Leigh Bros. and these were the *David*, the *Swift* and the *Nora*. In 1920 a motor vessel, *Wight*, was built by Groves & Gutteridge. Between the wars the firm became modernised still more and motor transport replaced the horses. In 1931 the firm also became tobacconists.

By courtesy of A. L. Baigent

Mew Langton Van

24

In the Second World War both the Portsmouth and Southampton branches were destroyed but each has since been rebuilt. The last of the brewery horses, 'Old Tom', was retired to Ringwood. In 1964 the firm merged with Strong & Co. By that date 17 members of the Mew family had been actively engaged in the business and 4 Langtons.

Regarded as 'one of the family' was Mr. A. L. Baigent, who retired on 31st December 1966 on the same day as the Lymington depot closed down. He had been with the firm for 46 years. Mr. Baigent was born on the Island and joined Mew Langton as an office boy when office hours were from 8.0 to 5.30. His first job was to take a bottle of champagne to Groves & Gutteridge for the christening of the motor vessel *Wight*.

In 1933 at the age of 28 he was appointed manager of the Southampton Branch. He and his family had just moved out from living on the premises when three weeks later they were blitzed. He was able to carry on working from his home in Shirley for 18 months until alternative premises could be found. The bombing took place at Christmas time and all the wine and spirits in the store were broken and ran down the cellar steps in a stream of different colours. His wife still cannot stand the smell of the stuff. Mr. Baigent later served in the Royal Artillery on anti-aircraft radar and became a sergeant in the personnel selection staff.

On leaving the army in 1946 he took over as manager of the Lymington Depot from Dorothy Armstrong's father. Her father had moved to Lymington from Newport in 1902 and lived in Brewery House before moving to Stanley Road on his retirement. Mr. Leonard Mew then moved into the Brewery House after him. Dorothy Armstrong, a well-known Lymington character, had worked for the brewery for 50 years, finally retiring in 1959 some thirteen years after her father's death. She was a member of the Lymington Community Centre and a keen bowler. Peg Carruthers, formerly of the Ship Inn, remembers Dorothy Armstrong although she had never met her father. "She was a sweet little soul, two foot nothing and a very 'ye olde worlde' but a very efficient secretary. She was a wonderful little woman and right up to almost the end she used to help all her neighbours, who were less able to get around than herself."

Mr. Leonard Mew was a member of the Royal Lymington Yacht Club and owned a yacht called *Quiver*. Mr. Frank Mew, Colonel Mew's father, owned a yacht called *Coral* at Cowes and it was the mate of that yacht who took over as skipper of the *Wight*, Mr. E. J. Foley. Colonel Francis Mew was also a member of the RLYC and was a founder member of the Lymington Harbour Commissioners. He had four daughters and that was one of the main reasons for the Company merging with Strong.

Lymington had a self-contained depot and Mr. Baignet was responsible for supplying all the licensed houses, clubs and retail distribution as well as two off-licences – one in High Street, Milford and one at 82 High Street, Lymington, where there was also an office. The shop manager before the war was Mr. Cull, who lives in Pennington as does Mr. Stevens, the manager at Milford. Weekly deliveries were:–

Monday	Brockenhurst and Sway
Tuesday	Lyndhurst, Brockenhurst, Milton
Wednesday	Burley, Sway, Hordle, Pilley
Thursday	Fawley, Hythe, Beaulieu Manor
Friday	Lyndhurst, Brockenhurst, Milton, Highcliffe and Boscombe

Milford and Lymington and district were daily.

Mr. Baigent saw a good deal of the Carruthers at the Ship Inn and said they were a remarkable couple. They were both real characters and he used to wear a monocle. Tom Morris rented the old Yacht House from Mew Langton; most of the property round the Quay was owned by the firm and Mr. Baigent had to collect all the rent. Another 'character' was Dumbie Murray, so called because he was deaf and dumb. He was employed as an odd job man and used to light fires and help generally. Mr. Armstrong had been able to converse with him in deaf and dumb language.

The last Beer Barge

XXXX took its name from Mew Langton's prize-winning brown ale and was built by J. Samuel White of Cowes in 1948 to replace the *Wight*. She carried beer from Newport Quay to Lymington Quay for 18 years and her skipper was F. A. L. (Les) Chiverton. Only a few months after her first trip (not when Les Chiverton was skipper) the vessel sank at Lymington Quay. Mr. Baigent was woken at 7.0 a.m. by a fellow calling out, "What shall we do, the *XXXX* has sunk!" Fortunately he summoned the fire brigade and the barge was pumped out and refloated!

In the hard winter of 1963, when the Lymington River was frozen up, *XXXX* used to break its way through the ice three yards at a time, making a passage too for the ferries. The two-mile trip up river took 3 hours instead of the usual half an hour.

XXXX was known as the 'Booze Barge' but she was a good sea boat and the pride of the Medina River for speed and handling. She had a crew of three, and her hold could take 140 tons of barrelled and bottled beer which, without the containers, amounted to 90 tons of beer. She visited Lymington twice a week from Newport. Despite the temptation, the crew never once sampled some of the beer during their crossings from the Island! "We never drink when we are on duty," said the skipper. The decision to cease operating *XXXX* came with the merger with Strongs, and from 1964 onwards the beer from the Island now came to the mainland all the way by lorry in the Solent ferries. The last sea-going motor barge owned by any brewery in the country had made her last voyage and Lymington River was the poorer for it.

Shell UK Administrative Services

Shell UK Administrative Services, one of the successors to Shell-Mex and BP Ltd. wrote to me on 19th May 1981 as follows: "From the records we still hold, it would appear that there was a depot at Lymington from about 1913; some old personnel records show that a supervisor and a driver were employed there. This depot would presumably have belonged to the original British Petroleum Co. Ltd. Another source indicates the 'Shell' Marketing Company (a forerunner of Shell-Mex and BP) had a Can Store at Rickmans Coal Yard in either Station Road or Quay Road, Lymington in 1920. We cannot say whether these were separate sites or not. A Can Store would have held supplies of motor spirit, or petrol, in two gallon cans for distribution to local garages as the sale of petrol from roadside petrol pumps had not been introduced at this time."

Brookes & Gatehouse Ltd.

The first practical echo sounders were constructed in France as long ago as 1918 by Paul Langevin and the first British "Asdic" system for the detection of submarines was developed in 1923. The advent of the transistor brought about a revolution in the design of echo-sounding and radio equipment for yachts. The meter presentation system for use in yachts was produced by Brookes & Gatehouse in 1958-1959. Many of the echo-sounding trials were carried out during the winter in Major Gatehouse's yacht *Wavecrest II*.

Major R. N. G. Gatehouse, founder of the electronics firm of Brookes & Gatehouse Ltd., designers and makers of navigational equipment, was born in Reading on 19th May 1918, the son of Brigadier Gatehouse. As a boy he was fascinated by electronics and worked first for Marconi and later served as a Radio officer on South American shipping routes. He was at sea when war broke out but he served in the Royal Artillery engaged in perfecting radar. In 1955 he left the army to form a partnership with Ronald Brookes to develop and manufacture a new radio-direction finder for accurate navigation. He was interested in flying and held a pilot's licence and enjoyed sailing small yachts. He took part in the Junior Offshore Group races and his interest in navigation developed from racing and cruising *Electron*.

He became a Fellow of the Institute of Navigation and was awarded their Gold Medal in 1975 for his outstanding contributions to the improvement of small craft navigation. Not long before he died, he kindly prepared these notes for me on the history of the company which are set out as he wrote them.

"1955. During the first year of its life the Brookes and Gatehouse partnership operated in rented accommodation at Selsey in Sussex. Points of particular interest were the location of the company's premises right on the tip of Selsey Bill with an unobstructed view over water of the Nab Tower. This was an ideal situation for testing the accuracy of the Heron DF aerial during its development, taking advantage of the radio beacon installed on the Nab. The company designed and built some special short-wave versions of the Heron for use by Dr. Vivian Fuch's Trans-Antarctic expedition. These enabled sledging parties on reconnaisance to 'home' in on to Base. Production of the standard long-wave marine Heron was started in February 1955.

The partnership became incorporated as a Limited Company in May 1956, shortly after having moved to Shirley Holms, near Lymington. Here the 'Homer' receiver was developed; reputably the first transistorised DF set to appear for sale in the world's marine market.

1957. The Company moved to an ancient building, believed once to have been a small village or 'dames' school in the garden of the Gatehouse's home in 5 Captain's Row, Lymington. Richard and Penelope Gatehouse were joined by a cousin, Major Peter Bailward, who had also recently retired from the Army. The production of the Homer receiver was started.

1958. Hecta echo sounder went to production. This was the first transistorised echo sounder to appear on the market and, as with the Homer, it was powered by four miniature torch battery cells. Both instruments were housed in the same grey nylon-coated metal case which afforded complete protection against moisture and spray. The bulk of the production work was carried out by a 'cottage industry,' largely comprising friends scattered about the Southern Counties and working in their spare time. The majority were already skilled craftsmen and craftswomen and required no training in electronics assembly technique.

1960. The Hermes speedometer went to production. This was novel at the time in that it used a diminutive nylon impeller driven by the water-flow beneath the hull and could be withdrawn into the hull for cleaning. Another retired Army friend, Lt. Colonel John N. W. Hearn, joined the company to look after production and sales, and in the Autumn of 1960 the company moved into comparatively spacious premises in Bath Road, Lymington. The building resembled an aircraft hangar and was said to have been built in the 1930s by Messrs. Walls for use as an ice-cream storage depot. Offices and workshops were built on the 3,000 sq. ft. of floor space by stages as the business expanded. The 'cottage industry' continued to play an important role.

1961. The Harrier combined log and speedometer went to production. This used the same little nylon impeller as Hermes and was housed in the same grey metal case as Homer and Hecta. As with the other instruments it was powered by four miniature torch cells. Harrier proved to be the most popular instrument manufactured by the Company.

1962. Hengist/Horsa launched. These are precision instruments for the measurement of wind direction and wind speed respectively. An important feature of Hengist is the close-hauled indicator which gives a magnified reading ($\times$ 4) of the wind direction within the windward sailing sectors.

1963. John Hearn joined the board. The staff at this time numbered about 20. There followed a period of consolidation and the up-dating of designs to take advantage of the silicon transistor which has many advantages over the geranium type. Another floor was built inside the factory, literally by raising the roof, and this had to be achieved without interfering with the business of the company! Half an acre of land immediately to the rear of the building was bought for further expansion.

1965. A subsidiary company, Brookes & Gatehouse, Inc. was established at Larchmont, N.Y. for the purpose of marketing and servicing the company's products in the U.S.A.

1966. *Gipsy Moth IV* was fully equipped with Brookes & Gatehouse's instruments for Francis Chichester's single-handed circumnavigation.

These are on permanent exhibition at the Science Museum, London.

1967. The Hestia electronic course indicator went to production. This was a form of transmitting compass in which the navigator dialled the desired heading and the helmsman simply had to steer the boat in such a way as to keep the pointer of a meter in its upright, or vertical position. It incorporated an off-course audible alarm which enabled the skipper to take the helmsman to task if ever he should take 'forty winks' and allow the boat to wander!

1968. Production of the Hadrian distance-off-course computer began. Hadrian accepted data from the Hestia electronic compass and the Harrier log and displayed the *distance* by which the boat had wandered from the specified track due to errors in steering. From this data and the distance run from Harrier it is possible for the navigator at any time to plot the boat's D.R. position. Hadrian was probably the world's first marine D.R. computer.

1970. Donald J. Mudie joined the board. A house called 'Four Shells' in Queen Katherine Road was purchased for the Accounts Department. The garden of this house bordered on to the company's Bath Road property so that the site now had entrances in both roads. In 1971 a new stores building of 3,200 sq. ft. was constructed and in the same year a machine shop of 3,500 sq. ft. was purchased as a going concern. This is near to the railway station, in Waterloo Road, Lymington.

1972. Production of the Horatio sailing performance computer began. The development of Horatio, which was carried out in collaboration with Southampton University, took several years to complete and was believed to be the first instrument of its kind to be manufactured commercially. As with Hadrian its use while racing under RORC rules was banned by a Special Regulation which remains in force today.

1975. The Halcyon electronic remote-reading compass went to production. It was probably the first compass ever designed which senses the earth's magnetic field directly, without having to make use of a pivoted magnet system.

1978. Commander J. R. C. Turner joined the board of Brookes & Gatehouse Ltd. as technical director on his return to the UK, having held the post of executive vice-president of Brookes and Gatehouse for 3 years. In July the Brookes and Gatehouse Group was purchased by Unitech. Ltd., a public company. Messrs. P. A. M. Curry, Chairman of Unitech, P. J. Price, Group Executive, joined the board. At this time the strength of the company had risen to just over 100.

1979. In January Hecta echo-sounder (200 metres

range) went to prodction. This instrument provides a digital display on the instrument case and an analogue display for use in the cockpit. In May Messrs. A. C. P. Gale, C. C. Kirkman and P. S. Thomas were appointed to the board. Richard Gatehouse resigned as Chairman and Managing Director, and was appointed President. P. J. Price was appointed Chairman and J. R. C. Turner was appointed Managing Director. J. N. W. Hearn became deputy Managing Director.

1980. In January the Hercules multi-function data computer was demonstrated at the London Boat Show. Using a microprocessor, an LSI chip and other up-to-the-minute technology the arrival in the market of Hercules was a major milepost in the history of the company."

In 1981 the firm was awarded a Design Council Award for their Hercules electronic data system, which introduced computers to every-day boating and in 1982 received their second Design Council Award, the first marine electronics firm ever to gain two, for their Homer 5 marine radio receiver.

This latter award was presented by Prince Philip at a ceremony in London only hours before the death of Major Gatehouse on 28th April 1982, at the age of 63. In his obituary in *The Daily Telegraph* the following day he was described as "a navigational pioneer whose inventions over the past 25 years revolutionised small boat sailing." As a navigator one could hardly have a finer epitaph than that.

Mariner Electronics

I called at the offices of Mariner Electronics at Admirals Court, Quay Road, Lymington on 13th July 1982 and talked with Mr. J. Bell, one of the Directors.

"Mariner Electronics has a background of instrument making going back thirty or thirty-five years," he said, "and we really came into this market as a wing of instrument making, having been designers in that field since the late forties. We first started in the photographic field making cameras and projectors and then moved into the educational market with similar mechanical electronic optical devices in the field of overhead projection and micro-projection. This was a complete break really – a change of scene and really a question of marrying a technical background with a rather more pleasing environment.

"At the time I was sailing a Contessa 36 and, needing some equipment and not liking the prices being quoted this led me to try it out on the drawing board and make one for myself, which I did. When Jeremy Rogers saw it, he and his brother, Jonathan, invited themselves out for a sail and he was so impressed with it that he suggested we should exhibit it at the Boat Show which we did. He even offered to make a little display stand for it. That is really how we started.

"When we first saw these premises they were just a hole in the wall and earmarked as a boatyard and slipway. However, the flat owners in Admirals Court above had not paid £100,000 for a flat just to have the noise and smell of a fibre-glass boatyard beneath them; it was not really viable. Even so it took us two years to get planning permission for a change of use and we have been here now for eight.

"We have passed through the various facets of instrumentation for yachts from the simplest speed indicators through depth sounders, radio direction finders and everything that the racing or cruising yachtsmen needs in order, we hope, to arrive safely at the other end. The range is now quite large, covering specific designs for boats of different sizes. In the past few months we have even fitted one unit to the Q.E.2! We have also installed our gear throughout the UK in all the HM Coastguard stations.

"Last month we received the approval of the Council of Industrial Design for one of our new instruments. Despite the depressed state of the market today we seem to satisfy the smaller boat owner while our friends down the road, Brookes & Gatehouse, still look after the bigger ones – and a very good job they make of that too.

"We try to stay in what we call the 'enthusiasts market,' the person who enjoys his sailing for sailing's sake. People tend to start with first buys, such as a simple depth sounder which gets them to the top of the river and back in safety. Next they stretch their legs and go round the Needles, and then they suddenly realise that they need a compass, so they go off and buy one. After that they want to sail faster than their friends down the quay, so they buy a speedometer and having gone round the Island they latch onto the idea that even they might be able to take the family across the Channel, so they need a means of distance recording. Having missed Cherbourg by five miles and finished in Alderney the next time out, they latch on to the radio beacon and buy a simple little hand-held radio direction finder, which is a good start and teaches them a great deal and is very good indeed provided that the sea is reasonably flat and the sun is shining.

"However, as so often happens, they may run into foggy conditions when they need something to help them sail more accurately in these conditions and this divides them: there are the people who sail in the Solent for 20 weeks in the year and might go as far as Poole and back, and those who jump on the boat every Friday evening and hare across the Channel for coffee and croissants in the Café de Paris in Cherbourg. But at the end there will always be the intrepids who battle it out every weekend around the cans and they are a breed to themselves and their requirements for instrumentation are rather different, although restricted by the regulations of the Royal Ocean Racing Club, which dictates that no instrument can compute any two parameters.

"Today one hears so much about satellite navigation and the interesting thing is that it has tended to have gone full circle and we have now gone back to a smaller version of the Decca navigator, which of course has been used in commercial shipping since the Second World War. Of all the systems today that is probably the one which has the greatest advantages from a small boat's point of view.

"In any yacht you really need more than one system to cover for failure. The natural tendency there is to home on to local beacons using the VHF radio and to do the distance work by radio beacons using satellite navigators or, in fact, the Decca navigation system and then to qualify it by entering the manual market, which we are all used to, by taking readings from the basic instruments on board. With a 3-shot system you ought really to be within yards of the target even in the thickest fogs and it is very easy to use.

"We have been getting increasingly nervous recently when people take their families across the Channel simply because they have got all the gear but if the gear fails them they really will be lost. It is surprising how few of them can repair their diesel engine, climb a mast and ship a fouled halliard at sea, which are really basics to seamanship. It is the breed of the professional men who are not usually noted for picking up screwdrivers or getting their hands dirty who buy all these fancy toys and quite rightly expect them always to work. But sadly, because they are made by other human beings, they do not always do so. We gain each year in reliability but there is still a long way to go in marine navigation before we can effectively fight the elements with electronics in a salt water environment. We are one of the few companies in the world who fill all their meters with dry nitrogen. It has taken us something like ten years to establish our reputation for navigational instruments and this does not come easily.

"We deal with thirty-nine countries currently through about fourteen leading overseas agencies and up until recently we exported to Argentina." (My interview with him was at the time of the Falklands War.) "We deal with Singapore, Hong Kong and the Trucial States," he continued, "and odd corners of the world in addition to the major European nations. There is a ready market for English goods in this sphere. We seem to have the reputation of being the Number One country to generate a quality product but how long we can sustain it, of course, is another matter.

"Everything is designed here, developed here and tested here and then subsequently tooled. Most of the interim work is put out and then it comes back and we control final assembly and test the quality of the goods before they go through the door. We also provide for after sales service from here. We do all the servicing in the Lymington area but we have agents around the coast of the UK and overseas to do long distance work.

"It is difficult to see where we go next. We have had in the past two or three years the 'fashion' for installing electronic tiller steering systems; then we had the 'fashion' for VHF radio and we have just come through the 'fashion' for satellite navigation and one wonders really what the next 'fashion' is going to be. If we could all crystal-ball gaze we would be a lot more successful than we are now. It is a 'toy' market and people tend to follow advertising and the boat shows in an effort to have the latest and greatest.

"We are tending to see a lot more specialisation nowadays. Companies like Brookes & Gatehouse, for instance, used to have speed meters, radio direction finders, satellite navigators, radio communication receivers and compasses and cover an enormous spread but there is a tendency today to see companies specialising in one field and one field only. There is a company which does nothing else but steering systems; another which does nothing else but magnetic compasses; and another which does nothing else but metering systems and so on. We are all tending to find our own little niche in the market, which allows us to cover a much greater product range within a specified area and therefore helps to keep the overseas people overseas!

"Nowadays we see more and more younger people coming into the market place, buying their boats second-hand or new and the aim invariably is to equip them to a much greater standard than we older people ever did before. There is a tendency for the 'bits and pieces' which decorate the boat to be viewed as the first requirement rather than the second. Therefore you tend to get maximum sale of 'bits and pieces' every time a boat changes hands. I think too that the advent of the small pocket calculators have introduced the 'key pressing' factor. People do not just want to look at a display they want to play with it, and it follows the logical pattern of the toy market that the more buttons there are to press the more people will enjoy pressing them! So we are seeing more and more devices being integrated into block units, which is interesting from Mariners point of view because that is how we really started business.

"In 1971 we brought out the first combined metering system for a boat, and that was really what got us into the market, and since then we have developed it through four different models. Currently it is the Micro 5 system which, as its title suggests, has five different systems within a single valve. This is the way it will go because it is much easier for the boatbuilder and cheaper to instal; and it presents the information at one spot and allows the helmsman to keep the crew out of the way, and there are advantages in many directions. But it is a different concept so that people have to re-learn an old game.

"In addition you get some significant gambit with the change from meter systems to digital systems and the younger element are looking more and more for the numerical approach whereas the elderly yachtsmen really prefers the needles around the dial principle with which they have been indoctrinated for goodness knows how many years. So there are different approaches for different people and age is significant; type of sailing is significant; size of boat used to be significant but no longer is because we see boats from 90 ft. down to 20 ft. doing very well in longer distance races such as the Round Britain and so on. So people can enjoy it just as much on a small budget as on a major one.

"Instrumentation and navigation-offered performance record is really basic: it is only its packaging which allows it to be used more effectively in boats of different sizes and configurations. Style is very much a factor too because people do like a choice. In the marine field people today have got an enormous choice of 'goodies', and a lot of the rubbish seen in the past has gone, because the companies have not been able to stay the course. So we are left on a much more solid base than we have had hitherto, certainly during the high-flying days of the early Seventies.

"As to what is going to happen round the corner, well inevitably things will get much smaller and more complex and will become easier to use. I sometimes wonder really whether it is not taking an edge off sailing because it would be quite feasible to equip a boat to sail from Lymington to Cherbourg and back again without actually leaving your armchair, which is rather ludicrous! So there must come a point in time when people realise the fringe advantages are really not worth the additional expense.

"Tape recorders today are being used for recording the weather forecasts and there are quite a few gadgets that are around for allowing them to work automatically on a pre-set timing, so you can forget all about it and still have a good recording. Another factor is the arrival of the cheaper weather facts machines and that could very well set another fashion, if someone can currently break the price barrier within that territory. Everyone who goes out sailing any distance is very conscious of the weather, and if they can record and print the pattern of it days previously they would be in a much better position to dictate what is going to happen in their own specific area, rather than listening to a generalisation, which might cover the entire area from Lands End to John o' Groats. So I think that is one of the future uses of electronics. Various items are now available to do just that but current prices are a little too high for the yachtsman's pocket. But that is very much a matter of time. I do not really see basics disappearing. I think the nominal items, speed, distance, wind direction, wind speed, depth will carry on for many years. Presentation might vary but the efficacy of them currently is at a very high level and any failings on their accuracy are largely dictated by violent movements of the boat through the water rather than to any deficiency in the equipment itself.

"People will still jump on little boats, have coffee and disappear over the horizon and will do so for many years to come. We just hope that within our little sphere we can help them to arrive safely without too much effort and yet without taking too much fun away from sailing itself. We do not want to remove the total adventure factor by making it fully automatic but at the same time we feel that many yachtsmen, particularly newcomers, do need a hand to hold and we aim to provide just that."

RIVER INNS

"I had worked in the City in a luncheon Club but had no residential experience and Paddy had had no experience at all. But you can learn the hard way!"

PEG CARRUTHERS

Fifteen inns are associated with the Lymington River, of which only four still exist today. Edward King has gathered from the Town Books, the licensing records, churchwarden's accounts and vestry accounts the description of the inns contained in his book *A Walk through Lymington,* written in 1972 and I am indebted to him for much of my information.

Waggon and Horses

The Waggon and Horses was in use in 1800 and used to be a thatched inn and the ceiling of its old tap room was covered with coins. Before the bridge was built in 1731 it used to be a stopping place for waggoners waiting for the ebb tide before crossing the ford. Country people would leave their donkeys and carts there before taking the ferry for their weekly shopping in the town. It was rebuilt in 1908 and is a convenient stopping place for passengers to and from the Sealink ferries to Yarmouth.

Swan

The Swan, later known as the Bridge Tavern and later still as the Freemans or Freemasons Arms, dates back to 1791. It was situated on the tollbridge and the gatekeeper who used to collect the tolls was also the landlord. Edward King recounts an amusing incident when Lord Montagu was taking King Edward VII for his first drive in a car. "Lord Montagu called to the landlord: 'Hurry up and open the gate; don't you see that His Majesty the King is with me?' 'I know them Kings,' he replied, 'two of your sort slipped by me only this morning. Pay your 6d. and then you'll have to wait until I've let the donkey cart go through.' And wait they did, to King Edward's considerable amusement'."

Harlequin

The Harlequin Inn in Bath Road just past the shipyard was reputed to be the headquarters of the Press Gang circa 1800. A ferry once ran from there to Blakes Dock on the opposite side of the river now the site of the ferry terminal.

Mayflower Hotel

The Mayflower Hotel, situated in King's Saltern Road, used to be on the opposite side of the street in what is now 'Old Inn Cottage,' dating back to 1868. In 1883 its landlord was Captain James Cutler, who was formerly skipper of the yacht *Rita.* It closed on 21st July 1927 and the present Mayflower opened the same year. Although the sign shows the ship that carried the Pilgrim Fathers to America being watched rather suspiciously by a Red Indian brave, the hotel was actually named after the vessel in which Marconi tried out his first experiments with wireless telegraphy in the Solent.

In 1951, when Anna Chitty bought her small terrace house 'Isle View', opposite the Mayflower, the proprietors then were a Mr. and Mrs. Stevenson who were great characters. She recalls that: "Mrs. Stevenson was a very handsome lady with beautifully coifed grey hair, elegant clothes and strong personality, who was known affectionately as the 'Duchess.' He too was always immaculately groomed, and never seen without a flower in his buttonhole. The great bone of contention was that, being a passionate horse lover since his boyhood, nothing would induce him to have a car. Every year they set off in a hired Rolls in great style to the Adelphi in Liverpool for the Grand National, waved on their way by all their neighbours."

Fisherman's Rest

The Fisherman's Rest in Woodside was formerly a house called Grattens Cottage. A licence was first granted in 1870 to James Bran, the father of George (Monsey) Bran. Smuggling was carried out in his time and George (92 years of age in 1951) remembered seeing one of the small 3 gallon kegs which were used by the smugglers. 'Monsey' Bran was at one time the landlord there.

Sloop

Another smuggling inn was the Sloop situated at Brook Cottage, Brook Road, Waterford which closed as a licensed premises about 1850. I was told of a raid made by the Customs and Excise officers in that vicinity, perhaps at the inn itself, where they found only an old lady sitting knitting by her front door. What they did not know was that she was sitting on a keg of brandy that was hidden under her long skirt!

Another inn of this name was situated on the far side of the river but its exact position is not known. However its records go back to 1791 and it provided beer to celebrate the Peace of Amiens in 1814 at the end of the Napoleonic wars.

Dukes Head

Now No. 3 Dukes Head cottages, this inn was probably named after the Duke of Wellington and was the site of the old Coastguard Station at the Salterns. It closed in 1870. 'Monsey' Bran, who was born in 1859, just remembered it being open when he was a boy.

William IV

Its records go back to 1851 and it was almost certainly named after King William IV who was crowned in 1830. Its royal name was changed to the more mundane The British Workman in 1885. (Willie Gallagher would have approved!) It later became the Lodging House for the Quay.

Kings Head

The Kings Head (quoted as Kings Arms by K. B. Haig) is situated at the top of Quay Hill and dates back to 1836 if not before. There is a tradition that a room in the old inn was occupied by Charles I and, if this were true, it might explain why his ghost can still be seen walking in Walhampton. It is more probable that the inn is called after Charles II whose 'King's Arms' were set up in the church in 1676. Hence the suggestion that it was King's Arms and not King's Head.

Dolphin

This inn was known as The Blue Anchor and later as The Railway Inn in 1858. It changed its name to The Dolphin in about 1883 and was situated on the right-hand side of Quay Street opposite the 'Yacht Inn' where the clothes shop 'The Birdcage' is now, and it had a skittle alley. Like The Sloop it also provided beer to celebrate the Peace of Amiens in 1814. The licence expired on 11th July 1911 and it became a private dwelling house later to be occupied by Mr. Renouf.

Yacht Inn

Opposite the Dolphin on the corner of the Quay and Quay Street was the Yacht Inn which dates back to 1863. It closed on 28th December 1911 just five months after its neighbour. Several other pubs closed at the same time and these closures were attributed to changed in the Licensing Laws in 1911.

Alarm

The Alarm goes back to 1830 (although the building itself is c. 1680) and was named after the famous yacht of that name built by Thomas Inman for Mr. Weld of Pylewell that year. The building itself is much older and painted on it is 'The Old Alarm'. It was at one time a marine antique shop and is today a hairdressing salon.

Solent

This building at the foot of Quay Hill facing the High Street has reverted to what it originally was in 1700, a gentleman's residence. The inn had a bowling green at the back of it and until about 1880 they brewed their own beer. The landlord at about that time was William Stephens, a man of strong character and strong physique, and his grandson remembered a family story that he used to urge the drayman to save time by dropping the barrels on his chest. It closed on 2nd February 1939. Today No. 5 Quay Street has been converted to become Old Solent House Galleries, belonging to Denys Brook-Hart.

Chequer Inn

The Chequer Inn can hardly be defined as a 'River Inn' and nor for that matter can the Fisherman's Rest but both are so closely inter-linked with our story that they are included in this chapter. 'Chequers' inns exist all over the country, mostly at sea ports, and they were the places where tax was collected. For this reason it seems certain that our Chequer Inn was the headquarters of the Salt Duty Collectors at Lower Woodside, as there were 22 salt pans in the immediate vicinity. Apparently in the Middle Ages small change was often so scarce that innkeepers and merchants often made their own halfpenny and farthing tokens, many bearing the inn sign on the reverse. It is known that 13 different kinds originated in Lymington.

The inn sign itself is said to be the oldest in the world, a chequered flag was discovered during the excavations at Pompeii. The Chequer Inn dates as far back as 1759 when John Serrel was landlord but the inn sign itself was stolen, although fortunately a photograph taken in the early 1900s can be seen in the pub. There is a similarity between it and the coat of arms of the St. Barbe family, the Lymington bankers and owners of many of the saltworks, but no explanation is given.

The article on the 'History of the Chequer Inn', published in the *Lymington Times* of 13th November

1982 recounts the very close links with the smugglers and how very highly organised smuggling was in the Lymington area. Sometimes 200 – 300 horsemen and 20 – 30 waggons loaded with kegs could be seen. Not only spirits but silks and tobacco, playing-cards, raisins, figs and gold sovereigns worth 10,000 to 12,000 guineas were brought into the country this way. The reward offered for the capture of a smuggler was between £500 – £1,000, an immense sum in those days. The Riding Officers on the other hand were only paid £20 a year to catch them.

Ship Inn

Another survivor and dominating the Quay today is the Ship Inn. Three cottages have been knocked together to produce the present premises but formerly it consisted of only one. Records go back to 1784 and in 1805 The Stoney Cellar was assessed for rating at £4.00. It used to have a 6″ board bedded in clay just inside the door to keep out the high tides. Long before the Carruthers went there after the war it used to be *the pub* of Lymington because of its perfect position for yachtsmen.

The Ship Inn

Herbie Rand once told Peg Carruthers that Paddy was the only man he knew who had started the war with a naval rank and ended it with army one! She explained to me how this had come about. "Paddy joined the RNVR in the First World War as a Sub-Lieutenant and worked his way up until just before the end of the war when he was minesweeping in HMS *Nepaulin* and she was blown up. He was sent on sick leave and was then offered a job at Princes Risborough, shipping ammunition from there to Dunkirk for which he was awarded the French Croix de Guerre. This meant being seconded to the army and he only agreed to this provided he held the equivalent rank to Lieutenant-Commander. So that was how he was made a Lieutenant-Colonel!"

When the Second World War started he could not get back into uniform quickly enough and joined up again in November 1939 and went back to mine-sweeping. But because he was a bit older and his eyesight was not good enough for him to go to sea, he was given shore jobs. The Carruthers were living in London at the time and when they went into the Trocadero at Piccadilly the bartender would say: "Good evening, Colonel," even when he was wearing naval uniform, and everyone would look hard at Paddy and wonder if they had heard correctly!

"After Paddy retired and there was nothing for him to do, he thought of running a pub and applied to Mew Langton. He was offered the Ship in Lymington and accepted. I had worked in the City in a luncheon club but had no residential experience, and Paddy had none at all – but you can learn the hard way!"

By courtesy of Peg Carruthers

The Ship Inn

A little room was turned into the cocktail bar and Paddy had a half dinghy built for the bar. This was known as 'The Tender' and the lifebelt bore the name of the minesweeper in which Paddy was blown up. From here there was access into the Residents Dining Room, and any casuals for lunch or dinner, and round the corner was the visitors lounge, a huge room. There was also a saloon bar and a public bar. The latter was Paddy's 'baby' and he was always very fond of the public bar. To the side were some garages which belonged to Mew Langton and the directors used to park their cars there. With an eye to the future, Paddy had three more single and one more double room, with beams, built over them with their lovely outlook onto the river.

The hotel was a 'gold mine', especially during the season with the yachting crowd and some of their regulars became very good friends and Peg has still kept in touch with them. Another lot of good friends were Herbert Rand and his gang of 'Figgy' (Alan Figgures) and 'Ozzie' Luce, amongst others from the

Lymington Town Sailing Club. They used to frequent the saloon bar. The 'boys' often used to come to the Ship and were, with the exception of Herbie Rand, confirmed bachelors. However, after one of Peg's curry dinners, Alan Figgures got engaged and so did Jerry Palfrey. They both said it was her curry dinner that had spurred them on!

In the Ship there were about a dozen photographs by Beken in the cocktail bar and the dining room but of all these the *Suzanne* was Paddy's 'pet' because he was great friends with the original owner, Sir Robert McAlpine, and had been on a short trip in her. She had a crew of 23 in those days and carried 75,000 sq. ft. of sail. When Peg heard of her last, about seven or eight years ago, she was in Greek waters. However, recently in a TV programme on the 'J' class, the *Suzanne* was mentioned but whether she is still around or on the scrap heap she does not know. The photograph is now in the hall of her home in Kingston Park and is much admired by everyone. Peg believes that Roy Coombes did a painting of the *Suzanne* which was exhibited in the Dolphin Galleries about four years ago.

King's Lea Guest House

Horace and Catherine Bashford lived in Surrey originally and after the war, being a bit unsettled, they decided they were going into catering and were looking for a café rather than a guest house; but in fact it developed on that side, which was much more interesting. They came to Lymington in 1953 and ran the King's Lea Guest House in King's Saltern Road, whose Deeds go back to 1832. Surprisingly, although it looks small from the outside, there are plenty of rooms at the back but no space for expansion. But it was large enough for the two of them and part-time helpers. The 'Smugglers Haunt' Restaurant could seat about 30 and later when it was converted into a small house, Jennie Murray, the Southern TV personality lived there. Commander Torlesse ran a tea and coffee company called 'Aroma' and the Bashfords made quite a feature of tea and coffee and he would recommend what blend he thought right. He always told them: "If tea and coffee is good, people will excuse some short-comings in your cooking!"

"Our semi-basement, 'The Smugglers Haunt,' was sticky in wet weather," Catherine told me, "because of the salt in the plaster: it used to come out like little flowers. In those days there was nothing that you could do about it. We used to have to do our tea room nearly every year as it got spoilt during the winter because it was so damp.

"Then there were the floods in 1954. We had 2½ feet of water: it just trickled over the top step and when the tide went out, so did the water – it went through the floor. They started pumping but they didn't get it all. The Butchers lived opposite us then in Bath Lodge and of course Doug was a weather-wise man – he had been a sailor – and he came over to King's Lea and said, 'There is going to be a very high tide tonight. If it comes up to us, can we come over to you?' We said, 'Of course you can.' They had already sent the children up to his mother because there was an east wind, a lot of rain water coming down the river and the Spring tides: a formidable combination.

"The banks were not half as well built up as they are now and the water began to come over by the Club. Somebody came rushing in to us. We had an elderly couple staying with us who were looking for a house. Luckily all our rooms were above the basement so although it was flooded, everything else was perfectly all right, even the kitchen. So we were the only people who had gas, electricity and phone working. In the houses in Bath Road all the electricity meters were sizzling as they were covered with water. We had firemen travelling in and out and we were making cups of tea for them.

"Then all of a sudden we thought of the old gentleman's car which was out in the car park and the water coming over like nobody's business. We called out to the Butchers across the back and he said, 'Go and get the keys and we will drive it up the road.' So I went and tapped on their door and said, 'Can I have your car keys as there might be a little water coming over at the high tide and I think we had better move your car.' 'Oh, yes, my dear,' he said and the old lady opened one eye and said, 'We shall be all right," and turned over and went to sleep again. It was lovely.

"In the morning I had laid a table for them in the lounge to have breakfast and got a fire going because it felt a bit cold. She said, 'Aren't we going down to the dining room?' and she opened the door and there was water, black water, sitting on the bottom. She was absolutely amazed.

"The Mayor came to visit us – he wore ordinary shoes and had to borrow some wellingtons – he met all the distressed people and saw that they were all right. Somebody got out a boat and the WVS served hot dinners; it was really very well organised. In those days everybody was geared to it and in an emergency would turn out and help."

Herbert Rand recalls the extensive flooding from the 26th to 30th November 1954 with the tide coming over the bank five nights in succession and the floor of the LTSC covered with 2 inches of water. In the Figgures house the water came in through their windows. "The saddest sight," he told me, "was to see

By courtesy of Anna Chitty

Flood at RLYC, November 1954

BATH LODGE
Tea Room
MORNING COFFEE
11 AM to 12.30 PM
AFTERNOON TEAS
3.30 PM to 5.30 PM

By courtesy of Anna Chitty

Flood at Bath Lodge, November 1954

books, swollen up by the water until they had burst their bookcases and even damaged the walls. Nearly all the houses already had salt marks on the walls from previous floods. We were taking up the carpet at Bath Lodge for Doug Butcher's mother-in-law and she was picking up the tacks of the carpet which went ping, ping, ping against the walls!"

Anna Chitty remembers watching the flood water from the river slowly creep along King's Saltern Road and meeting the flood water from Harpers Lake exactly in front of her home, the highest part of the road. The Mayflower Hotel car park was flooded to a depth of 3 inches. At Harpers Lake, there was a 6 ft. drop from the sea wall on to the Marsh and it looked like a mini Niagara Falls. It flowed so strongly that it lifted all the sheds in the Boatyard and washed them into a field. Hugo Duplessis had to replace them with Nissen huts from the old Beaulieu aerodrome and used the deckhouse of an MFV as his office!

In 1963, on the other hand, the winter was very cold and the river froze over. The ferry had to lift and drop its bow flap to break the ice and even so she took half an hour to reach the pontoon from her berth, which she normally did in two minutes. A mast and sail was fitted to two planks on wheels for ice sailing on Hatchett's Pond!

CHAPTER 6

THE OLD QUAYITES

*"It was beautiful on the Quay. We had nothing at all but we were always happy.
I don't know why people said that they were afraid to come down here. It might
be that we were a bit rough and they used to call us the 'Quay Roughs' or the
'Old Quayites'."*

J. CLEALL

Jim Arnold and Joey Cleall

The first two 'Quay Roughs' whom I had the pleasure of meeting – I certainly was not afraid of them – were Jim Arnold and Joey Cleall! We met at the Arnold's home at 1 Quay Cottages, Lymington on Saturday, 20th March 1982 over a most welcome glass of sherry. Apparently they had been born next door to each other, although a year apart, in the two cottages nearest to the water where the Ship Inn is

By permission of T. Doe

The Quay, Lymington

today. Jim's birthplace was No. 1 The Quay and sometimes called the 'Coffee Cabin' because his parents took it over from some Italians who had run a small coffee cabin there. Jim Arnold later worked in Wellworthy and Joey Cleall worked at Berthon.

They both could remember when the big timber barge called *Dag* used to come up to the Quay. She was a three-masted or four-masted schooner and they knew all the hands. The cook was a man called Cookie Nestor and he was either a Norwegian or a German, more probably the latter. There were a couple of Germans on board who were arrested when war broke out. "In 1912 we were both five and six years old and on the Quay there was timber as high as you could see, not just timber but whole logs, big trees. They used to pile it up as high as this ceiling and we kids used to wriggle in and out and it was a wonder we were never killed."

"The old coal barges used to come up too," continued Jim Arnold, "the old windjammers – and

if there was no wind they would have to push them with big poles all up the river and then tie up at the Quay. There was an old man with hair all round his face and we used to call him 'Beaver'. The barges used to bring about 100 tons of coal. Sometimes the gangers, who were unemployed, used to row out to meet these boats and that was how they got the work. There would be six in a gang – two were inside the boat – and they would unload a hundred weight at a time. They would have a winch handle and wind it up and another chap would get it on his shoulder and they would run up to some big sheds with it. They were given 3*d.* a time to share between the gang. They got such a thirst on them that they used to go straight over to the 'Ship' which was open early in those days.

"But to get back to the coalyard: there was a crafty lot there. Every now and then someone would loose a bagful of coal but there was always a chap ready to come round with a grapple and go after it! We never bought any coal. Many a time I have seen a sack come off the old crane on the Quay! Every time a barge unloaded there was so much dust about that you could write your name on the pillows!"

Joey Cleall was out in the Far East during the war. He was captured at Singapore and was a prisoner-of-war of the Japanese. He served in the East Surrey Regiment and worked on death railway – and survived! He and his mate, Chitty (no relation of mine) were two of the lucky ones. He came home in 1945 and the troopers called in at Colombo where a great reception awaited them. Amongst those waiting to meet the boats and look after the ex-POWs was Leading Wren Chitty, who found it a most rewarding experience. We were the first white women that some of them had seen for years.

Jim was at Wellworthy in the war when Mr. Howlett organised the Home Guard and the fire-watchers. He went to Wellworthy at the age of 14 when there was just Mr. Howlett and another chap called William Gray. He joined in 1920 or 1921 when the firm started up in the old livery stables at the top of the town. He told me that you could see the rings on the walls where they used to tie the ponies. "I have seen it expand from nothing," he said. "We made about 8,000 piston rings a week then and when I left the output was about 80,000 to 150,000 piston rings a week. That was back in the days when there were those little Austin 7s and we were churning the piston rings out by the million. I earned 2½d. an hour when I started. You had to go there as there was nothing else except the Berthon and the Berthon was only a seasonable job."

Joey remembered how just before the summer started they would get all the yachts out. "They only had a small gang then of about 60 men. They were not all skilled men; a skilled man in those days got only £2 9s. 0d.

"The Bethel used to be a Seaman's Mission," he continued, "and we kids when we were small all had to troop in there and sit down with some of the old seamen although we never knew why we went! In World War Two it was occupied by the Navy and was pulled down afterwards; it was an awful shame. Many other cottages were pulled down within 50 yards of Quay Cottages, including some belonging to Berthon Boat Company, the traces of which can still be seen. There used to be a yard with timber and grit and, as the years went by, cattle too.

"In the summer there used to be a proper Lido on the Quay. There were half a dozen boats belonging to a man called Billy Cruse and they would make about 6d. per hour. There were only about three fishing boats in those days but there must be about fifty now.

By courtesy of E. M. Knight

Quay Road, Lymington

"We used to live in the water as children; there were about 30 or 40 kids out there, some with costumes and some with nothing at all! We would go off the end of the quay one after another – it was like the Serpentine. Sometimes we would go into all that mud over there when it was low tide and slide right down as black as anything. But by the time you had swum back here again you were nice and clean. I don't think we ever had a wash under the tap, certainly not in the summer time; we were in and out

of the water all day. You would not even put your feet in there now, it is so dirty."

Jim Arnold continued the story. "Every summer the 'Beanfeasters' used to come on a boat from Portsmouth. They would drive in four-in-hand carriages and would come and throw pennies into the water and we used to dive over and get them. It shows how clear the water was then. Boxing classes used to be given at the St. Lawrence Boys Club further along down at Marsh Lane. It was where the old Isolation Hospital used to be – and now it is a Council yard.

"I used to be in charge of the little orchard behind my present home. Joey used to work for a Mr. Jordan up on the hill and was on a milk round and I used to hop over into the orchard. Once when I was picking those apples somebody said, 'Have you got enough then?' I looked around and suddenly there was Mr. Clements from the coal yard. He added, 'You'll hear more about this later' but being a nipper of 14 years old he did not say any more about it. But we never used to break the tree down. The only time any damage had been done we never had any change! They were beautiful days. We used to play football and somebody would kick the ball into the orchard and one of us had to go in and fetch it, hadn't he?"

Joey remembered other games they used to play in the street – there was no traffic in those days. One was called 'Ukky cat'. You had two sticks, a little bit of string and a wooden reel and you would throw it up and catch it again. You could not do that outside now.

"Where Tom Morris lives on the corner we used to play a game called 'Hollie Collie.' There were about 20 kids all throwing their tennis balls up against the wall and catching them and someone would have to run and the ball would be thrown at him. Sometimes it was a cricket ball. Imagine if you were throwing a ball up against someone's house now they would be chasing you away. We knew the old lady, Mother Lance, she was deaf and was a real old character.

"Old Jack Woodford used to live in the third cottage from here and he used to sleep on Sunday afternoons while we used to go out and play 'Kick can policeman.' There was a big can; it rolled down the quay and another boy had to walk slowly to the can, pick it up and walk back and put it down and we would all have run away. You had to run and kick this can three times. Old Jack used to come out and swear then!"

"I must say it was rough," mused Jim. "People used to be afraid to come down here but it was just kids' devilment and there were so many of us down there that there was always somebody to play with round the back of the 'Ship'. The 'Ship Inn' was only a little place then. We used to play pitch and toss back behind it and that is where we used to undress and go into the water. Before the restaurant was built there used to be some garages.

"My Dad was the ferryman and he had a wooden leg. It used to be ½d. over and ½d. back. Nearly all the men were either invalids or had something wrong with them. There was another man called Billy Cruse who was paralysed in both legs so we never had a really fit man there. Once when there was a timber boat at the Quay, there were two chaps who had either had a night out or too much to drink. They got on the slipway and fell overboard. My Dad rushed out and managed to save one but the other was drowned. The one my Dad saved was taken to our house, which is where Shipmates is now. It used to be a lodging house and we moved into it when I was about 7 or 8.

"We used to go swimming down at the Quay and when the ferry went over, whether it was my father or anyone else we would creep up behind and hang on to the stern of the boat before he realised that anyone was there. 'Let go,' he would say, because having no legs he couldn't get out of the boat. It was rather cruel perhaps.

"The ferry went to the Quay from where the laundry used to be on the other side, taking 17 or 18 laundry girls and only one man rowing it. It used to be a thing seeing these laundry girls going over, some of them big women and the water would be up to the gunwales. There used to be a little man called Ollie, he was a navy man, and one day his oar broke and they started back to the Quay and finished up down the road. It was a wonder they weren't drowned! They were screaming away and he was only a little chap and instead of getting off at the Quay they got off at Berthon!

"Where the restaurant is now is where they used to board the ferries. They pulled it down and lost all the beauty of the place. They said they were going to put the stones back but they never did. The ferrymen used to keep their two boats there; one in the water and the other drying out. We kids used to go there and sit round the fire. We were very cruel in those days, when you come to look back at it. We would sit round the fire and all at once we would tip the fire over!"

Joey Cleall recalled some of the characters who used to live near the Quay. "There was poor old 'Buzzy' Saddler, who took bad here and old 'Broody' Lane. We children used to call him 'Red Top Cherry Hole Long Arse Buzzy' and he would reply, 'I don't mind you calling me Red Top Cherry Hole Long Arse Buzzy but don't chuck stones at oi!' because we used to chuck stones at him. Then there was an old

man called Billy Payne, who lived to 102. He went up a ladder and fell off it when he was 100! He used to read to Jim Arnold from an exercise book but he is dead now and so is his daughter. There was another chap, old Joey Rawlings, who used to keep South Hayes. He was a miser really and that is another place we used to whip stuff off. If you picked up a foreign coin and if you wanted to change it you took it up to Joey Rawlings and he would give you an English coin for it. South Hayes was a massive great place like a castle but it is split up now. He was mayor of Lymington and used to own all Flushards. In our time there were no houses there and no Queen Katherine Road then, just a little path and we used to run for miles; all the children did, even the little girls. No fear at all. They can't go anywhere today, though. People are sometimes afraid to open the door."

Joey Cleall told me that past the yacht marina in Bath Road there used to be a rubbish dump and then a marsh and a man called 'Fatty' Gold used to put his cows out there. "You could always get a penny off old 'Fatty' Gold if you helped drive his cows back to the milking sheds. Just behind the Arnold's house there used to be a stables, Crampton's stables. There was also a big pear tree and every October the pears were so thick that they just had to be thinned out! I used to get up in the tree and shake them down. They were lovely pears!

"Then there was a little man called Dumbie Murray, a deaf and dumb mute. But he would get around and worked like a horse and they used to think the world of him at Mew Langtons. We used to mimic him but he couldn't say anything but 'bugger, bugger, bugger.' My Dad was the driver for Mew Langton. Once Dumbie took me for a walk and let me fall overboard at the Bridge and brought me back wet through. My mother told me that. But little Dumbie Murray, he was a real character and would work like anything bottling the beer. When he wanted you he would call 'hubba.' As children we would go round bottle washing. We used to turn these bottles upside down and the water would squirt up and sometimes it went all over him. Then he wouldn't give us a lemonade. He wasn't very old, about 60 I should think, and the girls used to be frightened to death of him.

"Joby Phillips used to go down and pick up winkles and when he came back he would be rowing with the oars level with the water and there would be all these great big sacks of winkles. Then he would send them up to London and get about 2/6d. for them. That is how he earned his living.

"Then there was old Basil. He used to go out on the mud; it was mainly weed there until all this oil killed it all. He used to have a long pole with hooks on the end like a spear and you could see him walking on the mud, he had mud pattens on and he would go and spear eels. All along the edge of the river there was grass growing like corn, a sort of rice grass looking something like bootlaces swaying about in the water and they said that fish used to clean themselves on it. It has all gone now."

Jim Arnold joined in again. "Where the Assembly Rooms used to be next to Tesco there was an old picture-house there but we couldn't afford to go to the pictures. It cost 1d. or 1½d. and the films were of cowboys and indians and we were always given a stick of rock. If you couldn't get a penny to go to the pictures there were some tears then – but we always got in.

"At the top of Nelson Place there used to be a fair and there was a machine called the Joy Wheel and it would start spinning and in the end it went faster and faster until it slung the lot off. Oh, it used to be good! Where Travis & Arnold are now was a theatre called Hayes Theatre. (Before the laundry on the other side of the river there was going to be another theatre but it never opened up). There are still Hayes about now. They put on damn good shows. Mr. Hayes played golf and was always knocking golf balls about. We used to pinch them and when we took them back to him he would let us go in for nothing!"

Jim Arnold's wife came from Eastleigh and she worked in the laundry for five years and was there with Joey Cleall's wife. The Arnolds got their present house when they married and have lived in it now for 45 years. Joey Cleall's wife was a local girl whose father was a shipwright at Berthon and came from Shoreham. The laundry used to go round by horse and cart as far as Beaulieu but the laundry closed down because the water ran out. When John Howlett set up at Ampress they started sucking up all the water and although the laundry put in artesian wells the water never seemed to get there.

It was now Jim Arnold's turn to reminisce. "There used to be another laundry on this side," he said, "David's laundry it was called. It was the Imperial Hand Laundry and it was not very big. Then there was the old man who used to work at a laundry at Waterford, 'Push-up' George. He used to push these big baskets and sometimes we would help him and at other times just called out 'Push-up George' and then he would swear!

"The Southern Railway over there used to take all the cattle over to the Island. There used to be a big jetty across there. There was a tug called the *Carrier* which used to tow six of these horse boats although they could take anything, cattle and pigs as well. It was a proper heyday when they brought the pigs over

because when they unloaded them we would chase them around. We just waited for one to slip overboard! We used to pass them down the alley way and when the gates were open all the cows went out. They used to take circuses across as well. The last one-horse boat went down when there was some rough weather, cars and all on board. The old *Jumsie* came next. The paddle boats, the old *Lymington* and the *Solent* used to tie up at the Quay.

"There was a big flood in 1915 or 1916 and the tide came right up. At my home (where Shipmates is now) there was a step and my mother said, 'Jim, go and put another mat there,' just to stop it coming in. That is how high it came up. People were taking rowing boats from the river and rowing them right down by Waterloo Road. A chap called Dimmick used to have a coalyard there with stacks of coal and coke. Coke floats and a whole lot of it came floating along all down Mill Lane; it was a heyday for us because we salvaged it.

By courtesy of Helen Figgins

John Dimmick

"Where Golden Produce is now used to be Lance's rubbish dump and he used to keep chickens there but what became of them I don't know. My father was rowing the ferryboat at the time and said to me, 'If a policeman comes round, tell him that all your father has got are two or three empty boxes,' but what else he had got I never knew. You had to live by your wits in those days because you didn't know when the next meal was coming."

Joey Cleall told me that the mill wasn't working in their time but they remembered the building. It was a large building near SCATS and they used to make concrete bricks and curb stones there. Jan Hicks was working for them and the barge used to come up and unload cement. SCATS took it over later.

"There was a place at the bottom of Quay Hill which was owned by a man called Billy Winkworth and there was a little cubby-hole where we used to sell bloaters and red herrings in those days. In the living room you could buy rabbit skins and you can imagine the smell of that lot. He was about 80 or 90, poor old man. There was a barber's shop where Laurent Giles is now and a Singer sewing machine shop at the top of Quay Hill owned by Mr. Osborne. Next door was Fanny Hall; next to that a butcher's shop and then there was Hardings, a general shop where he used to sell paraffin and there was old 'Soldier' Webb's for ice creams. I have seen him come out of the Ship half drunk and go straight over to the Alarm. It used to have a sawdust floor with spittoons. Up in Quay Street where it is tarmac now there used to be stone slabs and we would play hop skotch on them!"

Jim Arnold remembered how some old tramps used to come round the Quay and tap on the door. "Sometimes they would come in and we would give them a cup of tea. There were also some rough customers up in the Lodging House – 6d. a night. Once a Welsh bloke came along and started swearing at my Mum and luckily my Dad came home and told him off. The next morning half a brick came through the window!"

After our long talk, which I found fascinating, Jim Arnold had kindly arranged for me to meet an old lady of 92 called 'Gran' Perry and her daughter, Joyce Harrison, who lived at Veryan. It is a lovely old house behind the Birdcage and probably the oldest in Lymington, going back four or five hundred years. In the old days it was called Newgate House and they used to keep French prisoners-of-war there. It is connected with the Catholic Church by an old secret tunnel. Prisoners were also brought down from London and stayed there before going to Australia. They showed me the crux of the original old beams in the roof which enabled people to claim squatters rights.

The Quay had plenty of character in those days. It still has some now but most of it has been lost. How sad for the 'Old Quayites.' It was the passing of an era.

Bob Cook

Bob Cook, the organist and choirmaster of St. Thomas' Church, Lymington and a very hard-working woodwork instructor at the Lymington Community Centre, is another 'Old Quayite.' He and his twin sister were born in a house called 'The Steps' (now the Old Customs House) and placed in a small drawer for a cradle. From the family papers he thinks his people have been there since 1700 because an ancestor was the first pilot appointed by Trinity House in this part of the Solent. They were associated with coastguards and customs as well as boat-building and his father was a boatbuilder in Salcombe, Devon.

Bob Cook told me something of the life on the Quay in the old days. "The Harpers used to live next door to us and they had a fish shop and always had winkles and things like that, all lovely and fresh. This was before the war. All his sons were fisherman too. Harpers Post, down the river, is named after them. Then there is Samuel's adopted son, Ozzie, he was a good pianist and was a cripple. They used to own a West Solent; it was about 30 ft. and did not have much accommodation and was more or less a dayboat. It went quite fast and I think he was skipper.

"Then, of course, all the timber used to come on great big black barges belonging to Travis & Arnold. Old Cecil Keeping, a very great character locally, used to have the job of transporting the timber from the barges to Travis & Arnold's timber yard in his long timber waggons. When the barges were in there was continuous activity down at the Quay. It was a very busy port, very busy indeed, with all the coal and the oil coming in. A firm called Fraser & White used to handle the coal.

"In the old 'Ship Inn' there was a chap called Buck Stacey. He was a great character and had a fishing-boat. He always kept it painted up well and one day there was mud all over the boat. Well, usually during the week I would have been the guilty one although there were lots of us kids down on the Quay. However this happened on Sunday and he came up to my mother absolutely furious and said, 'Your son has been down there again!' – but I was singing in Evensong so it wasn't me that time!

"There were two big rowing boats and they ran from the old Quay to what was the old laundry. It was a big building, turretted with battlements round the top. The ferry was mainly used to take the laundry girls from Lymington to the laundry. My uncle couldn't walk; he was paralysed from the hips down and invalided out of the navy. My father used to carry him down and he stayed in the boat all day. I can remember as kids, he had a dog that used to go with him. This was Bill Cruse. Then there was an old sailor called Sally Miller. I don't know why he was called Sally but he was a proper old sailor with earrings and I think he was the last boatman." (Rob Smith told me that Sally Miller used to live in the cottage which is now Doc Slatter's surgery. "He was a relation of another family of Millers who used to live on the Quay. He had what seemed like dozens of kids but they weren't his – I think they must have been his daughter's – living in appalling conditions.") "The ferry was owned by Badcocks, the Estate Agents, but it went downhill and was given to old Sally Miller in the end. I suppose he retired when he was about seventy. Then there was one called Tomkins, 'Buffy' Tomkins, who drank on the ferry and I think once had had too much. Well, when the ferryboat was not running they would be in the 'Ship Inn,' so whether he had had a drop too much but anyway he fell out of the boat and drowned. The current when it runs down is very, very strong there and it was hard work.

"Another day I can remember well, when I was still a youngster, was screaming laundry girls – I say laundry 'girls' but they were anything up to seventy years old – and they were standing up in the ferry because they were anxious to get home for their lunch time. There was a little chap, 'Oldie' Winkworth I think it was, and the tide was running out – there had been a lot of rain or it was a Spring tide – and the ferryboat was going round and round in circles all the way down the river. He couldn't do anything about it, I imagine he was drunk, and somebody had to go and pull them back in. There was a staging and a little hut on the opposite bank and people would cross in the Spring and go up around the old monument and pick primroses and walk back across the tollbridge. The ferry stopped thirty years ago now.

"When we were kids we never wanted to play anywhere else except in the Station yard because the transport of cars was done by a string of barges pulled by a tug and they used to tow up to three at a time. But best of all the cattle, the sheep, and the pigs all used to come over and run all round the Station yard. At the end, on one of the last trips, one of the barges sank at the mouth of the river with cars on board. The *Lymington* was the first paddle-steamer, *Kraut* as we called her because she was a German boat that came in about 1938 and almost went off to the war towing the barges. Good fun."

Bob Cook became a choirboy at St. Thomas' and later his father also became a chorister there. His mother played the piano so music was part of his life and he went from the piano to the organ, when Harry Wakefield was the organist at the church for nearly fifty years.

"There was a clergyman in Lymington called Fletcher-Jones, who has now retired and ended up as an Archdeacon in the Liverpool Diocese. He had been to Australia and had done a lot of youth work there and then in the war he formed his youth fellowship. There was already a big youth club in Lymington, under the aegis of the County and it used to meet in the Literary Institute. But Fletcher-Jones, against a lot of opposition, particularly from his vicar, formed this youth fellowship, about fifty or sixty strong, mainly from church-going people, and

it met at the Parish Hall. It met nearly every day of the week all the year round and was a fabulous thing; dancing played a big part with a social evening once a week and dancing classes as well. I didn't dance but I took to playing for whatever it was, folk dancing, ballroom dancing and American Square.

"By the time I was seventeen there was always a call for dance bands and I used to have a trio. It enlarged to a 15-piece band by the time we had progressed to mainly Old Tyme dancing. It had to be absolutely spot-on and all good players, because we played in the Guildhall in Southampton and were given quite a good write-up; although it was a bit nerve-racking with all the judges standing round on the edge of the dance floor. We had a good reputation because a man called Latimer, who used to run the BBC 'Those were the Days' programme of old tyme dancing thirty years ago, used to come over to Lymington.

"In Southampton we found that dancing almost ceased to be a pleasure and became too professional: there would always be officials with stop-watches timing the band. Once somebody came up at the end of a tango and said, 'You were half a beat too many in that minim.' Fair enough, I suppose, as a lot of the dancers were gold medal holders. We used to play regularly and it was super in Southampton on a Saturday evening. I was on the grand piano but I never knew who was going to be on the fiddle or who was going to be on the drums but they were always tip-top musicians and we used to play Palm Court stuff. It was good music and had to be played properly.

"I remember that the M.C. used to be all smiles, his wife was also all smiles, but as soon as they got away from the microphone and off the floor they had literally a cat and dog existence – it was awful." (Shades of *Hi-de-Hi!*) "They had six children and eventually parted. Dancing is an expression of pleasure and relaxation and something to do for the fun of it, but in competitions they became so finnicky: the bands had to be just right. Really, one saw the other side of it. Still, it got us away from Lymington!

"I went to South Baddesley when I was 16 and was there about ten years, and then I packed it up and went singing in Lymington for a while: it was too much of a tie and the kids were of an age to take around. Then the organist at South Baddesley left and they were stuck, and they asked me if I would go back, so I went there for two or three years. Then the job at Boldre became vacant, and I put in for it. Despite what they say about lack of organists, ten of us applied for it and it was short-listed to three. It was on a bitterly cold afternoon that we played it off and I had on a shirt and the keys were like icicles but I landed it and stayed there for fiteen years." Canon John Hayter, writing in the *New Forest Magazine* in January 1962 reported the appointment of Bob Cook as organist at St. John the Baptist, Boldre in these words: "I am particularly happy about this – and I know this view is shared by a great many others – not only because he is such a capable musician and choir trainer, but also because he is already well known to many of us. We are lucky to have him."

Bob felt it was then time for a change and, when a vacancy turned up at his own parish church in Lymington, he became the organist there in 1977. However, it has been a bit of a tustle and he would have thought that by now they would have had a choir of about 40 whereas they have only got 28. They should have been at a good standard by now.

"My father was working at a place called the Lymington Slipway & Engineering Company which was run by Jack Beagley in the middle thirties. It is where Golden Produce is now. The firm had a factory which made components for aircraft during the war and developed into laying up of boats and boatbuilding. I went there as an apprentice at the age of 14 and was lucky because they were building whalers and Admiralty cutters and I worked under my father. So where all the other nips skived around I was made to work!" By the time he was sixteen he had built his first whaler. He did a seven-year apprenticeship which finished when he was 21.

"After the war, Ian Carr bought the company and it changed to yacht building. He was quite successful because he was a keen yachtsman and there was an architect called Brian Kennedy, one of the up-and-coming designers, who designed some very good boats. *Pinker* was one of them, which was quite revolutionary. Suddenly his partner pulled out and in one day they were all given the sack. They went to work in the morning and at 11 o'clock everyone was given notice.

"Old George Smith bought it with a chap called Les Marshal, who died quite early on, unfortunately, and then old Parker, foreman at Berthon Boat came to be foreman with the company. We had quite a good programme of building there but then the place folded up. I then went to the Berthon for about nine months and we were on minesweepers and yacht work. It was O.K. but I wasn't very keen really.

"One day somebody talked about a joinery works that wanted two chippies. Not that I knew anything about joinery work, always having been in boat-building, but it was good money for those days I got the job. The foreman must have taken a liking to me and asked me to find another chap and I persuaded another joiner who was a bit dissatisfied to join me

and we were there four or five years I suppose. I was about 24 or 25 then. While I was there the lady who used to run Vicars Hill School wanted somebody to take the kids in the evenings for woodwork. We had slackened off a bit and the foreman, knowing that I was studying for an outside course in mathematics and woodwork said, 'This seems to be up your street,' so I went there for a couple of evenings a week. I had some very good years there and then I went on to Rope Hill.

"Then the chap who was doing woodwork and pottery at the Community Centre found that it had got a bit too much for him, and came to see me one evening, and that is how I started there; it must be eighteen years ago. I do one session a week now for the unemployed, which was over-subscribed at the beginning but as they get jobs they move out and somebody else comes in. It is quite interesting, but a bit sad really, as it is a problem for which there is no answer until more work appears. It does keep them occupied and they seem quite happy. On the first morning I had a talk and went through the tools and they seemed content to just sit or stand and do nothing and not show very much spark. Some of the older people popped in, seeing the place was open, and said, 'Crumbs! What a shocking lot you had in on Wednesday morning.' Well, of course they all had coloured hair and the kids get labelled purely by appearances. It is sad because when we were eighteen we had somewhere to go but these lads have no idea what is going to happen in the next week or the next year. They have no money: they live on sub-sistence. But I don't think full employment will ever come back again, quite honestly, not here. I think there will always be up to a million out of work."

Tom Turrell

It was Wendy Carrington who put me in touch with another 'Old Quayite,' Tom Turrell and I had the pleasure of visiting him in Trafalgar House, Hythe on 26th January 1982. When he was a boy, there used to be a place called Gowans Machinery, which closed down because it went bankrupt. It used to be next to the Pierside laundry, close to the ferry boats. "Years ago, long before the war," he told me, "if a stranger came there, they either swam, caught the train or ran! It was a rough, terrible place. The 'Ship Inn' then was a little place no bigger than a match box. Where the car park is now used to be a coal yard and David May's garden is now what used to be B.P. and Shell Mex.

"I was born in Lymington in a place called 'The Bethel' but it has gone now. My mother died when she was nineteen of tuberculosis when I was a month old.

I had two sisters, one brother and an Uncle Fred. Her mother, my grandmother, could not afford to bring us up and I was put into one of the Dr. Barnardo's Homes. We children never met again until I was about sixteen. My brother was in the Navy during the war and I haven't seen him for about forty years. I used to live in what is now the 'Boathouse' and our back garden reached where the Ship Inn car park is now.

"When I was a young boy I took the trade of butcher. But first I started in a grocer's shop where there is a jewellery shop today. I worked for Eastman's just up by the bus station and earned 5/- a week. Then I went into the army; first in the infantry and then I transferred into the Royal Army Service Corps which is now the Royal Corps of Transport, and I passed a test and became a butcher in the army.

"When I came out of the army I had nothing to turn to, my grandmother had passed on and I walked around for thirty years all over England. Unfortunately, in 1959 I contracted tuberculosis but got over it O.K. I then went down with chronic sinus. I did all manner of jobs around the country and have been to Scotland and Wales.

"I did some gardening with some people in Somerset and I worked for a little Catholic church in Chard. I was a porter at Milford House Hotel, although I didn't finish the season there. I have also worked in the Queen's Hotel in Brighton, the Atlantic Hotel in Bristol and at an hotel in Newquay, Cornwall.

"Not quite two years ago in April I had a torn cartilage and in June I broke my ankle. I went down with arthritis in the ankle and now I have got it in the spine. I was off the road for a time and had tablets to kill the pain which helped a bit but it is something you have got to live with.

"I worked for Joe Sanders, the sailmaker in Bath Road, for fourteen years. His son now does the sailmaking – he started there as a boy – and his daughter is a riding instructor in Walhampton School.

"I did one or two burials at Pennington and I did several burials up in Lymington churchyard as well. I also did four cremations. The last person I buried in Pennington was a three-day old baby. There were hundreds of flowers there for young Moffat; seventeen years of age he was and a footballer. I don't know if he passed away of leukemia or not. Then at one time I used to do all the hedging along there. I also worked at Our Lady's Primary School in Lymington.

"I knew 'Flounders' when it was a grocer's shop belonging to Mr. Travers and when he passed away

his daughter took it over and her husband was in the army. Next door to it, the 'Lentune Restaurant' used to be Mr. Harper's Fresh Fish Shop and on the other side, the 'Old Alarm,' which is now Christian, the hairdresser's shop, belonged to Mr. Biddle, my uncle. He has passed away now but where there are some little shops further down Quay Street there used to be cottages which he owned too. He had a lot of land but he drank all his fortune away.

"My mother's sister's son, who works in the rescue launch, Alan Coster, is the Assistant Harbour Master. He is a good boy. He married Mr. Goodall's daughter. He is a farmer and Alan has taken over now. They grow strawberries next to Elmer's Court.

"Part of the author Dennis Wheatley's old place is a home for old people and part is flats. Along there, at one time, many years ago, there was a little foot-path used to go up the Grove that we called 'The Monks Walk.' There used to be a monastery there years ago. Church Lane and Normandy Lane, when I knew them, were all fields. The population at Pennington used to be about 8,000 people and now it is becoming quite a large place. It goes with progress. A lot of people grudge the marinas but there is no need to do so. They bring in the money and without them there would be nothing in the town at all – it would be finished.

"I used to live in a tent by the Monument; you are not supposed to be over there and the police used to come and see if I was all right. I spent two winters out there but Dr. Rogers, my doctor, got me moved here, as I probably would not have survived another winter."

Apart from being a great story teller, it was he who told me about the ghost of Charles I walking in shackles at Vicar's Hill. He is also a great reader and was a familiar figure in the public library where he spent so much of his time. Tom still manages to come over to Lymington from Hythe to look up his many friends. He was chatting to Tom Bradley the other day about a kind of snail that eats away into the shells of oysters, which the fishermen fear will return again. I think he put it far too modestly when he ended by saying, "Quite a lot of people know me." They do indeed and one could not meet a nicer fellow.

Tom Morris

Another, but more recent 'Old Quayite' is Tom Morris, who sadly sold up his chandlery on the Quay in the Spring of 1982. He first came to Lymington in 1935 but was only passing through. "In those days it was quite an unfriendly place down on the Quay," he told me, "and I think Jimmy Arnold is the only one that is likely to give you the names of the old people who were in this area in his childhood. He has lived here, I believe, all his life. It is a most interesting part of Lymington and has plenty of history.

"I have been in Lymington since 1946. I have always been down at the Quay, because I operated passenger boats at one time from 1948 until about 1958. We went to the Needles, to Cowes to see the 'Queen' liners at Southampton and to Portsmouth and all over the place. I used to take them out alongside any predominant liner that was coming. The 'Queens' of course were the favourites, but there were several others; there was the *Olympic* and quite a number of troopships at that time. We carried about 54 to 58 passengers in the launches. I changed to chandlery before that – in about 1955. When we first came my wife had the Yacht House as a café and it was not a success at all: she worked very hard but all for nothing. I inadvertently got hold of her bank statement – dear, dear! The café closed the next day! It was a shame after all the hard work but there it is: that is life and that is business!

"Lymington Quay was a very different place in those days. There was a Shell Depot here and that was the only one left as Esso were back here and they closed. There were two of them, Esso and Shell. Esso closed just after the war. Wood had a coalyard this end and, of course, the 'Stone Cellar' was here and that was run as a café in those days. After we came here it was opened as that. Claude Halifax was living there then and he ran charter boats. As a matter of fact he came by last summer and looked me up. He is living on the East Coast somewhere now. A nice fellow. He was a disappointed man from the Indian Army. However it was one of those things.

"Dan Sutcliffe bought 'Veryan', which was Newgate House and was the link with Newgate Prison. It had a dungeon which was filled up and it was reputed that there was a tunnel to the Quay. We know there is a tunnel from there to the High Street – with a call at the Catholic Church! Well, they were masters at smuggling! He had Deeds going back to 1200 but they had a very mysterious disappearance. They were on parchment and were in copper-plate writing, beautifully done. Apparently a Bishop lived there at one time and sometimes the locals would call it 'The Bishop's House' but that is a very long time ago.

"After that it became linked up with Newgate Prison with the transportation of prisoners. They were brought down here to wait for a ship to come in, because this was quite a shipping port at that time. You could get to Lymington three days before you could get into Southampton, if you kedged. You could only kedge on the tides; they would run the anchor out in the dinghy and pull it in and the boat

with it, so Lymington could have been very popular.

"Certain schemes were put forward, I believe, as long ago as the 1700s to make a pier out into the Solent for the ships to tie up to but they never materialised. Lymington was probably influenced by about four families and whatever the four families thought, Lymington did! I suppose they wanted Lymington as it was for their pleasure and not commercial. So they just had the old sailing barges coming in and of course coal, wood and everything else came by water. There was a timber pond opposite the custom quay and there are traces of the old piles now. The Customs House was on the Quay where the car park is now: it was not in Quay Street.

"Before Aquaboats came the place belonged to a Mr. Lant, who was a quarry owner, and he imported road stone, building stone and stone of all sorts. He also rented a piece of land on the other side of the railway from the Lance family and made breeze blocks there. I think the poultry people have got it all now. But the buildings are still there, what is left of them. Coasters used to bring in gravel and all kinds of road dressing. I believe they made concrete blocks as well as breeze blocks because there was quite a good crane there at one time and a weigh-bridge. It was all properly fitted out. Apparently he was quite an old character, old Mr. Lant.

"I only knew of him from Mr. Lance, the scrap merchant and the man who reclaimed the land, where the poultry place and Rogers are now. I never knew the father but apparently he was quite a clever man and was a pioneer in haulage contracting. I think Leonard said that they were the second people to own a steam waggon in the South. Bournemouth Gas Works bought one just before them, and it was called a St. Pancras, after the place where it was made in London. The father must have been quite a unique fellow. He came to Lymington as a porter on the railway but moved on to more exciting things. I knew both the Lance brothers and they are extremely nice people, but their father was the man who went ahead. They had the mineral water works in North Close. One ran the mineral water works and the other ran the yard and the contracting side of it. The Lances lived in No. 7 Station Street which were the offices of Nautical Publishing and now Laurent Giles.

"Dumbie Murray worked for Mew Langton but he was also a famous cox. He was the cox of the famous boat owned by Mr. King which won 40 successive races in a row. They rowed in Lymington, Yarmouth, Ryde, Portsmouth and Southampton. It was bought by Mr. King when he saw it up on the rafters of what was Camper & Nicholsons. He knew the lads; there was 'Mush' Goodman, 'Monsey' Bran and two other fishermen. They were all fishermen, or made their living more or less by the sea, and Murray was the only one who didn't because he was deaf and dumb. So he became the cox. If he wanted them to go to port, he put his thumb out and the same with starboard. He never dared touch the rudder because of the drag pulling the boat back. They would have been fairly sharp-tempered old fellows, I should think. 'Monsey' Bran certainly was; he was a 'cank,' a very precise old man. They never had a moment's practice apart from when they took the boat out and rowed it.

"The story goes, as 'Mush' told me, which I am sure is true, that they went to Fyffe's yard, quite a famous yard, with Mr. King. He took the five of them along and they had a look at this gig. When they got it down, it was covered in black soot, because there were coalyards not far away, and they took it down to the water's edge, washed it and brought it out of the water again to dry it.

"Mr. King looked at his watch and said, 'Well, there is just time to pull round to Royal Pier, lads' – it was Southampton Regatta Day and he timed it beautifully. They decided that as they were there they might as well have a go, and so they got on board and away they went. The boat was bone dry; that was how well the clinker-built boats were built. They pulled round the corner of Dock Head and there was a shout through the megaphone of 'Come on, Lymington! We can't wait for you all day,' and they were about three boat lengths away when the starting gun was fired and they went whish! straight through, and won. They did that every time afterwards.

"The great story was that of the last time they ever raced. They had packed up; 'Monsey' Bran was not going to row any more and neither were the others. But one day 'Mush' Goodman was walking along the High Street when Mr. King came out and said, 'Yarmouth Regatta is next week, Mush.' 'We have finished and have put the boat up, Mr. King,' was the reply. However Mr. King offered to put up another three pounds on the prize money and asked 'Mush' to try and persuade the others to row just once more. So he went down to the Fisherman's Rest, where 'Monsey' was the publican and after a couple of drinks they eventually decided to go.

"When they got to Yarmouth it was a case of 'Good old Lymington, come and have a drink' and these boys kept buying them drinks, but they wouldn't drink too much so that they kept their heads. Their opponents were big, strapping men with arms bigger than their thighs. It was a four-mile race up the Solent towards Hamstead Ledge and back, and they did the same thing and passed everybody, and stayed in front so that they could see

them. I don't know what the others were like but 'Mush' Goodman was so smooth that you did not feel that you were in a rowing boat with him. His action was fantastic and the blade was never covered, it went just above the water. 'These big boys were pulling away and of course we could see them digging the blades right in and knew that we could hold them and we won.' So with Mr. King's extra £3 they won £8 which was a very useful sum of money in those days. But that was the last time the boat went out and it was sold about 1948.

"'Mush' Goodman often used to come out with me because he was bored stiff with nothing to do and he was getting quite old then and I took him to Hamble by car. We got to Luke's yard and were walking round looking at various boats, neglected and otherwise when 'Mush' said, 'Tom, there she is,' and there was the old gig just rotting away in Luke's yard. Poor old man, there were tears in his eyes. So that was the story of the Lymington Rowing Club of those days!

"Billy Morgan was a professional boxer at the age of 15. His father owned the laundry. I think a chappie from South Wales drifted in to Lymington and started working locally and formed the Boxing Club. Bill was one of his protegés because he was getting such a terrible time in school. The locals were picking on him because he was very small. Apparently this man was a most diplomatic fellow and was an ex-champion at welter weight. So he taught Bill how to look after himself and he became a professional boxer. 'That is when I had some peace and quiet,' he said, 'I didn't have it before. It was a harrassment to go to school.'

"Tommy Turrell, well Tommy Turrell is a legend. Through his mother's side he was related locally, I think that she was a Phillips but I am not sure. His father came from elsewhere and the story has it that he was a terrible man, an absolute horror. He used to work at Berthon and was a big strong fellow. Had this chappie who started the Boys Boxing Club been around when Tom Turrell was being beaten by his father, he would have stopped him for sure. Although he was a big, strong man it would not have made any difference to him at all – he would have got the measure of him.

"It was because Billy Morgan remembered the childhood that Tommy Turrell had had that made him try and get him somewhere to live. Tommy was sleeping out at the Monument and all over the place: he slept at the bus depot and just anywhere. He was supposed to be at the Monument but was not often there. Billy Morgan went to Lyndhurst to try and get him proper accommodation and when Billy Morgan gets going, he gets going, and he finally found this hostel at Hythe where Tommy is living now.

"There were quite a number of these old characters when I first came to Lymington but they have all gone now, unfortunately. Lymington has changed greatly; it has changed in every way. When I first came here I was paying £17 5s. 0d. rates and 5/- of that was water rate. Now it is over £1,500 and the drains are blocked up solid!"

'Don't forget the diver' was the catch-phrase used by Tommy Handley in the wartime radio show 'Itma' – and I have very nearly done just that. By the very nature of his job, M. J. Foot ('One Foot Under'), the diver would seem to qualify for membership of the 'Old Quayite' fraternity, as he too is in and out of the water all the time! He is kept very busy, particularly in the summer, checking to see if hulls are damaged or need scrubbing down, clearing fouled propellers and picking up objects accidentally dropped overboard. He can be contacted at the office of David Kane, the marine engineer whose workshop is down on the Quay.

OLD LYMINGTONIANS

"My grandfather used to tell me tales, because he heard them from his grandfather, and he knew where they used to hide the loot in the sea wall and various places on the marshes."

JACK BLACHFORD

"I had a fascinating talk with Jack Blachford at his haidressers shop in the High Street and he told me more about his grandfather, 'Monsey' Bran. George 'Monsey' Bran, no-one knows the origin of his nickname, died in June 1954 at the age of 95 and another fine old character has been lost to Lymington. The Brans have lived in Lymington for generations and if you go back 150 years the whole of Woodside was the Bran family. There were very few other people in the village apart from a few Spaniards.

'Monsey' Bran could remember the bitterly cold winter of 1881 when an iceberg about 30 ft. long drifted into the East Lake, 2 miles from Lymington, and afforded good shelter for wildfowlers. His earliest memory though is being sent at the age of nine to get a wheelbarrow load of salt from the old salterns at Oxey to salt a pig.

He first went to sea at the age of 14 in the $10 \times$ tonner *Pauline,* and at the age of 17 he sailed in a $2 \times$ ton racing yacht from the Solent to Naples for an Italian prince. He was sailing in the $300 \times$ ton yacht *Australia* when three men, Mr. Inman, Mr. Shutler and Mr. Springer were washed off the bowsprit and were miraculously washed on board again at the stern! For ten years he served in the *Shark,* belonging to the Duke of Rutland. His contemporary and 'mate' Jack Hayter was on board a private yacht off Cowes and saw an angry Edward VII fell the Kaiser on the club steps!

Although 'Monsey' used to go to sea in private yachts during the summer months, he was primarily a fisherman and in those days, with more fish in the Solent, it was possible to make a living from it. He used to fish at night and would often row the catch to either Cowes or Southampton to get the best markets.

Jack Blachford also told me the story of King's gig which is slightly different from that of Tom Morris and is well worth repeating. "Mr. King, Mary King's grandfather, owned a racing galley, which was a four-oared gig. My grandfather, George Bran (or 'Monsey') was the skipper and his friend, 'Mush' Goodman, another well-known character who was around in those days, was a member of the crew. 'Mush' used to play the accordion or concertina – it

didn't matter which it was – and he could play anything. He was known all along the South Coast for his playing. He really was quite a character. The other two members of the crew were the two Hayters: one was old Jack Hayter and the other was his brother. There were four members of the crew.

"Old Mr. King used to have a little steam yacht and they used to go to all the regattas along this part of the South Coast. In all the years they were racing they were never beaten. One memorable occasion they were racing at Yarmouth Regatta and the Royal Engineers had a team and these sappers were huge men – I remember my grandfather telling me the tale – and their arms were as thick round as my body. Apparently they met in the final and the local fishermen, our boat, beat them all ends up, and there was a row afterwards because they said that King's boat was a better boat. So our crew said, 'Fair enough, we will re-run the race and we will change boats.' So they did and still beat them!

"Another little tale he used to tell me was when they had been to Cowes racing and they were coming back when down came a thick fog. So they went along the Island shore until they got to Yarmouth and then decided that, if they steered due North, they would probably hit Lymington River. They steamed across and when they gauged they were very close to this side my grandfather, being a local fishermen, knew every inch of the shore and only had to look at the mud to know where they were. He decided that they would anchor and he would row North until he came to the edge of the shore head. He was thinking they were probably no more than a hundred yards off the Park Shore. Anyway by the time he had disappeared into the fog he hoped he would be able to see the shore and sure enough he could see Jack-and-the-Basket 100 yards to the East. So he rowed back to the boat and in they came, 100 yards East and straight up the river. How about that for dead reckoning!

"Another little story I remember him telling me was when they were getting on a bit and decided that perhaps it was time for them to retire. A new crew of younger men was formed and in their very first race, which was at Lymington Regatta, they lost; they were

Regatta

soundly beaten. While they were rowing up the River old Mr. King was watching them with his glasses and my grandfather, who was standing beside him, said, 'Ah, thee'll need a strong pair of glasses to see her today, Guv'nor!'

"Jack Hayter and my grandfather were both 92 and during the war he used to ride a tricycle even at that age. He lived at Woodside village and my grandfather lived at Poles Lane, just down the road. The old boy used to go down on his tricycle and have a glass of whisky and a smoke with my grandfather and then at lunch-time he would go home. My brother and I were both at home at the time because we used to come in and help father when we were on leave. We were cycling home and met old Jack tearing up the road on his tricycle and when we got back we found that grandfather was not at all well. So Ted said, 'Aren't you feeling very well?' and he answered, 'No, I am not feeling at all well today,' so Ted said, 'Well, you are not as tough as your old mate. We have just seen him going up the road on his tricycle.' 'Ah well,' he replied, 'he baint as old as I be.' There was only three months between them!"

'Monsey' Bran celebrated his 92nd birthday by sailing with three generations of his descendants on Lymington River on a blustery day. He sailed the 20 ft. sailing boat *Dunlin,* built by his son-in-law, J. C. Blachford, with his customary skill and without any assistance. He still raced and competed in a Lymington Town Sailing Club event a few days later.

Jack Hayter

Both 'Monsey' Bran and Jack Hayter could recall stories of smuggling in the olden days that had been recounted to them by their grandfathers. In fact, Jack Hayter's grandfather was captured by the coastguards and died in prison. It was said that 100 men were carrying kegs at the time: they used to wear braces which supported one keg in front and one behind. Two thousand kegs were hidden in the mud offshore.

Contraband was often dropped at Pitts Deep and kegs were sunk into the mud at a place still known as Brandy Hole. Later they would be taken inland by horse and cart and hidden in the New Forest. Ghostly sounds of kegs rolling across the floor were said to be heard in Pylewell Farm House, which was once used as a hiding place.

"My grandfather's grandfather was the local smuggler and he lived in Woodside. William Bran, who is buried in the churchyard at St. Thomas, was the local smuggler leader, and he operated between Keyhaven and the Beaulieu River and the whole of that area. My grandfather used to tell me tales, because he heard them from his grandfather, and he knew where they used to hide the loot in the sea wall and various places on the marshes. It was quite a story.

"The 'Fisherman's Rest' was not around in those days: it was a private cottage and that belonged to old Mr. King at one time. My great-grandfather and my great-grandmother lived there, and she used to have a little cottage laundry. In those days you either sold boiled sweets or you had a little laundry, and they had a sort of little one-room pub. That is all they ever did in the village to make a little extra money, I suppose. So she decided to get a licence and turn it into a public house and, of course, all the Bran family, being fishermen, it was called 'The Fisherman's Rest' and they took out the first licence in 1870.

"My grandfather took over from them and he did a little bit of smuggling too because he was a yacht skipper as well as a fisherman, and he and the owner of the yacht used to sail for Boulogne. They would load up there and used to buy a lot of tobacco and stuff in France to sell in the pub. They would come back at night into the Lymington River and their mooring was Crooked Lake, next to Oxey Lake. Strangely enough, years later, I had a 6 metre and she was moored in exactly the same place.

"Over on the marsh just by Crooked Lake there is a brick barn and that was there in those days. They would come in at night. Grandfather used to row through Crooked Lake to the sea wall, carry the loot across the marsh and hide it in the Solent and the next morning at daybreak you would see the yacht beating down the Solent and she would come down the river and straight up to Customs – as they had Customs in those days – and of course they didn't have anything to declare as they had already got it ashore! As soon as they cleared Customs, the owner used to go home, and my grandfather would take the boat back to its moorings. He would go back to the Fisherman's Rest and either take his donkey trap or the wheelbarrow, depending on how much they

were taking, down to the barn on the marsh, fill it up and chuck a piece of old fishing net over the top and back to the Fisherman's Rest. The next day the owner would come along in his trap, have a drink and take his share of the loot. It was rough and tough in those days but grandfather used to do it just to get the better of the Customs. It was like that in everything he did."

'Monsey' Bran's son-in-law, J. C. Blachford, was a very skilled boatbuilder, being the originator of the Oxey Birds. There is a photograph of him in *The Bournemouth Daily Echo* of Wednesday, 17th May 1950 at work on his new and biggest boat yet, the 20 ft. half-decker *Dunlin*. With him was his 91 year old father-in-law who celebrated his 92nd birthday by sailing in it with his family.

'Monsey' Bran and J. C. Blachford

"My father started this hairdressing business in about 1924 or 1925, and then in 1935 I left school and joined him, and 18 months later so did my brother, and we have been here ever since – well over sixty years now.

"I have been doing my family history and we can go back to about 1200. We originated at Ringwood. There is a little village called Blashford, and there is a lake there called Blashford Lake and they sail boats there. They spell the name slightly different as Blashford, and that is a corruption by some clerk at one time or other. Originally it was Blaeccasford, Blaecca was Anglo-saxon and he was our ancestor and then in the Norman invasion with the two languages it became Blacheford with another 'e' on the end and that is where we started from.

"We had a Founder Member of the Royal Yacht Squadron too. Pope Barrington Blachford was a Founder Member and there were only 20 of them, I think. It makes me laugh now when I go to Cowes – I am not allowed to step on the hallowed lawns, though I doubt if any member today has an ancestor who was a Founder Member!"

Jack Blachford told me that he and his brother Ted taught their boys to sail when they were very young. "My boy used to sail on the River when he was six years old, in a little boat like a miniature Cadet which I made for him and he used to sail it up and down. Then I made him a 12 ft. catamaran and later Major Hibbert came along and started the Sailing Club at the Salterns, and so of course they went into the British Moths then and gained quite a reputation.

"Tony was the British International Moth champion. He has come into contact with three crowned heads I think it is now. He raced in the European championships in Norway and the King presented the prizes. The young King of Siam decided he wanted some Moths to start a little private sailing club of his own, and he wanted to race the British champion, and that happened to be Tony at the time, and he was only a young lad and he didn't know what he had to do. He said, 'Do you think I dare beat him? You must not beat a king or he might have you beheaded!' The third time was a little while ago when he sailed with the King of Spain, so he has been getting around.

"My son, who works at Berthon, is quite a helmsman too. He is nearly always in the first three in any sort of boat from an ocean racer down to a small dinghy. I have got a lot of cuttings and write up the stories. One of the Lymington Regattas, when they were still Juniors, held the National Junior Championships and the youngsters from some of the London clubs came down to compete against them and they had four races. It was rather a hectic week because it blew harder and harder as the week went on and for the final race it must have been blowing a gale. I think about three boats finished out of about forty odd. But it was rather funny as Gerald won all four races and Tony, who was three years younger, was second in all four races. I think they revelled in the rough conditions, being local boys. That was four races in a row and then they had the Junior Regatta at Lymington and there were four more races for that and he won all four of them.

"Then there was the Lymington Regatta; there were 3 races for the Junior and 4 for the Regatta. He won the 3 as a Junior and on the last day they had a big turn out, there must have been about 60 British Moths that turned up. Many of the lads came from the London clubs, all the National champions and all the rest of them and none of our youngsters had ever beaten any of them before. They had raced against them but they had trailed behind and so at the final race there were too many to race in one go, so the best of the Saltern boys were told that if they wanted to they could race with the Senior Group. So Gerry thought, 'Well, I have got to have a go at them one day,' and he had already won about 8 races in a row, so he said he would go in with the seniors. The others decided that, with Gerry out of the way, they stood a good chance of winning and they all opted for the Junior race! So he was the only one and he won the race! Altogether it made eleven races in a row so it was quite a remarkable feat and the first time that a local youngster had beaten outsiders. So then they all thought, 'Well, if Gerry can do it so can we,' and they began to beat them quite regularly. Eventually Tony became the National Champion and he was second in the European championships; he was unlucky as he was leading by miles on points and in the last race his mast broke – but he still had enough points to be second even so. But in boat racing that is the sort of thing that happens"

CHAPTER 8

THE FISHERMEN

*"If anyone lives near a harbour or river or anywhere there are mud flats, he could
have quite a bit of fun and quite a few fish if he knows how to go about it."*

GEORGE SMITH

George Smith

George Smith was born on 6th January 1903 at
Hermitage and the Emsworth Channel of
Chichester ran nearly up to their back door. So
George was born with boats. His father was a
fisherman and a yacht hand and used to fish with
the Emsworth Oyster fishing fleet. It was as skipper
to the Russells of East Grove, Lymington that he first
came here with them in the summer of 1914 and
prospects seemed so good that he stayed and his
family joined him.

George left school at the age of 12 and at one time
joined his father as yacht-hand on board the Russell's
yacht with Jim Smith (no relation) as boy. Jim Smith
continued to work for the family right up to about
fifteen years ago when he went back to work full-
time at Berthon. George fished with his father all
through World War One up until 1931 and in their
spare time they fitted out small yachts and laid
moorings. George married and had three sons, Jim,
Bill and Rob and they lived in 'Alexandra' in Bath
Road, next door to his father.

When his father died, George started a small
boaytard but he kept up with his fishing. His eldest
son, Jim, fished with him commercially up to World
War Two, making the third generation and Rob
would go out and fish with him too – but only for
pleasure.

In World War Two he was too old to be called up
and he closed his yard and started fishing again but
there were too many restrictions. Then he joined a
Southampton firm, Westminster Dredging Company, which dredged out slipways for landing craft.
At the end of the war he started the yard again but
continued to fish and would occasionally go out with
his mates to keep his hand in.

When George Smith first went fishing he often
had to row two or three miles, but if he had to go out
further, he would sail in his Itchen Ferry *Star,* towing
a dinghy. Then if the wind should drop he could
always row home again and he kept straw in his
boats to keep his legs warm. He used Don Howard's
jetty right up until the marina was built. Two of his
sons, Bill and Rob, worked with him but in the 1950s
he sold out to Hugo Duplessis who later went into

partnership with Peter Webster. Don Howard
remembers that he used to ride round Lymington in
a Rolls Royce and top hat and was a real character.

Although in the the First World War the government gave grants to fishermen to help them instal
motors, his father was too old and he was too young
to make the change. However, probably no fishing
boat did instal motors much before 1930. In those
days you could put down a couple of nets and leave
them safely there all night, knowing that all that
could happen would be that someone would row
over them. Today you are lucky if a speedboat or the
outboard engine of a yacht doesn't snarl up your nets
and tear them to pieces.

George Smith did fish with motors later but he
really always preferred sail. "On a still night under
sail you could hear the water lap on the shore and a
nightingale singing in the woods." But with no motor
there was no electricity and as all fishing was done at
night this meant using torches or a candle lantern.
The advantages of a candle lantern was that if they
were knocked over they immediately went out and
they also acted as a hand warmer on cold nights.
Paraffin was not used in case it came into contact
with the catch.

In these sailing boats there often used to be a little
coal stove in the cuddy and they would make tea
there. Often George Smith would crawl into the
cuddy to get warm and drop off to sleep but they all
kept an eye on each other and he would soon be
woken up! Fishing then was hard work with little
sleep, as on coming ashore you had to take your
catch to the market and then check over your gear.
The one night nobody went out was on Saturday
night because there was no market on Sunday and
few people had fridges. How he fished, collected
winkles and cockles, caught eels, crabs and lobsters
is admirably recounted by him in the booklet
Secrets of George Smith, Fisherman, written down and
illustrated by Maldwin Drummond and published
by his Ilex Press. It is probably one of the few of its
kind about fishing in harbours and estuaries and it
makes fascinating reading.

It was George Smith who told Maldwin Drummond how to walk on mud for the thesis he was

writing for Southampton University. George Smith used to make his mud pattens from either English elm or waterproof plywood ⅜″ thick, cut into two pieces about 12″ square and with the corners cut off, rather like snow-shoes and they used to skate along the mud with them. There were no long 'wellies' in those days and one wore leather boots, so it was essential to keep oneself dry. There was a special way of walking on them to prevent them tipping up and the secret was to have your foot over the front.

Roger Bayzand

Roger Bayzand was born on the Isle of Wight so he supposes he is still a 'foreigner,' as it takes a long time to be accepted by the old families in Lymington, even though he came over here at the age of five years.

"The Gates, the Phillips and the Mapes are three of the old fishing families," he told me. "They have been fishing for generations. It was only part-time fishing then and they would also work at the Berthon Boatyard or the Ropewalk Boatyard. Ron Gates is the only member of the Gates family still fishing part-time; he works in the boatyard at Aquaboats and he is a good boat painter, but he will go oystering once the season starts up and do a bit of trawling now and again. George Phillips is still fishing: he is not too well but works for Eric Whitcher."

Roger Bayzand started working at Peter Webster's Boatyard in King's Saltern Road and then worked on yachts in the Mediterranean for four years. On his return he went back to boat building, this time with Chris Carrington in the Bridge Boat and Crane yard by the 'Ship Inn.' He has been a part-time fishermen for some years and has had his own boat for nine years; fishing and lobster potting for his own pleasure. Five years ago he thought it was time to make a move from the boat business as it seemed to be slackening, mainly due to the fact that moorings have reached saturation point, and he then became a professional full-time fisherman. For the last year he has been Secretary of the Professional Fishermen's Association.

Roger Bayzand very kindly came round to my house on a March evening in 1982 and we had a long talk about fishing and also about the Professional Fishermen's Association. "As Secretary I am very involved in all the problems that variously come through the Association," he said. "People approach you with a problem and you have to try and sort it out. There are two ways we do this. Every Association in this area, which stretches from Selsey Bill to Lyme Regis, sends a representative to the Fishermen's Council, which meets monthly. They then make recommendations to the Southern Sea Fisheries, which is the regulating body of this area and makes its by-laws. These include fish sizes, enclosure of oyster beds and net sizes and we advise what we think is the best thing for this area. Southern Sea Fisheries also give grants to help fishermen buy their own boats and it is also running a publicity drive for fish.

"The Professional Fishermen's Association did apply for representation on the Marshes Management Committee but I last heard that the committee was only concerned with the area within the sea wall and had nothing to do with the water outside of it and therefore we were not entitled to be represented. But there are some aspects of it that we would be in conflict with sometimes. There are some of our members who keep their boats round in Oxey Lake and have done so for generations. Maiden Dock and Moses Dock have been used by sporting fishermen, but fishermen nonetheless, and it will be a great shame to see them closed up and will also deny small boat owners pleasure. There is going to be restriction of access there; you never quite know how fishing is going to turn but you might want to go down and gather cockles for bait for long rod fishing from the foreshore.

"Fifteen years ago there were hardly any fishing boats. The build-up started first with the potting boom – and there have been several booms. Lobsters were found in the Solent and round the Isle of Wight and several boats started working there. At the same time there were angling parties going out from Lymington and most of the full-time commercial fishermen started that way. People came down from all over the country to go fishing and sea angling in this area – the Isle of Wight and the Needles in particular are world-famous.

"Most of the boats on the river are now full-time; there are some part-time boats but no so many in this area and sometimes they are just used for pleasure. Some of the fishing boats still take angling parties out, which are not classed by the fishermen as part of the fishing occupation but as charter hire business, but to my mind they are all fishermen in one form or another. We have fifteen or sixteen boats going out from Lymington. This doubles in the winter and you get the oyster boats coming in from Mudeford and Poole and sometimes from as far away as Weymouth.

"A boat normally carries a crew of two or three for most forms of fishing. Working from here on a daily basis there is only one boat that stays out more than one day at a time. She is a potting boat and pots for crab mainly with a by-catch of lobster and works the grounds to the East of the Isle of Wight and may stay away for several days but the rest of the boats are in and out every day.

"The times we go out and come back depends on the type of fishing we do. Trolling is usually done at night and therefore the catch is landed early in the morning at 6 or 7 o'clock. The crab and lobster potters go off early, about 4 o'clock to 6 o'clock and they are back around midday. The oyster fishing in the winter is usually done by about 4 o'clock. The season is at present from November until the end of March and we have a by-law regulating the time we fish from 8 o'clock to 4 o'clock. Also we are not permitted to take anything smaller than about 2½". These restrictions are designed to keep the amount of fishing effort down.

"In the beginning we lived through the winter on the proceeds of lobster potting. But the summer is not as good as it used to be with lobsters and crabs being over-fished. It is funny how these industries go up and down. We have a problem with lobsters at the moment because the Canadians can produce lobsters a lot cheaper than we can. They grow more lobsters over there and have been supplying the French market with tons and tons of lobsters, which has tended to reduce the price and made the lobster market unstable.

"Then the oysters started nine years ago. Most of the fleet have got their boats through oystering and that is why we have got such a large fleet in Lymington. If it was not for the oysters I think you would only have about six boats here working full-time.

"There are two 'Orders,' one at Stanswood Bay and one at Calshot, which are basically co-operatives of fishermen that have been allowed to cultivate a portion of the seabed and grow the oysters and improve the stock. Stanswood Bay has been running since 1974 and Calshot has just started up and has caused many problems. There is a lot of feeling that others should be in it and of course people have fished that area for some time and have now been excluded from it.

"Unlike in Britanny, we have not got oyster pens but I believe 'SeaFayre,' the local fish merchant, has a piece of land up by Solent Boom and they are laying oysters in bags down there, and clams from Southampton Water are also being stored there. They are stacked loose on the foreshore. But we have not got the real space to lay stacks here. The advantage of stacks is that you can retrieve the oysters at the right time and as it is such a fluctuating market we could then be sure of a good price.

"The main market used to be France. At Christmas and Easter there is a vast demand for oysters there. The oysters we gather from the Solent are known as seed oysters; that means that they are meant for re-laying and fattening up. It depends where they go, and the size when they are taken, as to how long they lie on the beds. Some of the oysters we sent to Spain last year, a fairly new larder for us, were on the beds a month. They were laid in shallow, warmish water and the meat content trebled in about a month and they were fit for consumption and were put on the market straight away.

"We sell direct to a merchant on the Quay or to a factory on the Stem Lane Industrial Estate at New Milton and they are transported in hessian sacks in a truck. Quite often at the beginning of the season, when a lot of oysters are being shipped, a French articulated lorry turns up at the Quay and then they go direct to France or Spain. There is also a market in Holland. They eat far more shellfish on the Continent than we do and it is not a luxury food there.

"We now have a clam fishery in Southampton Water with five local boats working there: two are temporarily based in Southampton and three steam up there each day from Lymington. The clams are sent mainly to France and some are exported to the United States from where they came originally. The story is that they were brought over by trans-Atlantic liners. They carried live clams on board, and at the end of the trip they were tipped over the side into Southampton Water and they naturally seeded there. There are also slippy limpets, which also came over from the States, attached to the clams, and now we have slippy limpet beds all the way along the Solent.

"We also do trawling. It used to be quite a popular thing locally. There is a lot of sole fishing. Dover soles are very popular. We also get skate and plaice but sole is the most valuable fish and we get the best return for it. Trawling has really dropped off because of the price of fuel and people are turning to fixed net fishery.

"Fixed net fishery consists of gill nets and trammel nets which are fastened to the sea bed and they catch the fish at rest. The fish swim into the net – you are not taking the net to the fish – this saves fuel. Also you catch less small fish by this method. The trawl will take pretty well everything that is on the sea bed and will gather up small and large fish. But the fixed nets, which have been used for generations, have come back into their own because they use less fuel and select the right size of fish, which is becoming more and more important. You cannot carry on just taking everything, because once a fish has been trawled there is not much chance that it will be returned alive and most just die. They are trying to restrict the gill net fishery in this area with pressure, mainly from the angling lobby, because it is the time of year when we are fishing for bass.

"Bass is a fish that locally had no value at all when local fishermen sold it, but again our friends the French regard it as a valuable fish. People started fishing for bass from the shore on the shingle beds to the West of Hurst Castle. This is another form of fishing that has come into the area. So those are three markets which would not have got off the ground so quickly if it had not been for the French I don't think that the French fishing can supply them with enough – it is not because we are supplying them at a cut rate. It is a strange thing that fish that you cannot sell in England, the French would consider as a delicacy. It is a shame. Fish eating in England has declined, unless it is in a packet. People seem to have lost the art of cooking fish to a great extent. So the Sea Fisheries Board which has been set up to take over the old white fish authority, is running a scheme to promote fish through advertising and hopefully the fishing industry will receive a boost because it certainly has declined over the last two or three years."

Graham Butler

"I have been in Lymington about eighteen years but I was born and bred here. My family came from Bournemouth originally and I started fishing there and used to go out part-time fishing from Poole.

"When I came to Lymington I started working here with John Perkins. He had a boat here and I worked as crew on her and then skippered her for a couple of years until I bought my own boat. John Perkins had a sort of fishing company – he was a man of many interests. He had a boat built by David May, called *Tamarak,* to take his angling friends out and he bought a half share in her and formed a company.

"We did not want to get involved in the angling side and stuck to the potting side of it. In those days it was only ourselves and a few other boats working lobster and crab then and you did not need to go so far out – just round the Needles. After I left they had another boat built at Exmouth and then they had three boats with a couple of skippers running them for three or four years. When the original partner with John Perkins retired – he was getting on a bit – the boats were sold and the company folded up.

"We used to keep the lobsters in those days at the Salterns Sailing Club. Major Hibbert used to let us keep them in cages in his lake. Brian Macnamara was also potting at the time and he had a boat called *Shelhorne.* One day he did not tie the lid of his cage firmly enough and the lobsters got out and crawled

all round the pond. I know that the Water Board workers used to walk along the sea wall and were for ever poking down with a stick for these lobsters. The lobsters used to get in a hole by the sluices there and the men would put down a stick and hook them out. They lived there for a long time, for years. The lake was drained in the winter but there was always enough water to keep the lobsters alive. That was before it was sold by Major Hibbert."

"He gave John Perkins permission to keep his cages there and they floated around but the water used to get too warm at the surface and so we had to sink the cages and keep them down. There were also some 'old timers' who would go down there along the sea wall and hook lobsters out of what we call 'turrets' but I think that is a thing of the past. All along the shores of the Solent there are the 'turrets,' which are fossilised trees, when it used to be forest, and if you go down between the river entrance at very low Spring tides, you will see them there right at the lowest tides. There are not so many lobsters in the Solent nowadays.

"The boat I originally had was called *Torbay Pearl,* built by Jack Brabham, and I had her for eight years and four years ago I had a boat built at Appledore. I concentrated exclusively on lobsters and crabs and I have not gone in for oyster fishing which is seasonal. Basically you can fish all the year round with lobsters and crabs. Originally we used to fish sprats in the winter from September to December or January: that was up to 1970 which was the last year we made any good catch in sprats but we found some shoals two years ago in 1980 by the Island. We were crabbing at the time and we saw some of these shoals, so we told the Mudeford men; they went out and caught some and so we decided to put the nets on and had a go ourselves. Last winter, 1981 was very good and we caught a lot of sprats then. But basically we crab all the year round. When we first started potting we would put the pots out from March to September but now we have got so much money tied up in it that we pot all the year, apart from a refit.

"I have got a crew of two on the boat. We sell mainly for the markets in France and Spain through a merchant, who used to come over on the ferry to Southampton. But now we have heavy lorries coming over with tanks which are refrigerated and they take the catch still live over to France. I usually meet them at Portsmouth or Southampton; they do not come down to Lymington Quay. If they do it is for oysters but that is a different type of lorry, an ordinary transport lorry.

"My wife is Tom Morris' daughter and we used to

live in the top flat over the chandlery. Then that little bit was infilled and we thought why not sell there. People always used to come down to the quay to see if we would sell them crabs or lobsters and so we decided to sell them retail. We started up one Saturday morning and called ourselves 'SeaFayre' and it built up from there. It is ideal. It is right by the quay and people know that we catch our own stuff and I think we have got a good name for it. We had to wait quite a long time to get planning approval and it took six to nine months to get it through. It has been quite a successful business. It is open full time on Saturdays and Sundays; we do not want to do it seven days a week. We have stuck to shell-fish – we do not sell white fish.

"We do not tread on Foot's toes and he does not tread on ours and we get on quite well and I have sometimes sold him crab. We do get more than enough crab to keep him going but he has always dealt with a Christchurch wholesaler and they bring the stuff to him.

"I have not been on one of the courses run by the Fishery Training Scheme although Lionel Seddon Jones has tried to twist my arm a few times about it! The only ones that would be relevant – I have been fishing a number of years now – but launching a life-raft and things like that are very, very useful. The actual training courses are basically for people who have just come into the game. Not always – but, of course, there is always something that you can learn: there is net mending, wire net mending. He is running a good thing and he is a good bloke for it. He has put a lot of time into it and certainly some of the courses he has done have been very successful. He has not managed to get me along yet but he keeps trying!

"In Bill Gates' time they were not only fishing but they would be boat painting or boat building or any other activity to which they could turn their hands, because there was not enough money in it as far as they were concerned. It was more or less part-time fishing. That is what they did – or trying for trout above the iron bridge and dodging the bailiffs!

"The whole Solent area is basically sheltered water, not like the open sea, and it has altered the fishing scene considerably in the past ten years. When I first came there were probably not more than 15 to 20 boats full-time fishing boats. Now there are probably 200 or more. Basically what has happened is that all these boats have been brought in for the oyster fishing and the more traditional trawling fishermen, who caught soles, plaice, crabs and lobsters have been over-fished because you have too many boats chasing too little fish. They do oystering in the winter and then in the summer when

the oyster season closes they have got to turn their hands to something on a boat to earn some more money. The area can only support so many boats because there is not the amount of fish to expand the fleet. They use the oysters to subsidise the rest of the year's work.

"I have never fished oysters and do not regard it as fishing as such; anybody can do it – you do not need to have any knowledge. You can just go out there, provided that you have got a boat, and dredge them in. It has affected me inasmuch as I have had to buy a bigger boat and steam further out to sea. I go about 30 miles out now because in the Solent there is so much gear work round the shore that we are working 15 or 20 miles off St. Catherines to get a reasonable living beside the inshore grounds. George Smith would have had some yarns. He said that the dredging had ripped up all the kelp and left the seabed looking like a ploughed field! It has certainly ruined the Solent fishery for many people."

Dave and Kay Mitchell

Those who have driven to or from Beaulieu on the Walhampton Road will have seen at the Portmore cross-roads a notice outside the corner house stating that cooked crabs are for sale. To find out more about it I went to see the Mitchells at their home on 21st August 1982. Kay Mitchell told me that during the war Five Ways had been the Village Stores and Post Office, and there had been a thriving village at Portmore then. This was why she did not need a licence when she started selling crabs at her kitchen window and why she could put a sign up outside her garden gate.

Dave Mitchell used to dredge for crabs during the winter but then noticed that no-one was selling crabs. So they started selling them from their home. He originally owned a boat called *Callisto*, which had overturned once at Calshot and her skipper had been lost, but later he needed a larger boat so he now owns *British Raj*. The business thrived and they had an idea, which had been at the back of their minds ever since they came to Lymington, to have a trailer and sell from that. The children were growing up and it meant Kay need not stay at home; it was a case of either getting a job or working for herself.

"We designed the outside of the trailer," she said, "and I asked Lush Signs to make a sign for me. Everybody knew me as Kay and they all knew it was Kay's shellfish and so to keep my trade and my customers I used my own name so people would know who we were and associate us with 'Five Ways.'

"I then approached the Angel Hotel and asked Mrs. Perrett if I could keep the trailer in the Angel car park, and got her permission to do so on Thursdays.

This was so successful that I then sold there on Fridays as well and, when business continued to increase, I applied to the Council to have a stall at the market on Saturdays. I even ran a stall at Hythe market but it was very expensive to run, as a year's rent cost £250; but I may go back there again just for one day a week, probably Tuesdays. People have been coming over from there on a Thursday to Lymington and buying two weeks' fish in one go and freezing it and returning again in a fortnight. It is a lovely market there, an enormous market." "Perhaps," she added wistfully, "I may even have my own shop in a couple of years."

"Twelve boats go out fishing full-time from Lymington and I buy from most of them. I have got two pens in the Beaulieu River to keep the crabs as the Lymington River is so polluted. I feed them on mackerel. Sometimes I go over to Poole for whole cod and large plaice of up to 5 lbs. because they go out fishing deeper from there. My customers like to see a whole cod dressed for display on my stall. In the trailer underneath the display I have got an in-sulated cold box and even in the hot weather it kept to 32 degrees with the ice. You have to box all your fish, which takes a long time, several hours in fact, because you have got ice, fish, ice, fish and it keeps beautifully. When the trailer is in the Angel yard some of the old ladies come and I just don't charge them the full price because they are on pension. It is a good thing I am not a shop!

"I asked the Council if I could go to Lymington Quay with a trailer but was told it would cause a hitch. Mrs. Butler runs 'Seafayre' there now and Tom Morris, her father, did up the garage for her. She only opens on Saturdays and Sundays but when the children are on holiday she picks four weeks and opens Thursdays and Fridays as well. I had to do everything myself.

"In the beginning, when it was small, I could manage on my own but now I need the girls to help me. They all skin fish and clean them and dress the crabs for me. Mandy runs it here on Saturdays when I am in the High Street and another daughter comes with me into Lymington. You need a full team. Dave has been fishing with his Dad all holidays. He loves it and cannot wait to get a boat of his own next year. It is good for them: you do not find many family businesses these days, especially just starting up."

Rescue of Colonel Jardine

"Man grabbed from inferno – helpless as fire crept nearer" and "Quick acting fishermen save Colonel's life" were the headlines in the *Southern Evening Echo* of 28th August 1981 and *The Lymington Times* of 5th September 1981 respectively. Colonel Jardine,

father of the famous Jardine Twins, was up in his bedroom when his dressing gown caught fire from his bedside lamp. He thought he had extinguished it but as he could not turn his head he did not see that flames were spreading upwards and setting the roof alight.

As Dave Mitchell was returning home from a fishing trip in *British Raj* with two of his crew, Wayne Grouse and Paul Phillips, he saw what he thought was a bonfire in the grounds of Walhampton March but then saw that the roof of the house was on fire. As they dashed up the drive they could see Colonel Jardine, who is disabled, sitting in a chair in the front room. Dave Mitchell was luckily able to kick down the front door, despite the Yale lock, and he and Wayne Grouse and a neighbour, Chris Parker, entered the house and only just got Colonel Jardine out in time. Smoke was coming down the stairs and shortly after the roof went up and tiles were falling all over the place.

Colonel Jardine seemed more concerned with his medals than with anything else and not only did they manage to save them but with the help of Fred Blunt, a local builder, they also rescued some of his furniture as well. In the end twenty firemen were tackling the blaze but the upstairs of the house was completely gutted and downstairs was extensively damaged by water and smoke. Colonel Jardine was taken by ambulance to Lymington Hospital with shock but an hour later he discharged himself and went to spend the night with neighbours!

One is very conscious of the words "Old soldiers never die, they only fade away" and this is exactly what happened to him; he 'faded away' and died eighteen months later. In the meantime, one of his sons, Lieutenant-Colonel Stuart Jardine, Royal Engineers, took over command of the Army Diving School at Marchwood from Lieutenant-Colonel Peter Chitty in July 1982 and so was able to be near his father and help him in the months that were to remain to him.

Lionel Seddon Jones

Lionel Seddon Jones came to Lymington sixteen years ago in 1966 from London, where he had been a Marine Superintendent. The Seddon Jones had been looking for a property on the South Coast and happened by pure chance to drive into Lymington. They took one look at the High Street and said, "Right, this is it; it looks just the place we are looking for" – and so they decided to settle here. Lionel Seddon Jones started a yacht brokerage at No. 9 High Street and from there opened up a Sailing School, which he ran for ten or twelve years before feeling the time had come for a complete change. So he became a Fisheries Training Officer in 1981.

"Although I have entered a totally new sphere in my life," he told me, when I visited him at his home on 31st March 1982, "it is naturally still connected with the sea, very much so. Apparently, up to about eighteen months ago, the sea fishing industry had never had a training scheme of its own, unlike most other major industries such as the oil companies, the Post Office and the banks. So a training scheme has been set up, which is financed by the Manpower Services Commission with a head office in York, being pretty well the centre of the country and close to such places as Hull and Grimsby.

"The British Isles has been divided into eighteen areas and I am one of about eighteen Training Officers with an area from Selsey Bill to Lyme Regis. We have in this area somewhere between 1,000 to 1,500 fishermen.

"I have been in the job only since May 1981 but already we have had some 70 fishermen do a special one-day sea survival course; we have had them on the fire prevention course and we are running first-aid courses, as this is an industry which is very accident prone. Conditions can be pretty awful on occasions. When the weather gets bad they do not stop fishing; a lot of them will carry on into a gale if they are out there and regard it as commonplace.

"I was sent up to Aberdeen recently to become an instructor on giving sea survival courses because the big nautical colleges, who do have a Department of Trade approved sea survival course, do not like coming out to the fishermen. On the other hand the fishermen, being self-employed, are loathe to give up a day's work and go to the colleges. So that is a new angle we will be pushing.

"Last week (March 1982) I was over on the Isle of Wight and the Sea Fisheries Authority had a large mobile classroom, a great big 50 ft. long trailer that can be taken to every little port, cove and cranny. We did courses in specialised engineering, hydraulic and acoustic courses and recently we ran for the men a special net mending course. Many of them knew the basics of it but like everything else there is a right and wrong way of doing everything. That went down extremely well. The net mending course was attended by Lymington and Keyhaven men but some did come from Poole and as far afield as Hull.

"We have just sent four Lymington men to Lowestoft to perfect their long-lining abilities. There is a lot of experimental work being done in this field; fishing boats can have lines out astern of them anything up to 4 to 6 miles from the boat. If they go to Hull then at the moment they get £8 a day subsistenace allowed but that does not go far. We are hoping to get more money from the government in due course.

"I do not lecture myself, although I can, of course, lecture in navigation and seamanship. I did this for a number of years at Lymington Community Centre and at New Milton Further Education Centre, and I also lectured on astro-navigation. I was recently asked if I would like to lecture at Calshot Activities Centre near Fawley, but regretfully, due to current commitments, I could not do it. We actually ran a VHF Radio Operators one-day course out at Calshot for fishermen and we had an exceedingly good attendance. They were mainly Lymington and Keyhaven men, although a few came from Mudeford and 4 even crossed from the Isle of Wight, so we are hoping to get another similar type of course done in this area fairly soon.

"If we cannot get one of the nautical colleges to run a survival course, then now that I am an instructor we will run our own course. In fact I am being supplied with a ten-man life-raft so we will be fairly mobile. I do see an opening here and we have been giving it some thought. If we are short of fishermen on a course we could proffer one or two places to local yachtsmen. I think if for nothing else the recent Fastnet Race tragedies showed up the need for a little more guidance in the safety direction.

"I do rather take the RYA's attitude "Educate not legislate.' I always think myself that one of the tragedies of the Boat Show is that for the complete beginner it looks so easy: just buy the boat, launch it and sail off. I think if there were even a few short evening classes on basic safety and possibly the theory of boat handling, it would be a great help to the complete beginner and save the coatsguards and lifeboat services some trouble. I would not like to see the law too rigid, because it would take a great deal of pleasure out of what we nationally regard as a sport.

"Under a local by-law in Lymington and, I believe, in other ports such as Christchurch and Poole, fishing vessels often take angling parties out and if they do then they have to be licensed to carry up to twelve anglers. If they are licensed, then they have to be inspected, and I am an inspector of local boats. I go on board to see that the boat is in a seaworthy condition and I also insist on it being slipped so that I can have a look at the bottom. I check that the vessel carries basic life-saving equipment such as life-buoys, life-jackts and distress flares and I also see if they have a compass and a chart, which many small yachts do not carry, mainly because they do not have to but also due to inexperience. So I think that the local harbour authority could slightly tighten up inasmuch as they make it a similar by-law for yachts in the river to have to conform to a safety standard. I am sure that many of them do but there is always the odd one that does not.

"One good thing about our training scheme is that we have introduced a new entrance scheme, which means that youngsters of around the 16 to 22 age group are sent from here to Falmouth for a special 12-week introductory course to the industry. The first two weeks they do things like survival, fire fighting and first aid courses. They are taken to fish markets, fish sales, see fishing boats built and are given a general background to fishing. Then the third and fourth weeks they are put on board selected local fishing boats and go out with selected skippers. They then go back to the Nautical College to finish off their twelve weeks and cover such things as seamanship, rope work, wire splicing, net repairing, a little bit of meteorology, a little bit of basic navigation and a little bit of the rule of the road.

"In twelve weeks you cannot do everything but it gives them a good basic grounding and they cover a fair range of the different types of fishing. They have to keep a work-book for the examination and provided they reach a certain standard the Sea Fisheries Training Council issues them with a certificate and then hopefully the Training Officer in their district can place them as crew on board a fishing vessel. They also do a few days' cookery because even some of our smaller inshore boats can spend sometimes two to five nights at sea, so to be able to cook basic meals is an essential part of the health of the crew. If you have got a healthy crew you also have got a safe crew – as well as a happy crew.

"Fishermen are very much a one-off type of individual by virtue of their hazardous profession and by being self-employed. I would like to see in this harbour a little more done by local authorities for them; they only have a small quay here to land their fish. In fact, I believe they are not allowed even to sell their fish over the quay – it has to be taken away. Yet in other ports a few miles away, like Mudeford, you have your fish stalls where local people can come down and literally buy fresh fish instead of having it imported.

"I believe shortly, once the industry has some more money injected into it, there is going to be a big television campaign mounted like 'Drink a pinta milk a day' and 'Eat more cheese.' I think the modern generation of younger housewife firmly believes that fish-fingers have gills! The term 'wet fish' tends to put the modern housewife off. Fish in itself, with rising prices, is no longer the cheap meal it used to be: it costs more. Much more is trying to be done to improve presentation in shops. Supermarkets are starting to open up fish-stall type counters inside. There are more mobile fish-shops going about and, of course, there are the fish and chip shops. They have been hit by Chinese 'take-aways' to some extent but I think there is going to be a big fight-back from the industry to regain some of their lost markets. A large number of fish and chip shops change hands every year but only a few people go and learn how to run one: you do need experience before you start frying, as in everything else – like running a pub. I think something like 900 million tins of fish are sold in this country of which about 890 million of them are imported. So we have got a situation that is possibly getting more political of buying fish abroad instead of using what is in our own waters.

"I think we could do a little more locally on presentation of fish. Most yachtsmen will agree that when they cross the Channel and go out in the French ports in particular they all love to wander around the local markets and see the amazing variety of fish on display there and in the restaurants in the evening. I am not saying that the restaurants here do not have beautiful fish in the evening but you do not get the display, which again brings me back to the fact that they are not allowed to sell fish over the quay.

"Some years ago at the Ship Inn in Lymington, before it was modernised to its current form about seven or eight years ago, you could always buy fresh lobsters in the bar. There was a set of watertight drawers, rather like a merchant-ships' chart table or that of a large yacht, and you could literally pull out a drawer and there were live lobsters inside and you could select the one of your choice. I have not seen its like anywhere else round here but perhaps it will come back one day."

THE FERRIES

*"We used to carry livestock and sometimes you would be washing and scrubbing
down three or four times a day. The decks of the old "Lymington" would come up
like a yacht's with so much scrubbing."*

CAPTAIN L. T. CHAPMAN

I am indebted to Captain F. T. O'Brien of
Bramshaw for kindly allowing me to use material
from his book *Early Solent Steamers,* published
by David and Charles, Newton Abbot.

Until 1930 the passage between Lymington and
Yarmouth had been made by rowing boats or under
sail, a crossing which could be hazardous across the
main tidal stream. A well-known boat at that time
was the sloop *Hoy* which gave its name to an inn in
Gosport Street, Lymington and to the naval cry of
'Ship Ahoy.' Sailing vessels also voyaged from
Lymington to Portsmouth, calling at Cowes and
Ryde for, despite the tedium and discomfort
involved, most passengers preferred this mode of
travel to an overland journey in view of the appalling
state of the roads.

In 1829 it was announced that a steamer service
would be inaugurated between Lymington and
Yarmouth and the *Duke of Buccleuch* was built at
Cowes for this route but she joined the Cowes to
Southampton service instead. So in March 1830
three enterprising Lymington bankers, Charles and
Samuel St. Barbe, who owned many of the salt pans,
and Edward Hicks, purchased the *Glasgow* from her
Newcastle owners. She was a clinker-built steamer of
51 tons and 16 h.p. and her Master was Captain
Robert Dore, who was to command her for 18 years
until his death on 12th March 1848 at the age of 59.
She went into service on 5th April 1830 and took 30
minutes to make the crossing on only half-power.
She also did the Lymington to Portsmouth run
calling at Yarmouth, Cowes and Ryde for three days
and to Southampton calling at Yarmouth and
Cowes for another three days. She crossed only to
Yarmouth on Sundays.

In 1835 the *Glasgow* was lying at moorings in
Cowes during a gale one night when the steamer
George IV rammed the pilot boat *Jane* before finally
colliding with the *Glasgow* and bringing her mast
down.

Even with the introduction of steamers, crossings
to Yarmouth were still made by local boatmen,
sometimes with tragic consequences. In April 1837 a
23 ft. wherry boat capsized in a squall while taking

the mail to Yarmouth, drowning her 12 passengers.
The mailboat man, John Webster, owed his life to
hanging on to the mailbag by his teeth while holding
up a small girl who died in his arms.

Another Webster was also involved in a tragedy.
The *Yarmouth Hoy,* belonging to E. Webster, was
discharging her cargo of cattle there when a bull ran
amok and gored to death the local shoemaker and a
dentist called Andrews. Perhaps as a result of this
incident the *Glasgow,* in May 1836, decided to
provide both more comfort and possibly more safety
for their passengers by transferring horses, cattle and
carriages to barges towed by tugs and this practice
was still in operation right up until 1938. But when
the tow boats were not in use – they would be
cancelled in bad weather and were often used for
towing other vessels in and out of the harbour – then
the passengers would still share deck space with
farm animals of all shapes and sizes much to the
discomfort and dismay of the former! It became
worse when, in September 1849, the *Glasgow* was put
up for sale and eventually broken up in October
1852, leaving only the *Solent.*

In June 1841 the iron-built *Solent* was purchased
and the Solent Sea Company was formed to cope
with the anticipated influx of passengers being
brought by the railway. She was 61 tons, 82 ft. long
with a 15 h.p. engine and was built at Northam. Her
saloon had some fine panelling depicting local
scenes. Her Master was J. M. Gibb. Both steamers

Our first steam boat *Solent*

were called Royal Mail packets but *Solent* took over the passages from Lymington to Southampton and Portsmouth with the *Glasgow* now sailing to Yarmouth on weekdays as well as Sundays.

In 1842 the *Glasgow* took hundreds of sightseers to Totland Bay to see a dead whale, 71 ft. long, which had been found on the beach. The skeleton was removed and it was later reconstructed and exhibited at Blackgang Chine at 1/- a head and is still there today.

In 1844 the engineer in the *Glasgow* was thrown overboard when the vessel made a sudden lurch during a stormy crossing. Miraculously, he clambered back over the bulwarks as dry as a bone, having landed on the sponson outboard which saved his life.

On 27th March 1851 the *Duke of Buccleuch* was in collision with a 15 ft. Lymington yacht owned by J. Barfoot called *Sea Dog*. The steamer was off Calshot, when the yacht suddenly tacked and ran across her bows. Captain William Calpine put his helm hard over and stopped the engines, but a collision was inevitable and the yacht sank within seconds. A boat from the steamer picked up the three crew but the owner was missing. Fortunately, Captain Calpine heard a faint cry and plunged overboard with a life-line and was able to save him. Mr. Barfoot accepted full responsibility for the accident, the first in the steamer line.

There were other hazards on board the steamers besides cattle. In the summer months they were tightly packed with passengers and pickpockets were rife. In May 1848 on board the *Pearl* on passage to Lymington, a Mrs. Hayes of Southampton had a handkerchief containing more than ten gold sovereigns taken from her pocket. The thief was caught redhanded and was sentenced to three months imprisonment by the Lymington magistrates and ordered to be privately whipped.

On another occasion it was discovered that the *Solent's* mooring ropes had been cut, when she was tied up at Lymington, and it turned out that a retired member of the crew, described as 'an old Solent Sea Dog,' had crossed to Lymington to collect his pension, and had caused so much trouble that he was charged for his passage. This *riposte* earned him a fine at Lymington Magistrates Court!

In June 1852 the *Solent* rescued seven survivors off the French brig *St. Barbe,* which had foundered on the Needles, and took them to Cowes. In the following year off Portsmouth, three men and a girl of 5 were out in a skiff when it was swamped by the wash of the ferry. Two men drowned but the third, who kept hold of the little girl, managed to cling to the waterlogged boat. The *Solent* came alongside and a seaman threw a rope to the man, while Captain Edward Webster, with great bravery, hung over the bulwark by one hand and foot and just managed to grasp the child by the tip of her fingers with his other hand. The *Solent* was held responsible at the inquest that followed but the skiff had obviously been unseaworthy.

During one of her excursions to the Needles and Alum Bay, the *Solent* managed to salvage an empty horse cart floating on the waves but what had happened to its driver, horse and cargo was never known. This same year, 1857, marked the cutting of the first sod for the Lymington-Brockenhurst railway after years of delay.

Lymington had been facing stiff competition to her salt industry from the Cheshire salt mines, and her trade had gone into a decline. This was partly due to Lymington River silting up after the construction of the tollbridge, and to the fact that Southampton was now developing into a large port. So in 1844, a far-seeing Lymington Town Council decided that its future prosperity would now be linked with the railway, and they asked if Lymington could be joined to the proposed Southampton and Dorchester line. This was approved and the land was surveyed, and on 2nd July 1847 the necessary powers had been obtained but, due to land purchasing difficulties and other problems, these were allowed to lapse.

On 1st June 1847 the Southampton and Dorchester railway was opened, and on the same day so was a station at Brockenhurst. In August 1853, a public meeting was held in Lymington and negotiations opened with the London and South Western Railway (which had taken over the Southampton and Dorchester Railway). On 7th July 1857 (13 years after the original decision by the Council), an Act of Parliament authorised a branch line of 4 miles long from Brockenhurst to Lymington Town Quay. The Company was also empowered to purchase the road tollbridge across the Lymington River and the Town Quay and ferry at a cost of £5,000. George St. Barbe was one of the directors and Alfred Mew, of Mew Langton the brewers, was the Company Chairman. There was further delay while the old mill pond was drained so that the station could be sited there and a temporary one was built near the tollbridge.

On 8th May 1858, there was a private trip for railway officials, but the public took over and the train made several two-minute trips, garlanded with laurel leaves, whilst over a hundred navvies drank Mew Langton ale, conveniently supplied by the Chairman! The Board of Trade inspection was to its satisfaction, and on 12th July 1858, the first train departed from Lymington at 7.15, while the Town Band played and the church bells pealed. The horse bus between Brockenhurst and Lymington was was withdrawn. On 17th September 1859 the new station was completed, with a new approach road, Station Street.

In June 1858 the wooden-hulled 54 ton *Red Lion.* with a 29 h.p. engine, joined the *Solent,* having been bought secondhand from the Admiralty, with a passenger capacity of 100. She passed almost un-noticed, with the railway due to open the following month. She maintained the service single-handed for two years, when the *Solent* was withdrawn in 1861. A new railway jetty was opened in July 1861 but the *Red Lion* could not always tie up alongside at low tide, and passengers had to scramble over coal and other boats tied up at the jetty. It is probable that the "Red Lion" at Boldre was named after her.

On 3rd November 1863 another wooden-hulled paddle-steamer, built by Thomas Inman at Lyming-ton, entered the service and was also called *Solent.* She was 94 feet long, weighed 61 tons, had a speed of 12 knots with a 32 h.p. engine and could carry 230 passengers. She was single-masted and smack-rigged with a square stern. She was transferred to South Shields in 1880.

On 22nd August 1881, the first train crossed the river on the new 70 yard viaduct and continued to the new Lymington Pier Station. In 1884 the London and South Western Railway (LSWR) took over from the Solent Steam Packet Company and purchased the two paddle-steamers, four horse and cargo boats and some other boats for £2,750.

In July 1886 the *Mayflower* joined the fleet. She was 98 ft. long, 69 tons, iron-hulled, sloop-rigged with two oscillating engines producing 40 h.p. Her accom-modation was luxurious and boasted stained glass. Her master was Captain Doe and it was this vessel that ran aground on a mud bank one evening. His son was Tom Doe's father, who was later to be drowned rowing a passenger back to Yarmouth late one night, who had missed the ferry. His widow lived in 'Isle View,' King's Saltern Road and at her death it was bought by Anna Chitty in 1951 for £2,000 and has been her home ever since.

In October 1889 Tennyson composed his immortal poem, *Crossing the Bar,* on one of the ferries crossing between Lymington and Yarmouth and more fame came to the fleet when in 1897 the Italian engineer. Marconi, experimented with ship-to-shore wireless communication from on board the *Mayflower.*

Robert Hole wrote a short article about it for *The Galleon,* Volume 2, No. 10, Christmas 1937, price 4d. the magazine of the Lymington Sea Scouts.

"In 1897 a certain Signor Marconi, then an unknown young man, chose the Royal Needles Hotel at Alum Bay as a good place from which to experiment with a new way of telegraphing without wires, which he was hoping to perfect. With his home-made apparatus, he had demonstrated across a room before the Postmaster-General that such signals were possible and now he set himself to increase the range of sending.

"After much disappointment Marconi achieved a distance of half a mile – from the Royal Needles Hotel to the coastguard cottage on the hill behind Totland Bay. But soon his range increased and on December 6th, 1897, he chartered the *Mayflower,* installed his receiver on board – the first ship in the world to carry wireless apparatus – and while she steamed out into the Channel he was able to keep communication with her up to a distance of eighteen miles.

"So history was made, and I like to think that the modern wireless facilities with which great ships are now equipped, direction finders, wireless telephones, broadcasting, radiogram services and the like, had their origin in the little S.S. *Mayflower* of the port of Lymington."

A friend of Marconi was Mrs. Tillyer-Blunt of Priestlands House. She made her own wireless sets and is said to have 'gone on the air' herself. She was a cousin of Colonel David Sylvester-Bradley, a Lymington Councillor, and taught him all about radio when he was a boy. He consequently joined the Royal Corps of Signals.

In 1893 the *Lymington* was brought into service, built at Northam Ironworks, Southampton and larger than her two predecessors, with 130 tons, 120 ft. long and a speed of 11 knots. The main saloon was panelled with birds-eye maple. She carried 311 passengers in the summer and 236 in winter. One of her Masters was Captain Seymour, and Seymour's Post, at the end of the Long Reach, is named after him. The *Solent 2* now became the spare vessel, before being sold to Holland in 1901 for breaking up.

In 1902 she was replaced by another *Solent,* built by Mordey, Carvey & Co. of Southampton. She was 161 tons, had a length of 135 ft. but could only carry 250 passengers. In 1910 the *Mayflower* was with-drawn and broken up in 1912. With the increase of motor traffic both the *Solent* and the hired tug *Jumsey* used to tow the barges as did the *Carrier.* An LSWR poster called 'Motoring in the Isle of Wight' in-dicates how quickly cars had established themselves.

Roger Pinckney recalled a most amusing incident when a lighter, being to towed across to Yarmouth by the litte tug *Jumsey,* broke adrift and drifted slowly up to Cowes. On board was a huge, expensive car

On the *Lymington* – 13th August 1909   *By courtesy of T. Doe*

By courtesy of E. M. Knight

Captain T. Seymour

with a chauffeur sitting in front at the driving wheel staring passively out into space!

Another story was told to me by Bill Smith. "Once a whole string of barges, with old Arnold's spare equipment and some cars on board were being towed, when the skipper thought he could weather the bow of a big merchant-ship, which was moored just outside Yarmouth. With a hard tide running, they should have gone round the stern, but instead they went round the bow, and the lock part caught round the chain of his boat and, with the tide sweeping up, it rolled the whole lot completely over and that was the end of that! So there are still some cars out there! Of course, with the old tug *Carrier*, you could never tell what that boat was going to do. You could put her hard astern and put the rudder hard aport and she would still go on in the opposite direction!"

In World War One, the branch line was of considerable strategic importance, carrying troops and armaments to Lymington to be ferried out to shipping in the Solent. After the war the LSWR was incorporated into the Southern Railway on 1st January 1923, and yachting and family holidays in the New Forest and the Isle of Wight became increasingly popular with more and more people travelling down now by car.

The *Freshwater,* built by J. Samuel White at Cowes, was launched on 3rd May 1927. She was 159 ft. long

Paddle steamer *Solent* pulling a barge

with a gross tonnage of 264 tons but could still only carry 300 passengers at 12 knots. Her promenade deck went three-quarters the length of the ship from two staircases either side with the wheelhouse in front of the funnel. *Lymington* now became stand-by ferry and was sold in 1929. Prior to buying her, Southern Rail had spent £18,000 (nearly as much as the vessel) on dredging the channel and the pier berths at Lymington.

In 1938 Lymington copied the Portsmouth-Fishbourne route by ordering her first double-ended car ferry with the Voith Schneider propellers at each corner of the vessel so that she could move sideways and turn in her own length. She was nicknamed very aptly 'The Crab.' *Lymington 2* could carry 516 passengers and 16 cars and set a trend for the future type of marine transport. The practice of towing barges between Lymington and Yarmouth now ceased. Tom Doe always used to say that passengers and cargo did not mix but now there was no other option. They used to carry pigs, bullocks and sheep, with the passengers on the top deck looking down on them. In his opinion, they should have either had a passenger boat or a cargo boat and not have mixed the two. *Lymington 2* was in service for 36 years and then was transferred to the Clyde, where she was built.

Because of restrictions of movement on the South Coast of Hampshire and the Isle of Wight, the number of passengers using the ferry route in World War Two dropped to about 50,000, though motor vehicle transport increased, and *Lymington 2* handled most of the sailing with *Solent 3* as standby. In 1940 the *Freshwater* was requisitioned for war service whilst the *Solent 3* was used as a troop carrier during D-Day preparations. The slipways in Lymington were doubled so that two tank-landing craft could be loaded simultaneously.

After the war the three vessels returned to Lymington but in 1947 a paddle version of *Lymington 2* was ordered from the William Denny yard at Dunbarton. She was called the *Farringford* and weighed 498 tons, had a length of 178 ft. and had diesel-electrically driven paddles and could carry 32 cars and 320 passengers. Despite independent paddle-wheels she was unwieldy and not popular with local yachtsmen, because she took up too much of the narrow channel into Lymington. This is hardly surprising since on Whit Monday, 17th May 1948 a Montagu Sharpie called *Micawber,* owned by the School of Infantry, was run down by the *Farringford* and one of the crew, Major Rickman, was caught in the ferry's revolving wheel and lived to tell the tale! Miss P. Clarke, another crew member, could not swim but also survived. *Micawber* originally belonged to H. A. E. Russell of East Grove, Lymington, who called it *Micawber* because when he was busy taking exams, it was 'always waiting for him to turn up!'

Solent 3 was now withdrawn and *Freshwater* was laid up in the winter months. In June 1959 another Voith Schneider ferry was introduced, also called *Freshwater* and the old *Freshwater* was withdrawn. In 1966 Lymington was the sole surviving branch line of the railway in the South of England to use steam, but on 1st June 1967 it too became electrified.

Tom Doe recalls that when the new *Freshwater 2* came into service the skipper asked the Marine Superintendent for a staysail. "The reason was that in a paddle-boat the paddles are in the middle of it. When they are out of the water directly the wind got into that paddle-box – and there was a heck of a space in underneath – over she used to go. Then she used to run up towards the bank, and the only way you could stop her was to give her a paddle astern, put your staysail up and let the wind blow her off."

Captain Chapman explained that with old paddlers like that you could not go ahead on one paddle and astern on the other, so you had no control that way. They were then either both ahead or both astern, and you had no steering power until you were moving. Tying up was an even more complicated process.

1968 saw the last of the 'Round the Island' trips which had been so popular in Victorian and Edwardian times and, indeed, the ferries had carried 'fashionable persons of both sexes round the Isle of Wight for 145 years.' But the cry 'Any more for Round the Island' can still be heard – in Yarmouth coach park or at the Island Sailing Club, Cowes!

In 1972 British Rail ordered three new car roll-on roll-off vessels to be built at a cost of £1,800,000 from Rob Caledon Shipbuilders of Dundee, and the MV *Cenwulf* and MV *Cenred* were delivered in September and November. *Cenwulf* made her maiden trip in October 1973 with about one hundred civic dignitaries on board. The *Farringford* and *Lymington 2* were withdrawn; the former was fitted for sideways loading and joined the Hull–New Holland line and the latter was renamed *Sound of Sanda* and went to the Clyde. *Cenwulf* has a gross weight of 703 tons and can carry 756 passengers (double the previous number) but only 52 cars. Between them they can carry as many passengers in a week as were carried in a whole month in 1830. In 1976 a new terminal was built with increased parking arrangements and a covered walk way and automatic gang-planks. In 1979 the ferries conveyed 1,323,056 passengers, 217,567 cars, 29,351 lorries and 640 coaches.

Saturday, 7th June 1980 marked the 150th anniversary of the Lymington–Yarmouth ferries and the 'Great Day' was celebrated in style with the ferry dressed overall. Crowds gathered in Lymington and Yarmouth and an article in the *Lymington Times* the following week recalls that as well as vintage cars on board there were also "penny-farthing bikes, ridden with great determination and courage on and off the ferry, also a Whitbread dray hauled by two magnificent white shires, Hengist and Horsa, though the driver muttered a few oaths as the ferry captain blew his sirens when the vessel moved off, startling the horses! On board there were the Knightwood Oak Morris Dancers, with children in Victorian dress, in some cases originally worn by their great grandparents, spontaneously joining in. The Lymington Borough Military Band appropriately struck up with 'Anchors Aweigh' on the top deck" – they were off!

At Yarmouth a short speech was made by the M.P. before the cutting of a ceremonial ribbon, and then selected guests were given lunch at Farringford, where Captain Leonard Wheeler read out a telegram from the Royal Lymington Yacht Club. On the way back there was a parade of veteran cars to Yarmouth, where a Ferry Boat Fayre was in progress; the old steam locomotive *Freshwater* of 1876 was there and maypole dancing and gymnastic displays were taking place. It was a most enjoyable and memorable day.

By courtesy of E. M. Knight

Captain H. Doe and Pilot J. Andrews

Tom Doe is the grandson of Captain Doe, who was Captain of the ferry boats, the old 'paddlers' – the old *Lymington,* the *Mayflower* and the old *Solent.* Pilot Bill Andrews worked on the Lymington River some sixty or seventy years ago. He was skipper of the tug *Carrier.* Tom Doe left school on the Friday night and on the Saturday night he was a deck boy on the cross channel boats. He was paid 7/- a week and all he could eat! "The more you could eat the better you were paid," he said! He used to go to France and the Channel Islands from Southampton. He then joined the Island ferries in 1935 where he was a Mate and finished up as Dock Foreman when he retired in 1958.

Captain Chapman, whom I talked with at his home on 16th November 1981, told me that he was not a Lymingtonian but was born and bred a cockney. "I came here after the war in 1948 when I was 43. I had been in the Merchant Navy before the war but finished with deep sea in the slump, and after that I went into business. I was in the fire service at Mersey Docks during the war and ended up second in command for that area.

"The big attraction of coming to Lymington was that it was a shore job and my children grew up with their father home every night. I worked 22 years with the ferries, until I retired at 65 in 1970. We used to carry livestock and sometimes you would be washing and scrubbing down three our four times a day. The decks of the old *Lymington* would come up like a yacht's with so much scrubbing. You put a bit of sand down if you had a load of sheep. They would bring them in cattle trucks to Yarmouth and they always had a drover to drive them off at the other end.

"You never stayed in one ship – you went round all the ships in turn in rotation, the Masters and the crew members. We used to work a shift system. The old *Freshwater* took some manoeuvring to bring her alongside. It was an operation known as the swinging flood. You had to come up as close to the boats moored on the west side as you could; then, when you got nearly up to the pier, you put the helm hard astarboard and then stopped your engines – you had got a fairly good way on her. Before you got there, you had a long rope known as a 'swinging rope' on this sponson and it was passed round by hand up into the bows and the mate was up there with a heaving line. So you had to swing her round and then go full astern, the art being to stop her with her stem as near to the pier as possible. Then he pulled his line up and they got the eye on the bollard. You came astern on it, and it was fast on this and she swung round on it until you got round to where you could go ahead and tie alongside. It really was a work of art.

"She was a pretty little ship. We used to go out to Cowes on firework night and we had a lot on board for the Coronation Review at Spithead. Before the war they used to run a sort of summer trip in the old paddle-steamers to Totland Bay. I think it was 1/6d. complete with a strawberry tea.

"I was returning from Yarmouth in the *Farringford* one Sunday afternoon and we had just go to the mouth of the river and I said, 'Isn't there something on fire up there?' and I got my glasses out and said, 'Good Lord, it is Dan Bran's shed.' By the time we were up to it it was near enough finished: it just went up like that. I don't know what caused it, but the shed was full of paint and tar and stuff. It was his whole existence. It just went up like tinder. I suppose from the mouth of the river to his hut was about quarter of an hour and in that time it was more or less burnt out by the time we reached it.

"The story was that Dan Bran used to have his fire going and had a big log and each day he would push the end of it a bit further into the flames. I believe he opened fire on a ferry with a shotgun once because it had rocked his boat!"

Fire at Dan Bran's Shed

Captain Chapman does not sail but he has done some compass adjusting off the mouth of the river until he had a heart attack in May 1981. He held an extra Master's Certificate, the highest one.

Monty Knight remembered embarking on the steamer and "proceeding down an almost deserted river into the sparkling adventure of the sea beyond. Here, particularly in August, if we were very lucky, we might catch a glimpse of the royal racing yacht *Britannia,* her slim black hull and clouds of snowy canvas posed between sea and sky!"

Mr. P. W. Penny, Manager of Sealink ferries, gave me an account of the present-day running of the ferry service and its future prospects, when I visited him in his office on 9th June 1981. He has always been in the shipping and docks side of the railways, having started in Southampton Dock with the then Southern Railway. When the docks were closed in the war he went to the railway workshops at Eastleigh, before going into the forces. When he came out, he went back to Southampton Dock and then Portsmouth Dock before coming to Lymington in 1968. He finds the specialised work at the terminal extremely interesting and all embracing, because there is liaison with the railway and contact with a broad spectrum of the public.

"We have a very good understanding with the yachting fraternity of the river," he told me, "and the only occasional trouble we may have is usually with a visitor, who is not familiar with the river and who comes up on the wrong side of it. We also have a very good rapport with the yacht clubs. In fact, one of the annual events is our sailing competition with them, when the Royal Lymington puts on the X Class races and they invite one or two of our Masters to man the X Class craft. The telegram of congratulations on our 150th anniversary on 7th June 1980, which we received from the Royal Lymington Yacht Club, is framed and hanging on the wall of my office.

"We have got three ships on this service, which is a combined passenger and car ferry service. The *Cenwulf* and the *Cenred* are sister ships and are absolutely identical and there is also the smaller *Freshwater*. They all have this Swiss Voith Schneider propulsion, with a unique type of propeller which can be feathered as in an aircraft. There is one propeller at each end and you can literally turn the ship round on the spot and also crab her sideways. So these are ideal for this type of work in the river, which is very restricted and where there are many yachts. Another advantage is that in the river, where there is a lot of silting, the propellers skim and scour the bottom. Whereas before 1965 we had to have a regular dredging programme every four or five years, we have not needed to dredge since then.

"The kinds of traffic we carry are many and varied, consisting of rail passengers, car passengers, coach passengers and lorry drivers. Coach passengers are sometimes local people, from Bournemouth, who are brought by firms such as Shamrock, Rambler, Excelsior and the Hants & Dorset and passengers perhaps from Leeds and York, who come in long-distance coaches. Long-distance coach passengers used to have to de-coach and pick up another coach on the other side, but under a recent Transport Act, they can remain in the same coach throughout the entire journey – a great boon.

"As far as the commercial aspect is concerned, there is a complete community on the Island and while obviously there are some things they can produce for themselves, such as dairy produce, most of the food has to be imported as well as such items as coal, timber and building materials. The number of people on the Island doubles in the summer holiday season and hence the commercial requirements do as well.

"In order to keep up with demand we then introduced larger vessels in 1973 – the *Cenwulf* and the *Cenred*. When we reached capacity again we introduced the mezzanine deck, a lifting deck. This is another deck, superimposed over the top of the car ferry deck, and is operated on ramps, so that it lifts off the bottom deck to half-way between that and the under side of the bridge. On that deck, with link chains either end, it is possible to carry an additional 24 cars as well as the normal 50, which is virtually another half a ship's load. The only limitations are that you cannot ship a mixture of lorries and cars, because of the height, and you cannot, for the same reason, put more than 13 or 14 caravans on it. So we had mezzanine decks put in the *Cenwulf* and the *Cenred* and that made a considerable saving.

"From 1978 onwards we have been running an hourly service in the winter and from Whit Saturday we run a half-hourly service on Saturdays right throughout the day until the first week in September. Then in July and August we also run half-hourly services on weekdays as well to cover the peak period of traffic for the holidaymakers. On Sundays our service is hourly but augmented by relief services with the small *Freshwater* at every two hours. In normal circumstances in the river we would not have been able to do this. But in 1976 we dredged out a passing area in the bend by the Cocked Hat, so the timeable is very carefully planned. The crossing is half an hour in both directions, and this means that both ferries cross in the river: the one leaving Lymington 7½ minutes after departure and the one from Yarmouth 22½ minutes after departure. This enabled us once again to compete temporarily with the increase in car traffic.

"When we reached capacity again, we introduced a night service on Fridays and then increased this to two ships. The final way we can increase capacity is to bring a third ship, the *Caemond* from Portsmouth, when they get two new ships on that route. She is a sister ship of the other two and would replace the *Freshwater*. We would have preferred a new one, but at a cost in 1980 of £1¾ million, it was out of the question. So that is the ultimate. At some stage, bearing in mind the other two routes to the Island are on the increase as well, the Island will reach saturation point, and I would feel that the controlling authority there would say, 'Well, sorry, but that's the limit for the season' and that would be it!

"In line with this we have increased car parking facilities, most of it reclaimed from the sea six years ago, when we purchased the land from the Crown Commissioners. We intend to get it re-surfaced and landscaped and it should hold 140 cars. This is still not sufficient in the summer, so we have an overflow field owned by Mr. Goodall, the farmer. We do not pay rent but split the proceeds with him. He pays for half the cost of the staff and, when this is deducted, we split the income in half again for maintenance of the car parks. We hope in the future to reclaim more land and square it off and then we could cease to use Mr. Goodall's field.

"Development ashore has to keep up with development of the actual ships and service, and we are not in a good position office-wise, now that the passenger service has moved further away to the new terminal. We had to extract the ticket office to go there and ultimately hope that the offices and, particularly, the toilet facilities will move there as well.

"We are also installing a system of cameras. This has been made possible by a firm wanting to use this small port, not only to assist Sealink but also to provide a working shop window for their products. So it will benefit both them and us at the same time.

There will be panning cameras at various points that will sweep the car park. The watchman will not only regularly do his rounds on the ships, but he will also have a little repeater monitor here, and if he sees anyone prowling amongst the cars at dead of night, he can immediately phone the police. We have had a few break-ins at Goodall's field at Easter (1981) with things taken from cars, so we hope to have a camera there as well."

Sealink are obviously extremely well organised to meet any demands that may be made on their services in the future and we wish them every success in their next 150 years.

LYMINGTON SEA SCOUTS

"A man who can 'use his hands' is never dull. He may be a keen gardener, he may
sail a boat and fit her out himself, he may like to make things – but time is never
going to hang heavy on his hands."

ROBERT HOLE

Baden-Powell started an experimental camp for boys on Brownsea Island in 1907, but the Scout Movement did not officially start until 1908, when the first official camp was held in Yorkshire. That same year the 1st Lymington Scouts were formed but it was not until 1922 that Robert Hole formed the Sea Scouts, the 9th New Forest (South). In 1925 a District Association was formed and there were by then ten Scout groups in Lymington.

Charles E. Turner, the present Group Scout Leader, has written a brief summary of the history of the Group, which has been helpful in compiling this chapter. "The first Sea Scout to be officially enrolled into the troop was Arthur Wright, who for many years ran a taxi business in the town and was for some time the official chauffeur to the Mayor. He now lives in retirement in Pennington.

"Robert Hole, who founded the troop, was known as 'Holy Joe' as he was a retired schoolmaster from a very religious school, Stowe," recalls Bill Martineau. "Miss I. E. M. Billings then became his secretary at Delawarr and did practically everything with the Sea Scouts. In 1935 she was Guide Lieutenant and Assistant Editor of *The Galleon*. She stayed with Robert Hole until he was called up in the war. After the war, when he founded the Lymington Community Centre in 1946, she could have been the first Warden, if she had not had an invalid mother to look after. As with everything, he soon involved others in his work but he would never ask anyone to do something he would not do himself."

In addition to Robert Hole, a very great part of the Group's success was due to the hard work of Frank Claridge, who lived to his mid-90s and died only in August 1982. He was a retired Naval Gunnery Chief Petty Officer, and for some years used to be responsible for training the Portsmouth field gun crew for the Royal Tournament. When he left the Navy in the 1930s, he was employed by Robert Hole as chauffeur/gardener but, in reality, he quickly became a very full-time Cub-Master, Scoutmaster

and boat repairer for the Sea Scouts: in fact, he *was* Lymington Sea Scouts for many years!

Mrs. Hole (Dorothy Harding) was Assistant Scoutmaster of the Group, as well as being Cubmaster, before she married 'the boy next door.' Robert Hole lived then in Heathcote House. He wrote, "If it had not been for her carrying on when my work took me away from Lymington, the 9th Lymington Sea Scouts would not have been in existence now. She was also the Hampshire Training Commissioner for Cubs, so she has the skill as well as the necessary powers of endurance!" When they married, the Scouts towed their car from the Church to Heathcote House and were given a good meal afterwards. Frank Claridge then took over as Cubmaster from her and for 7½ years did great work with the Pack. His successor was Mrs. Hole again!

The Galleon of Christmas 1937 reported "Unfortunately, owing to ill health, Mr. H. L. Iddles has had to give up the Hon. Secretaryship of the Group after all these years. He saw us through the building of the Headquarters, through the first and all the subsequent Sea Scout Fairs, the Shows and the many other hectic times, and has always added a cheerfulness to his energy and efficiency, which has made working with him particularly pleasant. It is good to know that he will still be helping us in many of his former capacities, and particularly in that of Box Office Manager for the Shows."

Mr. Lyon, who had been acting as Scoutmaster of the Nelsons for nearly a year, had been promoted to District Commissioner on the retirement of Mr. Fullerton. The Group were very proud that it was one of their own Scouters who got the job and the Nelsons made him their Honorary Scoutmaster, to show how they valued his help.

Mr. Laurent Giles, the well-known yacht designer, became Vice-President of the Scouts in 1937. He had often helped them in the past and he had recently designed new sails for *Gipsy* and the new gig.

In the Christmas 1935 issue of *The Galleon* an article stated, "We welcome to the fold of Scouters some old faces and one new one. Mr. W. M. Martineau has taken up the job of Rover Scout Leader, and the number of nights on which the Rovers rove these days testify to his popularity. An experienced seaman, who sails and maintains his *Wilful* single-handed, he has been connected with the Scout movement in Andover for many years, and came to the Sea Scout course here this summer after settling in Lymington.

"He brought with him a wooden hut which is now being fitted out by the Rovers as their Den. He also gave a small sailing dinghy, *Porpoise,* and the canvas Berthon boat used by the Cubs. Major Allott, a Vice-President and a firm ally on the River Committee of the Council, presented us with a 14 ft. boat only a few days ago."

Herbert Rand remembers that "We first met in a room behind the King's Arms and then moved to an old loft over Robert Hole's garage at Heathcote House in St. Thomas Street. In 1933 the building that is now in King's Saltern Road, and our third headquarters, was opened by Lord Hampton, the Deputy Chief Scout, who was welcomed by the Mayor, Alderman E. A. G. Stone, and thanked by the Group Scoutmaster." Reporting on the ceremony in only the second issue of *The Galleon* in the Autumn of 1933 (price 4*d.*) Robert Hole described how hard everybody worked to finish off the building and tidy up the surrounding ground.

"The Rovers are panelling the inside, doing the electric lighting, fitting shelving in the store and kitchen and fencing the ground. The Troop is painting the outside work, lining the roof of the boat store and making other improvements there, and making up the gravel paths. The Pack has the flower beds to look after. The parents are painting the inside. So we shall have a job to do towards making our new possession the smartest and best-cared-for Headquarters in the country.

"We have settled down already to a busy season of handicrafts. The Rovers, besides the panelling and the other work at Headquarters, are making tables, chairs, a carpenter's bench and other things as well as a new gangway for *Albatross* and the usual work on the boats. The Troop is organised into three sections, taken by Mr. Hole, Mr. Claridge and Mr. Wilkins. The first party are making trugs (wooden gardening baskets) in Mr. Hole's workshop, and they are also going to manufacture wasp scissors, an ingenious article for dealing neatly but firmly with that insect! Mr. Claridge's party, working at Heathcote House, are doing bone work, while Mr. Wilkins is running at the Headquarters the toy hospital, that is part of our Christmas good turn. In fact, there is plenty doing! . . . The Group has also got its own

library, from which many instructive and interesting books are lent out for the small sum of ½*d.* per week . . . A camp bank is being run to collect money for next year's trip to Holland, and you can pay into it at the same time as you pay your subscription."

In the summer of 1935 Mr. Claridge was taking classes for the Coast Watchman, Pathfinder, Pilot and Pioneer badges, besides Second and First Class Work. Mr. Marshall ran a capital course in First Aid, and for the Rovers, Mr. Wicks at Keyhaven Coastguard Station, has been right through the syllabus for the Board of Trade Coastwatcher. This latter was to come in extremely useful only four years later. Swimming classes were arranged by an old Member of the Group, Mr. R. V. Montgomerie, Vice-Captain of Lymington Swimming Club.

The autumn programme gives woodwork by Mr. Wood and Mr. Rhodes, miniature ships by Mr. Iddles at his home, canvas work by Mr. Claridge, Junior physical training and Senior physical training by Mr. Butcher and at 8.00 p.m. on Fridays Robert Hole took 'Songsters.'

Handicrafts in the spring of 1936 took the form of painting Coronation decorative shields with Mr. Anker, making trug baskets and the wood part of the shields in two classes with Mr. Vaton and the G.S.M., and Borough arms ship models with Mr. Stevens. The articles were sold at the Caravan Stall in the High Street on May 1st in aid of the Lymington Hospital.

Many of the activities, reflecting the history of pre-war England, were written as articles for the house magazine, *The Galleon,* by the Scouts and very interesting reading they make too.

In the summer 1935 issue, Patrol-Leader Ken Isted wrote, "The outstanding feature of the Jubilee revelry in the ancient Borough of Lymington was, without doubt, the Historical Pageant. It comprised a thirty-one lorry tableaux portraying landmarks of English history since the time of William the Conqueror. The groups were the work of many local organisations. Ours was 'Nelson' and it was said to be one of the best. It was manned by the Patrol Leaders and Seconds of the Troop and it was a novel experience for us. Lord Nelson is ordering his famous message to be hoisted by the Yeomen of Signals just before the Battle of Trafalgar. Captain Hardy and Mr. Pasco stand by. The seamen stand ready and the gunners and the powder monkeys are prepared to action . . . The carefully marshalled procession covered about 30 miles and crowds of spectators lined the route, which was through Everton, Milford and Barton to New Milton. At New Milton the performers all received a free tea, and then the colourful pageant made it way home via

Ashley, Hordle, Everton and Pennington. It was led into Lymington by the Town Band and heralded by a peal of bells from St. Thomas Church. Then the procession dispersed in the High Street, after the singing of patriotic songs and hearing a speech from the Mayor, which was relayed from loudspeakers up and down the street."

This next article appeared in the *Lymington Chronicle* of 19th July 1935 and was written on board the *Lady Belle* (Robert Hole's yacht) at Spithead by the skipper. "Everyone is keyed up to concert pitch and the ships are looking their smartest and cleanest and brightest under the sparkling sunshine for, in a short time, H.M. The King will be here to review the greatest gathering of ships since 1914. From the East Brambles buoy off Cowes, as far as the Horse Sand Fort, off Southsea, eight lines of grey hulls stretch into the distance. There are 243 ships charted, and many more must actually be here. Every ship is gaily dressed with bunting. There is a constant passing and repassing of pinnaces and other small craft and yachts of all sorts, with their metal-work highly polished and reflecting the sun as they slip by.

"*Lady Belle* is at her berth in Area B off Stokes Bay, dressed overall and proudly representing the Sea Scouts of Great Britain. Her crew had the time of their lives, sailing four times down the lines of anchored warships, and meeting naval officers and rating and merchant seamen and yachtsmen galore. In Portsmouth, Admiral Campbell, Lord Hampton and the Rev. L. Spiller ('The Sky Pilot') came aboard, and we also received visits from Deep Sea Scouts from the Navy, and from Sea Scouts of Portsmouth and Southampton.

"Yesterday was, perhaps, the peak day of our experience when, at the invitation of Captain Elliott, lately come to Lymington, more than twenty of us went on board the *Royal Sovereign,* lying near the east end of the line, and were shown all over her. And how we were looked after by our hosts! Memories remain of spotless decks and paint work, of the wonderful workshops, the engine room, the bakeries, the fighting tops, BBC engineers, mess decks, iced lemonade in the Captain's cabin, and above them all a general air of friendliness everywhere. Before our crew left the *Royal Sovereign* in the *Tarafal* and the *Black Pearl* we were given a sumptuous tea. It was not seemly to cheer Captain Elliott on his own quarter-deck, but we shall certainly do so when he next pays us a visit at King's Saltern Road.

"Lots of friends have greeted us and we have made new ones . . . Harry Eales was on board the *Black Pearl* and *Wilful* (Bill Martineau) of Lymington is lying alongside as I write. Our happiness will now be complete if the *Freshwater* comes along close enough for us to exchange greetings with her and to dip our ensign in salute. The 1300 gun has just gone and this letter must be posted. Another hour till the Navy greets the King."

Patrol-Leader Jack Clark completes the picture and describes the illuminations later that day. "Hundreds of searchlights at first stabbed the sky and, when we all had more or less become accustomed to the sight, they all faded as with one switch. The fleet had gone, vanished before our eyes and all that was left was the moon hanging low in the sky! Suddenly, without any visible or audible signal whatever, the ships were there again, this time lit with a thousand red, white and blue stars from the Jubilee rockets. At twelve the Fleet again finally 'blacked out,' left us and was not seen until the red sun of dawn crept high enough into the sky to show it steaming out into the Channel for exercises.

"After breakfast we started beating back against a strong sou'wester, but we shall never forget that trip, one more on the list of things we owe to scouting. It's a fine thing. Thank you, B.P."

Our same young reporter also wrote this article: "Never before has such a title as this been printed in *The Galleon* and I only regret that I cannot do full justice to it in recording these few facts about our trip to London to see the celebrations.

"This outward and visible sign of the designation of our King and Queen has surely surpassed all other ceremonials within the annals of our country, and above all in the unparalleled display of loyalty. It has been a happy and memorable occasion, engraved in the minds of everyone and, not least of all, in the memories of three of us, who had the good fortune to be standing in Constitution Hill on the morning of May 12th 1937.

"Everyone was awake in the Horticultural Hall (where we were billeted) by 6.0 a.m., at which hour London's streets were crowded with hurrying ticket holders, marching soldiers, bands, policemen, and cars all bent on one purpose. Seven o'clock found us, a thousand strong from all over the Empire, marching through the grounds of Buckingham Palace and along part of the Royal route to a merry song from our Canadian friends. The eight-hour wait for the procession gave us ample time to get to know some of our brother scouts, who had shared the same roof as ourselves that night. I was particularly interested in the chaps from the Gold Coast. They suffered a great deal from the weather and, when I sat up in bed next morning, I saw one of them in bed with every stitch of clothing on, including his raincoat and gloves. By the way, there will be several copies of our magazine sent to the Gold Coast this year.

"The remainder of the time was spent in whistling

to cordons of policemen as they marched up and down, cheering lone telegraph boys, and other policemen on bicycles, etc. A few community songs were also slaughtered!

"It would be quite unnecessary for me to try and describe the procession. I finished up the day by sitting in the most expensive stand in front of the Abbey Annexe, looking out on the heart of the Empire with its swirling traffic splashing through a steady downpour, listening to the King speaking to his peoples. And Long May He Reign!"

One day in 1935, when all the Scouts were wearing their oldest clothes, a Rolls Royce pulled up outside Headquarters. 'Stosh' went to welcome them and left Robert Hole and Bert Rand working dutifully and idly speculating on who the visitors could be. They were Lord and Lady Baden-Powell, no less. "Somebody suggested that the Chief should sign the visitors book, so we all trooped up the stairs talking excitedly, and while Stosh was fetching the book, the Chief Scout told us about some Scouts he had visited in Western Australia. Not to be outdone, we explained how our Rover Crew act as Coast Watchers and belong to the Intelligence Department of His Majesty's Coast Life Saving Corps. The Chief then remarked how very lucky we were, living near the Solent, and told us that he obtained his first experience of yachting at Yarmouth, Isle of Wight, a favourite haunt of ours. Of course, he wanted to know all about our boats, how many we had, how they were rigged and so on. . . ."

Here is a description of the Annual Fair held on 31st July 1935. "Once again the Rovers gave their life-saving rocket apparatus demonstration to the delight of the watching multitude. Everything ready, the first shipwrecked mariner came gliding through space from the wreck (a tree) with the greatest of ease. Captain R. Elliott, RN, OBE of the *Royal Sovereign* was rescued (not from the *Royal Sovereign* by the way) and many others had the thrill of their lives as they jumped into the breeches buoy and embarked on their swift journey to safety, whilst the Rovers, capably carrying out their motto of 'Service' vigorously pulled on the warps. I must add, particularly brave was a young girl, who joined in the fun – after climbing the tree she made a gallant leap for the breeches buoy – the crowd awe-stricken – then a burst of laughter when she showed 'how it should be done'." Bill Martineau recalls that the girl was Sylvia Marshall, who had "awfully nice legs and both she and the legs were admired by the boys as she swished down off the cedar tree." The breeches buoy was a canvas seat with two holes through which you put your legs. Sylvia later married Les Marshall.

"The Crazy Circus and Funfair in 1936 was opened from the roof of Delawarr House by Lady Kerr; the Mayor and many members of the Town Council being present. Soon the air was filled with the cries of the stall-keepers and the screams of the people enjoying the thrills of a Rocket Ride erected by the Rovers with the Rocket Life-Saving gear.

"It was a gay scene, the big, close-cropped lawn dotted with the brilliant colours of the awnings over the stalls and festoons and strings of flags everywhere. As the time approached for the opening of the Circus, the crowds left the stalls and side-shows and gathered around the arena. Mr. Butcher, the Ring Master, opened it with a crack of his whip, and from thence until the final grand march of the entire group, our audience was kept amused with one turn after another, following in quick succession. The P.T. displays of the Golden Arrows were fast and thrilling and, considering that this team consisted mainly of juniors, was an admirable tribute to Mr. Butcher's training. The acts were many and varied, and were spiced with touches of humour added by the clowns, Pecker and Leo Carrol, commanding much applause and laughter by their antics on and off and half off their bikes.

"The Alterte Brothers gave a snappy five minutes of the more advanced tumbling and diving, but although they had that extra polish, they would have found it difficult to eclipse the neat little displays of their younger brothers, or the rhythmic movements of the Cubs' club-swinging.

"The horse and the bull who got mixed up, as befits a crazy circus, caused roars of merriment followed by a strained silence while Don Taylor, Don Samways and Wilf Veal performed on the tightrope as the Streamline Troupe. The Cycling Celestes gave a scene of gay colour and pleasing movement, as they circled the ring and crossed and inter-crossed, and indicated to the crowd that Sea Scouts are capable of handling a bike with the best Landsmen.

"The final scene brought in the whole Group marching with flags to the strains of a rousing march and forming itself into a catherine wheel, which finally untwined itself, and showed us off in all our splendour and made us feel quite proud of ourselves. As soon as the Circus performance ended, the stalls got busy again until the second show started.

"In the evening we wound up with a giant camp-fire composed of the Group, and everybody else present. It started off, as camp-fires always do, with a chilled atmosphere until Ralph Reader had said about six words, and then the whole crowd was drawn into eager response by that magic touch of his. We all sat there and ate his words until we were hoarse. Good old Ralph! He certainly knows how to handle 'em, and brought the first day of our Fair to a triumphant close with a drowning riot of fun.

"As for the second day. Well, it wasn't anybody's fault but it just rained and rained all day long. So we contented ourselves with making £51 17s. 6d. on the first day."

Robert Hole was a first-class producer and in addition to the Annual Fairs the Scouts used to put on wonderful 'Gang Shows.' There was *The Forty Thieves and their Swag* in January 1934 with an orchestra consisting of five violins, a viola, drums and a piano under the Musical Director, Mr. H. Wakeford, FRCO, MRST, and the Stage Director was Mr. F. Claridge, Stage Manager, Mr. D. Wilkins and Business Manager Mr. H. L. Iddles. The lighting was by Rover Sea Scouts A. Figgures and H. Rand and the scenery was painted by Mr. F. Claridge with make-up by Mr. F. H. Humphreys.

In 1935 there was *Sinbad the Sea Scout,* complete with acrobats, rehearsed by Mr. H. Bell. Curtains were loaned by Ford & Co. and Stowe School and this time the Stage Manager was Mr. L. L. Marshall. This was followed by *Bumps* in 1936, with the music arranged again by Mr. H. Wakeford and pianists Mr. H. Jenvey, A. Lord and R. Ridett, and *Eight Bells* in January 1937 with a cast of 74 and an extra chorus as well. These shows, written and produced by Robert Hole, were sometimes held at the Parish Hall and sometimes at the Lyric. After a few years at the Lyric, they cut the stage back to make more room for the people and, as it was not large enough, they started using the Parish Hall. Admission was 3/6, 2/6 and 1/3 including tax. (Scouts and Boys Brigade half-price in uniform at the Saturday performance). There were six performances of *Bumps*. Tickets from King's Library, Lymington.

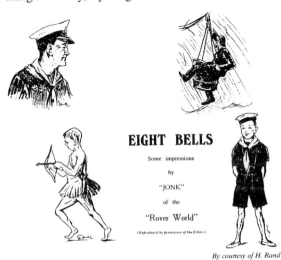

EIGHT BELLS

Some impressions

by

"JONK"

of the

"Rover World"

(Reproduced by permission of the Editor).

By courtesy of H. Rand

Eight Bells

It is not possible to report fully on all these activities but mention must be made of an extremely interesting foreign cruise well described by Rover Sea Scout H. Rand. In June 1936, *Wilful* and her crew set off from Lymington for a cruise in Holland, visiting Ostende, Middelburg, Vere, Zierikzee and through the estuaries of the Scheldt, Rhine and Maas to Dordrecht and on to Rotterdam.

Amongst many other visitors during the summer and autumn of 1937 was a party of 33 Czechoslovak Scouts who had attended the 5th World Jamboree in Holland. The march-past was taken by HRH Queen Wilhelmina and Lord Baden-Powell. The Czech Scouts then came over to Lymington in August to spend three days with our Sea Scouts. They were received by His Worship the Mayor, given a presentation album of photographs and a model of the Lymington Borough Arms Ship, taken on cruises in the Solent and to Brownsea Island, and visited the Gang Show film and the Shipyard. Sir William Seeds gave them all lunch in his garden one day, and the 3rd Poole Sea Scouts gave them lunch on their visit to Poole Harbour.

In the summer of 1938 Robert Hole took a party of Sea Scouts on a return visit to Czechoslovakia, where they spent two weeks as the guests of the Prague River Scouts. This was very shortly before the Germans invaded Czechoslovakia and the atmosphere was tense when they were right inside the frontier positions. Herbert Rand remembered how very friendly and hospitable they had been and so pro-British. It was very sad. Jean Vernon-Jackson, the daughter of Robert Hole, told me that her father was asked to look after a Czech Scout, as war was imminent, and he did so in Lymington for the duration of the war.

As we have seen, the Group rapidly rose to success and quickly became one of the leading Sea Scout units in the country, very well known in these pre-war days, not only for their wonderful 'Gang Shows' but also, following Robert Hole's appointment as Assistant Headquarters Commissioner for Sea Scouts, for their training. The Troop was frequently used as a 'guinea pig' when new ideas for Scouts were introduced, and most training manuals were illustrated with pictures of the Lymington boys in action. Robert Hole wrote a book under the name of 'Gilcraft' and a copy is in the library of the Royal Lymington Yacht Club.

As early as the spring of 1934 they had participated in a film that was made: Jeff was played by Jack Clark, Mr. Marsden by Mr. Blake and Mr. Harland by Mr. Day. Les was the policeman and Mr. Weston, who was a CPO in the Navy, was appropriately played by Frank Claridge. Mr. Marsden's home was partly filmed at Bucklers Hard and partly at Delawarr House. The cave was mostly made of a lathe and plaster shell put up in the 'Studio' and you can guess where the Sea Scout Headquarters was situated.

On 13th October 1937 Mr. Hole took three Sea Scouts to Alexandra Palace in London to be filmed on television. The Boy Scouts Association had been invited to contribute to an interview in the 67th edition of *Picture Page* and Lymington were selected. The discussion between the announcer and Robert Hole was mostly about the *Discovery,* which had been handed over to the Boy Scouts Association. After the interview, Rover Sea Scout Jack Clark had to dance a hornpipe and ended up in a sitting position which caused some amusement. Luckily this was only a rehearsal. After it was all over they were taken round the building and "gazed into rooms filled with the most confusing switchboard and great things like steel lockers, each containing some weird valves about 4 feet in height in which tiny blue lights danced, like so many trapped flies." Such was television in those days. This same Scout presented himself at the Scala Theatre and sold programmes at *The Gang Show 1937* but had some difficulty making his way back to Lymington in the early hours of the following morning.

At the outbreak of war, many of the older boys – and there was a strong Rover Section at the time – found themselves in uniform, mostly in the Navy, but even the boys not old enough for actual active service became members of the official Coast Watching Service and found themselves doing regular stints on lookout at Keyhaven. A number of ex-Sea Scouts failed to return from the war and it is a pity that no form of 'Roll of Honour' was ever kept.

After the war it was some time before things got back to normal. Robert Hole severed his connections with the Sea Scouts and devoted his time to establishing the Lymington Community Centre which, like the Sea Scouts, immediately became a great success under his leadership and a pattern for similar centres all over the country. Frank Claridge made gallant efforts to keep things going, which he did for some years but eventually not only was RN recognition (so proudly awarded in the 1930s for Sea Scouts of outstanding achievement) withdrawn but the unit actually closed down.

Fortunately, in 1967 quite 'out of the blue' Charles E. Turner, a very experienced Scouter with a great ambition to re-establish the troop back to its pre-war glory, came to Lymington. After a great deal of hard work, numbers rose from 23 to 50 and they were once again given Royal Navy recognition. In the ten years 1968-78 Lymington Sea Scouts have participated in every single event organised in the District, and in the various competitions held annually, and were the overall winners of the Camping Competition 5 times, First Aid 3 times, Swimming Gala 4 times, 'Signpost' Competition (General Scoutcraft) 3 times; Handball Competition twice. In the Solent Area Scout Regatta, which is open to all units from Poole to Portsmouth, Lymington have been the overall champions 3 times and runners-up 3 times. At the present time there is a very successful Cub Scout Pack of 24 8-11 year olds, a Scout Troop of 24 11-16 year olds and a small Venture Scout Unit of 16-20 year olds. There are 7 leaders with two regular instructors.

The Troop has 8 canoes, 6 10-ft. pulling dinghies and 1 16-ft. 4-oared pulling boat. For sailing they have a Wayfarer 26-ft., S/Scout 11-ft. dinghy, a Mirror dinghy and 2 11-ft. Gull dinghies and 2 G.P.14s. They also have a 12-ft. motor launch with an inboard motor, and complete camping equipment for 8 Scout patrols, as well as a 30-ft. × 30-ft. marquee and a Ford 35 cwt Transit van.

'Tibby' Turner said that naval recognition was a struggle each year but it meant that the Scouts could go on various sea cruises organised by the Navy. Should they lose this official recognition, it would probably mean a wait of fifteen years before they could apply for it again as, out of 800 troops, only 100 were officially recognised. But with Herbert Rand as their President and Dr. Chris Lawn as Chairman of a very active support committee of eight, devoted to fund-raising, and with 'Tibby' Turner as Group Scout Leader this surely would not happen to the 9th Lymington Sea Scouts!

CHAPTER 11

'CONFLICTS IN AN ESTUARY'

"The history of the River is one of conflict, one interest overriding the other."
MALDWIN DRUMMOND

Maldwin Drummond, Verderer of the New Forest, Hampshire County Councillor, past Chairman of the Solent Protection Society, author and yachtsman, is also a Member of the Marine Biological Association and Director of an oyster company. *Conflicts in an Estuary,* written in 1974 about the Lymington River, was his thesis for Southampton University's Certificate of Environmental Science, and few can be as well qualified as he to examine these conflicts and attempt to resolve them. These include road and rail transport against water transport; recreational use of the river against commercial use; wildfowling against wild life; water ski-ing against angling, passive enjoyment and bird watching; cultivation against conservancy; and waste disposal and effluent against shell-fish farming to mention only a few of them. These conflicts of interest are so inter-related that to strike a correct balance between them all is the most that can possibly be achieved. This book is compulsive reading for all those interested in planning, management, ecology and enjoyment of our estuaries.

The most important problem connected with the Lymington River today is siltation, affecting yachtsmen, commercial fishermen, the ferries, the marinas and boatbuilders and repairers. There are many reasons for this. A copy of a chart dating back to 1795, when the first survey was carried out, shows that the river had been navigable for two miles beyond the present tollbridge for vessels with a 10-ft. draught. The tollbridge was constructed by Captain Cross in 1731 and there is continuing evidence of the siltation problems caused by the construction of this causeway. Unfortunately, after much legal wrangling, it has been allowed to stay. There is a very detailed thesis in the Harbour Commissioners' office on how long it would take for the River to scour if the sluice gates there were enlarged. This is a scientific treatise prepared by a student at Southampton University and covers the physical side – the geological and the hydrographical – and in itself is of tremendous interest.

The Lymington River Commercial Users Association also started to carry out some research and invited Dr. D. S. Ranwell, of the School of Biological Sciences of the University of East Anglia to give them a talk. According to Dr. Ranwell, one of the reasons why silt is deposited in the river is because the fresh water coming from the New Forest has a negative ion, and salt sea water has a positive ion. So where they meet there is an ion exchange and the silt particles are deposited.

The Spartina grass on the salterns is dying off, mainly because it is asexual and can no longer replace itself. The result is erosion of the salt marshes with the mud on the banks subsiding into the river. A study of photographs taken early this century with recent ones illustrates this only too clearly and the river is now practically double its original width and correspondingly much shallower. Dr. Ranwell reported on an interesting experiment up in Scotland where a new strain of spartina grass had been bred. That country was chosen because it had the worst conditions they could find. This grass can actually be sown and this means that the banks could be bound and the loss of mud into the river prevented.

Spartina grass has become increasingly widespread around the coast of Britain, although it was completely unknown a century ago. Maldwin Drummond wrote that this hybrid spartina was first noticed in Southampton Water in 1870 because of an accident to an American ship. It is believed that the American grass was emptied over the side, having served as packing or filling for the passengers' bedding. It arrived in Lymington in 1892 and colonised the whole estuary. It was therefore particularly apt that a Symposium to discuss current work on its origin, present ecological status and economic value was set up in Southampton University in August 1964. It was chaired by Dr. C. E. Hubbard from the Royal Botanic Gardens at Kew and Southampton; Dr. J. M. Lambert and Professor W. T. Williams from Southampton University, and Dr. Ranwell for Nature Conservancy. The causes of die-back were studied and one was due to the "slipping of soft mud back into the channels and thereby bringing neighbouring marsh surface down to a level too constantly flooded for healthy spartina to grow." Another cause of river bank erosion is the wash caused by passing vessels, particularly that of the passenger ferries.

A View of Lymington River – 20th Century

By courtesy of Marcus Associates

Professor F. W. Oliver, one of the pioneer investigators of Spartina in Britain, realised that the British grass could not only be used for reclamation, as has been carried out in Holland, Denmark and Germany and on a smaller scale in the Wash, but also as a crop; its food value being equivalent to a medium-quality hay, which could be cut and used as silage. Its disadvantages include choking minor channels used by yachtsmen, invading mud flats near holiday beaches and, from a conservation angle, there is a danger of the loss of certain forms of wildlife, due to other salt-marsh plants, the feeding ground of wintering wildfowl, being eliminated. So the continual study and experimentation with spartina grass is of vital importance to Lymington River and its neighbouring marshes.

Fred Woodford, the Harbour Master, considered that we need two breakwaters in about ten or fifteen years to prevent further erosion of the marshes. These should be situated, probably in the vicinity of Seymour's Post, Naish Point and Pylewell Tar Barrel area. They would then protect the Inner Harbour and also make possible the extension of the Yacht Haven marina or even the creation of another marina lower down the river on the east bank which would take care of erosion as well.

In the meantime, thousands of tons of silt are deposited in the river at the Lymington Marina and at the Yacht Haven and elsewhere; to a lesser degree, there is trade effluent discharged from Golden Produce chicken factory. The Town Quay, where visitors' berths are sited, just dries out and becomes a sea of mud and yachts have difficulty in getting in there to tie up and difficulty again when they get out. An example of this was when a famous French yachtsman, Eric Tabarly, brought his 74-ft. ketch *Euromarche,* with a draught of 11-ft. into Lymington River to have her equipment checked by Brookes & Gatehouse, Hood and other Lymington-based firms, before the start of the Whitbread Round the World Race. Half an hour before low water she ran aground opposite the Haven Marina, delaying the ferries for up to twenty minutes, and an hour after refloating with the tide at 8.0 p.m. she ran aground a second time abreast the ferry slipway. She eventually berthed at Lymington Marina. Not a good advertisement for Lymington River, particularly with a foreign yacht on a commercial visit.

A. Vernon Sainsbury, former Chairman of the Harbour Commissioners, talked to me in his home at Normandy Cottage, Normandy Lane, Lymington on 10th May 1982. "Broadly speaking," he said, "the position over dredging is that dredging of the river, the 80 ft. middle channel down the river, is the responsibility of British Rail and they obviously consult the Harbour Commissioners as to when it is necessary to dredge and at what time of year. The two marinas are responsible for their own dredging, under the guidance of the Harbour Commissioners, and the Harbour Commission itself dredges the rest of the river, as necessary. Our real problem is that what we call the special area, the moorings up and above the ferry station, is a constantly silting area and a constantly rising price. When we dredged about ten or twelve years ago the total cost was about £4,000; the last time we dredged the total cost was getting on for £80,000 and that is just for our portion."

Don Howard had also stressed that the cost of dredging the river is astronomical: the Yacht Haven spent £90,000 on dredging one tiny patch in 1980. British Rail, as we have noted, has an obligation to dredge but have not done so properly for the last twelve years. Their argument is that the Voith Schneider propellers on the new ferries are able to drive through the mud so that in effect they are dredging it continuously, except that the mud they churn up is deposited elsewhere!

The dredging firm, Yacht Harbour Services, and Lymington Marina were prosecuted by the Ministry of Agriculture, who had granted the dredging licence, with dumping in United Kingdom waters between 10th October to 11th November 1980 and 11th February to 12th March 1981, contrary to the Dumping at Sea Act 1974. Evidence was given by Mr. Woodford, the Harbour Master, that he expected the spoil to be dumped out at the usual dumping ground by Hurst Narrows, and he was concerned at the over-spilling in the river. The level of the river bed had been raised by 3 ft. and craft using the channel were impeded.

Graham Butler, Chairman of the Lymington Professional Fishermen's Association, said that the silting was so bad that even boats with shallow draught had been unable to get up or down the river one hour before and two hours after low water. Boats had gone aground and there had been damage to equipment.

Captain Leonard Wheeler, the Isle of Wight Services Manager for Sealink said that at low water the ferries had been unable to use the lay-by, stand-by and slipway berths at low water.

Captain Michael Dunkerly, a Director of Dunkerly Marine and Hydrographic Surveys, told the Court he had carried out surveys in the Lymington River over a long period and said that there had been a serious silting problem for many years and described Lymington Marina as a "perfect silt trap."

It was the first time suction dredging had been carried out at the Marina at a contract price of £36 an hour and a total amount of about £30,000. The collecting barges had filled too quickly and substantial overspilling of thousands of tons had occurred. But Lymington Magistrates acquitted both Yacht Harbour Services and Lymington Marina.

Dredging in the Lymington and Keyhaven Marshes would require the permission of the Crown Estate Commissioners and local landlords. Don Howard said that in his opinion and that of the Lymington River Commercial Users Association, it would be an excellent thing if the river was also cleansed. It was not so long ago that children were swimming all day in the river and you could stand on the quay and watch the fish swimming over the gravel, the water was so clear. Quite apart from being a good advertisement for Lymington as a yachting centre, he considered that there should be a commitment to yachtsmen to keep the river navigable. He would like to see a clean river and some of the area pleasantly landscaped as at Christchurch, but here again it was a matter of cost.

It was largely as a result of the discharge from Fortuna Dock and the yacht berths that the Lymington River Commercial Users Association was formed and started to carry out some research of its own. They invited Dr. Ranwell to give the report we have already noted. It was the purpose of the Association to exchange ideas, disseminate information and also to maintain a list of people who were totally undesirable in Lymington. Their Secretary was elected to serve on the Harbour Commission and at present (1981) this is Don Howard.

"The Harbour Commission is a very strange body," said A. Vernon Sainsbury, "and was set up by Act of Parliament in 1951 and the Commissioners are half elected and half appointed. There are six appointed members of the Council; three elected members of British Rail; two elected members representing the yachting interest (one from each yacht club) and two elected members representing the Lymington River Commercial Users interests. Their job is to manage the Harbour within the Harbour limits which, broadly speaking, is a good slice of the river down on either side. The Harbour Master is appointed by the Harbour Commissioners and is their Chief Executive and the Clerk deals with the administrative side.

"The Habour Commission has no capital: it is one of these strange semi-government bodies and if you wish to do capital intensive work, you have to go to the bank for it. That is absolutely splendid except that it puts at least 25% on to the cost of doing it! The bank is very good and so indeed is the Council and we can borrow quite a lot of funds from them. They have not go much income but they have got a lot of capital. The expenses of the Harbour Commission are charged to the rates.

"We have no security except for the income from moorings, which is somewhere around £60,000 a year. £60,000 does not cover dredging half a mile of river and this is the sort of problem we are up against!"

Don Howard would like to see fees on the river put up. He keeps a 35 ft. boat on the river and pays approximately £130 a year but in the Marina he would pay £1,200, and he considered that the river moorings should be doubled.

Fred Woodford issued a leaflet on the 'Code of Conduct' for the river and the idea was that every boat should have one, at present conduct is very poor compared to the past in terms of elementary knowledge of the Rules of the Road. It includes a little chartlet on the buoyage of the river and on the back there is a list of useful companies.

Lymington Harbour Commissioners are the lighting authority for Trinity House. Last year (1980) they were the first to use solar panels at Jack in the Basket. "These were highly successful and they may well go over to all solid state solar panels," Fred Woodford told me. "Originally they used gas lanterns until 1946, then battery-operated mechanical lanterns in 1967, and the first solid state solar panels in 1980. So the lighting has changed from gas to solar in less than twenty years. In the old days as soon as it blew at Force 6 the lamps would blow out and I had to go out and relight them," he said.

Tom Doe remembered seeing the old oil lamps. There used to be four of them and each had three burners and a thick magnifying glass. They could be seen from a matter of 3 miles away. There was one on Cross Boom, one on Seymour's Post, one on Cocked Hat and one on Harper's Lake and when you passed there you could see the Board of Trade light on the pier. They were long-burning oil lamps, which could last a fortnight but it depended on the state of the weather because the posts were always on the shake.

"The complex system of salt marshes, mudflats and creeks between Pitts Deep and Hurst Spit, and the marsh pastures and pools which form their immediate hinterland between Lymington and Keyhaven, comprise a landscape of rare aesthetic appeal and an ecological system of great biological interest and nature conservation value. At the same time the marshes are valued and have a long tradition of use by fishermen, bait diggers, wildfowlers, walkers, birdwatchers, small boat sailors and others, and thus serve important social functions in the local community." So reads the first paragraph of the Introduction in 'The Lymington-

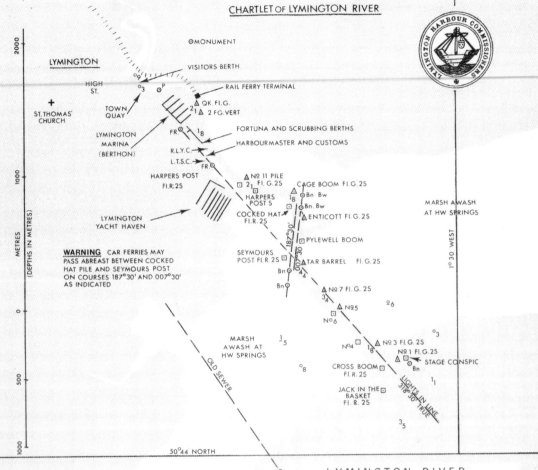

CHARTLET OF LYMINGTON RIVER

LYMINGTON RIVER

CODE OF CONDUCT

1. MAXIMUM SPEED = 6 knots. (This is a max. speed; NOT a norm.)

2. Pass Port to Port.

3. Maintain course on Starboard hand.

4. Overtaking vessels keep clear. Sealink car ferries excepted; see 6 below.

5. DO NOT cast off or leave berth without ensuring all clear - dock or berth at <u>minimum</u> speed consistent with safe steerage headway.

6. All craft must give way to Sealink ferries (Byelaw). Maintain lookout for ferry movements and anticipate own course, position and speed accordingly.

7. Use of autopilots in Lymington River is NOT permitted.

8. All river users - particularly dinghy sailors - please note that the British Rail Sealink ferries cannot stop their Voigt Schneider propulsion units; they can be put into neutral but continue to rotate, therefore aquaplaning and windsurfing are strictly prohibited (Byelaw).

Produced from portion of Ba Chart No. 2040 with sanction of the controller H.M. Stationery Office and of the Hydrographer of the Navy. Note: This chartlet may not include the latest information published by the Hydrographer of the Navy.

Keyhaven Coast: Policies for Future Management,' the Report of the Review Group to Hampshire County Council and the New Forest Council of March 1982, ratified in May of the same year.

A Study was carried out jointly by a group of Councillors from Hampshire County and the New Forest District Councils between January 1980 and November 1981. Separate meetings were arranged with 44 local organisations and written comments were received from 78 local people. The lists of both were attached as Appendices 4 and 5, and give an indication of the trouble taken to consult with everyone deeply concerned with the marshes and their future management. Previously, in December 1979, a re-drafted Report, 'The Future of the North West Solent Coast,' largely compiled by C. R. Tubbs, of the Nature Conservancy Council, had recommended that the coast from Pitts Deep to Hurst Spit should become a local Nature Reserve but this was not accepted although it forms the basis of the second Report of 1982.

The decline of the Little Tern is a national problem and it is now regarded as a threatened species. This is often due to small boat sailors landing on the shell banks occupied by breeding terns and waders, whose eggs can be trampled unwittingly. These sites will be wardened with explanatory signs placed at appropriate places. This system already exists within the Hampshire and Isle of Wight Naturalist Trust Reserve. This conflict is all the more important because the terneries on our marshes are the largest in the South of England.

The sea wall stretching 6½ miles from Lymington to Keyhaven is popular with walkers, fishermen and others but is in need of restoration. Horse riders, cyclists and motor-cycles will be prohibited from using it and stock must be kept away from the sea wall. It is hoped that anglers, who have the largest stake in its future, will participate fully in its protection and management.

Moorings in the Lymington River are controlled by the Lymington Harbour Commissioners and there is provision for just under 1,600 boats:

72	–	above the railway bridge
30	–	fishing boats in the Town Quay area
56	–	on piles north of the Ferry Station
300	–	in the Lymington Marina
79	–	in the Fortuna Dock
450	–	in the Lymington Yacht Haven
600	–	on river moorings
1,587		

In addition there are variable numbers of moorings, approximately:

9,000	–	visitors per annum using the moorings at the Town Quay
20	–	small boats moored by their own tackle in Moses Dock with the permission of the Harbour Master
20	–	small boats moored at Tanners Lane (and a few at Pitts Deep Quay).

The Harbour Commission's moorings are reserved for those with property within 7 miles of Lymington Church and the present waiting list is 420. Largely because of the density of yacht traffic in the river and the increased displacement of the British Rail ferries, the Harbour Commission's policy for some years has been not materially to increase the present number of moorings within their area of control.

Although no detailed records are kept it is estimated that Lymington, which has two slips, launches more than 350 trailed boats in a season. Any material increase in the number of launchings increases the density of river traffic and it is difficult to identify offenders against river discipline. Another way to deter too many trailed boats was not to improve access roads.

There are some 200 dinghies at Lymington kept in dinghy parks and belonging to local residents. Although a great increase in numbers might cause concern these dinghy parks already come under the control of the District Council and no recommendation was as yet necessary.

Excessive bait digging can de-oxygenate the mud and so reduce intertidal fauna which is the food of estuarine birds. There is no evidence that worms are fewer than 20 years ago nor have bird numbers declined. It was decided that bait digging can continue provided it is not on a commercial basis.

Little commercial fishing is carried out in this study area although both Lymington and Keyhaven provide moorings for fishing vessels. There is no objection to fishing in tidal waters.

The South Hampshire Wildfowlers Association has a lease from the Crown Estate Commissioners over intertidal land east of Lymington. The Lymington, Keyhaven & District Wildfowlers and Marsh Users Association has licences from the Hampshire and Isle of Wight Naturalists Trust and the Lymington Harbour Commission over intertidal land between Lymington River and Hurst Spit.

Doug Baverstock is Chairman of the Lymington & Keyhaven Wildfowlers Association and told me that is was founded about ten or twelve years ago because the local people were going to lose the use of the marshes for their shooting. "We went to see the Harbour Commissioners and the County Council and were granted licences to shoot on the marshes by both organisations. Not only do we shoot but we also rear quite a number of birds each year to keep the population going. There are a lot more birds here now than there used to be so we do a little bit of good! Mostly we shoot mallard, widgeon, teal and sometimes an odd goose, which is allowed, but not very often. Most of the geese down here are Brent Geese which are protected birds. We have about 80 wildfowlers today.

"When the weather gets cold there is always a ban on shooting nowadays. Years ago they never used to but now they impose a temporary ban on it for a few days and I think they are right. The birds come down to the Solent from countries where they have been frozen out because it is a little bit warmer. So it is a shame to pursue them and shoot them when they are tired and hungry birds. We go out and shoot just before 4.0 p.m. in November; the night flight is about this time and you can carry on until it gets really dark. They do show up when it is a sort of half-light although you cannot shoot when it is really dark."

Colin Mudie told me that Doug Baverstock had some very interesting old shooting gear which today are collectors' items and are of considerable antique value. The gun is an 1¼ inch bore and fires about a pound of shot. It is about 7 ft. 6 ins. long and weighs about 70 odd pounds. It is too heavy to carry so he puts in in a crutch in a big double-handed punt with breeching ropes back; the same sort of principle you can see in a picture of Nelson's cannons which also had breeching ropes back to stop them jumping about in the boat. It is a good looking set of gear which he has not yet had time to use.

Lymington and Keyhaven Wildfowlers Association has been criticised for their annual fox cull on Sturt Meadow, Milford, which they have carried out for the past ten years. It is said that the shoot upsets the balance of nature, had an adverse effect on the ecology of the area and that there was a danger from the discharge of firearms.

On the other hand in July 1982 they released 60 8-week old Mallard ducklings into the river and marshes as part of a rearing programme. In the four years since it started, 248 ducklings have been reared and released in the area.

The South Hampshire Wildfowling Association, which shoots on the foreshore to the East of the Lymington River, was formed in 1952. At this time it was realised that if wildfowling was to survive at all, people would have to get together as part of an organisation, as in all field sports.

Their Secretary is Captain Peter Bevan, a Senior Trinity House Pilot in Southampton. In theory, his territory stretches up to Lymington, but in 30 years he has never got up to here. However, in his leisure he is up and down the river all the time, as he has kept his boat here for the past years.

"In 1964," he told me, "a Colonel A. Phillips of Lymington, a keen and interested naturalist, approached the Association to seek their assistance in controlling the shooting in the Lymington area. The land east of the river from Naish Point to Sowley is owned by the Crown Estates Commissioners. We obtained many signatures from local people; no one at that stage opposed us because, I am told, in that area on a Sunday morning, it was like the opening barrage of the Battle of Alamein – anything that moved was shot! There were all sorts of plastic bottles and tins full of shotgun pellets lying around. Three years later the Crown granted us a lease of the shooting rights.

"Although we have very close relations with the Nature Conservancy and the Hampshire and Isle of Wight Naturalists Trust, at present we do not have a conservation scheme. We have tried changing the habitat on the foreshore at Lymington but the mud and spartina are gradually going back into the sea and what is left is clay and gault which is no use to breeding anything.

"Another reason is the opposition from inshore, apart from a few like Mr. Whittaker of Pylewell and Mr. Hammond at Sowley, who have been a great help to us. The inshore estates are so well keepered and the flight ponds are so heavily fed, that there is already a terrific amount of duck and we would really only be helping them.

"We have always had a notice board in the grounds of Shore Cottage at the bottom of Tanners Lane that states we own the shooting rights. An old chap lived there named Archie Phillips, who used to phone me if he saw anything odd going on. The present owner wrote and told me she strongly disapproves of shooting and loves watching the birds on the foreshore and is not prepared to help us. The geese she mentioned, that were so tame they would practically come and talk to her, were the Barnacles, introduced to Newtown on the Isle of Wight by Arthur Adam, who was Deputy Surveyor of the New Forest, and these get very tame and then have to be fed. Of the geese on the foreshore at Lymington, Brent Geese have built up because of the extraordinary rearing situation in the last few years in Northern Siberia; White Fronts are drifting in from Southern Ireland where they have a big crowd and the others, the Canada Geese – now almost a pest – and the Greylags have been introduced by us.

"You can only shoot wildfowl if you know what you are going. Once Derek Mullins of East End and two of his pals, went down to the foreshore when the weather was reasonable and for six days they could see hundreds of birds flying up and down about a hundred yards from the edge of the foreshore. On the seventh day, when the wind had increased to gale force, these birds came two hundred yards inland and they had the best bag ever. That is because they waited till the weather was right.

"The Lymington-Keyhaven Plan will now only apply to the west side of the Lymington River and as far as we are concerned, on the east side, it does not really affect us. However we have told the Nature Conservancy that we will help them in any way we can, provided it does not affect our interests. It would be a far better thing for wildfowl if the public realised that black-headed gulls, which are protected, do a terrible amount of harm and if they were shot there would be far more of the duck that they want to see breeding. But if you shoot a gull on the foreshore of Lymington – be it a black-headed gull – there would be a court case against you!

"As well as the lease on the foreshore we do try and organise other kinds of shooting. We are working with the Hampshire and Isle of Wight Naturalists Trust over the control of rabbits. They have purchased an enormous amount of ground that was not wanted for cultivation by its previous owners with the result that you start getting large numbers of rabbits, who now live above ground since myxomatosis. We have a shoot up at Romsey, which covers about 12,000 acres and it costs a deal more money than wildfowling because anybody who wants a pheasant shoot today has got to breed the birds; you cannot just go and shoot them indiscriminately. We have very good deer shooting as well and we also take that on."

Their national association, the Wildfowlers Association of Great Britain and Ireland (WAGBI) has now changed its name to the British Association for Shooting and Conservation (BASC). This in itself is significant and shows that both can be compatible, not only in name.

Colonel Peter Hawker, the famous 19th century wildfowler, is the great-great grandfather of Daphne Bruce. In the period covered by his Diary, 1802 to 1853, he found 29 different species of wildfowl at Keyhaven and shot 1,327 Brent Geese, 2,211 Widgeon and 1,329 Dunlin. It seems unbelievable to us today. In 1833 he wrote his famous book *Instructions to young sportsmen in all that relates to guns and shooting,* which was also published by Richmond Publishing.

It is proposed to attempt to strike the correct balance between long grass and shrub, associated with small mammals and song birds, and short grass grazed by cattle, which nesting birds like Lapwing, Redshank and Yellow Wagtails prefer. Where intertidal food resources have become inadequate, Brent Geese have taken to feeding on farmland, where they cause damage to cereal crops and, as they are a protected species, this causes many problems.

It is interesting to note that there is a proposal to excavate 10 acres of shallow lagoons on Normandy Farm, using existing fresh water. It will have some islands, covered with shingle, to encourage nesting birds, particularly terns. Access to the public may be restricted to the use of hides or screens.

Since early 1960 the Hampshire and Isle of Wight Naturalists Trust has employed a Warden to prevent disturbance to the breeding bird colonies in their Reserve. In 1973 the Trust Warden has also been employed by Hampshire County to look after its land. To find out more about his work, I visited Eddie Wiseman, the Nature Ranger, at his home in Normandy Farm on 13th January 1983 and had a most interesting talk with him.

Eddie Wiseman told me that he had been born at the other end of the county in Portsmouth. His great grandfather was a fisherman and his paternal grandfather did all sorts of things. His father was a farrier and worked for a firm called Curtis, which hired out horses to the dockyard. He was responsible for all 150 of them and used to take them through the town to the Yard and back again. But his son did not follow in his father's footsteps. "I don't like horses very much and they don't like me," he said. "I have never got on with them."

Eddie Wiseman had always been keen on birds, even when he was at school, and he admitted that he used to collect eggs like most small boys in those days. This was before the 1954 Bird Protection Act when it was not illegal but egg collecting, except by professional collectors, was becoming outdated in any event. The headmaster of his school advised him that there was no future in earning a living with birds, and said the same of his second choice of a career, which was to become a thatcher. That was regarded as a dying trade although, in fact, today there are more thatchers than ever. "At 13 or 14 you accept what they say and that was really knocked out of me," he said.

So when he left school he did an apprenticeship as a sheet metal worker, and for the last year he worked in the drawing office, which he found quite enjoyable at times. He then was called up for National Service and spent two years in the army. He returned to the firm but after a month he felt that if he was going to make the break this was the time to do it, so he left and went into forestry. The Forestry Commission land he worked was to the north of Portsmouth near Rowlands Castle. There was about a thousand acres there and they also worked at the Queen Elizabeth Forest, near Petersfield. He did that for five years and gained experience in using hand tools, ditching and fencing work that would stand him in good stead should he ever work on a Reserve.

Then the opportunity came to go to Shetland and to Fair Isle and work at the bird sanctuary, something he had always wanted to do. It was summer work and the following autumn he went off to Sweden and Lapland and hitched around in Scandinavia, returning to Fair Isle the following July and spent another year there. The work involved trapping and ringing migrant birds and our own nesting birds and he did this for two years.

He had always hoped to return to Hampshire, particularly as there were so many people there and therefore a lot of pressure on the countryside. In 1960 the Isle of Wight and Hampshire Naturalists Trust was formed which had reserves all around the county and in 1962 they agreed with what was then Lymington Municipal Borough to take over the salt marshes on the outside of the sea wall, mainly in order to protect the Little Terns that were nesting there. In 1966 they advertised for someone to take on the job of looking after the Terns as a spring and summer job and he thought that this was a start and he wanted to get back to Hampshire. So they wrote to him in Fair Isle offering him the job. "I realised that it was going to be a fairly difficult job because I had known the place since about the mid-1950s and I had seen the pressures on it," he told me. When I got off the bus at Milford a man walking with a rucksack asked if I was the new Warden and warned me that 'they were a rough lot down in Keyhaven'."

Protecting the Terns finished in August each year and so he usually went off for four or five weeks holiday in the autumn and then did Forestry work in the winter, mostly with the National Trust in West Sussex and at Selborne, and he did this for the next four or five seasons.

Finally, in 1973, Normandy Marsh came on the market and the County Council purchased it jointly with the New Forest District Council; later they also bought the Salterns and later still, Oxey and Pennington. That year they advertised for a full-time Warden and he tried for it and, quite naturally, got it. So he had come full circle round to what he originally wanted to do and had become extremely well qualified for the job on the way. He still looked after the Naturalists Trust land as before and worked them together.

The County then put forward a coastal plan. Many people were nervous that the sea wall was going to be closed and various rumours went around but what the County had proposed was the formation of a local nature reserve and this was simply a device whereby the local authority could give it the strongest protection. But there were strong objections to this plan and it was changed to a conservation area which is what it is today.

What made the job particularly interesting were the various people who used the marshes for one reason or another. The first group he met were the local lads collecting gulls eggs. There were four boys doing this at Keyhaven on a semi-professional basis. The Isle of Wight and Hampshire Naturalists Trust had taken the view that it was all right as long as it was done sensibly and did not harm the gulls. "If you egged them right on through the season," Eddie explained, "and took practically every egg that was laid up until June, then in ten years the colony would probably have gone away." So they came to an agreement that they collected for about a month each year and then stopped.

So marsh users, who were particularly anxious that their right to use the marshes would not be curtailed by local by-laws, were the Lymington & Keyhaven Wildfowlers Association, who were formed in order to protect the rights of its members. "I am not anti-shooting, although I don't like seeing birds shot," he confessed, "but I can see wildfowlers go out for much the same reason as I do basically. They like being out at dawn and dusk but the main difference is that they shoot and I don't – I watch. It is perfectly legal and people have shot over the marshes for years, rightly or wrongly, but there has been illegal shooting unfortunately." The Ranger's job is to try and ensure that the place is shot within the law and is essential shooting and, secondly, that it is to as high a standard as possible. Wildfowlers would themselves agree that you cannot shoot every square inch of the marshes and you have to leave sanctuary areas, where birds can go fairly undisturbed.

The dividing line between the Hampshire and Isle of Wight Naturalists Trust and the Hampshire County Council is the sea wall: the County land is on the inside and the Naturalist Trust land is on the outside, the mudlands and the salt marshes. The nesting sites of the Little Tern are particularly important in the Solent area because they are our rarest regular breeding sea bird in this country. Nationwide there are only about 1,800 pairs left and of these, 200 pairs live on the Solent. It is also good for waders, duck and wildfowl like geese.

"The impact of yachts is really two-fold," he said, "and the main problem from the large boats is really the growth of marinas to berth them. They are entitled to take some of the land but quite often it is mudlands and salt marshes and there must be a limit on how much they swallow up. But once in the water, the large boats are off racing or sailing and are no threat to the environment at all. It is the small dinghy sailor who can cause a lot of damage. They go out for perhaps half a day and then decide to land on one of the Tern sites. The trouble is that Tern eggs are extremely difficult to see so someone could land there and trample around and break half the eggs without knowing that they have done so. It is usually entirely unintentional. But there again if you point out to people that there are Terns there and the importance of them then they are usually reasonable."

By far and away the largest group to visit the conservation area are the anglers. Eddie Wiseman has seen as many as 400 of them out on the sea wall holding their competitions. He is not anti them but one must realise that these competitions are organised with large cash prizes and draw people from all over the country. "There was a match not long ago and I chatted to a couple of chaps and asked them where they had come from," he said, "and they told me they had come from Buckinghamshire. It had been advertised in the national angling press." So these are not necessarily local people.

Probably the smallest bunch of people who come to the marshes are bird watchers. "I try to steer clear of large groups of bird-watchers," Eddie continued, "because it can turn into a bit of social activity and half of them chat most of the time! I would rather take round half a dozen at a time, as I think you can get more out of it that way. Still, this is one of the modern trends these days and more and more people are becoming interested in bird watching. They enjoy doing it that way but I would rather just be out on my own, or with one or two friends."

During the spring and summer Eddie is out all the time watching nesting sites. In addition to this he also does a lot of survey work, recording migrations and he keeps notes for the whole area and collects them from other people. It is something that he has always been very interested in.

Eddie is equally busy during the winter months from October until about March. Most of the management work is done then, jobs like fencing and ditching work. "Many people don't realise what happens if you just leave land alone," he told me. "It only stays the same because of man's activities. If you left the marshes to themselves they would soon end up as copses and grow to outwood eventually. This can be extremely interesting as when the land changes, so do the animals, the birds and the insects. So you have to decide at what stage you want to hold the land. Down here I think we are trying to keep a balance between the open grassland, the open marshlands and the scrub. The scrub here is very good for small birds and all sorts of animals and insects but equally you have to keep your open grassland with water areas for waders and wildfowl

and if you left that it would virtually grow in. So it all has to be maintained with that in mind."

Another extremely important aspect of his work is, of course, that he is responsible for his employers' property and the fact that it is the County Council does not make any difference. "County Councils and Councillors have the same rights and responsibilities as any other landowner and I do the job because I think the County is taking a responsible attitude towards it which is very good for natural history. It is of high value from that angle. The law says that if you own land which is a site of special scientific interest (SSSI) then you have to be very careful what you do with it. If the nature conservancy feel that an operation is damaging to the scientific interests of the site then they have every right to intervene. "I don't go out of my way to upset people," he went on, "but equally I don't see why we should all do exactly what we want to do in an area like this. We are all governed by the law of the land I think it should be adhered to; the laws are made for good reasons and I hate to see land like this abused. I have always liked this county; it is worth looking after and I have enjoyed every minute of it." So speaks a happy and contented man doing the work that he always wanted to do and doing it really well too.

We must now return to the last, but not least, of the users of the river and its estuaries, the marinas. The word 'marina' was coined in 1928 by the American National Association of Engine and Boat Manufacturers to describe modern waterfront activity for recreational boats, although the term 'yacht harbour' was often preferred in the U.K. Marinas spread rapidly in America, South of France, North Europe and Scandinavia but were slower to take off in this country, partly due to the conservative tastes of our yachtsmen and partly, and much more importantly, due to planning constraints and finance.

Since 1947 controls have been in force as in the Green Belt Policy and the 'Coastal Preservation and Development Circular No. 56/63. This was followed by 'Operation Neptune,' launched by the Duke of Edinburgh in 1965. Lymington Yacht Haven (Harpers Lake) made applications between 1963 to 1970 and David May too was subjected to considerable delay but met with speedier success when he opened the Lymington Marina in 1968. Lymington Yacht Haven was not to open until June 1972. The long delays were due to the fact that eight separate authorities in the case of Lymington had to be consulted and we had "conflicts of interest" at Council level as well. The bodies concerned were:–

(1) Department of Trade and Industry (Coastal Protection and Navigation.

(2) Harbour Authority (responsible for conservancy).

(3) Crown Estate Commissioners (responsible for the estuary or the sea bed).

(4) River Authority (drainage and coastal protection).

(5) Highway Authority (access and traffic).

(6) District Councils.

(7) Police Authority (traffic).

(8) Adjoining planning authority (if near boundary).

Recommendations would then proceed upwards from the District Council Planning Committee to the Divisional Planning Committee to the County Planning Committee and thence consultation with the Secretary of State for the Environment and public enquiry.

Maldwin Drummond in *Conflicts in an Estuary* then goes on to give the criteria set by Hampshire County Council for the establishment of yacht harbours as:-

"(1) Areas of high landscape value should not be chosen.

(2) Priority should be given to sites linked to existing boatyards.

(3) Adequate road access should be made available or proposed.

(4) New yacht harbours should provide public access to the water and tender dinghy parking for other users.

(5) Ancilliary features such as cabins for yachtsmen, hotels or cafés, would not seem to be needed unless associated with urban areas.

(6) The prime consideration should be the effect upon navigation and on hydrographic factors, such as the effect of the proposal on river banks, tides, currents, silting, etc.

(7) Vessels should be able to leave their berths at all states of the tide.

(8) Proposals should not encroach upon navigable waters in such a way as they reduce the area available for use by small boats, or which would result in the displacement of existing public moorings."

Both marinas managed to conform with most of these requirements with the exception of the siting of the Lymington Yacht Haven in the saltings. It is interesting to note too that the Chapman Report to the Harbour Commissioners (1960) stated that there would be a general improvement in the width and depth of the river if the tollbridge restriction was removed, despite initial disturbance but again it was the expense factor that prevailed.

Between 19th and 21st April 1972 a Symposium was held at the University of Southampton and its proceedings are contained in 'Marinas and Small Craft Harbours,' edited by N. B. Webber and published in 1973 by the University Press. At this time Lymington Marina had already been built in 1968 with 300 berths and the Yacht Haven was to open two months later in June 1972 with 250 berths. J. R. Bryans, a former Commodore of the Royal Lymington Yacht Club, represented the Royal Yachting Association and put the case for the yachtsman at the Symposium.

He concluded with these words: "I have touched on the main features which a conscientious yachtsman will look for before he is prepared to commit himself to using a marina for any length of time. These main points cover location and physical limitations, services, access, security, hygiene, safety, noise and financial stability. I hope that it will be remembered that it is the yachtsman who is doing all the paying. Not only has he bought, or built, his yacht, but he is providing employment and bringing business to the promoters of marinas, designers, construction engineers, dredgers, marine architects and planners." In other words it is they who 'pay the piper' where marinas are concerned.

To find out more about the Lymington Yacht Haven, I went to see Dirk Kalis, a director, on the 5th August 1982 in his office. Dirk Kalis went to University and read law. Then he became a dredging contractor for six years and had some experience of holiday work on dredgers before returning to law to practise at the Bar for five or six years. He came to the Lymington Yacht Haven when Commander Dent retired.

"My father, who was a Dutchman, with a background of boat dredging, met a chap called Linaker, who was trying to build a marina because he realised that there was a great lack of facilities. Originally they wanted to build the marina in Poole and took borings there but the local people had an oyster bed in Poole and were frightened that the oysters would be upset by the yachts, so that fell through. Then they decided to try and start one in Harpers Lake.

"Peter Webster owned Ropewalk Boatyard which he sold to us as they had fallen on hard times after the imposition of the 25% VAT. Boatyards have been up and down and, fortunately, Peter sold us his yard before these very hard times and I think he was lucky that he sold out when he did. He is a 3% shareholder and can look forward to a comfortable old age. We have been running the boatyard simply as a repair yard. We did build some new yachts there but have given that up.

"So they measured up the marina but all the interested parties and 'curry colonels' thought that it would be absurd to have a yacht harbour near to yacht clubs. They did not want any boating for the masses: it was only for people with 40 ft. yachts and over! But times change and there were many objections that the waves would be too great in this piece of water and that they would have to build a huge sea wall round the whole marina. Finally, after I think two appeals, they got planning permission in about 1970, after waiting nearly twelve years. Then we had some right-of-way difficulties but these were sorted out and we got going in 1972 with construction.

"We were only able to do this because Westminster Dredging Company, which was our family firm, built the harbour and then said we could pay them back later. To do this we borrowed £5,000 from 121 of our customers and gave them special cheap berthing rights until 1992. So we were in business. We found that there was a terrific demand for berths and there has been ever since we opened, despite local opposition and public opinion.

"Commander Dent was introduced to this marina by my father, who left the country as a tax exile. He was here all during the construction stage and got it all going and then left the country. I think we have probably got enough boats in Lymington now. Saturation is very difficult to assess really. When you look at some of the busy waterways in Holland, they have got a lot more traffic, but in Cowes Week it certainly is busy. Lymington has a lot to offer: it is still an attractive place.

"The yard has 23 people and in the offices we have nine. We are open seven days a week and close only on Christmas Day. We do not need to but I think people expect a certain amount of service and help in sorting out their problems. Visitors take quite a lot of parking. We have many visitors but we never turn any away. We get them to come to the office and then we try and find empty berths whose owners are away cruising.

"We have just opened a yacht harbour in Swansea where we have rented the docks down there. They were put out to tender and we offered to make it a marina and were selected to do it. There is not one marina in the whole of Wales. It has got a lovely coastline and furious tides in the Bristol Channel but there are no facilities for yachting at all. We are stirring them up in Wales!"

The Lymington Marina dockmaster's office now maintains a listening watch on VHF radio Channel M (37) during manned office hours. The call sign is *Lymington Marina* and it was stressed that Channel M is subject to normal radio-telephone procedure and traffic of a personal nature would not normally be accepted.

These then are the 'Conflicts in an Estuary' today and the formidable problems they pose to those connected with the administration of the Lymington River and its marshes. As Maldwin Drummond has so succinctly put it: "It is important to identify these conflicting demands on the estuary, against its geography, history and present role, to assess the future trends. By this method, multiple use of the estuary will be possible, without unforeseen changes that can damage the estuary's resource." We have looked at the 'conflicts': all that remains is how we can reconcile and resolve them.

CHAPTER 12

THE BOATBUILDERS

*"Dan was a craftsman who relied almost entirely on eye. He had no drawings
but a wonderful eye for the lines of a boat."*

E. M. KNIGHT

It is known that there was a shipbuilding industry at Pylewell Hard as there is a record that Charles Guidott sold it in 1688 to John Coombes, shipbuilder. Prior to 1820, shipbuilding in Lymington was limited to trading vessels up to about 60 tons and revenue cutters for the government.

In 1821 yachting, and yacht racing, which was a comparatively new sport, received a boost when the Royal Yacht Squadron was founded at Cowes in 1821 with 50 members. Amongst these was G. A. Fullerton of The Grove, Lymington, who had been out sailing in *Zephyr* in 1806 when she was chased at the Needles by a French privateer. Another was James Weld. Joseph Weld, the owner of Lulworth Castle in Dorset, used to spend six months each summer at his other residence at Pylewell House, adjacent to the Hard, and was himself a skilful yacht designer. These gentlemen used Lymington as their yachting base, along with other members of the Club and, as many of their yachts were laid up in the Lymington River, they were looking around for a local boatbuilder to maintain them and, later, to build new ones for them.

Thomas Inman

Thomas Inman had been a boatbuilder in a small way at Hastings in Sussex. He could see that yacht racing was coming into its own and also the great potential of the Solent, so in 1819 he brought his family of wife and six children in his own boat to Lymington and set up business here. The yard at Pylewell Hard was transferred to his own yard but he also wisely set up as a part-time farmer and timber dealer at his farm at Vaggs Lane, Hordle until he became safely established in boatbuilding.

This he did very quickly as in 1820 he built his first yacht, the 20 ton *Hind* for N. Polhill and between 1820 and 1889 the yard was to build 118 yachts in all (see Appendix 5). Besides the local gentry his customers included several members of the English and French aristocracy, although the latter may well have been emigrés who had settled here. They included Lord Listowel, the Duke of Bedford, Lord Grosvenor, Comte de Damrimont, Vicomte d'Estampes (who did live in Spring Road, Lymington), Comte de Botmilian, the Earl of Shrewsbury and the Marquis Raggi.

Three of the most famous yachts were those owned and designed by Joseph Weld, the man who really established Thomas Inman's reputation as a boatbuilder. The *Arrow*, a 113 ton cutter built in 1823 was later bought by F. Chamberlayne, who raced her most successfully, winning the first Gold Cup at Cowes, the King's Cup in 1826, 1850 and 1852 and the 'Round the Isle of Wight' race for 100 guineas in 1850. Her last and most famous victory was over the *Formosa* in 1879. She was a splendidly built boat and after 58 years was still 'the most formidable cutter afloat.' (A point of interest to present-day owners who often change their yachts year after year.) The *Lulworth*, a 127 tonner built in 1828 for £14,000 won the King's Cup in 1828 and the Ladies Cup the same year.

The third yacht was the 193 ton cutter *Alarm* in 1830 and the largest vessel in her class. She won the King's Cup in 1830, 1831 and 1832. Afterwards Mr. Weld had her cut in two, lengthened and converted into a schooner of 148 tons. She was one of the few English boats to beat the *America*, which took the Queen's Cup to America, where it has remained ever since. He won the Ladies Challenge Cup three times, thus becoming the champion of the Royal Yacht Club. The name is still mentioned with pride in Lymington and an inn at the foot of Quay Hill was named after her. So was a fire engine! The mast of the *Alarm* was used for making pews in the Baptist Church. In addition to paying £30,000 for these three yachts Joseph Weld, always Inman's best customer, paid £1,200 a year for their upkeep.

In the seventies, two more famous yachts, amongst others, were built. The *Australia* in 1875, a schooner of 212 tons and the *Fortuna* the following year in 1876. She was the largest vessel ever built at Inman's Yard and her berth in the river is still called Fortuna Dock today.

Miss Freda Inman, now living in Chichester and writing the family history, told me when I visited her there on 19th February 1982, that Thomas Inman was no relation to the Inmans who established a famous shipping line in Liverpool. That enterprising firm, if one is permitted a digression, organised trips from England to the Crimea, in the iron paddle-steamer, *City of Glasgow,* at a cost of £5 per head for a fortnight's travel and accommodation, including visits to Constantinople and the battlefields!

Thomas Inman retired from business in 1845 and was succeeded by his son George, who served on the Railway Company, and his brother James. They traded as 'G. & J. Inman.' By now the yard included the whole of the river front from the coal yard to the Baths. Here the site was used for stores and apparently its boundaries were lined with mounted cannons taken out of yachts and other vessels. Their property also included land to the north of Bath Road and the present Drill Hall was the 'mould loft.'

Sadly, James became mentally ill a year or two later and George Inman remained as sole proprietor. His son, Edwin, was to help his father later but never became a partner in the business. George became extremely prosperous and was a notable figure in Lymington, becoming Mayor in 1852. For the next twenty years Lymington was the most important yacht building centre in England. George Inman died in 1883 and his son, Edwin, died two years later, leaving a sister Alice.

Unfortunately both George and Edwin had been rather too easy-going in business latterly and sadly the firm ended up in the hands of mortgagees. When Edwin's widow died in 1887 the Inman estates were sold. After the death of the Inmans the business passed successively into ten different hands before finally being purchased by the Berthon Boat Company in 1918.

Dan Bran

If 'The River is within us' is true of anyone in Lymington then it is true of Dan Bran. His whole life centred on the river; he worked and lived by the river and he will be remembered for all time by the river. He is the River!

He was born in Waterford in 1868 and inherited his father's love of boats. His father, George Bran, served in the crews of such famous yachts as the *Alarm,* the *Australia* and the *Fortuna.* Dan was apprenticed in the Lymington Shipyard and then went to Poole for some years as a spar maker. He returned to Lymington in 1910 and started building on his own in a hut beside the swimming baths.

"Dan was a craftsman who relied almost entirely on 'eye'. He had no drawings, but a wonderful eye for the lines of a boat." He was the designer of the famous Lymington Scow and the Lymington Pram and built his first 11 ft. Pram in 1912 for Captain Nicholson and a class of six was formed with some

Dan Bran (1950)

keen racing only ending on the outbreak of war in 1914. In 1925 he produced his first 14 ft. Pram and at one time there were 50 of them on the river and they were very popular with yachtsmen from both clubs, many of whom he had taught to sail. The Lymington Pram was known all along the South Coast.

Monty Knight once asked him if he had the measurements of the Prams he built and he pointed to his head and said, "Yes, I keep them up here." 'Buffy' Springer, who worked with Dan Bran for a time, told Tom Morris that Dan would draw lines on the floor while looking at the person concerned and that was the only measurement taken. They made the dinghy, finished it, and turned it upside down: it fitted the chalk marks exactly. He was very, very good and a nice old man.

Dan Bran lived in Rope Walk Cottage, King's Saltern Road, conveniently right next door to the Mayflower Hotel. Roger Pinckney remembers him as "a striking and bizarre character who drank like a fish and every now and again he used to imagine that he had bought the Solent. 'I am not going to have any bloody skippers on my Solent,' he would mutter and would then go down to the end of the pontoon and shoot at them!"

Tom Morris recalls too that he was 'quick on the trigger.' Dan could be found on the river and marshes at all hours of the day and night and prided himself that he needed very little sleep. He used to take his flat-bottomed dinghy out and there were certainly no thieves on the river in those days. Dan had a twelve-bore gun and if he pointed it at you, it was not far off. And he would pull too! He also had a keen sense of humour as the following story will show.

Once Tom Morris was scrubbing down his boat about 3 o'clock on a summer morning and heard a shout. "That sounds like Dan Brand, I thought, and then I heard another shout followed by a bang and said, 'My God, he has shot someone!' There in a dinghy on the far side of the river was a chap who had obviously got on board for a sleep. Presently in they came to the quay with Dan just standing up in his punt and paddling with an oar with the gun under his other arm. I took his painter and tied it up but Dan still had his gun on this fellow and kept saying, 'What have you taken? What have you taken? That boat doesn't belong to you.' That fellow was really frightened and he had good reason to be. Dan said, 'I don't know whether to shoot you here on the spot, let you go or take you up to the police station. But I don't feel like walking up to the police station with my old rupture, so it has got to be let you go or shoot you.' The fellow never waited to find out which and raced up the slip with a shower of chippings behind him. I bet he never came back again!"

"Dan used to go to Yarmouth in his flat-bottomed boat," Tom Morris continued. "It was just the state of the tide; he always worked his tides beautifully. He did not row fast but he moved nicely riding the tide. I can remember one day when it was rough in the Solent and I caught up with him at the Spit buoy and called out, 'Are you all right, Mr. Bran?' 'Of course I am all right,' he replied. 'I am going to Yarmouth, you old so-and-so. You watch me. I'll hit the end of Yarmouth Pier.' And he did! He knew his tides. He also knew every answer about yacht building – there was nothing that he did not know. If I had any problems I would go to Dan and he would know the answers. He was a great old man."

Monty Knight once said to him, "Dan, these tides in the Solent are the devil!" His answer was, "Yes, they may be, but if you will only learn them, you will find them staunch friends."

Dan often used to go wild and live out on the marshes. It was always best to keep upwind of him! When they moved him to hospital and washed him, he died on 23rd December 1950, and his wife died a week later. At his funeral at All Saints Church, Woodside, in addition to his relatives there was the Harbour Master, Mr. H. E. Thomas and the Baths Superintendent, Mr. R. V. Montgomerie, also a character in his own right. There were floral tributes including wreaths from both the yacht clubs and also from present Pram owners. Monty Knight summed it all up: "We shall miss him on the river."

Berthon Boat Company

The Berthon Boat Company was founded in Romsey in 1877 by the Reverend E. L. Berthon and three solicitors 'to build boats and other floating machines.' Berthon was a parson at Romsey of whom it was said, and I quote Roger Pinckney, "St. Peter left his boats to follow His Master but the Reverend Berthon did it the other way round!" He was a Peer of the Realm and also a Member of Parliament as well as an Officer in St. George's Volunteers.

The Royal Lymington Yacht Club's 50th anniversary souvenir states that: "As well as punts, skiffs and other craft for the use of 19th century sporting gentlemen, the Yard also built the famous Berthon collapsible boats. These folding boats, built with a double skin and divided into six sections with an air space between the skins, were unsinkable and were widely used by the Navy as well as by private yachtsmen throughout the world."

The establishment of the Lymington Yacht Club in the late 1880s and the setting up of The Lymington River Sailing Club Building Company Ltd. on 30th January 1924 (to build premises for a new Lymington Yacht Club with a membership of some 400 members), gave a fillip to yachting and yacht building in Lymington. The Berthon Boat Company improved its yard and could provide space for 70 vessels of all sizes to be laid up during the winter. This firm also designed and built some 40 racing 7-tonners for the West Solent Restricted Class of which 10 remained on the Lymington River, 13 went to Burnham-on-Crouch and 6 to South America – of all places. Other ships turned out by this firm included *Nefertari* and *Nefertiti* for Mr. W. F. Perkins of Boldre Bridge House, father of John Perkins, the Editor of the *Southern Evening Echo,* besides several of the 'X' Class, 4-ton racers and two 6 metre boats.

Mr. George Courtney, during his time, built the *Braemar* (50 tons) for Mr. Paxton and the barge yacht *Four Marys* for Mr. John Princep. He and his successors, H. G. May, who bought the Berthon Boat Company in 1917 and the Lymington Shipyard the following year, were engaged by the War Office and Admiralty in building 50-ton drifters, sea-plane hulls, pontoons and at least 1 ambulance craft in World War One.

Gauntlet was the first of the Gauntlet Class which were so successful in small class ocean racing. Designed and built by the Berthon Boat Company, the waterline length was 33' 6", the beam 9' 6", the draught 5' 6" and she carried 595 sq. ft. sail area.

Gauntlet was owned by the Royal Naval Engineering College at Plymouth. Bill Smith served his apprenticeship in Berthon Boatyard in the days of David May's grandfather, H. G. May, and was there when the first *Gauntlet* was built. "It arose from a challenge. The boat was drawn by Mr. Paul, who was the naval architect of the firm in those days, but a customer decided he would go to Phillips of Dartmouth instead to get her built. Then there was a challenge of whose would be the best boat and, of course, *Gauntlet* excelled in her day. That was how the Gauntlets started and then they were upped to 14 tons, 18 tons and 24 tons. One of the first ones was owned by a Mr. Capper and he called it *Maiden Light.*" Bill Smith thinks she is still going somewhere and may have been involved in some smuggling about a year ago (1980).

Then on 12th January 1982 I visited Bob Blunt at his home in 45 Waterford Lane and was fortunate to have had the opportunity of a long talk with him as, sadly, he died three months later.

"I was born in Lymington but my father was a Sussex man and my mother came from Staffordshire," he told me. "My father was in the Navy; he spent 12 years in the service and that was in the days of the old tall-rigged ships. You may have heard them talk of the *Warrior,* well, he was on her. Then he joined the coastguards and was stationed at Southsea, Stokes Bay and finally at Pitts Deep. He finished there about 1904 and shortly after that they closed the station. I believe there are still some ruins to be seen there.

"I started working at Berthon Boatyard in 1923. In those days you left school at the age of 14 and I had to do two years' probationary period at 5/- a week. At 16 I got a 1/- rise and became an apprentice then, but of the 6/- I earned, 1/4*d.* came off for insurance There was a five year apprenticeship.

"Fortunately, when I started I worked with men who were perhaps 60 years old with plenty of experience. There were two at least who came up from Shoreham, George Courtney, I think, was one of them and there was another bloke, a Cornishman, who came from Philadelphia in the States: he had spent a lot of time out there. Then there two Devonians and also an old boatbuilder of the name of Fred Cook (Bob Cook's father) and he was one of the eight who had worked for the Reverend Berthon who came down from Romsey. He was a marvellous craftsman. There was a 40-ft. National which was cut in half and he mended it as if nothing had happened to it! Eventually he went to work for Elkins down at Christchurch and finished his days down there. He was the oldest.

"I knew both Parkers. Fred, the old man, was the yard foreman when I joined and he had been there for about two or three years before I started at Berthon. He came from Whites at Woolston, Southampton and his son, he was only a youngster, 'Young Fred' as we called him, he was still going to school. He was two or three years younger than me. Then he worked for one of the well-known designers and in the end he became a designer himself, mostly of big boats of about 200 or 300 ft. long. His father's brother was Tommy Parker and he played back for the 'Saints' and then from the 'Saints' he went to Arsenal and played for them." (His son, Frederick R. Parker, a director of the firm of that name comprising naval architects, surveyors, yacht brokers and insurance consultants in Guisborough, Cleveland, in a letter of 6th May 1981 confirmed that his father, 'Old Fred,' had been yard manager at the Berthon Boat Company and wrote that he lived at Seaforth, Bath Road and later at Redcroft, Queen Katherine Road, Lymington.)

"I know H. G. May," Bob Blunt continued, "but he never had much to do with anybody. He used to breed dogs, I have forgotten the breed, but they were brown, shaggy dogs. When work was short, we used to make dog kennels down at the side of a small garden that used to be there. One of his dogs, Googie, was really a prize dog. He would win First, Seconds, Thirds and Commendeds. I can remember seeing the old gentleman coming up the yard and he would always have one dog on a lead and there were sometimes five, six or ten of them running beside him. Sometimes we had to stop work and catch them. At the lower end of the yard there were some old stores built on stilts and every time there was a good tide it would come through the bank – there used to be a pond there – and that would bring out all the rats. Sometimes there would be as many as 40 running about!

"We used to start work at 7.30 and you were allowed two minutes after that and then you lost pay. The reason for the two minutes was that in the docks at Southampton there would be such a queue that they would allow them a few extra minutes to clock in, and we did the same at Berthon.

"We built dinghies, those Prams and nearly all the boats built there had their own dinghies. The son of the Devonshire man worked mostly on the slip but the old man himself and a boy of 16 or 17 could turn out a 12-ft. dinghy in four days. It was marvellous. Nowadays it would take weeks and weeks if anyone could do it. Those old boys used to drink quite a lot but they could turn them out!

"I think I am right in saying that Major Martineau had *Saluki* built there and it was the first boat built after the war. I helped build her actually and when I became the foreman I had quite a lot to do with Major Martineau. A sad thing that he lost his sight.

"David May's father used to visit us sometimes but I don't think that he was all that keen. He was an accountant and had his own business up in London but when the old gentleman died, he used to come down perhaps once a week. There used to be a garden where most of the marina boats are now, a lovely garden and there was a bungalow and the Mays would spend about six months there in the summer. Then, unfortunately, he died and at that time David was working in Southampton; it was his father's intention that he should work his way up from the bottom but it never happened and he got brought in at the top. He took over three or four years after I had been made foreman."

Allan Raines and his wife Vera, who have lived throughout their 50 years of marriage in the 350-year old Cottage 'Rosedean' in Woodside Lane, Lymington, celebrated their Golden Wedding in January 1982. Allan was born in Portsmouth, the only son of Allan Angus, a Chief Petty Officer in the Royal Navy who later became a coastguard, so when he was 12 Allan went to live in Coastguard Cottages. He worked on a milk round for Aldridge's dairy before becoming an apprentice shipwright in Berthon for 2/6d. a week. In the 1920 slump the shipwrights were sacked and he found employment on the Beaulieu estate doing building and carpentry work. He even appeared in tin armour as a yeoman in a film made on Lord Montagu's estate, called *The Virgin Queen*!

He returned to boatbuilding and became foreman at the Slipway Engineering Company. He again went to work at Berthon and helped build some thirty 79-ft. coastal defence motor launches and then went back to the Slipway until he had a heart attack and was off work for five years. He helped Major Hibbert at the Salterns Sailing Club and built yachts for the children to sail there. Allan Raines has constructed several most intricate models; one of a 100 ton fruit clipper called *Mary Ashburton* took him three years to build and he has made several models of old Bristol cutters. There is an excellent photograph of Allan Raines and his wife and the *Mary Ashburton* in an article in the *Lymington Times* of 19.1.82.

Another well known character, who has been skipper and shipwright, is Jim Smith, whom I visited at his home, 'Home Port,' 51 Western Road, Lymington on 19th November 1982 and had a most interesting talk with him, followed by a video film of the Tall Ships.

"I am a native of Shanklin," he told me, "and went back there when I left school at the age of 14. My father was in charge of a shipyard at Wootton Creek and I started there as the boy. It was an old-fashioned yard with bits chucked here and there but some very nice little yachts. Later we took it over. My father was a great model-maker. The model of the *Cutty Sark* in Blackgang Chine was made by him and he also made tiny models of lifeboats as well.

"My first introduction to Lymington came through being the skipper of a yacht called *Joyce*, which belonged to George Dearie Russell, the father-in-law of the present Mrs. Russell. George Smith was a member of the crew at one time. *Joyce* was a 70-ton vessel of World War One vintage and she was built in Bayonne in 1917. I was her skipper for many years. We used to lie at Pylewell Creek and had to moor her fore and aft because she was a big boat. Even so every time a paddle-steamer went by she used to jerk about. The *Joyce* was later sold and I took her round to West Mersea. After that Mr. Russell had a smaller yacht built in the yard at Berthon, which I worked for 42 years. At that time the Russells used to live in Guildford and the yacht was used purely for weekends.

"When they came to live in Lymington at the Grove, we built this yacht *Lentune*, which is another name for Lymington, and he gave her as a wedding present to his son. They sailed off in her on their honeymoon and I went with them as skipper. Later, when the two children went out with them, I used to sleep in a hammock slung under the boom. We used to cross to the other side and go up the Seine and all down the estuary; that was an alternative cruise to Skye. We never visited the East Coast much: it was always such a long slog from Lymington right up to Dover, where we would make a stop, and then cross to Flushing and Walcheren Island.

"When I worked at Berthon I would still go out with the Russells for pleasure in their boat *Maya*. I brought her down from the East Coast in the winter – there was snow and ice that Christmas – and worked her up into really good condition. She was a lovely boat built in West Ireland.

"Mr. Russell was second-in-command of *Ark Royal* during the war. He used to love to go out in his large garden but one day he got pricked by a bit of ivy – and he died. He was the smartest chap you ever saw. The boat was sold before he died to four New Zealanders with a baby of about four months old; I constructed a cot up in the focsle and this baby went all the way to New Zealand. Could you imagine a worse place than being in the focsle but they got out there and had no trouble whatsoever.

"At one time I was skipper for Kenneth Moore. He used to live in a little cottage up the Beaulieu River. Kenneth Moore had a boat called *Jenny*

Spinner, which had a flush deck and no raised cabin top, only what you put on when you went to sea. We rigged up something from the stanchions and toured all up the North Sea and up the Dutch canals. I remember one very good trip there when we were going up the Scheldt and, remarkably at sea, we took a fair wind all the way up it. Every buoy is marked on your chart and all you had to do was to strike them off. We made one or two trips up the East Coast but there are not very many good harbours and it was not our hunting ground at all.

"Then Kenneth Moore had another boat called *Red Gauntlet* and we used to go down to the Scilly Isles, a very nice hospitable place. They used to say that half the population got drowned and never reached old age, which I can imagine because there was no proper harbour: you just had to go round to the back of the Islands and take shelter.

"I joined Berthon and worked in the shipyard under Mr. H. G. May as a shipwright and shipwrights are usually associated with the sea. We used to build a craft every year and go in for the Channel Races and the RORC Races and, being a new boat just off the stocks, she always used to capture the prizes. But he never kept any of his boats. Someone would say, 'That's a good boat,' and he would sell it. I might be cutting out a stem or a stern or some of the keel of a boat and he would say, 'There is a race on this week-end,' and we would have to down tools and go! There have been some remarkable changes at Berthon. We built hundreds of yachts and some of them really good vessels and well-known names. In 1929 we built a big yawl called *Elaine*: she was an absolute beauty.

"Across the water there is a red house which was at one time owned by a man called Chris Heseltine. He was a brass hat in the war and his wife was a lady-in-waiting to the Queen. Mr. May had a boat called *Pegasus* and Chris Heseltine would come down from the War Office and would charter her for fortnight. He had to go to Yarmouth first and get permission from the Guard Ship to go through the boom and then off we would go for the day. You had to report as otherwise you might get blown up on the mines. There was only a little gap to let the ships through; all the rest were buoys, hundreds of buoys.

"I had to remain as a shipwright during the war, although I tried to get away to sea three times, and on the last occasion I was taken to Court by the tribunal. I wanted to go into the Merchant Navy. But at Berthon I would take the vessels out on trials and sometimes half the chaps would be seasick, even the naval crew. We had to take them out with us so that they would get used to the boat. We used to turn out a minesweeper a month; it would take twelve months

to build one now. We had 150 women working with us just to keep things going. It was called the 'Madhouse' down there with all the noise! We used to work from 7.30 a.m. to 7.30 p.m. and then after that you had to do Home Guard training three nights a week. People may have thought that we had a sheltered trade but it was very hard work and often you might come home to an all night air raid.

"During that time I had a lot to do with Mr. May, although our priorities were war vessels but after the war yachting suddenly came into its own again. For instance, prisoners of war coming home would often buy boats with their gratuities. One ex-P.O.W called his yacht *Release*. We have built a lot of big ships down there and some real nice ones too. A few years ago we built a lifeboat for Padstow called *Trevose Head*. She was donated by Crawford, the biscuit firm. I had to collect eight chaps from the yard and take them to sea for eight hours a day. We used to go out in all kinds of weather, including Force 9 gales. I used to protest that I was not a lifeboatman but they said that a lifeboat goes anywhere! I can remember coming up behind the *Winston Churchill* once. She was ahead of us and going like blazes and so were we but we couldn't catch her! She was a lovely sight.

"I was skipper at one time for the Hon. Henry Guest of Guest, Keen and Nettlefold, the brass screw company. He was a funny man and I never won any prize money with him because he was so courteous. He might be in front and well ahead and he would say, 'Oh, skipper, you can't go in front like that, there is a lady there. Slow her up again.' Of course we didn't win! We were placed sometimes but never first. There were a lot of ladies sailing in those days, including The Hon. Mrs. Cecil Brownlow. She used to live down here and was Commodore of what is now the Royal Lymington.

"I used to fit out all Major Tilman's boats. He had three, *Mischief, Sea Breeze* and *Baroque*, but they were all in a rotten state and I used to have to do a lot of work on them. He was a foolish man. On his last trip he didn't go in his own boat but went with a fellow who had bought an old tug over in Holland. This tug had capsized when she was built apparently, and you just cannot convert a tug into a sailing vessel; it is impossible. When they went missing near the Falklands the *Endurance* searched for them for six months but never found a trace. I think *Baroque* is up in London now and they have rebuilt her. If he had gone in her he would have been all right. He was a wonderful man.

"One of the last jobs I did in Berthon was to take the name off Clare Francis' boat and put on another. She is a wonderful boat. Clare Francis has sold her house and gone to live in London but she is still keeping her boat here."

Jim Smith is a keen photographer, as is his son, and he has all kinds of cameras, as well as ciné. Now that he does not go to sea any more he goes up to Chester instead and cruises on canal barges. "I love the sea; I always did," he said.

Berthon Boat Company has changed a great deal since those days. An article in *Yachts & Yachting* of 17th July 1981 describes how the latest interspray centre was opened on July 3rd by Clare Francis. Capable of handling yachts up to 50 ft LOA, the centre will be one of the largest purpose-built paint spray booths so far completed and will provide owners based in Lymington, Yarmouth, Beaulieu and Poole or further afield, with the facility to restore the topsides of older boats. Those with newer boats will be able to transform them with personalised colour-schemes.

Berthon report that with the usual spring refits and repairs now almost past, work has been started on the fit-out of a 70 ft. glass fibre ketch for a Hong Kong businessman. Smaller boats nearing completion include two levi-designed motor yachts and a 32 ft. sloop with a ferro-concrete hull, teak coach-roof, teak decks and an attractive interior, again incorporating a good deal of teak. The covered slipway has been in almost constant use since before Christmas with yachts up to 90 ft. in length having major refits, normal scrubbing and so on. That then is a quick sketch of Berthon in 1981.

George Smith

Rob Smith recalled that his father bought the ground and built up the boatyard at Rope Walk in 1935 and Bill Smith (no relation) helped him develop the site and worked with him for a long time. Harveys, the builders, built the first premises on the site, a wooden building which was destroyed by fire in 1963 when owned by Peter Webster.

"When my father had that yard they said he couldn't build anything more than 6 ft. high," Rob told me when I visited him at his home at 5 Samber Close, Lymington on 3rd February 1982. "I remember there used to be a bit of garden – it was literally an old lady's garden that was stuck in a triangular shape between the original Rope Walk Boatyard and what was part of a farm. This old lady would not sell to anyone who would build anything on it and my father bought it from her on that understanding. She had never been allowed to even build a shed on it for her garden tools and yet today there is a chandlery, a workshop and everything else, all on the bit of land that they really did try to save.

George Smith and Leslie Marshall

"A chap called Marshall took over from my father for a short time, and then Hugo Duplessis, who used to come from Norley Wood, took it on and Peter Webster joined him. Hugo Duplessis then bowed out of it and is now living in Bantry, in Ireland.

"I was originally apprenticed to my father when he had another yard, where Golden Produce is now, but in 1954 or thereabouts they went into liquidation and work got scarce and so I went over to Bucklers Hard. After I came back from there my father had finished at Rope Walk but I worked for Peter Webster and I suppose I set up on my own in 1972. I work where the job is: I haven't got a yard of my own. Where they want me, I go. I am prepared to go anywhere and do anything, any bit of carpentering that comes my way. It is not like my father's day when you could ply your trade. Now everyone wants to grab for himself. Down at the Yacht Haven they take a percentage of what you earn. The marinas do not offer work as a general rule. I thought that before they opened, and I wrote to the papers against it although you might have thought it was in my interest. Very few of the people who come purchase anything here: they do not buy from the local shops and bring it all with them.

"I think you ought to live where your livelihood is: nowadays anyone working near the water has no chance of living near it because someone wants to live there just to look at the view.

"I spent my national service in Germany as a lorry driver with the RASC and never went anywhere near a boat! It was the luck of the draw really. Some were called up and some were not. It was how it struck the man who was in the Lymington office, I suppose!"

His brother, Bill Smith, also worked at the Haven for a time, continued with Peter Webster and then went to Berthon where he was made redundant. At one time he was Harbour Master.

Bill Smith

Bill Smith (no relation) is now the oldest boat-builder in Lymington and has a yard off Mill Lane, which he started in 1954. He spent all his boyhood in the Woodside area and his family were farmers. "Our family used to control the farming right through Pennington, the Lower Pennington area right to Sadlers; that would be my father, my uncles and my grandfather, and there are relations still farming down at Lower Woodside and Sadlers Farm. My interest in the sea, or mucking around with boats, came from my mother's family and I am the only one who took to the sea. My grandfather (her father) was 'Monsey' Bran, who lived to 96 and he was very active and was sailing a small boat at 90, believe it or not. So if his age is anything to do with my age then I still have a lot of time! My mother is still alive and she is 86.

"My grandfather was landlord at the Fisherman's Rest, which they have recently done up and his father before him, in the 1800s. It used to be a beer house in those days. My grandfather, so my mother told me, was known in those days to have done a bit of smuggling. I have been told they rolled an barrel of rum all the way to a house which adjoined it and then when darkness fell again they got it up to the pub and sold it!

"I used to walk round the sea wall as a boy and often walked across the marshes with my grandfather. But now it is all fenced off and you are not allowed to set foot on this path or that path. There used to a very fine 18-hole golf course down there too which closed in 1938.

"I used to sail in the Sea Scouts when Bert Rand was also a scout and I knew Bill Martineau and Robert Hole very well indeed. I have sailed with Bill Martineau in the *Wilful* and also with Roger Pinckney in *Dyarchy,* the first one.

"After I had served my apprenticeship with Berthon I went to join George Smith start up the Rope Walk Boatyard in 1935. Three years later, in 1938, I went to sea with the Union Castle and served as a chippy for some time and, when war broke out, it did not seem quite right to be in a big outfit like that, so I came out and worked for Scott Bayne at Hythe. I was then offered a job at the Berthon and worked there for a couple of years and then I joined the Navy in 1942 and served until 1946, so I don't know much about what happened here.

"The Navy took over the Ship Inn, the place where the present Slipway Restaurant is and, in fact, the whole Quay was taken over by boom defence. I knew that they had a resident shipwright on the site here and I thought that it would be nice to come home and get that job – but not likely, the Admiralty would not play that one and I was sent as far away from Lymington as they could send me! Derry (Derry Seaton, his assistant, and Chairman of the New Forest Association) was here during the war. The Montagu Arms was turned into a Wrennery and Balmer Lawn was taken over the army. A concrete harbour was built on the Beaulieu River and before it could be towed down river Derry had to blow up the banks of the river to make room for it. Derry was at Yarmouth for D-Day and went across from there. They also made decoys out of old oil drums and Jerry used to come over and blast away at them!"

Derry told me that the *Dulcibella,* of *The Riddle of the Sands,* was broken up here in Bill Smith's yard. Apparently Maldwin Drummond is writing a book about the *Dulcibella* and followed the identical course she took in the Baltic.

Bill Smith took up the story: "I have always liked Devonshire. When I sold up on the Quay in 1970 I almost decided to go and live down there; there was a nice old farmhouse with a few holiday caravans on it at Sticklepath on the main A.38, but I think my wife realised that she would be losing a lot of her friends so I bought a house on the Milford Road and bought this yard in Mill Lane. Then Derry came along as an assistant. Before that I would work at the yard all during the day and then in the evening I would write and type and it got too much for me. Now I can take a fortnight off every year and that is when I go to Devon and Cornwall.

"At the yard we carry out specialist work using the best materials – for a special customer. It is not the time to spend on building any boat as a spec job now. I have not gone into speculative building very much anyway. We recently did a good job for an American. He probably could have bought the boat much cheaper elsewhere but he would not have had the workmanship that we put into it.

"Derry and I also run All-in-Yacht Transport. Trailaway Boats used to be next door but they have moved now to the Yacht Haven. Chris Harridge runs that but I don't think you can do in five minutes what has taken me a lifetime to do. A boat is a delicate piece of equipment and you have to know what you are doing with it. I remember those big yachts back in 1973. I then decided that we should abandon the idea completely and we can think again whether we have another go. It will never come back to what it used to be. It is a shame just to fizzle out overnight. I remember when we used to take boats to France, Switzerland, Germany and all over the place. We always used to do the Boat Shows. So that is another thing that has gone for the present and we just have to concentrate on the yard here and keep it ticking over. We do a lot of repairs.

"Just after the war there used to be all that rye grass growing along the banks where the Fortuna Dock used to be, and we used to slip the boats alongside the banks: it was so hard that you could walk around on this grass. The river was not so wide in those days and was much deeper. The river has got so much wider and it has all slipped into the middle. If there was no ferry here I think it would close up. There is only one way to cope with it and it would cost a great deal of money, and that would be to ship all this mud down on to the east side and do what the Dutch do,

reclaim land. I have been saying this for years. There is going to come a time within the next ten years when that mud will disappear completely. It is the east wind that does the damage here and once the mud goes it will just be open and the sea will come rolling in straight over Naish Point right into the yacht club. I cannot see how they are going to stop it unless they put an arm out there. The Yacht Haven realises this and so do the Harbour Commissioners.

"I think the trouble went back a long time ago when they allowed these sand dredgers to suck up the shingle. When we were boys we used to out there scouting and play on this shingle bank; it was like a big mound. You were out of the water fifteen or twenty feet and when you decided to swim from there it would drop suddenly just like that. The sand was a natural barrier all along on that spit there."

Lymington Slipway & Engineering Company

Bill Smith remembered that "the Slipway Yard was started by Alderman Beagley in 1934 or 1935. He was connected with the Community Centre and was Mayor in 1952 and 1953. He was an engineer and had an engingeering works down where the Waterford Stores is today. That is how he started and he founded the yard the same way and later he was joined by Mr. C. E. Linaker. His sister used to be keen on sailing and they had a house down Nor-

The Slipway

95

mandy Lane on the Salterns ground, now King-fishers and later occupied by Dr. Allan and at present by Mr. H. Nelson Ewer."

After returning from the Army, Mr. Ian Carr, a lifelong resident of the New Forest, bought the Lymington Slipway and Engineering Company from Alderman Beagley and Mr. Linaker and it was in his time that they built the Lymington 5-ton Slipways. Mr. Carr was a member of the Royal Lymington Yacht Club since 1932 and celebrated his Golden Jubilee as a member of Brokenhurst Gold Club which he joined as a boy. When he died on 26th April 1981, his daughter, Elizabeth Carr, flew back from Hawaii, where she left the boat in which she was making a round the world tour. The shipyard was sold to the Caulcutts and became the Golden Produce chicken factory.

Lymington Bridge Boat & Crane Company

Chris Carrington served his time in the Berthon Boat Company and then he and his brother and an uncle got together and took over part of Lance's yard to use as a boatyard. The firm was originally called Carrington, Carrington & Chambers. Amongst other boats, they built an Extension, designed by Van der Stadt to beat the Rule! Then they teamed up with Dick Carter and built a Carter ¼ tonner and also six ¼-tonners called Dingbats in Sammy Sampson's organisation. Both Sammy and Dick came down to Lymington to supervise from time to time.

In the meanwhile, Colonel Mew had sold off his brewery on the Isle of Wight and the Lymington Bridge Boat & Crane Company used Mew's yard, next to Aquaboats. It then lay dormant for a while until a man called Johnnie Jacobs started up Pegasus Boats. He left for Guernsey rather hurriedly and his partner then teamed up with Chris Carrington. The yard closed in 1979 and is derelict now.

Since 1979 Chris Carrington has been skipper of the yacht *La Vague* and in 1981 took her to the Mediterranean when she was sold to a new owner in Palma. His wife, Wendy, went out there for the winter to join him but will be back again in Easter for the *Water Rat* trips.

Wendy Carrington told me that Chris had been in the RNLI since it first started in Lymington about fifteen years ago and is still a member of the crew. There are 12 in the crew and 3 go out at a time, so when the maroons go up there is a lot of dashing about and the first three go out. They can hear the maroons quite clearly in their home in Nelson Place. Chris got a letter of commendation from the RNLI but it was a long time ago, probably when they were living on the houseboat *Kelana,* which is still moored just above the bridge.

Peter Webster Limited

Peter Webster comes from an old Quaker family in Yorkshire. His father started up the West Riding Sailing Club, the first dinghy sailing club in West Yorkshire and they used to sail on old reservoirs. John Hay, another mining engineer, who lived in King's Saltern Road until his death in January 1981, joined him in the venture and they raced National Twelves. The family used to holiday in Cornwall and Peter's first boat, given to him when he was 7 years old, was built down there.

As Peter could not find a suitable dinghy he designed and built his own in the cellar of their home in Yorkshire. It was so successful that he received orders for six more and part of a warehouse they owned was set aside for boatbuilding. So that was how he started – building boats as a hobby.

Pat Webster remembers washing the cotton sails, there were no nylon ones then, on Monday mornings after she had taken in her household washing and it seemed strange to see sails hanging on the line so far inland. Incidentally, the Websters were one of the first to use coloured ropes and these were dyed in a boiler in the kitchen!

Part-time building of small glass fibre dinghies in Yorkshire was not enough and in 1960 Peter Webster took the big step of moving down to Lymington, a place they had visited when motoring back from Cornwall. Peter stayed at the Mayflower Hotel, then run by the Stevensons, until they were fortunate enough to be able to purchase their present home at 6 Solent Avenue from an old lady of 96.

He then went into partnership with Hugo Duplessis, who had taken over the Rope Walk Boatyard from Smith and Marshall and George Smith (the fisherman), whose son, Bill Smith, continued to work for him for a time. A previous partner who left before Peter bought the yard was Mr. Hammick, whose two daughters went to the same school, Fernhill School at New Milton, as did the Websters' daughter, Elizabeth. The two Hammick sisters took part in and completed the Two-Handed Trans-Atlantic Race in 1981, sailing in *Miss Alfred Marks.*

Peter Webster created a brand new organisation to build large glass-fibre offshore craft – the first ever constructed in Lymington. "The layout of his 'factory' was impressively simple and compact," wrote Anthony Churchill in *Yachts & Boating Weekly* of 9th December 1965. "In one shed two hull moulds and two cabin moulds are kept at constant temperature and once the hulls and decks are ready they are wheeled a few dozen yards to a second shed for joinery and finishing."

In addition, the yard provided an emergency repair service open to any yachtsman, day and night – a boon to those on short holidays who could waste hours waiting for repairs to be carried out. The chandlery also gave a 24-hour service, 7 days a week.

His designer was Kim Holman of West Mersea, Essex and the first Elizabethan 29 appeared in 1960 and the Elizabethan 35 in 1965. Twelve of these craft were built each year and several were shipped to the United States where Lewis Marine were the US agents for the Elizabethan 29. The Americans found in this yacht "all the advantages of resin-glass plus a standard of materials and finish, due to the skill of our shipwrights, that cannot be found elsewhere." In 1963 they were also being built by Henry Waquiez-Mouvraux at Roubaix in France. Their advertisement quoted that this yacht had sailed in 15 races

and had been winner of 9 as well as winning the Queen's Cup at Cowes.

The *Bournemouth Evening Echo* of 1st April 1963 gave a very good write up of the Elizabethan 29: "... Since making an impact on the yachting world at the 1962 Boat Show, the Elizabethan 29 had made marked steps forward and is the main product from Mr. Webster's Ropewalk Boatyard at Lymington. Already a dozen have been built. There are prospects of a sufficient number being moored at Lymington to form a class of their own and they are finding their way into the export market. Two of the three have been ordered by Americans and the third will be shipped to Malta. Collaboration between Mr. Webster and designer C. R. Holman, brought off the drawing board this handsome craft. The price is a little over £2,500. . . The Elizabethan 29 is 5½ tons

By courtesy of P. Webster

Liz of Lymington
Peter Webster, Roy Parker, Ken McIntyre and Ken Wreyford

Thames measurement and has a main sail area of 177 sq. feet with two jibs of 136 sq. feet and 58 sq. feet, a spinnaker of 320 sq. feet and a Genoa of 212 sq. feet, The accommodation is convenient for family cruising . . ."

The Websters knew Ross Coles, son of Adlard Coles, and Peter used to sail in his Dragon at Scarborough and later sailed with him in *Blue Bottle* when she was up in Yorkshire. They sold their own Dragon to a Devonian who later was to buy an Elizabethan 29 from them in Lymington.

The Websters owned six *Liz of Lymingtons* over a period of 20 years and in 1963 the new Top Hat class yacht *Panache,* with builder-owner Peter Martin, was set to challenge *Liz of Lymington,* manned by Barry Perry and John Oakley.

Between the mid 1960s and early 1970s Peter won the Round the Island Race outright and also won the Junior section; in 1963 he won the Queen's Cup at Cowes and was 1st or 2nd every day of Cowes Week; and he was a member of the British team which took part in the Half Ton World Championships in Sweden and the Three-Quarter Ton in Plymouth in 1976 and La Rochelle, 1977. He has also won the Potter Ship at the RLYC.

On 10th July 1963 thousands of pounds worth of damage was done by a fire which swept through the office block and chandlery stores. These were built of timber in George Smith's time and soon burnt out. So fierce was the blaze that flames could be seen for miles around. "People over a wide area were awakened by explosions caused by tins of paint bursting, self-fired rockets and the crackling of the burning timber and many turned out in pyjamas and dressing gowns to watch," wrote a reporter of the *Bournemouth Evening Echo.* When the alarm was raised four fire engines arrived but it was all that they could do to contain the blaze. Some boats stored nearby had their paintwork blistered but the firemen managed to move many of them to safety. The roof of one of the Sea Scouts' huts was slightly damaged. Fortunately, this did not affect the boat construction and later two new large buildings were completed to speed up production. A new chandlery store was opened in April 1965 in time for Easter; it stocked admiralty charts, ropes, screws, paint, yachting shoes and every type of garment. The firm continued its emergency service.

In 1964 the local firm of of *Sea Ventures,* with their headquarters at 33 Highfield Road, Lymington, had three yachts available for charter and these were kept at Peter Webster's yard. There was no limit to the cruising range of these craft.

In 1961 Mr. Linaker had applied for planning permission for a marina. A public enquiry was held in the Town Hall and "there were dire warnings that there would be dancing on the marshes if the plan went ahead!" A new consortium was formed and Noel Cowper acted for the company and negotiated with the Crown Commissioners, who own all land between high and low water and hence, when it dried out, Harper's Lake. The Websters owned the only freehold land. The planners wanted to alleviate traffic on the river by using Oxey Lake but the dredging costs would have been too great.

On 23rd July 1963 a *Daily Mail* reporter wrote that "when the tide goes out at Lymington, Hampshire it leaves a desolate expanse of evil-smelling slime, rotting hulks and a sewer. It is known locally as Harper's Lake and lies on the port hand going up the main channel. It could be turned into a marina with accommodation for about 400 yachts and water at all states of the tide." But Lymington Borough Council refused planning permission on the grounds that it would "create an undesirable intrusion into an area of great scenic and landscape value included in the proposed Green Belt." It also considered that the concentration of so many yachts would bring serious navigational hazards and aggravate the silting of the river. Hems Kalis, a director of Westminster Dredging Company, who was prepared to spend £350,000 on the marina, appealed against this decision and lost.

Peter Webster was finding that the shortage of mooring space in Lymington was serious enough to threaten his livelihood, which is why he concentrated so much on the export side of his business. The Websters' solicitor in Yorkshire helped with ideas for raising the money and Hems Kalis and Commander Dent tried to obtain funds from the City. Commander Dent's father was a retired Admiral who lived at Beaulieu and his mother, an active Conservative, served on the Women's Advisory Committee for the Forest with Pat Webster.

The struggle for planning permission had continued for 10 years but in the end the planners won their case and dredging started in 1971. There is a painting of the dredger by the marine artist, Stuart Beck, in Dirk Kalis' office at the Yacht Haven. The Websters remembered that crowds would turn up on Sunday afternoons to watch the barges coming in with gravel which they pumped out and care had to be taken that a child had not climbed into one of the large pipes. As soon as the piles went up there would be clusters of yachts tied up to them, not waiting for the pontoons to be built and there was soon a waiting list. The Lymington Yacht Haven was born!

Jeremy Rogers

This history of Jeremy Rogers' career was very kindly prepared for me by his wife, Fiona, in February 1981 and is included in its entirety. She handles all his P.R. and is also Editor of the Company journal *Jeremy Rogers Logbook*.

"Jeremy Rogers first found his love of the sea and boats at the age of four, when he lived near the Ottawa River in Canada during the war, and throughout his school days in England he sailed and built his own racing dinghies. He considered boat-building as a possible career when he was at Clayesmore School.

"This career started with an apprenticeship at Chippendale's in Fareham, and in 1960, at the age of only twenty-three, he started to build a 25 foot 'Folk-boat' at his house in New Street, Lymington. This boat, called *Dysca*, owned by Dr. David Carnegie, was the first of four yachts built by Jeremy's yard for the same owner, the latest being *Dysca IV*, a Jeremy Rogers Contessa 32. During the time in which *Dysca* was being built Jeremy acquired some land at the bottom of East Hill at the junction with Gosport Street, and he quickly obtained permission to build a shed on the site. It was there that the business started properly. Jeremy had a handful of men working with him, amongst whom was a painter, named Dennis Crouch, who still works at the yard. Another early employee was Mr. Hoare, the Lymington school-master, who retired and came to run the office and the book-keeping for Jeremy; he had taught most of the men who worked at the yard in those days, and

although he left the office over ten years ago and in spite of being well over eighty years old, he still pops in from time to time as he goes by on his moped. And he always comes with his wife to the Christmas party.

"In the first five years of business Jeremy's yard produced seven hundred dinghies, of which most were OK and Finn dinghies, and seventeen Folk-boats. The first of these boats was beautifully crafted in wood. Then he decided that glass reinforced plastic (or glass-fibre, as it is more commonly known) was the answer for the future and he led the way where others have continued to follow since. He never forgot the beauty of wood, and a hallmark of all Rogers boats is the superb joinery which goes into the interior of each GRP yacht.

"The wooden Folkboat was replaced in 1966 by the GRP Contessa 26; this boat was basically a GRP Folkboat with a masthead rig, designed by David Sadler, for whom Jeremy had built a similar wooden yacht called *Contessa of Parkstone*. As she had literally walked away with all the prizes the previous season, the name Contessa seemed as good as any to give to the new type of yacht. So popular was this yacht that by 1968 the yard at Gosport Street had to be enlarged. The work-force now numbered twenty. It is interesting to note that in 1970 Mike McMullen took his Contessa 26, *Binkie*, into first place on handicap in the Round-Britain Race.

"Next came the Contessa 32. This was the first boat ever designed by David Sadler, and he was to have the first boat. The second, *Red Herring*, was Jeremy's own boat which he built at home at weekends during the winter of 1970 with his younger brother, Jonathan, who was by now a local doctor. After she was launched in 1971 *Red Herring* was successfully campaigned for two seasons by Jeremy, Jonathan and their wives, Fiona and Ann. *Red Herring* put the new class of yacht on the map, and the Contessa 32 has been the best selling yacht built by the yard. Over five hundred of them have been built to date. Contessa 32 successes include being voted London International Boat Show 'Boat of the Show 1972', countless race trophies, and the good fortune to be the only small yacht to finish the ill-fated Fastnet Race of 1979. There is a very active class association, and racing, particularly in the Solent, has reached unofficial one-design status; fleets of over seventy are regularly entered for the Round-the-Island Race, and the class has its own start during Cowes Week and also during Burnham Week on the East Coast. These yachts are to be seen racing and cruising literally all over the world, and they are generally regarded in Britain to be the class 32 foot yacht.

"In 1971 the yard was extended to include a new factory unit of over 14,000 sq. ft. in Waterloo Road, Lymington. The production area had reached over 18,000 sq. ft.

"By 1973 a new yacht designed by Sparkman & Stephens of New York, was introduced. By this time the work-force had doubled. Two of these new 38 ft. yachts were campaigned in the One Ton Cup World Championships held off Scandinavia that year. Jeremy's own *Thunder* was one of these two, but sixth place was not what he wanted, and after seeing the best boat in the championships, *Ganbare,* designed by a completely unknown young Californian called Doug Peterson, Jeremy decided to ask Doug to design a production yacht to the lines of *Ganbare.* At this stage Jeremy was joined by an old friend, Bill Green, an American and a good friend of Doug Peterson's.

"The following year Jeremy's yacht, *Gumboots,* a 35-ft. Peterson design, won the much coveted One Ton Cup. It was the first time that a British boat had achieved this, and later in 1974, Jeremy was voted 'Yachtsman of the Year.'

"In the autumn of 1974 the Labour government put 25% VAT on yachts, and the buoyant home market died overnight. It was a bitter blow to Jeremy Rogers' yard. It should have been a time to reap the benefits of racing success. However, the overseas market began to grow as quickly as the home market died, and over 80 of the new yachts, called the Contessa 35, were built over the next four years, and these went mostly overseas.

"The yard weathered the 25% VAT and because of its generator the 'Three-day Week' of 1974 was no great problem either.

"It was in 1974 that the production of a 25 ft. Quarter Ton Cup yacht, to be designed by Doug Peterson, was first considered. Over the following two years twenty-four of these boats were sold, but with the introduction of the 43 and the 28 in 1977 it was decided to take the 25 out of production.

"By now the work-force was approaching one hundred, and to meet ever-growing demand for Rogers yachts Jeremy Rogers purchased the Leonardslee Industrial Estate (between Lymington Town railway station and the Lymington River). Early in 1977 a new moulding shop of about 10,000 sq. ft. was built on the new site, and with growing production the administrative staff needed more accommodation, so that the old public house, called 'The Britannia,' on the corner of Station Street, Lymington, was purchased and renovated to provide offices for the staff.

"During 1977 two 43ft. yachts were built and entered for the Admiral's Cup Series. One of these

yachts was Jeremy Rogers' own *Moonshine,* which was the top scoring yacht of the victorious British team; she was narrowly beaten into overall individual second place. The other yacht built at the yard, *La Pantera,* sailing for Hong Kong, came eleventh overall.

"Despite so much else happening yet another yacht was produced at the yard later in 1977. This was the first of the popular Contessa 28 range. In the three years since then a further 150 have been built.

"Meanwhile a new fitting-out shop was being erected on the Leonardslee Estate, and this was ready for occupation early in 1978. By this time the work-force had increased to 150. Now the yard was building four types of yacht: the 43, 35, 32 and 28; the Contessa 26 was found to be no longer economic in 1977, and the moulds were sold to be used elsewhere.

"Ever mindful of change, and feeling the need to remain at the forefront of yacht building, Jeremy Rogers decided to invest in a revolutionary new moulding process which had previously been used by Colin Chapman of Lotus Cars but had never been used for yacht building. The process, vacuum-assisted resin injection moulding, was perfected at the yard after many months of set-backs and hard work. The results were the best hulls yet produced by the yard, and probably the strongest and most refined yachts yet to be built anywhere. Two types of yacht have so far been produced by the new method; the OOD 34 (Offshore One Design 34) and the Rogers 39. In 1979 five Rogers 39s were built, three of which competed in the Admiral's Cup Series of that year. Jeremy Rogers' own *Eclipse* was selected to represent Great Britain and won the trophy for the best individual yacht in the series. The other two 39s represented Ireland and Switzerland. *Eclipse* was voted 'Yacht of the Year' by the Royal Ocean Racing Club as a result of her racing success in 1979, the year of the Fastnet storm.

"In 1980 business was badly affected by the world-wide recession, yachting being a luxury which must be foregone by many of those hit by the recession. It was necessary to reduce overheads and keep the business buoyant, so the original Gosport Street premises and a recently acquired garage near the Britannia offices were sold.

"Amid the general gloom of 1980 there was a pleasant surprise for Jeremy Rogers in the Queen's Birthday Honours List: he was appointed M.B.E. He was also invited to lunch with the Queen and Prince Philip in May 1981.

"Throughout the latter part of 1980 and the early part of 1981 the Rogers yard has continued to innovate and research, particularly in the field of injection moulding techniques. A Custom Boat

Division was set up for the construction of specialised one-off yachts for both the racing and the cruising markets: the first product of the new department was *Apollo V* for Australian Alan Bond of America's Cup fame. Industrial mouldings are also being produced at the yard, where there is a wealth of talent ready to be tapped; a contract was signed late in 1980 for building panels for a training centre at Esso, Fawley, and other contracts are likely to follow.

"With three more Admiral's Cup contenders to build, the normal production run of yachts to manufacture, and a large number of building panels to deliver the Rogers yard will not be idle in 1981."

"Jeremy Rogers has been one of the most prolific builders of high class cruising and racing yachts in the country," stated *Yachting World* of July 1981. "He is currently going through a quiet time with the recession, but as the producer of boats as successful as the Contessa 28 it would be difficult to see him emerging from the recession in anything other than a strong position." Fateful words, but it was to become much worse before it got better again.

The recession hit Jeremy Rogers very badly indeed and what was described as 'trimming off excess fat' meant selling his offices in Station Street, the fitting-out shop in Mill Lane, the joinery shop at the bottom of East Hill and his factory in Waterloo Street. At one time a Receiver was called in but in June 1982 it took on a new lease of life when the firm was purchased by Contessa Yachts. The Managing Director and Chairman is Mr. Bown with Jeremy Rogers as his second-in-command, and Bill Green, a bearded California, General Manager. They eventually hope to build the company up to where it was before – and beyond – and they are succeeding!

John Claridge

"I learnt to sail at the Salterns Sailing Club; I suppose I started when I was six and progressed right through there till I had to leave at sixteen (the top age limit) which I joined the Lymington Town Sailing Club," John Claridge told me when visited him at his yard at Sadler's Farm on 5th June 1982. "I think I am an 'Old Salt.' Anyway, I try and help the kids as much as I can because I got a lot out of it when I was young and I like to put a bit back into it. Major Hibbert started the Salterns Sailing Club in 1960 and it is a marvellous scheme: the children run the Club although the parents have a guiding committee. He has helped many people and there is a large number of good helms today who owe their initial start to him.

"Nowadays I find it very hard to be competitive against the youngsters because they are so much fitter and younger and they have much more time. So it is very difficult. I like to think that I am still competitive but I have a sneaky suspicion that I am fighting a losing battle! I think I was lucky; it all happened at the right time. I happened to be building the right boats when I was young. I had faster boats than anyone else and I was probably a bit keener. That is really what got me going.

"I started off boat-building in the back garden and then I moved down to Major Hibbert's house – he had an old shed at the back. That is another way in which he helped me very early on. I then moved to where Jeremy Rogers is now and later spent two years at Joe Sanders in Bath Road. We moved here to Sadlers Farm, Lower Pennington Lane, six years ago in 1976 and hopefully we will remain here. Certainly the overheads are very low.

"Usually I have friends to whom I sub-contract work but I have got one youngster working with me at the moment, but he concentrates mainly on building sailboards. We did sell our sailboards at the Quay and Tom Morris kindly let us use his chandlery but now he has sold it so it has closed our operation down. It would be viable to open up a shop but I decided, and decided very quickly in fact, that I am not a shopkeeper so we are selling them mainly by word of mouth although we do use the occasional advert, and that side is going quite well.

"We build mainly Moths but I have probably built a fair amount of other boats as well: I have just finished an Osprey and an International Canoe. But my main work is Moths: it is the thing I do best, I think, and I am set up to do it. I can turn out a Moth relatively quickly. I think a complete boat takes me about two weeks but most of the boats go out in kit form. We prepare them in kit form because Moths tend to appeal to young people and young people have not go much money, so that the more they save the better. I can probably make two kits in a week, possibly three. Certainly, from an economic point of view it is slightly better anyway because although the sum obtained is smaller there is a higher turnover. I quite like doing kits as you meet more people that way.

"My kits go all over the world. I am just doing five for Japan at the moment (June 1982): it is the first time we have exported to Japan. They never import much and it was very strange. I was quite surprised when I got the order. But the Worlds will be there in 1984 and I think they want to get the top boats just to see them and be competitive. They will have a job building one as light and stiff as I do because of getting the materials. Also I have 12 years' experience. We have exported to Australia; quite a few boats have gone to Switzerland and they should be ideal for the lakes there; and they have also gone to

Holland, Sweden and all over Europe except France. Import duties tend to stop them and it is difficult to get boats into Australia and New Zealand. Now they are building them under licence. I think Australia had 50% import duty and New Zealand had 100%. They are over protectionist.

"With the Moths, within the limits of 11 ft. long and 7 ft. 4 ins. wide, you can have any shape you like; it is a free design. But the Moths I build are generally designed by my brother-in-law, Mervyn Cook, so it has become a family enterprise. He is a very talented designer although he is really a civil engineer and does boat design on the side. He was well ahead of the rest of the designers when he designed the original Moth. It gave us a big advantage over everyone else but now they are catching up and we are looking round for the next big development in design. Everyone thinks that they have reached the limit but I have been in the Moth fleet for years and years and what the next development will be, I don't know. It could possibly be in weight – we are building them much lighter now with plywood; or rigs – they could go faster that way; or possibly a slightly more stable hull shape. It is all faster. We are very lucky that measurements are so simple, which makes building them so simple. The boats I build probably weight about 60 lbs. for a semi-complete boat and there are no weight limits but the lighter you can get them, and they still hold together, the faster they will go. It is a limited market but quite a good one. We are also looking to build boats for the Speed Week and that is something where strength is very important. There is a good chance that we may be doing that soon.

"When it comes to sails it is rather embarrassing for me. I have been in the Moth fleet a long time and so has Richard Hargreaves and he makes very good sails. But I have also used Pete Sanders' sails from the Lymington Sail & Tent Company and I have won a lot of championships with them. It is a difficult choice because I know them both personally; they are both excellent sailors. Richard Hargreaves is in Winchester and his sails tend to be more popular and the class probably have a loyalty to him but Pete Sanders is nearer to me and he makes a lot of sails.

"I have been all over the world for the Moth Championships. That is a nice thing about the Moth Fleet – it is an international class. The championships are in a different country each year. I was very lucky and went to Australia, but I missed out on Japan, and I have been all over Europe. We used to do absolutely ridiculous things. I used to have an old Wolsey 1500 and we used to load it up and travel over to Switzerland. How on earth we ever got away with it I will never know. I think when you are young you can get away with a lot more; we did things that I would not contemplate now. We had fantastic times and the Moth fleet is very friendly and everyone settles in well together. I have twice won the International Moth European Championships, the UK Nationals and finished second in the World and have won the prestigious Burnham Icicle, Hoo Freezer and Draycote Water events as well as countless Area Championships and Open Meetings. I did *not* win the Ladies World and European Moth Championships – but one of my boats did!

"Of course, there is a snag to all this success; I am not getting any younger and so many helmsmen have got our boats, that I am finding it increasingly difficult to win! It is most frustrating to be beaten by a boat you have built, but then I can still surprise these whipper-snappers occasionally, and it is some consolation that at least the boats are still winning World, European and National Championships as well as dominating most Open Meetings.

"This year we are raising money, £1,000, to send a youngster to Australia. Because Richard is a sailmaker and I am a boatbuilder we can put a lot of expenses down to the business but when we came back and worked out how much it had cost we were both absolutely horrified. We realised that there was no way a young kid could have done it and we thought the Class ought to do something about it. I put up a boat and Richard put up some sails and all sorts of firms chipped in, like Joe and Pete Sanders, and we had a big raffle and made quite a lot of money out of it, with the result that we are putting up the money for a youngster to go. I am not on the Class committee – that would be bad being a boatbuilder – but this is a separate Trust away from the Class and I am one of the Trustees and so is Richard and a couple of other keen 'Mothers'. But it will not be easy to select one person and we are basing it on a series of races this year and we will see who comes out best and who is most deserving too. I think the experience is so useful – they will not necessarily do particularly well but that is not the point. To actually go to a World Championship, particularly in Europe, gives you a great deal of experience for the future. As I have already said, I have been very lucky and many people helped me when I was young and I got a lot out of it. Now I want to put a bit back into it."

What a nice person! His great-uncle is Frank Claridge, of the Sea Scouts.

Aquaboats Limited

Aquaboats Limited was inaugurated in 1960 with the original company being formed by three directors, Mr. E. R. W. Eyre as Chairman and Joint Managing Director with Mr. C. A. P. DeVeulle, and Mr. R. E. Horning as the third Director. I went to see Chris DeVeulle at their office in Mill Lane on 1st December 1981. "When we came to this site," he recalled, "it was empty and owned by a company called Saturn Gases, which I think was a subsidiary of Air Products at Fawley and before that, somewhere along the line it was part of Shell. I understood from the locals that during the war it was reinforced with piles and acted as some sort of emergency repair point for motor torpedo boats.

"The intention of the Company then was to market small speed and ski boats, small sailing dinghies and accessories, including a very limited amount of protective and sailing clothing together with chandlery, sports goods and fishing tackle.

"The demand for small craft was growing continuously and the need to offer after-sales service was very obvious. At this time a small repair workshop was opened in Highcliffe to carry out repairs and refits, including painting, to the smaller type of motor cruiser. This was found to be insufficient for the increasing demand and in 1964 part of the present premises at Mill Lane were purchased and turned into a boatyard, which was further expanded in 1965 with the purchase of Lymington Light Craft Ltd. They rented the old Lymington Ferry Slip from British Railways, used for the original Isle of Wight ferries. In 1969 we purchased the old site of Scats Warehouse, thus making Aquaboats Ltd. into its present size.

"In 1970 the Company became a member of the Sea Corner Group Ltd. The Group owns two garages as well. We have got our Group offices in 20 New Street and we bought the site from Tiffins, the builders, who used to be in New Street some years ago behind the Community Centre. It used to be called Gabriel's Yard some years ago. We run the three businesses entirely separately but they are administered by the Group and the three principal directors are the three who inaugurated Aquaboats in 1960.

"In 1975 there was a change in Company policy and it was decided to close the Highcliffe branch as from 30th September 1975 and move it to Lymington to enable the Aquaboats entire operation to continue under one overhead. On 30th August the Chandlery and Boat Sales departments were transferred in their entirety to new premises at 2 Gosport Street, Lymington and the month of September saw a run-down on the clothing at Highcliffe, as it had been decided to discontinue this side of the business altogether. Therefore from 1st October, brokerage facilities were available from Gosport Street and the actual boats for sale were displayed at Aquaboats yard at Mill Lane.

"I am sorry to say," said Chris DeVeulle, "that many years ago I used to hate Lymington and thought what a dreadful place Lymington was and how I would never like to go there. We used to live at Southbourne, Bournemouth and I think Bournemouth rather spoilt me. Then we bought this property and I thought, 'Well, Lymington is not such a bad place' and then it has just grown on me and I do not want to go anywhere else now, it is just fantastic!

"As far as sailing is concerned, I do a mixture of things, if you like. I go boating from Beaulieu at weekends with a friend of mine and I 'X'-boat sail here on Thursday evenings. I have got my own boat which I have not used this year (1981) and it has been laid up in the yard. It is a Freedom. But I have done some cruising. Chris Carrington is the skipper of a big boat down at Palma called *La Vague*, an 80 footer, and I went with him on part of the delivery trip. However, when we got to Benodet we ran out of time because the weather was so bad but he has gone down there to supervise some work and Wendy is going out to join him. We have got the *Water Rat* in the yard here.

"Fred Woodford told me a little while ago that if he has his way he will not have another marina opening into the river as there is enough traffic. He reckons that if there is another one it will have to go straight out. Silting of the river is a permanent problem to us. We did our own dredging some eight or ten years ago but it has got silted up and needs doing again. Until the Harbour Commissioners decide to dredge up here there is no point in us doing it, as we would just dig a hole and it would all fall back in and they would benefit more than we would!

"We do not get many customers from abroad but during the summer we get visiting yachtsmen but that is all. We used to build boats here – *Ebblake IV* is one of them – but we have not built any for some years now and just repair and service boats, which is work and very welcome the way things are nowadays. We store boats – somewhere between 70 and 100 boats during the winter. At the present time we employ about 8 staff but before VAT a few years ago were up to 27. We have run down through natural wastage over the years and it has worked out very well and we can keep them occupied most of the time."

It was good to read in Pat Pocock's column in *Yachting Monthly* of November 1982 that Aquaboats had appointed Chris Carrington to be their new manager, in place of Ray Jones, who died suddenly earlier this year. "Chris has spent the last few years as skipper to various owners of large motor cruisers, both in the Mediterranean and in UK waters, but he has plenty of experience of boatyard management, as he used to run the Bridge Boat & Crane Company, just above the Ship Inn. Aquaboats offer excellent refit and repair facilities and they also concentrate on the hulls damaged by osmosis." Their boatyard facilities include craning up to 10 tons, pressure-scrubbing and washing, wood and GRP repairs, and painting by skilled shipwrights and engineers.

CHAPTER 13

SAILMAKERS AND SAILING SYSTEMS

"As you sit at your sailmaker's bench, John
With palm and needle and thread,
There are ships that are sailing the seven seas
With sails unfurled to catch the breeze:
Sails that you made in your shed."

L.S.

Hood Sailmakers (UK) Limited

After the war, designers started to concentrate on developing a new type of yacht, the cruiser racer, which would combine the strength and sea-worthiness of the pre-war cruiser with the speed and grace of the modern ocean racer. But not only yacht designs were to change. Even in the 1950s sails were largely made from traditional materials of canvas and Egyptian cotton. Here again the pressure of the developing ocean racing scene produced a revolution in sailmaking and a totally new type of cloth emerged.

Ted Hood in his loft in Marblehead, Maryland, USA had pushed conventional materials to their limits and was looking for a technological break-through. Fortunately, his father, Professor Ralph Steadman, was a leading chemical technologist who soon realised the enormous potential of the new synthetic material. Father and son now combined their talents to "weave sailcloth from the new synthetic fibres on looms which they had developed themselves. The end result was a cloth with such stability and toughness yet with soft handling that it really revolutionised sailmaking." Ian Thurgood described it as "the sort of cloth which distorts much less under load than any of the competitors' cloth and that is one of the reasons why we have been pre-eminent: the sail keeps it shape and therefore the boat performs that much longer." Under the stimulus of ocean racing, Hood technology has progressed every year and today they weave a huge range of dacron and nylon fabrics.

The Company that started in the sail loft at Marblehead twenty-seven years ago (1955) rapidly expanded and spread to the major sailing centres in Australia, New Zealand, Japan, Canada and Europe. Hood Sailmakers (UK) Ltd. set up in Lymington in Bath Road in 1967 and Ian Thurgood is European Financial Controller for the Company. There is an associate company in the South of France and they have franchises in Germany and Sweden but they are franchised to the American parent company and not to Hood in Lymington.

On 21st December 1981 when I visited his office, Ian Thurgood said that "certain people have wider-ranging responsibilities. I have had responsibility for the Irish cloth manufacturing company since the early 1970s and on and off I have been to France, Sweden and Germany but my responsibilities in those three locations are virtually mil. The cloth is manufactured by fellow associates in Eire and in Marblehead. The latter is in the same town as Hood Sailmakers but in a different building. So you have got two sources of supply for Hood cloth.

"Chemistry is an ever-changing area of development and the chemists, who provide the finishing coating for our cloths, are always coming up with new, improved coating. Then, of course, there are always new yarns like Kavlar, Laminar and Nylon. Kavlar is not new but the other two were in the past few years. It is a progressive industry from the point of view of a developing product – and it will not stand still.

"We have an associated company, Hood Yacht Systems, which make masts and head stays. We do not make them in Lymington but we do market them. I must say Hood Yacht Systems is certainly a very integral part of our business and a big contributor to our profitability."

It is interesting to note that the rise of the aircraft industry in the twentieth century saw the need for accurate calculation of strength/weight ratio, particularly cutting down weight while maintaining strength. This led to a more widespread understanding of lamination, hollow construction and later to the use of metals and light alloys. This technology spread to yacht masts – a far cry from the primitive yachts made of tree trunks on which sails were tied at convenient intervals.

Hood were the first sailmakers to offer a professional back-up service and although this service was designed with their customers in mind it is available to all yachtsmen, irrespective of make of sail. The service department is a separate section of the loft – around 2,800 sq. ft. – and is fully staffed by professionals under the expert direction of Ted Kimball.

Hood operates van collection/delivery service to all leading marinas in the Solent area and for customers further afield; they have a contract with Securicor or sails can be sent by Red Star to Brockenhurst station to be collected by them. All repairs, rebuilds, and alterations are undertaken and advice on sail care is given. Hood run a comprehensive conversion service to furling headstay systems, either their own 'Sea Furl' or any other make and conversions to slab reefing are organised. They maintain a register of secondhand and demonstration sails and will even personalise a standard spinnaker with the customer's own logo design.

At the end of the season Hood will check sails thoroughly, including stitching, patching, chafing, eyelets and marking. They can then be expertly cleaned in their 'in-house' laundry. They have a giant industrial washing machine and they charge 35p per pound (dry weight) for a complete wash. The sails are cleaned with specialised techniques to remove fuel oil stains and most other marks. Finally, they will be properly stored in their warm, dry loft for protection against damp and mould damage and are ready for the new season.

As the sailing world of Hood expanded, so the Hood team grew up from leading sailmakers and sailors who combine a tremendous balance of sailmaking skills and traditions with performance talents. This is clearly illustrated by the appointmen of two Managing Directors at Lymington in March 1981: Peter Bateman and Bryan Axford. Peter Bateman had previously been a director of Bruce Banks Sails and had also been the British Olympic Yachting coach. He will look after sales and the external affairs of the company. Brian Axford had already been in the Lymington loft for a number of years and will be responsible for the internal affairs, but both will come together on the product development and design.

It is indicative of the important role of the sailmaker that more and more of them now form part of the crew of a racing yacht and so are able to assess and offer their expertise at first hand. The Hood Group have built up a dominant position in the racing world, winning every major racing event – America's Cup, Admiral's Cup, Southern Cross Trophy, Round the World and the Two Ton, One Ton, Three-quarter Ton and Half-Ton Worlds.

Although most people connect Hood with top-notch racing yachts, they are the first to emphasise how much they are involved – and increasingly so – in cruising. The recession has increased the share of the market that cruising boats have taken out of their total sales.

In spite of the continued development of mathematical means to calculate sail geometry, the final result lies "with the sailmaker's skill on the loft floor and the adept handling of the flowing sail by the seamstress." Sailmaking continues to blend the mystical qualities of art and craft.

Sanders Sails

Joe Sanders told me that "about five years ago (1976) we chopped the sailmaking away from the rest of the Lymington Sail & Tent Company and gave it to my son, Pete, who has since made a success of it under Sanders Sails. It is entirely his company and he has built it up from very little. He shares the building with us, and works upstairs, and my wife does the accounts for both companies."

John Claridge was full of praise for Sanders Sails. "Pete has done very well for a relatively young man; he is three years younger than I am, and he is getting better all the time."

"Hood tends to be in a larger bracket," Joe Sanders continued. "They make the very expensive sails and for quite some time they did not do the sail repair side which Pete specialises in, whereas now everyone does it; there is not so much new work around. Pete has got a very interesting section, a wide cross-section of dinghy sails whereas Hood do not generally do this. He makes a lot of cruising sails and is very competitive with Hood but I think they both have a case. I suppose they are in competition but not to a very great extent; there is room for both of them. Hood send their sails to places all over England and export to Europe too, whereas Pete is a much more locally-based person."

Pete Sanders originally helped start the Lymington Hospital radio and is still the Treasurer. "There were four of them and they raised all the money to start it," said Joe Sanders. "They raised about £6,000 by running discos at school dances and other functions and my son was one of the disc jockeys. The hospital radio basically plays for the elderly who are bedridden and my eldest daughter was in a group of Brockenhurst College who used to go round on Saturdays and Sundays, handing round the tea and chatting to the old dears. They made the boys go to the Women's Ward and the girls went to the Men's Ward and all these seventeen-year-olds cheered everyone up tremendously. The staff too appreciated that the youngsters could serve tea for them and take some of the petty jobs off their hands. It was a very good thing and I think they still do it."

John McMullen

Captain Colin McMullen told me that his son had been a sailmaker in Lymington. "He was really grinding himself and was not making much out of it and he has left now and let the premises in North Close to that up and coming firm of glass manufacturers, Lymington Glass Mystiques Ltd., and has got a job in a large electrical firm. I think he now probably feels that he should have expanded but when he started up Hood arrived and so there were then three sailmakers in Lymington. My present No. 1 jib which has been all across the Atlantic was made by John."

To a Sailmaker . . .

I was looking through some old copies of *Yachting Monthly* in the library of the RLYC, and in the 1934 May-October issue, Vol. LVII, page 94, I found this rather moving little poem, written by L.S., evocative of bygone days.

"As you sit at your sailmaker's bench, John
With palm and needle and thread,
There are ships that are sailing the seven seas
With sails unfurled to catch the breeze:
Sails that you made in your shed.

Have you ever been aboard a boat, John
And left your rambling shed
With its crazy roof and old red tiles
And cobwebs and stored-up sails
On the beams which bump your head?

Have you ever made sail at the Sunk, John
In a bitter easterly breeze?
Past Kentish Knock and Isle of Wight
And on down Channel to Longships light
And the broad Atlantic Seas?

Have you ever sailed in the Trades, John
Where a good breeze never fails?
Do you ever feel proud that by your skill
A ship's alive? Do you feel a thrill
Because you made the sails?

Have you ever roamed 'neath your sails, John
On any sort of boat?
Or have you worked in your shed,
With your sailmaker's palm, your needle and thread,
And never been afloat?"

Stearn UK

On 8th December 1982 I had a talk with David Barrow, European Manager of Stearn UK, who has worked for this company since it was formed in Lymington in 1977. He looks after the hardware side of the business throughout Europe.

Tim Stearn was an American who was born in Sturgeon Bay, 'a backwater ditch' off one of the Lakes about 200 miles north of Chicago. He founded Stearn Sailing Systems in 1973 in the States and it has been a major innovator in rig and rig system design ever since. A new breed of designer/builder/engineer had come to the fore including names like Doug Peterson, Ron Holland, Gary Carlin and Tim Stearn, and they were all working to find new ways of making boats sail faster. The Company started with the twin stay and David Barrow told me quite an interesting story about it. "Tim Stearn had the twin stay manufactured and put on one of the boats he was sailing in the One Ton Cup at Miami and it won the first race. Orders literally came in there and then by word of mouth, from boat to boat, for the next race and they sold a lot of twin stay from the dock and that is how the company started!

"From there the company entered the spar market and started selling them and the first one was for a boat called *Pied Piper*. In 1975 they moved into the hydraulic field and that is the area they cover today, although they have diversified quite a bit since then. At present they are making mainsail reefing systems as well by mounting the dynafurl behind the mast and they are involved in the rigging side of the building too, mainly from external sources but they are buying the rigging and giving it to the customers as a package.

"Stearn UK was initially set up by Stearn Sailing Systems in Lymington in April 1977 to provide a servicing side for the spars they had sold to their customers who would be competing in the Admiral's Cup series that August. So they set up an operation over here which was very small and with very little finance and away we went. There was John Green, Phil Crebbin and a month later, in May, myself. We imported the spars from the States and sold them in Europe. The same eventually happened with the Twin Stay Dynafurl.

"One day Commander David Balme, the owner of *Hephzibah,* came into our office, at that time housed in a Portakabin, and said, 'I want to buy one of these furling systems you sell.' The company at that time was mad keen on racing and was not so interested in these old cruising fellows who used to hang around at meetings but we said, 'Well, we have got one somewhere; sure, we will sell you one,' and we dug one out of our stock, covered in cobwebs from the old potting shed which served for our store! We fitted it to *Hephzibah* and David Balme said, 'I like it,' and then his next door neighbour wanted one and then another chap from the same marina wanted one and so on – word of mouth again – and we realised that there could be something in this and started to promote it. In 1982 we sold over 600 of them just to ordinary cruising boats, ranging from a 25 footer up to just under a 98 ft. cruising boat in Spain, which had five large ones installed on her."

As we have seen they started with quite humble premises: if a potting shed was their store then a Portakabin at the end of Jeremy Rogers' factory was their office. There were three people in the Portakabin, and when numbers increased to six "and secretaries were sitting on people's laps typing out letters" they felt that the time had come to move, so they went to Brockenhurst. This was a period of consolidation for them and also the company in the States had some financial problems to get through and they could not spare money for development. Then when Phil Crebbin left they were joined by Geoffrey Hand, who had been able to help at the takeover in the States and was well qualified educationally and financially in business matters.

"Moving here to Jeremy Rogers' factory," David Barrow continued, "has changed everybody's attitude as far as the company is concerned. We were a bit stuck in the place in Brockenhurst, which we leased from Redmayne Engineering, and we kept hoping to move but were held up because of Jeremy's problems and the lease kept falling through. Then suddenly it all happened and we are here! In our present spacious premises we can now build spars for the European market and build them inside. In Brockenhurst we had to work outside and it was a bit traumatic in the winter.

"The company has got three main, really active agents in Europe. One is in Sweden and in 1983 they will do about 100 dynafurls and also market the spars for them; one in Germany which will do about 200 or so furling systems and again will market the spars; and one in Italy. We have sub-agencies from the Swedish agency in Norway and Denmark and we are also looking at Finland as well. We are also hoping for agencies in Holland, Spain and Portugal, although Portugal has not really started yet. Looking further afield, we have also dealt with South America, Australia and New Zealand and quite a bit with Hong Kong.

"Everybody is really an interesting client for the production of the competition side because anybody can build an Admiral's Cup boat – it shows a certain degree of wealth. We have done work for the Aga Khan, Baron Rothschild and, although we have not put masts on Edward Heath's boat, we have carried out work for him. We have also provided masts for the King of Spain. Most of the top Admiral's Cuppers like the Dunnings and the Aishers come to us and generally, in the past, three Admiral's Cups, 77% and 85% of the masts have come from us. That has been our bread and butter up to now!"

Harold Cudmore is not a member of the firm but he has sailed quite a bit with their spars, especially in the 12 metre boat *Victory*. "Harry is an interesting person to sail with," David Barrow continued, "and you very quickly find out about your parentage! It is his way of life." Phil Crebbin, another Olympic helmsman could no longer be associated with the company because of conflicting interests (the spars come from Stearn) and also because he is completely dedicated to the America's Cup and that demands total involvement. While he was still working for the company, he was interviewing applicants to join the *Victory* syndicate. An MA from Cambridge, who had practical talents as shipwright, engineer and welder as well, Phil Crebbin gave up an enviable salary as a business executive to dedicate his life for the next 18 months to the *Victory* syndicate. In a profile on him Tony Fairchild, in an article in the *Daily Telegraph* of 25th March 1982, quoted Phil as saying: "Skippering *Victory* in an America's Cup campaign is the second most important thing; the first most important thing would be *winning* the America's Cup." An Olympic Gold Medallist and reputed to be one of only two world class yachtsmen, we must all will him to succeed although disappointingly perhaps, not in the *Victory* designed by Ed Dubois and launched by Princess Michael of Kent.

CHAPTER 14

NAVAL ARCHITECTS AND YACHT DESIGNERS

*"To yacht design Jack Laurent Giles brought a high degree of mathematical
and engineering knowledge combined with an original artistic sense so true that
his boats were conspicuous by their practical 'rightness' of form and line."*

JACK LOWIS

Jack Laurent Giles was born on 22nd June 1901 in Scarborough, Yorkshire, the son of a local doctor. Educated at Winchester and Magdalene College, Cambridge he read engineering and took an honours degree.

He served his apprenticeship with Vickers Armstrong in Newcastle-upon-Tyne but early in the 1920s his love of sailing and yachts led him to join Camper & Nicholson in Southampton. Under the direction of that famous yacht designer, Charles E. Nicholson, he developed his flair for yacht design. He had lost an eye in an experiment while he was at Winchester but could do more with one eye than most people could do with two!

By courtesy of P. Woolass

Jack Laurent Giles at No. 4 Quay Hill, Lymington

In 1927 he founded his own firm of Laurent Giles and Partners with G. R. Gill and, later, with Humphrey Barton. Two years later he married Elizabeth Falconer and had twin sons and a daughter, Tamsin, who later married Stephen De Mowbray. In 1930 he became a member of the Royal Ocean Racing Club and the influence of the experience he gained there showed in the many cruiser-racers he designed in the 1930s, including *Maid of Malham* and the 'Channel' class. But cruising boats remained his prime interest and during this period he designed the famous *Dyarchy* for Roger Pinckney and the classic class of the 5 tonner Vertues.

During the war he was first in charge of the Small Boats section of the Department of Naval Construction and later he served in Washington D.C. on aircraft construction.

After the war he designed such famous boats as *Myth of Malham* for John Illingworth, which was the outstanding ocean racer of the post-war period and the 24 ft. waterline boats for the Royal Naval Sailing Association. He produced *Miranda IV* which swept the board in racing events in the Mediterranean. In 1936, nine years after he started his partnership, he was approached by Dick Kindersley of Guernsey and asked to design a 5 tonner which would be suitable for serious offshore cruising. So it was that he designed the famous *Andrillot,* which became the forerunner of a class of small cruisers which, by their exploits, were to cause many a raised eyebrow amongst the diehards!

A very good description of Jack Laurent Giles is contained in the book *Vertue,* written and edited by Peter Woolass. "In 1951 Jack Giles received well-deserved acclaim when he was appointed to the Faculty of Royal Designers for Industry. Looking through examples of his work it is easy for us to appreciate why this honour was bestowed on him – there is a common theme of purity of line combined with practical purpose which few other designers have achieved. Shortly before he died in February 1969 he laid down the lines of one of his most important commissions – a 25 ft. four-masted schooner.

"Despite the demands of his work, during his life Jack Giles took a keen interest in other fields – he was a great supporter of the Lymington Players Amateur Dramatic Society, a keen Rotarian and a staunch upholder of Lymington and its traditions. He was also a dedicated family man." Peter Woolass, author of *Vertue,* has kindly allowed me to include this tribute by Jack Lowis, who was one of his colleagues for many years, "Jack Giles was first, and always, a very kind person. He was ambitious, brilliant, determined, far-seeing, but none of these qualities impaired at any time his gentle kindness. He was a splendid companion. Alert, witty, observant, understanding, and possessed of a forceful, dominant personality which in conjunction with his unfailing charm enabled his associates and those whose business it was to give effect to his designs, to do so with enthusiasm and in full appreciation that they were helping to fulfil the inspiration of the Maestro.

"To yacht design he brought a high degree of mathematical and engineering knowledge combined with an original artistic sense so true that his boats were conspicuous by their practical 'rightness' of form and line. He set new standards which were appreciated and accepted on all sides, and which brought about a general advance in practice and quality.

"Inevitably he had friends without number because no one could meet him or work with him without appreciating his nature. And to all of them his practical down-to-earth kindness was his most outstanding characteristic. As someone said from the other side of the world, 'He was a very fine person!' "

To find out more about the firm of naval architects on Quay Hill, Frank Webster took me to meet Jack Lowis on 22nd February 1981 in their office and he not only told me all about the company but also showed me round the building.

Jack Giles founded the firm of Laurent Giles and Partners Ltd. in 1927 and became its Managing Director. His partners were George Gill, who remained with the firm well into the 1960s and Humphrey Barton, who was the surveyor. Roger Heron handled the brokerage side and joined in the 1940s and Jack Lowis entered the firm in November 1949.

Jack Lowis had spent half his service in the Indian Police from the end of 1924 to the beginning of 1936 and in February of that year he transferred to the Political Service and remained there until 1948. In 1939 when he was lucky enough to be back on leave, he bought a boat called *Dorado* on Humphrey Barton's survey but had to scrub her on the outbreak of war. His wife, daughter of the Goodharts, had fortunately been able to join him out in India in 1940, just before ways of getting out of England were stopped for the duration.

"Humphrey Barton spent all his time running about the place surveying boats for chaps who wanted to sell or who wanted to buy them," he told me. "Sometimes the surveyor would go out with clients if they did not know very much about sailing and very often he would rope in some odd chaps to help pull the strings. After I had been sailing with Hum for about 18 months or so and was contemplating getting a job in East Africa, my Guardian Angel must have been flying low at the time because out of the blue Jack Giles rang me up and asked if I would like to join his firm.

"What the hell did I do here? I knew nothing about drawing and could not even draw the square of a box – and still cannot do so," confessed Jack Lowis. "But I became a kind of administrator and dealt with correspondence from owners. This delegation of work enabled the designers to spend all their time on designing. Jack Giles used to like going out and seeing how the boats he designed behaved and I sometimes would take out new boats on sailing trials which was enormous fun."

He then explained the procedure involved in designing a new boat for an owner. "An owner would write saying he would like to have a boat and a Proposal Drawing would be done. This would be run off fairly quickly in about a week to ten days. The owner might then alter it and suggest changes. Jack Giles usually drew the lines of practically all the designs and George Gill drew the interiors (G.A.s and sail plans). Then the draughtsmen would take over the 'nitty gritty' of the smaller stuff, usually one draughtsman to each boat. In response to the first approach, or possibly as a result of the Propsal Drawing and discussion on it, the firm might say, 'Look, one of our existing designs seems to be very close to what you want,' and we would then send him prints of drawings of that design which had already been published, and at the same time one could also quote there and then what our charge would be for use of the design. The Preliminary Drawings for Quotation would include a Construction Plan, General Arrangement Plan and a Sail Plan."

There would also be specifications which could run into 25–30 pages according to the size of boat and multiplicity of detail. Jack Lowis often did the specifications which contained everything down to the minutest detail, in order to relieve the design staff from "wasting their far more valuable time on it."

The Preliminary Drawings were sent off to several yards for quotations and then there was a great deal to discuss such as proximity to the owner's home, besides the price.

The Building Contract laid down the stages of building and the accompanying times of payment of the building cost. The first payment was on signing the Contract; the second on completion of deck and deck works; the third on completion of basic interior accommodation and basic engine installation; and the fourth on completion of the yacht in all respects and satisfactory trials under sail and power. "Our own fees were paid in 25% parts at these times. The boats were built all over the world and many of the famous Vertue class were built in Hong Kong. Jack Giles, or occasionally others, would visit yards in Europe but further afield we were guided by circumstances. Sometimes the owner knew some qualified person who could do the job, sometimes (in Hong Kong, for example), we knew a firm of naval architects and surveyors who would take it on."

Roger Heron was in charge of the Brokerage Department and, having been an accountant, he also did the accounts. Later in the 1950s, he left to become a Company Secretary with another firm. Various people in succession took over either the accounts or the brokerage and the latter was held for a time by Captain James Crawford. It was when Peter Barrett was running the brokerage that the Yacht Haven got into its stride and he arranged to do the brokerage of the Haven at the same time. From 1961 to after Jack Giles' death, the back office of Laurent Giles and Partners was shared by Vernon Sainsbury, who had been Commodore of the RORC, and Jack Lowis.

The first Vertue was designed by Laurent Giles and Partners in 1936 for Dick Kindersley. The class took its name from a boat or its owner who had achieved some notoriety by winning a race on the East Coast. The famous *Vertue XXXV* was built in 1950 and was sailed across the Atlantic by Humphrey Barton and Kevin O'Riordan. Jack Lowis was later to send written advice to the Vertue Class on how to adjust standard rigging.

In 1937 the Fastnet Race was won by *Maid of Malham,* an auxiliary cutter, which was designed by Laurent Giles and built for Captain John Illingworth, who was then Commodore of the RORC. "He was a vigorous and charming man," recalled Jack Lowis, "who must have been in and out of the office breathing down Jack Giles neck two or three times a week while she was being built." In 1947 *Myth of Malham,* also designed for John Illingworth, won the Fastnet.

There had been a tradition of racing to Spain before the war and when the Santander Race was revived the first year after it ended, 'Hum' Barton suggested Jack Lowis as crew and to Jack's delight he was accepted and he joined the yacht at Brixham. John Illingworth was on board at that time." *Myth of Malham* had previously crossed to Bermuda," continued Jack, "followed by another race back across the Atlantic but had not been particularly successful. She carried a crew of 8 which was quite a crowd for a yacht with a 33 ft. waterline. A crew member said that they would not be taking a reef in the main, as it was so stiff but in 24 hours it had been taken off and they continued with a storm jib! It was one of those years!" Jack Lowis raced a few times in both *Myth* and *Minx of Malham,* an auxiliary sloop designed by Laurent Giles and Partners in 1949.

John Illingworth, although very much tied up as Commodore of the RORC, came to the conclusion that it would be a good idea to have a class aimed at offshore racing of a smaller size than *Myth of Malham.* His boat, *Minx of Malham,* had a 24 ft. waterline, which in those days was the minimum waterline length accepted by the RORC, and it was one of the first. And so the Junior Offshore Group was started in 1950 and they made very strict rules that yachts had to be kept to about 16 ft. or 17 ft. Jack Lowis remembers when he joined Laurent Giles in November 1949 watching Colin Mudie drawing a tiny boat. She was called *Sopranino* and she was the founder of JOG. Her owner was called Wells Coates and he and Colin sailed her across the Atlantic. Wells Coates was instrumental in getting Jack Giles the distinction of R.D.I.

John Illingworth also founded the RNSA and *Samuel Pepys* was specifically designed for them by Laurent Giles. Later, Commander Erroll Bruce was to race her against Adlard Cole's *Cohoe* for first position in one of the most exciting Transatlantic races of all time.

Jack Lowis then took Frank Webster and me round the offices and showed us some of the designs, a Drawing Register and a Data Book. There were many photographs of yachts, including *Blue Leopard,* designed for and pretty certainly still owned by Desmond Molins, the famous *Dyarchy,* designed for Roger Pinckney, and *Wanderer*, designed for Eric Hiscock. Sadly, in 1982, the famous offices in Quay Hill were put up for sale and Laurent Giles and Partners moved to No. 6 Station Street, Lymington, next door to the Royal Ocean Racing Club Rating Office in No. 8.

The story is now taken up by Richard Stower, a Director of Laurent Giles and Partners, who brings us up into the 1980s. My visit was on 19th May 1981 when they were still at Quay Hill.

"We took over from Jack Laurent Giles in 1969 and four partners carried on the partnership of which Jack Lowis and Vernon Sainsbury were the last of the old partners. Then we also took over a number of clients, who were going at that time, but we also attracted quite a lot of new business and did quite well.

"I think the most significant thing was that we got a contract from Westerly Marine Construction to design a boat called *Centaur*, which was actually in train just before Jack Giles retired. She was a 26 ft. glass-fibre so-called Marine Caravel type boat, which just happened to be very successful at a time when there was quite a number of badly designed glass-fibre boats about. This really got Westerlys going in a big way and they increased their turnover fairly rapidly between 1970 to 1974, when they suffered a bit of a recession, which fortunately did not last long. Then they got going again and in the meantime we designed a 38 ft. boat, a 23 ft. boat, a 21 ft. boat and then another 21 ft. boat and they were all pretty successful as cruising boats.

"Then about that time they decided to build a bigger boat, a 36 ft. boat, a Conway, and that proved highly popular as well. In the meantime Westerly expanded and became much more competitive and had at that time started to export to the United States. We also carried on doing some quite big one-offs. We had done quite a number of glass-fibre boats, including a 44 ft. motor sailing boat, a Caribinier. We then did a 52 ft., a 63 ft. and, more recently, we have done a new one, a 134 ft. Grenadier and we have just done a smaller version of that. Westerlys have been fairly quiet at the moment on the design front but we did do a 30 ft. motor sailer and a 29 ft. Consort motor cruiser, which has also proved extremely popular. In addition we have done quite a number of one-offs, getting on for a dozen offshore over the last few years, mostly fairly large ones in the 50 to 79 ft. range.

"Then we designed two steel motor-sailers for Bonetti in Italy – quite nice boats – and many odd boats in between. We designed some boats for Seamaster. We designed another boat called the Giles 38, which has proved reasonably popular. We did a glass-fibre Vertue, which unfortunately has proved a little too expensive. We have also done some racing boats: we did two for Westerlys – one was a ¼ tonner and one a ½ tonner, a GK24 and a GK29 and at the moment I am doing a 33 ft. centre-board for Terry Erskine Yachts in Plymouth (later called the Dulcibella 33) and have got a new 38 ft. on the board for Westerlys, which is still in the formative stages."

"There are only three of us at the moment working full-time. The length of time it takes to design a boat depends so much on its size and it can take anything between three months and a year. The drawings would not take that long but it is supervising as well. A boat of any size takes about a year to build; even with production boats it can take almost a year to produce the moulds.

"We have not done much racing; nor have we hit the headlines in the last couple of years but probably more boats have been built to our design than almost any other firm in England.

"It is very hard to make money designing racing boats. I think designing racing boats is a way up the ladder; once you have got to the top you really do not want to go much further. The IOR Rule is difficult and it is one of the reasons why I am not worried about not designing racing boats. I know one young designer who finds the Rule a bit inhibiting as there is so little room for manoeuvre. It is something that you have to be doing all the time to really grasp it.

"One of our main problems is the continuation of the firm as the older directors retire. It is very difficult to find young people who are sufficiently trained. They lash out on their own with not much background. Obviously, if you are going to design boats where there is a lot of money involved, owners may be rather reluctant to invest designs of some of these youngsters. So I think there is going to be a bit of crisis in yacht designing because it is becoming economically far more difficult to make it pay because of high wages.

"The trouble is that a few years ago you could get a draughtsman who was content to work as a draughtsman, probably for years for a fairly modest wage. Nearly all the draughtsmen were brought up through the apprentice system and had to have practical experience. Now all these chaps go to University, come out with a degree in ship science with practically no professional or practical background and, of course, because they are well qualified they expect to be paid extremely well. I think basically there are too many well qualified people and not enough with practical experience. Five years was the normal apprenticeship during which time, in the early days, they went to evening classes and day release courses at Technical College.

"The days when a yacht designing firm would go on and on for a long time are over. Perhaps they never really existed. I think that normally, design firms are started by someone with ability and then they usually peter out. In our case it was unusual that we were able to take on from Jack Laurent Giles and make a success of it for a further period of ten or fifteen years. I think we are an exception because obviously younger designers will take over, even though most of them are only capable of designing racers. There will always be a demand for large cruising yachts but the difficulty is to know who is going to design them!"

We then went on to discuss his connection with *Dulcibella* of *Riddle of the Sands*. Not only did his uncle own the original *Vixen*, but Dick Stower was responsible for the conversion of a lifeboat for the film and advised on its production. *Dulcibella* has many links with Lymington and will have a section to herself in a later chapter. Dick Stower also contributed to the historical postscript on *Dulcibella* in the famous Bowker edition of *Riddle of the Sands*, published in 1976.

Ed Dubois

Ed Dubois is such a busy and elusive fellow that although he works in Kew Cottage, No. 13 Station Street, Lymington, just across the road from the Royal Ocean Racing Club Rating Offices, I am indebted to the Editor of *Yachts & Yachting* for permission to use material from articles by Strahan Soames and Malcolm McKeag that appeared in the August 14th 1981 issue of the magazine.

Ed Dubois was born in Croydon in 1952 and has three sisters, all as creative and artistic as he is himself. Catherine is a concert pianist, Sarah is a graphic designer and Elizabeth trained as an artist. They are all married but he is still a bachelor.

As a boy he used to sail model boats in the Round Pond in Kensington Gardens but his only link with the sea is a somewhat tenuous one through his mother having been a WRNS officer during the war and having encouraged his interest in boats. Later he went to a Sailing Camp in Wales and returned there year after year. "I had this passionate desire to sail and I suppose that I enjoyed sailing more than any of the boys there," he said. "I spent all the time I could on the water and I just went berserk over it." At the age of 15 he bought a half-share with his parents in his first boat, a Hornet, and finished 4th in the Class Junior Championships and 11th in the Nationals.

Ed Dubois went on the then new course in yacht and boat design at the Southampton College of Technology and gained practical experience on release to Alan Buchanan in Jersey. "I used to think that I was a tremendously gifted drawer but when I got there I realised how hopeless I was at it. For draughting you need a certain ability, and after that it is just practice," he confesses very modestly. He qualified in 1974 and then went back to work for Alan Buchanan as a design draughtsman. While he was there he went sailing with George Skelley which was to make a considerable impact on his career when he set up on his own.

But before doing that he applied to work for Sparkman & Stephens in the United States to gain more experience but, unfortunately, he was unable to get a work permit. He applied for and was taken on as, an editorial assistant at *Yachts & Yachting*. In the meantime he had persuaded George Skelley to order a ¾ tonner to his design and through the good offices of the editor of *Yachts & Yachting* he was introduced to John Oakley.

John Oakley persuaded Ed Dubois to design boats for him and this was a golden opportunity to have John sailing his boats. As John Oakley often told him, "The design is one thing and the other is that you must have somebody to point the boat in the right direction – it is no good going fast in the wrong direction!"

Ed's first boat, *Borsalino Trois*, was launched in April 1976 and was tank-tested at the Wolfson Marine Technology Unit at Southampton University. A 'bit of a rule bender,' its success in winning the Three-Quarter Ton Cup trials, the Solent Points Championship and the RORC Class 3 championships encouraged him to persevere. The follow-up, *Nadia*, won every race in the Level Rating Week in 1977 and then came the famous 2-tonner *Vanguard*, the Hong Kong Admiral's Cup yacht, which was to make his name.

Up until now he had been designing at home and taking his work for John Oakley to see in the office but with clients like George Skelley, Bill Turnbull and, most recently, David Lieu of Hong Kong, all of whom had taken risks in supporting a new and up-and-coming young designer, he felt the time had come to go it alone and involve himself in finance as well as design. After the 1977 season and the great success of *Vanguard* in all but the Fastnet, Ed Dubois parted from John Oakley and came to work in Lymington in September 1977. Once again his good luck held and Peter Bruce and Peter Johnson found him his office in Station Street and also a flat. Three months later he was employing a part-time assistant and when he advertised in *Yachts & Yachting* for a permanent staff member he got 90 replies! From a short list of 15 he chose Stephen Wallis, who is principal draughtsman in his office today (1982). He later bought Kew Cottage (No. 13 is omitted although he can afford not to be superstitious!) and he bought a house in Boldre.

Even with a staff of four Ed Dubois makes sure that each yacht that bears his name as designer really has been designed by him. He does the concept work and personally draws the lines plan and the sail plan so that the concept of the boat is firm. During construction he will visit the builder at least once more and will attend the sea trials. If she is an IOR boat he will usually try to race on her to see for himself how she goes, and he travels extensively.

Names of some of the yachts designed by Ed Dubois include *Santa Evita* and *Honey*, both ½ tonners; *Schwanensee* and *Nadia*, 1 tonners; *Pink Panther*, ¾ tonner and the famous 2 ton *Police Car* which helped ensure that Australia won the Admiral's Cup. For the 1981 Admiral's Cup, seven out of his nine boats were selected. *Victory* and *Dragon* for Britain; *Pro-Motion* for Holland; and *Vanguard*, her sister ship *Uin-Na-Mara* and *La Pantera* for Hong Kong. Although not selected *Panda* had a successful season, as did *Winsome Gold*, designed for David May. His most prestigious yacht is the 12 metre *Victory*, which he designed for the Peter de Savary syndicate and which was built by Souters in Cowes and launched by Princess Michael of Kent. The fact that her future as the contender is in some doubt need not prevent us from wishing her all the luck in the world.

Ed Dubois now enjoys an international reputation, rivalling only that of Jack Laurent Giles and it is therefore consistent that he should now largely have taken over from Laurent Giles and Partners in designing for Westerly, in particular the Griffon, Fulmar and GK24 designs. Although he is best known as a racing yacht designer who can command fees from about £2,500 for a ½ tonner and up to £6,000 for an Admiral's Cup yacht (they can reach the £15,000 mark), it is important to remember that he has designed many cruising yachts from a 65 ft. schooner and a luxury motor yacht to production cruising yachts.

Some of the yachts designed by Ed Dubois in 1982 with the most interesting names are *Beach Inspector* ('the Aussie name for a lifeguard – those macho types who swim very strongly and rescue fair sheilas from the jaws of snapping sharks'); and *Smuggler*, which was top boat overall in the Southern Cross Cup and, appropriately with that name, she has never been caught! *Bimblegumbi*, Australian built and Hong Kong owned, was top boat overall in the China Seas Series during April; *Framboise*, a 1 tonner, won the Lymington Spring Series and her class at Cowes; and *Geriatric Bear*, a Westerly GK34, was winner in Class I in both the East Anglian Offshore Week and Burnham Week.

Ed Dubois is the first to acknowledge the tremendous support he has received from his parents and sums up his his success with these words: "The reason that I have been able to make my living out of designing boats is that I wanted to do it so much and I have been lucky in that respect." He has certainly put Lymington once again in the forefront of yacht design.

Michael Pocock

Michael Pocock was born in 1931 and is married to Pat, daughter of the famous Humphrey Barton and who, with her twin brother, did so much to put Lymington to the fore in the sailing scene in the 1950s, as did Michael himself. He crewed for Robin Aisher in the Coppa D'Italia in 1957 and for Stuart Jardine in the Flying Dutchman Olympic Trials in 1959. He was skipper of *Rose Rambler* when she crossed the North Atlantic from Antigua to Salcombe, 3,700 miles in 33 days. Their son, Richard, following the family tradition, is no mean yachtsman too.

Pat Pocock told me that "after a formal training and ten years in practice in conventional architecture, Michael joined the yacht industry in 1967. After six years in the yacht charter business, he became associated with Einar Ohlson of Sweden. Michael was particularly successful in developing and marketing the Ohlson 35 in England. In 1974 he introduced the Mark II version of the Ohlson 35 and with his own yacht, *Flashlight*, won the RORC Class IV championship.

"In 1975 Michael Pocock designed *Starlight*, a modern Half Tonner, which was immediately successful in winning the RORC Class V championship in 1976. Michael built the original Starling in Lymington, using C Flex but the production run of over 30 boats were all built in Jersey. At the end of 1976 he accepted an invitation to become a partner in the well-known design office of Laurent Giles & Partners, working on a variety of designs but particularly on the Westerly GK29. This design, of which 150 or more have now been built, has been very successful as a sensible cruising/racing yacht of simple concept with a large interior volume, and she has proved economical to build.

"After two years in the partnership, Michael Pocock left Laurent Giles to return to independent design. In addition to IOR competitive designs, he has drawn several production yachts for a Spanish boatyard and more recently a 38 ft. LOA yacht for the 1981 Two-Handed Observer Trans-Atlantic Race. This yacht, named *Blackjack*, is for Rodney Barton (no relative of Humphrey) and Michael is going on the race with Rodney. Michael is currently drawing a 56 ft. LOA yacht for the 1982 Round Britain Race and various IOR designs for both UK and abroad are in hand." There is a painting of *Blackjack* which was exhibited at the Royal Lymington Yacht Club when the Lymington competitors discussed the Two-Handed Observer Trans-Atlantic race there, under the chairmanship of Erroll Bruce.

"In 1982 two new designs by Michael Pocock were launched. One was *Greased Lightening,* intended for IOR racing offshore in the Irish Sea, and her owner, Bernard Cox, finished second overall in the ISORA championship. The second was *Micro Metalsmiths* (originally *Quicksilver*), a 56 ft. LOA designed as the prototype of the Supercruiser 56 class and for her owner, Christopher Shaw, to race in the Round Britain Race. Although she came 27th she achieved the fastest time of any monohull from Lerwick to Lowestoft and had a best day's run of 225 miles.

"Michael Pocock's most satisfying project is *Lumberjack,* a 45 ft. centreboard yawl being built in Poole for Rodney Barton as a successor to *Blackjack.* It is a prototype of the Migrant 45 class, 'a tough, no-nonsense design for shorthanded racing and comfortable cruising.' Rodney Barton is intending to race *Lumberjack* in the 1984 OSTAR.

"Complementary to design work, Michael Pocock has been a regular correspondent for *Yachts & Yachting,* covering design, the IOR Rule, Boat Shows and various aspects of racing offshore." Pat has been writing 'Around the Coast Notes' for *Yachting Monthly* and covers the Keyhaven, Lymington and Beaulieu area. She has also started contributing to a new trade magazine (1981), *Boating Business.*

MacAlister Elliott & Partners Ltd.

I went to talk with Gowan MacAlister in his office on 5th May 1982, which is situated across the road from St. Thomas Church. I particularly remember the date because the church bells were tolling for the funeral of Major Gatehouse which took place that afternoon.

"We lived in America for five years at Marblehead, a super place on the East Coast," said Gowan MacAlister, founder of the firm of naval architects and fisheries consultants. "I was working for General Electric as an engineer designing jet engines," he continued, "and I started designing boats as a hobby. I even put the lines of my first boat and had them cleared out in the General Electric computer, and designing and building my boat meant pretty well full-time part-time work, as it were!

"In 1972 we decided to come back to England and start building little boats so I needed to be by the sea. My wife is a doctor (Dr. Anthea MacAlister) and fortunately patients are everywhere, so we had an easier choice. We arrived one day at Lymington, quite by chance, and thought 'Well, this is a nice place. Let's live here!' So we literally stopped the car, got out and walked into a house agent. I am ashamed to say that I bought a house for £5,000 and it was only ten years ago. I nearly did not buy it because it was only 12 ft. wide!

"I found a microscopic works in East Boldre in an old bakery and started building little launches, the punch-line being that they were built in ferro cement, which was fairly novel at the time. I built boats 15 ft. long, which I named the 'Mac' range; then a 24 ft. Mac boat and after that, as usual, one builds bigger and bigger ones. I then moved to New Milton and took on a financial partner and we built a 28 ft., a 30 ft., 34 ft. and 40 ft., all fishing boats. Probably more ferro cement fishing boats were built in New Milton than anywhere else in Europe and most of them are still fishing in the Channel Isles and around the Scottish coast but we also have one in the Sudan and another fishing in West Africa.

"In those days the price of resins had gone up very dramatically all of a sudden, due to the oil crisis, and the price of labour had not caught up, so in the first instance we had a very real advantage. But labour rapidly caught up with the cost of oil and it seemed to us that trying to compete with glass-fibre was very difficult (glass-fibre was an excellent product too). So then we started MacAlister, Elliott & Partners, specialising in the developing world. If you take the same material and apply developing world economics to it, materials are cheap; the process is labour-intensive but in the developing world labour is very cheap and now we have a process that can be simply done almost anywhere, producing sound but very low-cost boats.

"We are now working in a large number of countries and have produced some fascinating boats, all built locally in the various countries. We have built West African Pirogues – they are essentially canoes but they are the traditional boats, some of them 60 ft. or 80 ft. long. We have also built Jehazis, a sort of small dhow, and Sessi, which were originally Lake Victoria canoes but now are seen all along the East coast of Africa. We are working with Markips, which are marvellous sailing/fishing boats in North Egypt and we have developed from the ferro cement into all sorts of appropriate boatbuilding.

"We look at a country where there is a need to expand its fisheries and find out the most suitable materials and suitable methods of use, and then we send in a team and try and set it up. For instance, on the north coast of Somalia, many boats given by various aid organisations have come to pieces. We are sending a team to refurbish them and to teach the fishermen how to use them better and to remember to change the engine oil every few years!

"There is no doubt that the developing world is very under-developed; in fact it is surprising how backward and deprived some of these places are with no water, no transport system and no food.

There is just nothing. In some places in West Africa you only get rice to eat and even in an international hotel in Kampala there were no knives and forks! In India we are going to Bombay to reintroduce sail to fishing boats. Sail development is quite a major part of our activities in several countries because fuel is so expensive – and it is even more expensive in the developing world because of logistic problems. In somewhere like Malawi, the only way they can obtain fuel is by it crossing Tanganyika and Tanzania and they are fighting with them! Fuel comes out at £3 or £4 a gallon which, in terms of their incomes, is an astronomical price.

"In Somalia we have done a project with the Food and Agriculture Organisation (FAO) of the United Nations and we are looking at all sorts of different sails, including junk rigs, which turn out to be very appropriate sails. We are also looking at sails in Egypt and in India and we may introduce a dipping lug rig. It is fascinating studying all these sails because you come up with all sorts of reasons why a boat sails the way it does.

"The great dhows with their latifs which are essentially trading sails. You go down the coast in one season and come up the coast in another. Consequently they are marvellous reaching sails but trying to tack with them is impossible; you would have to take the boat to pieces and rebuild it again on the other side. If you look at our own traditional sailing fishing boats you can almost tell by looking at the rig where their home port must be. You can tell if they have had to beat back into it or whether it is a port where the prevailing wind allows them to reach in and out and so on.

"We have been here, in what used to be the Electricity Showroom storage, for only about 8 months. We survive on a small number of quite big projects and you never know what is going to happen to you when one of them comes to an end. However, usually something seems to turn up, mostly funded by aid organisations, international banks and some religious organisations. Because, generally we are working with the poorest level of developing world fishing communities and it means we are trying to teach them to build boats. For instance, in Tanganyika, boats come out at about £200 each – so we are never going to make any money out of royalties and we don't really want to either. So in Tanganyika it is the European community that will fund the project.

"We travel around quite a bit and it is a very strange business being a little company and yet when you go abroad to some of these small countries you are dealing at ministerial level. You are whisked off the aeroplane and whisked into the official car. I did not know even that there was a minister in one country! But we also have many fascinating people who come and visit us here. We had a king who came in the other day, King Ndosi and he pulled out a chair and sat right in the middle of the room and said, 'I am a king!' Not the sort of person you expect to see in Lymington but occasionally a car draws up outside with a flag on its bonnet and an entourage gets out.

"Most of our staff are overseas at any one time. They live here but we send them out, sometimes for a couple of years, and they come back and then go out somewhere else." He showed me a photograph of himself taken on safari which reminded me of Dr. Livingstone and, in fact, there was a plaque by the side of the road close to where the photograph was taken saying that was where Dr. Livingstone and Stanley had met! It was quite erroneous but it was put there for the tourists!

Gowan MacAlister concluded by saying, "I have got a boat which I use as much as my commitments and my family permit. Being married to a doctor I do not get out much but I think you have got to own a boat if you live in Lymington. Somehow you would feel as if you were missing out if you did not!"

Freeward Marine

This firm of contracting naval architects has its offices at Freeward House, Gosport Street, Lymington and Maureen Davin kindly sent me the following review of their work.

"The objective of the three naval architects running Freeward Marine, Gordon Wyatt, David Freeman and David Palmer, is to achieve as wide a field as possible within the design environment, drawing from their collective shipbuilding experience to produce conventional and functional vessels ranging from the Fairways Fisher motor sailers to Middle East crew boats, steel tugs and fishing vessels.

"Freeward Marine has now been operating for over ten years and are well known for producing good looking boats that work. On the commercial side over the last year a number of interesting design projects have been completed, generally for commercial yards, a notable example being the design work and calculations necessary for producing a prototype assault craft for the Ministry of Defence in conjunction with a local builder. Survey and building supervision work is undertaken in the UK although this is now restricted as far as possible to within easy reach from Lymington.

"The Freeward 35 GRP hull and superstructure mouldings available for private and commercial builders to complete have been produced steadily throughout the year leaving the moulding shop at approximately 3-weekly intervals. One or two of these are completed under Freeward Marine's supervision and sub-contracted to local yards, a typical example being a fishing boat for the Middle East with a considerable amount of long-lining equipment to allow the vessel to lay 10-mile lengths of line each carrying approximately 1,000 hooks.

"Freeward Marine are versatile in their design and often find that the design of one particular vessel develops into a series of similar vessels or even an established class of vessel. A particular example of this follows the construction of a 10 metre multi-chine steel fishing vessel last year, the design of which was subsequently modified to a mini-tug arrangement and this has drawn another order from the Crown Agents for three of these vessels to be completed in the early summer (1981).

"These tugs, destined for the Tema Port Authority, Ghana, are 10.5 metres overall length, 3.8 metres breadth and 1.3 metres draft. Scantlings are all to Lloyds requirements for this type of vessel and each tug is fitted with a Lister Marine JW6 MGR marine diesel engine of 138 bhp with 3 : 1 reduction to give a free speed of around 8 knots and a static bollard pull of 1.3 tons. The boats are to manoeuvre barges within the estuary and harbours and will also be used as general work boats and for coastal pilotage duties when required. Each vessel is fitted with substantial fendering particularly around the bow for pushing purposes and a heavy cruciform towing bollard is fitted for pulling duties. A small open-backed wheelhouse is positioned over the engine casing and with the twin funnels and unobstructed working decks should prove to be most functional little tugs."

Rob Humphreys

At the end of the sailing season I went round to see Rob Humphreys in his home at 5 Curzon Place, Pennington on 13th October 1982. As usual he was very busy indeed but he kindly stopped to tell me something about himself and his work.

"I was born and brought up in North Wales and my father was a pharmacist with no connection with the sea at all but my two uncles owned a boatyard so I used to help out in the summer. One of them was a lobster fisherman who has, unfortunately, since died. I learnt quite a bit about boats from them and also used to sail from there. I then went to Art School to do industrial design at Leicester, which is as far from the sea as you probably can get, and was there for four years. It was a good course and gave me useful experience although there was nobody there to advise me on boats, except on a general level.

"Then I went to Yachts & Yachting as an editorial assistant. That was very good from the point of view of experience and making contacts and I also learnt about design. When I was there I designed Midnight Special, a quarter tonner and we went to Deauville for the Quarter Ton Cup. I do not know where we were placed when we finished but it was great fun even if we did not do very well. We had been third or fourth in the British trials before we went. I was with Edward Hyde and we shared the boat together.

"I left Yachts & Yachting after about three years and I decided about then that what I really wanted to do was to design boats. I felt in a way that as I was earning more money at Yachts & Yachting it was getting more and more difficult for me to leave. I left in the autumn of 1975 and then as I sailed in the Solent I moved to Bursledon where I lived for three years. While I was there I designed three boats: two mini tonners and one half-tonner but nothing very distinguished until Roller Coaster in 1978.

"She was designed in the spring of 1978 and built that winter, or at least the plug was, but Roller Coaster herself was built in a great rush in 1979. We had to bring her up to Lymington from Devon to complete because about three weeks before the British trials there was nothing in her – she was just a shell! The keel was on and that was all! We finished her with the help of Berthon and a great deal of effort by the crew, which included Simon Richards and Harvey Bagnall from Lymington.

"We worked through the night and had half an hour's rest from 2.0 a.m. to 2.30 a.m. We had to leave at 3.0 a.m. and floated down the river with the tide as there was no wind. All of us were very worried and wondered when we would get there and then a little breeze came up from the north and we reached up to Cowes. We had to find Revolution and drop a French girl off and had just turned round to get to the starting point when the gun went off. We had not been on the wind at all at that stage so we reached back down the Solent again to Hurst and round the Needles and again a reach to St. Catherines. It was at St. Catherines we first came on the wind and we won the Round the Island race, our first, by fifty minutes and won overall in the rest of the selection series.

"Then we went to Holland about two weeks after that for the Half Ton Cup. My son had not been well but I decided that there was not really an awful lot I could do at home but I did not sail on the boat in case I had to return to Lymington. We needed to be fourth and we came fifth. Still, that was a good result obviously and it brought more work.

"In the same year Gems had its first season and the previous autumn we had sailed the boat in the Autumn Series in Lymington and won our class and it won the production division of the micro class in France that year as well. She was built by Mike Parry at Sadlers Farm and they built about 75 boats altogether.

"That winter *Roller Coaster* was sold to a Greek and that was very important and led to other things. I had a phone call from this chap at about 11.0 p.m. very apologetic, saying that he had just arrived at Heathrow and could he possibly come down and see me. He arrived the following morning with another Greek and two English friends of his. He had been at Exeter University and spoke perfect English. We chatted in general terms about design and then, that very day, he decided to go down to Devon and buy *Roller Coaster* and take her back to Greece. There was also a half-tonner called *Harmony* who had two disappointing seasons but this year she has done very well.

"*Roller Coaster* did extremely well in Greece and won the Aegean Rally overall, the first time it had been won by a small boat and that year Mr. Alafouzos, the new owner, commissioned me to design another half-tonner to tune up for the Half Ton Cup in Greece this year (1982). I designed two boats, *Glafki III*, the Greek one, and *Scorpio* which is an English charter owned by Paul Gatrill and they both sailed in the Half-Ton Cup. *Glafki* was third and very nearly won it. Paul Elvström was pretty dominant really but *Glafki* was second on points in one race. They had a bad broach in the boat which was very unfortunate from my point of view as the sail virtually wound round and the only reason that she broached was that they were pushing their luck so hard. If it had been a bit hairy they would not have been doing that. Also one of the crew appeared to be badly injured although fortunately, in retrospect, he was all right and they were lying sixth at the time. They still carried on sailing and finished the race but came 19th. Had they finished sixth I think they would have won.

"Last winter I designed *Roller Skate* and *Countdown,* two three-quarter tonners and another half-tonner production boat for a Norwegian company which is not quite finished. In fact there were two: there was a half-tonner for a New Zealander this time last year. After *Harmony* I had a half-tonner built for a Hong Kong owner but she was built on the river and is sailing out to Hong Kong. *Roller Skate* in particular was very successful: *Countdown* was also successful really, but *Roller Skate* was RORC Class 4 and Solent Points Class 3 and *Scorpio* won her Solent Points class and *Glafki* won the Greek half-ton trials at the Aegean for the second time so it was three times generally overall.

"*Roller Skate* was built in Lymington; she was locally built by Neville Hutton and Steve Etheridge at Mount Pleasant, toward Sway, and *Countdown* was built in Calshot by David Blachford, who lives in Lymington. He is the younger brother of Tony Blachford, who works for North Sails and lives a few doors away from me here in Curzon Place. Unfortunately, David had rather a rush on and he was not able to do as good a job as he would have wished but both the ratings have been satisfactory: *Roller Skate* in particular. *Countdown* was really launched before she was properly finished and had lots of teething problems. Unfortunately, there is usually a mistake and it is always far more difficult to finish a boat in the water. It never is really finished and that is the truth of it!

"I have visited Greece a lot really; I have been there six times this year, partly because Alafouzos is in shipping and it is easier for him to send me out there and I fly out for a few days. I have got to go to Norway fairly soon and I would like to go to the SORC series this winter. At present I am designing a boat for the Admiral's Cup in 1983, some more three-quarter tonners and also a half-tonner being built in Scotland as a production boat. I also have a 36 footer to design for another Greek and the same design for a Spaniard. The problem is getting it all done and going away.

"If I was actually working on one boat solidly I would probably do the design work in about five or six weeks but it tends to be spread out and you usually find you work on different boats at different times. Obviously, for the lines plan I have really to crash through; you need the continuity but what generally happens is that an owner usually takes quite a bit of time to make up his mind whether to commission you or someone else. Once he has decided, he wants to start building straight away and you are left with very little time to complete the lines plan. Usually there is a bit of a contest but most of the designers are my best friends and yet you find you are in competition with them. All the same it is very amicable and we still get on; it is a *c'est la vie* thing: sometimes you win and sometimes you lose! What I tend to do sometimes when an owner decides to go ahead is to design the deck first and then they can start building and it gives me more time to work on the other lines. I take the lines to a fairly advanced stage so I know what the deck outline is going to be and I can work for longer optimising the other shapes. You tend to follow the other drawings and hope that you keep ahead of the builder.

"I always follow through after a boat has been sold to give the best sell that I can and, rightly or wrongly, I do not make a charge and treat it as part of the original design. I have also done many other ratings as a consultant. Last year I was on the Admiral's Cup Selection Committee, which was interesting and from the designer's point of view it was fascinating as you could see things from the other side of the fence. I have also been on the committee of the British Level Rating and my term is up next year.

"I have done quite a bit of writing but it has become progressively less as I am finding it difficult to find things to write about and it is not easy to write about oneself!"

Rob Humphreys has converted a double garage into his drawing office and there was just space for two drawing boards. He had a young assistant attached to him from college and he was contemplating whether he would take a partner. In the corner was an Apple computer which works off his television screen. But his 'brain child,' Tacticalc, is better described by Malcolm McKeag in *Yachts & Yachting* of 16th July 1982.

"He (Rob Humphreys) developed the idea from his own use of a computer for his design work and, indeed, for solving other problems (As an Admiral's Cup selector last year he somewhat surprised and delighted his colleagues by taking his computer afloat and using it to produce not just corrected time positions at each mark in each race, but relative performance evaluations on each leg of the race and on each point of sailing for all the trialists, showing which yachts did best on which point of sailing). Using the computer to evaluate actual sailing performance, led Humphreys to develop a programme which could be used on board while racing and which would enhance his service to his design clients, giving them a tool by which they could get the best of the design they had bought from him and it was in this way that Tacticalc came into being: only when the idea was a reality did Humphreys and his collaborator, John Fulker, decide to make it generally available . . ."

Yachting World of November 1982, completes the account. "Both programmes Tacticalc 1 (T1) and its big brother, Tacticalc 2 (T2), come with the hardware necessary to run them, namely the Sharp PC - 1211 pocket computer for T1 and its bigger relative, the PC - 1500 for T2. The computers also have the advantage that either the programme can be downloaded (computer slang for 'stored') on cassette tape so that they can be used for other functions. At about £100 and £300 they are a relatively cheap addition to the permissible electronic paraphernalia of the modern performance boat; indeed, *Yeoman XXIII* used one in the Sardinia Cup."

All this is a far cry from the more leisurely days of Jack Laurent Giles and it seems unbelievable that any one designer can undertake such a workload and under such constant pressure too.

A. K. Balfour (Naval Architects) Ltd.

When I had visited Graham Butler there was a line drawing of his new fishing boat, being designed by Sandy Balfour, in his sitting room and so I went to see him at his home in Brockenhurst on 1st October 1982 to find out more about his work.

"I came down from Scotland after the war," he told me, "and came straight to Lymington in 1947. At that time I had been in Harland & Wolf in Glasgow and was an outside Manager there and, as I was interested in yachts, I decided to come down here.

"I became Manager at Berthon back in the days when 'H.G.' was there: he was the grandfather of David May. David was just a small boy, about 11, then. In the period 1947 to 1950 the yard built wooden boats and quite a few of them were the Gauntlet Class, which was a favourite boat in Lymington.

"I designed my first boat for Berthon in 1949, a yacht called *Northerly*. She was 52' 6" and by pure coincidence in 1960, when I was invited back again to Berthon to be a co-director by David May, a Glasgow man saw this *Northerly* on the Clyde, liked it and wanted a similar boat for himself. So I brought the order down with me! Today in the yard there would probably be about 50 men working but from 1960 to 1970 we employed as many as 100.

"My boys joined the Salterns Sailing Club around 1972 and they were sailing Moths there. It was a wonderful place for children to learn to sail. I do not think people realised how much Major Hibbert did for them. They have gone off on their own now but they still do a bit of sailing whenever they get the opportunity. I had a boat up to about two years ago and was a cruising man.

"I designed a boat we built at Berthon called *Dodo IV* in 1961 and we sailed her up to the Clyde for her owner, the Chairman of Teacher's whisky. Another fairly large boat of mine, a 60 ft. ketch, was built for a Canadian called George McKee and I sailed her round to the Med where he was going to pick her up in Greece. She was a beautiful boat. David May has to keep up with racing boats and he is in the fortunate position that he can have a new boat and sell the old one nearly every year. You could not alter a wooden boat and the Rules were not so involved in my time. There are very few pretty little boats nowadays.

"Graham Butler approached me to see if I would design him a fishing boat which I am just in the course of doing. He hopes to start building it before the end of the year (1982). I think he is probably one of the more successful fishermen. He is going to employ his own labour to build it; there are plenty of local shipwrights about who are working on their own.

"In the marina they are putting up a new building. They are going to dismantle one of the old stores to provide more room for winter lay-up and the new stores will be beneath the offices; one of them will be David May's new office and the brokerage will move there too. My daughter works in the Berthon brokerage.

"We started up our own firm of A. K. Balfour (Naval Architects) Ltd. five years ago and a co-director, Charlie Rossiter, was with me at Lloyds. I was with Lloyds for 17 years and ended up as Senior Surveyor in charge of planning programmes in Southampton. Charlie Rossiter is a lot younger than I am and his father is a yacht builder in Christchurch. Now Charlie is running his father's yard and I give him work as and when available. The other director is an old friend of mine who has got a house in Brockenhurst, Hamish Roberts. He is a Master Mariner and a Fellow of the Institute of Arbitrators and he is also a barrister. So they are useful people to have for advice – they can help me a great deal. It is a big advantage knowing people who are in the trade.

"I do most of the surveying in Lymington but there are others. I know Alastair Easton, Hugh Marriott and Peter Barrett. There are one or two smaller, young brokers like Dennis Law. He has got an office in Waterloo Road and then another who has started up quite recently and is most progressive is Ian Driver at Sway but he does brokerage only on motor yachts.

"I carry out condition surveys for purchasers. I am doing one now; the boat is 10 years old and the owner thinks it time that I had a look at it. I do the supervision of new construction, the supervision of repair work, as well as the design work. It is mostly for sales. One other job we had quite recently was as consultants on the breaking up of the *Ark Royal*. Now we are working on a project for a floating restaurant for Ford Park. It is an authentic replica of the Mississippi River boat. I get quite a lot of variety and these are the things which really give you a tremendous interest."

Colin Mudie

I spent a very pleasant afternoon with Colin and Rosemary Mudie when I visited them at their home, Bywater Lodge on 15th November 1982.

Colin Mudie was born in Edinburgh in 1927 but was partly educated in England and came to Hampshire to become a design apprentice at the British Power Boat Company at Hythe. After the war, when it started packing up, he went to work for Laurent Giles and Partners in Lymington for about five years until 1956.

His first impact on the yachting scene was with *Sopranino*. "I would not put myself down as her designer even in the humblest manner," he told me, "but I did do the drawings." *Sopranino* has been described as "a big decked over canoe with a fin keel which had a big blob of lead on it just like a model yacht," by Humphrey Barton, who sailed her for a short time in the Lymington River and considered that she was not the sort of boat he would like to take out in the Solent on a windy day! Yet her owner, Patrick Ellam and Colin Mudie crossed the Atlantic from east to west in her, the most remarkable voyage across the Atlantic ever made using the Southern Trade Wind route (Humphrey Barton again). *Sopranino* sailed from Falmouth on 6th September 1951 and had many strange adventures before the actual crossing of 2,670 miles in 28½ days from Casablanca to Carlisle Bay in the States. The voyage was described in *Atlantic Adventurers* by Humphrey Barton as "a cruise in an ultra modern boat, brilliantly executed by two highly intelligent and experienced yachtsmen." Furthermore, which would please the older members of the Royal Lymington Yacht Club, "they sailed into Carlisle Bay immaculately dressed in their best whites and yachting caps looking as if they were coming ashore from a 200-ton yacht!"

Colin told me that he had learnt cut away drawing illustrations from the great Max Miller, the inventor of them and one of his heroes. He then worked for Iliffes which, *inter alia,* published *Yachting World* and also with Uffa Fox, helping him design his boat *Flying Fifties*. Rosemary recalled how amazed Iliffes were when he wanted to leave – and give up his pension! He then worked for Robert Carr, the principal designer of *Carthia*, his first job on his own.

Colin and Rosemary then set up their own independent yacht design firm, first in Westminster and, since 1968, in their home in Bywater Lodge in Lymington. On Uffa Fox's principle that no one makes a living in yacht design, they planned to support themselves in the early years by other work: writing and public relations by Rosemary and writing and illustrating by Colin.

Colin was asked to design a gondola for a hydrogen balloon which was going to make an Atlantic crossing. "I suppose we have always had an interest in the sheer jolliness of ballooning," said Colin, "but in the end it is a straight-forward design job the same as any other." In 1958 Colin and Rosemary and Arnold Eiloart and his son, Timothy, set off for an air/sea crossing from Tenerife to

Barbados in the *Small World.* Humphrey Barton again described their voyage in his book *Atlantic Adventures.* "After four days aloft when they were 1,200 miles on their way to the West Indies they were forced to release the balloon and drop onto the water. The remaining 1,500 miles was successfully completed in 20 days. They arrived in Barbados on 5th January 1959 after being towed across the reef by a fishing boat." This record held for the next eighteen years. *Small World,* incidentally, was the first British plastic foam boat.

In 1968, the year he moved to Lymington, Colin was awarded a Winston Churchill Fellowship in order to investigate certain aspects of yacht design, construction and, in particular, computer application in the States. "I took a great portable pendulum with me and dangled it on all sorts of boats to prove something in which I was interested," he remarked, "and also covered 13,000 miles doing this."

It was his designs for exploration and expedition boats that I found the most interesting. These included *Rehu Moana,* a 40 ft. catamaran for Dr. David Lewis, the first multihull to circumnavigate the world (1967-68). For Tim Severin he designed *Brendan,* a 36 ft. leather boat replica of the 6th century curragh in which he followed the believed route taken across the Atlantic by St. Brendan.

He later designed *Sohar,* an 87 ft. replica of a mediaeval Arab dhow in which Tim Severin followed the route of the legendary Sinbad the Sailor from Oman to China in 1980/81. Tim Severin had been put in touch with them by the Royal Geographical Society and by Mike Ritchie of the Royal Institute of Navigation. Colin regarded archaeological boats "as an extension of our normal trade. There are the same sort of problems. You first of all establish parameters and then draw lines round them. It is a straight forward jobbing problem that a jobbing boat designer can do anyway."

Another very interesting boat was *Acali,* a 40 ft. transatlantic research craft for the Mexican anthropologist, Dr. Santiago Genoves. Eleven volunteers (6 male and 5 female) of different nationalities, religion and races had made a slow voyage across the Atlantic in 1973 to study interpersonal relationships as affected by family patterns of behaviour, attitudes to sex, race, racism and verbal and nonverbal communication. His second transatlantic voyage was to be the very converse, a single-handed one in conditions as remote from the world as possible and his idea was to have a completely underwater glass cabin, so they designed him one. "We were frightened of him getting isolation madness," said Colin, "and we arranged with Nassau to have a forty-eight hour satellite communication check." The outcome was very sad as the boat was dropped from a lifting crane in the African departure port and completely smashed.

"It had some practical points about it in that it had an outboard motor which could drive him out of the way of other vessels. We tried the model out at the mouth of the Lymington River because the speed was terribly important – it had to be 1¾ knots at an average speed in certain wind conditions and we ran our model with an 'Action Man' to give it scale! The reactions of people coming up the river were quite fantastic and ranged from 'Get your toys out of the fairway' to 'How interesting – what is it?'"

Then they showed me a photograph of Dr. Genoves' boat and I could see why people may have thought it a little strange. It consisted of slatted boards which could be removed so that you could adjust wind speed by the number of boards you had up. It was self-directional because of the shape of the tripod and it was self-righting because there was a float on the top and this great buoyancy ring round it. "The Royal Cruising Club chaps had the most sympathetic approach and a much more sane one; it was the racing element who felt the model was an affront! It was very useful having a test tank close to hand!"

Colin Mudie has designed a wide range of craft, both power and sail, for pleasure and commercial use, and some which came from his drawing board included *Royalist,* a 76 ft. sail training brig for the Sea Cadet Corps, winner of the Lloyds Award for best design and construction in 1971 and winner of the Tall Ships Race to Lisbon in 1982. Her sister ship, *Varuna,* was built in Bombay in 1979 for the Indian Sea Cadet Corps. *Avila,* a 62 ft. sports fishing motor yacht for HM King Baudouin of the Belgians, was another, to name just a few. His Shetland range of power boats from 15 – 25 ft. won the Queen's Award for Export Achievement in 1978. His Dabbler Dinghies, a range of general purpose dinghies, were the first British vacuum formed dinghies (originally called Durafloat).

The boat which arouses the most interest today, not only in this country but in Holland, Norway, Germany, Sweden, South Africa and Australia, is the *Lord Nelson,* which Colin designed for the Jubilee Sailing Trust. The imaginative idea of a sailing barque for a disabled crew came from Christopher Rudd, a teacher and sailing instructor in Sussex. He envisaged an Offshore sailing vessel to be partly manned by physically-handicapped people, irrespective of their disability, sharing with half an able-bodied crew. A Trust was set up in 1977, Jubilee Year as its name implies, with Sir Max Aitken as President and with Vice-Presidents

By courtesy of Colin Mudie

T.S. *Royalist* – Designed by Colin Mudie, FRINA for the Sea Cadet Corps

including Sir Douglas Bader, Norman Croucher, the mountaineer, and four Round the World yachtsmen, Dame Naomi James, Clare Francis, Robin Knox-Johnston and Sir Alec Rose.

It sounded a fascinating venture and a real challenge to Colin's designing skill, since special aids were needed to help those in wheelchairs, not only to get about the decks but also up the mast, as well as visual signals for the dead and audio compasses for the partly blinded. In addition to permanent officers, including a doctor, there would be accommodation for 30 trainee crew, half of which would be disabled and varying in age from teenagers to geriatrics. The 135 ft. barque, nearly twice the size of *Royalist*, which has participated in some of the preliminary trials, is capable of cruising at 10 knots and carries a maximum of 10,000 ft. of sail.

"Disabled people taken to sea on trials have visibly improved whatever the criteria used," said Colin, "although obviously very marginally in the people who are very badly damaged. Nevertheless, it has extended their scope beyond their original terms of reference to include those who are mentally-handicapped, in the sense of brain damage rather than congenitally mentally-handicapped, but even there the options are open. People formerly unable to communicate have now communicated that they want to go to sea again and, quite extraordinarily, so do the able-bodied crew, some of whom may perhaps have been slightly reluctantly drawn into it in the first place. It is very odd the way people's attitudes do change, once they get a little practical experience."

In 1982 three events occurred that definitely overshadowed fund-raising as far as the *Lord Nelson* was concerned and they were the Penlee lifeboat disaster, the Falklands War and subsequent South Atlantic Fund and the raising of the *Mary Rose*. So although a moderate amount of fund-raising has gone on, it was not the large amount that was needed. "But it is really starting to move again now," said Rosemary, "and we keep saying it is a modest sum, two million compared with all the other millions but it is difficult to raise when people are committed to more immediate causes. Enthusiasm for the project increases all the time and the more people get involved in it the more they say how it is so worthwhile." They aim to set up a regional fund-raising scheme and soon hope to announce that the keel will be laid. In the meantime they are planning further equipment trials on *Royalist*. Colin made a model of *Lord Nelson* which was on display at the Boat Show and also made one of the *Mary Rose*, which was exhibited as part of the raising ceremony at Netley.

It is worth digressing here to remind ourselves that A. Kavanagh, a remarkable Irishman who was born without arms or legs (before Thalidomide had even been heard of), married and produced a perfectly normal family. He could read, write and shave himself and became Member of Parliament and Sheriff for Co. Carlow. He was a keen shot, mostly duck, and could drive a four-in-hand using two stumps and his mouth and, most important of all to us, he also went out sailing from Lymington. His yacht *Eva*, a schooner of 40 tons, was built for him by Inmans. Mr. Harper, the Harbour Master at Lymington, was his personal attendant and had a testimonial written and signed by Kavanagh and he could personally vouch for Kavanagh's capabilities.

THE HARBOUR-MASTER. LYMINGTON.

ROBERT I GROVES.

Colin Mudie is a Fellow of the Royal Institution of Naval Architects and Chairman of RINA Small Craft Group and is also a Fellow of the Royal Institute of Navigation. He is a Past President of the Yacht Brokers, Designers and Surveyors Association and a member of the *Mary Rose* Recovery Committee and the Steering Committee of the Southampton College of Higher Education, Yacht and Boat Design Course and many other committees. He is also a chartered engineer.

He is particularly interested in the Yacht and Design Course at the College of Higher Education as he was pretty well in at the start. "It is a very good course and I am very keen on it and I promote it all I can: it is doing a marvellous job. It is the first course that yacht designers have ever invented that is worth a damn.

"People are not prepared to take apprentices nowadays," he continued. "one of the reasons we do not have draughtsmen any more is that you spend such a long time teaching them and a lot of time out of the individual day. Then they want to go off on their own, particularly in this line of business, so we find we take specialist consultants when we need them rather than have four or five draughtsmen. One thing the Southampton course is doing which is exceptionally valuable is that it is producing a knowledgeable climate about boats for once. It has all been mystique and so forth up to now, whereas it is a very straight forward engineering situation. We have got 15 chaps in this country every year joining the trade and if one becomes a yacht designer, very good, and if the other fourteen criticise him, it is even better! They will go into other parts of the trade, into building, surveying and that sort of thing, where it is very useful to have people who do know what they are talking about in a professional manner.

"Apprentices are becoming increasingly less useful because the work for them to do is nil. So many of the tasks you once gave to an apprentice to keep him occupied, as well as to make him earn, no longer exist. They have been put out by computing, for one thing, and you do not need someone to sit and make calculations which the machine will do for you. What you need is somebody who knows when they get the answer whether it looks right or not, or whether there has been a misfeed somewhere, and you cannot leave that to an apprentice. People are coming into the trade at a far higher level of awareness, that is the thing. They come in with the right bag of tools to do their job and then it is up to them."

Colin has written some extremely good books, such as *Motor Boats and Boating,* now in paperback and illustrated by Roy Coombs. "His illustrations were just right for the book," said Colin, "charming, cheerful illustrations for a cheap and cheerful book! We supplied every reference for him and checked all the drawings so in effect it was a very good combination because his particular style, which he does so well, particularly in colour, worked out excellently. Living and working in his studio at home in Lymington, Roy could just go down the river and see for himself the type of craft he was to illustrate."

Colin has also written *Power Boats* and, of course, *Sopranino* (with Patrick Ellam) and two with Rosemary, *The Story of the Sailing Ship* and *Power Yachts.* In addition he has been Editor of *Yachting World Annual* and illustrator of the *Yacting World Handbook,* and has contributed many articles and illustrated many of them in various books and journals in the UK and overseas.

In the immortal words of Eamonn Andrews, I feel I should say, "Colin Mudie, yacht designer, engineer, yachtsman, editor, illustrator, author, model-maker, yacht expedition and exploration boat designer, pioneer in sailing for the disabled, balloonist and multi-committee member and Fellow – This is your life!"

THE CLUBS

"I believe that in the absence of war or National Service the community has a responsibility to channel the aggressiveness and exuberance of youth into sporting activities. Sailing is but one of many such activities, but one which brings out the best qualities, and one which is particularly suitable for this locality.

J. A. HIBBERT

Pre-Lymington Club Sailing

We have already covered the racing days of the Weld family in their famous Lymington-built yachts, *Lulworth, Alarm* and *Arrow* but almost unbelievably we can now go back there in time again and follow the fortunes of George 'Monsey' Bran, fisherman, yacht-hand, smuggler and publican and surely one of Lymington's most famous and fascinating characters.

An article in a local paper, dated 20th June 1951, to celebrate his 92nd birthday confirms that his physical and mental faculties were hardly impaired by advancing years and he can still spin a fine yarn about ships of years ago, smuggling and the changes which have taken place in Lymington since he was a boy.

"Since 1873, at the age of 14, 'Monsey' Bran has followed the sea. He first sailed in the 10-tonner *Pauline* and at 17 sailed a 20-ton racing yacht from the Solent to Naples for an Italian prince. Another of his ships was the 300-ton *Australia.* While racing her round the Isle of Wight they encountered bad weather off St. Catherine's." Jack Blachford, his grandson, now takes up the story as he heard it first-hand from his grandfather.

"She was a big schooner: I have a feeling that she was a three-masted schooner, and when they had set headsails they always needed men out on the bowsprit. On this particular day there were three local men out on it, Inman, Shutler and Springer. They were just off St. Catherine's when a big wave washed them off but fortunately it sort of curled round and washed them all back on board again at the aft end of the boat. There were no life-jackets in those days and they were dead lucky!

"There was another yacht he was on, I don't think it was the *Australia* and I cannot remember the name of her now, but she used to 'work a lot,' which means that the deck planking when she was really going would open up. My grandfather told me that when you were sitting on the weather side of the boat and they were beating along, the seams opened

up a bit and your trousers could get nipped in the crack. Then if they went about a bit quick and you were not ready for it you would find you could not get up as your trousers were pinched in the deck planking. So on the next tack when you were down to leeward and probably the waves were coming along the deck you nearly got drowned! Boats were boats in those days and if they did not 'work' they reckoned they were no good." 'Monsey' then shipped for ten years aboard *Shark,* the Duke of Rutland's yacht.

The next time that we read about him was when he went sailing on 17th June 1951, on his 92nd birthday, with three following generations of his family and, refusing the aid of anyone – in fact, he would have been most annoyed if assistance had been offered – he handled the 20 ft. *Dunlin* up and down Lymington River in blustery weather with the touch and skill acquired through a lifetime of experience at sea. With him in the boat were his son-in-law, J. C. Blachford, a daughter, a grandson, Gerald Blachford, aged 5, and 2-year old Tony Blachford, his two great-grandsons. The boat he was sailing was built by his son-in-law and grandson. A hairdresser by occupation, J. C. Blachford and the members of his family share 'Monsey's' love of the sea. J. C. Blachford is a very skilled boat builder, being the originator of the Oxey Birds which find so much popularity with yachtsmen on the Solent.

Oxey Lake Sailing Club

Jack Blachford continued his stories about his family. "When I was a boy, Captain Nicholson was living at Creek Cottage and he started the sailing club in Oxey Lake, the Oxey Lake Sailing Club, and all the boats that sailed there were known as Oxey Birds. The club burgee was an Oxey Bird painted on a white flag. The first lot of boats were just odd dinghies and boats that had been altered so that they could sail and some of them went and some did not! Eventually some of the chaps started building their own and my father thought that he would have a go and get a bit of help from one of the local boat builders. He must have had good ideas and his boats were so successful and the prototype was so good that twenty years later, when they started the Lymington Town Sailing Club, they used it as the basis of their club boat. I used to help my father build them and I think we built about ten or twelve of them. We did a lot of boat building – or used to. Then my brother and I used to sail the Oxey Birds and he was very good. He had a boat called *Mermaid* and I think she won every cup that she competed for two or three times over. He was brilliant."

Jack Blachford showed me photographs from his mother's old albums of some of the boats they used to sail in the Oxey Lake Sailing Club, including the one that he and his brother first raced in when Ted was aged 8 and he was 10 years old. "She was just a 14 ft. dinghy and father put a centre-board in and the old grandfather was then around 80 and my father used to let him sail his boat first. Then my cousin, Bill Smith, who has a yard down on the Quay (his mother was a Bran too) used to crew with my grandfather in his Oxey Bird. The following year he wanted to sail it himself which left the old grandfather high and dry. So my father thought that we could not do that to him because he would be broken-hearted, so he suggested to him that he should take the two young ones out and teach them to sail. We used to keep the boat in Maiden Dock on Oxey because it leaked so badly that it would not stay afloat any more! So from the time we started to race I had a great big saucepan and I would be down in the bilge shovelling the water out."

Herbert Rand now takes up the tale. "Before the war there was a fair amount of dinghy sailing done both by Scouts in 14 ft. dinghies and Rovers in 17 ft. whalers and a small class racing mostly for 14 ft. dinghies at Oxey. Some of these were modelled on 14 ft. Nationals and the early ones were built by Jack Blachford and his father and 'Monsey' Bran. The Oxey Lake Sailing Club closed down in 1935 or 1936 when the Hurst Castle Sailing Club was formed. Several boy scouts, who pre-war had sailed in the whalers and dinghies, got married and could not take their wives out in the Scout boats any longer, so they decided that they had better get boats of their own. So for this reason they decided to form a sailing club.

Lymington Town Sailing Club

"A public meeting was called in 1946 at the Town Hall," continued Herbert Rand, "and Major Martineau, who had been, pre-war, the Leader of the Rover Scouts and was a Vice-Commodore of the Royal Lymington Yacht Club, took the chair and there were about a hundred people present. The idea of forming a new sailing club came about because it was thought that there was room for a club for people who were shipwrights, builders and shopkeepers who might not wish to join the Royal or possibly they could not anyway! So an artisans club came to mind and Stan Lamb, who, I think, was the only Labour councillor that Lymington ever had, was chairman of the Rover committee at the time and he thought it would be a good idea to try and get the use of the old Baths.

"There was considerable discussion on the name of the club. There had been a Lymington Sailing Club before the war, where the Slipway Restaurant is now on the Quay, and this was 90% a drinking club and not much else, so to be different from both that and the Royal, we decided we would call it the Lymington Town Sailing Club and we embodied the ship of the town seal in our burgee."

Bill Martineau was elected 'Captain' and Herbert Rand was elected 'Mate'. The ranks of Captain and Mate were taken from the Oxey Lake Sailing Club. Seventy members joined in the first year and five years later there were between 250 and 300 members. After two years the Club decided to fall into line with most other sailing clubs and appointed Flag Officers. Herbert Rand became Commodore, Alan Figgures was Vice-Commodore and P. Blachford was Rear-Commodore. Stan Lamb, who had been Chairman of the River Committee, became Club Secretary.

"The suggestion of using the Bath House was approved by the Council, thanks to Stan Lamb," continued Herbert Rand. "It had been used as a coastguard observation post during the war and it was very neglected with very low rooms and there were two rooms without fires in them. Anyway we got access to the top room for £5 a year!

"Bath House was built in 1835 and it had plunge baths out at the back and two old tiled baths in the wings of the building. There was a mysterious old Colonel, who was said to have drowned in the plunge baths, and he had been heard coming up the stairs and going through a door, which never moved, but he has never been seen! Later the plunge baths were pumped out and this also drained a pond in the garden of the Mayflower Hotel.

"A great deal of work needed to be done in the Club and more and more rooms were cleared. The floors were put in by the Club members themselves and the Rovers helped. (Incidentally, after the war, Robert Hole wanted me to become Group Scout Master but I was involved in the Club and wanted to build that up.) We managed to buy 30 old planks for £30 from an 80-year-old barge, which was being broken up at the Quay, provided we moved them by 3.0 p.m. that day – and we did. All these planks had wooden fastenings so the wood could be sawed in any direction; there were no metal castings in them at all.

"When the Club started we used to go to the Mayflower Hotel but later went to the Ship Inn. The landlord was Paddy Carruthers, the only man I know who had been a Colonel in one war and a Commander in another! Eighteen months after we were founded we applied for and obtained our own licence and Paddy presented us with a firkin. Mirrors were fitted in the bar to give a periscope effect which enabled members to look through a window four feet above their heads and see what was happening on the river."

Bill Martineau recalled that "We had some awfully good names in the Lymington Town Sailing Club when you think of chaps of the calibre of Herbert Rand and there were several who were top Rovers. Roger Pinckney played a major part in designing the Club, and I think, in those days, Ralph Montgomerie was in charge of the baths and he was one of our Rovers. He swam across to Yarmouth – I think he did it twice – which was quite an achievement. He worked the tides carefully and could not go wrong.

"I think they did a great deal of work themselves to save money and with capable people like Rand and Alan Figgures and Roger Pinckney behind them giving advice the Club soon took shape. They were naturally determined to keep the subscription level lower than the Royal Lymington – and did. We had very good people like John Humphreys, who got a very good award in the war. There was a 'JBB' who used to write up the notes in those months but who 'JBB' was I am not absolutely sure.

"After Sir Alec Rose sailed round the world in *Lively Lady* he was invited and was delighted to accept becoming an Honorary Member and we already had got Eric and Susan Hiscock. We also had Bill Tilman: he vanished with his entire crew but he did a lot of very stout sailing and was a fine and courageous engineer. I think we had Professor Finch as a member and he was very useful in giving his analysis on anti-fouling. He had a very great skill. Colonel Tobin, Secretary of the Central Asian Club and an Everest man, was a member too. The Creagh-Osbornes were members and supported the Club and so did Derek Pitt-Pitts. Adlard Coles, too, joined the Club. There were some wonderful names."

"Racing fixtures and social events soon got under way," resumed Herbert Rand, "and a barbecue organised by Alan Figgures became a tradition of the Club. We had a pretty good one this year (1982);

we had three birds and cooked one in front of the bar and accommodated about a 100 people. Another barbecue is held at Hurst, when a dinghy is burnt, reminiscent of the Vikings. There were also picnics at Alum Bay and Christchurch if the weather was good.

"When the Club started there were dinghies, some ex-fishing boats and three Rover Scout whalers, two from Lymington and one from Oxey. In 1948 we raced to Hamble and a keel boat came along as escort-cum-rescue boat. This was the beginning of the Hamble Scramble. I won the Hamble Scramble in 1955 both ways because nobody else finished and it was the only way I could win the race! Richard Creagh-Osborne did ring up *Daedalus* at Lee-on-Solent when we got back, as he was in the Fleet Air Arm then, and it recorded 38 steady, gusting to 52 mph that afternoon! So driving a 14 footer back to windward in a Force 8 – 10 was a bit of hard going. The race should not have started really but I had a wrong forecast from Calshot when I rang them up and they told me that a gale was forecast from 12 o'clock onwards that it was going to be in the south-east; it was not, it was south-west. South-east we could have reached on quite happily but south-west was a different story and it came on a bit earlier. Another boat nearly got home and was within 50 yards of the finish and another Oxey Bird, which was a bit ahead of me, went over just before the line. I was about a mile behind and everyone else had put in ashore at different places. Nobody was in trouble at all although one or two capsized."

Herbert Rand's yacht was No. 7 *Silver Spray*, and he painted her that colour with paint scrounged from the Navy when he bought her in March 1946. These Oxey class boats were built by Smith and Marshall at Rope Walk Boatyard. The first one built there was No. 12 which sailed round the Island in 10½ hours. Once they sailed to Newport Folly up the Medina River and slept overnight in their Oxeys. Returning to Lymington it blew very hard, about Force 7-8, and three girls, Olive, Moo and her sister Kathy, were awarded the Martineau Trophy.

"In the 1950s we first raced to Alderney and used to meet in the Rose and Crown there," said Herbert Rand. "Once someone passing us in a smart Huntress type motor-boat asked us, 'Which way to Alderney?' and were told 'Straight on!' The Lymington Town Sailing Club was the first club to race there and the inhabitants of Alderney were so proud of us that they presented us with a trophy which is raced for every year now. There used to be a cement factory down by the harbour which caused the boats to become covered with dust but it was pulled down."

Bill Martineau remembered that the "race to St.

Peter Port was one which was popular with both Clubs and at times it was considered a risky race but I can't think why because you could see the French coast (it was 60 miles across) long before you got any hazard risk which a boat should take according to what the tide was doing when you got there. That was the interesting part – to calculate what the Alderney Race would be doing as against the Casquettes entrance, and you had to protect your crew by making the rules very much on the safe side. There was a very risky bit of tide rip at the far sound of Alderney. When you made the approach the exciting part was that if you went through the Alderney passage with the ebb taking you through, you could see the Navy coming in from, say, the West Casquettes and you would be heading for this approach to St. Peter Port and it was a neck and neck race to see what the Army and the Navy could do. We had in *Saluki* a fast boat and she won quite a number of times. I presented a silver salver for the St. Peter Port Race."

"Roger Pinckney had always been a good friend of the Club," said Herbert Rand, "and it was appropriate that when the Solent Room was extended upstairs, five or six years ago, that he should have been the architect. There used to be a chimney up which the lift from the galley used to go to the Octagon Room, although it only had six sides, and sometimes people went in it as well! They used to clean the chimney by firing a rocket up it!"

The most recent event started by the Lymington Town Sailing Club was the Autumn Circuit two years ago (1980) which brought a lot of publicity to the Club. There were at least 100 starters and it ran for seven weekends. No other club had raced so late in the season before.

At the age of 72 Lionel Rose, Secretary to Lymington Town Sailing Club for the past ten years, decided it was time for him to retire. He had seen the membership of the Club grow from 500 to 1,400 during his time in office. The biggest landmark was the Solent Room.

In appreciation of all the good work he had done for the Club – he twice turned down requests for him to take on the post but "capitulated at a lifeboat social evening when the wine flowed a little too freely!" – he was made an Honorary Life Member and now looks forward to pursuing his favourite work of poetry. He has had several poems published in the past and two years ago he wrote a booklet of verse which was sold at the Club and raised £90 for the RNLI.

The Club is considering appointing a full-time secretary to meet the growing needs of the Club.

Royal Lymington Yacht Club

In 1972 on the fiftieth anniversary of the Royal Lymington Yacht Club an excellent booklet was written by authors who remain anonymous, but I am deeply indebted to them for some of the early history of the Club.

Captain H. H. Nicholson founded the Club in early 1914 to race Lymington Prams (later called Scows) and he was the owner of the very first one built by Dan Bran at a cost of £20. Weekly races were arranged for a season from 15th May to 15th August but it was never completed as on the 4th August World War One had broken out and the Lymington River Sailing Club closed down.

After the war, in the autumn of 1921, a member of the Royal Yacht Squadron, Major Cyril Potter, called a meeting of interested men and women at his home in what is now Ferry Point to discuss the suggestion that a sailing club should be formed and so it was that in the spring of 1922 the Lymington River Sailing Club had its second birth. Captain Nicholson, rather surprisingly not connected with its re-formation, then founded the Oxey Lake Sailing Club four years later.

The coastguards had for a long time maintained a boathouse and slipway at the end of Bath Road. The site was owned by the Lymington Town Council but in 1924 the lease was transferred to the Lymington River Sailing Club in April 1923. A limited company was then formed and in 1924 the Club bought the boathouse, slipways and site at a cost of £600. After many fund-raising events, several improvements had been carried out but in 1928 with 384 members the premises had to be enlarged and further extensions were done between 1935 and 1938. A flag staff and signal guns were provided for the Club.

In December 1925 the Admiralty Warrant was granted and in April 1926 the Lymington River Sailing Club changed its name to the Lymington Yacht Club. The Duke of Gloucester became Patron in December 1931 but a Royal Warrant was not granted until 3rd November 1938. This was nearly jeopardised by the Steward, Francis, preventing the Duke from landing on the slipway by saying, "You can't land here, sir, if you are not a member," to which came the speedy reply, "If I don't land here then this club will not become Royal!"

Next there was a good deal of discussion as to what type of ensign they should apply. Patrick Beesly recalls that his father, Gerald Beesly, was in favour of the defaced Red Ensign which we now have because it is the senior flag. An Admiral of the Red was senior to an Admiral of the Blue to an Admiral of the White and a squadron flew one of the ensigns depending on whether the Admiral was of the Red,

White or Blue. Gerald Beesly suggested that it would be more unusual and distinguished to have a defaced Red Ensign than to have a Blue Ensign like all the other Royal Clubs, so that is part of the reason why the RLYC has a defaced Red Ensign.

"The Club was very much more stand-offish and snobby then," Patrick Beesly told me. "The men wore white-topped yachting caps and nobody would have dreamed of coming into the Clubhouse without getting out of their sailing things and putting on a reefer jacket. If they had not been sailing in a collar or tie they jolly well had to put them on. The correct rig was white rubber-soled either canvas or doeskin shoes, and if you were running up to Cowes you wore white flannels. It was not a very practical proposition in small boats but certainly you went ashore in Cowes Week respectably dressed!"

In January 1924 Francis, a former Royal Marine, was appointed Steward and his duties included those of gunner and boatman. In those days, probably because most members were living in the near vicinity of the Club, all that could be obtained in the way of refreshment was afternoon tea, one of its special features. An ex-member recalls: "Alcoholic drinks could be obtained, but only with difficulty, from the Club steward, a splendid man, a veteran of Zeebrugge, who took his duties seriously, if slowly. A thirsty member would first have to locate the Steward (it was not *de rigeur* to ring for him); then having placed his order, there would be time for the member to nip across to the Mayflower for a preliminary snifter." There was no proper bar and you just got a drink in what is now the Reading Room, if you were lucky. The first bar after the war was downstairs but since then it has moved upstairs and is being extended yet again so that now, at one end of it, yachtsmen can come up in wet clothes! (*Pace*, the old members of the twenties!).

It was the Commodore, Major Cyril Potter, who introduced the West Solent Class in 1924 and its success was largely instrumental in the success of the Club. They were 6-ton sloops, designed by H. G. May and built at Berthon, and each boat had a paid 'skipper.' Mrs. Russell remembers how her parents-in-law owned a West Solent called *Dart.* "They shared a World War One ex-ML with, I think, somebody called Hampshire and they used to go round from port to port or regatta to regatta, live aboard and sail West Solents."

Gerald Beesly, father of the author Patrick Beesly, was a very keen yachtsman before the war. One of his friends was Admiral Cardon, who had been Commander-in-Chief of the Dardanelles in World War One, and another friend was Angela Brownlow, who became the first woman commodore of the RLYC.

"The first boat my father had was a rather nasty half-decker called a Solent Seabird, which he didn't keep very long and then he got an X boat called *XDecision,* which he raced for a couple of seasons. The X-Class was a good class even in those days. Then he bought a yawl called *Eve,* which he raced in a handicap class but although the handicapping may have been good, the racing was poor, as the class was so varied in size and performance. After that he got a West Solent called *Jade,* which he raced extremely successfully. In fact he was Cock Boat for a number of years until his doctors told him that he had to give up as he suffered from a gastric ulcer.

"Then he took to *Black Pearl.* She was a dockyard pinnace from Portsmouth, built by Phillips of Dartmouth in 1900 and, I think, there were about 35 or 36 when he bought her and he did a few little cruises in her up to the West Coast of Scotland and down to Torbay. Basically he could not get racing out of his blood, so he used to watch all the races and used to tow his friends, particularly those in the West Solent Class, up to Cowes and so on. There was racing very often, I think on four days a week.

"In those days the skippers used to sail the boats up single-handed either the night before the regatta or very early in the morning according to the tide. The owner would usually go by car. So that if they were racing off Hythe. when the regatta finished, the owner would come ashore and motor home to tea and the hand would take the boat on to Ryde or Cowes or wherever the next regatta was being held. The West Solents were very good boats," continued Patrick Beesly, "and one of the rules was that they had to carry a W.C. to prevent people stripping the boat down completely. In fact no-one had them shipped because the boat performed better if they were stowed in the fore peak or somewhere inaccessible. So there was a W.C. on board but nobody could use it! This new-fangled sanitary apparatus, called the 'Admiral,' was treated as rather a joke and the paid-hands used to greet the 'sissy' newcomers with significant gestures of the art of chain pulling!

"The Navy took *Black Pearl* and used her, I think, as a boarding launch and after the war, when my father was 75 or 76, he decided it was too big for him and too expensive to run, so he commissioned a smaller boat, *Mana of Poole.* She was based on the design of a Poole fishing boat with a fairly powerful diesel engine and my father continued using her right up until 1953. He died in February 1953 and was not quite 83 but he had been out in the boat almost every day, still with Harry Eales, who did all the work for him.

"Harry Eales stayed with my father all that time and he was a marvellous chap, very good tempered. My father was a very particular man and there was only one way of doing things and that was the right way. He was also rather hot-tempered, so if anything went wrong there was an absolute blast of anger which Eales, who became very fond of my father, put up with very well. Jobs were not easy to get in those days; most of the hands were just engaged for the season, even though the same hand was engaged next season. He would have to look after himself throughout the winter and they used to then go and work with the Berthon Boat Company or somewhere like that, often on a building site.

"Quite early on father arranged with Eales, I think by paying him a few bob less during the season, but he maintained the wage throughout the year, although he did not call on Eales' services during the winter, so he could go and get another job in the winter if he wanted to.

"Dan Bran was a marvellous boatbuilder and he could neither read nor write. My father got him to build the first 14 ft. Lymington Pram which was more or less taken off a boat owned by Captain Nicholson, who would sail round in her to do his shopping. This once made him late for the start of a Pram race at a regatta but his boat, full of parcels and, later, with a girl he had rescued when her boat capsized sitting on top of them, managed to overhaul the fleet of 20 and still come in first! My father was very struck with this boat and got Dan Bran to make one for my sister and myself. I was at Cambridge at the time and decided I wanted to do other things in the summer vacation so in the end it was given to Mrs. Brownlow for her daughter, Daphne. I think it was No. 1 or at any rate the first boat in the Pram class which because extremely popular. There were 35 or so of them in the late 1930s.

"They were very good boats for beginners and my father's idea was that most of the Club members were getting rather old and there must be something to introduce the younger generation to sailing and a large number of them did learn to sail in the Prams. They had only a single mainsail, no jib in those days, and they carried an awful lot of weather helm so they had their disadvantages, but they were almost impossible to capsize and were quite good little sea boats. You could sail across the Solent single-handed to Yarmouth or out to the Shingles. More of the Shingles was showing than is the case now and at low Spring tides, if it was a calm day, people would go out and picnic there but I have never seen that done since the war.

"It was quite an adventure in those days to race across to Yarmouth or sail to Yarmouth and race on the other side, and the danger was, of course, that if the wind dropped and the tide was ebbing you could go sluicing out to the Needles. However, my father used to stand by with *Black Pearl* and would tow about half a dozen of them home when the wind had failed and they had been rescued just in time."

Mrs. Russell told me something of the other great class, and in some ways the better boats, the Montagu Sharpies. "The X-Class was going strong and the West Solents was going strong," she said. "This was all pre-war and there was no handicap class as well and it was rather fun racing; people did not take it too seriously. The boats were named after the late Lord Montagu because a small number had been built for the Beaulieu River Sailing Club and were adopted as a class in 1938. Mr. Russell had a Montagu Sharpie called *Micawber*, so called because at that time he was busy sitting exams and it was 'always waiting for him to turn up.' In 1949, like the Pram, the class gave way to the Firefly.

"My parents-in-law had an old X-class *Ajax*, which up to four years ago was being revived. She was No. 22 way back and it is a very popular class which has gone from strength to strength. They all had 'X' in their name, such as *Excalibur*.

"My father-in-law had built *Lentune*, which was a Gauntlet. The reason for the Gauntlet name was because old Mr. May, David's grandfather, was challenged to build a boat by another yard and that was 'throwing down the gauntlet' for him. Two of the small Gauntlets were called *Foxglove* and *Mitten*."

On his retirement after thirteen years as the Founder Commodore, Major Cyril Potter in 1937 presented the Club with a beautiful silver wine coaster, fashioned as a model of a royal sailing galley. The trophy is awarded to the winner of a mixed race and is competed for annually. He also donated an endowment to provide prizes for three other classes.

Mrs. Russell went on to tell me that her father was at one time Secretary of the Yacht Club and when he retired they made him and her mother, Honorary Life Members. His name was Corbet. "We came down here," she said, "because he was rather good with horses and after he left the army at the end of World War One he was made remount officer for Hampshire and Isle of Wight. He had to see that these army horses were not starved in the Forest area or broken-winded on the slopes of the Island. We originally came from Shropshire, further north.

"My father, being a Secretary of the Yacht Club, had the unenviable job of starting the races from a dreadful launch. Fortunately, he had a cast-iron stomach, because it bobbed up and down so much and then they had to hold out great boards to show who was over the line. He had for some time put forward the idea of building a starting platform, and it was only finally taken up when he nearly sank without trace! The Club launch was out of action and the Russells had kindly loaned one of their launches and Jim Smith with it and when one of the starting guns went off the wad went through the bottom of the boat!"

After the war the Club Secretary was Captain Mostyn-Williams, MC, who was confined to a wheel-chair with polio and lived in Bath Road, facing the Recreation ground. He was an energetic 'new broom' in the post-war Club. "The days of white trousers and brass buttons have definitely gone," he said firmly.

When Commander Brown (Larry Brown) joined the Club in 1953, he found that they wanted a new pier for the dinghies and was told that there were some good pontoons being sold off by the Admiralty at the Boom Depot at Portsmouth. Fortunately, he had been shipmates during the war with Commander Stanwitz, who was then the Boom Defence Officer and was very pleased to help. They were refitting the Sowley Boom and so Larry asked if the Boom Defence Vessel would bring a pontoon every morning and drop it casually into the Solent and he would be there with a boat to pick it up. He was advised to write to the Admiralty at Bath and offer £2 each and so for £12 they got six enormous pontoons. His navigation was to come in very useful.

"One pontoon was dropped every morning out there and Doug Baverstock and I would go out in the launch (and Vernon Sainsbury would go out if I could not), and we would tow these things in from Sowley Boom and would aim at the beach and by the time the tide was right we just made the entrance to the harbour. So for £12 we had a new jetty which we then had to moor and we had a wonderful time mooring it.

"Vernon Sainsbury, Ted Barraclough, Doug and myself laid all the anchors and things out in the mud and went on working until the tide was right down. I was wearing waders and I went over the side and started sinking and had to shout for help and they slid a dinghy across the mud to me and caught me just before I disappeared! In those days the Club was so poor that we had to do it all.

"The posts that held up the verandah were lovely pitch-pine and Doug had a look at them and said, 'Just what we need for the deck of the Club launch but nobody will cut it up because there may be some nails in it.' However, Larry offered to do this on his circular saw and every time they came across a nail they had to change the saw blade, as it got blunted and had to be re-sharpened. Eventually they did get enough planks for the fore-deck of the Club boat!

"Doug Baverstock had been working at Adams' boatyard at Keyhaven as a shipwright and when they had to economise it was a question of last in, first out. So their loss was the Club's gain and Doug has been boatman here ever since. Frampton, his predecessor, then became a Mate on the ferries."

Larry Brown remembered the catering side of the Club in the 1950s. "Jane Creagh-Osborne was a Councillor and she used to organise the wives of members of the yacht club to do things. For instance, lunch used to be prepared by Miss Hayles and she would cook lunch for 12 people and you had to ring up early and book it. If you were the 13th you did not get any! When Miss Hayles was off sick, Jane Creagh-Osborne would get one of her 'Sink Officers' (as opposed to 'Flag Officers') and Doll went there one day and was asked to cook lunch and was just given a leg of lamb and some potatoes and left to get on with it!

"At one time we had a caterer called Freddie Borran and she complained about the state of the tables in the kitchen. No lunches were served at the weekends so I went down one Saturday with some sheets of formica, planed off the top of the tables and put the formica on and when she came in on Monday there were some 'nearly new' tables. Everybody at the Club used to pitch in and help."

Two of the 'Sink Officers' told me some amusing stories about the Club. In the Regatta celebrating 800 years from the Granting of the Charter to Lymington in 1950, there was a take-off of the Mayoral Party, which included Jane Creagh-Osborne who was Deputy Mayor. They went by on a raft and some joker pulled the bung out and it slowly sank. They were dignified to the last and then had to swim for it!

On another occasion there was a re-enactment of the French invasion of Lymington when they landed at the Quay and fought their way up to the Town Church. Boat loads of French sailors went by and the 'Women's Lib' of that day, not wishing to be left out, dressed up in period costume and followed them up river. However, some of the men turned the fire hoses on them when they reached Berthon which dampened their enthusiasm in more ways than one!

At one of the Club regattas, Major Hall and his Australian wife were stepping off his motor launch when was moored alongside the pontoon when she missed her footing and fell between the boat and the jetty. Her lovely hat floated slowly down the river. Undaunted she swam around to the far side of the boat, climbed on board, quickly changed into practically an identical outfit and came ashore again as if nothing had happened. It was a wonderful example of British – or Australian – *sang froid.*

The last story is about the time when the late Freddie Borran was cook/caterer at the Club. It was the Regatta Ball and in those days volunteers used to make simple food which was served as a buffet supper. On this particular occasion it was decided to bring the meal up to Hunt Ball standards and many were the lavish concoctions brought that evening. Two of the 'Sink Officers' noticed that some of the aspic jellies had gone 'off' and to save hurt feelings they crept to the end of the pontoon when the dancing was in full swing, and slipped them into the river. By the time they had drifted down to Dan Bran's shed unfortunately the tide turned and to their horror they saw these aspic jellies, just submerged beneath the surface of the water, slowly floating upstream again. It was at the supper interval and several of the young had gone out along the pontoons for a breath of fresh air. "What a lot of Portuguese man-o-war," remarked one young fellow, looking at the 'jelly fish' with considerable interest. "You do not expect to see them here!"

In the 1950s afternoon tea was still served at the Club and the Mayor and Mayoress had been invited to attend. There was a right of way through the Club forecourt and one elderly gentleman walked in and said that it was his right to do so. "Yes," replied the Club Secretary, George Edwards, "it is your right to walk through but not your right to sit down and have a cup of tea," so after walking up and down a few more times the 'right of way-er' finally gave it up and left!

The 1950s and 1960s saw the rise of several yachtsmen of outstanding ability who brought fame to Lymington and to the Royal Lymington Yacht Club in particular, putting her in the forefront of international racing. For a decade RLYC members such as Richard Creagh-Osborne, Derek Pitt-Pitts, Graham Mann, Adrian and Stuart Jardine and Michael Pocock represented their country at national and international championships including the Olympics at Naples and Tokyo. These were golden days indeed although by 1967 dinghy sailing was already on the decline due to congestion of the river. Pressing hard on their heels were the Rogers Twins and the Bagnall Twins who later moved on from dinghy racing to the 'big boys' in international offshore racing.

Finally, on 6th November 1982, I went over to the Royal Lymington Yacht Club and had a talk with Doug Baverstock on a quiet Sunday afternoon.

"I was born around Lymington and have always lived here. I went to the old Pennington School and after leaving at 14 I was fortunate enough to get a job even during the war when there was a shortage of work. I became a general apprentice, which means you have a go at pretty well every trade in the yard and finish up as a shipwright and boatbuilder. I was with Bob Cook at the Lymington Slipway: we were apprentices at the same time although he is a little younger than I am and he only joined the yard at the latter part of the war.

"I stayed there all during the war. The qualified shipwrights and boatbuilders were building clinker type boats like whalers, 27 ft. Montague whalers, 32 ft. motor cutters, 10 ft. tenders and dinghies and repairing, assisting to repair numerous small craft for the Navy, War Department and Air Force. It was great fun. Sometimes we got a few delivery runs for a change anywhere in the Solent which added a bit of interest to life. If you left this river you had to get the daily two-flag signal from Yarmouth because up at Sowley there were a boom laid right across the Solent. We went through two gates (two ships made a gate), got our flags and then went on up to the Eastern Solent or to the West. Civilian craft could not be at sea after the hours of darkness and they had patrol ships out there. The Solent was very heavily mined.

"We carried on when the war finished and started building yachts: one was the Lymington Slipway 5-tonner. We had done all sorts of jobs on that, such as mast making, making up the stem and stern framing and sometimes helping on the planking. You might even be in the loft making the decks. We did all sorts of little jobs as we did not have a fixed job at all. I carried on there until September 1951, when the company went into liquidation and that was the end of the Slipway.

"After that I moved off to Keyhaven and worked in the Keyhaven boatyard doing repairs for small yachts. There was more general work down there and we did everything, engineering, painting, fitting out and the general yard work. I did approximately five years down there. I was getting a little fed up with the routine when Captain Barraclough asked me if I would like to come and work at the Club and here I am after 25 years."

I asked Doug if he had talked with Princess Anne. "The first time I met Princess Anne," Doug told me, "was a couple of years ago when we were asked to keep a place reserved on the pontoon as the Royal barge would be putting in. We placed a reserve notice and many members asked why we had to keep this bit clear and we could not tell them or otherwise you would have had every boat on the river on it. So then I went and put on a clean jersey and came down and met Princess Anne outside: it was one of these unannounced visits. She was going on from here and meeting the Queen on the Royal yacht after some engagement she had just carried out.

"The next time we met her and were presented to her was when the Princess came to our Annual Dinner two years ago. She was a very pleasant person and very nice to talk to; she made you feel at ease immediately. In 1981 she came down and sailed in the Potter Ship and went in *Quiver*. It is good to see members of the Royal Family visiting the Club. She was informal then and wore a pair of washed jeans looking just like any other member. It was terrific.

"We do not have anything to do with the parcels for the Needles Relief; we steer well clear of that and they are carried by one of the RNLI boats! All we do is to take the launches over – it is quite a ritual each year. We take the big boat over on the previous Friday so that we do not get hung up by bad weather and at least we have got one boat there. We have done it for many years now and it is the same each year. We take the little boat over on the Saturday morning and one of the bigger boats tows us the best part of the way across the Solent and we go on and finish. All we do is to ferry the people from their yachts to the shore where they go and get the appropriate refreshment and then when they are refreshed we bring them back again. Sometimes they are a little bit noisier when we bring them back than when we took them off. Sometimes you could not think that they have any legs! We put them all back aboard their boats and we all have a merry day. It is a worthwhile day when you get lots of Club members together again with their boats all over in Yarmouth. It is great fun.

"The extended season makes the year go quicker. The average week you get Saturday and Sunday being busy and on the other three days one or other of us is on and we can do quite a lot of work. At one time you would stop at the end of September and it used to go dormant and you would lay everything up and you damn near forgot where everything was when you started up again on the 1st April! It was like wakening a garden up after there had been some snow on it. It was a wasted period too. All these boats are a very big investment and people want to get the most out of their investment and if they can sail nine months of the year or even ten months it is a better return for their investment.

"One highlight of the season is the barbecue wherever it is; sometimes it is on the beach at Hurst, sometimes on Mrs. Tew's beach or James McGill's. We always get involved in that, running people about in the launch except if it is at James McGill's place when it all done by motor-car. We still go and burn our fingers with sausages. This, the Potter Ship and the Needles Relief are all highlights and with the Regatta help you through the season and they are something to look forward to and it makes it all worthwhile.

"I have had 25 happy years here. I look round and often think, well, you might have been able to get a little more money but I would not have got the satisfaction from doing this job. You help a lot of people too. It has been a jolly good time working here and the Club has treated me well. It has always been first class. I had a bit of a spell when I was ill and they looked after me very well and saw that I did not return to work until I was really fit. I could not wish for better."

Salterns Sailing Club

In 1973 Major Hibbert wrote to the members of the Salterns Sailing Club and the Old Salts Association informing them that, regretfully, after sixteen very happy years in Lymington, he and his wife would be selling the Salterns. As some members did not know the whole story of the Salterns Sailing Club he thought that perhaps he should start at the beginning and this is where we join him.

"When I came here in 1957, the Salterns Lake was an expanse of evil smelling mud. With bulldozers and dragline I dug out the lake, built the islands, strengthened the banks and put in sluices. When the sluices were opened a shallow lake three feet deep was formed, and my own and some local children bought British Moth dinghies and started sailing. By 1960 we had six boats and we formed the Salterns Sailing Club.

"I bought an old cabin cruiser which we used as a Clubhouse and a caravan as a changing room. Over the next three years the membership expanded rapidly ... In 1963 the Clubhouse was bursting at the seams. Through the energetic and generous support of John Perkins and of his friends, the magnificent sum of £437.40 was raised. With this money and with many hundreds of hours of voluntary manual work by the members and their parents, and by the members of the Old Salts Association, we were able to build our present Clubhouse.

"This enabled us to expand our membership and from that day the Club, supported by the Old Salts, has stood on its own feet financially. The Club has never had any lease, nor has it ever had to pay any rent or charge for the land and water it uses."

The aims of the Club were to encourage and organise sailing and racing for helsmen between the ages of 4–16 and to give its members practical experience and responsibility in the organising, administration and financing of a club. An inaugural meeting was held at Major Hibbert's home, Salterns, Woodside at 5.30 p.m. on Saturday, 23rd April 1960.

St. George's Day, with its strong connections with youth, was a most auspicious founding day! Those present were Niall Robertson, Gerald Blachford, Christopher Hibbert and Carolyn Hibbert with Major Hibbert in attendance.

The following were invited to act as Club officers and Committee members: Commodore, Niall Robertson; Vice-Commodore, Michael MacMillan; Rear Commodore (Sailing), Gerald Blachford; Rear Commodore (Entertainments), Nigel Hallett; Secretary, Christopher Hibbert; Sailing Committee, Tony Blachford and Gavin Turcan; Finance Committee, David Soames and Ian Deighton; and Entertainment Committee, Clare Hallett and Carolyn Hibbert. The entrance fee was £1.00 and annual subscription of £1.00 and a dinghy park rental of £1.00 was also charged. It was also agreed that a limited number of visiting boats could use the Salterns and that 5/- per week per boat would be charged. Temporary members could be accepted at a subscription of 5/- per week. It was agreed that Walhampton School should be offered special membership terms in view of the large numbers involved and the fact that many of the members could use the facilities only in term time. A reduced subscription of 15/- per head per annum was recommended with no entry fee. Major Hibbert stated that he would approach 'J.B.' about this.

At the first Executive Meeting on Saturday, April 30th, 16 full members and 2 temporary members were elected. "Membership increased to 100 members and the number of boats to about 50. Due to a most successful appeal launched and organised by Mr. John Perkins, we were able to build a very substantial Clubhouse and this has now been followed by a new lavatory block.

"We have interested a lot of children in sailing and have taught them to sail, who otherwise might not have had the opportunity. We have given a lot of children a chance of helping to run a club, which will have taught them how a club is run, and the majority of retiring members have now become members of the adult sailing clubs in the area.

"We cannot expect all the members to become top racing helmsmen, but I think we can claim that, in relation to the size of our Club, we have had more than our fair share of success. Last year the S.S.C. President, Tony Blachford, won the UK National Championships of the International Moth Class, against very hot competition, and the S.S.C. Commodore won the Junior National Championship. During the same year Tony Blachford won just about every available schools trophy in a variety of classes up and down the country. In the last three years past and present members of the S.S.C. have represented Great Britain 15 times in European and World Championship events. . . ."

The Solent Moth Association (SMA) was formed as a parents' association to give technical and administrative advice and assistance to the Salterns Sailing Club. One of its original aims was also to promote the formation of British Moth Fleets in the Solent (For various reasons the aim proved not to be practicable.) Its main function was to act as an advisory body to the S.S.C. Executive Committee in such matters as obtaining plans and quotations for the Clubhouse and lavatory block, preparation of audited accounts, organisation of voluntary parent labour, etc. The S.M.C. has also helped to build no less than 30 British Moths for S.S.C. members, with a saving in cost of 20%. The present members of the S.M.A. are: Chairman, Alf Claridge; Secretary, Josie Davies; and Sandy Balfour, Ted Blachford, Jack Blachford, Tony Hibbert, Russell Linsell and Pat Webster.

The Old Salts Club was formed as a fund-raising organisation to raise finance for the development of the S.S.C. and also as a form of Supporters Club. It was felt that it would be in the interests of both to amalgamate and this they did, forming the Old Salts Association.

Membership was open to parents and relatives of members of the Salterns Sailing Club and to all persons who wished to support the Salterns Sailing Club. Members were known as 'Old Salts.' The Officers of the Club held the salty offices of 'The Skipper,' a 'Bosun,' two 'Bosun's Mates' and a 'Scribe and the owner of the Salterns was to hold *de jure* the rank of 'The Ancient Mariner' with a vote on the Council of Old Salts!

The Skipper's report to the Annual General Meeting of 24th November 1973 reported that to save the future of the S.S.C. an Action Committee was formed, under the chairmanship of R. D. Pretty, to explore the possibilities of assistance from the Borough Council, County Council and others to secure a permanent safe sailing area. The tremendous effort put in by the Action Committee and Major Hibbert was finally rewarded when His Worship the Mayor, Alderman W. Symons, negotiated with the County Council and the Salterns Estate was purchased by the County and the amenities secured for the town on 31st October 1973. The constitution was then amended to allow the Major of Lymington, and later, the Chairman of the New Forest District Council, to hold the *de jure* rank of 'The Ancient Mariner,' with a vote on the Council of the Old Salts.

Mr. A. C. Claridge was invited to present to Major Hibbert a watercolour of the eight acre lake by Stuart

Beck, which had been commissioned by the Old Salts Association and a table lamp from Match-makers to Mrs. Hibbert. In making the presentation Mr. Claridge spoke as a long-standing member and former Skipper of the O.S.A. and said nobody knew better than he did how much Major and Mrs. Hibbert had done to help to bring the Club to the position it is in today.

Major Hibbert said the occasion was not so sad as it might have been as he felt he could leave the Club in good hands. He paid tribute to the Officers and Committee members of the Club and finally asked the Mayor, as 'Ancient Mariner' to accept, on behalf of the Club, the remaining 18 years of a lease of the Four Acre Pond given by the Harbour Com-missioners and a cheque for £2,000 which the O.S.A. was to hold as Trustees for the Club. The Mayor said it was difficult to find words to thank Major and Mrs. Hibbert for passing on the Lease which the Council would honour and their farewell gift would enable the Club to make a capital expenditure when the time came.

At the Annual General Meeting of the Old Salts Association held in the Clubhouse on Thursday, 28th November 1974 at 8 p.m. the 'Skipper' (in the chair) was Mr. S. Power and the Town Mayor, Mr. W. Symons, 'Ancient Mariner', and Stella Cookman, 'Honorary Scribe', and Jean Halliday as 'Purser.' The latter replaced Mrs. Reddrop.

The Purser's report confirmed that the Salterns had been purchased by Hampshire County Council and Lymington Borough Council (now the New Forest District Council) and the acquisition of the lease by the Salterns Sailing Club. Many new members were welcomed and Mr. Chadwick, Pennington Junior School representative and 'Bosun's Mate,' took on special responsibility for the interests of Group members.

The Old Salts Association gave permission for deprived children from a camp run by Brockenhurst College students to be given a taste of sailing and rowing on two July evenings. S.S.C. Committee members took the children out in their Moths while Mr. Green manned and gave rides in the safety boat. Mrs. Halliday undertook the general arrangements for the evenings which were much enjoyed by all.

The BBC was given permission to use the facilities of the Salterns to film an episode for a Christmas film of the *Little Mermaid* by Hans Christian Andersen. This proved a profitable venture for the Club and also an interesting evening for those members who watched from the bank.

The Skipper outlined the many meetings with the County and New Forest District Councils which had taken place and the various conflicting interests of the Council and the Wild Life Conservancy scheme. In addition, following the O.S.A.'s pro-posals for expansion, possibly into a 17 acre field and Oxey Lake, the Royal Lymington Yacht Club and the Lymington Town Sailing Club made it known through Major Gossage of their interest in Oxey Lake due to the congestion on the river. Major Gossage had been pressing for a decision and had also been successful in securing pontoons for positioning in Oxey Lake for use as a starting point for racing.

On the suggestion of the Old Salts Association, Major Hibbert wrote a booklet giving all the basic information which a member would need during his membership of the Club. It contained the Salterns Sailing Club Rules and its By-Laws and also gave details of the sailing and seamanship tests devised for members of the Club so that they would only sail under conditions in which their ability and know-ledge had been tested. The tests were in four stages: Blue Pennant, Silver Pennant, Red Pennant and Gold Pennant. The Club organised voluntary tuition and coaching to help members pass these tests and also provided the examiners.

Perhaps it can all be summed up in the last paragraph of Major Hibbert's letter to the members of the Salterns Sailing Club and the members of the Old Salts Association: "Finally, a special word of congratulations to the Officers and Committee members of the Salterns Sailing Club, past and present – you have proved, over the years, that boys and girls in their early teens, and even younger, can accept the responsibility of running and administer-ing a club entirely on their own, often more efficiently than their elders. I have been proud of you. I have every confidence in leaving the Club in your capable hands. Good luck and good sailing."

Royal Ocean Racing Club

After World War One most English yachtsmen had never heard of an ocean race and were content to race round short courses in sheltered waters. But in 1924 a British yachtsman and writer called Weston Martyr had taken part in a New London – Bermuda race, organised in the States and was so thrilled with all the excitement that an ocean race can provide that he came back determined to introduce this new dimension in yacht racing.

With the help of leading yachtsmen of the time he announced a race from the Solent around the Fastnet Rock. The first ever Fastnet Race started off Ryde on 15th August 1925 with 14 entries. The Royal Victoria Yacht Club at Ryde handled the start and the Royal Western Yacht Club was responsible for the finish.

It was after this first British ocean race that the Ocean Racing Club was formed in the dining-room of the Royal Western Yacht Club with the object of racing the Fastnet annually. It received its Royal Warrant in 1931. Until the Ocean Racing Club was formed yachts had raced for large sums of prize money and most of the crews were paid hands. Now not only could owners no longer afford a large number of paid hands but there was a restriction on their number on each yacht. A new type of yachtsman was also emerging; the keen, adventurous, amateur young gentleman sailor. As the type of owner changed so too did the yachts themselves and a compromise was reached between the huge inshore racing yachts and the heavy displacement cruising yachts and this led to the new cruiser/racers that we know today.

At the same time the Club devised a system of measuring yachts afloat and arriving at an appropriate handicap by using a simple formula. This enabled yachts of different types to race together and was also to give a fillip to yacht design. Yachts were now being built to the Rule and a Technical Committee was formed to keep a watching brief on new design. The first Measurer was Major Malden Heckstall-Smith and he devised a new ocean-racing formula which was a compromise between the International Rule and the Sewanaka Racing Rule. He measured the very few yachts which at that time took part in the Club's races.

The purpose of the Technical Committee was to see that progress continued and that some brilliant new design is not prevented by the Rule from reaching its 'just rewards.' It is interesting to recall that a case in point was the Laurent Giles designed *Myth of Malham,* which was considered an 'outrage' when she first appeared on the racing scene after World War Two.

As ocean racing developed the number of yachts which were measured became much greater and more measurers had to be appointed and trained. Ray Barrett was Chief Measurer from 1945–1955, after Major Heckstall-Smith had to resign in 1955 due to ill health. Brigadier 'David' Fayle, a Royal Engineer, who had been sailing the RE Club boats for many years, offered to help the RORC and in 1957 did a great deal of work on analysing proposals for modification of the Rule of Measurement, the results of which upset previous Time Scales. He was called 'David' (his initials were L. R. E.) because apparently he could recite all the Psalms!

In 1957 a new modified Rule of Measurement and Rating was agreed and David Fayle worked out the ratings for many hundreds of yachts which had been measured to the old Rule. He then became Chief Measurer for the new Rule. The RORC Rule did not recognise it and continued to use the CCA Rule. As more and more British yachts crossed the Atlantic to take part in races in the States, the CCA then appointed Brigadier Fayle to measure to their Rule in the United Kingdom.

It was obvious that the two Rules had to be combined and who better to organise this than David Fayle who worked under both systems. Commander Brown recalls that "the Americans did not like our Scantling allowance and we did not like their inclining but eventually we had to give way and adopt their inclining procedure, and on those terms they agreed to reduce the International Offshore rating."

In fact, it was Larry Brown who laid on the first inclining experiments in this country to prove that it could be done, and they did it by moving men instead of hanging weights on the end of the spinnaker boom. Charles Hay said that this was not entirely reliable as it depended on how much roast beef they had eaten and whether they had remembered to take their sea boots off!

In the late 1960s the Offshore Racing Council had been formed to control ocean racing world-wide. It appointed an International Technical Committee to devise a rating rule and co-opted Major R. J. de C. Glover, MC as its technical adviser, which he still is today (1981).

David Fayle was responsible for welding the final rule together. Measurement to the RORC Rule ceased on 31st August 1970 and the International Offshore Rule was adopted everywhere from 1st January 1971. David Fayle was appointed Chief Measurer to the Offshore Racing Council and as such was responsible for implementing the Rule world-wide. He also became the first Rating Secretary.

Later the calculation of ratings to the RORC Rule was done by computer and a new programme was written for the IOR but David Fayle continued to re-write personally every input sheet submitted by a measurer and to check every intermediate calculation on it. The change over from the RORC generated a tremendous amount of work and this further increased in 1971 with the Admiral's Cup series but he refused to compromise on his system and his health suffered as a result.

To trace the start of the 'Lymington Connection' we must go back a few years to the time when Captain Barraclough was Measurer under the RORC Rule for the South Coast. He was also acting Secretary at the Royal Lymington Yacht Club and now that he was living in Sway he used to invite Larry

Brown to sail with him. They had known each other when both were Vice-Commodore and Rear-Commodore respectively of the Royal Naval Sailing Association (RNSA). Larry Brown takes up the story. "One day Barraclough said to me, 'Look, I have got to measure a boat,' so I asked him what it was all about and he said, 'Would you like to do it? I will ask David Fayle.' David Fayle happened to be measuring a boat in Lymington the following afternoon and invited me to join him. He took a measurement of the freeboards and said, 'It is quite easy. You'd better come over and see me at my office in 72 Belle Vue Road, Bournemouth.' So I went over there and he produced a pile of books and a set of rules and said 'Off you go!' So that is how I became a measurer for the Royal Ocean Racing Club for West Solent and Poole. My number was K7 and I was the seventh measurer to be appointed. David Fayle sent me boats to measure and every time I measured a boat and sent him the results he sent them straight back again and said I had done them wrongly!"

In 1971 Larry Brown invented 'Brown's Patent After Girths Angle Measurer,' known as 'Larry's Level,' and these went into production straight away and the following year he constructed three Manometers. A circular to all Measurers of 1.6.72 stated: "Amongst the papers being sent out now is information on inclinations being taken with the measurer not on board the yacht. This is Measurement Instruction dated April 1972 and paragraph A.4 states that 'The Bucket and Pendulum' should be replaced by the 'Manometer' method." The famous 'Larry's Level' meant that under the new Rule, when measuring the girths, you had to measure the angle of the hull, the angle which the tangent to the hull made with the horizontal and so Larry Brown invented 'Larry's Level' for doing that. The first one had a spirit level and this was then adapted merely to have a pendulum hanging to give the vertical.

Charles Hay reported that "the Rule itself is continuously changing and from time to time new instruments are required to make these changes. A number of Larry's devices are still in use. They do date from the cost-conscious era and tend to be practical and primitive rather than the sophisticated and electronic towards which we are moving now." Joe Sanders confirms this as he remembers in the early days of the RORC working with Brigadier David Fayle and providing him with some wire to which he attached pieces of copper at regular intervals. "This wire could be hauled up the mast of a yacht for measuring purposes instead of stepping it for measurement. Measurement was not so accurate and exact as it is now with computers," he said.

"After a couple of years," Larry Brown continued,

"they wanted more and more measurers and David Fayle upgraded me to Instructor. One of my first trainee measurers was Major Charles Hay, whose name had been put forward by Colonel Jardine. He became K19.

"In the meantime, the work of the Bournemouth office was getting too much for David Fayle: there were only two local girls beside himself, who did the typing and accounts but they had no technical knowledge at all. I suggested that he should take on an assistant, who would work part-time in the office and take some of the weight off his shoulders and David, who used to work all hours, eventually agreed. So Charles Hay went over three mornings a week and got to know how the office worked, which was just as well as shortly afterwards, in November 1971, David had a heart attack and luckily Charles was there to cope in his absence. He came back for about three weeks after Christmas and then died in early 1972.

"Measuring was less detailed under the old RORC Rule and one could actually measure a boat in the water in about 2½ hours and there was no need to take her out as there is now for some measurements. On one occasion, I remember, I left Lymington and caught the 8 o'clock ferry to Yarmouth with my measuring instruments and was met and taken to Wootton Creek. I measured three Folkboats and had a bottle of beer and some sandwiches for lunch and the first boat was aground before I finished. I was back in Lymington at 8 o'clock at night having measured three boats. It was for the Round the Island Race."

Charles Hay told me that "Ron Matthews (W. R. Matthews, Ch.E., F.I.Mech.E.), arrived in April to become the second Rating Secretary and I had been running the Rating Office single-handed. He had been Gunnery Officer under Mountbatten during the war and was an engineer by profession. Ron had been skipper on Sir Maurice Laing's yacht (Sir Maurice being the Admiral of the RORC) for many years and had been a member of the Club since 1957. He moved down from Norfolk and took a house in Burton, near Christchurch. I think Ron developed financial records in which the number of yachts was stated year by year. My recollection is that there were probably 400–500 new yachts a year at that time. As new yachts were measured a great many of the previous year's were not kept up so there was quite a large turnover in the fleet but the number of rated yachts was fairly constant, between about 1200 and 1600.

"In the old days measurers had to work out a certificate with logarithms. By the time I started it was all on the computer – I never had to do that myself. I remained as Assistant Rating Secretary from March 1972 when Ron came until December 1973 by which time I had become an Instructor. It had become clear that somebody with technical expertise was required in the office and Ron sought around for a suitable person. One of the lecturers at the Department of Ship Science at the University of Southampton recommended Keith Ludlow, who joined the Rating Office as Assistant Rating Secretary straight from Univesity. He was an expert on computers and it was Wellworthy Ltd. in Lymington who kindly gave permission for him to have some time on their computer.

"The lease came up at the end of 1976 at the Bournemouth office which was fairly remote from the scene of activity anyway. Lymington was quite the opposite; it was very much in the heart of things. It was also felt in the RORC that a Lymington address would give added prestige." It was very convenient for Charles Hay, who lived at Sandy Down and very convenient for Keith Ludlow as he would be so near to the computer. No. 8 Station Street was rented from Richard Creagh-Osborne on 15th November 1976 and the first rent of £59.50 payable on 15th December 1976.

Keith Ludlow then became Rating Secretary and a small sub-committee to run the Rating Office was set up under the chairmanship of Commander Erroll Bruce, with Captain Hugh Wilson, Dr. Jonathan Rogers and Ron Matthews, who continued to come into the office a few mornings a week as a consultant and back-up to Keith. He also did the accounts, but in April 1977 they were fortunate enough to get Rex Reddrop to do them which he does without the use of a calculator! He had been Manager of Lloyds Bank in Lymington and is very active in the community, serving as Hon. Treasurer to the RNLI and Save the Children and assists at the Citizen's Advice Bureau.

The other Lymington Measurer, besides Charles Hay, was Captain Nigel Hallett, DSC, RN, or 'Buster' Hallett as he is generally known. He was born at Pyrford, Sussex on 14th March 1913. Although his elder brother, Geoffrey, became a surgeon and followed his father in practising at Lymington, Buster went to the RN College at Dartmouth. He served in the Royal Navy from 1930 to 1967 as Seaman Officer and Aviator (Pilot), retiring in the rank of Captain.

Buster had a fine wartime record and served in the Mediterranean as a Naval fighter pilot, escorting convoys to Malta and also covered the North Africa landings. Later he flew on close air support for the invasion of the South of France and then served out in the Pacific.

After the war he was involved in training young Naval officers but one of his last appointments was as Naval Attaché in Chile, Peru, Ecuador, Colombia and Panama. He reads, writes and converses confidentally in Spanish and retired to Spain from the Navy and owned his own yacht brokerage in Puerto Banus, Marbella.

Buster has always been keen on sailing and was Fleet Sailing Secretary and Founder Chairman of the RN College Sailing Association. He served on Mountbatten's staff as Fleet Aviator Officer when John Illingworth was Fleet Engineer and they both played polo as well in a team called 'The Shrimps,' named after Mountbatten's first ship.

He trained as an RORC Measurer under Charles Hay in Lymington and his Spanish came in useful when some of the Spanish contenders for the Admiral's Cup called at Lymington. When he and his wife, Joanna, moved back to Sussex, he continued as a measurer in Brighton but had to give up measuring in 1982 for health reasons.

Since the autumn of 1973 Annual Measurers Conventions were held at the weekend at the Royal Lymington Yacht Club and sometimes on site at a sailmakers or boatyard, when the latest measuring techniques could be demonstrated. Measurers from all over Britain and Ireland could meet each other and exchange views. Most of them stayed at the Stanwell House Hotel but some were put up at the Mayflower and the Angel, and General Morris based himself on the Railway Inn, run by a fellow gunner. Measurers could exchange faulty measuring instruments and stock up with stationery from the Rating Office. These Conventions were also attended by the Secretary of the RORC, Alan Green, who at one time had been a measurer himself in Malta.

Another extremely important part of a measurer's job was to help at competition checking before International, National and important Regional regattas. They had to measure all the sails and check that everything on board a yacht was in the same position as it had been when she had been measured. Cowes Week and the Admiral's Cup Series every second year were the highlights of the summer and the local Scouts were of great assistance.

In July 1978 I joined the staff as a secretary/ receptionist at the Rating Office, after having been a Medical Librarian at the Royal Devon & Exeter Hospital in Exeter for nearly ten years. I was also fortunate in being able to transfer from the Exeter Bench to the Ringwood Bench. Fiona Terras replaced Janet Davies, who had been in the old Bournemouth office and stayed on in Lymington until her marriage in 1978. Fiona's father, Alasdair

Terras is a captain in the Merchant Navy in command of modern tankers, and when he is home on leave, he has been building a Colvic 28 in the garden of his home in Bingham Drive, Lymington, often helped by Fiona.

Jonathan Hudson came as Technical Assistant to Keith Ludlow in September 1980, straight from Oxford University, for by this time the Rating Office had its own computer and was also handling a great deal of work for the Club in London and the Offshore Racing Council. Charles Hay was still Instructor and trained newly-appointed measurers and was also responsible for writing the *Measurers Notebook,* which was updated by *Memos to Measurers.*

This then was the set up in the Rating Office until September 1982 when the shadow of the measurement and rating of *Victory* (challenged by the Americans and found to be incorrect), fell across the Rating Office and with it the resignation of Keith Ludlow as Rating Secretary, although he continues to act as a consultant for the Offshore Racing Council. Eileen Caulcutt, a Rear-Commodore of the RLYC and well-known and well-liked in the sailing fraternity, was appointed Assistant Secretary (Ratings) to 'bridge the gap.'

British Level Rating Association

The British Level Rating Association was formed at a meeting of interested people in Cowes in July 1973 and it is an association of yacht owners. It has no clubhouse and meetings are usually held in London, either at the Royal Thames Yacht Club in Knightsbridge or at the Royal Ocean Racing Club at 20 St. James's Place, London. It is of particular interest to Lymington because not only does it hold its National Championships here but its Hon. Secretary and Treasurer is Captain Hugh Wilson, RN, who lives at Norley Wood, Lymington. Hugh Wilson is a member of the RORC Rating Office Sub-committee and is a frequent visitor at the Rating Office.

On Friday, 13th March 1982, Hugh Wilson was interviewed by Bill Lyon on the BBC Radio Solent programme *Open Waters* and I am indebted to them for use of the transcript.

Hugh Wilson explained that "Level Rating is a particular form of yacht racing in that the owners can race their boats off scratch without having to have handicaps and all the nausea that goes with them. We are quite unlike the One Designs though, which are coming very much into vogue, in that a One Design is, as its name implies, a one design and is the same in every respect under very strict rules. All the level rating yacht has to do is to be of the same handicap, by the International Offshore Rule which gives a rating to all boats. As long as the boat comes out at the same rating it can, within obvious limits, be of any size or shape and be designed by any designer. So here you get the advantage of scratch racing with no handicaps; no waiting at the end of the race for the times to be worked out and your handicap time to be applied. If you go ahead you are winning and also you have the freedom to mess about with your boat within limits – put on a different sort of halyard or different piece of new equipment – provided you do not put your rating above the limit.

"There are six sizes of boat, coming down from the big 2-tonners, which are big enough to go in for the Admiral's Cup, down through four other sizes, 1-ton, ¾-ton, ½-ton, ¼-ton down to the little mini-tonners which, though they probably won't like it, are basically dinghies with lids on, but, by golly, they go! So there we are: the owners race with no handicaps, they do not have to hang about, they look over their shoulders to see who is behind them – or vice versa – and know exactly where they are all the time and this leads to a very needle, very competitive racing and a different form of racing to the handicap man.

"We have our Level Rating Open Championships, for all the six classes, at the end of July and this will form the Selection Trials to decide which boats can represent the United Kingdom in Cork in the One Ton and in Poole in the Half Ton World Championships. We can only have six 1-tonners and ten ½-tonners because you cannot have too many of those sizes on the line. So that week of racing is very much modelled on the World Championship style; Olympic courses, a short offshore race and then the Channel Race just before Cowes Week as the long offshore. That is going to be a pretty needle and competitive week as well.

"I am not directly involved in the rating organisation. The RORC Rating Office, which is the National Rating Office for the United Kingdom, is in Lymington, which is nice and close for me. But it is a direct exchange between the owner and the Rating Office.

"We do not as an Association of owners actually organise very much in the way of racing because our owners, being owners, want to race themselves and one bloke in a boat waving a flag and blowing a whistle is not really good enough to run this sort of racing. So we do lean very much upon the Royal Thames Yacht Club particularly, which has always run our Open Championships and we run a series inside the Solent Points Championship which, of course, all the thirteen clubs organise.

"The only thing we do organise and we are going to do again this year and the coming season is a little

Match Racing, with ½-ton yachts, just six of them. Each race against the others, just like the Lymington Cup and very like the America Cup except there are six boats. This was very successful and it was fascinating to see six boats of different designs fighting each other two by two. So this year we are going to run it again on three Sundays, six boats on the first two and the best six on the last Sunday. If this really catches on, which I think it may well do, perhaps we shall have to ask a Club to organise it on a bigger scale for us in the future; we will see how it goes. However, it is an addition – and a very exciting one – to the level rating field and it has not been done before."

Lymington Amateur Rowing Club

The Lymington Times of 12th June 1981 published an extremely interesting article on the history of the Lymington Amateur Rowing Club in its Centenary Year (1981). In that year they managed to achieve one of their best results by reaching 3 finals out of 4 with their Junior/Senior, Junior 'A' and Novice 'A' crews. The competition was held on the Lymington River but this may well be the last time that it is held there. Congestion on the river is forcing them too look elsewhere for their Spring Regatta. They were considering holding it in the sea opposite the 'Needles Eye' café on the waterfront at Milford-on-Sea. There is no doubt that Lymington's loss would certainly be Milford-on-Sea's gain.

The other notable achievement this year was that the Junior 'A' crew went on to become County champions for Hants and Dorset, only the second time that the Club has won it in the hundred years since it was formed. The crew was Adrian Bull, Terry Woolford, Peter Woodford and Dave Gale and it was coxed by 10-year-old Stuart 'Straight' Lane, nicknamed after the courses he steers.

The article continues: "Their original two boats were the *Victoria*, clinker-built with fixed seats, which had been constructed in 1878, and *Alexandra*, built for the Club by Mr. George Watkins in 1880. Their boathouse was alongside the Coastguards slipway, now the Royal Lymington Yacht Club site – and the Town crier was often summoned to proceed along the High Street announcing the day's racing."

In 1890 the local M.P., the Hon. John Scott Montagu was elected President; Dr. Pithie became chairman and Mr. Edward Elliott, whose father, George, founded the Lymington Clothing Mart, now Elliott's (New Forest) Ltd., was to be the Hon. Secretary for the next 20 years.

Many clubs participated in the 1890 regatta and in 1891 Lymington had its first win over a 'foreign' boat when they beat the Southampton Club's *Black Cross*.

Mr. C. T. King (Mary King's grandfather) loaned his steam launch, *Kelpie*, to the umpires.

As early as 1891 the Club first purchased new sliding seat boats at a cost of £35 each (towards £3,000 today). They were the *Florence*, launched by Mrs. H. St. Barbe, the Lymington banker's wife and the *Lady Cecil*, called after the President's wife and launched by Cllr. C. T. King. A few old club boats, but not the original two, *Victoria* and *Alexandra*, were then sold off at an auction at Inman's Yard for ten shillings and four shillings respectively. The crews at the time included such well-known names as Totterdell, Bran and Hayter. Incidentally, wagers were placed on those two boats and in 1891 *Alexandra* beat the favourite, *Victoria*, in 12 minutes 46 seconds over a 2½ mile course!

The Rowing Club also organised aquatic sports on the river which included cask races, duck hunts and swimming races – for men and boys only. On one occasion the only swimmer to participate in one of the races was Frank Totterdell, as he was so good that no-one competed against him. "Prizes were regulated according to the amount of entrance money taken at the gate, 3*d*. for adults and 1*d*. for children being the amounts to be charged."

Fund-raising was carried out in those days and a 'smoking concert' was often held in the Assembly Rooms (next to the Angel Hotel) where one could enjoy violin and singing recitals. At a dinner in 1894 the Chairman emphasised the importance of rowers being able to swim and urged the County to appoint "a competent man to educate children in the art of swimming. It would be of great benefit to the nation as a prevention to drowning."

In 1897 the Club boasted of 23 Vice-Presidents, amongst them Colonel Cornwallis-West of Newlands Manor and Ingham Whitaker of Pylewell. The Vice-Presidents contributed to the funds of the Club in amounts varying between 2/6*d*. to £1 a year.

The Club went into abeyance before World War Two and it was not reformed until 1948 by two Town Hall staff, Eddie Austin, the present Chairman, and Bert Wilshin. At the Centenary Dinner a photograph was taken of them with Archie Campbell, who had been a shipwright in Berthon and had helped build the famous J Class yachts in the 1920s. He personally built 3 Fours, a Pair and a Sculler for the Club which are being rowed today. A surprise presentation was made to him at the Dinner.

In 1950, Mr. H. G. May, Managing Director of the Berthon Boat Company, offered the Club a derelict site on the corner of Nelson Place which needed to be cleared of debris as it had not been used since World War One. On this site, at the foot of Nelson Place, women workers from Berthon had stitched canvas on their sewing machines in World War One to produce the original Berthon Boat, invented by the Reverend E. L. Berthon, Vicar of Romsey. It was a collapsible 28 ft. lifeboat which folded up to 2 ft. width and was capable of carrying 75 men. However, owing to its poor state of repair and dampness, varnishing of the Club boats had had to be done on additional hired premises and they are looking around for some land on which to build a new clubhouse.

Together with the Lymington & District Sea Fishing Club, the Lymington Amateur Rowing Club have been pressing the Town and District Councils to allow them to build joint club premises over what was originally a children's paddling pool, and later a storm water overflow, down by the river adjoining the Harbour Master's Office. It is essential that the two clubs combine together as the project has been costed at up to £50,000, as it would have to be built on piles. The idea is that the ground floor would be a fishermen's weighing room and a place for the stowage of rowing boats with a club upstairs and possible spectator area for walkers on the roof.

Lymington Swimming Club

The Lymington Swimming Club, formed ten years after the Lymington Amateur Rowing Club, celebrated its 90th year in December 1981 and has 400 members. They had a successful year in water polo and two Juniors, David Rose and Mark Keeping, represented Hampshire at swimming. The Club instructs its members, ranging in age from eighteen months to the mid-seventies! The Lymington Sea Water Baths is one of the largest open air seawater baths in the country and we are indeed fortunate to have this facility. In the 1960s it was possible for many 'locals' to swim there as early as 8 a.m. on summer mornings and have the baths to themselves.

The Lymington Swimming Club coach, Graham Glazpool, deplores the lack of an indoor pool and we hope that they will get one well before their Centenary in 1991.

RESCUE AND PROTECTION

"If only the nation would take a leaf out of the RNLI, where people are unselfish, brave and work together, what a marvellous example that would be."

ADMIRAL GRAHAM

It seems almost unbelievable to us nowadays that sea rescue and lifesaving in Lymington, even immediately after the war, was left to private enterprise and public-spirited yachtsmen such as George Power, who ran his own rescue service, and Charles Munro who, in his seven-ton fishing boat *Telima,* built 50 years previously at Salcombe, often towed in yachts which had got into difficulties. Indeed, on one occasion he and his crewman, Ted Blachford, were out in *Telima*, and had to call on the assistance of the Yarmouth lifeboat! The *Lymington Times* of 18th February 1982 reported that: "The pair were off the Needles with Charles merrily singing "If I were a rich man" in none too melodious tones when – horrors of horrors – *Telima* struck a rock and was left with a gaping 3 ft. × 2 ft. hole. Slamming the engine in reverse, they wriggled back into Scratchell's Bay, where Charles and Ted looked a forlorn sight, sitting on the wheelhouse roof, which was a foot below water, waiting for amused Yarmouth lifeboatmen to release them from their predicament!"

One rather unusual rescue, which took place just after the war, was related to me by Lieutenant-Colonel Mark Goodhart. His branch of the family first came to Lymington in 1947 just after the war but he had visited it earlier when he used to stay with his Aunt Nell, who lived at Keyhaven Lodge, where Jack and Jean (her daughter) Lowis are today. His uncle was Captain B. H. Goodhart, MC, who was Mayor of Lymington twice in 1936-1937 and again in 1945-46, when he died in office. He was very active as head of Civil Defence during the war.

"I had just come back from Libya," Mark told me, "and my brother James and I were looking out of the window at Weston one morning at about 10 a.m. when we heard an aeroplane which was clearly in trouble. It forced landed on the marsh just south of what is now the Yacht Haven Marina. We still had a little motor-boat in the water for duck shooting and we ran down to the yacht club, whether on our bicycles or not I cannot remember, and managed to reach the crashed aeroplane, a Gruman Avenger. Thankfully, the crew had got out and were all right and they got into the launch and we were about half-

way back to the yacht club when the rescue helicopter arrived from Lee-on-Solent. It lowered a winchman and hoisted them up and they said 'Thank you,' and away they went. The pilot was Lieutenant Victor George Sirrett and the observer Sub-Lieutenant Richard Edward Vanderplank.

"The only thing that was slightly ironic was that I had spent the previous 2½ years in the Libyan desert waiting to pick up aeroplanes which had crashed there and I had not been home for more than a week when one crashed right on my own front door-step! Later they sent a gang of aircraft fitters to dismantle the plane, float it to the sea-wall and take it back and it took them at least a month. Luckily the aeroplane landed on a fairly firm bit of the marshes because they can be very squishy indeed."

Lymington Sea Rescue Service

Through an introduction by Colin Mudie, I visited George Power at his home, Wychwood, Harbridge, Wiltshire on Saturday, 4th December 1982, to find out about the Lymington Sea Rescue Service which he formed in 1963.

The younger son of a Baronet, George Power was born in London in their home at 38 Belgrave Square (loaned to the Belgian Government during the war) but for 30 years his family lived at Newlands Manor, Milford-on-Sea and he grew up there. Today Newlands Manor, sadly, has been divided up into sixteen maisonettes but when the Powers lived there it comprised of 56 bedrooms and needed a large staff to run it. King Edward VII had stayed there once. It even had its own cricket pitch. "You might say that I was born with a silver spoon in my mouth," he said.

George Power had been very keen on boats since he was 12 years old and joined the Keyhaven Yacht Club. He then went to stay with Lord Plymouth, near Cardiff, at the age of 17 years in order to study estate management with the intention of taking over the estates at Newlands and managing them. Unfortunately, both the war and finance were to put an end to that scheme.

With war imminent, he had tried to join the Navy in 1938 but they were full up and so he became commissioned into the Royal Welsh Regiment on the recommendation of Field Marshal Sir Cyril Deverell, who had retired to Lymington. He was posted to the Glamorgan battalion which then changed to searchlights. Much to his chagrin he was then sent to Filton "when to my horror I was promptly promoted from 2nd Lieutenant to Major and pushed into the position of Controller! It seemed rather odd that they had not decided whether they would have an RAF Controller, who would keep the planes out of the way of the Army or an Army Controller, who would stop the Army guns from firing at the RAF planes!" Then, unfortunately, he caught double pneumonia followed three days later by getting cerebral spinal meningitis, which put paid to his army career and he was invalided out.

Very enterprisingly he then bought himself a trawler and was allotted five Merchant Navy crew. "I think she was the last sailing trawler in England at the time and I fished off Aberdovey. Shortly afterwards, the army arrived in force with 'boffins' and proceeded to shoot out all over his fishing grounds. Realising this they said, 'You had better join the War Department fleet,' and they made me a Captain in charge of a War Department vessel so I did eventually get to sea during the war after all!"

After the war, he returned to Newlands and his father had written a rather sad letter saying that although he had got an income of £67,000 a year, a colossal sum in those days, he was left with only £5,200 after taxation and the idea of continuing to stay in Newlands was out of the question. The housekeeping bills alone came to £3,000 a year. His father brought architects down to see whether they could make it into a school but in the end it was sold on 9th October 1949 to a local builder. "I never thought in terms of knocking bits of it down," said George. "If I had done so I should have been there now." So George Power bought a little place, 'White Lions' in Woodside, so-called because there were two white stone lions on either side of the gateway. His father was to die in France on 9th June 1950, and they got a civilian pilot to fly his body back. But the French pilot decided, with characteristic French logic, that his passenger could not be in any hurry, so he stopped off en route to visit his mother-in-law and arrived a day late! His father was buried in Milford Church.

George Power, with plenty of time on his hands, and very conscious that when you are rich you have a responsibility to the community, decided that he would like to go into Parliament, (his father had been M.P. for Wimbledon) but his health precluded this. So then he thought of the local council and was elected as an Independent, becoming a Conservative candidate three years later and he served on the Council for about 18 years. "I was, I think, the most unpopular councillor in Lymington," he confided, "but I was completely without any bias at all and if something came up that was good I voted for it and if it was bad, I did not!" He was very keen that Council meetings should be held in the evenings so that local tradesmen and working people could have the opportunity to participate in its deliberations. Indeed, on 20th December 1952, a most amusing poem was published in *The Lymington Times* called 'Wakey, Wakey!' He tried unsuccessfully to be elected to the County Council but was beaten by Robert Hole.

While he was on the Council he served on the Harbour Commission as its representative. The Chairman was 'Purple' Blatch of Moore & Blatch, the solicitors, and the Executive Harbour Commissioner was Commander Larry Brown. David May was also a Harbour Commissioner at that time. George was in favour of a yacht basin near Rope Walk and visited it with some Council members, including Major Hall. He even offered to build a wall there "free, gratis and for nothing" and got estimates for dredging that would cost about £75,000 but the Council turned this down! "I was 20 years ahead of my time," he said.

George Power then inaugurated a new inshore rescue sea service entirely at his own expense which, in the words of the *Bournemouth Evening Echo,* "met a very long felt need." He announced the scheme to the Lymington Harbour Commissioners and called for volunteers to crew a 5-ton craft which he was having built privately called *Torshaunt,* which was capable of 25 knots. Not only was the vessel his private property but he had gone to the additional expense of equipping it with rescue equipment costing between £500 and £600 for the inshore rescue. In January 1963 he reckoned that the Lymington Sea Rescue Service cost him what would today be in the region of just under £250,000. There were five boats, amongst them *Torshaunt,* a little boat called *Seeker,* capable of about 30 knots, *Maid of Baltimore,* capable of 20 knots and their chief rescue boat, and *Huntsman,* which was a 28 footer. Robert Pretty was President and George Power was Chairman.

The Lymington Sea Rescue Service soon ran into "whacking problems." The main one was over communication. Rockets were provided at first but one of them went through someone's roof, so maroons were obtained instead and here too they ran into difficulties. The first maroon fired by the police happened in the middle of an operation in the Lymington Hospital and was rather a shock to the surgeon in the operating theatre, who was not expecting the noise! After discussion the Hospital decided that in the cause of saving lives the noise of an emergency signal could be accepted.

However, the Ministry of Transport had different views and gave orders that maroons were only to be used by the RNLI and coastguards. The Committee of the Lymington Sea Rescue Service felt that they should not offer a service unless it was really reliable and speedy. A press article stated: "As they cannot achieve this amongst volunteers without an efficient means of call they have unfortunately been forced to withdraw the service for the present. Councillor Power told me that a long telegram had been sent by his committee to the Minister but the reply caused even more indignation than the original veto on the maroons. It apparently stated that the noise of maroons might inconvenience local residents but this has caused quite a few of them to feel very strongly that if Whitehall thinks that the inconvenience to the residents by the harbour comes before saving lives at sea then someone else ought to be in charge of that Ministry! Meantime, I sincerely hope that no one will drown who would have been saved but for a bureaucratic point of principle which has effectively stopped volunteer citizens from performing a really worthy and thoroughly efficient voluntary task. The Lymington Sea Rescue Service is typical of the spirit that made Britain great: the action of the Ministry of Transport is not!"

Here again George Power used great ingenuity in getting round this ban. He first had 12 people put on to the telephone at his expense and then rang up Sweden and got three horns flown over. They were about 2 ft. across and fixed at about the height of the Church. He then installed a compressor in a cellar with an automatic link to the police. They turned a handle which set off a mercury switch and the compressor tank blew the horns. Incidentally, they could be heard as far away as New Milton if the wind was right. So much for the noise of maroons!

The RNLI were not really in favour of the Lymington Sea Rescue Service. They were experimenting with different types of craft and were also concerned that local collections would go to this Service rather than to the RNLI. George Power then gave them an undertaking that he would not collect outside the Lymington area.

There was a volunteer crew of about 20 with a different cox each week and 4 were on duty each day. George Power could not get anyone to man the boat at weekends so he undertook this himself and continued to do so for three years until he was forced by his doctor to give it up on health grounds. In the first three months the Service rescued 9 people and

over 50 were saved in the three years that the Service was operating. The volunteers received no payment and could only make salvage claims with the written approval of the committee, which would only be given in exceptional circumstances. They were all men who really knew local waters well and had frequently been afloat about their own affairs.

The press report continued: "The boats belong to George Power who also receives nothing for their use but the committee received from the RNLI a normal reward when called out to rescue. When a boat was on call it was used for nothing except Sea Rescue Service. The whole organisation had been inspected by the RNLI and the coastguards. The Chief Inspector of the RNLI himself told me that the Sea Rescue Service at Lymington set a very high standard of efficiency."

A postscript to this story is rather ironic. When the RNLI started up in Lymington in 1965 they decided that the only practical way to call the crew out was by firing a maroon and they have been doing so ever since! No wonder George Power feels rather bitter. He was a man ahead of his time and a great 'philanthropist manqué.'

Royal National Lifeboat Institution

Rosemary Mudie is Press Officer of the Lymington RNLI Committee and is very highly qualified to do this for them. She started her career in journalism and was film critic and editor of the British Film Institute's *Film Bulletin* and then became public relations executive with the London Press Exchange. She has been a partner in Colin Mudie's naval design firm since 1958. She is a Member of the Institute of Public Relations and was awarded the first Jubilee Trust Medallion for her services in 1980–81 as public relations adviser to the Jubilee Trust. She is also joint author, with Colin, of several of his books, and of course is a regular contributor to national and local newspapers and journals.

There was an RNLI lifeboat first stationed here in 1965 and then there was some local fund-raising but there was not really an established branch until 1967, although a Flag Day and house-to-house collections were organised on an ad hoc basis. In December 1967, Rosemary Mudie recalls, there was a meeting at the Ship Inn with Robert Pretty, Herbie Rand, Rex Reddrop and Bernard Foxen, amongst others, and they decided that there must be a proper RNLI Branch. Robert Pretty was the first Chairman; Bernard Foxen arrived late at the meeting to find that he had been elected Secretary and he carried out these duties until October 1978. Rex Reddrop was handed over a stamp and £3 4s. 2d. which was all the money that remained from the previous volunteers and he was made Treasurer and has been Treasurer ever since.

Robert Pretty was Chairman until March 1974 when Derek Hobson took over; Derek gave it up in October 1981 and Brigadier Douglas Bright is now the Chairman. Pamela Keen took over as Secretary from Bernard Foxen in October 1978. The first President was Derek Steele-Perkins and he was succeeded in that office in October 1980 by Sir Bernard Scott, with Mrs. Pleydell-Bouverie as Vice-President. It is interesting to note that Douglas Bright has strong family connections with lifesaving and is a direct descendant of Archbishop Manners-Sutton, who sponsored the first legislation in the House of Lords for the setting up of a lifeboat service. His wife, Rosemary, is related to Captain George Manby, the inventor of the breeches buoy.

Derek Hobson was awarded the RNLI's statuette of a lifeboatman on his retirement as Chairman and Rex Reddrop was awarded the Institution's silver badge in recognition of their services. In addition, Branch members presented Derek Hobson with a watercolour painting by Charles Munro of the view of the marshes from their home. Since 1965 Charles Munro was the deputy launching authority, firing maroons from his home at Bywater House and later carried out the duties of Secretary for four years. He was presented with a decanter, engraved by Richard Fitzwilliam, and showing the RNLI lifeboat at full speed – suitably filled with whisky!

"The Station is a separate entity within the Branch and deals solely with the crew," said Rosemary Mudie, "and the running of the lifeboat and its launching. It is run by the Hon. Secretary and an admin. chap who looks after the finances, petrol returns and that sort of thing. Keith Bacon was the Hon. Secretary of the lifeboat station at the beginning; then Alan Roxburgh, then Charles Munro and now Graham Webb. A large viewing window by an anonymous donor has been installed at the lifeboat house so that visitors can see the Atlantic 21 lifeboat inside, which creates even more interest. Any time there is a call out I tell the local papers so that people know why the maroons went up. Otherwise, in a town like this it is infuriating if you hear the maroons and never know what happened.

"We have got a very good crew and there is a good crowd waiting to come forward. Jacques Redon, husband of Clare Francis, is a helmsman and when he returned from the Whitbread Round the World Race in early 1982, his colleagues in the lifeboat planned to rendezvous with his yacht *First Co-operative,* off the Needles. But to take on board wine and food during the race would have meant dis-qualification: it would have been a disaster with the finishing line so near at hand after circumnavigating the world.

"Graham Webb was a helmsman until he retired and Alan Coster is an absolutely super chap. Chris Carrington is another helmsman and so is Simon Chalk from the Harbour Master's office." The *Lymington Times* of 11th April 1981 reported that three Lymington lifeboatmen had been awarded medals for bravery in rescuing two fishermen from their sinking boat at the mouth of the river during a gale on 17th December 1980. They were helmsman Alan Coster, aged 35, and the Assistant Harbour Master, who received a bronze medal; Simon Chalk also on the Harbour Master's staff, aged 21, and Peter Harvey, aged 40, employed at Elmer's Court Country Club and Time-Sharing project, who both received bronze medal service certificates.

When they could not get their 21 ft. lifeboat alongside the fishing vessel, Alan Coster swam 20 yards in 7 ft. high waves and led the fishermen half a mile across the treacherous sedge marshes in pitch darkness to Pylewell shore, where the lifeboat picked them up. The two fishermen who were rescued by Alan Coster were on the oyster dredger *Al Mor* and

By courtesy of Rosemary Mudie

Alan Coster – A helmsman of the Lymington lifeboat

although very young were very frightened and hypothermic. The citation read: "Coster showed fine seamanship, good judgement, dogged determination and displayed great courage and self-sacrifice in clearly risking his own life."

On another occasion, after rescuing a fishing boat *Tracy Ann*, in difficulties off Hamstead Ledge, east of Yarmouth and towing them back to Lymington, the crew of the lifeboat were rewarded with two fine cod as a thank-you.

At the Lymington RNLI Social Evening following the Annual General Meeting, Admiral Graham praised the work of the lifeboatmen, saying, "If only the nation would take a leaf out of the RNLI, where people are unselfish, brave and work together, what a marvellous example that would be." In 1981 the Lymington lifeboat crew had carried out more rescues than in the three preceding years added together!

"A separate entity, but interlinked, is the Ladies Guild, which is now just called the Lymington Guild because they decided that there are not so many ladies any more!" Rosemary told me, "but I understand that one of the reasons was because two men's lib had joined it! The Guild is entirely responsible for fund-raising and souvenir selling." Rosemary keeps a summary of annual results, including subscriptions and donations, Flag Day and House-to-House, as well as all their special events organised by the Lymington Guild. Attendances at these functions have been recorded from 1968 and events like sponsored walks, film shows, bridge drives, etc. which were later not so well attended were replaced with visits to the Boat Show, Sotheby's Antique Fair, car boot sales and 'Operation Moonshine', to name a few. In 1968 the total money collected amounted to £560 and in 1982 it was £9,909, including £2,000 donated to the Penlee Disaster Fund. "We are always searching for new ways to raise money," said Rosemary. "The Beaulieu Boat Jumble has been marvellous and we try and get as much variety as possible. In 1981 the Guild raised £6,000. A very touching donation was that from Captain Colin McMullen, who gave the fee he received for an article in *Yachting Monthly* about the sad disappearance of his son, Mike McMullen, in the Trans-Atlantic Race of 1976 to the RNLI."

Twelve years ago one of the original lifeboat crew, Doug Baverstock, now their Hon. Bosun, organised the first sprat supper at the Ship Inn as a social occasion for lifeboatmen and local fishermen and 30 attended. It became so popular that it was then moved to Bath House. In 1981 197 attended a Sprat Supper at the Masonic Hall where £200 was raised for local charities; they do not only collect for themselves. This year they were loaned the Solent Room at the Lymington Town Sailing Club free of charge and 9 stone of sprats were consumed, which were donated by John Chandler of CFR Fisheries.

The flotilla of about 60 boats which accompanied the RNLI lifeboat from Lymington River to the Needles Lighthouse, carrying Christmas parcels for the lighthouse keepers there on the Saturday before Christmas, may sadly be the last, as the lighthouse is expected to be fully automated by December 1983. The 'goodies', which included a Christmas tree, had to be transferred by breeches buoy "after a line had been fired with commendable accuracy to the lighthouse steps." A *Lymington Times* reporter wrote that before turning for home the lifeboat made a call "alongside the £400,000 floating 'gin palace' being skippered by Chris Carrington" and was given a welcome half bottle of whisky. "With the reporter now so paralysed as to be insensitive to the elements, Coxswain Alan Coster showed the inflatable's paces passing the Yarmouth *Arran* at 30 knots on the homeward journey, taking a short cut inside the mainland creeks and sending gaggles of Canadian geese hurriedly airborne."

One Sunday morning, early in 1982, six youngsters from Lymington and Milford went out in the Lymington Atlantic 21 inflatable and then transferred to the Yarmouth 52 ft. lifeboat at the mouth of the river to take them to the Needles. They had previously been training in the lifeboat station and the final instruction for their Silver Duke of Edinburgh Award Scheme medals was breeches buoy drill and depth sounding at the Needles lighthouse. Some of them perhaps will be the lifeboatmen of the future.

Two senior officials of the Spanish Red Cross of the Sea Lifeboat Society visited the Lymington lifeboat station in January 1982 and inspected the Atlantic 21 ft. semi-inflatable and her crew. They were so impressed with it that they have ordered three Atlantic 21s for their own fleet. Quite a compliment to Lymington!

The Marine Police

At 11 o'clock on a fine winter morning on Sunday, 17th January 1982, there was a loud knock at the door and there was a Sergeant in the Marine Police. Sgt. Feist had called to take me to see over their launch *Ashburton,* but I got some strange looks as I walked with him to the riverside, carrying a tape recorder and camera which belonged to me!

Sgt. Feist told me that he had been with *Ashburton* for 10 years. "Some of my colleagues are ex-Royal Navy and ex-Merchant Navy and some are amateur yachtsmen, but I served in the Royal Air Force on Air/Sea Rescue. We used fast launches so I have had plenty of experience with them.

"*Ashburton* is 10 years old and was built at Havant and fitted out at Bembridge in the spring of 1971. She is based generally on the design of a pilot launch although there are certain differences in the wheelhouse, to allow more height for policemen! She is 40 ft. long and powered by two V8 Cummins, which are American diesels and they have proved very reliable. We have a dinghy across the transom, which is for water work. The launch has a draught of 4 ft. which is not a lot when the tide is out, and there are many places that cannot be reached in her such as Keyhaven and parts of the Lymington River. We keep an outboard motor and extra fuel on board so that we can carry out quite an extended patrol in our dinghy. In fact, on many occasions, that is used for our rescue work as well. If there is a yacht aground in bad weather there is no way that you can reach her except in the dinghy.

"We have two large liferafts with a capacity for 12 persons which enables the crew to carry 8 passengers and if the boat were to sink the liferafts would automatically float off. The boat has been used in bad weather in the Solent and we have had some rough rides in anything up to a Force 12!

"We cover all the Hampshire coastline and we divide that into three areas: West, Central and East. There are three watches: an early watch, a late watch and one watch on a day off, so it follows on in a rota and we change over at Cowes. Each shift is nine hours so the launch is running eighteen hours a day at least, and is on standby for the remainder of the twenty-four hours. The watches are designated in colours of Red, Blue and Green and this watch is the Blue watch.

"Stealing from boats is very prevalent and in January 1981 quite a lot of boats in Fortuna Dock were broken into and stuff stolen from them. One of our most important functions is crime prevention. If we go to a place and there is little movement on the water, we then go ashore and walk the shore line so that we have a chance to speak to people, who are working on their boats or just in their boats, and we talk to them about crime. Many boat owners do not live locally, so we have to put them in the picture as to what is going on here and how best to prevent crime happening to them. Outboard motors and inflatable dinghies are two of our main headaches. We had 15 dinghies lost or stolen in Lymington last year (1980) and only 2 of them have been recovered. It is virtually impossible find them again.

"If we were to come across smuggling or contraband we would deal with it but it is specifically covered by the Customs and they have special powers that enable them to deal with it. As we cover the whole of the Hampshire coastline we cannot become tied up with one particular job, so we would turn them over to the Customs or local police. We do deal with rabies and bringing foreign dogs ashore though. In fact this launch had the first prosecution for that in this area, which occurred on the Isle of Wight two or three years ago now, when a Frenchman brought in a dog. We have dealt with three cases of Contravention of Rabies Order.

"We are also engaged in rescue work because we are in direct contact with the coastguard on our marine VHF, and quite often they will call us before the lifeboat because they know we are already out and about. Of course, if it is a major job then the lifeboat must be called but if it is a small boat, which it usually is in these waters, we often tow them back. Some are amateur yachtsmen, who don't really know what they are doing and so are caught out by the weather, or their gear fails, and they have no option but to put out a distress call. This launch is quite fast, 20 knots is her maximum speed, so we can answer a distress call quite quickly. Being out on patrol all the time, we get to know the area very well indeed.

"We have a very good radio system on board with two marine-band sets. So we can monitor three channels at once. There is Channel 16, which is the calling channel and distress channel; one working channel which in this area is normally Channel 12, the Southampton Port Radio; and on our other set we monitor Channels 6 and 7 which are the coastguard frequencies. We also have three police radios: the top one gives us direct communication with Winchester, which is the control for the County; then there is our personal radio base set for communication with our shore party or with our dinghy; and the third one is for communication with shore stations on the coastline, which today is Lymington Police Station. We have a code and if there is no one on board we do let them know by radio.

"We have been in touch with the army at Marchwood and they have been very good to us. There is so much rubbish about in the Solent, very often rope which people throw over the side and they have freed our propellers two or three times when we have fouled them. We have also run bomb disposal squads to the Island because the Sappers obviously do not like taking their stuff on the ferry! When we are in Portsmouth the Navy helps us and we are very fortunate in that respect. One of our crew members, a Sergeant, is a diver but he will be leaving the launch soon on promotion.

"We are also fitted with radar which enables us to operate even in thick fog. We could come down the Lymington River in an absolutely pea soup when nothing else was running and it gives us an all weather cover. As far as crowded rivers are concerned, it is very much the same wherever you go these days, be it the Hamble or Cowes but it is not so bad in the winter. Yachtsmen in general are very good but you do get the rogue one who still thinks that steam gives way to sail in all circumstances, which just isn't the case any more!

"*Ashburton* carries fire axes and bolt croppers for rescue if we need to cut away rigging. We have had one or two accidents in the Solent, which have been fatal. We also work with flares: we have red distress flares and white flares for illumination at night, if we need to light up the scene of a rescue or if we are searching for someone.

"We keep a record of all the owners we have spoken to: it is all written down not only alphabetically but sub-alphabetically as well. There must be something like 5,000 boats in this book and those are just the ones we have contacted. We make it easy for ourselves by taking the names and addresses of owners so that if anything happens to the boat in the future then we can contact the owner and let him know the score. Today we have two officers ashore and when they return they will write out their reports. Finally there is the log book for completion. Yesterday we spoke to six boat owners and we covered the whole of the western side of Langstone Harbour."

Long may *Ashburton* and her crew continue to protect us!

Coastguards

On Sunday, 23rd May 1982, after a very large Sunday luncheon, our intrepid author made a perilous climb up the iron ladders to the top of Calshot Control Tower, complete with handbag, brief-case and a tape recorder, to talk to Mr. G. B. Downing of HM Coastguard. But it was well worth it, as not only did I have a most interesting conversation with him, but the the view of Southampton Water and the Solent on a sunny spring afternoon was breathtaking.

Lymington is in the Needles District, where all the records are kept and Mr. Downing had often visited Lymington and given lectures on the work of the Coastguards. He had spent 35 years in the service and was sad that he had to retire on his 65th birthday on the 'Glorious Twelfth' of August 1982. He had served in Sussex, Lancashire and Cornwall – always on a cliff top – but never at a place like Calshot. It was a complete change and is quite unique. Calshot

Tower was built only ten years ago and already there was talk of closing it down.

"It is a great deal of responsibility for one coastguard on his own," he told me, "which is why today there is the tendency to have larger stations, regional control centres and district control centres where they have three or four men on watch all the time. But they have a very large area to cover and only time will tell if it will be more satisfactory than the singly-manned stations.

"Originally the service was part of HM Customs and Excise but between 1823 and 1856 loss of life round our coasts had reached a figure that caused this new service to be formed principally to cover life-saving. It was formed in about two weeks from extra naval personnel, which is why at the outbreak of war it came under the Navy. Today it is part of the Marine Division of the Board of Trade with a headquarters in London."

There used to be several coastguard stations in this vicinity. There was one at Pitts Deep and there are still traces of the old pier. Although it is silted up now craft used to be able to moor at it at half-tide and there were three cottages and a brickworks. William Allington used to visit the coastguard station there and it was often mentioned in his diary. Then there was a coastguard station in Lymington at King's Saltern Road and one at Keyhaven, where the Sea Scouts were trained before World War Two. There was another one at Lepe – the houses are still there – one at Calshot. (In fact, in 1959, Mr. Downing made a synopsis and apparently at that time there were more coastguard houses from the Thames to Southampton than there were coastguards in the service!) They were particularly useful in the war for carrying out observation on the convoys and patrols in case of an enemy landing. Today there are about 150 coastguard stations and about 150 auxiliary stations with equipment varying according to need.

"I think the minimum age for becoming a coastguard is around 27 or 28," Mr. Downing told me, "and an applicant should have had about eight or nine years service in a marine organisation, as well as qualifications in communications, chartwork and navigation. When he is accepted he goes to a coastguard school down at Brixham in Devon for 5½ weeks. They then put in six months at a coastguard station before going back to Brixham for a further 2½ week course, after which they become fully-fledged coastguards. There are about 550 of us in the service as regulars and we have to rely on approximately 7,000 to 8,000 auxiliaries.

"An auxiliary can be a man or a woman. They get trained for a few hours and then they come on duty but they always have a back-up system. They assist us in watchkeeping and life-saving equipment. This is necessary because many stations can have a quiet time one year and then the following year they can be very, very busy.

"Also all round the coast we have Reporting Members. They are responsible people who live in a house close to the sea with a telephone and if they see something they will ring us up. Equally if somebody reports an incident that is outside our vigil then we can ring them and ask if they could help us out.

"Most important of all there is the Auxiliary Afloat system. This is a two-fold system with the coastguards and yachtsmen working together and there must be about 250 people in the Solent area. These are all people who have yachts, usually cabin cruisers and they must have a radio so that we can contact them at any time. If they see an accident or incident then they inform us and tell us what they can do and what they must leave for us to do. This makes life rather easier because many incidents could not be seen from the shore, either by coastguards or Reporting Members, and so you have got yachts from Lymington, Bucklers Hard, all Southampton, Fawley, Hamble, Portsmouth, Ryde and Cowes ready to assist us. They must have training in radio up to Post Office stipulation and they usually visit the Station or I go down to the yacht clubs and give lectures there.

"The increase in yachting has obviously greatly increased our work and there are two important aspects of this. Firstly, the yachtsmen come to us for the weather and information connected with their leisure; and secondly, they tell us where they are going and then if we have an incident we could often call a yacht instead of having to send out rescue boats.

"We do a three-hour Met. Report for Southampton Weather Centre as we have our own met. equipment. Then we give the yachtsmen the shipping forecast and if they ask for the weather at Calshot then we give them that too. But we never give advice, just information. Otherwise, if we get involved with people's intentions and there is an accident they can turn round and say that the coastguards told them it would be all right. This is one of four hoisting stations where we hoist the weather cones for gale warnings.

"When we get a call we have to assess the situation, whether it is a boating accident, fire or illness and get the fastest help we can obtain and a helicopter is not always the answer, particularly in a gale. The public think we have access to helicopters at any time but this is not so. They are really for the use of service personnel and we are short of helicopters in the Solent at present as they have all gone to the Falklands. They are only too pleased to help as rescue is a diversion from their training routine and gives them experience.

"In the Solent we can call upon our friend, the marine police launch *Ashburton,* which plays a tremendous role and as far as life-saving is concerned they are probably more involved than any other craft in this area. We can also apply to the Harbour Authorities and they are always ready to help *if available.* Those are the key words, 'if available' because one day you can count on 30 or 40 people to help and the next day everyone is at work and you have nothing.

"We have always got the RNLI lifeboat to fall back on and there is one here at Calshot, one at Yarmouth and another big one at Bembridge; in Lymington there is the small rubber inflatable. It is a big area to cover for an individual lifeboat and we do need *time.* We have a '999' system which is very valuable as calls come through to us and we have a list of life-saving craft at our finger tips. Also we are manning the radio and can co-ordinate operations. We also have an inshore rescue volunteer group on patrol, like this afternoon when some wind-surfers got into difficulties. We always go back and tell those who have helped us what the outcome was and this way we increase co-operation and make many friends.

"We have to cater for patrols on oil pollution and we also patrol the foreshore and see nobody blocks up the access which we might need for life-saving." (Alas, the author's mother did just that, sitting out a heavy shower in the car at Calshot and was very quickly but courteously told to find a different parking position!) "If there is a wreck on the foreshore and we have to do life-saving for it then we also guard it on behalf of the customs or until a policeman arrives on their behalf to stop people from stealing. The watch is automatically set up by the coastguards and this is another instance when we use auxiliaries.

"Coastguards are also the local agents for Crown Commissioners. No one is allowed to build or lay anything below the high-water line and to save sending someone down from London they often send us a plan and we will commission the local borough engineer or the people concerned in the project. We go down and inspect it and see that it does not interfere with public or fishermen's rights. If it is a big project we inspect it periodically and pass word back to London. This is provided it is not too technical but usually in that case the borough surveyor or engineer will explain it to us in easy terms and here again we make more friendships.

"Another of our jobs is dealing with royal fish. If they are washed up on the beach we have to remove them but if they are needed by naturalists, we have wrap them up and put them on the train for the Natural History Museum, which is very interesting.

"In addition to all this work there is lecturing and visits to schools and clubs. I find you cannot convert the converted and if you go to yacht clubs and give a lecture and there is a bar, only about half of them decided to come and listen to it! From my own personal view I realise the children pass on information to their parents and many of them come to me and say, 'I am fed up with hearing what Mr. Downing has said about safety at sea.' In many cases they decide they are not as clever as they thought and they will come along to the coastguard station or invite a coastguard to talk at a men's club. If possible, and I try to make it possible, I tour the schools to instruct the kiddies in life-saving and I make many friends. It is surprising how many children are allowed to go to sea without proper life-saving equipment; it is really frightening. You can tell them at school that they must swim a hundred yards in three feet of water but the difference is that at school there is somebody to pull them out and at sea the deeper the water the colder it becomes.

"Then you start off with sailing and try to show them a film and get them involved with the lifeboat men and life-saving. At one time I talked to 500 or 600 children in an Assembly Room and they remember me and I get a lot of joy out of it. This is extremely important because children sometimes play, or try to play a hoax; that usually happens at the first break of holidays when they have access to radio and make hoax calls on it. You have to follow up calls as somebody might really be in trouble. On the other hand, put to proper use, children have sometimes saved their parents' lives if there has been an accident on board and they have been taught how to use the radio or fire a flare.

"We work with everybody – the lighthouse service, lifeboat service, customs service, the police, the fire service, the merchant service, the fishermen, dock masters and yacht masters and we are also in close contact with the three services. It is fascinating if you get involved with everything."

We all wish Mr. Downing a very happy retirement.

Lymington Weather Centre

In May 1981 a Weather Centre was opened at the top of the Stanwell House Hotel and in addition to yachtsmen it has proved a great boon to the RNLI, the Coastguards and, in particular, to the Southampton Weather Centre, one of whose officers, Ted Young, lives in Lymington. The project was not only supported by these organisations but also received the backing of local firms, such as Brookes & Gatehouse and Jeremy Rogers. The Weather Centre was opened by Admiral Wilf Graham, Director of the RNLI, who lives at Shirley Holms. In an article in the *Lymington Times* of 2nd May 1981, he said that "weather was the biggest single hazard facing yachtsmen and the need for such a Centre could be seen by the growing number of yachtsmen getting into difficulties. Ted Young emphasised that this service to yachtsmen was particularly appreciated by the Southampton Weather Centre, which provided information to many other organisations dependant upon the weather, such as farmers, builders and engineers, as well as to yachtsmen and they welcomed the enterprise.

The article went on to describe the service provided and the instruments used to give it. The weather point produced synoptic charts by facsimile using a Plessey receiver. Instruments included a barograph, tide tables, wind speed and direction instruments, both above the hotel and also from Cliff House Hotel at Barton, along with daily reports from the Needles coastguards. Copies of the charts are given to hotel patrons and sent to the Royal Lymington Yacht Club and Lymington Yacht Haven. Individual copies for race days can be obtained for as little as 15p and additional weather charts for places as far afield as the Mediterranean can also be provided, subject to four hours notice.

Admiral Graham thanked Jeremy Willcock, resident proprietor of Stanwell House Hotel, for his permission to house the Weather Centre there. Another facility provided by the hotel is a telephone service between the hours of 7.15 a.m. and 7.15 p.m. It is hoped that every opportunity will be taken to make maximum use of such an excellent back-up service to yachtsmen.

CHAPTER 17

THE AUXILIARIES

*"I have had a very interesting life and I meet some very interesting people and
and that is why I do this job."*

JOE SANDERS

Shipmates

Mary Campbell-Ross told me when I visited Shipmates on 26th November 1981 that her father had been in shipping and he had a bungalow at Dibden Purlieu which they used to visit. "I was married at Beaulieu at the end of the war," she said, "so I have known this area for a long time. My husband and I started sailing here in about 1956. We found a little boat and it was a new venture for us. We used to go to Tom Morris' chandlery for paints and varnishes and anything we needed. My husband, Bruce, was an agent in Dorset – we lived at Sherborne before we came here – and we thought we would like to start up in business on our own. Some friends told us that this place was for sale and we bought it. When Bruce and I first came here in December 1957 we used to say that the only thing that came down the hill was the rain, which used to pour down it!

"Two years later we were able to buy the house next door to Shipmates and we took down the wall, knocked a door through and built a flat. I bought the premises down on the Quay about eighteen months ago and we took our sailing wear down there and opened for Easter 1980. We are reasonably busy down on the Quay, even in the winter, because quite a lot of sailing goes on in winter time, such as the Frostbite Series. Some days when I see them out there sailing on bitterly cold days, I think they must have all their thermal wear on or else they will soon come to me and buy some! The season never completely stops in Lymington.

"We don't go to the London Boat Show but we do go to the Southampton Boat Show. I think London is too far away and I feel that Southampton is really better, besides being so near at hand. There is now a major Marine Trade Fair in Brighton at the end of October/beginning of November and I think most people are finding out that this is almost better, from the trade point of view, than the London Boat Show. There are not the crowds there and you can walk around and it is open for three days. But with the fashion wear side the representatives usually come to me. I do sometimes go to Bournemouth when they have their stock-rooms there and are showing their spring range. When I bought my 1982 spring range and had finished adding up the bills yesterday, I thought I would have all the reps back and cut them off! Prices really are terrifying these days.

"We do stock the main firms like Helly Hansen, Henri Lloyd, Ron Holland and Javelin. We have done Stuart Madeley but not at the moment and Sebago for their 'docksiders'. We also stock Douglas Gill and some of Evett – mostly casual wear – and, of course, Joe Sanders has Equinoxe. We can't stock everything, as for one thing there is not the room and for another it is a lot of money. We do not do chandlery but we do stock lifelines, harnesses and life-jackets, which are all greatly improved these days. The water-activated ones are very expensive but if you have been knocked out or are unconscious you do not need to do anything at all; it just activates itself.

"Guernsey sweaters have not really changed at all. I stock La Tricoteuse, who are the main people on the Island and I just ring them up and they fly sacks of them to Eastleigh Airport. I go up there constantly it seems to me but it depends on the time of year.

"There are definite trends in sailing fashion, particularly in boots. This year (1981) we have been selling a lot of blue boots, another year it is yellow and there is very much a trend for white boots at the moment. It is very difficult to crystal-ball gaze when you have to order a year ahead. My 1982 order for shoes and boots has already gone in.

"In my husband's day we used to fit out quite a few of the crews and still do a few private crews. But these days more and more of the manufacturers will fit out a crew; some of them charge a nominal amount, some do not. It is very good advertising for them, especially for Trans-Atlantic and Round the World races.

"I think people are becoming more safety conscious these days, definitely with life-jackets and life-lines, especially after the Fastnet Race of 1979. It is very difficult to enforce the wearing of safety gear:

you can't just go to them at sea and say 'You haven't got your lifeline on!' But something should be done about people who just buy a little boat and sail off, taking their families with them. There have been so many disasters out in the Solent and particularly off the Needles that need never have happened."

Mary Campbell-Ross became a boat's crew Wren during the war and used to cox at Dartmouth, Southampton and Portsmouth. This used to be the ultimate in the Service and everyone who volunteered to join the WRNS, like Eileen Caulcutt and myself, hoped to do just that. It was a great feather in her cap to have been chosen. She recalled: "We were paid 2/- a day when we first started. I have always sailed since I was a small child and my father sailed or motor-boated. I was drafted to Southampton about three months before D-Day. I was not there during the bombing but I was there when the doodle-bugs kept coming over. The place was all flattened when we were stationed there. It was very interesting at D-Day as we went out in small boats into the Solent taking the troops out to the troopships (All so vividly described in Nevil Shute's book *Requiem for a Wren*).

"I don't live 'over the shop' now and have got a tiny little cottage in Boldre and go home every night. Unfortunately, I don't have much to do with the village because I am hardly ever there."

Lymington Sail and Tent Company

A month later, on 9th December 1981, I went to see Joe Sanders at the Lymington Sail & Tent Company in Bath Road and he was a mine of information. "I have been connected with the sea all my life, one way or another," he told me. "I do happen to have foreign-going certificates from the Merchant Service. I did pre-sea training in a naval college, served during the war in the merchant service and after the war too. I have been a superintendent stevedore, a wharfing manager and all sorts of things. As a result, it means that I have very broad interests. I was Export Manager of the second largest plastics company in this country about the mid-1950's with £1½ million turnover in my department alone. We were a separate company in those days and that would be equivalent to about nearly £30 million today. The company soon ceased trading but I have done many things and something new always seems to turn up.

"I have had a very interesting life and I meet some very interesting people and that is really why I do this job. If I wanted to make money I think I would go back into import/export. I used to work in the middle of the West End and we had charge accounts and entertaining expenses – the limitless expense account. I used to have charge accounts at all the main restaurants and never used them because I am not that kind of person.

"I bought out Ben Boxall fifteen years ago in 1966, although the firm itself had been founded about 1951 on the site of Lance's Yard. Ben Boxall had this mentality that every time he had a new idea, he registered a new company for it! So we had the Lymington Wire, Rope & Rigging Company for the rigging side; then he started making covers and formed the Lymington Sail & Tent Company; and then he did a bit of upholstery so the Lymington Yacht & Marine Upholstery Company was founded. Every time he had a new idea he formed a new company!

"The Lymington Sail & Tent Company was the only company that was any good at all so I bought it with the auxiliary companies as make-way. However, we do a small amount of business under Lymington Wire, Rope & Rigging Company for specific purposes. About five years ago we chopped the sailmaking away from the rest of the firm and gave it to my son, Pete, who has since made a success of it under Sanders Sails.

"Last heard of by me, Ben Boxall was staying with a sister in Southampton. Ben was married twice; he was a tremendous character, our Ben, and a man of many parts. During the war he was in the RAF and commanded an air/sea rescue launch before going out to India. Then he came back and I believe at that time the Berthon Boat Company were building inshore minesweepers. He managed to get a sub-contract from Berthon for riveting work for them, as in the past he had been a trained boiler-maker and a riveter. He was a man of many parts and, to some extent, a misunderstood man. He had plenty of ideas but he did not have the necessary push to put them through."

Chris DeVeulle of Aquaboats had told me that "Ben Boxall had bought the brewery barge *XXXX* from Mew Langton, intending to run it as a general sort of cargo boat from Lymington to Yarmouth, but there was so much opposition and poor old Ben was not very proficient with that boat. I do not know what happened after that: both Ben and the boat just disappeared off the face of the earth!"

Joe Sanders takes up the story: "Ben Boxall owned property in Gosport Street, and fought for many years to get planning permission without any success, and it was not until the land was purchased by the Trafalgar Group of Properties, that they were able to do what he had tried to do ten years before.

"It is going to be the same with the Bridge Boat & Crane yard, that was formerly the beer store: they are fighting to get that as a block of flats. I shall certainly try not to let them because the whole appearance and livelihood of Lymington is changing and changing rapidly. The Ship Inn is being developed, and what is now the car park of the Ship Inn was formerly part of the original boatyard. I was personally interested in it at the time.

"I had just been burned down when all this was happening. I was round in Jeremy Rogers' yard and had this old wooden building on top of these piles and the two buildings, side by side, were burnt down. We then put up the new building which is still there – although the planning authorities told me it would not be allowed to remain there and, as a result, I had to sell it very cheaply! They allowed the change from the boatyard to the block of flats on the Quay – the 'magnificent Admirals Court' which is the biggest eyesore of badly-designed flats I have ever seen! Bill Smith used to have that boatyard at the head of the slipway and it came straight into his yard. To me one of the features of Lymington when I first came to the town was the fact that the car park on the Quay used to be filled with yachts in winter time.

"We were burnt down on a Thursday and Bill Smith very kindly offered his premises to me and made them available on the following Monday, and flooring to the tune of 2,000 sq. ft. was laid. All sorts of people turned up with a hammer and a bag of nails and we just did the whole thing continuously until it was finished. I have never seen a floor go down so fast. They were all very kind. Hood offered us the use of their sail lofts and machines in the evenings when they had finished. A very nice gesture. We were back in production within 24 hours of the fire and in full production a week later! I was most grateful to Bill Smith and his family because his youngest son re-wired the boatyard so that we had extra lights and power points just where we wanted them. He worked all night on them sometimes. They were very kind to us. There was only one customer who cancelled his order and his name will be with me for ever!

"This building is owned by Berthon Boat Company. Originally, I believe, it was the first power station for Lymington and we had to make good quite a bit in the building behind us, over the old pits where the engines were formerly. Then when they closed the power station down a firm called Multi-hulls bought it and started building catamarans there. I believe Major Gossage was a director of the company. That is where all this glass in the office with the little yachties came from: they put that in and it has been there ever since. In one of the many vicissitudes of the boat trade, they went bust and David May then bought it and it is from him that we rent it at present. He made it into the Lymington Marine Garage. One day I was in here and noticed

that there were too many chiefs and not enough Indians and so I went in next door and asked if I could have the buildings when the business went bankrupt – and I got them!

"We are the sole agents of Equinoxe. I am very friendly with Clare Francis, and have known her for a considerable number of years, and when she came back from the Round the World Race it so happened that one of my clients, who is a Frenchman, asked me if I would be interested in selling clothing in a bigger way for Equinoxe. I consulted Clare and apparently that was the type of clothing they all wanted to have for the long-distance races and they could not get it because it was only available in France. So that is how I became their agent. Apparently, the French had tried to sell it in this country by mail order and it had been extremely expensive. They spent a lot of money on advertising and I think they got a 2% return on their advertising budget. We are gradually getting better organised and have got out our English catalogue and considering that this year (1981) has been a very bad year generally, we have done extremely well. We had about 75% of the Trans-Atlantic Race using our stuff and for the Round the World Race I think we had about 60%. We have had Connie von Rietschoten, who owns *Flyer*, in here personally buying his Equinoxe equipment and a lady who was flying out to New Zealand to join the yacht there asked if we could possibly equip her quickly with Equinoxe. We have had more Equinoxe clothing this year on board Admiral's Cup yachts than any other manufacturer in the world. It is accepted as being basically the best. It is not the cheapest, because it could not be to stay the best but neither is it the most expensive. We play the Franc market fairly closely. You see last year (1980) with the Franc being weak we actually cut the price 10% and as everybody else in Britain virtually put theirs up 15% we had a sudden decrease of 25% in our prices which caused one or two heart-searchings. But I am a lucky person – these things happen to me.

"I work very hard as well. In winter I work from 7.0 a.m. to 6.0 p.m. but in the summer I often work till 7.0, 8.0, 9.0, 10.0 or 11.0 o'clock at night and before we got better organised I used to start at 5.0 a.m. in the morning. We didn't have much choice. Yachtsmen like the stuff when they want it and I have had to move house once because they became so demanding. When I got back at night I would find them on the doorstep waiting for me!

"I encourage people to call me 'Joe the Tent' because, for one thing, it is a gimmicky name that people remember easily and as such I am known all round the world. But in France – and I am particularly well-known in Northern France – 'Joe la

Tente' has a colloquial meaning which is entirely different! It means a gentleman of a limp wrist and I have got a large number of clients who love to bring their friends to me to meet 'Joe la Tente'; it absolutely kills them! I thought a lady from the French Embassy was going to have hysterics!"

Joe Sanders had recently been given a NATO contract. He thought that there must have been duplication or triplication of orders for rope by the Americans. Certainly, he had been asked to make fenders for 25 NATO tugs – each fender weighing 2 tons of rope. To use it all up perhaps?

Yot Grot

No one is recorded as having survived adrift for as long as Maurice and Maralyn Bailey, after their yacht *Auralyn* had been sunk by a sperm whale off the Galapagos Islands on 4th March 1973. They spent 118½ days in a small life-raft and rubber dinghy without being able to sleep properly, with little drinking water and no tackle for catching fish.

How they managed to stay alive until they were eventually picked up by Korean fishermen four months later is vividly related in their book *117 Days Adrift*, published in 1973 by Nautical Publishing, which they started writing on board the rescue ship *Weolmi*, using Maralyn's diary and Maurice's log book for their text. In the words of Sir Peter Scott: "The Bailey's story will give hope to many a castaway of the future, but more than that, it will give a lift of encouragement to people in countless other situations of adversity." Although on several occasions ships passed by without stopping, they never abandoned hope.

Maurice Bailey had always been keen on sailing from the age of 16, mainly in dinghies on the lakes and reservoirs of the Midlands. He also developed a passion for gliding and that took most of his time. When he came out of the army he chartered boats on the West Coast. In 1963 he married Maralyn when they were 41 and 32 respectively and Maurice worked as a printer's clerk and Maralyn as a tax officer. They settled down in their own home, although yearning for an escape from the tediousness of suburban life. Maralyn was frightened of flying so they spent their free time in the Lake District and Scotland, climbing, walking and camping.

Although they could not afford to buy a boat, they had always dreamed of sailing to far off places and so eventually they took the plunge, sold their home and decided to live on board. They moored their boat at Lowestoft but found cross-country travel from Derby to Lowestoft rather difficult so they moved to the South Coast and opted for Hamble

Marina and found jobs in Southampton, although every spare moment was spent on the boat. Finally, they set sail in June 1972 for New Zealand and for an adventure that would have lasted most people for a life-time. On their return to England, after their rescue, Commander and Mrs. Erroll Bruce immediately offered to share their home with them and later Mr. and Mrs. Adlard Coles and Major and Mrs. Bill Martineau placed their homes at the Bailey's disposal while they finished writing their book.

They then sailed to Patagonia in 1975-76 which is recorded in their next book, *Second Chance*, and a further voyage to the Mediterranean in 1978-79. Then even they had had enough of world travelling and they sold their yacht and bought their present home in Sway and their business, Yot Grot. Maralyn then wrote a book called *The Galley Handbook*, which was published by Nautical Publishing Co.

Maurice Bailey told me that Yot Grot had been run in a minor way as an offshoot of one of the chandleries. This chandlery had been accumulating a lot of second-hand gear and so decided to open a store to sell it off. Although in existence since 1978 it was not until the Baileys acquired it in October 1980 that it grew to its present form and the store moved from Quay Street to Bridge Yard. "We attempted to provide the middle ground for yachtsmen wishing to dispose of surplus and unwanted gear and those looking for good second-hand gear at a reasonable price," he said.

The Beaulieu Boat Jumble, held in early April, they consider a bit of a flash in the pan but they have a stall there and generally speaking it has not affected them very much. Nevertheless, other people are always ready to jump on the band-waggon and so take a lot of the gear that they would normally handle. "Once one is on to a good idea one finds other people trying to copy. The Chandlery on the Quay tried it for a while but have stopped now. People seem to have money to spare for second-hand gear but not much for brand new gear. Some of our stock comes from bankrupt stock although we do not like to cash in on other people's calamities."

Yot Grot will buy in from yachtsmen but if an item is too costly or of an electronic nature they will sell it on a commission basis only. Some examples of what they sell are: sails, wood-shell blocks, winches, self-steering gears, cookers, a brass-cased paraffin burning water heater, rubber dinghies, chains and warps, navigation equipment, foul weather gear and galley and cabin equipment.

In 1981 the Baileys purchased D.M.S. Marine, which deals with the servicing of life-rafts and life-raft hire. They have part-time help in the summer in Yot Grot but Maurice and Maralyn do all the administrative work. Although it is a little slacker in the winter there are still quite a few customers fitting out or building their own boats.

Customers come from all over the UK, particularly from Wales, but also from as far away as the United States. They have clients in France and Belgium, and Holland is one of the most prolific sources of gear. They have an agent on the East Coast to deal with second-hand gear business for them in Denmark and they exchange stock with them. Visitors have been attracted too from Switzerland. "It is a fine way of getting to meet all these interesting people but it is literally a seven-day week for 52 weeks in the year!" Maurice Bailey remarked, somewhat ruefully.

Tollbridge Trailers Ltd.

Tollbridge Trailers Ltd. was started by Lieutenant-Colonel Robert Butler, MBE, MC, who had previously been a regular officer in the Queen's Own Royal West Kent Regiment. When he met the author's mother, quite by chance, in the Royal Lymington Yacht Club he absolutely insisted that he be allowed to give her a drink. Apparently she had given him one when he called on her at the Depot in Maidstone as a new and rather nervous subaltern and he had never forgotten it.

He took over a limited company in 1955 which was virtually bankrupt and the premises consisted of a garage, a precision engineering works and a boatyard. It had also made some trailers. He then established a specialist firm in road trailers and called it Tollbridge Trailers Ltd. because of its proximity to the tollbridge. At one time his Sales Manager was Mr. Stone (now Stone's Insurance), who used to live on the houseboat *Linnette*, moored close by. Amongst orders they fulfilled were 250 trailers for the Post Office, 20 1-ton trailers for Hong Kong and industrial trailers for the Royal Navy. They also carried out precision engineering for De Havilland and Vickers. Colonel Butler held a pilot's licence and flew his own aircraft.

On 28th March 1963 they organised a combined demonstration with Peter Webster Ltd. and I. I. Gmach & Co. at Lymington and exhibited a selection of their range. This included the trailer which had carried Bruce Campbell's *Christina* over 30,000 miles on journeys between the Hamble and Cannes on the French Riviera.

An interesting article by F. J. Dalgety, published in Volume 6 of the *Hampshire Magazine*, describes Tollbridge Trailers of Lymington having led the country in the development of the modern boat trailer. More and more yachtsmen were using them because not only could their boats be kept in their backyards, thus making them easier to maintain and avoiding a mooring fee and possible damage at moorings, but they could be towed to different places each weekend. Some of the small cabin boats had even been used as caravans.

Tollbridge Trailers designed a trailer of rolled steel in the shape of an 'A', giving extreme rigidity and strength. The wheels and chocks were arranged so that the boat's centre of gravity was carried 10% forward of the trailer wheels, thus allowing high speed towing and braking without the danger of a whip. The suspension on all their trailers was by independent rubber torsion units and they evolved several methods of launching yachts without their owners have to push the trailer to the waterside and heave the boat into the water. The trailer had rubber rollers on a ramp which was pivoted above the axle and a winch was fitted to the tow bar with a cable running to the boat's bow. In this way loading and unloading were comparatively simple. The firm, unfortunately, became a victim of the credit squeeze and closed down.

All-in-Transport

Another yacht transport firm was All-in-Transport and I went to see Captain Hugh Wilson, RN, at his home at Norley Wood on 14th May 1982. Two years before his retirement in 1969, he had been Commodore out in Hong Kong and many mementoes of his time there could be seen in his home 'Rossenford.' He told me that after he had left the Navy "it was quite a struggle because 49 is a lousy age to get lost. I managed to get a job as yard manager with a yacht yard at the top of the Hamble River. It didn't work out very well – it was going to expand but, in fact, did not – and I stayed there for only six months.

Journey by Road, 1930s

By courtesy of T. H. P. Wilson

Journey by road, 1970s – All-in-Transport

I then went off for a cruise, where I met Brian MacNamara, who has lived in Lymington nearly all his life, and he told me that Bill Smith, who had run a boatyard here for a good many years, was thinking of expanding his transport business.

"After a very well-arranged and informal meeting with Bill in the cockpit of my Skog, we agreed that we would set up a partnership and this we did. This was in 1970 but by the time we had got the office going, advertised and so on, we really started off in April 1971 with one long vehicle and a special trailer which we all had a hand in designing. We kept ourselves always as a small firm but we got enough work to pay ourselves and plough something back into the business. Two or three years later we were able to buy a heavier tug unit and also some writing tables. I stayed in the firm for four years.

"Trade was starting to slide away and the recession was just beginning to bite and various people were withdrawing from the yachting industry. Hugh Marriott who ran Jackson, Jackson and Marriott Yacht Brokerage at this time, stepped out of that side of it and I saw various straws in the wind and I think Bill did too. He was very keen for his son Malcolm to take on this driving because he did not like messing about in the yard very much, so with perfectly amicable arrangements, he bought out at a price decided by our accountants.

"It was a fascinating job, in particular driving through London to the Earls Court Boat Show towing a trailer 14 ft. wide with a catamaran on and a policeman in front and another one behind. Until you got to the Boat Show you didn't realise what goes on before and after the Show. We used to go all over England, Scotland and Wales. I didn't go abroad but since I left they have been abroad quite a bit with the heavy vehicle but we found really enough to keep us going in the United Kingdom.

"When I was seventeen they had just brought in the driving test but, being seventeen, I got an all groups driving licence provided I passed a test some time. So I was very lucky. This carried on until 1971 when tests became compulsory and meant that Malcolm and I could drive without 'L' plates provided that by 1972 we passed the test. So I did a lot of driving and we managed to get a very good chap, who was in sales and heavy loads for Ford Engineers and who supplied our vehicle, to teach us a great deal in a few days. Before I really started driving I had two or three lessons too with a very good ex-army transport chap who showed me little gimmicks for backing. But if you take a deep breath and carry on doing what you have been doing the past six months then you should get through your driving test and, in fact, Malcolm and I both passed.

"So I was Heavy Goods Class 1 driver and I learnt a hell of a lot about all sorts of things for the next eight years. You have to have a medical at sixty so although my licence carried on just past it I decided that I didn't want to go on driving so I let it go.

"When I was still in the Navy, Jean and I shared the Hewlett's Skog with them for one year while I was running the Naval Staff College at Greenwich, and we went 50–50. Then Henry decided he wanted to go back to Darings and so we bought it from him. It was quite a story because his brokers at Bosham were on the point of selling it to a customer. I phoned the Royal Thames Clubhouse at Warsash and the boatman rowed out to Peter Beagley and lured him ashore and said, "Don't sell it to that Scotsman as Hugh Wilson wants it!' He then had to point out all the snags he possibly could until his unfortunate customer finally decided to withdraw his offer and so I got her!

"We then went to Hong Kong for two years and I kept her in the Hamble and continued to do so when I worked in the yard and even when we first came to Lymington, because here there was a waiting list of nearly three years. So for two years we had to drive over to the Hamble each weekend to race and then drive back again. Then they dug out Fortuna Dock and Fred Woodford, the Harbour Master, cleared his backlog at a stroke with 100 more moorings, so we got in here.

"Two years later we changed our Skog for an Arpege, which we bought from a very nice man at Poole, who had to give up sailing on medical grounds. She had absolutely every instrument you could think of, all from Brookes & Gatehouse, and a life-raft, dinghy and I don't know what else. We race quite a bit: we used to do Cowes and we always go Round the Island and we do some West Solent races and usually the Poole Race. I know Howard Lewis, the Secretary of the Royal Lymington Yacht Club, well as he was in Singapore with us in the 1960s. I am still keen on racing because I think if you go on racing you will then sail the boat nicely when you are cruising, and you get restless if the boat doesn't sail properly. We didn't put the boat in the water this year because of this Round the World lark!

"I was asked to take on with a new committee to replace the one with Erroll Bruce, which handled the first two races. So we organised the third race. We went to Cape Town but not to Auckland and we did go to Mar del Plata. The Argentinians were charming and I don't personally believe that any at that level, including the chaps in the submarine base there, had any idea at that time that anything was in the wind. We left there on 1st March just a month before they invaded the Falklands and we had a lovely time there. Then last week (early May 1982) we had this terrific Whitbread prize-giving with all the crews and now we are looking forward to the next one in three years' time."

CHAPTER 18

SEAMANSHIP AND NAVIGATION

"My wife thinks I should run a course for wives. I always reckon that it would be a very good idea in case someone's husband falls overboard. She ought to know how to pick him up or at least know how to navigate home if she doesn't want to pick him up!"

DAVID STRANG

Commander M. H. Brown, OBE, DSC, RN

Larry Brown was brought up in the Royal Navy in the days when it was less specialised than it is today and everyone knew a little of everything. When he was at Osborne he went to the engineering workshop and re-lined a bearing on an old engine. "The idea was that if the Engineering Officer reported that a job would take three days you could say, 'Don't talk rubbish! It can be done in one day!'

"My father was a parson and schoolmaster at Oundle and was a great carpenter and he used to make the bedroom furniture, the wash-basins – they didn't have running water in those days – and towel rails and wash-stands. He had a House of 48 boys at Oundle, he was the Chaplain of the School, and he ran a 'backdoor entrance' where he took boys of nine and they evaded the Common Entrance and got into the Senior School without it. My father did very well out of it! He also used to do all the repairs of the furniture in the holidays and was his own handyman."

Larry also took great pride in doing things for himself and he found working with his hands a great relaxation. When he lived at 'Birchcroft' he painted the outside of that large house twice and he and his wife together re-decorated the inside of it. He never needed to employ anybody to do household jobs apart from an electrician and a plumber. His skills were to be used to the full both in the Community Centre and in the Royal Lymington Yacht Club.

His last job in the Royal Navy was Queen's Harbour Master at Plymouth. Larry Brown was on the sailing committees of 11 yacht and sailing clubs at Plymouth. He was there for 4½ years and when he left in 1953 he was presented with a barograph by the clubs in recognition of his services.

The Jardine Twins sailed there for the Firefly Championships and the whole family would go down in a caravan. When Larry came to Lymington, Colonel Jardine came up to him and said, "Are you the chap who ran the Firefly Championships at Plymouth?" and when the reply was in the affirmative he was phoned the very next day and asked if he would go onto the Sailing Committee of the Royal Lymington Yacht Club. "In those days you could watch Richard Creagh-Osborne and all those chaps sailing in the river and I used to go out in the rescue launch and pull them out. It was fun!"

Shortly after coming to Lymington Larry was introduced to Robert Hole, who at that time (1955) was hard at work at the Community Centre. Robert was full of enthusiasm and if he could not get somebody else to do a job he would – and could – do it himself. Larry Brown soon found himself rather a 'willing horse.' He made the double doors outside the Wellington Room and installed the lift there and also made the front doors at the New Street entrance to the Centre. He took over from Robert Hole as Chairman of the Maintenance and Building Sub-Committee, which was known as 'Dad's Army' in the Community Centre and later he became Hon. Vice-President.

While Larry was helping at the Centre he met Lieutenant-Colonel Moxey, who was very ancient and was running the navigation classes and so he took over from him and instructed in navigation for 11 years. "I was a qualified navigator and I had done quite a bit of teaching at the Navigation School," Larry told me. "In fact, one of my trainees became the Deputy Master of the School of Navigation! Captain Crawford took over from me for a year and then I think he thought that there was a bob or two in it and he started up the School of Navigation in Lymington

"I taught for an evening a week in the Autumn and Spring terms only. This was before the RYA Courses. One of my trainees at the Centre was Chris Bowen, the last Commodore of the RLYC, who was very shy of navigating for himself. On one occasion he took his boat over to Holland with Mac Reynolds navigating. Mac Reynolds went sick and they rang up Lymington and tried to get the Secretary of the

Club to find somebody to go over and navigate them back. Nobody would go so, in fact, Chris had to bring her back himself! He rang me afterwards and said, 'I am back, Larry. I did what you told me and it works!' "

Commander R. Milward, RN

Commander Ray Milward is the Royal Yachting Association Instructor in Navigation for Hampshire Adult Education classes held at the Further Education Centre, Priestlands and at Lymington Community Association in basic 'Coastal Navigation' and the more advanced 'Yacht Master Offshore' and 'Yacht Master Ocean' (Celestial Navigation). He spoke to me at the Lymington Community Centre on 16th March 1981 just before the start of one of his classes there.

"The compass is obviously the main navigational instrument in a craft but it is often rather forgotten," Ray told me. "In the old days the compass was the only navigational aid carried by sailing ships and early steamships and nothing magnetic was allowed anywhere near it. That is why the bridge was surrounded with brass. A Quartermaster going up to the bridge would have to hang his knife on a special hook and woe betide him if he had gone to the compass with it. He would probably have been hung from the yard arm! As a result the compass was perfect in that it had no effective deviation.

"The Admiralty had a Compass Observatory at Slough and you could say that I was a graduate of it as, partly because of war service, I went there four times in my career in the Royal Navy, from Sub-Lieutenant to Senior Navigator.

"During the war an interesting thing happened in the compass world. The Germans introduced the magnetic mine and to combat it ships were fitted with anti-magnetic degaussing coils (DG coils). The effect of a DG coil on the compass had not been appreciated and when a sweeper in which I served as navigator sailed out of Harwich, I set the course and suddenly the helmsman called out, 'The compass won't settle, sir,' and the darned thing was going round and round! So we had to turn back. But the scientists were quick in coping with this problem and balancing coils were fitted close to the compass which compensated for the DG effect.

"I came out of the Navy in 1951 and became Harbour Master at Chichester for the next five years. I soon became concerned that yachtsmen, some of them with little or no experience, could put out to sea and then scream for help from the coastguards and rescue services (there were no helicopters in those days). Apparently the Royal Yachting Association had thrown up its hands in horror at the very suggestion of a form of 'driving licence' and took the attitude 'We must not have government compulsion' although a lot of countries did this. So you can still buy a yacht, take yourself and your friends to sea and drown the lot without any government regulations preventing it! You did not need to take out any insurance either unless you charged them, but if you took them for a free trip, it was all right!

"While I was at Chichester, the Elder Brethren of Trinity House inspected the Harbour and, shortly afterwards, they advertised for a Superintendent at Dover. I applied for it, and my name must have rung a bell as I got it! While I was at Dover I had been teaching a little navigation and doing some compass work so when I retired – and still feeling fairly active – I decided to take this up seriously. Otherwise it can be dreadful when you retire as suddenly no one wants to know you and you are finished. I had always liked teaching and realised that compass work in a yachting area could be of interest. So I looked at the map and noted that Highcliffe looked interesting and was well placed between Lymington and Poole. My wife agreed to move as long as there was a sea view and, indeed, we can see the light of the Needles Lighthouse from our living room. My area extends as far as Weymouth in the West and Littlehampton to the East and I am kept pleasantly occupied, though not excessively so.

"Classes in navigation at Lymington are very popular and I often have to turn applicants away in September when they enrol. I aim at a class of about 22 to allow for an approximate 20% fall away later on. Some yachtsmen usually think that all they have to do is to sit in and then I go round with a bottle marked 'Navigation,' unscrew a knob on their head and pour it in! When they find that they have to work – and work hard with papers to take home as well – they fall away. But the fall-out is small in the senior class, the 'Yacht Master,' as they have already been through the 'Coastal' class and know what is involved. The RYA theory classes are getting stiffer all the time and now there is an examination at the end as well. But it is all very friendly; I am not there to fail them. I start off with deviation and variation of the compass to get the 'grey matter' going and its importance will be obvious later on. Follow-up practical courses afloat can be arranged with most sailing schools. I am also an Examiner for the Joint Matriculation Boards."

Ray Milward has some amusing stories about his experiences as a compass adjuster and these are to be found in a later chapter.

Lymington School of Sailing

Captain Lionel Seddon Jones ran the Lymington School of Sailing from his office at 9 High Street (Quay end), Lymington which he also used for brokerage. The School itself, which was also residential, was situated in Bath Road and is now part of Brookes & Gatehouse Ltd. He told me that, "Following on the yacht brokerage we started the sailing school inasmuch as I bought a boat and, having been an ex-Master, I started actually giving navigation lessons. After the first winter of giving navigation instruction to a small group of people one of them said, 'I wish you could teach me sailing too.' So I said, 'Right, I have got a boat,' so I thought about it and gave him a course of sailing lessons. Very quickly he asked if he could bring a friend along and the friend brought a friend and that snowballed and we had a dinghy section as well. That we operated mainly in the school holidays, as this is not what I would call a dinghy sailing area, in the sense of Chichester Harbour; there are more cruising boats here. We ran the Sailing School for ten years and I suppose we had seven or eight dinghies for the younger element on the go at one time." He still continued to give private coastal yacht-master navigation and astro theory during the winter. The author, whom he described as 'his delinquent pupil of yesteryear,' went on a 5-day cruise in the Solent for the RYA 'Competent Crew' and 'Day Skipper/Watch Leader' course, and enjoyed it immensely.

A quick look at his literature gives a good idea of what could be learnt. "Dinghy instruction is carried out in 16 ft. Wayfarer dinghies, well proven boats and selected by sailing schools for ease of handling, safety and performance. Other boats used are the popular 18 ft. Seafarer and *Happy Days,* a 23 ft. open day sailer yawl. These courses are ideal for persons of all ages from 10 years upwards wishing to start sailing or to improve their standards. For those desiring to obtain a certificate we can issue Elementary, Intermediate or Advanced Dayboat certificates to pupils reaching the necessary RYA standards.

"For Sailer Cruiser tuition, courses operate from a 9.5 metre (32 ft.) Maxi 95, fitted with a 22 h.p. diesel engine, a well proven offshore cruising yacht providing ample living, cooking and sleeping accommodation for 6 persons, including separate toilet facilities. Latest navigation equipment includes radio direction finder, radio telephone, a sextant, etc. Coastal cruises courses in addition to practical sailing covers application of rule of the road (nautical collision regulations), chartwork, tides and tidal atlas, radio bearing, basic yacht handling, mooring,

anchoring, entering and leaving port, etc. The RYA Coastal Competent Crew/Day Skipper certificates are available to proficient pupils."

The Yachtmaster 5-day Practical Offshore Course is a "live-aboard course including food found with visits to English Channel ports. This course is primarily for those who have undergone (or are undergoing) Yachtmaster Theoretical evening classes. However, pupils of Coastal Skipper standard and those desirous of obtaining further practical 'sea-time' are welcome to join. The course includes an overnight passage and pupils take command for the planning and carrying out of a passage.

"Theoretical courses include one in Astro-Navigation: a special ten-lecture course to RYA Ocean standard covering sun, moon, stars, planets, traverse tables and sextant. The Yachtmaster (Offshore) Theory is a refresher course of lectures over ten days for those with sailing experience but lacking on theory. Conducted to the RYA Yachtmaster syllabus with supporting literature, visual aids, slides, etc.

"Residential accommodation is available at the School house. Other hotels and guest houses of a good standard enjoyed and approved by previous pupils are: The Angel Hotel, High Street, Lymington; John and Audrey Ball of the Railway Inn, Station Street, Lymington; Mr. C. M. Willcock, Stanwell House Hotel, High Street, Lymington and Mr. B. Baker of the Crown & Anchor, Captains Row, Lymington. We can also arrange for you to hire a modern residential caravan at nearby Milford-on-Sea. For families or groups this makes an ideal base and one can either self cater or use one of Lymington's many restaurants. Camping facilities are nearby in the New Forest."

Grosvenor Charters Sailing School

This sailing school, at 36 South Street, Pennington, Lymington is RYA recognised and offers courses to RYA syllabus for the practical qualifications of competent crew, day or coastal skipper and yachtmaster offshore. "Sailing is fun," they write, "the more so as your skills improve. That is why there are so many sailing schools. So why choose us? We don't claim our instruction is better than all the others but it is as good as the best. Where we do score is with our type of boat and her location. She is a comfortable 36 ft. Conway Ketch with accommodation in 3 cabins, which makes her good for mixed crews. We can take up to 7 but prefer a maximum of 5 clients. *Hoplite* has a hot shower, two heads, refrigerator, good cooking facilities and cabin heating. On deck there is slab reefing, headsail furling, cruising chute and mizzen staysail and a spinnaker for more experienced crews. She has a 42 h.p. Mercedes diesel so that we can tide cheat if necessary. There is all the safety equipment you would expect – 8 man liferaft, dinghy and outboard, lifejackets, harnesses and flares.

"For practising navigation *Hoplite* has a super chart table area with a large range of hardware including ship to shore VHF radio, full sailing and wind instruments, both Aptel and Sailor direction finders, 3 compasses, a sextant and an autopilot. We provide oilskins on free loan (for those of average build) and also sleeping bags and liners. But we ask that you bring deck shoes and wellies (black soles very taboo), toilet gear, warm clothing, and of course as many hip flasks as you wish.

"A bit about our food. The skipper believes an enjoyable cruise comes by courtesy of food and weather, and the first of these he can do something about. So *Hoplite* is actually victualled by our associates, Pennington Lodge Guest House – and they are professional caterers. By the way, if you want to stop over in Lymington before or after our trip, the Guest House would be pleased to oblige.

"Now about our location. Lymington is the best placed marina in England. *Hoplite* can sail at all states of the tide, day or night, and whilst in her home port can offer showers, shops, chandlery, and a private free car park all year at hand. The sheltered waters of the Solent allow us to sail in weather conditions when others are harbour bound. For instruction purposes, the strong tides concentrate the mind. It is just a short distance to the Needles and the open waters of the South Coast.

"We also offer informal tuition for people who want to learn to sail without feeling the need for certificates – or maybe for those who wish to introduce family and friends to the best sport in the world. If you talk to us, we can tailor our instruction to suit. Or maybe include you aboard when we are running a RYA course, and not press the certificate part. Who knows – you might change your mind. But whatever you choose, we remember that a course is your holiday, and you have paid us good money to have you aboard.

"Whilst mentioning money – our price for these courses and the dates available are listed on another page. *Hoplite* offers a 10% discount for block bookings of four or five people, and has no age limits. But we do just ask that people over 70 and under 14 are accompanied by a friend.

"Lastly, just a word or two about liability. As we said, the skipper's job is to run an enjoyable cruise, but the weather controls all, and the decision, where, whether or when to sail must be his. Safety is our watchword, and we don't take silly risks. We do hope you will come sailing with us this year."

Lymington Seamanship and Navigation Centre

Captain James Crawford wrote that "in co-operation with one Philip Harley, who lives in Pennington, I set up the Lymington Seamanship and Navigation Centre in 1973/74, after leaving Laurent Giles & Partners, where I had been in a brokerage capacity since 1966. I was pretty appalled at the standards of seamanship and navigation which I encountered amongst people buying yachts, and there certainly was an opening for responsible instruction here.

"We set up 'shop' above Elgar's, the paint shop, in really admirable circumstances and set our sights on 'top people' for top quality instruction. We had some really admirable classes and the affair was going well, with the right sort of clients, until the miners challenged the last Conservative Government. We suddenly found that all our 'top people' cancelled their courses – and of course the three-day week hit the country. My colleague, Philip Harley, had children to educate and needed to earn more – so, to cut a long story short, we closed down the operation until the storm blew over.

"We then re-opened in 21 New Street (where the Centre still is). Philip had gone to sea as a Master and I sold my shares in the business to David Strang, an ex-submariner, who is still running it now in New Street – with fair success as I understand."

David Strang, the present Principal of the Lymington Seamanship and Navigation Centre was Senior Cruising Instructor at the National Sailing Centre for four years. He is Yachtmaster Examiner and Dayboat Coach/Examiner. We take up his story in 1974 after James Crawford gave up the business.

"For my sins I am by way of being Secretary of the Federation of Sailing Schools," he told me when I visited the school on 13th December 1981. "It makes a lot of work and is a damn nuisance really in some ways as in the summer there is not enough time to get things done.

"I have known Lymington for years and my brother-in-law, M. H. E. Thoyts, is the dentist down below. I had taken Philip Harley on a course at the National Sailing Centre and was looking for a change of scenery when I met him in Lymington and asked him if he thought of expanding on the cruising side as I was wanting to branch out. He was thinking of closing the whole thing down: it was a bad time of year financially and the motor-boat fraternity were the first people to give up. Most of their instruction had been on that side and very little on the sailing side. So Philip and I decided to resurrect it but he had to take off and so I was left quite literally 'holding the baby' and it was a case of in at the deep end from scratch.

"Erroll Bruce has continued as Chairman and has been a great help throughout, even though he was busy with his nautical publishing. He still gives the odd lecture and comes up and meets the students and discusses things with them generally.

"The change of premises cut overheads considerably and I developed the sailing side; the motor-boat work was done in the students' own boats, which saved me the expense of keeping a motor-boat for the Centre. The whole thing was put on a sounder financial basis and from a fairly meagre first year in 1975, we virtually doubled our intake in 1976 and in 1977 I was looking for someone to help me. An ex-naval bod stayed with me for three years but left to go back into the Navy, but now I have an ex-National Sailing Centre instructor to help me. Running a sailing school is great fun although jolly hard work and financially it is not very rewarding. It is because the sailing populace is not prepared to pay the going rate, it is as simple as that, and if you do charge it then you price yourself out of the service.

"In the early days of the Centre they creamed off the locals in the Lymington area and consequently I had to look further afield for students. There has been a steady increase in the theory navigation courses and 60% of the students come from the Mediterranean. Professional crews come back and try to get more qualifications so the Centre provides concentrated navigation courses. Instead of doing a Yachtmaster throughout the whole winter at Adult Education Classes – I cannot compete with them financially anyway – they can take it over two weeks, but obviously they have to be experienced. The Mediterranean crews in particular need to learn about tides here, the British weather system and the way the actual weather forecasting is available to them in UK waters. Also they can brush up the plotting side and they are taught to advanced level for the yachtmaster offshore and because they have plenty of practical experience they often only need to put in one day at sea for the final sea examination.

"But some people just come for fun and to learn a bit at the same time. The advent of advanced navigational aids makes no difference. It is a lot easier if you have got one of these magic boxes but it doesn't help when the electricity fails and you still have to put a line on a chart. It is no use knowing how to work them all if you don't know how to do the basics. And that is what we have been doing: a mixture of concentration on *practical* courses in the summer and *theory* navigation in the winter.

"We sometimes go across the Channel and down to the West Country to ports like Brixham, Dartmouth and occasionally Salcombe and back. But it depends entirely on the weather although often the strength of the crew is even more important. Sometimes you have got the right weather conditions and the wrong crew, or too weak a crew; and sometimes you have got the right crew and the weather is all against you. From a teaching point of view it is better not to spend a very long time crossing shipping lanes and dodging ships, but it is fine if they have never crossed the Channel and want to work out the navigational side and do it once. You learn more by doing short, sharp passages up and down the coast going into two or three harbours a day, picking up moorings, anchoring and coming alongside and then doing the navigation and pilotage involved in that.

"Also in the Solent you have got one of the best areas you can find, as there are plenty of harbours and plenty of sheltered water. If it is blowing very hard with gale force winds you can usually operate in Southampton Water unless it is a NW or SE gale. Of course, one is tempted to say, 'Well, now is the time I would advise you heartily in these wind conditions to put your feet up and watch television, visit the nearest pub or do some work on the boat,' but you are expected to go out sailing every day and the pressure is on.

"The reference to medical matters in my brochure was put in after one of the bods I had taken out was very, very sick. The trouble was that he was a diabetic and having taken his insulin he was then sick and passed out five times on me. So the next day I didn't go to sea – the only time that I have not gone out – in order to let him get settled before we came back. I don't mind taking diabetics as long as I know beforehand and can plan accordingly. Also we eat very well and my wife prepares some lovely food and it could go to waste.

"There is no reason why one should not take disabled people out. You don't necessarily need more crew as disabled people are remarkably adept at getting around on a boat but you do need a special boat with plenty of extra grab rails. Also it amazes me how some of the blind people get on with special compasses and various other things but there must be one sighted person on board and again you need a special boat.

"I take non-swimmers with some reluctance as long as I know beforehand and can take precautions. I make certain that they wear safety harness all the time or a life-jacket and take that much extra care.

"I take out all age groups right up to 75 year olds. I do not like unaccompanied children under 13 or 14 but I have taken younger, mainly when there is a family on board. The 6, 7 and 8 year olds tend to tire very easily and they are not so ready to learn whereas at 13 or 14 they really begin to show an interest. The important thing is that they fit in with others.

"The number of students in a year varies considerably. To make ends meet you need about 80 or 90 but in a good year we have been up to 150. Usually the ladies don't come so much and I have a feeling that if the family is really feeling the pinch Dad might come on a special course and then teach the family. I think a lot of wives and girl-friends are put off by intolerable weather conditions. The husband or boy friend probably doesn't know 100% of what he is doing, gets a bit rattled and shouts, rants and raves a little bit, mainly because he is probably a bit scared himself. We also recommend beginners to come on courses in May or June when we get lighter winds and try to introduce them gently. My wife thinks I should run a course for wives. I always reckon that it would be a very good idea in case someone's husband falls overboard. She ought to know how to pick him up or at least know how to navigate home if she doesn't want to pick him up!"

Churchill Motor Cruising School

Henry Harris, founder and a director of the Churchill Motor Cruiser School, formerly served in the Royal Marines with the rank of Lieutenant. His Chief Instructor is a retired Commander RN, who had been in minesweepers, and he instructs in seamanship.

Henry was cruising in mid-Channel about ten years ago and saw a man waving widly from a motor cruiser, which had broken down and was wallowing helplessly in the heavy swell. The owner and his two small sons were in dire straits with no lifejackets, no radio and no flares. "I decided that I had better do something about it and it went on from there," he told me when I talked to him on board *Alda Trois* on a summer evening in July 1982. "We started off in Chichester ten years ago and came to Lymington as part of the course and we fell in love with it really – as everyone does, of course. We moved here about seven or eight years ago and have been operating from the Lymington Yacht Haven ever since. It is an ideal place." The Churchill Motor Cruising School is one of only five motor cruiser schools in the whole country and there are three on the South Coast.

"Henry Harris has little time for the owner who, he says, has probably bought his craft after a dazzling visit to the Boat Show," wrote Penny Gordon in *The Women's Journal.* "Blinded by visions of James Bond (or Erroll Flynn, depending on age), martinis at sunset, and bikini-clad lovelies on his deck, Mr. Average ignores the basic problems of sea life." He also ignores the hazards of busy shipping lanes, ferries and rules of the road in general. No licence is needed to drive a boat and it is not compulsory to carry safety equipment. Furthermore, there is still no test of competence in this country as there is in France and the United States.

The School has a twin-screw diesel Grand Banks 42 ft. motor cruiser called *Alda Trois*, which is ideal for teaching besides being a very spacious boat to live abroad, as students do on these courses. She has twin lever engine controls and all manoeuvres are conducted at 800 r.p.m. as the School stresses the importance of doing everything slowly.

The course makes sure that you have the necessary knowledge and experience not only to cruise in safety but to enable you to derive the maximum amount of pleasure from it. It is essential that everyone should have a working knowledge of seamanship, navigation and Rules of the Road and the ability to bring a boat safely back to port if there has been an accident. The School covers the syllabus of the RYA Motor Cruiser certificates and it also issues Course Completion certificates to those reaching a satisfactory standard. Students can also take the 6-day course for the Practical Section of the RYA Yachtmaster Certificate and also RYA Grade 2 National Motor Launch and Powerboat certificate.

For the owner and prospective owner wishing to cruise further afield, Henry Harris charters a motor cruiser in the Mediterranean, rather than take his own boat down there. From March to June and in September he runs an 8-day course on Seamanship based on Antibes and visiting such attractive ports as Cannes and Monte Carlo.

The 1982 charges for living demi-pension on board + VAT (inclusive of insurance) is £275 for the standard 5-day course, Monday to Friday, and for the 8-day course in the Mediterranean it is £400, no VAT (exclusive of air fare, food, fuel and berthing). Pupils can be instructed on board their own boats at weekends, Friday to Monday, at £100 for up to two students and £150 for three or over, with a maximum of five. These charges are per day.

"We had great excitement the other week," said Henry Harris, "when we went to see the *Canberra* returning from the Falklands. It was fantastic: there must have been about 1,000 boats out there. We also saw *Hermes* come in, and they were very pleased about that, and another week we watched the arrival of *Fearless* and *Intrepid.* A couple of years ago we helped get *Golden Hind* off a sandbank when she went aground. There was a tug there but we helped a bit. During our cruises we visit ports like Cowes, Poole and Chichester but there are limits to how much weather we go out in.

"John and Peggy Deighton, whose daughter, Jenny Welker, runs Elliotts in the High Street with her husband, joined a course about four or five years ago when they bought a boat. We became very friendly with them and still are: he is a great character, and so is she. They had studied theory with Lionel Seddon Jones in evening classes.

"Students come from all sections of the community and from as far afield as Derby and Nottingham. They may be company directors, engineers, chartered accountants and wives and girl friends no less. Surprisingly 20% to 25% are women and, according to their instructors, they are every bit as good as the men. (*Pace*, Women's Lib!). Furthermore they would often ask questions which the men were reluctant to ask, for fear of showing their ignorance, and their popularity rating positively soared as a result!"

The brochure of the Churchill Motor Cruiser School is entitled 'Live and Learn Afloat – as featured in thje ITV *Afloat* programme.' Henry Harris has appeared frequently on television; he has been on *Open Water* programmes a couple of times and three times on the Jimmy Young programme on safety at sea. One was just after the tragic 1979 Fastnet Race. "I was whipped off into this studio because I had already been asked about safety at sea, which was very interesting. I have also been on Nationwide television *South Today* on the safety aspect. I enjoyed that." So, I am sure, did the television viewers.

CHAPTER 19

"THE PROFESSIONALS"

"Having knocked about in boats for the last 59 years, I am quite happy to prop up the RLYC bar, be fed 'Bloody Marys' and talk boats to anyone who cares to indulge in this delicious pastime."

ALASTAIR EASTON

COMPASS ADJUSTER

Commander R. Milward, RN

In addition to being the RYA Instructor in Navigation for Hampshire Adult Education, Ray Milward is also Official Adjuster to the Royal Naval Sailing Association and Official Adjuster for Silva Compasses and covers the area from Weymouth to Brighton.

"Electronic aids will enable a relatively unskilled seaman to find out where he is and from that point of view they are a good thing," he said. "But they can create a problem, especially in smaller craft, as they tend to upset the compass unless they are kept a safe distance away. If it is too close you cannot correct for it and builders sometimes tend to put the compass in at the last moment with 'It looks nice there,' where it balances well in a line of gauges in the worst possible position for compass adjustment! All electronic aids throw out their own magnetic effect and so a change steadily takes place. I advise the owner to check on known courses and the compass can be reswung if errors are noted.

"The trouble with English compasses, although one must say in all fairness they are very fine instruments, is that the makers have not moved with the times. After the war the RAF came up with infinitely variable adjusters, which you could adjust with a non-magnetic screwdriver. You can vary the force by adjusting the magnets, so you can put infinitely variable correction on a compass. But the biggest British compass adjusters do not use this method and the whole adjustment then takes twice as long, as you have to pull out a magnet and push in another. If they don't look out they might well end up in the same position as the Triumph motor cycles did with the Japanese ones!"

It usually takes somewhere in the region of an hour to adjust a compass but this season (1981) he has a new adjusting aid which is a considerable improvement on the instrument last year. He has developed a system which originated in Sweden, of using an instrument for adjustment in yachts which obviates the need for external reference and is, as far as he knows, the only one of its kind in the United Kingdom. It effects a considerable reduction of time taken with adjustment.

It is also a help if he can adjust the compass just off the marina, in sheltered water, as out in the Solent you so often find wind against tide; the bumping about affects the compass and you cannot get a steady reading. He does the work at the convenience of the owner but, if a group is arranged by a yacht club, he then reduces the price, as he is transferred from boat to boat and this reduces travelling time. Despite inflation he does not intend to increase his basic charge for compass adjustment (one compass), which will remain at £15.00. This is much cheaper than the fee charged by commercial adjusters.

Ray has some amusing stories about his experiences as a compass adjuster as abilities of owners vary considerably. There is the owner who proudly invests in his new craft but can hardly handle it. He always warns the owner what is involved in compass adjustment. He then asks him to steer certain courses, although for navigational reasons and crossing craft his word should not be regarded as law! Before now he has found a ferry far too close for comfort! "Some owners, when asked to steer a course, do so come hell or high water and I have been aground several times. For this reason, if I do not know the owner, I usually choose a rising tide! Not so long ago, I had given my usual precautionary warning and the reply came, 'That's all right, it is my risk,' and on the way down river we got nearer and nearer to one side and, lo and behold, the craft came to a stop. 'Oh, that's nothing,' said this particular owner and put his engine full ahead announcing he could ride over the mud bank. But all he succeeded in doing was to drive her out of the water by another six inches and there we stuck on the mud. Whereupon his wife rounded on me and said, 'It's all your fault, compass adjuster,' which I thought a little hard, the more so since we were being laid over by passing ferries as a result of loss of buoyancy." The perils of compass adjusting!

Some interesting craft that Ray has swung have been concrete ones, difficult to adjust because of the steelwork net frame of the concrete, and the most unusual was a junk-rigged schooner in 1979. Ray is afloat quite a bit, especially in good weather in his own boat which he keeps at Poole, as Lymington is too expensive.

BROKERS

Yacht Haven Brokerage Ltd.

The Haven Brokerage is situated in King's Saltern Road, Lymington and the office is manned seven days a week. It offers courtesy, efficiency and service for buyers and sellers alike and has an enormous choice of boats. It is a member of the Central Yacht Brokerage Service, established in 1977. Peter T. M. Barrett who, with Dirk Kalis, is a Director of Yacht Haven Brokerage, kindly sent me this potted history, dated 16th February 1981.

"Laurent Giles & Partners operated a brokerage for very many years and back in 1972 when the Yacht Haven opened for business an agreement had been reached between the Haven and Laurent Giles for their brokerage operation to be moved to Lymington Yacht Haven. I joined Laurent Giles under Captain James Crawford, as assistant broker, with a view to my taking charge upon his impending retirement from brokerage.

"I had had a number of years previous experience in the West Country with brokerage and then I joined Deacons Boatyard as broker on the Hamble. In 1970 their brokerage operation was taken over by J. G. Meakes Ltd. and I was then employed by them. The opportunity to work with a company of the stature of Laurent Giles, combined with the chance to operate within a marine complex was extremely attractive, so I joined them. I took over the management of the brokerage for Laurent Giles & Partners in late 1973 when Captain Crawford retired. A few months later I was joined by Anne Jelley and about a year after that by Vanessa Hutton (as she became). The same team is still working together today, though under a different banner.

"In the summer of 1979 the period of the agreement between the Haven and Laurent Giles came to an end and the Haven decided that they wanted to operate their own brokerage. It was recognised that a known team of people would be an advantage to the new operation and we were offered the job. As Laurent Giles were uncertain as to the viability of operating a competitive brokerage outside the Haven, the old staff decided to move over to the new

company. So we continue to operate from the Haven with the old team and with all our friends around us."

Alastair Easton

"Having been knocking about in boats for the last 59 years, I am quite happy to prop up the RLYC bar, be fed 'Bloody Marys' and talk boats to anyone who cares to indulge in this delicious pastime!" writes Alastair Easton, who runs a yacht brokerage from his home at Little Belmore, Belmore Lane, Lymington. It was not a 'Bloody Mary' but a very strong gin and tonic that he gave me when I visited him after work on the evening of 16th August 1982 and the effect was lethal!

"I ended up my naval career appointed to *Britannia* to sail *Bluebottle* for the Queen and Prince Philip, and I did that for two wonderful years," he told me. "That coincided with the Navy cutting down and the 'golden bowler' scheme but as I was over 40 we were considered as 'natural wastage,' which is not particularly flattering. But after I had had that splendid job they decided that they could not have a silly old 'B' sitting around an airfield so they let me out three years early, when I was 42 and gave me three years pay. I thought I am not really capable of doing anything else so I learnt how to become a yacht broker.

"I learnt with Monty Bradshaw and I was there for nine months, six of which he was ill in hospital, and so I ran the thing myself. When he came back, I started up on my own in Fordingbridge, which is quite a long way from the sea but at least it crossed all the main roads and radiused most of the sailing places. So it worked all right. I probably know most of the boats in years past and I always try and look at them, but as I have boats in the Mediterranean and all over the place to sell, this is not always possible. So I end up, regrettably, mostly in the office with masses of paper work. I have also got a brokerage concession at Bucklers Hard!

"A yacht broker is not a dealer in any way at all: he is a broker and is very similar to an estate agent, except that I think you want much more technical knowledge and preferably knowledge of builders, designers and types of boat and so on. You need to be a user of boats, I think, and be an active sailing man yourself.

"We always insist that anybody who buys a boat, even a year old fibre-glass boat, has a survey and we arrange to put them in touch with several surveyors who live more or less in the vicinity, according to whether it is a steel boat, or an aluminium boat – we know one firm that is particularly good at that sort of thing. The younger surveyors now all have probably a lot of knowledge of fibreglass but if it is an elderly wooden boat, I usually advise people to go to someone who really knows about them, preferably someone who has been an apprentice in a boat-building yard years and years ago and has worked himself up and knows all about wood construction.

"Selling boats is not like the little 'black book' for motor cars. I think it is the most difficult question of all to ask a broker what price he ought to ask. Probably we go and ask one or two of our colleagues, anonymously as far as the boat is concerned, as two or three heads are better than one, and we come to a sort of mutual decision on the asking price. But it is very difficult these days to settle on a price. I think one thing we must do is not allow an owner to ask a stupid price to put people off. We try to advise them on a fair price and it is generally known that people like to bargain so we always advise them to leave a bit on top to bargain with. Sometimes you find an owner who asks and sticks to a set price and nothing else, and you know where you are, and the chap has to get up to that particular figure to get the boat, which is good.

"I had in fact been asked to run the big marina brokerage but it would have meant not working in my name, which I think I have established fairly well and I did not really want to work for anybody else. I have always worked from my old home and I think this is the way to do it.

"Most brokers seem to be very good friends and work together very closely. We all help each other; it is friendly competition. For instance, if I have a boat for sale and another broker in a marina has it for sale, I try and sell it before he does but if he sells it first, I probably congratulate him. It is a very friendly atmosphere and, unlike the American brokers, we have no cutting of commissions to do another broker down. This is the good thing about English brokerage: we stick to our proper standard brokerage as agreed by the two main Associations, the Association of British Yachtbrokers Agents (ABYA) and the Yacht Brokers, Designers and Surveyors Association (YBDSA). Both Associations are getting closer and closer together, having the same rules virtually and the same aims.

"I have been sailing since I was 2½ years old and that was years and years before I went into the Navy. I ran the naval team a couple of times and the inter-service competition and my name was put up and I was selected for an appointment to the Royal Yacht. The nicest job that any naval officer keen on sailing could ever have; it was wonderful. I think in two years I had three months off sailing. Otherwise I took *Bluebottle* round all the big regattas in Europe and had the most tremendous fun and keen racing.

"You could say that I was the Royal Sailing Master but actually I asked Buckingham Palace at one time what I was and they suggested that 'Royal Helmsman' was a proper title, because one was appointed to the Royal Yacht. When the Queen and Prince Philip went on a State Visit to Denmark, we took four or five Dragons. The Danes laid on special races for us in the Dragons and we had a lot of very good racing for a week. Then the Queen reviewed the fleet up in Scotland and from there we went to Norway, Sweden, France and Portugal, taking the Dragons everywhere with us and racing in all these lovely big international regattas, which for a sailing man is a first class life.

"Prince Philip raced with me, I think, two days in 1957 Cowes Week and two days in 1958. I have got several photographs of Prince Charles, one of him having his first sail. I took Uffa Fox as crew with me that day and so it is quite an interesting photograph. Prince Charles was, I think, eight years of age then. I had a paid hand who had been there for eleven years when I first had the job but he was not allowed to race in international races. Clive Smith was a wonderful chap to sail with and a real boat lover. We took old friends out, who were racing in Dragons fairly regularly, and some who had raced in *Blue-bottle* before under different skippers. I also selected odd chaps who were up-and-coming young helmsmen who possibly might be of interest to the Olympic committee, and it gave them good fun and good experience.

"I race a lot now with a chap I was at prep school with and I think when he came back from Burma, I sold him his first boat of any size; it was one of Dickie Bird's very good Heron boats which I had crewed in, and he has gone from strength to strength. I now race a 2-tonner with him which was built in England by Souters and designed in Norway in 1977, an Admiral's Cupper. I have my own X-boat, a beautiful varnished one, which I race as much as I get time for these days. We have got about 40 X-boats on the books in Lymington. I have raced Darings and the Dragons, but I think probably the X-boat class is the hottest competition of any Solent class at the moment. I used to race occasionally as crew to Barbara Payne and occasionally sail the boat at Itchenor, where I was a member for a long time. She had an 'X' which I think is No. 8 and I believe her parents had No. 1, which she gave to the Poole Museum. She wrote the *History of the X-Class* and is a great X-boat exponent."

Hugh Marriott

It was Hugh Wilson who put me in touch with Hugh Marriott and I went to have a talk to him at his home at Plough Close, Silver Street, Sway on Friday, 10th September 1982.

"Like so many people who have come down to this part of the world," he said, "I worked in London but did not want to bring a family up there. I was in advertising and thought I cannot really do that outside London, so I had the idea of doing something else, such as making toys for sick children and various other ludicrous ideas, none of which would make any money. One day I was asked: 'What do you know about?' and I said, 'I know a bit about selling' and it was the time when the boating boom was on and everybody was buying boats, so I thought it might be a good idea if I became a yacht broker.

"So I picked on the Solent as the best area to do it and I picked on Lymington as the best town in the Solent to do it from, because Hamble had already got some brokers. At that time in Lymington there was Laurent Giles and the Berthon Boat Company was doing a bit. The Lymington Yacht Haven had not yet been built and Alastair Easton had not yet moved to Lymington. So I thought, 'Right, this is the place' and then I thought 'Where shall I go?' and I looked at shops in the High Street and they all wanted £90,000 or something like that, so I walked along the frontage between the Town Quay and the Yacht Club. When I reached Hood Sails I knocked on the door and said, 'How about letting me have a corner of your loft?' and they told me to get lost! Unable to find anywhere to go and feeling rather dispirited I went to the Ship Inn and had a pint of beer there. It was at the weekend and I stood there on the Quay looking at Jackson & Jackson and thought, 'That is where it has got to be.' So I walked in and said, 'Come on, we are going into partnership and we are going to do yacht broking' and, surprisingly, they said, 'Good idea,' and so we did!

"Paul and David Jackson were ideal partners and very good indeed: they let me get on with it and they helped where help was needed and did not interfere where it wasn't and the two sides worked very well together. Quite a lot of people like to move into this area because they are interested in boating, and are probably looking for a house to buy or a weekend cottage and buy a boat at the same time. I did all right for the first year, did quite well for the second year, quite well for the third year and then we went bust with a large bang in the fourth year! So that is when I packed it up, in 1974.

"It was the year when the Chancellor of the Exchequer introduced 25% VAT and that was a bad thing. I was then faced with the problem of whether to hang on like grim death and possibly come through and then face exactly the same thing as when I started here. Probably other chaps would come down from London and start up in opposition, in which case I could lose some money and perhaps land other people in trouble as well. So the only alternative was to see if I could sell it. Alastair Easton very kindly bought the goodwill and so he took it over, although not the premises.

"I enjoyed yacht broking; it was a super way to earn a living because you met all sorts of people. Most people buying a boat had some sort of a dream; they were seeking perfection or imagined that they were going to escape and go to the South Seas.

"One or two brokers were most helpful and were nice enough to say: 'Here is our list of boats that we are trying to sell with the prices and where they are lying. If you can introduce a buyer we will split the commission.' So from Day One I started with a list of about 50 yachts and I advertised them like mad and that produced one or two buyers as well as one or two enquiries from owners wanting to sell. So that is how I started and to begin with it is difficult but you learn anything if you are really keen to do so. Obviously, we made mistakes but nothing too vital. Then there is the legal side. I had to do an awful lot of reading up about contracts and that sort of thing but it is not a hard-nosed sort of business, the yachting world. People are kind, so really I probably got away with murder!

"When I packed up the business I felt at a complete loss and a terrible failure. Then Peter Johnson came along and said, 'Write a book with all the answers to all the questions that people have ever asked you when you were yacht broking' – and that is what I did. The book is called *Owning a Boat – all the essentials of buying, running and even selling a boat today,* published by Nautical Publishing Ltd. in 1976. It was a great discipline because I would go down to the garden shed at the bottom of the garden, hammer away at a typewriter and I just worked an 8-hour day for three months and finished it. Today it is out of print.

"I am now back in advertising and it was the book that really started me on that again. Jeremy Rogers asked me if I would write a brochure for him and then I wrote an article in *Yachting Monthly* for International Yacht Paints. I was in fact trying to write another book, a thriller this time, but I started writing advertising copy, brochures and public relations stuff and so on. Then I became quite busy and turned away one or two people and so then I decided I must get some help and we got a girl to come in three mornings a fortnight. I can remember that was a big decision – three mornings a fortnight – and it went from there! I had eighteen months off so that must have been towards the end of 1975 and now there are ten of us working away and it is better than yacht broking!"

His firm, Marina Markets, did the 'public relations' for the Whitbread Round the World race. Patsy Ellis, who is half English and half Argentinian, was the translator out in Mar del Plata and got caught up in the Falklands Invasion. She now works for Hugh.

Hugh Marriott showed the same flair and imagination in the way he ran his boat. "I sail but I don't really like racing; I am not very competitive," he continued. "I had a boat, a 24 ft. one when I first started Jackson, Jackson and Marriott, but because I was working all hours, especially at weekends, I very rarely got to sail in her. So when some friends of mine asked if they could borrow the boat one weekend I replied 'Yes, provided that you put something right.' I left on board a book of things that needed doing, ropes to be spliced or holes to be patched, anything like that so that anyone could pick on one thing which was congenial and do it. By the end of the season the boat had never been in better condition. She looked absolutely sparkling! So I picked on three of them and asked them to dig into their pockets and buy a quarter share and suggested that we should run the boat as a syndicate. That was twelve years ago now and we are still going strong. I think perhaps that when I was in London I would not have liked to share my boat – then it was a lifeline. I used to come rushing down and jump into it. We kept her at Fareham to start with before we could get a mooring in Lymington. But living close to the water you don't get quite so possessive about the boat and the syndicate works jolly well."

Hugh Marriott had also been an interviewer with Southern Television for a time and had interviewed Adlard Coles amongst others. Apparently, when Adlard Coles was abroad he would not try and talk in a foreign language but would just draw what he wanted and got on much better that way! A man of many parts is Hugh Marriott.

Nicholas Edmiston

I went to see Nicholas Edmiston at Berthon International on 4th November 1982 at his temporary office in a 'portakabin' but now the brokerage has moved into some lovely new offices overlooking the river.

"I am fairly local," he told me, "and I lived at Bucklers Hard as a child so I have spent a fair amount of time down here, thirty odd years or so. I worked in the City after I left school and got involved in the yacht broking business rather by accident. I was a bit bored and then David May, whom I know quite well and whom I had met when I was ocean racing, invited me to come and work here at Berthon and at the time it seemed a good idea.

"I have been here for twelve years now. Yacht broking looks a glamorous job to most people but it is a seven-day-a-week job and often a 24-hour-a-day job. So unfortunately I don't get the same time for sailing as I used to have before, when I would sail every weekend. So that is where one has the difference in emphasis.

"I am responsible for the profitability of the brokerage department so really time off doesn't happen. I personally work on a profit share at the end of the year but, in fact, we can sell a lot of boats without making a profit. We are hit by the recession at present and it is probably the most difficult time I have ever had in the brokerage department. We probably sell more boats than most other British brokers but we have got four brokers here in Lymington and one office in London as well as a small office in Hamble, so it requires quite a bit of expenditure to keep them going.

"We co-operate a great deal with overseas brokers although we have never opened an office abroad. We have looked at the possibility but the cost of opening an office in the South of France, for instance, which is the main centre, is very expensive. But the time may come when we will have one down there. So we deal internationally but from England.

"The owner often suggests a price and the owner's price can be totally irrelevant to the value of the yacht. What happens is that an owner comes in to see us and asks us to sell his yacht. We then ask him to complete a questionnaire which provides us with all the information we need about the boat; where it was built, when it was built, what its equipment is, and whether it was built for Lloyds. We then hopefully have an opportunity to look at the boat afloat as it is very difficult to see it on land. Thereafter, judgement based on what similar boats have sold for recently and prevailing market conditions enable one to come up with an asking price. Invariably, the owner will say that his boat is the best maintained! Every owner says that and they cannot all be and some of the boats are appalling! At the moment boats are at a lower value than perhaps some owners would like. I am not a believer in agreeing with an owner if his price is unrealistic: it is a waste of his time as well as mine.

"The next stage is to type out the particulars, normally with some fairly good photographs of them, and then advertise in one of the yachting magazines, mainly in *Yachting World* where we take two pages. In *Yachting World* the brokerage advertising is something in the region of £15,000 a year. Our total budget ranges between about £20,000 and

£30,000 a year but you have got to do that. Hopefully, this produces the enquiries from the clients who ask for further particulars, which we post off to them, and we probably follow this up with a telephone call inviting them to come and have a look. Buyers often don't really know what they want and it really is a question of fitting what we have got with what they can afford. Some owners are quite experienced and know the sort of boat they want but others have an open mind and there is a lot of guidance that has to be given, rather more so than with an estate agent. I think an estate agent, whilst in a similar line of business, doesn't probably have to get quite so personal. A boat is a very personal thing, almost more so than a house.

"I think if we sell a boat within three months it is fairly quick. The copy date for the magazine is about six weeks before it is published, so by the time all that happens three months is quick. Occasionally you get the situation when someone will come and say that he wants to sell a boat, and I know in my head the right person and ring him up and sell it, but we have other boats that we have had listed for sale for about two years or even more. Normally, if it is that long it means that the owner is not taking our advice; any commodity has a market value.

"We sell a lot of ocean racers: we are certainly the leading ocean racer brokers in Europe and probably in the world, although there are some American brokers who do quite a bit. We have made our name in the brokerage market for selling ocean racers although it is a comparatively small part of the business. We sell other boats as well. We have sold ocean racers to people like Edward Heath, when he was Prime Minister, and Robin Aisher and Chris Dunning; most of the top Admiral's Cup boats get sold through our brokerage. At the last Admiral's Cup a year and a half ago (1981) we sold all the New Zealand Admiral's Cup team – two boats within a week of the Fastnet, and the third boat was sold within another six weeks.

"A lot of the boats we sell are being measured by the RORC now, and they are boats well worth over £100,000. Boats like *Yeoman XXIII* could have cost Robin Aisher something in the region of £175,000, and to replace it today would cost £200,000. It has become a very expensive game. When I say that we would not sell a boat under £30,000, £30,000 is a lot of money by comparison, but if you go down to the South of France there are all these people with large motor yachts costing millions of pounds.

"We do have all sorts of interesting clients, people like Sir Maurice Laing, of Laing Construction and Admiral of the RORC. We have dealt with several American film producers. One of the Vice-Presidents of Warner Brothers Film Company is quite a good customer of ours. On the boat building side we have just built a boat for over a million dollars for a Hong Kong owner, so we do get fairly interesting people. Selling the boats we have built is really done separately by the yard, but I am involved in doing a lot of PR for the whole company; I think I will become more involved in making decisions on what sort of boats we should be building now. It is a different form of selling. We get some very difficult customers but we also get some very nice ones.

"We also sell some Dutch-built boats, as I am involved in a company called Trintella, which builds some very good cruising yachts – a 53 ft., a 45 ft. and a 42 ft – in value from £100,000 up to about £250,000 for the 53 ft. and obviously I spend a lot of time when we get an order for one of those. It means going to Holland frequently. I suppose each boat involves probably about four trips there. This year I have been to the South of France, Italy and to Spain a couple of times, so I do get around.

"I had to go and value two large motor yachts for a divorce case earlier this year. One, based outside Genoa, was an 80 ft. day-boat with twin gas turbine engines, which I valued at about one million dollars, and a big motor yacht in Southern Spain, which was worth about two million dollars. I received all expenses paid plus a valuation fee. So we are recognised as experts in our field. I did not actually have to go to court, I just made a statement. But if one makes a valuation one must expect to go to court to justify it.

"We work on a commission rate of 6%, although the international commission rate is now 10%, and so if it is a boat lying outside England we work on 10% commission. I think it will go up in this country in due course, although many people think it is a lot of money. On the other hand, it costs just about £100,000 to run the brokerage."

AGENTS

Richard Bagnall

Richard Bagnall is a frequent caller at the RORC Rating Office and I eventually twisted his arm into allowing me to call and see him in his home at 19 Ambleside Road, Lymington on 1st September 1982.

"I was born in Lymington in 1946," he told me, "and we were really living round Keyhaven most of our early days. I have to say 'we' because Harvey and I went to the same school and we always sailed together." Richard Bagnall and his twin brother, Harvey, are very well-known racing yachtsmen and their sailing achievements will be included in a later chapter. It is Richard Bagnall, the Yacht Agent, who must be recorded here. Richard has always been very interested in the Lymington area and once wrote a thesis on Keyhaven beach – the shingle bank going to Hurst from Milford – and his parents read it out to the Milford Historical Records Society.

"I studied at the College of Technology in Southampton for the Yacht and Boatyard Management Course (not to be confused with the Yacht Design Course at the University of Southampton). Masses of people have been through it and most of them just enjoy the sailing during the course. But it was very, very interesting because we met people who had gone into business and then left to come to College, so you were meeting mature people. I had already been into advertising on the art side, trying to become an art director, and met all sorts of people there which I found very rewarding.

"I was working for Camper & Nicholson at this time. I started off at the Northam Yard and then went down to Gosport and there I was Personal Assistant to the Manager: in other words, 'general dog's body'!

"In 1974 I was in charge of a new project building a racing boat called the Nicholson 30 and the first owner was Peter Johnson. So there I was, suddenly realising that I had this boffin from Lymington coming over to check out on my first vessel! Peter Johnson described the hand-over in one of his books and a photograph reveals a thousand items on the pontoon still being assembled! But anyway he took it very well. I became Production Manager at the age of 33 and left the firm after a 1½ hour redundancy notice after 9½ years there. The Managing Director went the day before and I went too. Three of us were production managers and two of us left because they said that they could not afford us. I was surprised at that: no wonder, they were already in the red!

"1980 was a fantastic year for me. I did no sailing at all and I learnt wind-surfing and scuba-diving in Florida. I supervised a one-off Frers 65 for a Hong Kong owner and it was very special, and I mean extremely special, and was probably the most advanced interior construction at that particular moment when it was launched. It was built along-side the new *Kialoa,* so that was quite exciting stuff and things didn't go altogether too well and I had to take over from the builders and supervise the last four months. Well, I was looking after the owner's money and he was living in Hong Kong and I was getting rather anxious. In fact, I had good reasons. Anyway, we survived and I came back here.

"Then I saw this Greek vessel, which was the most expensive ½-tonner ever built, called *Don Quixote.* All very interesting and it was built in the same special construction we had chosen for the interior

joinery on the other yacht, the previous year. This is where I met the designer Bruce Kelly, a well-known designer now, although I think he had a few problems in Lymington. I am very pleased to say that when Harvey and I were on the boat it went well but they had a headache after that. We won the Cowes Week Level Rating for the Half Ton Series and then, for some reason, the Greek went off on his own to the World Championship at Poole and could not get his vessel to move because he had so many changes done that we had advised him not to do.

"The trouble is that it is so tempting to make changes and this is true of so many designers. I now speak of the ones who sail the boats they design without being too involved in the Rule. I see a boat going well and I then see them fiddling around with calculators and everything else and on paper it may well go better. But nearly every single vessel I have touched has been ruined if the boat has been tuned and is really going well and then is changed to go better. Usually it is the end of its days. Quite fascinating. Once it is going well, for goodness sake leave it. It is so tempting, you see, and it is impossible for someone who has got money to know when to stop. The owner thinks that he can buy speed and it doesn't work. I have always advised the designers that if they would only do one change at a time we could say yes or no – it is good or bad – but they never do and always want to know what has gone wrong and why. The answer is 'We don't know, because you have done too many changes.' So that is a shame. I do try and guide people.

"Anyway, after that I got involved for the first time with selling and I was invited to inspect the X.102 built in Denmark and become the manager and run the project in England almost entirely on my own, which is what I am doing now. Basically, I am not a yacht broker and now, I suppose, I am working for a yacht agency – we are agents for this Danish builder – so I am not actually selling secondhand boats, only the new ones.

"I have never been on the selling side before and it is quite interesting being on the other side of the coin. Having been a production manager I know the problems before I get the boat and when it comes I know what problems to look for! What is even worse is that my mind fills with all the disasters that can befall a production yacht! I find the Danes have a fresh way of boatbuilding and it is jolly nice to see the different ways people tackle a problem and usually come up with roughly the same answer and roughly the same mistakes.

"Unlike a car, a yacht is totally free and even with the most detailed rules it is really Joe with his hammer or screwdriver that is going to make a good or bad yacht. It is refreshing in that way but I cannot see it lasting much longer. Let's hope the boom comes back because we are going through hard times at the moment.

"Padrich Yachts is centrally based at 82 London Road, North End, Portsmouth, but as my base is here in Lymington, it was agreed that the best place to demonstrate would be in Lymington as well. So we have a demonstrator at the Berthon Marina and we use their facilities. It is really through advertising, contacts and, I suppose, the Boat Shows that we find clients. The Southampton Boat Show is probably our life blood and 75% of firms going there will actually depend this coming year (1983) on that Boat Show. It is frightening. Clients contact our Portsmouth office and they filter through to me here; there is about a 50% link with Lymington.

"I basically went to Art College at Southampton for a short while on the second year of an advertising and design course, but when I took my drawings of pussy cats and yachts they were not duly impressed, so I now draw yachts as a hobby! I haven't done it for a while now, which is a pity, and I suppose that is one of my major interests. I do special black and white scraper board, which I find is an interesting medium, and I think the famous seagull advert is probably the best example of simplicity in a few lines and the eye does the rest. That's why I like it but I never know where to stop, that is the difficulty!"

Fjord

I was not so successful in twisting the arm of the UK agents for Fjord but they were about to move from their premises in Quay Street, Lymington when I contacted them. Fjord, the Norwegian boat-builders, later announced the appointment of a UK concessionaire – *Fjord Boats of Lymington*. The company hopes that the new appointment will not only help those looking for new boats but also those who have existing boats and who need advice or spares. The company is headed by Christopher Harridge, who worked for Fjord in the UK from 1972-79 and therefore has a useful background in the field. Fjord Boats are now handling the full range of power and sailing cruisers from their new office at Lymington Yacht Haven.

YACHT CHARTER

Don Howard

Don Howard was one of the first people I interviewed in the Lymington Yacht Haven on 27th February 1981 and he could not have been more helpful. Don came to Lymington twenty years ago in

1961 to run a charter business. He had previously been Head of the Mathematics Department at Hardley School, Fawley (designed, incidentally, by Roger Pinckney) and left it when it turned comprehensive. Originally he rented a section of the foreshore adjoining that of Peter Webster just up river from the 'Royal' and today he operates from the Lymington Yacht Haven where he has an office.

He is a Founder Member of the Lymington River Commercial Users Association, which was formed in 1967 and as its Secretary he was then elected to represent the Association on the Harbour Commission. In addition to forming Sea Ventures Ltd., the charter company of which he is managing director, he is also a Founder Member and Secretary of the Yacht Charter Association Ltd., a national association based on Lymington, with its headquarters at the Lymington Yacht Haven. A man of considerable talent and many parts, and with a deep knowledge of and interest in the Lymington River, Don Howard *is* yacht charter in Lymington.

Convinced that there is a real need for a continuing sea-going charter business within the yachting industry as a whole, a number of UK firms formed the Yacht Charter Association Ltd. in 1962. To be eligible to join, a person has to make a living as a professional charterer; it cannot be a sideline. Private owners are not eligible to join unless their yachts are part of a YCA member's fleet.

It aims at ensuring high standards of maintenance, equipment and upkeep of yachts offered for charter, so that clients can do business with member firms with confidence, knowing that the craft they hire will be well-found and seaworthy. The YCA has set up working parties with – and is represented at – the Ship and Boat Builders National Federation (SBBNF) and the Royal Yachting Association (RYA) and liaises with local authorities and government offices.

Member firms of the Association agree to provide a certain minimum of equipment, without extra charge, to inspect their vessels regularly and to carry out effective servicing and cleaning between charters. It has accordingly raised the level of charter fees to one that would give a fair return to the charter firm. Another role it provides is that of a forum for the exchange of information and it helps reduce advertising costs by sponsoring group advertisements, which make considerably more impact than those of individual firms.

The Yacht Charter Association advises on starting a charter business. Statistics available to them show that the average life of a charter company is three years, and only two companies out of ninety-one known to have operated in the last eighteen years still survive (1981), although new companies mushroom up each year to replace those that have fallen by the wayside.

The use of the YCA Charter Agreement almost precludes the need for litigation, if necessary, as the Committee examines complaints and advises on arbitration methods. Insurance rates are less; its brokers have negotiated special rates for YCA members and special cover for charter work not available elsewhere. The Association does not interfere with the running of individual companies other than to require that their minimum standards are adhered to or, preferably, exceeded. They provide access to a list of unreliable gear and also circulate a list of unreliable people, running into three foolscap pages. In a recent case, a boat chartered in the West Country was found to have £250,000 worth of cannabis on board! Safeguards are essential and Don Howard – like the Mikado – 'has a little list'!

Lymington charter firms and firms for charter based on Lymington in 1981 are:–

Abbey Yachts.

Archimedes Yachts (a Harrogate firm) based at Lymington Marina.

Blue Peter Yacht Charterers (a London firm) based at Lymington Yacht Haven.

Festina Charter Ltd. (Lymington firm of Peter Morris and G. P. Green) based at Lymington Marina.

Jane's Yacht Charters (Purley firm) based at Lymington Marina.

Sea Ventures Ltd. (Don Howard's firm) based at Lymington Yacht Haven.

Shiphusbandry Services (Lymington firm of J. Oakley) based at Lymington Yacht Haven.

Trailaway (Lymington firm) based at Lymington Yacht Haven.

Of these, Blue Peter and Sea Free, relatively new, have now amalgamated; Shiphusbandry Services, headed by Jerry Oakley, started business a year after Sea Ventures (1962) and is the second oldest charter company in England; Festina charter for racing and have tied in with Archimedes; Trailaway are not so much in the yacht scene but go in for small boats (small as opposed to a top price of £97,000); and Grosvenor Charters. which provide a skippered charter service but are not members of the YCA. Sea Ventures have boats capable of racing but would sub-let to Festina if demand so dictated.

In addition to these charterers, the Lymington Centre of Seamanship and Navigation charter, as does the Churchill Motor Cruiser School; fishing boats may be chartered for angling or potting parties and individual boats, such as *Dartaway*, owned by William Payne, which is suitable for filming and photographic work, besides many others.

"With secondhand prices dropping and marine costs and maintenance costs going up," said Don Howard, "the yacht owner finds he cannot afford to keep a boat and cannot sell it, so he sometimes decides instead to charter for two or three weeks a year. Unfortunately these boats do not need to carry flares, an anchor, navigation lights and, worst of all, are not always insured. Incredibly, there is no legislation pertaining to safety on charter boats, and so people's lives are at stake.

"If an owner charters a yacht and declares that he does so, his premium may be raised. Also he would then have to pay a *commercial* rate of 25% or more to the Haven for his berth. This means that instead of paying £25 a foot he would have to pay £30 a foot, so a 30 ft. boat would be charged £900 a year plus VAT. Some owners, as a consequence, keep quiet about chartering and do not pay insurance, although with two boats in a collision costing £30,000 each there could be £60,000 damage done, quite apart from loss of life. Despite various working parties comprising of the RCA, the SBBNF and the RYA and most of the other bodies being set up, there is almost total opposition to licensing the charter boat. But the YCA policy is that anyone who runs a charter company should be registered, and it is trying to get licensing for charter operations, but after twenty years there is little interest. However, it will come and it would be better for an owner to accept YCA standards now rather than wait for EEC regulations to be imposed later and almost inevitably.

"There is an arrangement with the Yacht Builders, Designers and Surveyors Association (YBDSA) and a number of other surveyors to have charter boats surveyed but the survey, like the MOT test for cars, is only relevant at the time it is done. The YCA would prefer spot inspections instead and talks with the Royal Ocean Racing Club are in progress to see if these checks could be carried out by RORC Measurers" (but this was never implemented). "If an inspector turns up, wanders over the boat and sees everything is well kept and clean, it should be a sufficient encouragement to companies to keep their boats in good order and for the system to work.

"Many charter companies too are running into trouble because of the difficulty of selling secondhand boats. This is mainly due to berth deficiencies in the Solent and the long waiting list for moorings. Sea Ventures could foresee that the market was reaching saturation and people would be chartering privately, so they decided not to own all the boats in their fleet themselves but encourage owners to purchase better class yachts to invest with their company. Sea Ventures would then look after the boats, manage the charter properly and ensure a high standard. Some agencies, however, just take 10% commission simply for providing customers, the owners having to ensure that the boats are kept in good condition. This means that a boat could come in on Saturday morning for a change-over with something broken, but as yards are not always open for repairs at weekends and the next client does not want to lose any of his holiday, the yacht might be sent out again with little or no repair.

"A reputable charter company has the advantage of its own work force which can do repairs at the weekend when everywhere else is shut. Sea Ventures also carries about £21,000 worth of spares and can provide an efficient back-up service. Without this the public are open to some danger if private charterers have neither the ability to repair nor the spares for replacement, and this causes many problems."

Sea Ventures were to be the victims of a confidence trickster, but let Don Howard tell the story himself. "A man calling himself David Everitt, chartered a boat to take his father on a surprise holiday and paid cash down. References were not taken up as the father, Commander Everitt, was a broker in Littlehampton and known to Sea Ventures. Then, shortly afterwards, we received a call from his 'mother,' Mrs. Everitt, saying that her husband, far from being on holiday, would be visiting Lymington shortly and they had never had a son!

"It was alleged that a Hans Martin Sleyer had been kidnapped on the 4th September 1980 and on the 5th September a yacht called *Polly Douce* was brought over to Berthon from Holland and he was moved to the Sea Ventures' boat, as it was much larger. Then off they went round Gibraltar to the South of France. The pretext was that they were trying to keep Hans Sleyer safe but later he was found shot in the boot of a taxi in France. David Everitt was supposed to have had the boat as a perk.

"Everitt, whose real name was Pearce, came from Brighton and was supposedly involved in drug smuggling between Malaga and Morocco. The Westerly 36 was eventually spotted and he was put in a Spanish gaol, pleading to be sent back to England. But the Spanish police, for reasons best known to themselves, released him on bail and he disappeared again. He was believed to have gone under the name Van Damm in Jersey and Guernsey and he frequently used the christian name David, plus a false surname, in perpetrating his confidence tricks.

"He was a charming, plausible, well-spoken young man; the sort one would immediately offer a job. He was very clever indeed and had obviously done his homework. He must have done it all for the

excitement but what a waste of talent! He was finally caught in America and is presently awaiting extradition, so, hopefully, we shall hear more about him."

After twenty-one years as Managing Director of Sea Ventures, Don Howard sold the business in June 1982 to Wing Commander Peter Giddens, although he continued as a consultant for a few months. He is still Secretary of the Yacht Charter Association, to which he will now devote all his time and will run it from his home in 60 Silverdale, New Milton. Peter Gidden's wife, Angela, is the Editor of *The Bridge* – a monthly review of life in the Parish of Boldre.

Festina Charter Ltd.

Festina Charter Ltd. is a member of the Yacht Charter Association and specialises in top-placed racing yachts. In 1981 they have a fleet of ten yachts and their business continues to expand with great rapidity. This year they are chartering their Contessa 43 *Caerulia* to Neil Mooney, who is contesting a place in the British Admiral's Cup team; they are chartering Chris Dunning's *Marionette* to a group of bankers from Hong Kong, who expect to be racing for their Admiral's Cup team; and they are endeavouring to arrange a charter of David May's *Winsome Gold* to a South African syndicate for the same purpose.

In the ill-fated 1979 Fastnet Race they had three of their yachts competing: *Festina Prima, Festina Tertia* and *Fair Festina. Festina Tertia* was running back to England under storm jib, having abandoned the race, when at 1.30 p.m. on the Tuesday she was rolled 150 degrees by a cresting wave with tremendous force. One man was thrown so hard against the steering column that it broke and another man was missing, his safety harness tether still hooked to the boat. Sean Thrower stripped off his outer clothing and dived in to rescue him but Roger Wattas was dead, and Sean was pulled on board again, already suffering from shock and hypothermia. A helicopter took him off and later the remainder of her cold and exhausted crew received a tow into St. Mary's by a lifeboat crew. Despite these horrific experiences Neil Mooney and his crew sailed *Festina Tertia* in a very full season in 1980 and again in 1981.

Bygone Charters

Mention must also be made here of an imaginative new venture, owned and run by two experienced yachtsmen from Maidenhead but based in Lymington. They believed that there would a demand by charterers to sail in beautifully maintained wooden sailing craft, rather than in the glass-fibre boats which are so commonly available. Their aim was to charter to sailors, who perhaps were experienced in sailing but now no longer had a yacht of their own. Skippers were provided at no extra cost, so that those with little experience, or whose 'sea legs' were not so good as they used to be, would feel that they could charter from them with confidence. That this scheme did not become commercially viable detracts in no way from the conception of caring for and sharing these beautiful old wooden boats. Nevertheless, the fleet available in Lymington remain of interest and the histories of two of them will be recounted in a later chapter. They are *Tom Tit* and *Dulcibella*. I had a mug of coffee and a chat with John Atkins on board a third, the *Palagic,* on 20th April 1981 when he told me all about them.

MARINE INSURANCE

Tony Harris

Tony Harris and Chris Wilson started on their own from square one in 1978 under the name of Antler Insurance Consultants. In 1981 they wanted to expand and so did Thompson, Heath and Bond (Southern) Limited so they merged. They hope to expand still further, not only in marine insurance but also on the commercial side.

On 3rd November 1981 I went to their offices at 41 High Street, Lymington and Tony Harris told me something of the marine insurance carried out by the firm.

"Sailing is still a leisure activity and a yacht is not a necessity like a car. The volume of boats in the country compared with the water space is much greater than a car with the added protection that you don't have pedestrians! A boat test has been thought about very seriously but it is not a legal requirement and apart from infringement of personal liberty how would you police it? Mainly, I think, the skill comes in here not so much with policing or tests but with the broker – or individual insurance company – working out and ascertaining as much knowledge as he possibly can. Car rates are in a book – they have to qualify by certain requirements – but marine rates are not.

"The EEC Regulations will not affect us. Mainly France has had a slight problem in that most boats that got there now have to be registered, although that has been delayed for two years. The Finance Houses might require registration but no insurance company would ask for it. Marine law is very old and basically most countries subscribe to the same laws.

"I have been sailing for about fifteen years. I learnt at Keyhaven and have been sailing from Lymington for ten or twelve years and have been racing regularly ever since. I raced in a yacht called *Gadabout Kowboy* and this year I raced in *Indulgence*

which came third in the World One Ton Cup. I am racing at present in a GK 34 called *Straight Through*. It is very important in marine insurance that you are involved in the sport as you naturally understand much better what other people are doing. I also do quite a bit of teaching – we both do – as far as Charter International is concerned, which also gives us understanding when we meet clients. We did not have any repercussions from the 1979 Fastnet Race professionally but we had not been going very long. But, of course, we had many friends who were in it.

"Insurance is very much an individual thing. We specialise in that we have just brought out a family rescue scheme which we have negotiated with Lloyds and which was adopted by Westerly Marine. There is so much competition on the market that you really have to pick a subject and go for it although obviously you do everything that comes along in the meantime. It is better to specialise and be master of one than a 'Jack of all trades.'

"We have pioneered a scheme for personal accident. Once again it is placed in Lloyds. It is very difficult to make people understand their liabilities as most yachtsmen think they are covered by a yacht policy. But physical accidents, such as people getting banged on the head by a boom, can still happen on the water, especially when racing and most personal accident policies exclude racing of most kinds and also yachting outside territorial waters. So most RORC races are not covered for this and yet I have had three fractures of the skull when I was on a RORC race.

"Our Personal Accident Scheme was just something we put together and we thought it might be of interest to the marine world as such. It has been slow to take off but I think the interest now is just coming in. It is a revolutionary idea in some ways. It has been in all the magazines and I think people gradually are starting to think about it. It was something we wrote up as a policy for yachtsmen and it has completely new wording which we worked out together, knowing the problems involved. A policy for a boat would cost about £45 which would cover the whole of the crew.

"Life insurance is slightly different. For instance if you take up hang-gliding then it is best to do so after you have taken a life insurance policy out! There are some life insurance policies where you have to look back into them and see what the exclusions are and mainly our job is to sort out the conditions for exclusions. Each one is slightly different, especially when you are dealing with cruising ranges and people's abilities. It is up to you. You are acting as a buffer for the underwriter and he will give you a recommendation which you may or may not accept.

Then they take our advice which puts back the burden on the brokerage. Obviously, if you go racing a lot you have to take out a life insurance policy. Here again we find our experience of being on the water so much is quite invaluable. I think sailing experience is a real bonus."

Stone's

Ken Stone and his wife, Beryl, first came to Lymington 20 years ago quite by chance. He had been running a yacht brokerage in Weymouth for 10 years and was asked if he would sell *Kelana*, a houseboat on the Lymington River later bought by the Carringtons. Ken Stone liked her very much and wanted to buy her but "I was messed about so much that I asked who owned the houseboat next to her. I was directed to the Post Office in Lymington and was told that it belonged to one of their blokes at Milford-on-Sea, a Mr. Tempest. Although he was not prepared to sell her at first he relented when I said that I had come all the way from Birmingham. So that is how I bought *Linette* 20 years ago for £300. We lived on her for 17 years and had a wonderful life." *Linette* has got quite a history, including a fine war record which is recounted in a later chapter.

Ken Stone then worked for a while as salesman for Colonel Butler at Tollbridge Trailers at Bridge Yard. One of the perks was that he was able to have a power line run aboard *Linette* and he enjoyed 10 years' free electricity. *Linette* was moored off the western bank of the river just below the tollbridge and he paid 5/- a week to Mrs. Lance of Glastonbury, whose late husband had run a haulage business and a scrap-yard. She doubled his rent to 10/- a week but it did remain at that figure for the next 13 years!

He then returned to insurance and worked for Charles Bishop for a while. He had started in insurance in 1932 and after the war returned to it again, trying his hand in different aspects of insurance, such as hotels, pubs and yachts. In 1965 with a car and a capital of £200 he set up on his own in New Street, Lymington and since then the firm has gone from strength to strength.

"Marine insurance is a specialised job," he continued. "Most major companies do issue marine policies but in the main it goes to Lloyds. There is no test at all but in recent years the Underwriters are insisting on the age of the boat not being over ten years old without a surveyor's report. We issue separate policies for life and accident insurance and naturally passengers and third party are covered by these policies. We have a policy for water ski-ing accidents on the water and also cover boats being delivered across to the Caribbean and places like that; we insure them just for the passage across there.

"We do not get many claims as owners pay the first portion of a claim which may be from £25 to £100. So it is often better for them to pay it out of their pocket and forget it than lose their no claim bonus. When we do get a claim it is usually for a fair amount. Recently the no claim bonus rate has gone up, the percentage has been increased, which is unusual as most things come down. We are extending the European no claim bonus and the American one. It is good for insurers but bad for clients – that is freedom you see.

"We get the most peculiar claims at times which, in my opinion, are fraudulent. They send them in and then if we smell a rat we really investigate them. The insurance company sends a surveyor. We have had one or two which have been very dodgy. One yachtsman I know paid about £1,500 for a boat and insured it for £8,000. He did not keep his boat in Lymington. The Harbour Master told him that his ropes were too short and he kept sinking and sinking and then claimed £8,000! Well, everything about that was suspicious.

"(Sir) John Onslow, who used to live in the High Street, is a client and great friend of mine and he was appointed skipper of the King of Saudi Arabia's private yacht, with a salary of about £3,000 per month. We do not insure the actual yacht.

"When we were living on board *Linette* we were alongside the Carringtons in their houseboat. It was a wonderful life and I put my longevity down to it. I used to dive off the edge into the river and I used to spend every weekend there."

Ken Stone reluctantly had to give up his house-boat but now owns an "opulent 8-berth motor cruiser for his next home." It does 30 knots but uses 10 gallons an hour. His annual mooring fee at the Berthon was £700 – a big increase from 50p a week for *Linette's* mooring! Today he keeps his boat at Southampton; not only are the moorings cheaper but he can also go out in any kind of weather on the Itchen, the Test or Southampton Water before he even reaches the Solent. Now that he has to dress up and go all the way to Southampton he goes out in her far more than he did when she was near at hand in Lymington. He does not go out fishing and does not believe in fishing or hunting. "If I want a fish then I will fish for just one but I do not believe in fishing just for the sake of it. I do not regard that as a sport," he said.

CHAPTER 20

MARINE ART AND PHOTOGRAPHY

"From all my years of sailing I can claim to have a good idea of calm and gale, cloud, wind, sun and all the colours and lighting which should go into a respectable marine picture."

DENYS BROOK-HART

MARINE ART

Denys Brook-Hart

We were fortunate in having in Lymington a man of the calibre of Denys Brook-Hart; a man of great talent and sensitivity and an English gentleman in every sense of the word. He was not only a fine art consultant and a specialist in British marine paintings but he has written two of the most comprehensive books on British nineteenth century and twentieth century marine painting, which are both standard works of reference. He also ran a marine art gallery in the Old Solent House, for whose conversion he was awarded the European Architectural Heritage Year Award in 1975.

Denys Brook-Hart was brought up by the sea on a deserted sweep of shore in Sussex near to the cottage once occupied by Blake, the mystic artist, and acquired his enthusiasm for salt water writing and art at an early age. During the war he served in the 'Phantom' Section of British Intelligence on special assignments such as Dunkirk, North Africa, the invasion of Italy and, finally, D-Day and Arnhem. After the war he became an executive in the oil industry and eventually became chairman of an international consultancy with offices in London, Rome, Paris, New York and Toronto. During all his years of high pressure business activities, he still found time to sail and write and study the arts until, finally, he decided to come to Lymington fifteen years ago in 1956. My conversation with him at his home was on 15th May 1981.

"I decided to buy the Old Customs House, which is where Hawkes is now," he told me, "and had the idea of renovating it and selling it just to fill in time. This building dates back to c. 1780 and was used as a Customs House until about 1825-30 when it moved to the old Town Quay. It used to have a collector, a comptroller and a clerk and there was also a boat's crew and a small detachment of cavalry, as smuggling was rife in those days. Beneath the building were flag-stoned cellars and small horse shoes have been found there. The figure-head was discovered in a very dirty condition at Ringwood and is probably about two hundred years old; it came from a frigate or barquentine but no figure-head expert has been able to trace her origin.

"I had done quite a lot of design and interior decor in my business and half way through the conversion I suddenly thought the Old Customs House would be a marvellous place for an antique shop. I was very, very interested in antiques, paintings and so on and I started that mainly with early Staffordshire china, Staffordshire porcelain figures and marine paintings; certainly, everything had a nautical flavour and I also intended to do nautical antiquaria. But I soon discovered that people living by the sea don't want to buy anything to do with the sea! In fact, most of my clients came from places which are nowhere near the sea, such as the centre of Australia, America and the Midlands! The Staffordshire went on very well and we had an enormous collection of early nautical subjects on it; obviously Nelson and lesser known sailors who were commemorated. Then we discovered that the market went quite dead because the supply of Staffordshire began to run out. Where once there had been a sale every two weeks at Sotheby or Christies, they got further and further apart, so that there was only one a year. So I turned more and more to marine paintings."

To house his marine pictures, Denys Brook-Hart now bought Old Solent House at the foot of Quay Hill, which was originally built about 1700 as a 'gentleman's residence.' It has cellars from which tunnels run under the High Street to the Old Town Hall and they were said to have been used for smuggling. The building then passed to a brewery and the front room was used as a public bar and the property was called the 'Old Solent Inn,' but it returned to private use fifty years ago. The building was in a most dilapidated condition and technical reports on it were 'exceedingly gloomy and pessimistic.' Amongst other problems the main roof was on the point of collapse.

Denys Brook-Hart worked in daily contact with the builders and undertook all the design and decorative work, and it took from November 1972 until April 1974 for the conversion to be complete. The old bar parlour was converted into an art gallery and extends to the Old Customs House by means of a linking unit designed to be completely in character. Out of thirty-three nominations from Hampshire for the European Architectural Heritage Year Award, the Old Solent House complex was the only successful entry from Lymington. Today his picture galleries are known internationally and the building also provides a home for his family of the greatest charm.

Denys has written many articles on art and artists, particularly some of the lesser known nineteenth century marine painters and has brought them to the attention of the art world, so that today their work has become widely acclaimed. But his zest for writing really found its outlet in his two reference books, *British Nineteenth Century Marine Painting* in 1974, with a second edition in 1978; and *Twentieth Century British Marine Painting* in 1981, which are beautifully produced and are on display in the window of his art gallery. He told me how these had come about.

"I was, in a way, lucky with my first book because I had been making biographical notes on nineteenth century artists ever since I started the gallery. Every time I came across a new artist or one of some interest, I researched his background and made one or two sheets of notes about him. So I had that as a basis and then, of course, we had hundreds of photographs of all the paintings we have had, because every time we buy a painting we have it photographed and I was able to supplement them with photographs from the National Maritime Museum, the Tate Gallery and places like that. But it took me five years of just sheer dogged trudging on with it because with any kind of reference book the facts should be right. Although you may not think it there are thousands of dates which have to be checked because otherwise somebody immediately writes from Australia saying 'My grandfather died in 1899 not 1898!'

"My next book took less time, only three years, because there were so many people still living that I could go and see; so that it was easier to dig out the information. I should think I interviewed about fifty living artists; a fair cross-section from some very well known ones to young people who are just starting out.

"I have painted on holiday but with great frustration because I think you need to have a formal training to get the best out of it and to know how to mix colours and prepare ground and that sort of thing. Paradoxically, some of the best artists say that they would rather not have had any training but, nevertheless, I think it would be very suitable, certainly for an amateur. So I get a bit frustrated because if you want to paint that colour sky and you start mixing it up, it usually turns out rather different. The ones who have had training say they wish they hadn't had it and those who haven't had it say they wish they had! I paint in oils, mostly coastal scenes and I paint what I see.

"The last sailing boat I had was a 40 ft. yawl, which we kept here in Lymington only a stone's throw away at the foot of the garden. I found it enormous hard work maintaining it and then I actually discovered that in the Mediterranean you either have a Mistral, which is more or less a gale, or flat calm and it is a very frustrating business trying to sail there. So motor cruising is the answer and I now have a twin-engined motor boat called *Masterpiece* down in the South of France. We went down there 3½ years ago and we keep her at a place called Cap d'Agde, which is about a hundred miles west of Marseilles and we cruise from there. We went originally to the Balearic Islands and then we went to the Spanish Coast and then found this place which we liked very much so we are based there."

By a strange and, to me a rather moving coincidence, I was writing this section of my book about Denys Brook-Hart on the very day he died suddenly, on board *Masterpiece,* at Cap d'Agde on 18th August 1982. I would like to think that if his spirit returned fleetingly to Lymington, he may have seen – and I hope approved – of what I had written about him. When my first tape recording of our conversation went very faint he was so kind and patient in giving me a second interview, and it is his photograph of the Lymington River by Alfred Vickers that I have chosen as the cover for my book.

Three marine artists, born in the nineteenth century, have strong connections with Lymington, and they are Alfred Vickers, Sr., J. M. Gilbert and Wilfred William Ball. The author is very indebted to the late Denys Brook-Hart for permission to use the background notes he had written about them.

Alfred Vickers, Sr. (1786-1868)

Pride of place must go to Alfred Vickers, Sr. (his son was also an artist). Denys Brook-Hart described him as "a very distinguished landscape artist, at present much admired, whose pictures fetch fairly high prices and whose coastal views are sheer delight. He had a light, delicate style, almost feathery and some of his best sea work was done around the Isle of Wight and Solent areas." A fine example of this is the oil painting on canvas of the Lymington River, which is on the cover of this book. When he gave me the photograph Denys drew my attention to the fact that the artist had moved the high ground of the Isle of Wight more to the east in order to achieve balance! It really is a beautiful painting, even seen in black and white, and in its wildness is most evocative of the spirit of the Lymington River of past centuries, the river which is within us today. "His exhibition record was of course most impressive: 61 pictures in the Royal Academy, 125 in the British Institution and 81 in the Suffolk Street Galleries between 1814 and 1868. From his London addresses he travelled quite widely in the UK and occasionally on the Continent. Although his landscapes far outnumber his water pieces he took the latter in his stride and evidently painted them as the mood seized him."

J. M. Gilbert (fl. 1825-1855)

Denys Brook-Hart told me that after he had published articles about lesser-appreciated painters, the hunt had been on and up had gone the price. This in itself is a testimony of the high opinion held of him in the world of art. "One such barely recorded artist," he wrote, "was J. M. Gilbert, who painted a number of excellent pictures of the Lymington River and the West Solent, some of which were lithographed on stone by Louis Hage, at one time official lithographer to Queen Victoria. These very attractive coloured prints were executed mostly about 1840 and are now rare and desirable in themselves. The original paintings by Gilbert are, of course, even rarer and more desirable!"

Gilbert lived in Lymington and London and exhibited in the Royal Academy in 1825 and 1855, in the British Institution in 1827 and 1828 and two more paintings were exhibited at the Suffolk Street Galleries. Denys Brook-Hart continues: "It seems probable that Gilbert lived in Lymington between c. 1830 and 1845. In about 1840 when many of his Lymington pictures were being executed, five of his paintings came into the possession of the Rev. Thomas McCalmont of Lymington and about 130 years later I was fortunate enough to acquire these for clients." He bought two of them from a very old lady, introduced to him by her daughter, who lived in Lymington and wanted to sell them, and the other three came up in Bonhams in London.

"The soft colouring and skilful treatment of his sea pieces show that J. M. Gilbert was a truly professional marine artist of considerable merit. There is little doubt that good examples of his work should be bought, if found, and are likely to continue to appreciate," advised Denys in his book. Incidentally, the Rev. McCalmont lived across the river on the Walhampton side but must have retired to Lymington as he does not appear on the lists of incumbents of either St. Thomas Church, Lymington or on those of St. John the Baptist Church at Boldre. Be that as it may, it was interesting to hear old Tom Doe refer to McCalmont Quay when reminiscing about the river, and now I know why.

Wilfred William Ball (1853-1917)

Very little seems to have been recorded about this Lymington artist who painted, mostly in water-colour, marine and coastal subjects and landscapes. He exhibited in the RA, RBA, RE and RI. He was certainly living in Lymington in 1911 and his home was in Stanley Road. It is strange that he should have died in 1917 as far away from Lymington as Khartoum. His two watercolour paintings shown in this book are enchanting and I am grateful to Helen Figgins for lending them to me, after I had seen them at an exhibition which she had organised at an Annual General Meeting of the Lymington Society.

Stuart Beck (1903-   )

Stuart Beck first started to paint at the age of seven using his mother's oils on a piece of a shoe-box on board a cargo ship somewhere off Cape Horn. His mother was an artist and his father was in the Merchant Service, but his paternal grandfather, John Beck, a schoolmaster, was also an artist and so the amalgam came from both sides of the family. Added to this he had always been mad on boats so it was inevitable that he should become a marine artist. Indeed, he summed it up with the remark: "I couldn't really have done anything else, could I?" Unfortunately he lived inland and he told me, when I visited his studio at 5 Highfield House, Lymington on 5th May 1982, of many wasted years as a hack artist in London, when he should have been concentrating on marine painting. He studied at Rochester School of Art.

Stuart served as technical illustrator with the RNVR during the war for instruction purposes, from 1941-1946. He had written four books either on drawing ships or on the ships themselves, coupled with being 'on the borders of engineering' in order to be a technical illustrator without being an engineer. "I usually worked from the plans of ships." Stuart Beck had joined the RNVR with the aim of trying to go to sea "but I was getting a bit elderly even in those days for that," he said. But he did go to sea on gunnery trials and once made a trip in a mine-sweeper, escorting a convoy up the Channel on a seven days' leave.

"My sister-in-law lived in Southampton during the war and, when we stayed with her once, she

The Quay, 1914 – Wilfred Ball

Dan Bran's Shed – Wilfred Ball

180

brought us over to Lymington; directly we saw it we said 'This is the place we must live in one day, if we possibly can.' But the years went by until the house we were renting in Kent came up for sale and, as sitting tenants, we were able to buy it. This gave us the opportunity to move and we sold it and came to Lymington."

At first Stuart did commercial work in Bournemouth at £12 a week, which barely covered the price of his fare, but later he took an interesting job with Vickers. After he had been living in Lymington for seven years, the firm he had worked for in London invited him to return and work for them in an office they were opening in Weymouth. As Weymouth had plenty of boats, he accepted their offer and spent seven years there and made contact with the Weymouth branch of the RNLI.

Stuart Beck was invited to teach art in Portland Prison, which he declined at first but was persuaded to change his mind, and he found it extremely interesting. He though that painting might have had some therapeutic value but although some of his pupils there had talent most of them probably took up painting in order to get out of doing something else they liked even less! They were mostly young fellows and instead of starting with something simple, they usually wanted to paint portraits of their girl friends, which is one of the most difficult things to do. The prisoners were allowed to do jobs for their tutors: one prisoner was an expert on antique furniture and polished a table for Stuart which is in his sitting-room today. They were not allowed to be paid but they would accept cigarettes although you had to be careful about the brand as, otherwise, they would trade them against cash.

"One of the prisoners was a real 'spiv' type," he recalled, "who took up painting and then asked me if I could advise him on materials. As they got only a few shillings a week I really looked around and then mentioned some at a very reasonable price which I thought he could afford. His reply was, 'Don't you get worried about that, mate. What do you think I am in here for? Of course I can afford them!' "

Stuart Beck took me to his 'workshop' – he used that name rather than studio. There was a wonderful view over the rooftops of the Isle of Wight and the Solent – or would have been except it had clouded over. He told me it always did so when he invited friends to see the view and when he and his wife first moved into the flat it was a week before they discovered that you could see the Island! The window faces due east, which means that in the morning it can be very brilliant and he has to draw the curtains to cut down the light.

He paints in oils, watercolour and acrylic, nearly always marine subjects. He exhibited at the inaugural exhibition of the Royal Society of Marine Artists and many times since then and has exhibited at the RBA and SGA and held many one-man exhibitions. I was fortunate enough to see several of his paintings which he was collecting for four or five exhibitions. One of a tug was going to an international Towing Conference in London. There is a particularly fine and topical painting of a dredger working at night at the Lymington Yacht Haven, a copy of which is in the committee room at the Yacht Haven. Several paintings had been used as calendars by firms such as Wellworthy.

He showed me several extremely interesting and amusing cartoons, several of them dating back to the war. One showed the lengths someone went to in London trying to get a flat there just after the war when it was virtually impossible to obtain one. Another wartime one was of a sailor returning from the States and offering a mermaid some nylon stockings – a favourite 'bait' for their human sisters as well but this one did not seem very interested! Another, called 'Boat Drill 1968', was drawn in 1948, twenty years earlier, anticipating the use to which helicopters, "in those days more or less playthings and the crazy idea of inventors," might replace lifeboats on ships in the future and he had got pretty near it. How prohetic this cartoon has turned out to be! He confessed to a "twisted sense of humour" and only drew his cartoons when he felt like it. It would have been terrible to have to churn one out every week. Several of his cartoons appeared in shipping magazines. Stuart had spent a month aboard a weather ship and the crew had presented him with a meteorological certificate, so in return he gave them a cartoon of himself doing various tasks under difficult conditions, such as shaving or drinking a mug of tea.

One of his hobbies was making models, and on the mantlepiece of his workshop were two minute models which he believed to be the smallest plank and ribbed boats in the world. They were about two centimetres long and he wrote to the *Guinness Book of Records* about them. Apparently somebody had already submitted a 'smallest yacht' which, when examined under a magnifying glass, was found to consist of just a little triangle of boat with a tiny piece of paper for a sail and so they stopped having a smallest craft section. Perhaps if they had seen Stuart Beck's proper models they might have changed their minds. Framed on the wall nearby were some handwritten verses copied from Masefield's *Sea Fever,* by a lady in her 80s, who had been a tracer in his drawing office during the war. They were beautifully written although she had apologised for them!

Stuart can also be included as a 'local author' since he has written four books: *Ships, Boats and Craft* in 1950 or 1952; *How to draw Fishing Craft* in 1953; *How to draw Pleasure Craft* in 1954 and in the following year *The Ship – How she works,* which was published by Adlard Coles in 1955.

He has always been interested in the RNLI since he lived in Weymouth and has presented to RNLI Headquarters, now in Poole, several paintings which they used as Christmas cards to raise funds for their organisation. Buster Hallett sent me one called 'Home for Christmas,' showing some vessels at anchor in the Clyde, painted in aid of the British Sailors Society, which I have kept.

Later in a conversation about modern art, Stuart said, "One interesting feature is the contrast between people who are self-taught and people who have studied at University or the Slade. So few people nowadays learn to draw and it is the most difficult thing to go abstract if you have not done so. Abstract work is used more in design than anywhere else and I have not done any myself; I just paint what I see.

"In this respect art has a terrific advantage over photography as the camera is tied down to repro-duce exactly what is seen whereas in art there is the terrific advantage that you can leave out all sorts of horrible things, such as traffic signs, cars and yellow lines on roads. I have been sketching in places such as a street with cottages or a harbour and every ten minutes I would have to get up off my stool and walk over to what I was painting and look over the tops of cars. It used to embarrass me at one time when people spoke to me while I was painting but now I rather enjoy it and say 'Yes' or 'No,' hoping that I have said the right thing!"

His sense of humour and essential modesty were apparent again when he discussed his recent election as President of the Lymington Art Group. "I don't know why I was elected. I suppose being President is the most useless job in the Society that you can have; you just have to appear like a figure-head!" He then went on to discuss the difficulties of judging other people's work at competitions. "It is a little awkward when you know the people and can recognise their style. At a W.I. exhibition, I awarded first prize to the Chairman quite by chance. She was probably pleased and all the rest were furious!" Stuart is also teaching watercolour painting at the Lymington Community Centre, which is a wonderful opportunity for local amateurs to study painting with an artist of his calibre.

David Cobb (1921-   )

David Cobb, President of the Royal Society of Marine Artists, was born on 13th May 1921 in Bromley, Kent. He has drawn since he was quite small but became a naval cadet at Pangbourne Nautical College from 1935-1937 and then went on to read engineering at Cambridge.

He was called up as a reservist in 1940. He served in the Channel at Ramsgate and then as a First Lieutenant he spent two years (1941-42) with convoys in both the North and South Atlantic. He later commanded MTBs in 1943-45 and became a Control Officer MTBs in the North Sea. It was in 1943, when he took an MTB to HMS *Beagle* at Weymouth, the working-up place for newly-commissioned ones, that he first met Roger Pinckney, who was on the staff there. Roger came to sea with them and they hit it off and kept in touch. He didn't see Roger again during the war as Roger was later in the Hamble with an experimental boat.

All this time David had been seeing things at sea which were deeply fascinating to him. "I had been brought up amongst boats and it really was a continuing process," he told me when I visited him in his home, 'Woodis,' at Setley, Brockenhurst on 13th June 1982. "So at the end of the war instead of going back to read engineering, which is what I was supposed to be doing, I decided that I would try and be an artist and I still am trying to be one now!

"On the day I was demobilised I sailed from HMS *Hornet* in the family's little 4-tonner and went direct to Newlyn in Cornwall and started to try and learn to be a painter. This was before I met Jean and I had been there about eight weeks when I got a letter from Roger Pinckney saying, 'Can you crew us down to Brittany from Lymington?' Well, of course, I was thrilled and upsticks and sailed the whole way from Newlyn to Lymington non-stop in this little 4-tonner, 48 hours on end. I was jolly tired by the time I got here but I wasn't going to miss this, not for anything, and what a trip it was! None of the buoys were there and all the lighthouses were blown up. We were the first yacht down there after the war and poor old France was on its knees but it was full of interest and I have still got the drawings I made there. French tunny fishermen were still sailing then and there were coasters under sail. I was immensely grateful to Roger for that trip. He is such a good friend and so generous."

David Cobb's first home at Newlyn was on board a boat called *White Heather*, which had been owned by W. H. Watkins, a former Rear Commodore of the RORC, 1935-36. Watkins had bought her through Roger Heron of Laurent Giles and she was the forerunner, in fact the prototype, of *Dyarchy's* top-sail rig. David Cobb then met Jean Main, another artist, and told her that if she was going to marry him she would have to live on the boat! She agreed and they did so for the next seven years. *"White Heather* was a marvellous boat and large enough to play bears round the cabin table,"* he recalled. She meant a great deal to him and certainly seems to have lived up to her name and brought him well-deserved 'Good Luck.'

Jean Main was working at Street for Clark shoes and David Cobb wanted to live nearer to London, so they drew lines out to the coast and the point of inter-section was slap through Lymington. So they moved here and he virtually designed a Colt house which he and a carpenter built together. Upstairs it is all studio and, as he put it, "it is really a boat brought ashore – a sort of Noah's Ark. We were immensely lucky as it was the year before the Green Belt clamped down in 1954 and we should never have been allowed to build. But we regard ourselves as temporary and the real residents are the animals! We are still here 28 years later and it seems about five minutes. All we want to do is just go on living here until the bell strikes!" For a year or two afterwards they were rather broke but then bought another boat, an old 8-metre which they kept at Beaulieu for many years at a mooring fee of £7 10s.

He continued: "I have made my hobby into my career. It sounds bliss but it is not quite as easy as that because I had no teaching, no art training and had to teach myself. I believe most marine artists are self-taught and, in fact, the majority of the marine artists in the past have had some experience at sea first. Then they come ashore, moved by what they have seen and wish to report it in some way or other. I think you will find that very many of them in the past, but not so many of them today, have been of that type. Just after the war, of course, there was a great deal of sea experience that people were drawing on and that has tended to get less, and now we have got masses of people going afloat in boats with hardly any real interest in the sea at all, as I understand it."

Denys Brook-Hart wrote: "He is a yacht owner and keen yachtsman with wide practical experience of small vessels, both sail and power, and is a painter in oils of 'everything of any period that floats.' He has exhibited at the RSMA since its inaugural exhibition in 1946 and also at the ROI and RBA. He is a member of the Royal Cruising Club; a member of the Board of Governors of TS *Fourdroyant* and a Council member of the Society for Nautical Research."

It is significant that David was exhibiting in the first year he became a marine artist and so it was hardly surprising that 32 years later, in 1978, he was commissioned by the Admiralty to paint 17 oils depicting the Battle of the Atlantic and two further series on the Navy at war in the Mediterranean and the Pacific, all for the permanent collections at the Royal Naval Museum, Portsmouth. Denys Brook-Hart regards this commission as one of the most significant of its type in the history of British marine painting.

"Marine painting is a diminishing field, as this country's naval interest and global responsibilities have been diminishing," David continued, "and the merchant service has been winding down and running under a flag of convenience. I never dreamt that the Portsmouth commission would happen in my lifetime. I thought it was quite hopeless although I would love to have done it. In a way perhaps it has been a good thing that I have had to wait, because it is a very big technical exercise that needs an awful lot of knowledge of painting to even start it. I am not saying that I am the only person who could do it but there are now no more marine painters who are likely to come forward who served at sea during the war. They will be too old. I don't know of any more who are likely to come up; I can't think that they will now but, of course, we may have another war in view of what is happening in the South Atlantic."

David Cobb went on to discuss the Falklands campaign. "I have a number of naval friends, one of whom was the Naval Liaison Officer in Southampton, who had been responsible for the conversion of all these ships, at very short notice. Just before the *QE.2* was due to sail, he rang me up and said, 'Come and have a look at this lot; it really is rather fascinating.' This came at an exceptionally busy time for me anyway with various professional commitments that I had simply got to meet, but at any rate I went down and, in fact, watched her sail and I quickly did a number of drawings of her and some of the other ships, all of which had been fitted for the Falklands or for service at sea down there. When she came back I managed by other means to board her and met three of the survivors, the Commanding Officers who had lost their ships, which was rather a grim experience because one hardly knew what to say.

"I am now going to start to try and put together, with their help and the help of other people, some sort of artistic archive of the Falklands War. It is only in embryo and it has not been commissioned but I shall hope to find somebody who will buy something somewhere and get the thing formally accepted while it is still going on. It is a bit early. We are now into a missile war and nobody knows anything about it and there is a tremendous amount to be learnt and I have got to find out what it looks like. I know of no painter who was there when the heat was on but there may have been; good luck to him if he was and I want to see what he has been doing."

David Cobb doesn't do any showing normally as most of the work he does is commissioned. He has painted three times for the Royal Engineers; two about ten years ago and he has just done another painting of their landings in France, which was most interesting. "Painting for the Royal Naval Museum meant a great deal of reading and an immense amount of historical research. You have to get a whole lot of vanished equipment and you have to find out how to use it and how it used to work. You are very vulnerable as a painter, because memories are short and no two people will remember the same thing. But that doesn't prevent them from coming in and saying in a very firm voice, 'It was not like that at all. I know, because I was there!'

"I always make it clear though that when somebody has good reason to think something is adrift, I always want to know what it is and, if they are right and I wrong, I am only too ready to change it, provided they can really make a good case. But I try to get my evidence lined up – rather like appearing at a trial – you get things properly worked out beforehand. Though a lot is not just swatting up but what you can produce in your imagination as an interesting scene: your imagination and technique. Because nearly all sea painting, I think I can say all sea painting, is brought home in the mind and put together. You can't paint at sea, although people think you do. They want to fix you up with an easel afloat. Everything moves all the time so you come home and try and see if you can freeze the scene.

"I don't use models but I do use photographs for things which would take hours to draw but they don't contribute much to the overall drawing. They don't make the shape of a ship but they do allow you to make a quick and very complete note of a whole lot of details, which you could not possibly draw in the time you have available. But I never use photographs as a basis for a painting. That is not what it is about because the photograph has only limited power and one photograph is very like another but the painter is meant to be able to put something of

David Cobb

"Follow Me" – *Medusa* and *Dulcibella* in "The Riddle of the Sands" himself in as well. It is an aid but it is difficult to explain how you use an aid without relying on it wholly.

"I don't know enough about lenses and so on to know why but in fact you cannot photograph a ship satisfactorily from 45 degrees on the bow at anything less than quite a distance. Because there is a sort of malfunction or distortion that produces an immense bow and a tiny stern. I don't pretend to know why this is the case; if you do it with a telescopic lens it puts the thing flat so that bow and stern are equally distant and if you use an ordinary lens it produces a monster bow and a tiny stern.

"I have lived with *The Riddle of the Sands* since I was a small boy and I probably formed a lot of my ideas on life from it. Childers was certainly a versatile and interesting character and he wrote a marvellous book, an imperishable one. But for some reason, I can't really think why, nobody took much notice of it visually until about six or seven years ago and then in various quarters a lot of heads popped up, starting to write about it, talk about it and discuss it. My interest is obviously what it looked like because it has never been illustrated, at least I have never heard of it, and I am always looking for interesting ideas. Somehow this one took off and I thought 'the very thing – let's have a go at it.' So that is how I came to paint 'Short cut through the sands. Follow me.' The picture is in oils 18" × 26" and is in a private collection. Funnily enough, it is in the hands of somebody who has no interest in ships at all but likes painting, so you never can tell.

"Maldwin Drummond is writing what is rapidly turning into a major historical study of the run up to World War One, because, of course, it is all connected and the naval strategy of the time has still lived on up to World War Two. One of the aircraft carriers, *Courageous* I think, was in fact laid down as a shallow draught big gun cruiser, which would have been able to get into the German rivers in 1905. What I find so interesting is all Maldwin's researches. He is a marvellous chap because he is so methodical and he has got his own secretary and office and so on. So when Maldwin takes something up that interests him he can bring to bear a very powerfully-organised battery. The drawback is that he likes new things and some of them fall by the wayside."

Jean Cobb drew charts at the Admiralty during the war. "I was in Secret Section 7, which was all women, one man in charge and 13 women, and each of us had terrific connections with the Navy. They said that they had chosen women because they wouldn't go to the 'local' and get drunk and would keep their mouths shut. I couldn't get into the Wrens because I wheezed at my medical and I was called up

as a bus conductor!" Jean has done a wonderful job stopping oil exploration in the New Forest. She has recently taken up glass engraving with considerable success. The Cobbs do not watch television as they carry pictures in their minds and the image of an announcer opening and shutting his mouth would put them off! They wanted to think of their own images.

Rear-Admiral John Morrison Webster, RN (1932-   )

John Webster is still an 'amateur' painter and he is serving in the Royal Navy and lives at Soberton in Hampshire. His father is Frank Webster, a retired architect, who designed their present home at Lea House, Normandy Lane, Lymington and his mother, Kate, is very musical and organises 'Kate's Concerts' when a coach load of us go off to hear the Bournemouth Symphony Orchestra play at the Winter Gardens. The family moved here in 1955 when John was 23 and had already been serving in the Navy since 1951. They had sailed from Lymington several years prior to 1955 in their Vertue *Hussar* and a painting of her by David Cobb hangs on the wall of their sittingroom. Frank and Kate Webster are both members of the Royal Lymington Yacht Club and Frank was Chairman of the House Committee when Jack Bryans was Commodore from 1958 to 1963.

It was while sailing with his father in *Hussar* that John Webster first became fascinated with maritime scenery and had already started to translate it onto paper and canvas. He described this to me in a letter dated 9th July 1982 which I now share with you.

"The fleeting effects of light on water so absorbed me that I took a long time to draw properly (and still can't!), being more concerned with trying to capture transient situations in paint. The need to 'get something down' before memory faded often led to a difference of view between skipper and crew as my father was left to handle the boat while I ignored the imminence of maritime disaster and dug into the paint box! Of all the places we sailed to the Newtown River has fondest memories and gave rise to many sketches which are still providing material for paintings today. Lymington too, featured in the sketch book, but today is changed beyond recognition, at least on the waterfront, and has little attraction for the painter in me – the row upon row of plastic mouldings surmounted by forests of alloy tube are beyond my ability to make anything of, in artistic terms. So much for philosophy.

"As to being 'self-taught' I prefer the expression 'no formal training,' because I have picked up, plagiarised and otherwise plundered other people's ideas – some of which they have been kind enough to write down in book form. I owe a considerable debt to two fellow Lymingtonian painters, both professionals of long standing and high regard. Stuart Beck was most encouraging in the early days when I still lived in Lymington and could bore him with my paltry efforts in quest for criticism. Today David Cobb casts his eye over my stuff from time to time – and reaches for the rum bottle! It is this willingness to help others and pass on hard-learned lessons for which artists are not always well-known and for which I am particularly grateful to these two.

"I first exhibited with the Royal Society of Marine Artists in 1954, and although in subsequent years was often, quite rightly, not 'hung,' I am now a regular exhibitor and might, if I live long enough, even be invited to become a member eventually. I also exhibit regularly with the Royal Institute of Oil Painters and the Royal Institute of Water Colour Painters – this last one not this year (1982) because I have my first London 'One Man' show, which coincides with the RI and needs all the better work. It will be at the King Street Gallery, St. James's from 18th March to 3rd April 1982. I have had other exhibitions, usually after a period away at sea or travelling in some way. 'Meon to Mexico' in 1978 at the Old Granary, Bishops Waltham was one such. Perhaps the most significant one man show to date was held in the provincial Art Gallery of Nova Scotia in Halifax in 1976 – my family and I had spent three years in Canada which offered a wonderful change of scene.

"I am often asked 'How do you find the time?' with a naval career as well. My answer is that I don't play golf and try and make time for painting because it is a compulsion. It is also very compatible with a life at sea and ashore with the Royal Navy. The officers and men of two ships I have commanded have particular reason to be grateful to my 'hobby' as it has kept me out of their hair when otherwise I might have interfered and caused a shambles!"

John Webster mentioned that there was an exciting job in prospect at Portland "and, who knows, I might even do some painting." His is a name to watch.

Rodney Charman (1944-   )

The youngest marine artist in Lymington and the only indigenous Lymingtonian is Rodney Charman, who was born near Milford-on-Sea on 29th October 1944, the son of a naval officer. He was educated at Brockenhurst College when it was a County High School and took up a job with British Rail where he worked on the ferry service between Lymington and Yarmouth. Later he was employed at Wellworthy where he was Assistant Publicity Manager.

Although sailing is one of his hobbies, he has had little experience of deep sea sailing, except for a week on board the Sail Training Association's schooner, *Malcolm Miller.*

Chris Story had first come across Rodney Charman's work when he saw it in a gallery in Beaulieu and it was so obviously of a high standard, even in those days, that he enquired who was the artist. When the Storys came to Lymington they had hoped to open a business on the Quay but instead had the opportunity to open as 'Matchmakers,' 1 High Street, Lymington. Originally they were selling handicrafts, pottery, hand wood-carvings and then clothing and they thought they would like to supplement this by selling some of Rodney's work.

By a strange coincidence, when he came to Lymington in 1967 Chris had joined Wellworthy as a sales dealer and to his astonishment found that Rodney Charman was Assistant Publicity Manager to Ian Hodges. He told Rodney that he had always admired his work and asked if he could sell his paintings, to which Rodney gladly agreed. So in this way Rodney not only acquired an agent but also his own art gallery in Lymington. For Matchmakers opened in the summer of 1970 and by April 1971 they had started selling Rodney's paintings at about £20 each, which was a good price then. By the end of this year (1982) they are expecting to break the four figure barrier!

Rodney Charman did not take up painting seriously until 1966 and is completely self-taught, which has enabled his style and technique to develop quite naturally. He paints in oils, a wide range of marine subjects, particularly of sailing ships in interesting lighting conditions, and has painted Thames scenes at the turn of the century and Irish and Cornish fishing harbour scenes. But originally he specialised in horse paintings and was more interested in equestrian event horses. In the early days he painted a portrait of Marion Coates' horse which he sold to her. He also did a portrait of a racing pigeon which Chris Story described as being "fantastic how he got the rainbow colouring in the wings and I think the racing pigeon exemplified his constant desire for perfection in detail and authenticity and that is one of the reasons why for me his work has an advantage over Montague Dawson."

Rodney Charman was naturally influenced by the paintings of the world-famous marine artist, Montague Dawson, who latterly lived in Milford-on-Sea until his death in 1973. He is a great admirer of Montague Dawson but doesn't really like to have his work likened to him. "Rodney is a unique artist," Chris told me, "and his style is different and he is far more versatile with his choice of subject. Also

Montague Dawson often used artistic licence to get a splash of colour in a painting but Rodney will not deviate from authenticity. Alex Hurst, a leading writer on sailing ships, came into the Gallery and said that Rodney's painting of *Scooling,* a three-quarter deck sailing ship that used to sail the Southern Ocean, could only be faulted on one small deck detail and yet Rodney had never seen that ship. He had done it from ship's plans and photographs.

"He used a model for the *Cutty Sark* but he has got a tremendous library of books and many of them show the deck detail and the rigging detail and quite often he may spend two or three days study before he even starts painting, just to make sure that all the detail is correct."

Rodney Charman started to paint full time in March 1979 and continued to specialise in oils. But before doing so he had confided to Chris Story at Wellworthy, "that he was afraid that he would run out of ideas and might also lose his compulsive drive to paint," but of course, as Chris said, "he has gone from strength to strength. He is a hard taskmaster: he works seven days a week. He will work all day Sunday and quite often on Saturdays and in the evenings. When he gets an idea he does not need to sketch it because it is all in his mind. When I spoke to Stuart Beck, a charming man, he told me that he would go through books to get an idea but Rodney would never do this. His paintings are selling well and the prices are going up, and I suppose that is the true yardstick of an artist's progress.

"Several West End galleries are also selling his paintings as well as ourselves in Matchmakers, and a lot of his work goes abroad, mostly to Bermuda. We have got one or two collectors in America and a newspaper owner, for whom Rodney is working, has commissioned a very big painting of the Italian sail training ship, the *Amerigo Vespucci,* which he had seen at the 'Parade of Sail' in New York about four years ago. He has taken three or four other works by Rodney. There are examples of Rodney's work in most of the major countries such as America, Canada, South Africa, Germany, Malta and Bermuda and now possibly Australia. He has exhibited at the RSMA exhibition since 1973 and has a painting selected for the 1982 International Maritime Art Awards Show at Connecticut, USA.

"Rodney Charman has made arrangements to be out on the water at certain times when the Tall Ships are at Southampton and will probably do a lot of painting of them. He will take photographs just to keep a particular scene fresh in his mind. One of his favourite scenes, conversely, is of the *Queen Mary* leaving Southampton Water in 1967 to go to the States. He obviously found it a very moving ex-

perience. Another favourite subject is Milford beach, which has a special attraction for him and he has done half a dozen paintings of it. He has obviously got a feel for it because you can identify it at once. He has got that rare commodity of genius, there is no doubt about that." Rodney Charman is indeed fortunate in his Lymington agent.

Charles Munro (1913-   )

Charles Munro, strictly speaking, is not a marine artist but he has painted many marine paintings and is very much part of the marine scene at Lymington. He has been living in Lymington for about thirty years except when the ferry terminal spoilt his view and they went to live on the Isle of Wight. But in spite of this, they soon returned to that side of the River and have spent the last fifteen years at Bywater Cottage, Pierside, Lymington. He hated to admit it but he was a power-boat man but had sold his boat as it cost him about £20 every time he went out in her. Today he goes fishing every Thursday at Bicton Mill, near Salisbury. I visited Charles at his studio on 28th April 1981 and once again had trouble with my tape recorder but he also very kindly fitted me in again!

When he was younger Charles had obviously been an oarsman and a 'rider' as the following anecdote reveals. "We were once rowing at Henley and got knocked out rather early and some fool suggested that we should hire horses and go riding instead. There were nine of us on those horses, none of us had ridden before, and they were all fresh from the riding stables and went like the wind and how we kept on, I don't know!"

However, this 'riding experience' was to come in useful. Before the war he was out in India and worked for three years on Kipling's old newspaper, *The Civil and Military Gazette,* as the artist and political cartoonist. He joined the Punjab Light Horse in the Auxiliary Force and said that when he told people he has been trained to kill with the sword they did not believe him. But the Sergeant-Major used to say, "Sir, you only go 6 inches in – you don't want it flashing out at the back like Erroll Flynn!" If you went right through you couldn't get the sword out again! At the outbreak of war he went before a European Tribunal and was put in Category A, which meant he was reserved, but he managed to convince his boss that the paper had managed without an art editor and a cartoonist for a hundred years and could manage again for six or seven months. In the event it was six years before he was demobbed!

After the war he was attached to public relations, which he had avoided as they thought that if you could do cartoons you could do anything – which was probably true – and he asked to return to England and mount an exhibition at India House on India's war effort. This gave him a further six months in the army on a Major's pay and time to look for a job. In fact, he got one on his second day in London with the Central Office of Information.

When he came to Lymington he employed a staff of six: an assistant designer, Bob Baker, with whom he still works; a part-time secretary who is still with him; two draughtsman and a boy. That was about the limit for a designer. It was a question of whether you wanted a big design practice or an individual one. Exhibitions were his main job. He travelled all over the world putting them on in places such as Texas, USA, Germany, France, Moscow (3 times), India, and to Japan for Expo 70. But by the time he had paid all his extras and all his travelling expenses, income tax, VAT, etc. it just was not worth it. Another reason why he gave up exhibitions was because the space was getting smaller and smaller and £20,000 went down to £3,000. A small space took twice as much work; in a big job you could spread yourself.

In 1981 he was asked to arrange an exhibition at Cowes for Cowes Week and they were going to share space in Max Aitken's Museum but General Pigot got hold of a tobacconist shop which was empty. "It is very small but it seemed the better bet so I am laying it out now. It will be opened on 20th July 1981 for three weeks and there will be three big races on, a Maxi Race, the Admiral's Cup and Cowes Week. So we will see what happens. I am putting in about fourteen pictures and giving them 20% of the takings, which is about the same as a gallery would charge. There are going to be all kinds of things in there. We will be selling tee-shirts, balloons and God knows what else! It is not so much that we will sell pictures there but they will brighten things up and make it attractive inside. I am not holding out much hope at the moment. The trouble is that most of the customers are living on their boats and how are they going to take a picture back on their boat?" Nevertheless, in 1980 he did sell 'Spinnakers,' which was shown on local television, through a little art gallery in Cowes run by Mike Miller and it went to a London judge.

Charles Munro has painted many medical advertisements including a series of time and motion study and stress. One had sold 35,000 copies and had been submitted to the Royal Academy. He told me that they could no longer afford to send out these advertisements because of the price of postage so now he does rather cheapish things which go into medical magazines.

It was inevitable that Charles Munro would become involved in the Jubilee Trust as his next door neighbours are Clare Francis, a Director of the Trust, and Colin Mudie who designed *Jubilee*. The *Lord Nelson,* as *Jubilee* is called now, is a specially designed barque for a disabled crew very similar to *Royalist*, although of course able-bodied crew members will also be on board. Colin Mudie gave a talk at the RLYC and it was extremely interesting to learn of the imaginative way he had tackled this problem. Charles now paints a tiny *Royalist* on all his marine paintings as a signature symbol.

He designed the little exhibition stand for the Jubilee Trust at the Boat Show and then participated in a video film for publicity that the Trust Secretary, Peter Thompson, can show to interested firms as part of a fund-raising drive. It was shown on an appeal on local television and had obviously been a traumatic experience for him! "The film starts off with me painting, then Colin comes in and so does Clare Francis. It is all right talking to you like this but when I had a set text picking on this and that and I was reviewing my life – oh God! A chap was holding a script for me in front of the camera and I was painting his hand! It was not too bad and the bit I liked best was when Clare said, 'It is only two million pounds. Two million pounds may sound a lot of money but after all it is only the price of two footballers,' which brought the whole thing home. But when I saw the film I am sure they dubbed me in it: it didn't sound like me at all. They said that they hadn't but I don't trust them one inch! The plans are out for tender and they hope it will be built in the South. But it will probably be well over a year before she is completed. They could start – there was enough money to start – but not enough to carry on. That was why there was all this publicity caper!"

Charles Munro, as we have seen, is also extremely active and involved in the Lymington RNLI and has painted the RNLI launch at full throttle off the Needles, which has been printed as a postcard to raise funds for the Institute.

Roy Coombs (1910-   )

Like Charles Munro, Roy Coombs is not a 'marine artist' *per se* but he too has had many marine commissions and must be included in this chapter. A member of the Royal Lymington Yacht Club for many years, he is a well-known yachtsman and has owned and raced seven boats from the Lymington River; one of them, *Tre Sang*, a 30 sq. metre, was made famous by Blondie Hasler.

Roy studied art at Chiswick and Westminster Art Schools and especially the figure, under Mark Gestler. During the war he worked on aircraft design and produced a three-dimensional (drawing) handbook for installation of engines, enabling the untrained to instal in planes, and views of jet engines which were simply projects at the time. Roy said that these drawings were meant to convince the Air Ministry that 'we were getting on with the job.' He also painted murals in the underground factories near Bath for the Ministry of Works.

Between 1939 and 1949 he exhibited landscapes and figure at the Leicester Gallery, the Cooling Gallery, Alex Reid and Lefevre, and Leger. He held a one-man show at the Modern Art Gallery and exhibited at Leamington and Coventry. Many paintings were lent to the RAF and a mural he painted in Kenilworth Castle is still there!

In 1949 he moved to Lymington. For the famous yacht designers, Laurent Giles, he translated blueprints of yachts into paintings of the same boats sailing on the Solent and has carried out the same process for Albin Marine in Sweden.

He has illustrated many books, especially on nature, and books on wild animals, trees and flowers as well as some on boats, planes, space and oil rigs. He illustrated *Elvström Speaks,* written by Richard Creagh-Osborne and *Motor Boats and Motor Boating* by Colin Mudie. Roy Coombs also did the line drawings and a beautiful painting for the cover of a book by Ewart C. Freeston on *Prisoner of War Ship Models,* published by Nautical of Lymington. This was an illustrated analysis of the 'Napoleonic' ship models of 1775-1825, of which some interesting models were privately owned in Lymington. There are eleven photographs of models, submitted by Richard Creagh-Osborne. But the cover of the book consists of an oil painting depicting a prisoner of war making a model boat and wearing the saffron yellow prison clothes, stencilled TO (Transport Office) on the front and back. His light is a wick in mutton fat lying in an oyster shell. I love it.

Roy also designed and illustrated a book called *Fantastic Boats,* which were paintings of bizarre boats which were built and then were mostly never heard of again! This book appeared in many countries. At present (1982) he is illustrating the evolution or development of musical instruments since c. 1600.

Roy was one of the first in Lymington to make ciné films with sound from shots taken on his many trips abroad, and also was one of the first to instal a hi-fi system in his home to enjoy listening to music, another of his interests. He designed a complete music system for Elizabeth Taylor's yacht, when it was moored near the Tower of London and the equipment was built in sheds in Lymington! He has also been Commodore of the Model Yacht Club which races radio-controlled yachts on Setley Pond on most Sundays.

He painted a mural of yachts sailing on the Lymington River for the bar of the RLYC when this was downstairs and it is now outside the Reading Room. His most difficult job was to copy exactly an Old Master of two hundred years ago and the copy is indistinguishable from the original.

MARINE PHOTOGRAPHY

William Payne

William Payne and his family moved to Lymington in July 1977 from Salisbury, where he was working in a commercial studio. Before that he had moved round a bit, having started in Kent and then been in Wales and Slough. "I didn't have special marine photography training but I had photography training and then the marine developed as I went along," he told me when I visited his home at 98 Gosport Street, Lymington on 18th June 1982. The tape recorder worked this time! "You cannot learn photography from anybody else, it is a matter of experience. If you learnt from anyone else you would end up doing the same as the other person. When I came here I started from complete scratch without one client and it is quite satisfying now that it is going well and very frightening when it was not. Originally, I just photographed Lymington and hopefully I am going to get further and further afield. I did a job for a Mercury outboard brochure and they are based in Belgium but generally speaking my work is all in the UK. I have got quite a few London advertising agents now so it is picking up. But it is a slow process.

"I do not do very much private work for owners as such. I specialise in 'action' photography rather than boat portraits. Beken of Cowes is famous for his boat portraits – or that is what I call them. I like the 'wet' look." He showed me a book illustrating this. He was over at Cowes for the launching of *Victory* by Princess Michael of Kent. He thought she might fall in and was ready for both an 'action' shot and the 'wet' look!

Companies usually approached him for commercial photography, mainly close-up work for sail makers, mast makers and hull makers; with magazines he submitted photographs to them. "I started off just sending pictures to magazines as everybody does when they begin, and they were nearly all rejected! I think it is a matter of principle: that is how magazines work! But I do regular work for *Yachts and Yachting* and in the June 1982 issue of *Seahorse* (the RORC magazine), I had a centre spread.

Photo: William Payne

Admiral's Cup 1979

"I used to sail a lot, mainly dinghy sailing and cruising but I never really got into big boat racing. I did all my sailing in Wales and big boat sailing is something that doesn't happen down there in the way that it does here. It was something I discovered when I got here and since then I have spent all my time power boating and photographing sailing boats. I go out in my own power boat most of the time. She is an Avon Sea Rider and she is well kitted out and has VHF on board. My other boat is a ten-year old Aqua Bel called *Dartaway,* which will be available for charter soon. I do sometimes go out in racing yachts round the buoys but I am not keen enough to go on any distance races and also there is the time factor. I have to be here in my studio as much as possible to do clients' prints; these are still important to me until I am rich. Also I now look at the racing scene a little bit one-eyed, especially after various incidents!

"I went out in a hell of a blow last April (1981) when *Caiman* and *Victory,* the Admiral's Cuppers, were playing about, to get the first shots of them. *Caiman* lost somebody overboard and there was no way they could have got back to him. I was just there taking photographs and picked him out of the water in about 30 seconds and he couldn't even keep his head above water. What annoys me is the apparent callousness. They would have tried but their spinnaker was more important they had to get that on board first because they did a dirty big broach. Obviously they had to get the spinnaker on board before they could turn round anyway. But they weren't even looking worried. They never turned round to throw him a life-belt or liferaft.

"We then called up *Icebreaker* and just told them that we had picked somebody up. Then we went back to *Caman.* I said we would take this fellow back to Lymington and dry him up but they said 'No, we need him for the next race,' and just hoisted him on board and that was that. You sometimes want to leave them in the water to see if they do come back!"

While talking about rescues he showed me an excellent photograph taken by Beken of Harvey Bagnall being winched up by a helicopter and himself in his boat beneath, taking a photograph. "Apparently the helicopter could not take him off the yacht and so he was put into the rubber duck. Harvey had been hit on the head by the boom and was absolutely out cold all the time. I didn't recognise him, he was that bad. It wasn't until later when we were talking about Harvey that I realised in all that commotion that it was him. I tend to be involved in quite a lot of rescues because I am usually out there."

William Payne showed me his two underwater cameras which are very light-weight. He started by trying to use underwater housing but it was far too cumbersome because they are designed specifically for underwater use. His two cameras looked much like ordinary ones except they had a rubber seal all round them and they were armour plated, so you could drop one too. They were good in the sand and anything like that and the lenses were easy to change. He had used the camera under water abroad but here it was a waste of time because the water was so murky. He had done a fair bit of diving at college but was out of training now.

"I like black and white photographs better for my own satisfaction," he resumed, "because from a photographic point of view black and white has got more variables. I find that when I know I have got black and white film in the camera for some reason I seem to take better pictures – which is obviously psychological." He showed me a shot of sparkling water which looked very good in black and white but would apparently be very ordinary in colour.

"I take an awful lot of photographs sometimes. If I am doing it, say for *Yachts & Yachting* where they are not commissioning me, I don't take very many because I know what they want and I know when I have got it. Quality-wise every shot I take is usable. I hardly ever don't get a sharp picture. For commercial work you need to take many because there are little things that they would notice and I might not. The expensive side of photography is the time getting there and they would not be very happy if you took just one shot when they were paying: they would expect to have a good choice. Also I don't know which one they are going to prefer.

"I like a shot with a bit of wash in it but then they may not. They might prefer one to show off the hull better. When I started I thought I must get exciting shots and then they would say, 'That's no good. You can't see what the boat looks like.' So I aim to do a bit of both: what I want and what they want. For PR shots I usually have to develop and print them in a great hurry. That's another reason for taking a fair amount of photographs; having put a film in the camera which you have to process when you get home you might as well finish it up instead of wasting it.

"I don't go in for competitions actually. I always think I am going to but it is something I never seem to get round to. I think as time gets on and I get bigger and have got some profit to get rid of, then I might afford to do a lot of colour prints for myself. But it is very expensive. That is why I haven't got many in the office. There have not been any competitions for marine photography in the Master Photography of the Association but they have competitions and I would be able to submit. I would probably start off

Photo. Beken of Cowes

Rescue by Air. Harvey Bagnall at Admiral's Cup 1979 (with William Payne taking a photograph)

with quite a good chance because most of them are submitting portraits and wedding pictures and things like that. I don't get round to it; I am too lazy. It is like seeing a competition on the Weetabix packet: you are always going to do it but never get round to cutting it out and completing it.

"I am not very union-orientated but I think that it is particularly important that High Street photographers should become members of the Royal Institute of Photography. There are several associations – the Master Photographers Association and the Incorporated Industrial Photographers. Then you can become an Associate or a Fellow but basically the idea of that is just to have some letters after your name. This is something that really does not bother me at all. If I become good and make a name I will not need them and if I am no good letters are not going to be of much help. The best publicity that I can get is to have photographs published with my name on them.

"I have got about 2,000 transparencies and one of the outlets for these is through a colour library in London. He comes down or I go up there every couple of months and he looks through what I have got and keeps a very small portion of them. He is extremely critical and naturally will only take what he thinks will sell.

"People tend to think that sailing must be seasonal but from the photographic angle the main thing is to take as much as possible during the summer and then sell stock pictures through the winter. I have a cover picture that has only just been used and yet it was taken in 1980. So that is what stock pictures are about; they are not too bothered when they were taken.

"I am mostly working with boats and they have their own sort of character. They are much easier than people because you know that they are not going to do exactly what you want them to do but they will eventually! It is a very silent sport – a bit like bird-watching: that is why I enjoy it."

Brian Manby

I went round to see Brian Manby in his studio in The Square, Pennington on 16th October 1982. "I have always been a commercial photographer since I was sixteen," said Brian Manby, "when I was apprenticed to a firm in Bournemouth, but before that I was an amateur photographer like most kids. I took it up at about 12 I think and very luckily got my apprenticeship straight from school. I spent my National Service in the Royal Air Force – in photography luckily.

"I then came out and went on the ships, the *Orsova* and the *Orcades*, as a ship's photographer. That is how part of the marine side came in but all my family is Royal Navy, going back generations and my grandfather was a commercial photographer, though I never knew him. So having come out of National Service and done the cruising for one season I then managed to get a job with another commercial firm in Bournemouth and I was there for fourteen years as a Director. They started into marine photography in a very small way but towards the end I thought it might be an idea if I did this myself.

"I had the use of a small motor boat in Lymington, which was a good start, and in September 1969 I set up on my own, obviously in a very small way for a year or two. But within three or four years I was able to buy my own motor boat, or a half-share in a bigger one, and moved to these premises at Pennington in about 1976. I bought the place when it was derelict – it had been an old school – and it has been ideal.

"The marine photography side has been very tricky in the last few years with the recession and companies going into liquidation every other month and we are running now with only one-tenth of the customers we had give years ago. But we do other work too. At one time most of my work, 90% of it, was marine; now it is down to probably less than 50%. I can supplement with computers and light industrial work and just straight advertising. The main marine side that keeps us going are the military craft, Vospers and Thorneycroft and that type of thing because at least they keep producing those boats. We do our own processing here and we are the only firm in the area that does this and has it all on the doorstep. We employ three people but it varies a bit as sometimes we have a student part-time in the summer.

"The boat only does one mile to the gallon so it is a little bit tricky to do work on spec nowadays. She is called *Playtime II.* She is 12 litres of turbo-charged engines, so it is rather thirsty! Anyway, she is a very good platform. Lionel Byrne usually drives for me, though sometimes my staff will come out. It does need two to run the boat. We get called up to go out in the boat by radio contact, so we are very efficient, I feel.

"We are just doing ordinary photocopies of Denys Brook-Hart's oil paintings and watercolours, which is just a straight forward commercial copying operation. Nearly all of the paintings in his books have been copied by us, especially the big book which was published about six or seven years ago. But it was a great responsibility. We haven't done much work for him in the last two or three years before he died, mainly because the supply of nineteenth century marine artists is drying up. There are hardly any

LTSC Winter Series 1982

Photo. Brian Manby

around now and he had to diversify into bowls of flowers and all sorts of odds and ends.

"I am not a very good speaker but I have been asked to judge at Camera Club exhibitions and I have had my eyes torn out by the lady members! Also I have had students and camera clubs looking around these premises once or twice which was very interesting. I think one was the New Milton Camera Club. There were some yacht portraits in the window of one of the building societies here as part of a display by Lymington Town Sailing Club.

"We have done video filming about boatwork, though there have been rather limited demands for it, so at the moment that film has gone to London on permanent hire. We do not take slides normally; we only use large cameras. If we do slides then we produce them by another method by copying. We do not use 35 mm. Occasionally I do some work for magazines but normally have to be asked first.

"I went out for the Tall Ships and these photographs go to agencies nowadays in London except for one batch which went straight to Italy and they will be in an Italian calendar for 1983; that was just general sailing ships. I go abroad to collect material for agencies in London – not necessarily boats and mainly general scenes. I do a lot of background scenes for studio use or calendars and book tokens. I have had about eight weeks out of the country this year and I intend to double that next year. I also filmed for two weeks in Greece on a flotilla cruise and made some slides for their publicity. They are not always holidays, these trips, and are indeed often quite hard work!"

Brian showed me a photograph that had been taken 11,000 feet up in the Austrian Alps. He had not taken his skis up with him as everything was closed that day but it was taken at the top station looking down towards Innsbruck. "It is a very uninteresting open picture but the reason for leaving it like that," he explained, "was eventually somebody came along with an air-conditioning unit and we set it up in front of this on a block of ice and used that photograph as a back projected picture. Of course it looked as though we had gone up to the top of the mountain! With models in studios they use front and back projection nowadays but they still do quite a bit on location. Every time I go to Greece I find that there are two or three photographers, and half a dozen models rushing around in what to me look like handkerchiefs but I suppose they are dresses!

"We use helicopters quite a bit: the company normally charters them for me and they cost £300 an hour." Brian showed me a photograph taken at Rotterdam. A local firm made these craft for the port police in Rotterdam. He also showed me more of military craft, the great bulk of their work, and an aerial view of the Civic Centre at Southampton.

Naturally, Brian had been out in the motor boat to photograph the *QE.2* as she passed the Lymington River at the end of the Falklands War and he had a very effective shot of the *Canberra* arriving a week later on a very foggy morning, sounding her horn. I thought the view we had on television of the *Canberra* coming through the early morning mist was like a Turner seascape and quite beautiful.

The company did all the work on the America's Cup contender *Victory.* Designed by Ed Dubois, she was built in Souters at Cowes. They photographed her from the time she left the factory and nearly got stuck in the gateway of the yard: part of the gate had to be sawed away to get her through! He had plenty of photographs of the launching itself and all the jollification afterwards. Princess Michael of Kent performed the launching ceremony and took off her high-heeled shoes before she went on board *Victory.*

CHAPTER 21

MARINE AUTHORS

"We authors, Ma'am."
DISRAELI

Nautical Publishing Co. Ltd.

When one considers the many marine authors who are living in Lymington there is no doubt that the 'Big Four' are Adlard Coles, Erroll Bruce, Richard Creagh-Osborne and Peter Johnson. As all four of them were Directors of the Nautical Publishing Company of 6 Station Street, Lymington, it is appropriate to start with a short history of that firm, kindly written for me by Erroll Bruce at the time of the takeover.

"Nautical Publishing Company was formed as a partnership by Erroll Bruce and Adlard Coles in 1967, based in the Bruce home at 'Brackens,' Captain's Row, Lymington. Adlard Coles, until then chairman of Adlard Coles Ltd., moved his home from Bursledon to Lymington in 1968. Amongst its first publications was Sir Alec Rose's *My Lively Lady,* written by him almost entirely when staying in the partners' houses. 'Brackens,' at that time, became a meeting place of many other famous long-distance yachtsmen and authors, including Bill Tilman, Miles Smeeton and Bill King.

"Richard Creagh-Osborne, who had been editorial director of Adlard Coles Ltd., joined Nautical as a partner in July 1970, bringing with him special knowledge of Olympic and dinghy sailing, besides rare creative talent. Soon afterwards the offices moved about a 100 yards to Nautical House in Station Street.

"Adlard Coles suffered a serious illness following a lecture tour in Sweden and in July 1971 had to resign as a partner of Nautical on medical advice, but remained as a consultant and Hon. President. His place as partner was taken by Peter Johnson, whose book *Ocean Racing and Offshore Yachts* had previously been published by the company. Soon after this the partnership became a limited company.

"During this period Nautical had many discussions with European publishers in the same field and this led to the formation of United Nautical Publishers S.A., jointly owned by it and leading publishers in Germany, Holland and Italy. The first venture of this consortium was to make a set of instruction video cassettes in conjunction with coloured books. Creagh-Osborne, as producer, built a special little harbour from the Royal Lymington starting platform and acquired a fleet of dinghies; the actors and actresses were young people from the Lymington area, mainly students of Brockenhurst College. This project was aimed at several years ahead, as at that time video-cassette apparatus was scarcely available; meantime they proved in demand worldwide as ciné films and the accompanying books, written by Richard Creagh-Osborne had soon sold ¼ million copies.

"Many other full colour instructional books in the same series followed, besides other instructional books on navigation, seamanship, racing, boat building and design. There were also many pilotage books, extending in area from Adlard Coles' *Creeks and Harbours of the Solent,* besides the personal narratives of famous yachtsmen. A further range was Nautical's Historical Record Series, really beautifully produced definitive works covering specialized craft such as the Arab dhow, Fast Sailing Ships in the century to 1875 and Prisoner of War Models – of which some interesting models were privately owned in Lymington.

"The Directors travelled widely to find authors of distinction, and Nautical books had certainly achieved a worldwide reputation, with 65% of its turnover in exports, when it was shocked by the death of Richard Creagh-Osborne in 1980. Erroll Bruce, having been Chairman and Managing Director for so many years, was already well on in the 'Senior Citizens' age group, so it was felt that the objects of the company could best be maintained by joining up with some general publisher. Fortunately many leading London publishers were only too keen, so Nautical was ensured the continuation of Nautical Books under the general control of the famous house of Macmillan, which took over in 1981, with Maurice Macmillan as Chairman of Nautical Books and Sir Peter Johnson working at Macmillans in London; while Erroll Bruce became

Deputy Chairman and with Adlard Coles was a consultant, based in the Lymington offices."

In 1982 even the smaller office at No. 6 Station Street was closed and Erroll Bruce now works from his home at the 'Lofts,' Lower Pennington Lane so the 'Lymington Connection' still continues – and long may it do so.

Commander Erroll Bruce, RN

Erroll Bruce was born in 1913, the younger son of an Anglican parson. His father wrote poetry and many other books, mainly about dogs and horses and especially on breeding – he was a great student of Mendelism. His father had five children and said that he needed to write so that he could pay for their school fees. His son, Erroll, also had five children and presumably started writing himself for the same reason!

Over a cup of coffee at his home on 9th June 1982 he told me that one of his sisters, Verily Anderson, had also written a number of books. They started to write magazines at home when they were small children. "We wrote them out in longhand and then, when I was 13, I bought a little hand printing machine and we used to act together in the cellar. Her magazine was meant to be called *Useful Days* but she spelt it wrongly so it because *Usful Days,* and mine was to do with photographs. They were just for the family.

"One of the earlier books with which I was associated was not to do with the sea at all but with polo. That was really written by Lord Mountbatten anonymously and he asked me to help him with putting it together and dealing with a publisher, so horses and riding were very much an interest then. I had done a lot of riding both at home and in the Navy. In China, for instance, I kept polo ponies but early in the war, when I was in submarines, I broke my back and that really put an end to polo.

"When I was in China as a young Naval officer I had many adventures as we were mostly concerned with the pirate problem. One of the first times I was skippering a boat on my own, I was eighteen at the time, we had to put out a fire on board by letting the mainsail fall on it. My captain felt a bit apprehensive about allowing us 18-year olds to go off on our own and was not certain whether it was safer for me to have a pistol or whether it would be even more dangerous! In the end I was given a pistol with instructions that I must hide it!" Erroll Bruce once had to land to bail out his flooded boat on the beach of a Chinese pirate village. It was when he was disabled by a broken ankle that he first began to write for publication and since then he has com-bined writing with the life of a sailor right up to his retirement.

He has been influenced by his uncle, Scott of the Antarctic, and in many ways has had an equally adventurous life. He capsized in a native outrigger canoe among sharks and later broke his neck when he fell from a train. It was at the start of a holiday with his wife, Daphne, spent travelling with a donkey in the bandit country of the Aspromonte Mountains in 1958, although they did not discover this until later. Erroll has also lived on a coral island in the Pacific when they were letting off nuclear bombs!

In the war, with polo now out as a recreation, he tended more and more towards sailing as an interest, particularly in training young men, both sailors and officers, to be self-dependent and to be able to look after themselves if their ship was sunk. "I would take them off, perhaps for a day or two at night in an open boat so that they got familiar with that, and at that time I encouraged a very large number of men to go boating in various forms and it was really the beginning of adventure training. That continued later on when it was very much encouraged by Lord Mountbatten.

"When I came back to England from the Far East a year or two after the war, I became very keen on ocean racing again, having done a little before, and in 1950 I was put in charge of a very small boat with a naval crew of volunteers to race across the Atlantic and that was the beginning of my international career. The name of the boat was *Samuel Pepys.*

"Adlard Coles was then the leading ocean racer of the day and he became a close friend of mine and we went as a team to America in his boat and my boat and a third one and then raced each other back across the Atlantic. That was at a time when you could not get dollars, or very few, so we had to take everything with us, including most of our food, and I could only get limited leave from the Navy. So we signed on as deck hands in a tramp steamer and took the boats as our luggage.

"We did our practice sailing in Bermuda then sailed across to America and raced back from there. From then on I was really established. It was considered ridiculous that such small boats should compete and we were heavily criticised and every-body thought that we would be a long, long way behind. In fact, with many big boats, Adlard Coles was the winner on corrected time and I was about half an hour after him although I finished three or four hours before him but on handicap we were first and second. So that established that very small boats with highly-practised crews could race even across oceans.

"Since then I have raced several times across the Atlantic and the next one I did win. Adlard Coles did not compete again but our particular rival that time was a large American yacht, owned by a very wealthy man. He suggested we had some sort of bet on each other although he knew I hadn't got a penny in the world. His crew wore red socks and mine had little red hats, so it became the 'hats' against the 'socks' and we duly won the socks! It created a good deal of public interest when Britain was having a bit of a rough time and it was considered quite encouraging that a small British boat had beaten the Americans, the French and all the rest in bigger and more expensive ones.

"So my writing went on, and Adlard Coles wrote a book of the first Transatlantic Race but I co-operated with him and a lot of his material was quoting from my diary, so we worked together on that. Then in 1953 I was asked by Hutchinsons, the publishers, to write a sort of textbook on Deep Sea Sailing, which I did." This book has been described as one of the most brilliant ever written for yachts-men and has been reprinted three times; a revised edition in 1967 had also been reprinted three times and in 1979 it was published in paperback. Hardly surprising that Hutchinsons asked him to write various other books and he was really turning out a book every other year and he also wrote a lot of articles. "I found that in a naval career," he con-tinued, "there was no objection from the authorities, particularly if one was in a ship at sea. I really had quite ample time and on other occasions would normally get up at 4 o'clock in the morning to write before the day's work.

"Inevitably, I then got involved in voluntary administration: I was on the committee of various clubs and later was elected to the Council of the Royal Yachting Association, which was the con-trolling body for sailing. At that time my first cousin, Peter Scott, was Deputy Chairman and when he completed his time I took over from him, so we kept it in the family! It was very interesting and a new experience for me, learning about the administrative side and the finance. But I still went on sailing and at one time there was a proposal to challenge the America's Cup, started by Lord Craigmyle, and I was very much involved in that and was sailing his twelve metre regularly in the Solent.

"Before that, we had lived as a family for a time on an old trawler and when I was serving in an aircraft carrier we would sail it around from port to port, usually helped by one or two volunteer sailors with my family living on board. So my sons Peregrine and Peter, in their school holidays, were practically living in the water and, of course, became very keen.

Our then youngest, Errollyn, came on board at seven weeks and learnt to walk on deck. I never came into Lymington with the trawler because she was very clumsy to sail and I shied off trying to tack up the Lymington River but we did go to Yarmouth once or twice. She hadn't got an engine and with the bowsprit sticking out we were fairly guarded where we could go with a family crew.

"Before we came to Lymington, one of the places that we particularly loved living in was in Orkney. There I found myself in the lifeboat's crew in the Pentland Firth, where I learned a great deal about very difficult weather as we were frequently called out – normally for trawlers in trouble between Scotland and North End. Two or three years later the boat was lost with all her crew and that was the last major calamity before the recent one at Penlee and that was very sad.

"There was an appeal then but being in the North of Scotland it didn't have quite the same impact as Penlee although in some ways sadder. The boat was based on a tiny community at Lyness and really within this small community almost every man was lost. However, they got one going again and we were invited up there later when a new lifeboat was launched.

"I was in the Navy and commanding the naval base at Lyness so in fact the lifeboat's crew were all working for me but in the lifeboat I was, of course, the junior hand and I was very impressed with their courage and their seamanship. Then later the RNLI invited me to go on my own to a great number of lifeboats round the coast of Britain and Ireland and go out with them, particularly ones where there had been a service to yachts, so that I could hear from the coxswains what it was that had caused the yachts to get into trouble and how, based on their local knowledge, they considered that the yachts could best avoid it.

"That led to a sort of book called *Local Knowledge*, which was published in conjunction with the RNLI; it came out in parts in a magazine and this was then bound. I think if any one thing caused the accidents it was the seasickness factor really, but there were so many causes of problems and one of the books which I wrote very recently, called *This is Rough Weather Sailing*, was based on my experience from that. Much of it came from the lifeboats. I have always been terribly keen on lifeboats and have helped in any I can and have quite often been asked to lecture, mainly for fund-raising, and I have been in close touch – and still am – with the RNLI. Indeed, I was awarded some special trophy for services to public relations from lecturing and writing and that sort of thing.

By courtesy of Erroll Bruce

Rescue by Sea. Coxswain Ron Arnell at wheel of Selsey Lifeboat with Erroll Bruce

"When I was appointed to work in England, we settled in Lymington because we wanted to be near the sea for yachting and also because Daphne's cousin lived at Priestlands. My naval career had become a little limited: I had broken my back, my neck and, in one of the Transatlantic races, I had cracked my skull so when I was invited to become Editor of *Motor Boat and Yachting* I accepted. The Second Sea Lord, who was the top man in personnel, was involved in this and gave it his full support, so in fact I walked from a desk in the Admiralty one day to a desk in Fleet Street the next day!

"I was very fortunate and it was a marvellous experience and I spent six years editing that magazine. When the company asked me if I would become a director and give up as editor I thought I might as well direct my own firm, and so I started the Nautical Publishing. Combined with that, we found ourselves with a fifth child and did not really think that bringing her up in London was to the best advantage, whereas Lymington was a perfect place for a baby to start her life. That was Chloe. So we settled in Lymington and I have enjoyed it very

much. When Chloe was becoming interested in ponies, we move to The Lofts, Lower Pennington Lane from Captains Row. So that is about it!"

Sir Peter Johnson, Bart.

Sir Peter Colpoys Paley Johnson, 7th Baronet, was born on 26th March 1930, son of Lieutenant Colonel Sir John Paley Johnson, MBE. The baronetcy was created in 1755 at New York State and bears the motto 'Nec aspera terrent' ('Not even difficulties frighten me.') Debrett's *Illustrated Baronetage* records that "The 1st Baronet, General Sir William Johnson, of an ancient family in Ireland named Macshane, went in early life to America and conducted the expedition to Crown Point, and gained the battles of Crown Point and Niagara, for which services he was created a baronet and received £5,000 from the Government and also large grants of lands in the province of New York, then part of the British dominions. He settled on the Mohawk River and brought the Seneccas – one of the revolted tribes and inveterate enemies of the English – to a treaty in 1764. He was sole representative of Indian affairs for the northern parts of America for George II and Colonel of the six united nations, their allies and dependants."

Peter Johnson told me that there is still a family seat in up-state New York and he has been to see it. But he is leaving it to the family in America to write the history of the first two baronets – the second was also Superintendent General of Indian Affairs in North America and remained loyal to the Crown at the outbreak of the American Revolution – as after that, he claims, "they are not really a distinguished lot!"

Although amongst his forbears there were admirals and naval officers, he followed his father into the army, after being educated at Wellington and the Royal Military College of Science at Shrivenham. He served in the Royal Artillery from 1948 to 1960 and when he came out he joined a yacht fittings firm as a director of Sea Shore Ltd.

Between the age of sixteen and now (1982) he has owned about 15 boats over 34 years and when he was in the army he went off crewing and sailed with the army abroad in the Mediterranean as well as in the Solent. He did a lot of dinghy sailing but usually had a small cruiser himself for when he was on leave.

Peter Johnson was captain of the Junior Offshore Group (JOG) from 1965-68 and today is their President "which is pretty well an honorary job." He has sailed in about seven Fastnet Races, including the bad one in 1979 and this year (1982) sailed in the two-man Round Britain Race with Rodney Barton in *Blackjack,* designed by Michael Pocock. He has done masses of ocean racing and started the OOD 34 Class in 1979.

He has got two daughters and two sons, ranging in age from 22 to 5. His eldest daughter is on the administrative staff of the *Victory* syndicate at Newport, R.I. and has been on a cruise in a schooner to the West Indies. She is a keen sailor and his eldest son has already sailed in five RORC races, including the last Fastnet of 1981 with his father.

Peter Johnson told me that he had always written articles in an amateur way ever since leaving school and provided a lot of material for *Yachting and Boating Weekly* (now defunct) during the 1960s and then, subsequently, became Offshore Correspondent for *Yachting World* from 1970 to 1981. It was thus that he caught the attention of Adlard Coles and Erroll Bruce, who asked him to write *Ocean Racing and Offshore Yachts,* which he did in 1970, although he had written a book the previous year called *Passage Racing* and that is how he started his writing career. He was then invited to join Nautical Publishing in Lymington in 1970 until they sold out in 1980 to Macmillans, where he now works as publisher of nautical books.

We discussed some of his books and he mentioned that *The Guinness Book of Yachting Facts and Feats* in 1975 took him a couple of years to write. Since then he has published the *Guinness Guide to Sailing,* published in 1982. So although he publishes he also writes many books himself. Every year he writes for the Offshore Racing Council, keeping up their records *Passages under Sail.*

He has also edited other people's books and reckons that he must have done about 50 or 60 sailing books, sometimes adding to them himself. As a publisher he is entitled to do this as long as the authors are contracted and co-operative. Although he has written hundreds of articles, mainly ocean racing for yachting magazines – he wrote 123 articles alone in the series "In the Offing" for *Yachting World* – he is doing very little journalism today and is concentrating on publishing and working on the occasional book. He is chairman of the Yachting Journalists Association so he knows them all but is giving this up this year. He has now got a new project that he is going to write and we shall look forward to reading it.

Patrick Beesly

Patrick Beesly was born in 1913 and was educated at Oundle and at Trinity College, Cambridge. His father was Gerald Beesly, a very well-known yachtsman locally before World War Two. Patrick Beesly served in the Royal Naval Volunteer Reserve for 20 years from 1939 to 1959 and during the war from 1939 to 1945 he was attached to the Operation Intelligence Centre (OIC) of the Admiralty. After 30 years the security ban has been lifted and he has been able to write not only from personal experience but also from having access to top secret documents in the Public Records Office. The OIC worked very closely with the Government Code and Cipher School at Bletchley Park, which made a major contribution to the winning of the war by successfully breaking the German ciphers for the Army and Air Force and also, thanks to another local yachtsman, Lieutenant-Commander D. E. Balme, the naval ciphers as well. Patrick Beesly is married with two daughters and lives at his home in 8 Nelson Place, where I visited him on 19th January 1982 on a dark and very wet evening.

"I did not stay on in the Navy after the war as I was only RNVR," he told me. "I went to work in the Midlands in a firm making metal window frames. In fact, my firm made those rather extraordinary octagonal frames round the bar in the Royal

Lymington looking out over the river. I didn't get the order, in fact I was rather horrified when I saw it and I thought I know damn well something will go wrong with this – and it did! The estimator forgot to put a nought on the end somewhere so it cost my firm twice what we charged for it!

"When I retired we came to this house in 1971 and I didn't start writing until 1975. *Very Special Intelligence* took me two and half years to write. I suppose that is the time I do take but I think my current book will probably be completed in two years, and that is working very hard. I hardly sailed at all last summer in consequence.

"I get Xerox copies from the Public Record Office (PRO) and then I go up there and take written notes but there is such a vast amount of material it is not a very good way of doing it. The material is extremely ill-organised in the PRO. I don't think it is their fault, it is the way it is released by the authorities and you can't start at the beginning and work through. I am constantly darting about from this file to that file and the consequence is that one's notes are not in any logical order and I just have to remember them in my head. When I start to write a chapter I think, 'Oh, yes, somewhere I have made a note of it,' and that is why everything is spread all round my study. You have got to be very, very accurate or the experts will tear you to pieces if you make a mistake!

"I will have covered from World War One up to the end of World War Two. My second book, although it is a biography, is about the man who was Director of Naval Intelligence for the first four years of the war, John Godfrey, so what I didn't cover in my first book I will cover in the second. This third book I hope will be very comprehensive and will cover all forms of intelligence, particularly de-coding in World War One. Everything that was done in World War Two was done really exactly the same as had been done in World War One. I mean direction finding, de-coding and all the other things which were not specifically naval intelligence, like double agents and propaganda and so on. That was all done by the Naval Intelligence Division and no-one else, so I think I have got quite an interesting story there. (His third book is *Room 40*, published in November 1981 by Hamish Hamilton).

"I used to go up quite often with my father in Cowes Week and although I never sailed in any of them I can remember the J Class well. They really were a magnificent sight coming foaming through Cowes Roads, great enormous yachts with 20 or 30 chaps lying out on the deck. It was very exciting. I believe someone who went out in them was Alastair Easton, the broker. As a young man before the war, you could present yourself to the Royal Yacht Squadron with some sort of recommendation probably, and then you would get taken on, because although they all had a largish professional crew, for regattas they recruited a number of healthy young men to do the pullie haulie work! There were not the marvellous winches then: you had to sheet that enormous mainsail home and it was a question of having 10 or 12 chaps hauling on it.

"When I got my first little scow, I can remember this quite clearly, I suppose it was 1926 or 1927. I had sailed quite a bit with my father in his boats but I had never really sailed a dinghy on my own. It was tied up to the Yacht Club slip and my father said, 'There you are, my boy, off you go,' standing there with some of his friends. I thought, 'My God, I daren't disgrace the old man by getting into trouble in front of them all,' so I can remember rowing off into Harpers Lake until I thought I was out of sight, when I hoisted sail for the first time! You could sail through the Lakes then – well, you still can, of course – and it was very pleasant. According to the tide you could go out one way and come in another."

As I was leaving, Patrick Beesly told me another story about the origin of the name of Jack-in-the-Basket at the mouth of the river. He said that there had been an old pirate called Jack and his remains had been hung out there to act as a deterrent, hence the name. This could have happened long before the fishermen's wives started to leave lunches there so both stories are perfectly possible.

Captain Edward Murray Conrad Barraclough, RN (Rtd), CBE

I enjoyed a glass of sherry and a most interesting conversation when I visited Captain Barraclough on 7th March 1981 at his home 'Crosstrees,' Sway Road, Lymington. He was born in 1893 but had the enthusiasm and zest for life of a man half his age. Captain Barraclough is the author of four books, all of them on flags. "Flags and the way that they have been used had always held a fascination for me," he wrote in the preface of the 1978 Third Edition of *Flags of the World,* "but until I became editor of this book I had little idea how great a part they have played in the history of the world." This book, incidentally, has been described – and deservedly so – as a 'National Institution' and he is a world authority on flags.

He has also privately written his memoirs entitled *I was Sailing,* which he did at the request of his family, both the English and the American side, with the help of Jean Wilson. Jean has an Hons. degree in History and is the wife of Captain Hugh Wilson. Captain Barraclough very kindly loaned me a copy and very fascinating reading it made too. It was from his memoirs that I obtained most of his background history.

Ted Barraclough was born in 1893 in China, as was his mother before him. His father's family was an old Hanoverian family called Wedemayer, which came to England in the early nineteenth century but in World War One the name was changed by deed poll in 1916 to Barraclough, his grandmother's name.

He can remember the Memorial Parade of the Shanghai Volunteers on the death of Queen Victoria and he took part in amateur dramatics on the coronation of Edward VII. To his horror he was the little prince, son of Henry I, who was drowned in the White Ship. The first time he ever held a tiller of a sailing boat was in a sampan when he was ten years old. He was sent home to England and spent two years at Osborne and two at Dartmouth before entering the Royal Navy in 1910.

He immediately took up sailing and at Gibraltar once borrowed the Admiral's suit of sails for a pursuit race and came third out of one hundred boats which was quite an achievement for a junior 'snotty' and one of the memories he treasures most. When he was acting Sub-Lieutenant at Collingwood he met Prince Albert, later George VI, who was then a junior midshipman, and they often went ashore together, he as 'Jones' and the Prince as 'Johnson.' Ted Barraclough was one of the few Britons to have visited Petropavlosk, a great summer resort of the Russians, and was present when a monument was erected over the grave of Captain Clarke. This was followed by a terrific round of festivities.

"On 5th August 1914," he wrote in his Memoirs, "the morning after war had been declared, it was believed that two German cruisers were in the vicinity and action stations were called. But the Gunnery Officer could not supervise the preparation of the guns as the searchlight platform was occupied by a small, brown bear which repelled all-comers with friendly cuffs of its paw. Eventually a Marine, standing unsteadily on the rigging, enticed it down and back into its corral with a tin of sweetened condensed milk – and the war continued!"

Ted Barraclough was then posted to submarines and was present when the German fleet surrendered at the end of the war. Landing parties boarded the submarines and saluted their defeated opponents. The German officers looked so pathetic that in spite of everything they felt pity for them. Being sub-mariners themselves they knew only too well the stresses and strains they had endured and it had been a near thing between victory and defeat. His senior officer had difficulty weighing anchor and signalled him to proceed ahead into the harbour. So it was that U.138, under the command of Lieutenant Barraclough, led the long line of German U-boats into Harwich.

"I once had to carry out a very sad and unpleasant task. In practice a submarine was rammed by the target ship and sank. It transpired that when the destroyer hit the conning tower, she fractured the pipe to the whistle. The crew had forgotten to shut off the whistle valve. As each group of bottles of compressed air was connected to the main, the air went straight up the whistle pipe into the sea and so there was no air to blow the water out of the ballast tanks. When she was salvaged, Ted Barraclough had to go into her and found that the Captain must have survived for some time as he had left plenty of notes. It had a deep effect on him and was the day he grew from a boy into a man.

Ted Barraclough loved sailing in all its forms and was fascinated by models. He had met Engineer Admiral 'Alf' Turrell, a very fine designer of model yachts, who encouraged him to build his own, which he did. Model yachts pioneered two devices in particular: one was having a fin and skeg on keels, which were used by full-sized yachts fifteen years later, and the other was an invention of a Norwegian of the vane gear, later to be the new form of automatic steering. He entered for the British Empire Model Yacht Championships for 1 metre yachts at Gosport with little success.

In 1935 the Royal Naval Sailing Association was formed and a year later it adopted a sailing dinghy of the Island Sailing Club one design. Ted Barraclough became Commodore of the RNSA and one of these Admiralty dinghies, designed by Charlie Nicholson of Camper & Nicholson, was the famous *Samuel Pepys*. He chartered *Zenda* from the RNSA "for the giddy sum of four pounds per week" and ran her aground ignominiously plum opposite the Royal Lymington Yacht Club! He was shown great kind-ness but wondered if perhaps they had mistaken the RNSA burgee for that of the Royal Yacht Squadron!

In 1937 John Illingworth, who had been his senior engineer in Submarine XI, built the famous *Maid of Malham* in Coronation Year. Designed by Laurent Giles, she was the first yacht to have been built as an ocean racer. Later he lent her to Ted Barraclough, who has many happy memories of sailing in her; in one year he covered 4,300 miles. It was in *Maid of Malham* that he first got his nickname of 'Snow White,' partly because his hair had turned white in his early thirties and partly because he had a crew of "seven large and lusty young men" – hence Snow White and his seven dwarfs! A cup he had won at Dun Laoghaire, after forming a branch of the RNVRSA, is now presented to the RNSA yacht which does best in the RORC Channel Race. With World War Two imminent, he sadly had to leave the *Maid.*

He was later attached to the British Pacific Fleet and stayed a few days in Colombo and had dinner in the famous Galle Face Hotel, where he and Poppy, his wife, had formerly stayed to escape the coaling of the *Macedonia* when they were en route to Hong Kong. As in World War One, he was to be present at another surrender when the Japanese capitulated at the end of World War Two. When he was there he met Lady Mountbatten, who was Head of the St. John's Ambulance, and he was very impressed with her.

After the war he nearly became Secretary of the RORC, in fact, he was temporary secretary for six months, when he was offered the post of Admiralty Regional Officer for the Reading District, which he accepted instead. He was elected to the RYA and became Chairman of the Technical Sub-Committee of the RORC. He was there when the RORC Rule was adopted and also saw the first International Rule for the conduct of racing born.

Ted Barraclough had been an RORC Measurer with Larry Brown in Lymington in the days when ratings had to be worked out with logarithms and slide rules in what is done in seconds today on a computer. The Rating Secretary was a Major Heckstall-Smith, predecessor to Brigadier David Fayle.

It was when he was a civilian at Reading that he first started writing. The Admiralty had published *Flag Etiquette for Yachts* at the end of the last century when most yachts had at least ten paid hands. But the Director of Signals at the Admiralty was receiving requests for guidance from yachtsmen and passed them on to the RNSA at the time that Ted Barraclough was Chairman. (He and John Illingworth were Founder Members of the RNSA). So he wrote the book which was later re-issued by IPC as *Flags and Signals* as a BP Yachting Book. It gave him a tremendous interest.

Deciding to retire to Lymington, they were fortunate enough to buy his present house, 'Crosstrees,' from Helen Tobin, herself a yachtswoman of some renown, who then moved to No. 9 King's Saltern Road to be nearer to the Royal Lymington Yacht Club. Cyril Stephens, Chairman of the publishers Frederick Warne, then asked him to write *Flags of the World.* He still had much to learn and joined the Heraldry Society. He also saw the formation of the International Federation of Vexicollogical Associations (the word was coined by a young American, Whitney Smith, from the Roman flag *vexillum*). The Federation held congresses every two years and when he attended one in Boston in 1969 he met his two American aunts, one of whom was in her nineties. At the Sixty International Congress he was awarded a Medal of Honour to mark his long service to vexicollogy. He also formed the Heraldry Society's Flag Section and was its first Chairman.

In 1968 he became adviser to the Navy on heraldry and this appointment included designing badges for ships of the RN. One in his home was for *Lyness,* a stores and victualling ship, and he came up with the idea of a butter cask. Near Lyness is an Island called Butter and in the old days this was packed in old rum casks. Another was for a nuclear submarine called *Conqueror.* He used the dreaded Raven Flag of the Vikings because in the Bayeux Tapestry, William the Conqueror (descended from the Vikings) had a banner of a 'gonfanon' with a primitive bird believed to be a raven on it. He also designed flags and in Lymington one flies over his home 'Crosstrees' and another is at the Lymington Community Centre. In addition to his work as an author, Ted Barraclough has lectured in the USA and all over the world.

He was also a temporary Hon. Secretary of the Royal Lymington Yacht Club and engaged Doug Baverstock, formerly boat building in Keyhaven, as Club Boatman. A happy choice as Doug has been with the Club now for 25 years. In those days Miss Hale was the caterer and he remembered buying 12 ducks for her. A girl called Nina helped with the PAYE.

Ted Barraclough married his wife, Poppy, on 12th February 1919 and had two daughters. The eldest daughter, Joan, is a journalist and their second daughter became a doctor and married Captain Hewlett. They sailed *White Oryx* most successfully.

He finished his memoirs while the British Legion Festival of Remembrance was being televised from the Royal Albert Hall and as he sat and looked at the old soldiers and sailors, he could not forget the columns in the newspapers showing the casualty lists and remembered his own personal casualty list. The Memoirs end with a touching dedication to his wife, who died in 1980 after years of crippling arthritis. He writes sadly: "In our life it has generally been I who sailed away, but now it is the other way and so I can appreciate, just a little, how she felt when I went off in my ship and she was left behind." A very moving ending.

Humphrey Barton

Humphrey Barton was born in Wimbledon in 1900. In World War One he trained with the Royal Flying Corps but was too young to fly on active service. After the war he joined the firm of Callenders

Cables as an engineer and travelled round the world for them. He sailed whenever his work with Callenders Cables permitted and taught himself the skills of cruising in an open boat and had some hairy experiences. He once appeared "as a dripping apparition" on the pilot ship anchored off the Wash. Instead of dousing sail in a gale and rowing ashore he had turned and run before it and the pilot ship was all that stood between him and Holland! In 1930 he won the Little Ship Club's first North Sea Race and in 1937 raced in the first Fastnet Race.

He left Callenders Cables in 1936 and came south to Lymington where he became one of the original partners in Laurent Giles and Partners along with Jack Giles and George Gill. He spent most of his time dealing with marine survey and delivery work. For if Jack Giles designed the yachts it was Humphrey Barton who sailed them and he delivered them all over the world. He was closely involved in the development of the famous Vertue Class right from the start and sailed the very first, *Andrillot* (No. 1) to the Bay of Biscay in 1937 and undertook to deliver *Monie* (No. 3) to her owner in Wales. He collected her from the Berthon Boat Company and sailed off down the river, arguing with his crew whether to turn left or right for Wales when they reached Jack-in-the-Basket. In the event they turned left and sailed up the North Sea through the Caledonian Canal and down the West Coast to Wales! They had sailed 1,056 miles in 25 days, weathering 4 gales en route!

Humphrey Barton was a great friend of Roger Pinckney. In 1939 he and his wife, Jessie, and two young medical students brought back the famous *Dyarchy* from Sweden, where she was built, and passed through the Crinan Canal in Scotland. Then one year after the war they all sailed in her again when Roger left *Dyarchy* at Vannes in the Morbihan and the Bartons brought her back to Lymington.

In World War Two Humphrey Barton served with the rank of Major in the Royal Engineers in the Shetlands and Orkneys on defence projects. One of his most harrowing adventures occurred when he was up there. "He decided to sail a big Navy gig with a small army crew to the remote and rocky island of Foul in the Shetland Isles... On the way back a gale made him decide to turn and run for the shelter of Easter Sound directly under their lee. It was a terrible risk but the alternative was a night in the dangerous, dark and bitterly cold weather and a crew weakened with continual bailing. Nothing they could do prevented the sea breaking aboard or reduced their frightening speed. With less than an hour of twilight left they saw Easter Sound and it looked hopeless...

An enormous sea came along and was on the verge of breaking but miraculously it lifted the gig up instead and carried her along on its crest with gunwales awash and safely put her down in the smooth waters of the Voe." But unbelievably an even worse experience was to follow.

Humphrey Barton first hit the headlines in 1950 when he and Kevin O'Riordan sailed *Vertue XXXV* across the Atlantic from Falmouth to New York. This crossing is vividly described in his book *"Vertue XXXV"*, and some extracts are given below. "0605 26th May – It is blowing about 65 mph now, quite one of the hardest blows I have ever been out in. The wind is simply screaming through the rigging and the sea is all white. The crests are fairly being torn off. Barometer has dropped nearly one-tenth in the last hour.

"1300 – I took over from K.O'R. Conditions were absolutely shocking: the sort of thing one reads about but does not believe. A wind that has reached a state of senseless fury: a wind that soon numbs one into a dull state of hopelessness: a wind of absolute demon force that piles the sea into unstaple, toppling heaps. And with the wind came at frequent intervals the most blinding rain I have ever seen. It was impossible to face the wind and open one's eyes. Visibility was reduced to a little more than 100 yards. It became difficult to make out where the surface of the sea began and ended. There was, in fact, no clear dividing line with the atmosphere: sea and air had become inextricably mixed ...

"Forty-four days out – 29th May 0330 hours – There is a sad gap of two days in this journal but I have been too busy to do any writing. Furthermore, I have been in no fit state to write. In fact, I am not sure that I am now. I can still think of little else than those terrible moments when the end seemed so very near. The gale was blowing as hard as ever but there we were in our snug dry little cabin with an oil lamp burning as it was dusk, almost dark in fact. It came with devastating suddenness: a great fiend of a sea that picked the yacht up, threw her over on her port side and then burst over her. There was an awful splintering of wood, a crash of broken glass and in came a roaring cataract of water. Then the light went out. I thought, 'So this is the end and no-one will ever know how it happened. . . '."

This incident caused Jack Giles to re-design the structure of the doghouse and coach-roof to provide additional stiffness in later Vertues. Humphrey Barton was awarded the Vertue Cup for 1950. The citation ended: "This was a remarkable achievement and Humphrey Barton and his crew, Kevin O'Riordan, are to be congratulated."

In 1954 Humphrey Barton founded the Ocean

Cruising Club for the growing number of deep water cruising enthusiasts and became its first Commodore. Membership is restricted to those who have sailed 1,000 miles port to port in a yacht of not more than 70 ft. LOA. The Club now has an international membership of more than 1,500 from 30 different countries. He was later made Admiral of the Club and also regularly contributed to the Club journal, *Flying Fish*.

One of the most coveted awards for cruising is the Blue Water Medal which has been presented by Cruising Club of America since 1923. It is usually given for a particular voyage of outstanding interest or merit and it is significant that when this was awarded to Humphrey Barton no date was given as the merit had been established in so many different ways. Not least, he had crossed the Atlantic 20 times, more than any other living yachtsman, and his 20th crossing was made at the age of 75!

His wife Jessie, mother of the twins Peter and Pat, died in 1959 only days before Pat married Michael Pocock. Humphrey Barton then went cruising full time, living on board *Rose of York* and then his beloved *Rose Rambler*, which he built in 1963. Both were designed by Laurent Giles. He sailed 102,000 miles in her, which included five Atlantic crossings made with his second wife, Mary Banby, whom he married in 1970.

Humphrey Barton wrote three books, all in the 1950s. The first was *Vertue XXXV*, published in 1951 by Robert Ross & Co. (Adlard Cole); the second was *The Sea and Me* in 1952, full of autobiographical stories and the third, *Atlantic Adventurers* in 1955. which is an account of all the little boats under 30 ft. LOA that cross the Atlantic and the work of much research. Pat Pocock told me that this was the book of which he was most proud.

His writings are best summed up in an article by Bill Beavis in *Yachting Monthly* of February 1979. "Reading Humphrey Barton's books one rediscovers too that lost impeccability so typical of the men of this period. Inoffensive but not weak; humorous but not derisive; discreet but not guarded . . . His relationship with the sea is natural and professional. He talks of it in a knowledgeable, interesting way..."

The same author described Humphrey Barton's seamanship, written after his story of the Goodwin Sands adventures: "Fewer survived to graduate from this sort of school but those who did learnt a seamanship which was entirely to do with tide, wind and water, without the comforts of weather reports, sophisticated gear and rescue services. Naturally they attained a high degree but most of all developed a solid independence, a reliability upon self. Humphrey Barton is a seaman who has these

forgotten qualities and one which, you feel would not take unnecessary risks but sails always within the limitations of his craft and himself. That these limitations are far beyond what most of us will ever achieve is the mark of his professionalism. There is still a sharp distinction between him and some later acclaimed voyagers who have relied less on skill and experience and more on brute courage and luck. But not only do Humphrey Barton and men of his generation represent a higher standard of seamanship; they also – though we may not wish to admit it – were much tougher than we are today. Boats of their day were much harder to sail; gear was heavy or non-existent and comforts few and counted."

Humphrey Barton died of a stroke at Lyndhurst on the 18th October 1980 at the age of 80. If all that has been written about him is true then he was indeed a remarkable man and an inspiration for those who follow him. How proud he must have been of his 16-year old grandson, Richard Pocock, for being as unflappable and courageous as himself in 1979 in one of the worst Fastnet Races of all time.

Richard was on board *Windswept*, an OOD 34 owned and skippered by George Tinley and was the youngest member of the crew, if not of the race. However, he was given very high praise afterwards and had pulled his weight. The yacht had been knocked down and did a 360 degree roll but despite this they got themselves back to Cork with no outside help and were quite pleased. There were seven on board. George Tinley was very badly knocked about: he broke his wrist and had a bump on his head and was unconscious. Richard knew all about pyrotechnics having been attached to the RNLI rescue craft, although he was too young to have gone out with them. Perhaps young men today are as tough as those of preceding generations!

Barbara Webb

Barbara Webb is the daughter of Colonel Tobin, an experienced mountaineer of many expeditions in the Himalayas. He was a member of the Himalayan Club and was a friend of Major Bill Tilman, with whom he kept up a correspondence from Lymington so that Bill, being a bachelor, would always find some letters waiting for him when he arrived at his various ports of call in Greenland, Norway, Iceland or the South Atlantic.

Her mother, Helen Tobin, is remembered not only for her sailing ability but particularly for her courageous fight against cancer about which she never complained. It was fitting and rewarding that her last sailing season should have been her most successful as she won, amongst other trophies, the Round the Island Race in *Babar* in the summer of

1954 before her death. She nearly won it two years running, as in the previous year she had all but tied with Lionel St. Clare Byrne with seconds between them but Lionel, sailing *Pastime,* was just winner. She was the first woman ever to win this race.

Their daughter, Barbara, inherited her father's love of mountains and was an active member of the White Hare Ski Club at Andermatt where she met, and later married, her future husband, John Webb. John was a Director in the famous family glass firm and consequently they moved up to Wombourne in Worcestershire to be near his work.

From her mother Barabara inherited her love of sailing and she is an experienced sailor of both dinghies and keelboats. She continued to sail *Barbar* up to a few years ago and today the yacht is owned by the proprietor of 'Practically Perfect' in the High Street, so *Babar* continues to be a part of the Lymington sailing scene. But all the time she was living at Arbourtree House, Wombourne, Barbara continued to keep No. 9 King's Saltern Road, which she let out. It gave her a feeling of security that she always had it as a 'safety net' should she decide to live here permanently again. Unfortunately for her neighbours and friends in the road, she has decided not to return here and the house is up for sale.

In Wombourne Barbara became very interested in local history and did some research with a friend. They combined together extremely well because the friend was more keen on oral history and enjoyed meeting and talking to people, while Barbara liked unearthing and looking through ancient documents, the academic side. Yet surprisingly she has never been to university but has never allowed this to deter her in any way as the following story illustrates: "I had to go to Lambeth Palace (I was hunting for something about one of our priests, about 1596) and arrived with no letter saying I was a responsible person. 'What University did you go to?' 'I didn't.' 'Oh, dear! Nothing to authenticate you?' 'No, except a reading ticket for the Maritime Museum at Greenwich.' 'I'll see if that will do,' said the librarian and it did – and I got my information in ten minutes flat at which she said, 'Amateurs can sometimes be more efficient than professional researchers' – and my head swelled inordinately! But I do believe that enthusiasm counts for far more than qualifications" – and in her case it is most certainly true.

Continuing her letter to me of 31st March 1981 Barbara wrote: "As to my own literary activities, I started with a translation for Richard Creagh-Osborne (then Harrap's), of Joachim Schult's *Racing Tactics* and that led to my being asked to do the eight-language dictionary. Actually they just said "a multilingual dictionary" and the rest was up to me. It took

me about three years, when the kids were still toddling and I employed experts for each of the other seven languages, including a Spanish Admiral and a Duke, and an Italian Naval Captain and a Danish journalist. (I had to go and see the Admiral and the Duke because I could never get replies to letters! And when I came back I felt a bit grotty and immediately went down with mumps – never did hear if I had passed it to them!). Since then the Poles have bought the dictionary (but I haven't had the zlotys yet!) and I added Polish and Russian to make it ten languages."

It is worth noting that Joachim Schult is a Master Mariner, a consulting naval architect and Chairman of the German Institut für Segelsport. He has been an Olympic coach and editor of several yachting magazines. He has sailed for over 40 years, including a circumnavigation of the Atlantic in 1978/79 from Hamburg - South America - the Caribbean - USA - Newfoundland - Iceland - Norway - Hamburg. He is author of over 30 books on sailing and lives in Germany. A very useful contact for Barbara as it has turned out.

"From then on I did a number of translations, about 20 books of reasonable size," her letter continued, "almost all for Nautical or Adlard Coles and almost all from German – one and a bit from French, one from Dutch among that lot. I also wrote a little book called *The Beginner's Book of Navigation* for Ward Lock, to go with *The Beginner's Book of Sailing* which I translated from the German; the navigation book was designed to try not to frighten off those that look at navigation and say, I can't manage to add or subtract.' Then Peter Cook (Editor of *Yachts & Yachting)* and I edited *The Complete Book of Sailing* for Ward Lock – published in 1977 simultaneously in the US and over here. We wrote about a quarter of it ourselves, including the glossary, which was my baby, and the rest was commissioned from various experts such as Jack Knights and Eric Twiname."

Translations have ranged from children's sailing books to general cruising, racing tactics, square-riggers, naval architecture, diesel engines, self-steering gear and a vast tome of MTBs and MGBs of the world (Richard Creagh-Osborne – *Fast Fighting Ships).*

When my letter arrived at Arbourtree House in February 1981, Barbara was in the middle of "a fearsome session on the dictionary: first I had one of the Adlard Coles' editors up here for six days non-stop, then I received the first 200 pages of the dictionary in 'computer' form which is absolutely horrid to read when searching for printing errors, then I received the remaining 400 odd pages – all of which needed not only reading, and re-reading but correcting and cross-checking so far as italicised cross-references are concerned. I sent it off yesterday (30th March 1981).

"I have been working on it for three years. Originally German, compiled by Joachim Schult, 'extensively revised' and translated by me is what it says on the jacket, (assuming that they stick to what is planned at present) – and that is an understatement. I reckon I threw out a good half of it, and of the rest posted about a third to other definitions. Anyway it is a highly technical dictionary, aimed at the US as well as the UK. Jeremy Howard Williams' blurb reads: 'Specially written for both British and American readers, the common language which is said to divide us is here simply interpreted for all to read.' He also says that I have covered 'from astro-navigation to zone times and from arcane terminology to zany information' which amused me not a little."

I should add that it also referred to a "book of staggering comprehensiveness" and even Barbara had to have specialist help in aerodynamics, boat-building, electronics, meteorology, navigation and sails. The English language, having the richest vocabulary of any language in the world, meant that she not only had to find an English equivalent for every German term but had to try to include all those English terms for which there is no German equivalent. And this took only three years!

Michael McMullen

Michael McMullen was born in 1943 into a naval family, being the second son of Captain Colin McMullen, and learnt to sail, as one would expect with his sailing background, at a very early age. He was educated at Marlborough College. When he left school his first job was as a labourer on the new Forth Road Bridge in Scotland where his head for heights was to stand him in good stead later on.

He climbed for ten years in the Royal Marines and commanded a climbing wing and later became a Commando Arctic Warfare instructor in North Norway. Almost certainly some of the Royal Marine commandos he trained were to distinguish themselves later in the Falklands. Perhaps he was with them in spirit when they marched into history on May 26th 1982 with their epic 'yomp' of 50 miles from San Carlos all across the bogs with very heavy packs on their backs, not only living rough in appalling sub-zero conditions but fighting against the Argentinians on their arrival at Port Stanley on June 1st.

Michael McMullen has written only one book but the one he wrote is a 'classic.' He was an acknow-ledged expert on both racing and cruising in multi-hulls. *Multihull Seamanship,* 1976, was published by Nautical Publishing and became the authoritative work on the management at sea of catamarans and trimarans. The flap of the jacket records that "Mike McMullen has done as much as anybody to show that a good multihull properly handled can make coastal and ocean voyages in perfect safety. He built up an enviable reputation in short-handed races in monohulls before transferring to multihulls. In this book he is passing on his considerable experience which will provide invaluable guidance to the veteran and novice alike. His comments upon seamanship and safety should be hung up in every multihull's cabin." How portentious the last sentence of this review was to be.

Mike McMullen first hit the headlines in 1970 when he won the Round Britain Race sailing in *Binkie,* a Rogers 26 ft. with a fellow Royal Marine, Martin Read. Then in *Binkie II,* a Rogers 32 ft. Contessa, he finished thirteenth in the 1972 Observer Single-Handed Trans-Atlantic Race (OSTAR). There had been a large multihull entry and he admitted to a considerable latent curiosity about them. So after the race he accepted with alacrity an invitation to sail in an American Trimaran which had also competed in the race called *Three Cheers.*

He wrote: "We got to a speed of eighteen knots in a fifteen knot wind. I simply could not comprehend how a yacht could travel so fast. She was skimming across the water like a beautiful yellow bird with a total lack of effort that left me breathless." His cousin, Paul Mellon, bought *Three Cheers* for Mike and he then sailed her back across the Atlantic. She had successfully stood up to a very severe storm of near hurricane strength by lying ahull and all was now set for him to aim at winning the 1976 OSTAR in *Three Cheers.*

This ambition came even nearer when he won the Round the Island Race in 1973 in a record time of 5 hours 30 minutes. He followed this by coming second, with Martin Read, in the 1974 Round Britain Race only 1 hour and 12 minutes after Robin Knox Johnstone in the 70 ft. *British Oxygen.* During this race he was swept overboard and was heaved back by Martin Read with the aid of a halyard. This was to have the effect of making him even more careful with regard to safety precautions against going overboard again. Indeed, two chapters of his book are devoted to accidents, safety and heavy weather.

He and his wife, Lizzie, spent a great deal of time on the boat during the next four years. They had cruised together to Spain and then made an extended cruise to the West of Scotland. Colin

Forbes made a film of them for the BBC called *Three Cheers for the Hebrides.* The combination of Mike McMullen and *Three Cheers* now seemed to be unbeatable and as the start of the race approached he was favourite to win it outright.

As if jealous of their happiness and the golden future that seemed to lie ahead, Nemesis struck just four days before the start of the race. "Mike and Lizzie were working on the boat at Machford's Yard this morning," wrote Stuart Woods in *Blue Water – Green Skipper,* "when an electric drill fell overboard into the water. Mike shouted to her not to touch it but she did. They gave her heart massage and artificial respiration for half an hour until an ambulance could get her to Cremyl but it didn't help. She was dead on arrival at the hospital." A very moving account of a tragedy that was by no means over yet.

The stunned competitors sent flowers for her funeral in the Cornish village of St. Mellin, a few miles from Plymouth, which was attended, amongst others by Clare Francis. The Royal Western Yacht Club, the organising club of OSTAR, and *The Observer* contributed with the yachtsmen towards a magnificent silver trophy to be called the Lizzie McMullen Trophy and awarded to the first multi-hull to reach Newport.

Stuart Woods was to see Michael McMullen at the start. " 'Win it, Mike,' he called. 'I'll bloody well try!' he shouted back. He was smiling." Stuart Woods finished the race and was the sixty-third boat in. " 'Where's Mike McMullen?' 'He hasn't been reported since the start of the race.' I knew it. I think I had known it all along..." What made it even more poignant was that his mother and mother-in-law had both flown out to the States to be there to welcome him ashore.

"There was much discussion about what had happened to Mike McMullen. It was the concensus amongst those who knew him that he would not have taken his own life, even after having lost Lizzie. He seemed too good a yachtsman and too familiar with his boat and her limitations to have lost her in heavy weather. No collision had been reported."

The wreckage was washed up in Iceland four years later. He was believed to have taken the northern route and it was known there were about five hundred Russian fishing vessels in the Newfoundland area. A collision with a ship in fog remains a possibility. Alternatively, he could have capsized. We will never know. Somewhere in the North Atlantic the curtain finally came down on this modern Greek tragedy. All of us will ultimately have to make a single-handed crossing and of his one thing is certain: when Mike did make his last landfall, Lizzie was standing there on the eternal shore waiting to meet him.

Clare Francis, MBE

I was very fortunate in having an interview with Clare Francis on 7th December 1982, only a week before she left her home, Bywater Place, Walhampton for London.

Clare Francis was born in 1947 in Surrey, the daughter of a civil servant. She used to sail with her father during family holidays on the Isle of Wight. "He had a dinghy and the first time I went out with him I was very frightened because it tipped over and I thought it was unsafe," she said. But this experience did not prevent her from going out with him later and this time she wasn't quite so frightened and even thought it might be fun. She joined the Sea View Yacht Club and it was in Mermaids that she first gained experience in keel boats before going on to larger boats and longer trips. It was the Sea View Yacht Club burgee that she flew when she sailed round the world in 1978/79.

Another great interest was ballet and her teacher suggested that she should audition with the Royal Ballet with a view to taking it up professionally. "Ballet is a very pleasurable thing. They go on about the torture of it and I think when you are older it must be very difficult to keep going, if ever you reach the top. As a student, though, it is wonderful and it is great fun. The only unwonderful thing is that it is very competitive, which is not a good thing at an early age and only 10% of the students are taken on by companies after their training." So she left the ballet at the age of fifteen, but continued taking lessons for another two years after that. David Wall was a friend and Lesley Collier too.

Clare's father offered to finance her through university, and at the age of twenty she enrolled at the London School of Economics and obtained her degree in economics. From there she joined the market research department of a pharmaceutical firm and later worked for a jam and marmalade factory.

At the age of 26 she realised that she hadn't travelled at all and seen the world; her first thought was to go and live in the States but her second was to sail there instead. This idea turned into reality when a great uncle died and left her a legacy which she spent on buying a 32 ft. sleep called *Gulliver G* for £7,000. When others dropped out, she decided to make the Atlantic crossing single-handed for a bet, leaving Falmouth in May 1973 and arriving in Newport, Rhode Island, 37 days later. She was the sixth woman to have done so. She spent the winter in the West Indies chartering her boat but she had too active a mind to be satisfied with such an indolent life. She returned to Britain and entered for the 1974 Round Britain Race, sponsored by Cherry Blossom. It was the first two-woman crew ever to have participated and they came in third out of 61 competitors.

Clare next entered for the 1976 Observer Single-Handed Trans-atlantic Race in a 38 ft. sloop called *Robertson's Golly*, sponsored by her former employers. This was the race when Mike McMullen was lost but she believed very strongly that he would not have taken his own life. Afterwards she wrote her first book, *Come Hell or High Water*, about the race which became a best seller. She had also made a film for the BBC. Although this increased her value from a sponsorship point of view, she still had to write 50 letters and send a photograph of herself before BSR Turntable Company agreed to put up £250,000 so that she could enter for the Whitbread Round the World Race in the 65 ft. ketch *ADC Accutrac* in 1978/79. She came 13th out of 120 and held the record for a woman for four years.

I was surprised that she had had this difficulty in getting sponsored, when she was such a well known sailing personality. She told me that the main problem is that sailing is not a spectator sport and sponsors do not always feel that there is sufficient interest in it to get their money's worth, even if you make a film. "There are difficulties in filming as well," she continued, "as they tend to be rather insipid unless you get a camera crew on the boat to do a proper job, although they can get in the way of the crew. On the other hand, in France sponsorship is doing very well; everyone is happy about it and it is quite easy to get sponsorship there."

After coping with the problems of sailing single-handed she now faced the challenge of not only sailing round the world with a crew of eleven but being the skipper as well. "I had a clear idea of what I was searching for in my crew," she wrote in her second book, *Come Wind or Weather*. "Compatibility was the most important feature with sailing ability a close second. Enthusiasm, an easy-going nature and above all a sense of humour were vital to survive incarceration in a small space with eleven other people. Pure sailing ability would never be enough."

It was as skipper that she most impressed Erroll Bruce and her leadership which enabled her to complete the Whitbread Round the World Race without a change of crew, the only boat to do so. "I had a super bunch of people," she said. "We had our troubles, as everybody did, in differences of opinion and so on, but I think, being a woman, I bent over backwards to keep a happy family, whereas I don't think a man would have done so. Someone who has

done single-handed is not usually a terribly good skipper necessarily – although Chay Blyth is – as you are so used to thinking things out for yourself and making your own decisions, that you tend not to discuss it with the crew. That was my weakness at the beginning but then I got better. Also I was very sea-sick to begin with which doesn't help you to be a good leader when you are feeling desperately ill." They came fifth out of fifteen.

Although after the Whitbread Round the World race she and her husband, Jacques Redon, decided to spend two years of complete domesticity, it was only a fortnight after her return in March 1978 that she was approached by the BBC producer Michael Gill to make the six-part TV series *The Commanding Sea*. In July 1979, six months after the birth of her son, Thomas, she started filming. She not only presented the series, which involved travelling all over the world, but she later wrote the book of the series with Warren Tute, which was published by the BBC on 30th March 1981.

I asked her about some of the local Lymington people who had helped her with her sailing, in particular Joe Sanders and his son, Pete. "Joe Sanders is marvellous," she told me, "and is a very good friend. He is very kind to people setting out. Most people who supply equipment, if they see a rather 'green' newcomer coming along, might give them a hard time, but not Joe. He has always been immensely kind to people and helped them along and guided them in the right direction.

"Pete Sanders is really a super sailmaker and for the average sort of boat I think he makes the best value sails. I went to Hood for a big boat like *Accutrac*, which needed really big sails because Pete doesn't have the size of loft for a start."

It was through Joe Sanders that Clare found Mary Reid, who typed her second book *Come Hell or High Water*, and Mary held the fort and answered letters generally when Clare was participating in the Whitbread Rond the World race. She later wanted a full-time job so she went and worked for Ed Dubois, where she still is today (1982).

I asked Clare Francis 'to come clean' and let me know if she was really taken by surprise when Eamonn Andrews interrupted a committee meeting she was attending and invited her on to his programme, *This is Your Life*. "Strange things were going on and I wasn't quite sure what," she admitted, "but when I asked what I was told to shut up! So I was never told outright by my family but I did have an inkling that something was happening."

Clare Francis decided that she would no longer participate in races like the Route de Rhum or the two-handed Trans-Atlantic races. Sponsors do ask more than they used to and it could mean being tied up or away for three months, and she felt that was too long. "So when I had Tom," she continued, "I decided that I would not go on with that sort of racing. When you become a Mum you tend to lose your nerve in that you realise that it is not just yourself any more but your dependant too, in my case Tom, and that really changes everything. I might go single-handed again when I am a grandmother!" But she will keep *Gulliver G* in Lymington and hopes to do a bit of cruising next summer, possibly up in Scotland.

We then discussed her impending move to London, as she had sold her home, Bywater Place. She told me she would enjoy very much going to the theatre now and opera, her great love. "I am always disappointed that people assume that if you do a sport that that is your only interest and it couldn't be further from the truth. I am now writing full-time and being an author will be my profession. I shall not be writing any more sailing books but I have just finished a novel, which I hope will be published in the autumn. I hope to come down to Lymington whenever I can: it will probably drive me mad going backwards and forwards all the time and perhaps London will pall after a while. I want to try and get the best of both worlds but whether I will succeed or not is another thing."

Clare Francis, Jacques Redon and Dame Naomi James are Hon. Members of the Royal Lymington Yacht Club.

Adlard Coles

Adlard Coles was born at the start of the century in London and was brought up by his grandparents. At the age of six he used to wear a huge sailor hat and his ambition was to go into the Navy. He tried to join up in World War One but failed due to poor eyesight. He was first taught to sail by a friend when he was eighteen in a lugsail dinghy from Chidham in Chichester Harbour. Later he kept his own boat at Bosham and used to stay in rooms with a fishermen and his wife.

Adlard Coles read engineering at Clare College, Cambridge and then changed to economics for his last year. He rowed for his college in 1923. After coming down from Cambridge, he considered that there was little future in engineering and decided to become a chartered accountant. He became articled to a Southampton firm and after qualifying in 1926 he started up on his own in Newport; later he established another practice in Southampton, which he finally merged with a city firm, staying on as a Southampton partner. He specialised in company

and trustee work and in taxation, which was to stand him in good stead later on. He thought that being a chartered accountant in his own firm would allow him more time off for sailing – as indeed was the case.

During his last term at Cambridge he had planned a Baltic cruise. Not only had very few British yachtsmen ever sailed up there but also because he had fallen under the spell of Erskine Childer's *Riddle of the Sands*. After his marriage in 1924 he therefore sailed away to the Friesian Islands in his 7-ton yacht *Annette* on his honeymoon, with his wife's huge cabin trunk sticking out of the cockpit – it was far too big to go down below! Adlard Coles had also been influenced by reading Arthur Ransome's book *Racundra's First Cruise,* and actually bought the yacht off him in Riga. He was asked not to reveal her true identity when he wrote about her so he changed her name to *Annette II.* He and his wife were to cruise extensively in the Baltic in the 1930s.

His branch office in Cowes was opposite the Island Sailing Club and he would write up Cowes Week for the *Yachtsmen* when he was short of clients. He later bought the magazine just before the war for about £1,000 and owned and edited it for several years. He and his wife also owned a small publishing firm called Robert Ross & Co. Ltd. which changed its name to Adlard Coles Limited after the war. At the outbreak of World War Two he failed the Royal Navy again but, after being a chartered accountant at the Ministry of Food, he transferred to HMS *Excellent* where, as a civilian, he edited gunnery books.

His publishing firm weathered the difficult post-war years, which he attributed to keeping the company small and working long hours; sometimes when he was not sailing he would put in an 80-hour week. It started to grow and then in 1962, after an illness, he sold out to Rupert Hart-Davis. Later the company merged with Granada Publishing but Adlard Coles remained as Chairman until 1968. Deciding that he would prefer to be independent again, he formed Nautical Publishing in Lymington with Erroll Bruce, with the aim of publishing yachting books.

After the war he took up ocean racing and from 1947 until 1967 he was to the forefront, sailing in his *Cohoes* in most of the RORC races. In 1950 he won the Bermuda to Plymouth race in the most exciting Trans-Atlantic race ever, when the lead changed with Erroll Bruce in *Samuel Pepys* five times before he just came out the winner. In *Cohoe III* he won Class 3 in the 1957 Fastnet Race and became RORC points champion and was elected 'Yachtsman of the

Year.' He revelled in heavy weather sailing and his book *Heavy Weather Sailing* became the definitive work and sold 100,000 copies all over the world and was translated into Swedish, German, French, Dutch, Spanish and Italian. When he was not racing he still cruised extensively with his wife, sometimes covering 3,000 miles at sea in a year.

He wrote the first of his famous pilot books as far back as 1925 when *Creeks and Harbours of the Isle of Wight* came out at the vast cost of 2/-. Today it has been enlarged into the indispensable *Creeks and Harbours of the Solent,* now in its eighth edition. He has also written pilot books for North Biscay and North Brittany as well as the *Shell Pilot to the South Coast Harbours.* He produces new editions every three years. A great deal of work is involved, especially when they changed the datum on the charts, and it keeps him busy in his retirement. He is helped now by Dr. Charles Sergel and goes out in his yacht. In 1969 he was awarded the Royal Cruising Club Medal for services to cruising and in 1971 the Gold Medal of the Royal Institute of Navigation.

The Coles have a daughter, Arnaud, who used to go out sailing with her father when she was younger, and a son, Ross, who is carrying out medical research into deafness at Southampton University. He is a sailor and ocean racer in his own right and at one time was the sailing-master of the Royal Dragon *Bluebottle* during his service in the Royal Navy as a Surgeon-Commander.

This material is based on a *Profile of Adlard Coles* by Strahan Soames, which was published in the 6th September 1974 issue of *Yachts & Yachting*, and is reproduced by permission of the Editor. Strahan Soames concluded his interview with Adlard Coles with these words: "Now that I have met the author I can feel and see the manner in which he talks carefully but with ardour by means of written words. In *Heavy Weather Sailing* you know readily that he treats the sea with seriousness. He must do this because he is writing not so much about the niceties of sailing techniques but about life or death. Nevertheless, his manner is light-hearted in a very English and self-effacing way. 'I suppose,' he mused, 'that I have been lucky in winning in heavy weather but heavy weather doesn't worry me very much. I worry much more driving in a car on these damned roads!' "

Richard Creagh-Osborne

Richard Creagh-Osborne was not only an Olympic yachtsman but was also a well known author and publisher, being one of the 'Big Four' of Nautical Publishing. He can trace his family's links with Lymington back to the 14th century, which makes his the second oldest family in Lymington after the Blachfords.

It is at the beginning of the nineteenth century that we pick up their story and for this family history I am much indebted to his cousin, Pat Creagh-Osborne, who lives in Yarmouth. I went over to see her on 18th February 1981 and she produced several books of old newspaper cuttings about the family that had been meticulously kept by an elderly relative.

On his paternal side he is descended from the Croziers, who used to live at 'The Elms' and later at 'Delawarr House.' Richard's grandfather, Colonel Charles O. Creagh-Osborne (the name only became Creagh-Osborne in the *London Gazette* of 24th December 1867) was born on 20th December 1823 and later went to India. It was when he was home on leave that he first met his future wife, when she was sixteen. She was the daughter of Francis Henry Crozier of Delawarr House by his second marriage to Harriet, eldest daughter of the Rev. Sir George Burrard, Bart, born in 1846.

Colonel Creagh-Osborne decided there and then that she was the one he would marry – and he did, in 1866. Theirs was the wedding of the year and the local newspaper of 22nd November 1866 records that "from the profound and universal respect felt towards the Burrard and Crozier families the town was unusually gay on the occasion, numbers of flags being hung across the High Street and crowds of spectators lined the road to the church." A very handsome triumphal arch had also been erected at the west end of the High Street.

After the ceremony the couple walked on a carpet from the Church to the corner of the High Street and children from the National schools "bestrewed her path with bouquets." They listened to the band of the 1st Hants Volunteer Engineers and then sat down to a "breakfast replete with every delicacy of the season" under a marquee. During the afternoon "school children and poor persons were plentifully regaled with cake and wine." The couple left in a carriage and four for their honeymoon in Rome and later there was a display of fireworks from Mr. H. P. Burrard's yacht in the Roads. As a wedding gift to the town, the bride gave a splendid new flag for the church tower, the old one, presented by her mother, Miss Theresa Burrard on her marriage twenty years previously, being faded.

They went out to India with all their furniture by sailing ship to Egypt, transferred it to bullock carts (there was no Suez Canal in those days) and then took another sailing ship on to India. She bore him seven children and reared four there, despite never having gone to the hills in the hot weather. The eldest, Frank Creagh-Osborne, was born in 1867.

There was an article written about Richard's great-uncle in 1867, headed 'A Warning' which related that "another of these lamentable accidents from children playing alone by the side of the river nearly occurred on Saturday afternoon. A little girl, Mary Davis, aged seven years, whose parents live in the Bath Road, was playing with other children on the bank near the Baths, and fell into the river, the tide being high and ebbing fast. Mr. Burrard R. Crozier was passing near, and was attracted to the spot by the cries of the child and her little companions. He ran to the spot, jumped into the water, rescued the little girl, and carried her to a neighbouring house. Mr. Crozier had not long before returned by steamer from Yarmouth, and had he not providentially been going that way to Delawarr, the child would no doubt have been drowned, as no other aid was near. The surprise is that these accidents are not more frequent, and it is hoped this may be a warning to those residing near the river." Perilous days indeed!

Colonel Charles Creagh-Osborne died very suddenly at the home of his father-in-law, Mr. F. H. Crozier, on 17th August 1892 at Delawarr House. He was very fond of yachting and had only a month ago hired the steam S.S. *Ytene* for the remainder of the season. He had been out in a cruise in her that very day, returning about 6.0 p.m. and passing through the fleet of yachts moored opposite the baths – this being Regatta Day. He became ill at dinner but it was not thought serious and then he died before medical aid could be summoned. The first his friends knew of it was when they visited his yacht the following morning and found the flag at half-mast. He had been very popular with all sections of the community and particularly with the inhabitants of Woodside. He was buried at Boldre Church.

His eldest son, Frank, born in India in 1867, and Richard's father, joined the Royal Navy and was attached as a Lieutenant to the gunboat *Pigmy* when she attended the naval review at Spithead on 10th November 1889 before going out to Singapore. He invented the famous Creagh-Osborne compass, which many consider helped us to win the war at sea in World War One.

Both his sons, Richard and Francis, were to follow him into the Navy. Richard, the eldest, was to be dogged by ill-health and after being at Dartmouth College, he was later invalided out of the service when attending the Naval Engineering College at Manadon. He went on to study physics at Oxford but once again poor health intervened. He then took up market gardening and later joined up with the Caulcutts and ran a broiler house at Golden Produce.

He then found that he had a bent for writing – and publishing – and joined the firm of Adlard Coles where he rose to become an editorial director and later joined Nautical Publishing in Lymington. Perhaps because he had a Swiss wife, Augusta, he played a leading part in the formation of an international company based in Switzerland but administered from Lymington called 'United Nautical Publishers.' As an author his book *This is Sailing* sold 350,000 copies in five years, was translated into twelve languages and turned into an educational video cassette. This latter was very *avant garde* in those days. He was also Editor of *The Dinghy Yearbook* for several years.

Richard was three times a member of the British Olympic sailing team; five times National Finn Champion and National Champion of 5-0-5s, X-boats and the OK dinghies. It so happened that at the same time he was competing against the world's best helmsman, Paul Elvström, who took five Olympic titles and was virtually unbeatable. "The best sailor who has ever turned his hand to the sport," Richard wrote and as well as being a competitor against him in the Finns he also covered Paul's exploits as a journalist and considered him to be 'the greatest.' Richard was invited to be a tactician on a Japanese Admiral's Cup boat at Cowes Week and was tactician on Jeremy Rogers' boat *Gumboots* when in 1974 she won the World One Ton Cup for Britain, the first time ever. He was also a member of the RYA Olympic Committee.

Richard first met Paul Elvström at the Finn Gold Cup at Burnham in the Easter of 1956. The weather was bitterly cold and the sea froze on the decks. Elvström couldn't understand how some British boats could continue planing when he had to keep stopping and baling. The British had, in fact, developed the new Lewmar tube bailer which was at a distinct advantage in these conditions. "After the first two days racing Paul Elvström and other overseas skippers were to be seen, with numbed fingers, drilling holes in their boats and fitting these new bailers from a stock thoughtfully provided by one of the more enterprising British Finn sailors."

Paul Elvström was then to invent and perfect his own 'Elvström' bailer, which came into production in 1961 and which was promoted in Britain by Richard Creagh-Osborne. Later the bailer was further developed and became big business all over the world.

Richard also collaborated with Paul Elvström on all his books except his very first. *Paul Elvström Explains the Racing Rules* first appeared in 1965 and was edited by Richard until his death. It has now been re-issued by Adlard Coles Ltd. with Jonathan

Bradbeer as Editor. In his introduction to *Elvström Speaks on Yacht Racing* which he edited and published in 1969 with drawings and sketches by Roy Coombs, Richard wrote: "I must say that it is no small problem to work with Paul on a project like this. Having helped him with several books and frequently arranged to meet him at his home or at my home for us to do some work together, I have learned, from the experience of many frustrated hours that one has to use some degree of subterfuge to get his full attention." Reading and writing were clearly an anathema to Paul but, knowing that talking was his strong suit, Richard artfully bought a tape recorder which turned out to be a great success.

He described an occasion when he flew to Fornebu Airport at Oslo and was met by Harald Eriksen, the President of the Finn Association, "who led me to the end of the airport runway, where his large, fast, open-roofed motor-launch was tied up to a rock. We had climbed aboard, to be greeted by two beautiful Norwegian girls and a splendid table of refreshments. We then picked up two more Finn sailors from other points round the fjord, and so began in splendidly Scandinavian style an International Finn Class Technical Committee meeting. Thus it is that the very best class rules are made!"

Richard's mother was an extremely active councillor on Lymington Borough Council and was Deputy Mayor one year. She was an enthusiastic helper and organiser at the Royal Lymington Yacht Club. His younger brother, Francis, was killed when taking off from a runway while serving in the Fleet Air Arm and Richard was to die himself at the comparatively early age of 52 in August 1980.

The little Church of St. John the Baptist at Boldre was packed for his Memorial Service, conducted by the Rev. Canon John Hayter. Derek Pitt-Pitts paid tribute to Richard's life and work and, with a reading of Tennyson's *Crossing the Bar* and the organ softly playing 'Tom Bowlin,' it was a profoundly moving service. I shall always remember watching Richard sailing down the Lymington River at the height of his sailing career when he was truly 'King' of the River.

CHAPTER 22

THE MERRY MARINERS

"The Merry Mariners are bold and free
Say, my heart's sister, wilt thou sail with me?"

SHELLEY

None of the 'The Merry Mariners' was born in Lymington but in their retirement they have made it their home. Linked together by a common interest in sailing and love of the sea, each has brought with him a certain quality that has added to the prestige of Lymington as a yachting centre. "The Sea is all around us" is the challenge that they have taken up in their pursuit of sport and quest for adventure.

Nothing would appear to be more remote from Lymington than the mountains of the Himalayas, yet our first 'Mariner' found that mountaineering and sailing had much in common: both need and bring out the qualities of courage and endurance.

Major Harold William Tilman,
CBE, DSO, MC, FRGS, LL.D.

Major Tilman came from Cheshire but his home was near Barmouth in Wales because, being a mountaineer, he loved to be surrounded by mountains. He was born on 4th February 1898 and educated at Berkhamstead School and the Royal Military Academy, Woolwich. He was commissioned into the Royal Artillery in July 1915 and served on the Western Front during World War One and was awarded the Military Cross and Bar. After the war, in 1919, he took up coffee planting in Kenya and spent fourteen years there. On one of his leaves he bicycled three thousand miles across Africa in nine weeks living on mealie meal and bananas. This feat attracted the notice of Eric Shipton, who introduced him to mountaineering and he participated in expeditions to Mts. Kenya, Kilimanjaro and Ruwenzori, followed by ascents in Sinkiang, Afghanistan and the Himalayas. This included the Mount Everest reconnaissance in 1935 and he led the Everest Expedition of 1938. He was then awarded the Founder's Medal of the Royal Geographical Society.

In 1939 Major Tilman rejoined the Royal Artillery and served in France, Syria, Iraq, the Western Desert and Tunisia. He was dropped by parachute and linked up with Albanian and Italian partisans and actually established his HQ on the top floor of

the Gestapo building in Belluno! Later he was smuggled out in a coffin and buried in the cemetery, being resurrected later that night. Twenty-five years later he was invited back and granted the Freedom of Belluno. He was accompanied by his niece as he never married. There is a photograph of him sitting up in a high car all trimmed with flags. It was very difficult to get anything out of him about what he had done during the war. Once he was in a little armoured carrier and driving down a sunken lane when he was overtaken by motor cycles going three times as fast and discovered that it was the German advance guard – and they couldn't turn round in this lane! He was awarded the DSO.

After the war he became British Consul at Maymyo in Burma and climbed in Sinkiang and Nepal. On his return to this country he was made Hon. LL.D. of the University of St. Andrews. He later wrote: "When advancing years put the Himalayas out of reach my thoughts turned to sailing and the chance of combining this with climbing, two activities that have much in common." His voyage in his converted pilot cutters took him to the unclimbed mountains of the Arctic, Patagonia and the Antarctic. In 1954 he was awarded the Blue Water Medal of the Cruising Club of America, like Humphrey Barton before him, and in fact it was Humphrey Barton who went out with him and helped crew *Mischief* back from the Mediterranean. This is where the strong link with Lymington was forged.

Colonel Tobin lived with his wife, Helen and daughter Barbara (now Barbara Webb) in No. 9 King's Saltern Road. "The Major knew Colonel Tobin through the Himalayan Society," recalled the Bashfords when I visited them at their home at 40 Newbridge Way, Pennington, on 16th September 1982. "Colonel Tobin was an Indian Army man and he had done a lot of climbing in the Himalayas and probably met the Major at the Club in London. For a while Colonel Tobin edited *The Himalayan Journal,* or something similar, and he stayed once or twice with us because Mrs. Tobin and Barbara often used to go out sailing, particularly at Cowes Week. 'Well, I taught them how to sail but I am a bit past it now,' he told us, and Mrs. Tobin asked if we would have him to make sure that he ate properly. He would be bashing away on his typewriter sometimes to get his material ready for the Journal. He was a lovely person and we loved having him."

It was Colonel Tobin who, in 1954, asked the Bashfords if they would put up Major Tilman when he arrived in Lymington in *Mischief* and that was the beginning of a long friendship. His boats needed a great deal of maintenance and he spent much of the winter with them in Lymington in the years that followed.

"Colonel Tobin used to write to him regularly wherever he was going to be. He would find out his ports of call and he would drop him a letter – just something from home. When Colonel Tobin died, the Major said that he missed not getting letters from him so we said we would take it on and try to fill the gap, letting him know what we were doing and giving him local news. Of course we kept everything he wrote to us; he used to send postcards if it was a scenic place and occasionally an envelope with stamps on because one of his crew was very keen on that and knew that they would become valuable. 'Might bring in a bit sometime,' he said. It was very rewarding writing to him. Occasionally he used to write articles for yachting magazines and if we could we got hold of them."

The Bashfords not only have scrapbooks full of postcards and letters from Major Tilman but also some excellent photographs, many of them taken by Paul Curtis, who used to work with Myles Cooper. Afterwards he became a photographer on one of the big liners. The Bashfords also had a complete set of his fifteen books, several of them autographed. They went round the second-hand book shops and got them all. Many of them are now out of print.

"The Major wasn't a 'doggy' man but he loved cats and we had an old cat. In the season she would not go near the lounge but would go straight upstairs to our bed-sitter if she wanted to get away from everybody. But as soon as winter came on and we were on our own, although the Major used to come down a lot in the winter when he was refitting his boats for his expeditions, she used to go up to the lounge after she had had her dinner, look at him for a minute or two and then go and sit on his knees. She would spend the whole evening there. After dinner the Major used to try and complete the *Times* crossword.

"The Major used to come up when he was half-way through fitting out and we would all sit round together and work out what stores he should take with him. When Proctor, a great big skinny chap of 6

By courtesy of H. Bashford: Photo. Paul Curtis

Bill Tilman in *Mischief* on Lymington River

feet, who lived at Sway at that time and was later lost on a solo voyage round the world, went on a couple of voyages with the Major they had to allow six potatoes instead of three. It was a standing joke with the Major and he would say, 'Now how many potatoes ought I to take.' He would also get twice-baked bread from Jennings. When they were doing the 3 Peaks Race – the Major was the originator of it – Southern Television did quite a long interview with him.

"We used to get the Major to give us lectures on his voyages because he used to take slides; on one voyage he had a cameraman with him and there was a 16 mm film. It was the highlight of the season to have a lecture by the Major and the Lymington Town Sailing Club used to burst its sides. It may have been this that stirred them up into building the big room at the top. Anyway it was tremendous fun and we always used to invite the Club Officers to have dinner with the Major beforehand. But they were not very clever over their arrangements with the projector. One time we had to rush up and borrow the Vicar's! We used to have lovely social times afterwards. We ran the bar and he used to talk to everybody. When he had had enough he used to look at us and say, 'All right, let's go,' and we would go back to King's Lea and have a cup of tea to sober us up!"

In his obituary of Bill Tilman in the *Journal of the Royal Cruising Club*, D.L. wrote: "It is not easy to comprehend the full measure of Tilman's seamanship. Each one of his voyages was an outstanding expedition; any one of them would have placed his name among the immortals. The loss of *Mischief* off Jan Mayen and *Sea Breeze* off East Greenland in no way detracts from his remarkable record. His achievements were due solely to his superb seamanship.

Once, on their way to South America, he lost a man overboard and this did demoralise the crew who mutinied and thought that *Mischief* was no good at all. Alan Figgures once remarked: "I wouldn't sail down to the end of the river in *Mischief*, let alone go to Greenland or Patagonia. She was far to unseaworthy."

Bill Tilman started to have trouble with his crews. Life on board was spartan. His boats were not modern pleasure yachts and were pretty crude, and the crew had to put up with a good deal. A lot of them went with him for just that reason; they wanted to experience something really tough. "Many considered it a privilege to sail under one of the world's great seamen and were distinguished mountaineers and polar explorers in their own right."

The Bashfords often used to meet the crews who would go there for dinner every night, which gave them the chance to get to know and talk to them. "They admired the Major's character of course and wanted to be with him. But after that he began to get some layabouts and they didn't know what they really did want and expected the expeditions to be a pleasure cruise. You don't choose to go to Greenland for that for a start!

"We didn't have anything to do with his last voyage because the boat was at Southampton and the Major wasn't the skipper; he went as adviser because he knew the Southern Ocean so well." So in 1977 Bill Tilman sailed in a converted tug *En Avant*, under the command of one of his old crew members, Simon Richardson. They were last heard of leaving Rio de Janeiro, bound for the Falkland Islands where Bill Tilman planned to spend his 80th birthday – but they never arrived there. It was the way he would liked to have gone.

The Royal Cruising Club, which had already given him the Goldsmith Exploration Medal, now named a new one after him, in memory of his considerable achievements. The Tilman Medal is now given for voyages in high latitudes. He had sailed more than 100,000 miles in craft of 29 tons and 45 ft. overall, one only four years younger than himself. *Baroque,* a Bristol Channel pilot cutter, was built in 1902 and there cannot be many which have sailed to latitude 80° North or were still going strong at that age. Bill Tilman will never be forgotten in Lymington.

Captain Colin William McMullen, DSC RN (Rtd).

The first thing that I asked Captain McMullen, when I visited him at his home, 'Greenacres,' Brockenhurst on 24th May 1982, was whether he was related to the famous R. T. McMullen, who really pioneered single-handed sailing, partly due to trouble with his paid hands! Colin McMullen told me that several years ago a cousin had prepared the family tree and he had looked forward to seeing if he was related to him, only to find that he was not included anywhere in it. "I still claim him as a relative but it must be very distant," he said.

Colin McMullen was born in 1907 and joined the Royal Navy. During the war he was Gunnery Officer in the *Prince of Wales* at the time of her engagement with the *Bismark* and the sinking of the *Hood,* and is credited with a direct hit on the German battleship. He remained on board *Prince of Wales* until she was sunk by Japanese torpedo aircraft off Singapore. He survived and was awarded the DSC.

After the war he was attached to NATO in Paris and lived on board an old 80-ton Dutch botter called *De Bries* while he was there. When he was regretfully informed by their Lordships that they no longer had a use for his services, he retired in 1959 and as he could not afford to keep the old *De Bries,* he sold her and acquired the *Alexa*.

He had always been a keen yachtsman and in 1932 he was sailing back from France with two fellow officers in *Little Owl* and three more in *Wallop* when they were involved in an adventure which caused quite a furore at the time. This was before the days of the RNSA and there was not all that amount of naval sailing. "It was really rather amusing," he recalled, "and it ended happily but it might so easily not have done."

The Journal of the Royal Cruising Club recorded that they ran into a force 8-9 gale with driving rain on 21st October, Trafalgar Day, and *Wallop* was blown towards a lee shore but her crew were picked up by a passing collier. Colin McMullen and his two friends were in a small open boat in a full equinoxal gale and they removed the mast of *Little Owl* and put sea anchors out consisting of warps and kit bags. The boat filled with water and for three days they tried to keep her head up to wind by rowing. Fifteen miles south of Beachy Head they spotted a coaster and Colin fired his service revolver into the air to attract her attention. They were picked up and taken to Antwerp where they were treated as distressed seamen by the British Consul there and returned to the Naval Gunnery School at Whale Island only 1½ hours overdue from their leave! Both boats were lost in the storm.

Colin McMullen then purchased for £110 a sturdy West Country cutter built in 1893 called *Fidget*. "My younger brother Maurice, who is a Rear-Admiral and lives at Alverstoke was one of the original *Fidget* syndicate and another old *Fidget* chum was Vice-Admiral Joe Crawford. Twelve years later she was replaced by the new *Fidget,* a very nice little sloop built in 1938 by Camper & Nicholson. "Many is the song that has been sung in her snug saloon," records the RCC Journal. She has got a syndicate today similar to the one they had for the old *Fidget,* consisting of five naval officers including his nephew, Colin de Mowbray, who is serving in *Alacrity* in the Falklands.

"*Alexa* was a Hay, Harris and Butler 8-tonner and her first cruise was a single-handed one from Kyle of Loch Alsh to Carlingford Lough in Ireland. She was a long keeled, healthy boat – none of these fin-keeled jobs. The next trip was easy to Zeebrugge, where the Finn Championships were taking place, and I think about five or six Lymington entries, including my son John, were taking part and we were really a sort of headquarters ship for them. Then we went over to Harwich and up to Yarmouth and my sister, Louise de Mowbray, joined me for this trip and she has, since then, always been a staunch supporter of my boats.

"The most interesting cruise we did in *Alexa* was when we landed on the two extremities of the British Isles. On this occasion we went first to the Minquiers and the rock there called Faucheur, which is always showing and is the most southern point of Great Britain. We anchored off it and my son, Mike, made the landing in our rubber dinghy and we evolved a sort of technique doing this. The first thing was for the *Alexa* to be at anchor and for the dinghy to be on a very long line from her. The chap doing the landing had to have a long line round him, the end of which was made fast to the painter of the boat so that when he leapt onto the rocks and the boat went off he was still secured to it, so that we could pull him back again if he was washed away. It was just as well we did so because the lashing on one of the oars came undone and he lost an our.

"We then sailed round Ireland where I embarked three young Royal Marine officers and on to our second landing in Scotland. When they do these Round Britain races you always hear about Muckle Flugga lighthouse but in fact the most northern point of Great Britain is a rock off it called the Outer Stack. Lieutenant Alastair Troup, RM, made the landing this time with Lieutenant James Avenell,

RM in the dinghy, using the same method as before, and left a message in a bottle that I think ought to be recorded:

'Landing made on the Outer Stack from *Alexa* on 3rd August 1968. The following emblems have been embedded in the rock. Her Majesty the Queen's image in a new decimal and older coins and the following flags have been erected: the Union Jack, the White and Red Ensigns, representing the Royal and Merchant Navies and fishing fleets, the Australian, New Zealand and Canadian national flags and the flag of the Royal Commonwealth Society 1868-1968, representing all the Commonwealth countries. The burgee of the Royal Cruising Club, representing the thousands of boat owners, crews and others in our country who loves the sea and other waters. The following insignia have been installed: the Coats of Arms of Gibraltar, representing all Her Majesty's colonial territories; the Combined Operations badge, representing all three HM Services and the badge of the Royal Marines.

'A landing was made on the rock of Faucheur, part of the Minquiers, south of Jersey, the Southern point of the British Isles from *Alexa* on 2nd June 1968. The landing on this rock lying 780 nautical miles south of the Outer Stack was conducted by Mr. and Mrs. G. Gage, Lieutenant M. McMullen, RM and Captain Colin McMullen, RN (Rtd.). Similar flags, emblems and insignias to the above were planted with the addition of the flag of Jersey.

'These two landings have been undertaken as a small token of our loyalty to Her Majesty and our belief in the future greatness and unity of our country and the Commonwealth, whose trade and security must always be linked with the great oceans across the world. God Save the Queen. Signed, crew of *Alexa,* dated 3rd August 1968 – James Avenol, 2/Lt. RM, Hugh M. Blair, 2/Lt. RM, Alastair I. V. Troop, 2/Lt. RM and Colin W. McMullen, Captain RN (Rtd.).

"Well, the message is still there, I hope; it is hidden in a crevice and it is rather topical." (These very sentiments were included and were, indeed, the theme of the Queen's Christmas Message to the Commonwealth broadcast from the library in Windsor Castle on 25th December 1982). "It is a very difficult place to land on," he continued, "and we were very lucky because it was a fairly calm day but you still get a terrific swell on any rock. One of the great tips is, apart from this technique which I have described and which I believe in, is to choose a place where there is a vertical ledge with deep water. One of the dangers is that if it is not deep, in a swell the water suddenly disappears and a rock can be uncovered and then you capsize; so you want to choose a very deep vertical wall really to step out on. I have always been keen on landing on rocks but haven't done any recently.

"After that I thought I ought to have a more modern boat and I acquired the *Saecwen*. She is now about 20 years old. She was built in 1962 and there are about ten of them. *Saecwen* is a Saxon word meaning 'Sea Queen.' By this time I had been elevated to being the Commodore of the old Royal Cruising Club and so I thought I had better do a trip to play myself in, as it were, and so I did this first trip across the Atlantic via the Azores and then to Gloucester in the States and then on up to Halifax and home.

"Going to the Azores I had this very nice young bloke, who had done quite a lot of sailing in Scotland, and one of my son's bridesmaids, Trish, who was called 'Cross-Atlantic Trish' as she had been across it about five times. He was very seasick and was on his bunk for fifteen days so he flew back from the Azores and so I went on with Trish, who left when I got to Gloucester and stayed with these very good friends of ours, the Philip Welds. Philip had just won the last single-handed Trans-Atlantic race" (the one in which his son, Mike McMullen, so tragically disappeared).

But it was his trip in *Saecwen* in 1981 which was to gain him the Challenge Cup for the third time. The judging of the RCC logs was done by Hammond Innes. Colin McMullen left Lymington in September 1980 and returned in May 1981, having logged 9,673 miles with a cruise to the Caribbean, where extensive exploration of the islands was carried out, using only 57 engine hours. "The crew to Antigua was my old *Fidget* chum, Vice-Admiral Crawford and Mrs. Gill Lloyd, Chairman of the Lymington Lifeboat Guild."

The *Lymington Times* in its issue of 5th December 1981 reports that "near Tenerife a cruise ship was passing close by when Captain McMullen asked for their position. The liner obliged and, as *Saecwen* became the focal point for hundreds of binoculars, there was an added signal: 'My passengers are anxious to know the ages of your crew?' An answer was flashed back: 'Both men's ages are 73 – the lady's age I will not disclose!' Actually Mrs. Lloyd celebrated her 61st birthday soon after landing."

"Out there we were joined by various friends," he continued, "and my wife came out at one time and Helen Tew and the Lloyds daughter, Sarah and her husband. Captain John Lamb of Lyndhurst had replaced Mrs. Lloyd. But it was rather fun as the three old *Fidget* owners sailed her back from Bermuda, our fiftieth anniversary really, and we are still friends and still sailing." The combined ages of the trio on the return trip totalled 222 years. *Yachting World* of May 1982 provided the punch-line by emphasising that "it is a forceful reminder of cruising's wonderful capacity to be a sport for all ages." In addition to the Challenge Cup, Gill Lloyd, won the RCC Ladies Cup.

"I am still a marine consultant and very hectic at the moment (May 1982). I now have an associate helping me and what we try and do is to provide civil engineers with marine knowledge. We have just finished what we call a Master Plan of Poole Harbour and this has an enormous appendix with it, showing all the charts and surveys there have been in Poole Harbour since 1830. This was for the Poole Harbour Commissioners and was published this month, the May 1982 Poole Harbour Master Plan Study.

"In all these harbours you will find that there is a vast amount of reports and historical data that is never listed anywhere and now we have one and there are about fifty. At the back of the book, on the technical side, we have listed the reports affecting the hydrology of the harbour and have made a synopsis of each one, so that a person can refer to them. That was one of my things. I have been working at Poole Harbour – it is one of my clubs actually – for the last fifteen years.

"Most of the our work at the moment is in South Wales and we are just about to get involved in a harbour in Muscat in the Oman region, mostly with consulting engineers, but that particular one is direct with the Harbour Commissioners. This is the modernisation of the Mina Quabos, which is the port of Muscat. I have been doing this sort of marine work for twenty years now since I retired and it is a terribly interesting world because I have travelled more than I did in the Navy. I never went to Hong Kong in the Navy, never went to the Phillipines, never went to Australia, never went to Gambia and never went to America.

"One can do quite a lot of this sort of marine aspect civil engineering and I think one can play a part at the start of these studies. Once it comes to designing jetties, that is pure civil engineering, although one can sometimes help in the policy. It is rather like inter-service staff work in the Navy really, where each person has a contribution to make. There is not an awful lot of money in it but there is very, very great satisfaction because you feel you are doing something really worthwhile.

Vice-Admiral Sir Lennon Goldsmith

Another yachtsman to cross the Atlantic at the age of 70 was Admiral Goldsmith, who retired to Lymington after the war and bought a house in

King's Saltern Road, which he called 'Deadly Night-shade.' He too won the Challenge Cup of the Royal Cruising Club, on two occasions. He will be remembered most for his immense love of Greece, reflected by his many cruises there. Vice-Admiral Goldsmith is the father of Nausa and father-in-law of Roger Pinckney. I am greatly indebted to Alasdair Garrett and Trevor Wilkinson's *History of the Royal Cruising Club 1800 - 1980,* published by G. C. Buckley, for much of my information about him.

Captain Goldsmith joined the Royal Cruising Club as a naval member in 1925 and became Rear-Commodore in 1931, which he said he preferred to being Rear-Admiral of a Cruiser Squadron. It was appropriate that he became Vice-Commodore in 1936 in the same year that he became Vice-Admiral. A year later he was voted Commodore of the RCC at the Annual General Meeting of 1937 and remained in that office for 18 years. (His predecessor had been Commodore for 49 years and only retired at the age of 87!)

His first boat was a 20-ton transome-sterned cutter called *Rame.* He had waited 20 years before he had sufficient money to build a boat of his own (service pay was very low before the war) and he sailed her single-handed 2,400 miles from Plymouth to Malta, to take up his appointment as King's Harbour Master there. It was remarked that there was no ladies' cabin on board although his normal crew was a wife and four daughters, but they probably took over the whole boat anyway!

In 1927 he made an extremely interesting cruise in *Rame* among the Ionian Islands, tracing the voyage carried out by Odysseus from Corfu to Ithaca in his Phoenician galley 4,000 years before. "It appears that for a nautical almanac the Captain had a copy of Homer at his elbow. Like other Englishmen before him he was a passionate lover of Greece and although there was a tendency for his logs to be a kind of Hellenic tour, he recorded faithfully all there was to know about the intricacies of navigation often by means of small, roughly drawn charts of harbour plans."

In fact Captain Goldsmith wrote many and sometimes extremely long logs for the RCC Journal, some of nearly 70 pages in length, which led to problems of storage! One of the reasons given was that "he believed so sincerely in the evangelical call of the sea that his pen ran away with him almost as soon as it had warmed to the task."

In 1930 he bought another boat of 31 tons which he called *Oeniadae* and spent most of that summer cruising along the west coast of Brittany, with his wife and two of his daughters. Nausa (or Nausicaa, all of his daughters had Greek names) fell overboard but thanks to prompt action by her father she was soon picked up safely. "My wife was splendid," he said and apparently she "felt that she had to go sailing with the family because it was always so jolly unsafe!" Her daughter remembers that she was marvellous – always pulling the wrong ropes!

His retirement and promotion to Rear-Admiral in the autumn of 1931 delighted him as it enabled him to go on even longer cruises and make his home on board *Oeniadae.* After one voyage of 10,400 miles to the West Indies in his new gaff cutter *Madalena,* he refitted at Dartmouth and then went straight out to the Mediterranean. He was recalled at the outbreak of way, when he became a Commodore of Convoys and it is said that he lost only three ships from a total of more than a thousand. He was knighted for this.

After the war, he came to live in Lymington but in 1948 in another gaff cutter, *Diotema,* he sailed again for the Mediterranean with one daughter and Margaret Adams, and the latter went to the West Indies with him in 1950. In fact *Diotema* made two Trans-Atlantic crossings. In 1955 he died, as he would have wished, on board his boat, which was anchored off one of the Greek Islands. Appropriately, he was buried in Athens, the capital of his beloved Greece, under a slab of pentelic marble, "a fitting end to the active life of one of Greece's adopted sons."

Roger Pinckney

Although the Royal Cruising Club during the 1930s tended to be "dominated by the breezy figure of Admiral Goldsmith," Roger Pinckney, his future son-in-law, was already emerging as "a sailor of great renown and influence in *Dyarchy.*"

Roger Pinckney first came to Lymington 1920. He designed and built Rope Walk House in King's Saltern Road, which was his first job as an architect. "I bought seven acres of land but did not realise until after its purchase that there was 4 feet of water in the field, which is why I got it so cheaply and why the house is built on stilts," he told me. "Where the Marina is now there used to be 20 swans pairing in the spring." He remembered when he was a child climbing the style at the end of Captain's Row and walking through the fields (where Queen Katherine Road is now) and hearing 40 larks singing.

"Old Captain Dyer, who founded the Lymington River Sailing Club in 1900, lived opposite me in Westfield. I became a Founder Member of the Royal Lymington Yacht Club in 1922, which replaced it, and in 1929 I joined the Royal Cruising Club." When Admiral Goldsmith was Commodore and so often away, Roger, as Vice-Commodore, had to do much of his work. As the Admiral wrote to him: "No-one knows better than you who the fellow is who has literally filled my shoes for so many years. Thank you a thousand times for all you have done. Now, thank goodness, you will be able to act in your own right; and how well you will carry on." Roger Pinckney succeeded him as Commodore of the RCC and how right his father-in-law was about him.

"I bought my first boat, *Agnes,* with the proceeds of previous birthdays and had saved up these birthday 'tips' until I had £100." In 1926 he bought, as the 'senior partner' in co-ownership with his mother, an ex-Bristol Channel pilot cutter called *Dyarchy,* the Greek for joint ownership! She was 24 tons, 41 ft. overall and carried 1,200 sq. ft. of canvas. It was said that he really enjoyed his sailing and would sometimes 'heave-to, the more to enjoy an admirable breakfast!' In 1932 he sent the RCC Journal some "excellent notes on the north coast of Spain with harbour plans and notes as well as places where good victuals could be obtained."

Roger Pinckney used to sail *Dyarchy* over to St. Peter Port in Guernsey for a scrub at Easter. When he and his mother sailed there in 1934 one of his crew was Eric Hiscock and there was also Ralph Swann and Adelaide. Mrs. Pinckney was determined that the proprieties should be observed, and not only hung a curtain between the bunks but also attached to the lower edge of the curtain a row of bells "which at the least tremor would be set off tinkling. Ralph says he never felt better protected in his life and slept the sleep of the just!"

Susan Scalter, who celebrated her 21st birthday on board and was later to marry Eric Hiscock and an account of the race is to be found in his book *Wandering under Sail.* They had a most enjoyable time bathing and sun-bathing, smoking and eating – most of the meals were eaten on deck and no-one remained at the helm for longer than an hour. Eric Hiscock quotes Roger as saying when they encountered a head wind later on during the race, "After all, we are supposed to be out here for pleasure, let's go the other way!" Despite this *Dyarchy* was 8th on corrected time and apparently the race officials were more interested in Mrs. Pinckney's age than in inspecting the boat. After the race they cruised in the Baltic and returned to Lymington via Scotland and the Irish Sea, some 3,600 miles in just over four months. In a later book by Eric Hiscock called *Cruising under Sail,* he dedicated it – "To Roger Pinckney... who taught me and many others how to cruise without fuss."

Now for the story of a very different type of cruise in the Solent with the Lymington Sea Scouts, written by Troop Leader Jack Clark for the Sea Scout Journal *Galleon,* Vol. 2, No. 8 Christmas 1936.

"Everything was O.K. A good breeze, a good ship, and a good Skipper. What more could a Sea Scout want? As we rounded Cocked Hat, we stretched the mains'l and jib (the fores'l being already set) and cut out the engine. In such weather as this there was little wonder that the Solent was full of interesting craft. We passed very close to windward of a beautifully rigged schooner, and while Skipper was perched on the very end of the gaff, we took the bow wash of a Channel boat.

"In a few moments, as it seemed, a sea mist came in. The blue sky vanished as did most of the boats, particularly the schooner, which put about immediately. How those 'hands' must be fed up with the sight of the Solent on fine days. Tacking out through the bottleneck at Hurst, we met a decent swell, and with the rain came oilskins. Barely missing a larger motor yacht by a bowsprit's length, we were surprised to see a fast power boat bearing down on us, throwing up great sheets of spray as she caught the top of each wave. It really looked as if the Police were on our track at last. However, it turned out to be an RAF tender from Calshott, and it provided us with a most thrilling spectacle, for she was at times completely obliterated by spray.

"The South side of the Island looked very dull and uninviting, but steaming hot tea and buns held all our attention for the moment. A few seabirds, and an occasional cormorant, a smoky 'tramp' to starboard, and the rasp of the Needles fog-horn, so passed St. Catherine's, Ventnor and Shanklin, Sandown and Bembridge. The wind had fallen off quite a bit by this time and as we slipped into Portsmouth, faded altogether. We drifted up to Portchester Castle and there dropped hook. Mrs. Pinckney piped all hands below at ten o'clock to two huge steak and kidney pies, supper for six very hungry crew, one absolutely empty, having left the better part of his breakfast in the English Channel. And so to bed.

"We were awakened next morning by a splash and splutter. The Skipper had beaten us to it and declared the water was lovely. We got under weigh with but a light breeze, and it was past morning before we found ourselves out of Portsmouth. On the way out, however, we had cruised round Camper & Nicholson's yard, and had caught a glimpse of Mr. Sopwith's *Endeavour II* which was to be launched the next day.

"The return journey was very pleasant indeed, although the wind dropped completely in Cowes Roads and we just drifted down the Solent and in past the familiar old 'Jack' on the last of the ebb. Finishing up in masterly fashion, we towed a sailing boat off the 'putt' and up to her moorings before finally packing up our own. Tea on board ended that

By courtesy of R. A. P. Pinckney

Dyarchy

weekend cruise in which we had covered almost seventy miles, having circumnavigated the Isle of Wight.

"In the hope that Mr. Pinckney reads this *Galleon*, I should like to let him know how much we enjoyed that trip, and that we wish for nothing better in the coming season than that we may once again join his happy ship, and leave the rest to the elements. May we?"

In 1938 Roger Pinckney was having a new *Dyarchy* built, another Bristol pilot cutter, designed by Jack Laurent Giles and built in Sweden in the Sture Truedeson yard. She delighted her new owners and few boats have been admired so much; indeed she continues still to be admired to this day. She was also called *Dyarchy*. Roger had sold his old *Dyarchy* and "she was being sailed up Channel by a professional yacht delivery skipper when she ran ashore in broad daylight and with an offshore wind on the Owers and became a total loss. Many thought that she had committed suicide." Be that as it may, it is the reason why the new ship was called *Dyarchy* and not *Dyarchy II*, there only being one in existence.

After a preliminary cruise along the Swedish coast, Roger handed *Dyarchy* over to Humphrey Barton, who sailed her back to Lymington and was awarded the RCC Challenge Cup for so doing.

The war had come at a bad time for Roger Pinckney, just as he was becoming known as an architect. Roger himself referred to that period as 'Abortive Cathedrals Ltd.' as he won a competition for Sydney Cathedral, which was never built and then won another one for Colombo Cathedral, which was not built either, although there is one there now. He designed the West Front of Liverpool Cathedral, but was not officially the architect and was given no credit for it, although he did all the designs and had all the fun!

The *History of the Royal Cruising Club* takes up the tale again. "After the war *Dyarchy*, with dark topsides and wide, varnished oak rubbing strake, became synonymous with the RCC and the very best traditions of the Club. Roger Pinckney's ability to handle her under full sail in often very restrictged waters was an impressive sight . . . *Dyarchy* conjures up in my mind two distinctly different images. The

By courtesy of R. A. P. Pinckney

Dyarchy off Hayling Island

first is of a fine-looking ship under way but it is the man standing in the cockpit who catches one's eye. He is amiable, bearded, has no shirt on and is standing with his hands on his hips while the boat appears effortlessly to be steering herself." All of us who have seen him sail down the Lymington River will concur with that. In fact, Roger holds the speed record of 25 knots in the Lymington River for a vessel displacing over 100 tons and he doesn't think it will ever be beaten. He tried an experiment over a measured mile when the river was quite empty and the wash was breaking right down at Keyhaven!

"The fact that hospitality aboard the Vice-Commodore's yacht was legendary was in no small part due to the warmth and kindness of Mrs. Pinckney."

By courtesy of R. A. P. Pinckney

Roger Pinckney on board *Dyarchy*

We have already seen how good she was with young Sea Scouts. She was always one of the crew of *Dyarchy* although according to her son and co-owner "she steered a course very accurately, but had no idea how it all worked." The Bashfords remember seeing her pedalling along King's Saltern Road on a tricycle, rather solemnly, wearing a Queen Victoria dress. In her old age she suffered terribly from arthritis, but she would not give up sailing. She used to be hoisted aboard *Dyarchy* in a bosun's chair and she sailed each year until 1957, when she made her last crossing of the Channel to Cherbourg at the age of 91. She died shortly afterwards and her ashes were carried in *Dyarchy* to her old home, Guernsey, with a large party of her friends on board.

About six months later Roger married Nausa and they extended Rope Walk House to provide a home for Lady Goldsmith. They bought a little house in the Dordogne and motor down to stay there in May and September of each year.

Roger continued his work as an architect and designed the Wellington Room at the Community Centre. His major works locally were Brockenhurst School and Hardley School, near Fawley. These were in partnership with Arthur Grant. But his greatest monument must surely be the new extension to St. Thomas' Church. It was conventional in design and so much of a feeling of history did he manage to convey in a completely new building that it is possible to imagine monks eating and praying there. Just to confuse posterity, Roger told me that he even produced some designs as if, in fact, it had been an old Chapter House!

The 100th anniversary issue of the Royal Cruising Club journal perhaps summed up all that *Dyarchy* meant to its members with these words. "A facet of the Club which not only maintains a strong link with the past but also gives much pleasure to old and new owners alike is the way in which boats are kept in the Club by being passed on from one generation to the next . . . The faithful *Dyarchy,* now celebrating her 41st year, is very much in evidence in the ownership of our Rear Commodore 'Scrap' Batten. It was a splendid sight to see her alongside the pier at Greenwich for the Centenary Dinner in the Painted Hall at the Naval College – surely one of Europe's grandest rooms and a fitting place for the Club to hold that celebration."

Major William M. Martineau, MC

Bill Martineau was born in 1984. He served in the Royal Engineers during World War One in their 'Butterfly' Division – so called because they flitted about from place to place – and was mentioned in despatches. He was awarded the Military Cross in June 1917 when, blown up by a mine at Messines Ridge, he continued with his task although severely wounded in the head. After the war he ran a string of garages around Andover and Salisbury. In World War Two he was in uniform again, and was at one time in charge of the maintenance of all small craft and the training of their crews in India and Ceylon under Mountbatten.

He was sailing from Lymington as early as 1925 in his 4-5 ton cruising cutter *La Bonne.* From 1927 to 1936 he owned *Wilful,* an 8-ton cruising cutter which played such an active part in the training of the Lymington Sea Scouts. He can truly be called the 'father' of sailing in Lymington after World War One. He was a Founder Member of the Royal Lymington Yacht Club in 1928, later becoming Rear-Commodore 1946-47; Vice-Commodore 1947-1954 and Commodore in 1954-55 when he was sailing *Saluki,* a 14-ton auxiliary sloop. He was also Founder Commodore of the Lymington Town Sailing Club in 1946 and designed its burgee. In 1939 he joined the Royal Cruising Club. At one time he used to do quite a bit of writing for *Yachting Monthly* and each month would send up news of what was happening in these parts. Today, when he is blind, he can still remember and describe vividly races and cruises in which he participated in the past.

"One of the finest feats of seamanship on the Lymington River," he told me, "was that of a Polish Scout who was returning from a round the world trip in *Zuwar II.* The Lymington Scouts were alerted to give him any assistance possible, perhaps help him scrub before sailing back to Poland. We were there to receive him but he didn't turn up, and the next morning we found he had come in during the night, having been delayed by the tide. He had worked his way up the Lymington River in the dark right up through the Berthon frontage, past the pier and actually tied up where Golden Produce is now. When I remarked, 'Well, it is wonderful that you got here and tied up in the dark,' he said that it was only a small incident after some of the places he had had to nose in. I offered him a tow out but he answered, 'I am not used to being towed,' and he went off and did a thing I have never seen before.

"The wind was easterly, the tide was definitely flooding so he had very good rudder control but it was a contrary force. He came by the Berthon layout and did the bit where he had to go straight into the pier, as it were; you might say close hauled but there wasn't room really to throw a tack and he did it all on the port tack – it was wonderful. He relied on the tide giving him rudder control: as long as he got moving he felt he could do it but he hadn't got enough room on that narrow bit to the pier to come about and veer on the other tack. So he did a turn and carried momentum to a position where he could again use the same tack all the way out on the port tack right down the river. I have never seen it done before – it was amazing. I don't know if he did get back to Poland or survived after the war."

Another pre-war story concerned Herbert Rand. "My first introduction to Herbert, 'Clump' as we called him, was when he was diving under *Lady Belle,* an 8-tonner that was Robert Hole's boat and slightly bigger than the boat I had which was called *Wilful.* Herbert Rand was outstandingly good and quite unique in handling a whaler. At the time when the sea wall broke down and everywhere was flooded he ran up and said, 'Come and have a sail *over* the marshes on the old golf links,' so I let him have a reach which was down off what is now rather near Creek Cottage direction. I got in the whaler and we worked our way through there and the tide was still running and, of course, there was plenty of water. We sailed about but had to jolly well wait till the tide had stopped flooding so as to get out. It was coming in so

fast and we took a long time in getting out and I know we were rather pleased when we finally got back on the moorings.

"The Goodharts once spent a night opposite their home in King's Saltern Road facing the sea wall because they thought they couldn't get across and make a landing because there was some mud and water. They had to wait till the tide came up but the wind got up so strongly that they decided they had better stay the night on board and passed a very uncomfortable night. I said afterwards, 'What on earth did you do that for? When faced with mud, as one always is, why didn't you take the floorboards out of your boat and put them down on the mud and step ashore!'

"We used to like going to places where we met the Navy but we particularly liked sailing in Holland because the people were so charming and there were no language problems: they nearly all speak English and it makes it so nice when you get there from Harwich or an East Coast port almost direct. The thing to do was to take the Hook Race, which gave you a chance of some racing. I think Ian Carr was with me when we picked up a second place and John Illingworth, who was then Commodore of the RORC (1948-50) said to me, which was awfully nice of him, 'Bill, I do congratulate you. You know I take ocean racing really seriously and you are a cruising type, and yet you came in on this race and have beaten me by 15 minutes. I jolly well see that my crew do not bring heavy luggage and you are carrying coal, full tanks of water and oil. I regulate my fellows and here you are and I congratulate you.' I felt very honoured – it made the race worth while.

"Then we went in for the Cowes-Dinard-St. Malo race and I felt so encouraged as we picked up a second on that race. We ought to have got a first but I had a very nice fellow, I won't mention his name, but he was not a frightfully close-winded handler. We were well ahead but a boat did get in before us on the St. Malo-Dinard. We had been having lunch below and when we came up the boat which had been astern under our lee had worked its way up, close hauled, and was on our weather starboard bow. I gave a glance to dear Dick Linsell, who was with us and a sailing companion, and we didn't say much because this fellow was not close on the helm."

Bill Martineau practically invented automatic steering. His boat had what he called the 'Joan Wood' which were two little pegs rather like pencil tops on the wooden end of the helm. "We were going across West Bay at the time and I said to Dick Linsell, 'Just come and look at Joan steering the boat in her sleep. You know we could get elastic and a short cord to go round those two pegs in a figure of eight. Let's try it." We had elastic on what we called the 'cod line' and did a treble figure of eight round and if you wanted instant release you only had to flick up, and you could touch the helm and put the boat about if you were heading straight for a rock. It worked like magic. Adlard Coles was very interested when he saw it. He was teaching Charles Sergel to circle and on their way back across the Bay they were caught in a gale so he decided to give it a trial and found that they didn't touch the helm. They were more or less hove-to going steadily on. It worked wonders!

"The race to St. Peter Port was one which was popular with both Clubs and at times it was considered a risky race but I can't think why because you could see the French coast long before you got to any hazard risk which a boat might take according to what the tide was doing when you got there. That was the interesting part: to calculate what the Alderney Race would be doing as against the Casquettes entrance and you had to protect your crews by making the rules very much on the safe side. There was a very risky bit of tide rip at the far Sound of Alderney. And then when you made the approach the exciting part was that if you went through the Alderney passage with the ebb taking you through, you could often see the Navy coming in from the West Casquettes and you would both be heading for St. Peter Port and it was a neck and neck race between the Army and the Navy. *Saluki* was a fast boat and she won quite a number of times. We did have fun in those days.

"It is tideless off the Danish Coast and in sheltered waters like that you can therefore tie up and save the labour of putting anchors down or entering a small harbour. At the end of a day, we were in *Dyarchy* at the time, we were coming near an island that had a pier and a lighthouse. We decided to tie up there and old Colonel Pepper, who was one of the crew, said, 'I think we must have arrived in heaven – look at those beautiful women. What on earth are they doing alone on an island, rather remote from land, with only a lighthouse and a lighthouse keeper for company?'

"I was first ashore with warps to tie up and the lighthouse keeper came rushing down. Roger Pinckney was with us, of course, and was chatting about fixing everything up when the lighthouse keeper said, 'No tying up on this pier. This island is for women only.' When we queried what he was doing there he said it was different because he was the lighthouse keeper. Eventually he let us anchor but told us we could not land. The women sang to us and blew kisses: they were very attractive women too. So later we thought we would check up and see what

on earth it was all about and were told, 'They are not good women – they are all bad,' so we assumed it was a way of keeping prostitutes out of mischief, like a sort of prison sentence!

"From there we went into a placed called Rodwig, which was the last little harbour before entering Copenhagen itself. It was a good place to tie up. We sailed into Rodwig under full sail and a strong wind and there was the Harbour Master looking very worried and making signs to take the sail down. Roger, of course, is a very good man and knows what sail can do and he said, 'We are causing alarm, Bill. I think you had better get forward in case I want to do a quick turn and can't stop the boat's way quick enough to avoid ramming across to the lee side. If I want a quick turn we will do it on the anchor. We swished in and the Harbour Master put his hands up in a despairing way as much as to say 'This is ridiculous!' But we did, in fact, do the whole thing quite tidily and nicely without having to use the anchor to stop us. Roger judged it superbly. The Harbour Master admired what we had done but said he hoped there weren't any more like us!

"We then went to smoother water and there were some 8-metre boats there which decided to do the same. The Danes worked their way to windward without setting any sail at all or using an engine. It was extraordinary. It must have been that their boat had such a clean and slim hull that the weight of the wind, strong to gale, worked on the hull side aft of the mast and gave them just enough power to move without any sail. That was very interesting and we discussed it ashore with the Danes, who are very good sailors, and we had a wonderful time.

"Copenhagen is a place to go to if ever you get the chance. The Tivoli switchback was outstanding – through the Tunnel of Love, which is dark and draughty and all the ladies get their dresses blown up but being dark it is allowed! But you do wonder going for that rock face what is going to happen. I remember when Roger and I got off our little switchback car we quickly looked to see what had held us at these terrific speeds, and we saw there was another rail above ready to hold us down and we were pressed against that. It was a great relief and we didn't mind doing it a second time with another member of the crew, Colonel Pepper. He said, 'I wonder if it as good as the one at Blackpool.' The first dip wasn't very steep and he said, 'Well, we haven't really done a decent dive,' but at the third dive he was not only holding his hat on but I think he had taken his teeth out as well. He didn't realise that the art of conversation is to keep your mouth shut and hope to survive!"

Bill lost his sight when he was out in Canada

visiting his married daughter, Jo Van Valkenburg; bumping up and down on a bad road in a Land-rover caused the retinas of his eyes to get detached and he became completely blind. But being a very brave man and a very religious one, he has triumphed over this disability and is always full of cheer and ready for a yarn about his sailing. He and his wife, Joan, recently celebrated their Diamond Wedding.

Lieutenant-Commander D. E. Balme, DSC, RN

David Balme came out of the Navy in 1948 and worked full time in a family firm in the City. As soon as the Marina was built they moved their boat here and two years later, in 1972, they saw their present home, Lisle Court House, advertised for sale on the Walhampton side of the river. "It was very broken down," he told me, "and there was no sanitation, no nothing. When we arrived it had a loo in it – just a bucket. An old farm labourer who had lived in it had died and it was just left empty. When they had that Pop Festival on the Isle of Wight, vandals got into it and burnt it slightly. Today the house consists of three cottages – a Georgian one, a Victorian part which is now the drawing room and a third cottage which they added which is a dining room and kitchen. Outside was a lovely old stock-yard with a very old wall. Altogether, in such a beautiful and peaceful setting, it was an example of an English country house at its best. It was on the 4th February 1982 that I met him there.

"Sir Maurice Laing, Admiral of the RORC, had this boat which he tried to get into the Admiral's Cup but it was too well made – a bit too heavy," he told me. "So next year he sold her and we bought her second hand. He had christened her *Hephzibah,* which is from the Book of Kings and she was a beautiful queen. We had got to know the name *Hephzibah* and so we hung on to the name. This was in 1964/65 and we had her for quite a long time.

"Then after that we had a Phillips 43 and we now have a High Tension 36, which is slightly smaller. She is out of date now for racing but was very competitive the first year we had her (1978) and won quite a lot of prizes. But then all our children got married and all have babies so we have given up racing now. We only raced with a family crew, two sons and a son-in-law, but now they have all become very busy with their children and their jobs. Colin and Richard Chitty both came out several times with me.

"We raced ever since the boys were about 17 and 15, still at school, right up until 1981 when they are now 33 and 31. When they were quite young we always used to do the La Rochelle race, which was the greatest race, I think, of all the programme because it takes you to a beautiful place quickly. You wouldn't bother to go to it if you sailed gently because it is 350 miles from Plymouth. Then my wife used to come out in the car with my daughter, who was then about 12, and the crew used to take the car back and then the family of five of us used to have the most marvellous holiday bringing her slowly back. That really was the best way to do it.

"I am on the committee of the Royal Yacht Squadron and we had the Sea Scouts for starting the races, not pulling the guns but pulling out numbers. We have quite good fun on the committee doing the racing in Cowes Week and there is often a lot of argument amongst the competitors but not too much. There was a bit last year because it is so much more difficult when there is no wind because everybody grumbles. No wind is worse than anything.

"We walk quite a lot down Tanners Lane and all those places. It is jolly interesting and there are some lovely birds. Just across two fields from here, in a funny little cottage, lives a great character called Ken Parsons, who used to work with Billy Whittaker and was one of the labourers here and we still meet him. He is a great countryman and a bachelor who lives on his own and they say he reads Shakespeare and books like that. He might be a useful contact for you." He was indeed.

Ken Parsons lives in Corner Cottage and it was there I had a long talk with him in his home on 23rd March 1982. He told me an enormous amount about the river and, in particular, about the marshes and 'The Future of the North West Solent Coast – Proposals for the coast from Pitts Deep to Hurst Spit,' drafted by C. R. Tubbs of the Nature Conservancy Council in December 1979. Ken Parsons was very well read and steeped in the old history of the eastern bank of the river and particularly of East End, where he was born. He had press cuttings which he kindly loaned me and was able to confirm much that I had already heard. It was a great pleasure meeting him.

"Lymington is an amazing place with so many different things going on in the vicinity," continued Commander Balme. "Sue and I go hunting with the Buckhounds and literally half an hour from here is the most marvellous hunting country. Some people who come from very suave hunts say it is the best hunting country because, apart from Exmoor and Dartmoor, the New Forest is the only place where you can have natural hunting. Everywhere else is farm land and you can't go across crops and roads. Here you never see a car and you are never on a road. It is rather amazing. Some of these old keepers are marvellous people. One learns an awful lot by reading all these articles about the oil enquiry. Jean Cobb is doing a marvellous job. She really is the expert on New Forest wild life." This then is David Balme's life in 1982.

"Out of the blue in April 1981 I received this newspaper cutting in the post and it just said, 'Kind regards, Fritz' – no letter. It was from a retired German I employed for all the time I was in the City for about 20 years. We retired him when he was about 67. I send him a Christmas card every year but I hadn't heard from him at all other than that. Patrick Beesly translated it for me and then wrote to the editor of apparently one of the biggest Sunday papers in Germany, an awfully nice man of about 45, and he came over and interviewed me in London. As a result they published these articles, part of a three-week series with pictures and Penelope Chitty translated them for me." What was behind it all? What was the connection? To find this out we must go back to May 1941.

In the spring of 1941 Britain had reached a crucial stage in her history. France had been occupied by the German army for a year and only "a laughable strip of water 35 kms. wide separated Hitler's victorious army from the defeated divisions of His Majesty, whose heavy war armaments were now rusting away on the beaches of Dunkirk" – so wrote the Germans. Seen from the British point of view we had survived the 'Miracle of Dunkirk' and evacuated most of our army – in no small way due to the 600 craft ranging from open boats and motor cruisers to yachts and fishing boats, which assembled at Ramsgate and Dover. (Incidentally, the Cruising Club of America awarded its Blue Water Medal for 1940 to "The British yachtsmen who took part in this rescue, both those who survived the hazardous undertaking and those who gave their lives in the attempt.") Our young fighter pilots had smashed the German airforce in the Battle of Britain and with it the possibility of imminent invasion. But perhaps the greatest danger of all which threatened the British people at this time came from the German U-boats.

Out in the cold waters of the Atlantic the Germans had been sinking 300,000 to 500,000 tons of shipping each month. The Battle of the Atlantic now had to be won to keep the sea-lanes open between Britain and Canada and the United States for the transport of supplies vital to our survival. One thing was desperately needed – the capture of the Enigma coding machine with which every German vessel and submarine was equipped. We had already broken the codes of the German army and air force at Bletchley, but the German naval codes were far more difficult to decipher and, without an examina-tion of the coding machine itself, it would be virtually impossible to break them.

On 2nd May 1941 Convoy OB–318 left Liverpool with 17 ships and her escort of five ships; the number of merchantmen being increased to 42 as she passed the south of Iceland. Seven days later, on the bridge of the destroyer *Bulldog*, the convoy commander, Baker-Creswell, was taking sun sights at noon prior to confirming the position of the convoy with the commodore of the merchantmen. *Bulldog* was due to leave the convoy in four hours' time.

With him on the bridge was a former Dartmouth Cadet, Sub-Lieutenant David Balme, still only 20. He had his glasses trained on the *Esmond* when through them he saw a huge column of water spout into the air followed by an explosion; within minutes the stricken ship had tipped her stern into the sky, "her cargo of vehicles tumbling into the sea like toys tipped out of a box."

On 9th May 1941 the commander of the U-boat 110, Captain Julius Lemp, made his fateful rendez-vous with the convoy in the North Atlantic just east of Cape Farewell. Captain Lemp had fired four torpedoes: two ships were sunk, a third torpedo failed to explode and the fourth stuck in the tube. While he was looking through his periscope it was spotted by the alert lookout on board the corvette *Aubretia*. This was the moment of truth for the German captain.

Desperately he dived but the *Aubretia* passed overhead and dropped ten depth charges. The submarine was badly damaged but still operational. *Aubretia* made another run and this time the oil tanks were ruptured, the lights went out and the submarine sank like a stone, completely out of control.

Then, by a strange change in fortune, she suddenly "shot up to the surface like a cork out of a bottle," according to one of the survivors. Captain Lemp jumped out of the conning-tower and saw the two destroyers *Bulldog* and *Broadway* converging on him at full speed, *Bulldog* prepared to ram him. With the submarine settling in the water, he was exposed to the crossfire from the British destroyers, so devas-tating that one observer who saw it reported "the Battle of Trafalgar must have been like a snowball fight compared to this!" Captain Lemp conceded the situation was hopeless and gave orders to abandon ship. Within minutes the German seamen were swimming in the sea.

It was then that Baker-Cresswell realised that here was a faint possibility of capturing a German submarine and her charts and ciphers, but equally important, he had to do it without the Germans knowing. He gave orders for a boarding party and changed course and went hard astern so as not to ram the U-boat. Immediately, the Germans were dragged from the water they were hurriedly taken below decks.

In the meanwhile the boarding party, in charge of Sub-Lieutenant David Balme was approaching the submarine and it was then that he saw that there still one swimmer in the water. Captain Fritz-Julius Lemp had been the last to leave the submarine and for that reason had probably not been spotted by the boats picking up the survivors. Simultaneously, he could see that not only was the U.110 not going to sink but that the British were about to board her. Despairingly, he turned round and tried to swim back to the submarine and get there before the British. The next moment he had disappeared from sight beneath the waves and his death to this day remains a mystery.

David Balme told the editor of *Bild am Sonntag* that his prize crew of nine was equipped with Webley revolvers, calibre 45 from World War One. "Most of us had never fired a shot. We had no rifles and no sub-machine guns. When we were closing on the submarine there was still light firing taking place. I did not see Lemp swimming in the water and I do not know where he was at the time. For me there are only two possibilities: firstly Lemp was hit by a stray bullet from the *Bulldog* and died in the water; and secondly Lemp committed suicide when he saw that his U-boat had not sunk and was being boarded." He was not shot by any of the boarding party.

The boarding party came alongside the U.110 "twisting and porpoising drunkenly." David Balme drew his revolver and stepped on board and opened the hatch. This took great courage. Was there a party of German sailors still on board or had it been booby trapped? There was only a slight escape of air; otherwise everything was completely still. "The silence was positively eerie."

The telegraphist, Allen Long, went to work in the wireless room, making a note of all the frequencies and settings on the equipment and packing up coded signals and cipher documents. David Balme found maps with German minefields clearly marked and the channels swept for the U-boats, but most important of all, he found the Enigma coding machine itself, the size of a small typewriter. It took three hours to pass all the documents from hand to hand in a human chain and all were safely transferred. Captain Lemp's Iron Cross was returned later to his sister by Commander Baker-Cresswell in 1958 but David Balme kept his peaked uniform cap which he found in his minute cabin.

Bulldog then took the submarine in tow but, perhaps fortunately, she sank, as she should have done earlier, and for the rest of the war the Germans never suspected otherwise. Neither did they realise that what had happened out there in the North Atlantic was the turning point in the Battle of the Atlantic, and indeed of the whole war. When *Bulldog* arrived back in Scotland she was debriefed by Lieutenant Allan Bacon, RNVR, who worked in special liaison between the naval section at Bletchley and the Operational Intelligence Centre. Every page was photographed in case the originals were lost when being flown down to London. "The talented men and women and the eccentric geniuses who worked at Bletchley" succeeded in breaking the German naval code and gained an insight into the secrets of the Atlantic U-boats.

David Balme told me that within ten days they knew the significance of their capture but when Captain S. W. Roskill in 1959 wrote *The Secret Capture* he even then could not reveal what had been taken out of the U-boat. It was only in 1978 when Ronald Lewis wrote *Ultra goes to War – The Secret Story,*' that all this could be told. "The circumstances of this 'pinch' were so fraught with the possibility of failure and its consequences so crucial," he wrote, "that this was one of the exceptional occasions when history held its breath." It was the most important capture of the whole war.

David Balme was under terrific secrecy all this time and had to keep in touch with the Admiralty in case he was approached by the Russians. As a postscript it is interesting to note that living quietly in Lymington today are three people who were closely connected with this story: David Balme who made it possible; Patrick Beesly, who worked in naval intelligence; and the author, who was a Wren at Stanmore operating the 'bombes.'

Lionel St. Clare Byrne

Lionel St. Clare Byrne is a retired Company Director and a well-known Lymington yachtsman. He served with the Royal Artillery during the war and was taken prisoner. Shortly afterwards, when he came to Lymington, he was given 'The Local Facts of Life: Lymington sails, Milford-on-Sea bowls, Brockenhurst plays golf, Lyndhurst plays at hunting – and there is an iron curtain between each!' He became a member of the Royal Lymington Yacht Club in 1945 and later joined the Lymington Town Sailing Club.

Lionel owned a Slipway 5-tonner called *Pastime,* after yachts of that name owned by his grandfather, which he sailed and raced successfully between 1949–53. Another Slipway 5-tonner was *Babar (2),* presently owned by Mr. Shaw-Porter of Lymington but which formerly belonged to Helen Tobin. In

1953 Lionel won the Roman Gold Bowl in the Round the Island Race and Helen Tobin in *Babar (2)*, on the same handicap, was only a few seconds astern. "When, as often, *Babar (2)* had an all-female crew," he recalled, "they were known as *'Babar's* Bouncing Belles.' *Pastime* was sold that winter and Helen Tobin had a very successful 1954 season before she sadly died that year.

"After World War Two, Major Allott's father, known as Major 'Pop' Allott, suggested reorganising the Coronation Class. Coronation boats had been built before the war at a cost of about £100. Fortunately for all concerned this suggestion was not accepted and the famous X-Class were formed into a racing class instead. These were designed by Commander Westmacott's father and soon X-class yachts were to be found at clubs all along the coast from Chichester to Poole."

In 1963 Lionel St. Clare Byrne bought one of the famous Elizabethan 29 fibre glass sloops built by Peter Webster in Lymington. After a party at the Ship, the launching ceremony took place at the Quay and Patricia Webster named the yacht *Pastime II*. She recalls that the bottle of champagne did not break and she had to chase after the yacht into the water in order to do this at her second attempt. It was a very happy party that sailed down the river. As they passed the RLYC they realised they had forgotten the battens and dropped the mainsail just as the starting gun was fired and it looked as if the sail had received a direct hit! Lionel stayed the night in Yarmouth but Peter Webster, with Neil McIntyre and Charles Harding came back on the ferry. Their arrival at Lymington was hilarious. With Peter in the middle supporting the other two, who were still clutching wine bottles, they disembarked rather unsteadily down the gangway and along the terminal, preceded by a troop of very smart – and very sober – Sea Scouts. It was just like a scene in an old Ealing film comedy.

Lionel's grandfather and father were both naval architects; indeed, St. Clare Byrne, who died on 15th December 1915 at the age of 85, has been called the doyen of British yacht designers. He was originally a boatbuilder up in the Clyde but he returned to Liverpool to take up a new career as a yacht designer. Amongst many great ships which he designed was a large steam yacht called *Alva* for the American millionaire W. K. Vanderbilt, which was built in the USA. She was a screw composite three-masted topsail schooner, 285 ft. overall and 1,238 tons. In 1892 she was sunk in a collision off Martha's Vineyard and later broken up. Indicative of those days was the fact that St. Clare Byrne received the following laconic message: "Yacht foundered –

proceed with another twice the size," which he did!

The new yacht was called *Valiant*, one of the biggest in the world at that time, of 2,814 tons and given an auxiliary rig as a brig. She was particularly well-furnished below to impress, it was said, the 9th Duke of Marlborough, who was about to marry Consuelo Vanderbilt. *Valiant* was used by the Royal Navy in World War One and finally scrapped in 1926.

He also designed *Norseman*, which was later bought by the 5th Earl of Lonsdale, that wonderful sportsman and character, the 'Yellow Earl,' and other such famous yachts as *Maria, Erl King, Kethailes, Portia* and *Sabrina*. The most interesting of all of them was *Sunbeam*, which he designed for his first customer, Lord Brassey in 1874. She was 159 ft. overall, 27 ft. 6 ins. beam, 13 ft. 9 ins. draught and 532 Thames tonnage and was a three-masted topsail schooner.

Sunbeam was not only one of the first yachts to sail round the world, 1876-1877, but she did so in a style which is almost unbelievable to us today. There were 43 on board on that occasion, including a doctor, an artist, a ladies maid and a nanny as well as a crew of 30. There were also 2 dogs, 3 birds, and a charming Persian kitten belonging to the baby. Lady Brassey records this adventurous voyage: the yacht caught fire three times and on one occasion they were boarded by Chinese pirates. Her book, *A Voyage in the Sunbeam – Our home on the ocean for eleven months*, was written in 1891 and is full of drawings and makes fascinating reading. They came back with even more animals on board than when they left: 48 birds, 4 monkeys, a pig called 'Beau Brummel,' 2 cockatoos and a tortoise but most of them died when they reached the colder home waters again.

Sunbeam was used as a hospital ship during World War One and on Lord Brassey's death in 1918 she was offered to Pangbourne as a training ship but was bought by Lord Runciman, who had taught Erskine Childers, author of *Riddle of the Sands*, to sail and thus another tenuous but fascinating link with Lymington. *Sunbeam* was scrapped in 1922 after a life of 55 years.

Richard Bagnall

"My father had a clinker built dinghy built by Elkins of Christchurch in 1928 which he had at school. We were brought up on it before we were one and by seven we were sailing it on the Keyhaven River. When we had looked after it and painted it for a year, only then were we allowed to have our own dinghy. So the crafty devil got a free scrape for that year – that is one way of doing it! He is still sailing *Puffin* and you can see this little sail, No. 10, sailing out for Hurst nearly every weekend for the last goodness knows how many years. It was the first dinghy to start racing in Poole Harbour and that is the nearest he has ever got to big time racing.

"Our parents have supported us very much throughout the years and so we have been quite fortunate having a supporters club and it helps. We started racing in Cadets. Harvey and I were actually teased a bit about being twins, which gave us a tremendous advantage. One year my parents found out that some of the other families were offering their children something like £5 to beat us but we lost only one race in about 65 races!

"We were trained by Brigadier Hope and we used to compete in Portsmouth Naval Cadet week, which was the equivalent of the championships on the South Coast. We were towed from Keyhaven to Portsmouth, sometimes six little Cadets bouncing up and down behind *Gleam,* the Brigadier's boat. On board HMS *Excellent* we were under strict naval discipline and it was a subtle way of getting us to see naval life.

"Then we moved from Cadets to Fireflies and we went in for the National Championships ten years in a row and we never capsized in any of them, which I think is 'twinny' again. We got into the Gore every year, which was meant to be the top fifty in the first two or three races. In those days there were fleets of 160 to 180 and it was good racing. We once had a fourth at Falmouth but otherwise we were always in the first ten and were consistent but not outstanding.

"We later went in X-boats and all the early Contessa 26s but we never concentrated on one or the other of them for a season. We could do a Firefly meeting at Itchenor one weekend, an X race another weekend and then sail round the Island in a keel boat. That was the best thing we ever did because we did not have that sudden transition that happens today. You leave a dinghy and that is it. All this time we were looking at the big yachts, like *Drumbeat,* and the new revolutionary yachts and then came a fantastic opportunity.

"When I went to the Royal Lymington there was a draw from members only to sail on *Bloodhound,* which was being chartered to the Club. I think Ron Clarke was the skipper and everything started from there. I was one of the lucky ones so we went out every week and Helen Tew was on board as well.

"I was then asked if I would like to sail on this new yacht *Quiver V*; this was in 1969 or 1970 when I was working on the Yacht and Boatyard Management Course at Southampton and could actually see her being finished at Camper & Nicholsons. We were both invited on board and never looked back. We were now into the big yachts and Peter Nicholson

was the skipper and we learnt a great deal there and sailed in *Quiver VI* as well.

"In 1973 I helmed a Nick 45 for a very keen family that had only bought the boat to play around but we took part in the Admiral's Cup trials and were in the top eight and it was fun. The owner's two daughters, aged 13 and 8, were alongside me at the wheel, his wife was on the transom and we went like a rocket. We were run down once by a well-known yacht, who apologised afterwards.

"Then John Adams, who sails at Lymington, did the kindest thing in that particular year when he said, '*Sanjola II* is yours: you can helm it. I will watch from the shore and we will all go over to France. I will hazard the fish and the wine while you are racing offshore and we will see how you get on!' We were all quite young. We had John Channon from Hood, John Green from Stearn, and our navigator – and he was an absolutely marvellous navigator – was Simon van der Byl. We came 5th in the Worlds. There was a storm in the Bay of Biscay and none out of 37 got round; one completely overturned, three ran ashore and about 10 masts were broken. It was Ron Holland's first real attempt at Half Tonners.

"In 1975 we were lucky enough to team up with Ron Holland and he and I were joint helmsmen on *Golden Delicious,* owned by Peter Nicholson. We were lent this yacht and entered the Quarter Ton Cup in Norway and my brother delivered the yacht. We came second in the Worlds and this for Ron was quite exciting: it was the year of *Golden Apple,* one of his early ones, and he was full of hopes for the Admiral's Cup. We got *Golden Delicious* back to Cowes and just won the Three-Quarter Ton Series and were then off on the Fastnet.

"We were on quite a small boat and rumour had it that in the light airs the big boats had closed up and could not get round the point. Once you have stopped in a low wind you just cannot get enough momentum. We went out to sea to pick up the tide and a swell and we never stopped rolling down these waves and we won the whole thing. It was quite exciting. But it was the owner, Peter Nicholson, who got his name on the trophy even though he was on board *Morning Cloud!* Mary Pera explained that there was no precedent, as in the olden days the owners were always on board, and the only way round this was to charter.

"So I was the first one to tackle that problem and from then on I have always chartered and have been fortunate. Ron Holland had just about been in tears when his fine Admiral's Cup boat had been sitting for a day and a half off the Lizard and his dreams of success had gone, when suddenly our little boat came up with his design! So that was his beginning, although he did win the Quarter Ton Cup in Weymouth, which I sailed with Peter Bruce and my brother. Just the three of us.

"It was very hard work and if you went down below to pick up an apple or a Mars bar, which was Peter's offshore menu, you broached till you returned! Peter went down below to do some plotting on the navigation table and it was the most comfortable place on the boat. When we went down half an hour later, he had his head on the table and great apologies that he was trying to work out a difficult calculation. He was never seen to sleep again! When the skipper falls asleep then he is in real trouble!

"After the Fastnet I chartered a similar Three-Quarter Tonner, *Golden Delight,* and we went to Plymouth for the world championships and Bruce Banks won, sailing for Finland, and we came second, so we felt morally the first British boat. That was two second places in a row and we were beginning to be frustrated until I chartered *Silver Jubilee* in 1977, my best year. We won the Round the Island race on our second race out overall and then won the National Championships the following week overall. We thought we had the Fastnet again within our grasp but this time we were the ones becalmed at the Lizard. We actually went swimming and watched the race slip from our grasp!

"When Ed Dubois turned up I thought I must be loyal to British design and chartered *Honey,* which was being built in the Channel Islands but she was not completed in time. Luckily, I was asked by Richard Riggs to helm another beautiful boat designed by Ed Dubois called *Santa Evita.* We just got accepted for the trials and scraped in without upsetting too many people, as we had won the championships the year before and it was acceptable if we only participated in half the races; we came 5th and were the second British boat. It was fun and Ed was with us and it gave him his first taste of future success.

"When I was made redundant by Camper & Nicholson this gave me the chance to sail one of Ed's Admiral Cuppers, *Vanguard,* which was being built for David Lieu in Hong Kong. We were racing one weekend; flew out on the Sunday evening; raced in Hong Kong and won a race together and had a meeting with the owner; flew back on Friday and I sailed in a race that Sunday and never sailed so badly. I ran over the leeward mark at the beginning and got it wrapped round the keel and I nearly ran down Brian Saffery Cooper. I had to explain to him three days later that it was not as a result of alcohol but due to jet lag. It was rather dangerous and I was zonked out.

"Then the big event came and I was flown to Hong Kong and given the opportunity to select the crew, and get the yacht into the trials. There were 8 boats with all the top boys flying out from the States and everywhere else, and I was the only local Solent lad.

"My passport ran out while I was there and luckily I was able to pick up a temporary Hong Kong passport. The first time I walked into the yacht club I met my wife, Anne.

"We were selected, and back home, represented Hong Kong and were third out of nineteen teams, but my brother was injured in the second Olympic course, so it was rather difficult for me to sail well. When I left on the Channel Race they could not actually tell me whether he would be alive on my return. No-one had any idea. He had got hit by a boom when he was helming *Inishanier,* which was the Irish Admiral's Cupper, and it happened in the Solent. He was helicoptered off and it was almost a case of telepathy working, as I had heard a 'Mayday' on our radio, which we had kept going, and I had actually asked the crew to find out what was wrong. They told me it was *Inishanier* and after that everything went wrong: our sail blew out, a block flew off the deck and it was quite amazing because nothing else had happened like that before. Harvey recovered within a week and spent all his time worrying about me in the Fastnet, so it equalled itself out.

"Anne was working down at the Yacht Club in Plymouth and, because she is trilingual, she referred people to phone the police and other numbers, so she was actually given vital information. At the same time, some idiot, and we don't know who, said they had heard a call from *Vanguard* that we had abandoned the yacht, which was sinking and they presumed all were lost. So all these poor people were getting rather concerned and it was only 2½ hours before I returned to Plymouth that we were actually announced as being alive. So with the ups and downs we became engaged a week after that with the shock from the whole thing!

"Before I race in a charter yacht, I usually have one sail, perhaps two, to get used to it and then I usually try and choose half the sails rather than all of them. A boat is rather like a car – either it slides round a corner or goes round well. So it is either a stiff boat, in which case it can take a bigger sail plan, or it goes over on its beam ends and you can say 'help!' So actually I have been able to save a lot of money because in recent years boats are getting more and more tender. So we halve the number of sails – we don't need them. Sailmakers are not too happy about this but I find actually that it is much better to go straight in and get a boat tuned rather than playing around with the rigging. I usually complain of heavy helm or loose helm if the boat is not stable enough.

"I have no set crew and the result is that I have a worry every week. This is bound to happen in the middle of the thirties, because all your friends are married and going in different directions. I always like sailing with friends rather than get too involved with the commercial side, although they have always been very helpful. Also if I am happy in a boat I have usually been successful. At Cowes this year, (1982) which we were lucky enough to win, I had virtually a new crew and in the last two races we were picking up friends off the beach! The boat was going well and so long as someone could hold on to a rope occasionally, we kept in the right direction!

"Basically I like to sail something which is well fitted out below, so that I feel I am not in a shell. It is rather like having a car without seats. This year we were sailing with an oven and the whole works properly fitted out. I feel much better at the end of the day, even if I come second, because at least I feel I have beaten a few with no comforts at all! We even had fresh sheets and pillow cases instead of sleeping bags on *Quiver V*, and you kept your own bunk for the voyage. Of course, she was a fifty footer.

"Brother and I are always being teased because we like to get into our pyjamas if we are off watch. There was a famous occasion when we rounded the Ower light and there was David May in one of his *Winsomes* nearby and getting quite excited about trying to get inside us at the mark. The wind was very, very heavy and the boats got out of control with the spinnakers up and there was a cry of 'All crew on deck immediately.' On this embarrassing occasion I had my pyjamas on and they were slipping down, so I held on to them with one hand while once every three seconds the light flashed on me and there were wolf whistles from every direction and spray going over the top of us. That is what I call amusing sailing!

"Another thing, and I have told Keith Ludlow this, I hate communications from outside because I was brought up to sail alone. I like to sail a race with the weather forecast as your only information and not know where the opposition is; then you can make a decision without being influenced by what someone else is doing. I have had lots and lots of discussions about this. It can be very depressing listening in to where everyone else has got to and it is much more enjoyable going along and being totally oblivious that there is a problem. This was the old-fashioned way of sailing; you should not really get involved with communications because that is exactly what you are trying to get away from by leaving the shore.

"I think today the press is now getting excited enough by the crisis of the Fastnet that you will not be allowed to send boats out without radios. Also there is so much expense involved in rescue that sadly, if you go on an organised event, then you are going to be organised and herded as we were not in the earlier days. It has all happened in ten years."

CHAPTER 23

DULCIBELLA ET ALIA

"All this year I have had the sea thirst in me."
ERSKINE CHILDERS

Dulcibella

Mention the name of Erskine Childers and you will probably find that most yachtsmen will have read *The Riddle of the Sands,* not once, but many times, even though this classic book on sailing and espionage in the Friesian Islands was written in 1906. Who will forget *The Riddle of the Sands* and his famous yacht, *Dulcibella,* named after his sister. She was a legend then and has been ever since and is, perhaps, even more widely known today than she was then. *Dulcibella* has many links with Lymington, which makes her of particular interest to us, but let us now go back to the end of the last century.

Erskine Childers was born in London in June 1870, the son of a professor of oriental studies at London University and an Irish mother. By the age of thirteen, he had lost both parents and was brought up by his maternal uncle and aunt at Glendalough House, Annamore, County Wicklow. However, he was educated at Haileybury and later at Trinity College, Cambridge, where he took his law tripos and graduated as BA in 1893. Both these influences, the English and the Irish, were to confront each other later on with tragic results.

Two years later he entered the Civil Service and became a clerk in the House of Commons and joined the Royal Cruising Club, which had been formed in 1880. Its members were described as "so wrapped up in the salt water environment that they picked their teeth with marlin spikes!" Erskine Childers was taught to sail by Lord Runciman and, in 1896, he owned a boat called *Mad Agnes.* Hugh and Robin Popham write in their biography of Childers, *A Thirst for the Sea,* that "all that season, either alone, with Henry, or with one or more of his old and well tried friends, he coursed up and down the Solent, reached Poole again, sailed round the Isle of Wight, and weekend after weekend thrashed in and out of Lymington, Cowes, Beaulieu River, the Hamble and so on." "All this time I have had the sea thirst in me," he wrote to Lord Runciman in 1898.

Vixen was bought by him in Dover on 1st August 1897 and was fitted out for cruising in the Granville Dock. Ten days later Childers left single-handed for Boulogne, intending to cruise in the Mediterranean but fate in the form of a long spell of westerly winds persuaded him to sail to Holland and the Friesian Islands instead. His cruise in the Baltic from 11th August to 16th December 1897, on which *The Riddle of the Sands* is based, was the "longest and most arduous he had ever made."

There seem to have been at least two *Vixens,* possibly three, according to John Atkins, of which *Dulcibella* is *Vixen 2.* Certainly there appears to have been discrepancies over draught and whether she was a RNLI boat or an adaptation of a ship's lifeboat. The origins and measurements of two of the *Vixens* are investigated in considerable detail by Maldwin Drummond in an article "Telegrams and Tintacks" in the Royal Cruising Club Journal, which reads like a detective story. Bowker's Historical Postscript to the 1976 edition of *The Riddle of the Sands* also covers this very fully indeed.

Erskine Childers described her as "a cutter, 30 ft. overall by 7 ft. drawing 4 ft. to 6 ft. 7 ins. with the centre-plate lowered. Her ballast is 3 tons of lead, carried inside small pigs. Three comfortable berths are available and plenty of accommodation for stores and sails. A couple of small bilge keels make her sit nearly upright when on the ground, a feature which we found most valuable in North Germany."

This *Vixen* was laid up at Moody's yard in Bursledon in August 1898 and was sold for £12 in 1900. She became the housebot of George Newbury of Sarisbury and was then sold again to Claude Hapgood, a yachting journalist and owner of a small boatyard at Fishbourne, in the early 1930s. He writes in *Yachting World* of 26th May 1933 that *Dulcibella* was originally a 30 ft. lifeboat and confirms this with a photograph of her on the slip at Fishbourne. He had intended restoring her but had never got round to it. "She was moored in a mud berth at Wootton Creek," said John Atkins, "and nobody ever went near her. It was only the fact that these RNLI lifeboats were built of the best seasoned timber that she survived at all."

Then someone bought her and brought over to Lymington in 1938 and she was moored here just above the ferry. Jim Smith told me that in 1939 there was an appeal for donations to restore her, but with war imminent and the fact that she had deteriorated so badly, there was no chance of raising the money. Added to this she was hit by a bomb (or a very near miss) in 1943 and from then on she was doomed. According to Fred Woodford, the Harbour Master, she was eventually broken up and used as part of the foundations of Fortuna Dock, but Bill Smith told me that she was broken up and burnt in 1943 and this version is confirmed by Jim Smith, who said that someone had tidied up the yard and had burnt her. There seems little doubt that the *Vixen* in Lymington, photographed in 1942 by Group Captain Griffiths, was the real *Dulcibella*.

Her end was as sad as her original owner's, because Erskine Childers, torn between his loyalties to England and his loyalties to Ireland eventually smuggled arms to the Irish when they were fighting against us. In 1921 he was betrayed to our troops and was handed over to the Free State regime who condemned and shot him as a traitor. It is characteristic of the man that he first went round shaking hands with all the members of the firing squad.

But that was not the last of *Dulcibella*. In 1978 she was to rise again like a phoenix from the ashes and become even more famous and well-known. When Drummond Challis decided to make his excellent film of *The Riddle of the Sands* for Worldmark Productions Ltd. he contacted Dick Stower, who was not only Managing Director of the firm of naval architects of Laurents Giles and Partners but an authority on the *Dulcibella* since his boyhood.

Dick Stower's interest in the *Dulcibella* had been re-kindled, literally, in 1958 when he and his wife "spent a couple of months living in digs in Lymington and, not having any television and not having very much to do, I started doing a bit of research into the *Dulcibella*. This was because in the office, in those days, there were hundreds of old pre-war yachting magazines and also the original *Dulcibella* belonged to my mother's half-cousin, a chap called Claude Hapgood. He was retired from the Indian Army, I think, and he was yachting correspondent with the *Daily Telegraph* before the war. He bought *Dulcibella* so, of course, I got to know what she looked like and that is how it all started.

"Then, having prepared a paper on her, some

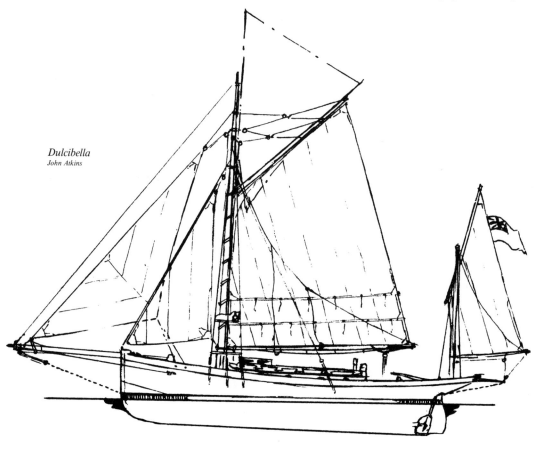

Dulcibella
John Atkins

years later, I supplied a copy of it to R. M. Bowker, who brought out a new edition of *The Riddle of the Sands* with an historical postscript in which my paper was quoted. That was got hold of by a film producer, who then came to ask me if I would do the conversion of a lifeboat for the film."

They used the Brook 35 ft. rowing lifeboat *Susan Ashley* as the basis of *Dulcibella*. *Susan Ashley* was built in 1907 and served at Brook on the back of the Isle of Wight for 30 years until the station closed. John Atkins received a call from Dick Stower asking if he would like to do a few detailed drawings as they were behind with a rush job. The owners wanted to get the boat finished as soon as possible for a film they were going to make on location in the Friesian Islands before the weather deteriorated. So that is how he got to know Drummond Challis, who had put up the money for *Dulcibella*. In the spring it only took Tim Bungay of West Wellow, eight weeks to carry out the conversion, including the addition of the counter and, with Harry Spencer's help, the provision of the masts and rigging. No expense was spared to render her authentic in every detail to the period of the first publication in 1903.

"They invited me out to see the film being made," continued Dick Stower. "I didn't actually go to the Friesian Islands but I went to Holland. They did quite a lot of shooting on the Friesian Islands but they also did quite a bit on the Isjelmeer as well. Enkhuizen was where much of the film was made – many of the town shots and the harbour shots were done there – but those showing marshes and sand dunes were filmed in the Friesians. The thing about the Friesians is that it is terribly tidal and making a film means that every day you are spending thousands of pounds. I think in six weeks they ran through a million pounds on budget with all these very expensive actors. So they used Enkhuizen because it is non-tidal there and absolutely ideal for the purpose.

"The film was quite a success, I thought: it could have been better but it wasn't bad. I think the person who directed it probably could have made more of the sailing shots. I suppose the thing is that of the average film goers only a tiny proportion are really interested in sailing and I think the film really fell between two stools: it didn't really satisfy the young audiences, who wanted something more active perhaps." The film had a special showing at the Royal Lymington Yacht Club and also at the cinema in the Community Centre in 1982, when *Dulcibella* was moored in Lymington Yacht Haven. John Atkins very kindly invited me on board to see over her and showed me where the rowlocks had been when she had been a rowing lifeboat.

John Atkins had contacted Drummond Challis and asked him whether he would like to sell *Dulcibella* now that the film had been completed. A friend, Peter Morton, put up the money and John Atkins did the work of restoring her. She then became part of the fleet of Bygone Charters. This imaginative concept did not catch on and, sadly, *Dulcibella* was sold. Today she can still be seen on the Dorset coast – she winters in Wareham and spends the summers in Swanage. *Vale, Dulcibella.*

Linette

As you cross the tollbridge from Walhampton, you can see a dilapidated wreck slowly disintegrating on its mud bank near the tollbridge, and it would be difficult to imagine that she was once a motor gun boat with a very distinguished war record. Yet that is what she was and her story is told in an article which was published in *The Lymington Times* of 7th January 1978. Her name is *Linette*.

She was built specifically for war, as she was one of the first motor gun boats built at Hythe between 1942-45 by the British Power Boat Company. This was the firm which in the 1930s had previously built Mitchell's supermarine aircraft, which won the famous Schneider Trophy before the war and was the forerunner of the Spitfire. Surprisingly, the boat's designer, Mr. Scott Payne, could not get a contract with the Navy to fit her with three Rolls Royce engines but, undaunted, he crossed the Atlantic and showed his design to the Americans, who ordered these gun boats for the US Navy. Later they were, in fact, shipped back to this country again under 'Lease/Lend' and then they were supplied direct to the Royal Navy.

Linette was Motor Gun Boat No. 77. She had a hull of 71 ft. 9 ins., a beam of 20 ft. 7 ins. and a 5 ft. draught. She was now powered by 3 Packard V.12 engines with three propellers and had a cruising speed of 40 knots. Each engine used 100 gallons of petrol an hour but they were particularly designed for speed. The petrol tanks held 2,789 gallons and were covered in rubber, so as to self-seal immediately if they were hit by German bullets. She had to modify her air vents, as in action stray German bullets had ricocheted down the air vents, wounding the crew who were witting beneath them to keep cool from the intense heat of the engine room. To counteract this, the cowls were made of canvas so that the bullets could now pass straight through them.

Her armament comprised of a pom-pom on the foredeck, which fired 2 lb. shells, a Swiss oerlikon turret aft and a Holman projector grenade made out of a drain pipe but nonetheless effective! She also carried four light machine guns, four depth charges and smoke-producing apparatus. Her crew consisted of two officers and ten ratings and was commanded by Lieutenant-Commander Hitchens, who was to add a bar to his DSO while serving in her.

Linette was first in action in the North Sea, then in the Channel, based on Folkestone, and in the summer of 1942, she was part of the 8th Flotilla down in the West Country, with the object of combatting the German E-Boats, which were active down there and achieving embarrassing success.

One memorable patrol was when Lieutenant-Commander Hitchens took three motor gun boats to the north of Alderney to lie in wait there for German E-Boats. As none showed up he then proceeded along the French coast to seek out German shipping. A small white light showed on the horizon and when they closed he could make out two large trawlers.

The three MGBs proceeded in battle formation of line ahead and were practically alongside before they were challenged. They immediately opened fire on the first trawler at practically point blank range and, taken completely by surprise, she offered little resistance. Lieutenant-Commander Hitchens then spotted a small tanker and realising she probably had escorts he proceeded to depth charge her and seconds later she exploded.

However, *Linette* herself had also sustained damage: her deck crew had been concussed by a terrific blast and she was on fire. The wheelhouse was ablaze, the flares had ignited and there was also another fire caused by escaping fuel. Lieutenant-Commander Hitchens and his 1st Lieutenant both managed to extinguish the flames, although she was travelling at 45 knots on a straight course away from the combat area at the time. The other two MGBs had sustained little damage and *Linette* went into the attack again. Sadly, when the action seemed over, Lieutenant-Commander Hitchens was killed by a stray bullet when he went into the wheelhouse.

After the war she was brought to Lymington from the Hamble by Tom Morris and became a houseboat moored on the Lymington River. The Carpenter family berthed her near the tollbridge and put wire netting all round the edge of the decks. Improbably, they bred dogs on board her and she became an "Irishman's Paradise," the gunwales improvising as a dog run. On one occasion she nearly sank, dogs and all, and Tom Morris came from his Quay chandlery and blocked all the pipes.

Another owner, Tom Tempest, who worked at the Lymington Post Office, spent at least two years renovating *Linette* and it was from him that the Stones bought her for £300 in 1960. They found her

full of beer bottles and believe she must have been used as a 'Fisherman's Rest!'

In May 1969 *Linette* was very nearly destroyed in the fire which burnt down the Lymington Sail & Tent Company and perhaps, in a way, it would have been better if she had: at least she would have ended her days fittingly for such a gallant boat with a Viking's funeral. But this was not to be. Many people from all over the country came to visit *Linette*, such was her fame, and one of them, John Phillips from Northampton, measured her meticulously with the intention of making a model of her as she once had been.

The Stones lived happily on board *Linette* for 16 years when, as a result of a change in the river flow, the mud beneath her keel was scoured away, with the result that her planking split and she broke her back. Ken Stone tried to sell her to museums but his offer was not accepted, as she was too big to transport by road and it was not possible to move her by sea.

So on 5th November 1976, sixteen years to the day since he purchased *Linette*, Ken Stone sold her for £80 to Waterside Marine of Fawley. "They took everything off her," he told me, "brass fittings, such as portholes, the lot. I understood they were going to move her or burn her but they have just left her lying there: it is terrible."

Tom Tit

John Atkins invited me on board *Palagic* at Berth 45, Berthon on Sunday, 8th March 1981 and told me about his yacht *Tom Tit*, presently laid up at Aquaboats. "Roger Pinckney has lent me some detail drawings of *Dyarchy's* rig," he told me, "so that he can help me with the rig of *Tom Tit*. Roger had had the original idea of setting his topsail from a track extended from the aft edge of the topmast on *Dyarchy*, thereby getting a really efficient fitting topsail. Whereas Roger's idea was to put a track on the outside, I decided to recess one in, starting about 6 ft. above the top peak halyard block. It would mean going aloft to lead the sail in but as long as it could be taken down from the deck in a hurry, that was all that mattered. I would have a fairly short, high peak gaff and have the efficiency of a Bermudan rig.

"The wind strength at the mast head is considerably greater than 2, or one-third that at deck level. But as soon as you got her off the wind, a gaff rigger has an advantage over the Bermudan rig, having more area – hence drive aloft. Also the advantage of this one is that, by having a maimast all in one, instead of having a separate top mast or fitting a jackyard topsail, one can set a masthead genoa. With a top mast, there is usually too much flexibility, even with running back-stays. to set a masthead genoa.

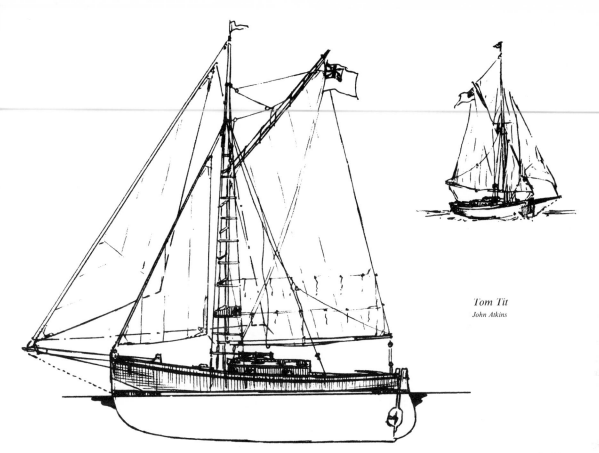

Tom Tit
John Atkins

This is the sail which gives you all the drive to windward.

"About five or six years ago I was asked by some friends to look over a little gaff cutter at Machford, in Plymouth. The owner was a Mrs. Studd-Trench-Gascoigne, who was incredibly rich and lived at Diptford Court in Totnes, Devon. For some unknown reason she had purchased this beautiful little cutter, 25 ft. and weighing 4 tons. It must have been a case of seeing her and falling in love with her. Anyway we went down to Plymouth to inspect her 'new' purchase.

"I recommended that the decks needed doing as well as a few other little jobs. Some 25 years previously, she had unfortunately been converted to Bermuda. It looked so wrong but I could not persuade the old lady to re-rig her back to her original gaff rig. The rest of the work was put in hand but, sadly, a year later she died, leaving an estate of about £4¼ million (what is a ¼ million!).

"I suggested her to a friend who went down to Plymouth and found that she was up for sale by the Trustees at a price of £2,750, as £1,800 had recently been spent on her. She had 13 sails, including 3 mains, and was in excellent condition but my friend lost interest when he learnt there was only 4 ft. 6 ins. headroom."

Tom Tit is an Itchen Ferry, designed and built on the Itchen by Cave & Son, a Southampton firm which no longer exists; she was built of Burma teak in 1894. When John Atkins was working on *Dulcibella* at Port Hamble, he came across an old man who had known *Tom Tit* in his youth. Just upstream from the Royal Pier at Southampton there used to be a boatyard and she was moored off there. An Association of Itchen Ferries has recently been formed. She was the only one which had been built as a yacht; all the other existing ones were strictly working boats. After 83 years it is incredible that she still has varnished topsides.

"When another friend would not pay more than £2,500, my mother put up the final amount of £2,200, and so today I am now the sole owner. I sailed her back to Lymington in practically the same time as a Contessa 32 which I had delivered, which is logical perhaps in view of both having the same water-line length. I am going to re-rig her traditionally, back to gaff, and I was fortunate enough to get the last bolts of tan cotton at Ratseys, just enough to make a suit of sails. A new gaff mast was quoted by Lallows for

237

about £400 and the sails cost £750 but all this was four or five years ago. I will keep her afloat as much as possible, as it is best for an old boat. She is now the sixth oldest yacht in Lloyd's Register and is in such good condition that she may well outlive some of her five sisters and become one of the oldest." Let us hope that *Tom Tit* will make a well-deserved century!

Sioux

The steam launch *Sioux* has been part of the Lymington scene for the past four years and I went to see Air Marshal Sir Arthur McDonald, KCB, AFC, MA at his home at 'Five Oaks,' Woodside Avenue, Lymington on 8th January 1983, to find out more about her. Sir Arthur came here in 1972 on retirement from the Royal Air Force. "We could have lived anywhere but we chose Lymington because we liked the idea of the place and the sailing in particular.

"I was introduced to steam in 1920 at a Caribbean sugar factory and it was for that reason that I became interested in the steam boat project. But the originator of the scheme was Commander Graham Mann, who formed a syndicate of about 50 people, who all subscribed £75, and decided in the summer of 1978 that they would like to operate a steam boat. I was not particularly interested from the user point of view at that time, because I had two other boats to maintain, and I reckon that that at least is one too many! Then I heard that people were playing about with nineteenth century steam machinery, which is what this is, and having been trained on that myself I offered my services as a consultant. And that was all. But as things have now developed I find myself, slightly against my will, as Chairman with the responsibility of dealing with the whole thing.

"We have now reached the stage when I am afraid we will have to give it up for lack of support. Of the 50 people who originally subscribed, the majority I think merely supported *Sioux* because they thought it was an interesting project, without very much idea of using her themselves. I gained that impression anyway. For some of them had hardly ever been in her; some of them never at all, I think. The number who are interested has dwindled down until now we haven't really got enough to operate her and pay for the maintenance and really keep her going.

"Four or five of us technically-minded people have had an enormous amount of fun out of her because when we got here, in fact before we bought her, I went over with a party to inspect her at Poole. I pointed out at least four fundamental faults, which could be put right without too much expense, and on that basis we bought her. Well, we have done those things and we have carried out ten or twelve modifications and all this was very interesting from

a technical point of view, but that process is more or less completed now.

"We have taken *Sioux* to the Steam Boat rallies at Beaulieu on at least two occasions and another at Christchurch, although in the case of Christchurch we had to trail her across because the boat itself is really a river launch, rather than an open sea launch, and we simply dare not take her through the Narrows. As far as the Solent is concerned, we have also taken her to Keyhaven, Yarmouth, Newtown and similar places, but we have to choose the weather for them.

"These steam launches were much used on the Thames and on Lake Windermere, those sort of places, at the turn of the century. The engine of this launch we think is about 1900 but the hull itself and the boiler is modern, only about four or five years old. As far as I can gather what happened was that somebody found this engine and, by the look of it, I would say that it had spent fifty or sixty years under a haystack or some rubbish dump. Then somebody found it and thought 'Well now, there is a sort of fashion, a nostalgic interest in steam machinery all over the country for locomotives and everything else, and this might be put together with a new hull and form a project which be of some value.' That is why I think it was done. So that is how we got hold of her. Now I don't know what will happen to her."

Water Rat

I had often seen the *Water Rat* going up and down the river and, in fact, had chartered her myself to take a party of us out to see the Queen Mother on *Britannia,* after she had been made Lord Warden of the Cinque Ports, but the weather was too rough. I went round to see Wendy Carrington at her home, 'Penny Farthings,' in Nelson Place on 8th December 1981 just before she was going out to the Mediterranean.

"I had the idea of running these river trips for some while," she told me. "I always thought it would be a good idea and then I was left some money by my father and so I decided to buy a boat with some of it and have a go! Fred, the Harbour Master, was not at all keen on the idea. Although he said I could do it, he didn't think anybody would go out in her, but my friends were very enthusiastic and Chris thought it a good idea and that gave me confidence. I am not sure whether you have to let the Harbour Master know but I thought it only polite to ask him anyway and although he said 'Yes,' he didn't hold out much hope for it.

"In fact I have done extremely well. Super. He has eaten his words – almost! Next year (1982) will be my fifth year: I started in 1978. I don't keep a tally of how many people I take out. I do Easter and then I stop and re-start at Whitsun and work right through until October. When the tide is right I can get in ten trips but then it is not always right but I can always get in something.

"It is a real mixture of people. Some foreigners, but mostly holiday-makers and quite a lot of locals. Quite a few grannies bring their grandchildren, which is lovely. We really do just the trips. My licence is just to the mouth of the river in this particular boat but it really entitles me to take 25 passengers 15 miles either side of the mouth of the river, either way towards Poole or Portsmouth and 3 miles out. I get my licence from the Department of Trade. The *Water Rat* was originally the Club launch of the RLYC and I bought her from them."

Kyra

The yacht *Kyra,* chartered from Sea Ventures of Lymington by Dr. Ian Marsh at a cost of £700 for a fortnight, became involved in the type of adventure that one associates with two hundred years ago and certainly not with the end of the twentieth century!

In August 1980 French fishermen set up a blockade of the Channel ports to try and get increased subsidies from the French Government for their hard-pressed industry. What happened is given excellent coverage in a article in the *Sunday Express* of 15th February 1981, which supplements what Don Howard, Managing Director of Sea Ventures, had already told me.

Dr. Marsh and his crew of two men and two girls decided to try and break through the blockade but within minutes of leaving their berth at the Marina in the Inner Harbour of Cherbourg, they were spotted and immediately surrounded by 13 fishing boats. Two fishing boats increased speed and not only rammed *Kyra* but the 'pirates' boarded her, armed with boat hooks, and not only threatened the crew but vandalised the yacht's fittings. Fortunately, the five Britons were able to scramble aboard a police launch for safety. The yachts was so badly damaged that the crew had to fly home and she was later brought back to Lymington by cargo boat.

The crew of *Kyra* had, nevertheless, managed to take the numbers of the two fishing vessels that had rammed them, and could also provide a pretty good description of the French fishermen. Furthermore, the affray took place in full view of the French police and a TV team who had filmed it all. The boarding of the yacht was the worst incident of the whole blockade, during which the ferries had been constantly harrassed and their passenger services interrupted. Yachtsmen everywhere were appalled.

But six months later no action had been taken at all by the Gendarmerie Maritime and no arrests or charges had been brought against the French fishermen. Efforts were made through the civil courts against them, not only for the cost of repairs and replacement of the damaged fittings of the yacht, but also compensation for the loss of charter revenue for the remainder of the sailing season. Whether their efforts will succeed or not remains to be seen.

Marlo's Barge

Marlo's Barge is moored just up river from the railway bridge at a site provided by Jeremy Rogers, off Bridge Yard. There is a covered gangway leading up to the port side of the barge with stairs leading down past cloakrooms to the restaurant in the hold. This has been beautifully panelled by Jeremy Rogers, as can be seen in the photograph, and there is also a tiled stove. Behind the bar at the far end is the engine room, which has a glass front so that you can see it, and it is in excellent condition, and the cabin accommodation is aft. This has been converted into an ante room, where diners can have a drink before their meal, and a hatch gives access to the deck above.

The galley is up forward with the focsle providing not only ample storage but also a safe play area for children. It was in the galley at 6.0 p.m. on 27th April 1983 that I talked with Marlo Johnston, after whom the barge is now named.

"The idea of a restaurant really started by my talking with Jonathan (Dr. Jonathan Rogers is her husband's partner) and Ann Rogers," she told me. "We thought 'Why not run a restaurant?' – and then we said 'Why not run a restaurant on a barge?' – so we went to look for one! Obviously a barge is much

MARLO'S BARGE

By courtesy of Marlo Johnston

Marlo's Barge

cheaper than buying property in Lymington High Street.

"We decided first of all that we would have a look at English barges but there weren't any that were suitable and in any case we could not afford them. They were too rusty, too big or too small. So we thought we would buy a French barge.

"We went on holiday to France and had a good look round. We searched in many different places and looked at a gravel barge near Fontainbleu but did not buy it. Gravel barges are not a good idea because having had gravel in the hold they are very dirty and spoilt. Then we visited Moret sur Loing and found this barge, *Maria II*.

"Monsieur Francois Cochin, whose barge it was, had decided to retire. His parents had bought *Maria II* for him when he was sixteen and he had lived aboard her all his life. However, his wife became ill and they could not manage any longer because there was only the two of them; they had no children. So he had bought a little cottage nearby and that was it. He retired on 7th July 1978.

"He brought the barge as far as Rouen and after that he handed her over and it was entirely up to us – and we were all extremely inexperienced! We had a Danish student with us called Olav, who did most of the work. He lived on the barge for the few weeks coming from Rouen to Le Havre. Then when we were ready to leave Le Havre, Jonathan Rogers and I were both there and we came with him. We meant to come under our own power but we could not do so. The French wanted us to be towed, so we started off that way, but we meant to drop the tow outside Le Havre. Unfortunately, we got the tow rope caught round the propeller so we were actually towed across the Channel. The tug was *Colass*, which normally dredges at the Marina but she goes up to Scotland quite a bit. She comes and goes.

"We had not checked the measurements of the barge with those of the railway bridge, which was a terrible thing! It was quite ridiculous that we got that far. So we went out with two dinghies and a clothes line and that was all! There was a large crowd standing on the Town Quay saying 'They will never do it; they will never do it' – but we did!

"We carried 50 tons of paving stones as ballast, which we brought over here and then sold. It was very difficult to find something that didn't cost a fortune and that could be disposed of easily on arrival. Fiona Rogers was with us at the start and so was the wife of another partner in the medical practice at that time, but they left, so she is out of it, and Fiona later left too. But she was very active in setting it up and we opened in June 1979, so we have been going for four years.

"I had done outside catering before but I am not a cordon bleu and had done nothing professionally before it all: just social catering and some cooking for Paul Jackson. Even so, we became recognised by Egon Ronay and Michelin too.

"Sunday evenings were always very quiet, especially during the winter, so we decided to show international films then with pizza or quiche and a glass of wine served beforehand. The films kept us happy and brought in many people."

Sadly, *Marlo's Barge* is now up for sale and will shortly be leaving Lymington River. *Bon voyage* and *bonne chance*.

*   *   *   *   *

It is always difficult to know how to end a piece of writing, whether it be a letter or an article in a magazine or book. So often everything that one has felt and wishes to convey is left to the final paragraph, sometimes to be left out altogether. Then Jack Blachford lent me an article in *The Bournemouth Daily Echo* of 17th May 1950, written by Ronald K. Palmer, a staff reporter, when Lymington was celebrating the 800th anniversary of the granting of its Charter. His words seem to me to convey it all.

"Time has been kind and unkind to Lymington. Time has taken away from her the motherhood of sea power. Time has robbed her of economic power.

"Instead, the gods who love men who live by the sea, have given her something to reward her for the sadness of memory. They have given her pride in achievement and skill in accomplishment, and the love of the endless waters.

"I would like to think that the greatest chapter in the Lymington story is not the sound and flame of battle, but the quietness of the river at dusk, with the lonely craft bobbing on the eternal tide, and a man on a boat in the middle of the river letting down his sail, and the opposite shore looking like Avalon through the evening mist."

That was written over thirty years ago and since then Lymington has emerged once again as a maritime town with a maritime history. Even the river has changed; in appearance perhaps but never in spirit. She may be more bustling and busy during the day but as the sun sets, she regains her tranquillity and timelessness. The past, present and future become one. "The River is within us."

CAPTAIN TOM JOHNSTONE 1772 – 1839

When I read of Tom Johnstone's fantastic adventures, which make those of the late film actor, Erroll Flynn, pale into insignificance, I did not believe them and even after reading his biography I still can hardly do so. That others share this view was confirmed to me in a letter about him from Tom Pocock that was published in *Country Life* of 3rd February 1983. He considered Captain Johnstone as "one of the most engaging characters on the borderline between naval history and myth" and added that "if even half of his adventures can be substantiated, he deserves recognition. That he did exist and must have enjoyed his own salty reputation is suggested by a portrait sketch of him in my possession."

By courtesy of Tom Pocock

Portrait sketch of Captain Thomas Johnstone

Here then is a summary of this colourful life and I leave it to my readers to decide whether it is a 'factitious' account of him or not. Although

Lymington was not specifically mentioned in his biography by James Cleugh, one must assume that the account of his early smuggling and the description of the Hampshire marshes must make this a distinct possibility.

As we have seen, he started helping the smugglers at the age of nine and by the age of 21 he was so conversant with the south coast of England and the coast of Hampshire in particular that he became a pilot.

Later he joined the Navy to fight the French in the Napoleonic Wars and was taken prisoner by them but released on condition that he took a secret package back to England. Once back in this country, he only just escaped from a Press Gang and resumed smuggling again, this time in Sussex. He was then captured but given his liberty in return for taking General Barrère, a prisoner of war, to France. Back in England he was later imprisoned in New Gaol in London but escaped by bribing his warder and became pilot to the British forces, embarking for Holland and given a full pardon. He now called himself Captain Thomas Johnstone and lived very extravagantly and so had to resume smuggling to pay his debts. In 1802 he was imprisoned for debt in Newgate but once again managed to escape and from Brighton made his way back to France, where he holed up with a French smuggler.

While staying in France, and this really is the part of his life which is of most interest, he met the brilliant young American engineer and inventor, Robert Fulton and actually worked in his drawing office in Paris, later visiting the prototypes of the new ships which would be driven by steam. He then smuggled English gold from Southwold to Flushing for Napoleon and it is to his credit that when Napoleon offered him his freedom in return for leading an invasion of England, he refused and was thrown into prison. Yet again he escaped and swam out to an American vessel, the *Lafayette,* and worked his passage to New Orleans. He worked as a clerk to the British Consul and was granted another pardon on condition that he returned to England in the frigate *Roebuck.*

Here he met Robert Fulton again and together they carried out experiments at Dover Castle testing underwater explosives. During the Walcheren expedition, he took one to Calais Harbour and exploded it, doing a lot of damage, but the Navy was not interested. He even swam to the Flushing ramparts with another explosive to blow up the enemy's powder magazine and for this dangerous mission he was given a pension of £100 a year and the command of HMS *Fox,* a revenue cruiser.

Now a Revenue Officer, he was pronounced a traitor by the smugglers and became a prime target for them. After several vicious attacks, in one of which he nearly lost his sight, he retired from the Navy and at the age of 44 married a squire's daughter from Somerset, Miss Constance Stonebridge, and settled down to bring up his family.

Five years later, as a result of his work with Robert Fulton on miniature submarines, some friends of Napoleon approached him and asked if he would rescue Napoleon by submarine, for a reward of £40,000. He started to build one but Napoleon died before it could be finished. However he managed to interest the Spanish Government in the submarine and demonstrated it on the River Thames with some Spaniards on board. When she dived, the submarine became entangled in the cables of a vessel and only just managed to surface again. The Spaniards decided not to buy it!

Surprisingly, Captain Thomas Johnstone died quietly in his sleep at the ripe old age then of sixty-nine.

THE FUTURE OF THE NORTH-WEST SOLENT COAST PLAN 1

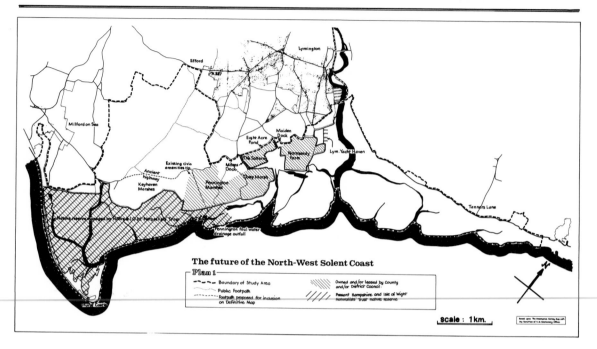

THE FUTURE OF THE NORTH-WEST SOLENT COAST PLAN 2

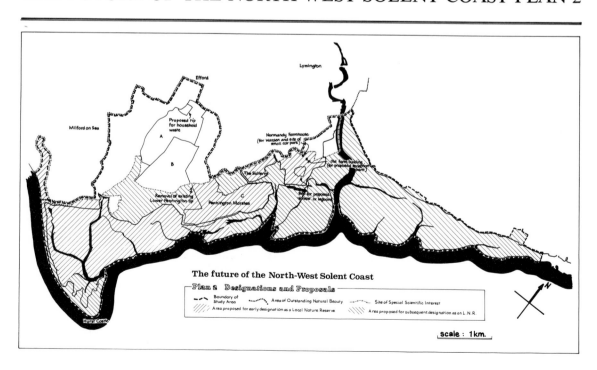

Allingham, William. Diary. Intro. Geoffrey Grigson
1967 Centaur Press Ltd., Fontwell, Sussex

Bailey, Maurice and Maralyn. Staying Alive
Lymington: Nautical Publishing Co.

Bailey, Maurice and Maralyn. Second Chance
1981 London: Weidenfield

Banks, Bruce and Kenny, Dick. Looking at Sails
1979 Lymington: Nautical Publishing Co.

Barraclough, Captain E. M. C., RN. Flag Etiquette for Yachts
pre 1900

Barraclough, Captain E.M.C., RN. Yacht Flags and Ensigns
1951 *Yachting World*

Barraclough, Captain E. M. C., RN. Flags of the World
1978 3rd Edition. Frederick Warne

Barraclough, Captain E. M. C., RN. Flags and Signals
1969 BP Yachting

Barraclough, Captain E. M. C., RN. I was sailing (Memoirs)
1980 Lymington: Privately published

Barton, Humphrey. Vertue XXXV
1951 Robert Ross

Barton, Humphrey. The Sea and Me (Autobiography)
1952 Robert Ross

Barton, Humphrey. Atlantic Adventurers
1953 Adlard Coles

Beesly, Patrick. Very Special Intelligence – Admiralty's
Operational Intelligence Centre 1939-45
1976 H. Hamilton

Boat World
1981 Haymarket Publishing Ltd.

Brassey, Lady. A Voyage in the Sunbeam
1891 London: Longmans Green & Co.

Brook-Hart, Denys. British 19th Century Marine Painting
Antique Collectors Club

Brook-Hart, Denys. 20th Century British Marine Painting
Antique Collectors Club

Bruce, Erroll. Cape Horn to Port
Lymington: Nautical Publishing

Bruce, Erroll. Deep Sea Sailing
1953 Hutchinson

Bruce, Erroll. Challenge to Poseidon
1956 London: Hutchinson

Bruce, Erroll. When the Crew Matter Most
1961 London: Stanley Paul

Bruce, Erroll. This is Rough Weather Sailing
1980 Lymington: Nautical Publishing

Chacksfield, K. Smuggling Days
1966 *Christchurch Times*

Childers, Erskine. The Riddle of the Sands
1976 Bowker & Bertram Ltd. (First published in 1903.
Historical postscript by R. M. Bowker)

Cleugh, James. Captain Thomas Johnstone
1955 Andrew Melrose Ltd.

Coles, K. Adlard. Channel Harbours and Anchorages
5th Edition Lymington: Nautical Publishing

Coles, K. Adlard. Creeks and Harbours of the Solent
1933 London: Edward Arnold & Co.

Coles, K. Adlard. Heavy Weather Sailing
1981 Adlard Coles

Cook, Peter and Webb, Barbara. The Complete Book of Sailing
1977 Ward Lock Ltd.

Corish, C. J. The New Forest and the Isle of Wight
1903 London: Seeley & Co. Ltd.

Creagh-Osborne. Scrapbook kept by Mrs. Creagh-Osborne of
Hove and owned by Pat Creagh-Osborne of Yarmouth
1866-1902

Creagh-Osborne, Richard. This is Racing
Lymington: Nautical Publishing

Creagh-Osborne, Richard. This is Sailing – A Complete Course –
More advanced technique.
Lymington: Nautical Publishing

Creagh-Osborne, Richard (Ed.). Paul Elvström explains the Racing
Rules. 5th Edition. First appeared in 1965

Creagh-Osborne, Richard (Ed.). Elvström speaks on Yacht Racing
1969 Lymington: Nautical Publishing

Crozier Family. Memorials of the Family of Crozier
1881 Lymington: Edward King

Doman, Henry. The Cathedral and Other Poems
1864 Simpkin Marshall & Co.

Drummond, Maldwin. Conflicts in an Estuary
1974 Ilex Press

Drummond, Maldwin. Salt Water Palaces
1980 Debrett's Peerage Ltd.

Elder, Michael. For Those in Peril – The Story of the
Lifeboat Service. 1963 London: John Murray

Ellam, Patrick and Mudie, Colin. Sopranino (A 10,000 mile cruise
in a 20′ Cutter)
1958 London: Rupert Hart Davis

Elvström, Paul. Elvström Speaks
1969 Lymington: Nautical Publishing

Fisher, Bob. The Fastnet Disaster
1980 Pelham Books Ltd.

Francis, Clare. Come Hell or High Water
1977 Pelham Books Ltd.

Francis, Clare. Come Wind or Weather
1978 Ipswich: W. S. Cowell Ltd.

Freeston, Ewart. French Prisoner of War Models
1973 Lymington: Nautical Publishing

Garrett, A. and Wilkinson, T. The History of the Royal
Cruising Club. 1981 London: C. Buckley

Garrow, David. The History of Lymington
1825

Grigsby, Joan. Lymington – The History and Today's Guide
Paul Cave Publications

Heaton, Peter. A History of Yachting in Pictures
1972 London: Tom Stacey

Hole, Robert H. Gilcraft
1925 C. Arthur Pearson Ltd.

Holford, Ingrid. The Yachtsman's Weather Guide
1979 London: Ward Lock Ltd.

Hosking, W. G. Lymington's Port in our Island Story
1946. Privately published

Howlett, John. The Guvnor
1973 Published privately

Johnson, Peter. Ocean Racing and Offshore Yachts
1972 2nd Edition: Nautical Publishing Co.

Johnson, Peter (Ed.). Offshore Manual International
Lymington: Nautical Publishing

Johnson, Peter. The Guiness Book of Yachting – Facts & Feats
1975 Guiness Superlatives Ltd.

Johnson, Peter. Yachtsman's Guide to the Rating Rule
1971 Nautical Publishing

Johnson, Peter. Boating Britain
1973 Nautical Publishing

Jones, C. P. History of Lymington
1930 Charles King

Jones, R. V. Most Secret War – British Scientific Intelligence
1939-1945. London: Hamish Hamilton

Jowitt, R. L. P. and Dorothy M. The Solent and its Surroundings
1978 Terence Dalton Ltd.

Kemp, Peter. The Oxford Companion to Ships and the Sea
1976 London: Oxford University Press

King, Edward. Old Times Revisited in the Borough and Parish of Lymington
1976 2nd Edition Winchester: Barry Shurlock

King, Edward. A Walk through Lymington
1972 Lymington: Kings

Lambert, J. M. The Spartina Story
Nature 1964 Vol. 204, No. 4964, pp. 1136-38.

Lymington Historical Record Society Papers
Best, A. M. Lymington versus the Tollbridge (14.2.58)
Haig, K. B. Some Lymington Inns (28.1.55)
Hole, Robert. A Boyhood's Memories in Lymington (17.1.58)
Jones, B. C. Illustrations of Lymington's Maritime Trade (18.4.58)
Lloyd, A. T. Lymington's History from Sources in London ref. Piracy and Smugglers (1962)
Phillips-Birt, D. H. C. Spithead and Solent in History (22.9.61)
Sandell, E. M. The Links between Lymington and Southampton (14.4.61)
Welch, E. Admiralty Courts 1199-1835 (19.1.65)

Lymington Town Guide

McMullen, Michael. Multihull Seamanship
Lymington: Nautical Publishing

Marriott, Hugh. Owning a Boat – All the essentials of Buying, Running and even Sailing a Boat Today
1976 Lymington: Nautical Publishing

Moody, Henry. Sketches of Hampshire
1846 Winchester: Jacob and Johnson

Mudie, Colin. Motor Boats and Boating
1972 Feltham-Hanly (Illus. Roy Coombes)

Mudie, Colin, Hales, Geoff and Handford, Michael. Advanced Sailboat Cruising
1981 Lymington: Nautical Publishing

Mudie, Robert. Hampshire – Its Past and Present Conditions and Further Prospects
1974 Alresford: Laurence Oxley

Mudie, Rosemary and Colin. The Story of the Sailing Ship
1975 London: Marshall Cavendish

Mudie, Rosemary and Colin. Power Yachts
1977 Granada

Nicholl, G. W. R. Survival at Sea
Adlard Coles

Nicholson, Ian. Surveying Small Craft
1974 Granada Publishing (Adlard Coles Ltd.)

O'Brien, F. Early Solent Steamers – A history of local steam navigation. 1973 Newton Abbot: David & Charles

Pasmore, Anthony. Verderers of the New Forest – A History of the New Forest 1877-1977
1977 Pioneer Publications

Paye, P. The Lymington Branch
1979 Oakwood Press

Payne, Barbara. History of the X-Class 1908-1981
1971 (2nd printing 1981)

Phillips-Birt, Douglas. Waters of Wight
1967 Cassell & Co. Ltd.

Popham, Hugh and Robin (Ed.). A Thirst for the Sea – the Sailing Adventures of Erskine Childers
1977 London: Stanford Maritime

Rayner, D. A. Safety in Small Craft
Adlard Coles

Roskill, S. W. The Secret Capture
1959 London: Collins

Rousmaniere, John. Fastnet Force 10
1980 Lymington: Nautical Publishing

Royal Lymington Yacht Club Report 1952-1972

Royal Ocean Racing Club. Fastnet Report and Race Card

Shute, Neville. Requiem for a Wren
1955 William Heinemann Ltd.

Smith, George. The Secrets of George Smith, Fisherman
Ilex Press

Solent Year Book 1980/81 and 1981/82
Solent Cruising and Racing Association.
Isle of Wight: County Press

Stevenson, William. A Man called Intrepid
1976 London: Macmillan Ltd.

Stuart Woods. Blue Water, Green Skipper – The Single-handed Transatlantic Race from Square One
1977 Stanford Marine

Taverner, J. H. Wild Fowl in Hampshire
1962 Winchester: Warren & Son

Webb, Barbara. Ready About – 8 Language Dictionary
1965 Adlard Coles

Webb, Barbara (Trans. Schult, Joachim). The Sailing Dictionary. 1981 Adlard Coles

Webb, Barbara with Cook, Peter. The Complete Book of Sailing
1977 Ward Lock Ltd.

Webber, N. B. (Ed.). Marinas and Small Craft Harbours – Proceedings of a Symposium held at the University of Southampton on 19-21 April 1972
1972 University of Southampton

Wood, Christopher. Dictionary of Victorian Painters
2nd Edition. Antique Collectors Club

Woolass, Peter. Vertue
1973 Woolas

INDEX